FROM THE PARTS TO THE WHOLE

ACTA OF THE 13TH INTERNATIONAL BRONZE CONGRESS

VOLUME 1

JOURNAL OF ROMAN ARCHAEOLOGY

SUPPLEMENTARY SERIES NUMBER 39

This volume is published with the support of Shelby White and Leon Levy

ISBN 1-887829-39-3
ISSN 1063-4304 (for the supplementary series)

 Printed by Thomson-Shore, Dexter, Michigan.
This and other supplements to the *Journal of Roman Archaeology*® may be ordered from:
JRA®, 95 Peleg Road, Portsmouth, Rhode Island 02871, U.S.A.
telephone (USA code+) 401 683 1955
telefax (USA code+) 401 683 1975 (fax only)
e-mail: jra@wsii.com
or via our Web site at: www.JournalofRomanArch.com

AN INTERNATIONAL JOURNAL

FROM THE PARTS TO THE WHOLE

VOLUME 1

Acta of the 13th International Bronze Congress,
held at Cambridge, Massachusetts,
May 28 - June 1, 1996

edited by

Carol C. Mattusch, Amy Brauer, and Sandra E. Knudsen

Portsmouth, Rhode Island
2000

Abbreviations

Abbreviations are based on the standards recommended by the *Journal of Roman Archaeology* and the *American Journal of Archaeology* 95 (1991) 3-16. Most abbreviations for ancient sources follow the *OCD*. Most monograph abbreviations repeated in the notes follow the form of author plus short title; most articles are abbreviated by author plus year. Only the lead museum name is normally cited for exhibition catalogues.

The following do not appear in the above works:

13th Br. Cong.	*Abstracts, 13th International Bronze Congress* (Cambridge, MA 1996).
Archäologische Bronzen	H. Born (ed.), *Archäologische Bronzen. Antike Kunst, moderne Technik* (Berlin 1985).
Art and technology	S. Doeringer, D. G. Mitten, and A. Steinberg (edd.), *Art and technology: a symposium on classical bronzes* (Cambridge, MA 1970).
Bol, *Bronzetechnik*	P. C. Bol, *Antike Bronzetechnik. Kunst und Handwerk antiker Erzbildner* (Munich 1985).
Comstock–Vermeule, *Bronzes*	M. B. Comstock and C. C. Vermeule, *Greek, Etruscan, and Roman bronzes in the Museum of Fine Arts, Boston* (Greenwich, CT 1971).
Comstock–Vermeule, *Sculpture in stone*	M. B. Comstock and C. C. Vermeule, *Sculpture in stone: the Greek, Roman and Etruscan collections of the Museum of Fine Arts, Boston* (Boston 1976)
Due bronzi	*Due bronzi da Riace: rinvenimento, restauro, analisi, et ipotesi di interpretazione (BdA* spec. ser. 3, Rome 1984) (2 vols.).
The fire of Hephaistos	C. C. Mattusch *et al.*, *The fire of Hephaistos: large classical bronzes from North American collections* (Exhib. cat., Arthur M. Sackler Museum, Harvard University Art Museums [Cambridge, MA 1996]).
The gods delight	A. P. Kozloff, D. G. Mitten *et al.*, *The gods delight: the human figure in classical bronze* (Exhib. cat., Cleveland Museum of Art [Cleveland OH 1988]).
Haynes, *Technique*	D. Haynes, *The technique of Greek bronze statuary* (Mainz 1992).
Master bronzes	D. G. Mitten and S. F. Doeringer (edd.), *Master bronzes from the classical world* (Exhib. cat., Fogg Art Museum, Cambridge, MA [Mainz 1967]).
Mattusch, *Classical bronzes*	C. C. Mattusch, *Classical bronzes: the art and craft of Greek and Roman statuary* (Ithaca, NY 1996).
Mattusch, *Greek bronze statuary*	C. C. Mattusch, *Greek bronze statuary: from the beginnings through the 5th c. B.C.* (Ithaca, NY 1988).
Pollitt, *Art of Rome*	J. J. Pollitt, *The art of Rome c.753 B.C.-A.D.337: sources and documents* (Cambridge 1983).
Pollitt, *Art of Greece*	J. J. Pollitt, *The art of ancient Greece: sources and documents* (Cambridge 1990).
Ridgway, *Severe style*	B. S. Ridgway, *The Severe style in Greek sculpture* (Princeton 1970).
Rolley, *La sculpture grecque*	C. Rolley, *La sculpture grecque.* 1: *des origines au milieu du V siècle* (Paris 1994).
Rolley, *Greek bronzes*	C. Rolley, *Greek bronzes* (New York 1986).
Rolley, *Die griechischen Bronzen*	C. Rolley, *Die griechischen Bronzen* (Munich 1984). French edn.: *Les bronzes grecs* (Fribourg 1983).
Small bronze sculpture	M. True and J. Podany (edd.), *Small bronze sculpture from the ancient world: papers delivered at a symposium organized by the Departments of Antiquities and Antiquities Conservation and held at The J. Paul Getty Museum March 16–19, 1989* (Malibu 1990).
Stewart, *Greek sculpture*	A. Stewart, *Greek sculpture: an exploration* (2 vols., New Haven 1990)
Walters, British Museum *Bronzes*	H. B. Walters, *Catalogue of the Bronzes, Greek, Etruscan, and Roman in the department of Greek and Roman antiquities, British Museum* (London 1899).
The western Greeks	G. P. Carratelli (ed.), *The Greek world: art and civilization in Magna Graecia and Sicily* (Exhib. cat., Palazzo Grassi, Venice [Milan–New York 1996]).
Das Wrack	G. Hellenkemper Salies, H.-H. von Prittwitz und Gaffron, and G. Bauchhenß (edd.), *Das Wrack: der antike Schiffsfund von Mahdia* (Kataloge des Rheinischen Landesmuseums Bonn, 2 vols., Cologne 1994).
Zimmer, *Bronzegußwerkstätten*	G. Zimmer, *Griechische Bronzegusswerkstätten: zur Technologieentwicklung eines antiken Kunsthandwerkes* (Mainz 1990).

CONTENTS OF VOLUME 1

[continued overleaf]

Preface

These two volumes represent the distillation of the work of the 13th International Bronze Congress over three intensive days at Harvard University from May 29 to June 1, 1996, during which 90 scholars presented papers about the results of their work on many aspects of Greek, Roman, and Etruscan small bronzes and large-scale bronze statuary. This congress provided a fitting culmination for many years of research into the technologies and styles of classical bronzes at the Fogg Art Museum of Harvard University. Already during the late 1920s, the scientific practice of conservation and analysis of works of art had begun at the Fogg Art Museum under the guidance of E. W. Forbes and P. J. Sachs, co-directors of the Fogg Art Museum until 1944. Soon, important results for the study of ancient bronzes began to emerge, as in R. J. Gettens's pioneering study of mineral incrustation on the interior of a large hollow-cast seated statuette of an Egyptian lion-headed goddess which came to the museum in 1943 as part of the Grenville Winthrop Bequest. Gettens's research also led up to his later fundamental studies of how Chinese ritual bronze vessels were cast, after he moved to the Freer Gallery of Art in Washington, D.C.

During the years following World War II, the energetic efforts of G. M. A. Hanfmann, Curator of Ancient Art, led to major exhibitions of ancient art at the Fogg Museum — *Ancient art in American private collections* (1955-56), followed by the first public exhibition of the Norbert Schimmel collection in 1964. In both of these trend-setting exhibitions, classical bronzes played a prominent rôle. However, the Fogg Museum's involvement with classical bronzes reached a new level of intensity with the comprehensive international exhibition of Greek, Roman, and Etruscan bronzes, *Master bronzes from the classical world,* which was shown in Cambridge, St. Louis, and Los Angeles during 1967 and 1968. The opening of the exhibition in Cambridge was accompanied by an interdisciplinary symposium, "Art and Technology," which set the stage for all future meetings of this kind including the series of bronze congresses that have been held in Europe (and now the United States) at regular intervals ever since.

In this ground-breaking symposium, which formed a critical beginning for the international effort to publish and study classical bronzes, the underlying emphasis was on how the manufacture of bronzes affects our understanding of their style. This was promoted, above all, by the leadership of the late C. Stanley Smith and H. Lechtmann of the Massachusetts Institute of Technology, which co-sponsored the symposium with Harvard University. In addition, the critical participation of leading European colleagues such as the late H. Menzel of Mainz, already widely recognized as the authority on bronzes from the provinces of Roman Europe, set the stage for the international effort to study classical bronzes that followed. At the initiative of H. Hoffmann, at that time Curator of Ancient Art in the Museum für Kunst und Gewerbe, Hamburg, H. Menzel had secured a number of the finest Roman statuary bronzes found in Western Europe for the exhibition. The proceedings of this symposium were published by Massachusetts Institute of Technology Press in 1970. Together this volume and the exhibition catalogue, *Master bronzes from the classical world,* have served as basic reference works for research in classical bronzes ever since.

Shortly after the exhibition, H. Menzel was host to a small gathering of bronze scholars at the Römisch-Germanisches Zentralmuseum, Mainz. This expanded into the regular series of bronze congresses that has produced a wealth of important scholarship on all aspects of classical bronzes during the decades since. At the same time, a library of definitive catalogues of collections of classical bronzes has steadily appeared from the Netherlands, Belgium, France, Austria, Switzerland, and especially from Germany itself, these last from H. Menzel's own exacting scholarship. In addition, new archaeological discoveries, such as that of the hoard of bronze statuettes from Weissenberg on the Danube in Bavaria, have provided exciting new impetus to this international wave of scholarly interest in classical bronzes. In the United States, interest was heightened by the exhibition of Greek, Roman and Etruscan statuettes, *The gods delight,* which appeared at the Cleveland Museum of Art, the Boston Museum of Fine Arts and the Los Angeles County Museum of Art in 1988 and 1989. The J. Paul Getty Museum, Malibu, sponsored an important symposium of small classical bronzes in 1989, with participants from many countries in Europe as well as North America.

It seemed to the organizers of the 13th International Bronze Congress that, for a fitting accompaniment that would recognize the pre-eminent rôle that technical studies of ancient bronzes had come to play in the laboratories of Cambridge and Boston area institutions, an exhibition should be organized examining and bringing together representatives of large-scale bronze statuary as a focus for the participants' discussions and the scholarly work of the meeting. This exhibition, *The fire of Hephaistos*, supported by a major grant from the National Endowment for the Humanities, was organized by C. C. Mattusch of George Mason University, H. Lie of the Straus Center for Conservation and Research, Harvard University Art Museums, and A. Brauer of the Harvard University Art Museums. S. Hemingway's internship enriched all aspects of the exhibition. As a result, we now know a great deal more about how many of the monumental Greek and Roman bronzes in American collections were cast and assembled. It also seems fitting that presentation of technical research on the casting of large-scale bronze statuary is prominent among the papers which we are happy to present here.

Among the many individuals to whom we owe enduring thanks for making this, the 13th International Bronze Congress, a reality, I must mention S. White and L. Levy for so generously supporting the publication of these papers. J. Cuno, Director of the Harvard University Art Museums, enthusiastically supported and sustained the planning of the congress and accompanying exhibition from the beginning. Without his guidance and support, the achievements of the 13th International Bronze Congress, including its definitive fruits which appear in this volume, would not have been possible.

David Gordon Mitten

Editors' note

All papers presented at the international bronze congresses are normally published in the *Acta* of that congress. The editor of *JRA* has graciously agreed to follow this procedure.

Introduction

In 1982 Dorothy Kent Hill came to George Mason University to lecture about ancient bronzes, enthusiastic about having just attended the 7th International Congress on Ancient Bronzes in Székesfehérvár: she was adding names to the mailing list for future congresses. She died not long before the Vienna Congress in 1986. Had she lived until 1990, when the 11th Congress convened in Madrid, she would certainly have been a member of the committee in whose behalf D. G. Mitten proposed that the congress meet in the United States in 1996. The members of that newly formed Planning Committee were B. Barr-Sharrar, E. B. Harrison, D. Buitron-Oliver and A. Oliver, C. Houser, J. J. Herrmann, Jr., D. G. Mitten, and myself as chair. D. G. Mitten, the most experienced American participant in the congresses on ancient bronzes, proposed that our congress be held at Harvard University in Cambridge, MA. J. Cuno, Director of the Harvard University Art Museums, generously agreed to host the congress, and A. Brauer at that institution became our tireless and multi-talented Congress Coordinator. Planning began with a seed grant from G. Ortiz, a regular bronze congress participant and, as our work progressed, we benefited frequently from the guidance of S. E. Griffin of the Archaeological Institute of America.

The 13th International Congress on Ancient Bronzes was held in Cambridge from May 28 through June 1, 1996. Ninety speakers and more than 200 participants came from Bulgaria, Canada, Denmark, England, France, Germany, Greece, Ireland, Italy, the Netherlands, Poland, Portugal, Russia, Spain, Switzerland, and the United States. One of the most delightful gatherings during the congress was at the magnificent reception hosted by Dr and Mrs. Jerome M. Eisenberg at the Museum of Fine Arts, Boston.

The major focus of the 13th Congress was large-scale bronzes, as had been the case in Vienna 10 years before. The papers published here include presentations of recently discovered bronzes, technical studies of statues well-known from the field of stylistic analysis, and a wide range of approaches to the study of ancient bronzes, both traditional and innovative. The organization of the *Acta* is generally chronological, though the papers were originally delivered in the following sessions: Athens; Early Greece; the Roman Provinces; Inscriptions, Coins, and Signatures; Vessels, Tools, and Implements; Post-Antique Bronzes; two sessions on Small Bronzes and two on Large Bronzes; and three sessions on Technology, Analysis, and Conservation. The session Chairs were E. B. Harrison, J. Neils, C. Houser, B. Barr-Sharrar, D. G. Mitten, A. Beale, H. Lie, J. A. Scott, J. H. Kroll, A. Oliver, S. Fabing, J. J. Herrmann, Jr., and myself.

The types and styles of classical bronze statuary, ancient technology, and modern research on the ancient bronze industry were the major themes of the exhibition, which was organized to accompany the Congress: *The fire of Hephaistos: large classical bronzes from North American collections.* The Berlin Foundry Cup, one of two objects in the exhibition not made of bronze, set the stage: it shows that technology did not drive sculptural styles and that styles were not dependent upon the medium in which they were produced. Scholarly collaboration was the key to the exhibition, and I worked with H. Lie and with A. Brauer in the conception and implementation of the exhibition. In addition to making extensive observations about the technique by which each bronze was produced, we had the alloy of each bronze analyzed and x-radiographs made of many of the bronzes. Lenders to the exhibition showed great interest in the project, and generously allowed us extended access to their bronzes. In particular, K. T. Luckner at the Toledo Museum of Art gave us expert advice on planning and organization, but, sadly, he did not live to see the results of our work. The exhibition traveled to Toledo and to the Tampa Museum of Art. The exhibition catalogue (Harvard University Art Museums 1996) included essays by B. Barr-Sharrar, A. Beale, B. R. Brown, H. Lie, A. Oliver, A. E. Raubitschek, and B. S. Ridgway. The editor, S. E. Knudsen (Toledo Museum of Art) worked tirelessly to ensure flawless production, and she is also to be credited with the far more difficult task of editing the *Acta* in these two volumes. A. Lilly and C. Schroeder managed manuscript preparation and extensive retyping. We are all grateful to J. H. Humphrey for taking on the publication of the *Acta* as a supplement to the *Journal of Roman Archaeology*, and to S. White and L. Levy for their generous support of this publication.

Carol C. Mattusch

The International Bronze Congresses and associated publications and exhibitions

1 1970 NIJMEGEN
Tagung über römische Bronzegefäße im Rijksmuseum G. M. Kam in Nijmegen von 20. bis einschließlich 23. April 1970, Hektogr. Niederschrift (Nijmegen 1970).

2 1972 MAINZ
H. Menzel (ed.), "Bericht über die Tagung 'Römische Toreutik' vom 23-26. Mai 1972 in Mainz," *JRGZM* 20 (1973) 258-82.

3 1974 BRUSSELS–MARIEMONT
Actes des IIIe journées internationales consacrées à l'étude des bronzes romains Bruxelles–Mariemont 27-29 mai 1974 (Bulletin des Musées Royaux d'Art et d'Histoire 46 [1974 (1977)] 5-217). Also printed separately.

4 1976 LYON
Actes du IVe colloque international sur les bronzes antiques 17-21 mai 1976 (Annales de l'Université Jean Moulin, Lyon 1977) 5-236.

5 1978 LAUSANNE
Bronzes hellénistiques et romains: tradition et renouveau: actes du Ve colloque international sur les bronzes antiques, Lausanne, 8-13 mai 1978 (Cahiers d'archéologie romande de la Bibliothèque historique vaudoise 17 [1979].

6 1980 BERLIN
Toreutik und figürliche Bronzen römischer Zeit: Akten der 6. Tagung über antike Bronzen 13-17 Mai 1980 in Berlin (Staatliche Museen Preußischer Kulturbesitz, Antikenmuseum, Berlin 1984).

7 1982 SZÉKESFEHÉRVÁR
Bronzes romains figurés et appliqués et leurs problèmes techniques: Actes du VIIe colloque international sur les bronzes antiques, Székesfehérvár, 1982 (Alba Regia 21 [1984] 5-136).

8 1984 STARA ZAGORA
Papers unpublished.
Ancient Bronzes (Exhib. cat., District Historical Museum, Stara Zagora 1984).

9 1986 VIENNA
K. Gschwantler and A. Bernhard-Walcher (edd.*), Griechische und römische Statuetten und Großbronzen: Akten der 9. internationalen Tagung über antike Bronzen, Wien, 21-25 April 1986* (Vienna 1988).
K. Gschwantler (ed.), *Guß + Form: Bronzen aus der Antikensammlung* (Exhib. cat., Kunsthistorisches Museum, Vienna 1986).

10 1988 FREIBURG
J. Ronke (ed.), *Akten der 10. internationalen Tagung über antike Bronzen, Freiburg, 18-22 Juli 1988* (Forschungen und Berichte zur Vor- und Frühgeschichte in Baden-Württemberg 45 [Stuttgart 1994]).
H. U. Nuber, *Antike Bronzen aus Baden-Württemberg* (Exhib. cat., Schriften des Limesmuseums Aalen 40 [1988]).

11 1990 MADRID
J. Arce and F. Burkhalter (edd.), *Bronces y religion romana: actas del XI congreso internacional de bronces antiguos, Madrid, Mayo-Junio 1990* (Consejo Superior de Investigaciones Científicas, Madrid 1993).
Los bronces romanos en España (Exhib. cat., Palacio de Velázquez, Madrid 1990).

12 1992 NIJMEGEN
S. T. A. M. Mols *et al.* (edd.), *Acta of the 12th International Congress on Ancient Bronzes, Nijmegen, 1-4 June, 1992* (*Nederlandse Archeologische Rapporten* 18, Provinciaal Museum G. M. Kam, Nijmegen 1995).

13 1996 CAMBRIDGE, MA
C. C. Mattusch *et al.* (edd.), *From the parts to the whole: acta of the 13th international congress on ancient bronzes, Cambridge, MA, 31 May–2 June 1996*, 2 vols. (*JRA* Suppl. 39 [2000]).
C. C. Mattusch, H. Lie *et al.*, *The fire of Hephaistos: large classical bronzes from North American collections* (Exhib. cat., Harvard University Art Museums, Cambridge, MA 1996).

14 1999 KÖLN
Antike Bronzen, Werkstattkreise: Figuren und Geräte, 14. *internationaler Kongress,* Römisch-Germanischen *Museums, Köln, 21 bis 24 September 1999.*

The casting process of the statue of Queen Napir-Asu in the Louvre

Pieter Meyers

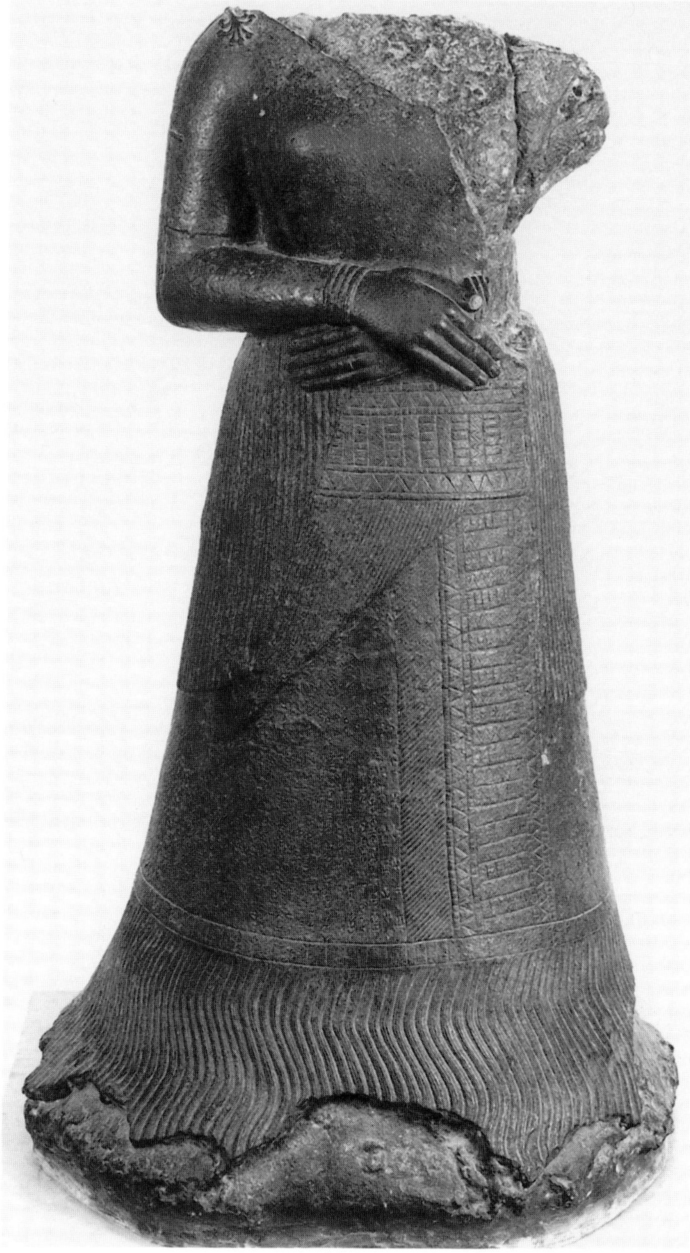

Fig. 1. Statue of Queen Napir-Asu. Middle Elamite, excavated at Susa. 14th c. B.C. Bronze and copper, h. 1.29 m; w. 0.73 m. Paris, Musée du Louvre, Département des antiquités orientales Sb 2731. (Photo: P. and M. Chuzeville; courtesy Musée du Louvre.)

Introduction

The statue of Queen Napir-Asu, dated to the 14th c. B.C., is a remarkable object in more ways than one (fig. 1). It is one of the largest and heaviest surviving bronzes from antiquity. Not counting the missing head, the statue stands 1.29 m tall and weighs 1,750 kg. The statue is also of exceptional artistic quality; the modeling is realistic and well executed, while the detailed surface decoration indicates superior craftsmanship.

The statue, now in the collection of the Musée du Louvre, was found in 1903 by the French archaeologist J. de Morgan at the temple site on the acropolis of Susa (western Iran).[1] Its significance and artistic quality were immediately recognized. The statue has been widely published and is generally recognized as a masterpiece produced by highly skilled workers in the Middle Elamite period.[2]

The identification as Queen Napir-Asu was considerably facilitated by the Elamite inscription on the front of the skirt that in translation reads:

I, Napir-Asu, wife of Untash-Napirisha. He who would seize my statue, who would smash it, who would destroy its inscription, who would erase my name, may he be smitten by the curse of Napirisha, of Kiririsha, and of Inshushinak, that his name shall become extinct, that his offspring be barren, that the forces of Beltiya, the great goddess, shall sweep down on him. This is Napir-Asu's offering ...

---

1 J. de Morgan, *Histoire et travaux de la délégation en Perse, 1897-1905* (Paris 1905) 121; G. Lampre, *Mémoires de la délégation en Perse* 8 (Paris 1905) 245-50.

2 P. Harper, J. Aruz, and F. Tallon (edd.), *The royal city of Susa* (Exhib. Cat., The Metropolitan Museum of Art, New York 1992) 132-35, no. 83.

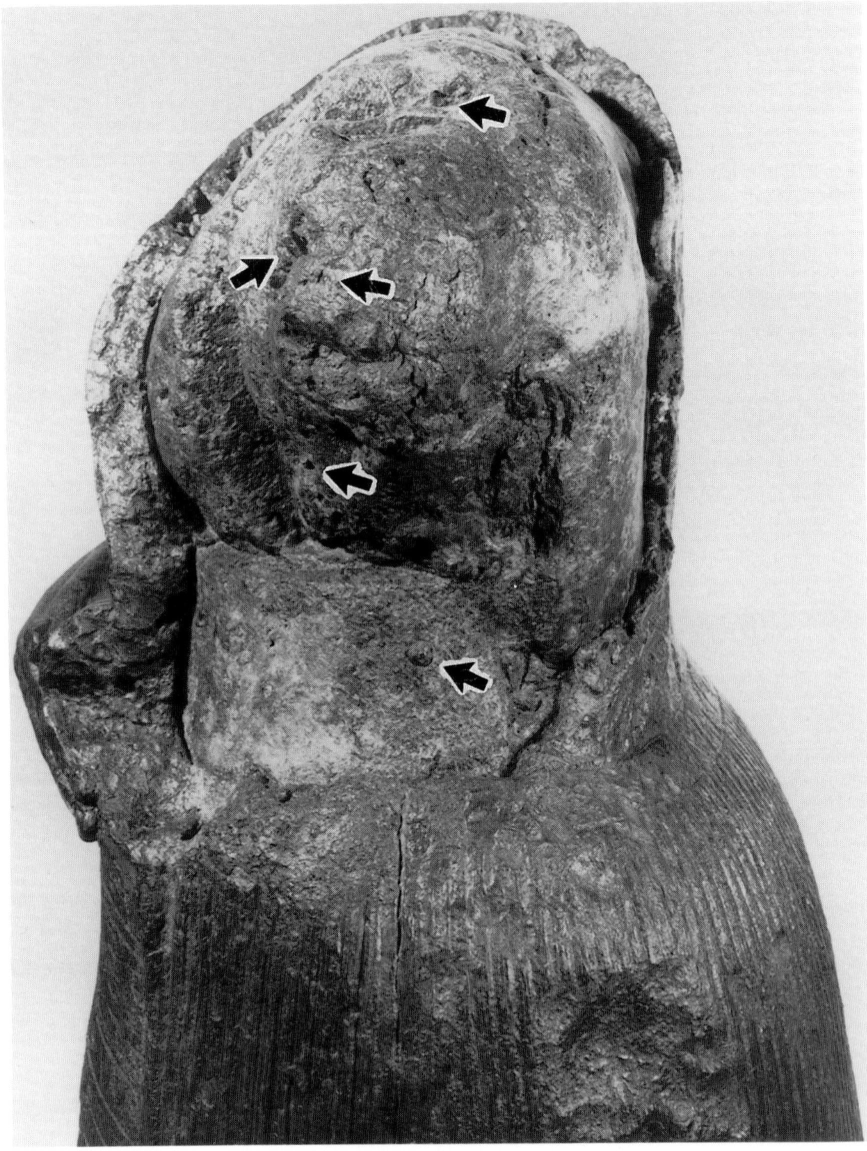

Fig. 2. View of exposed bronze core in area of left shoulder. The exterior surface is seen separated from the core with air space in between. Arrows indicate the location of chaplets (core pins). (Photo: The Metropolitan Museum of Art.)

The inscription has a special significance, since it appears to provide an explanation for part of the manufacturing process (on which see below).

The seemingly solid statue is missing its head, left arm and shoulder, and adjacent sections on the chest, neck, and back. Also missing is the bottom edge of the skirt. The losses expose a solid interior mass (core). The exterior surface, typically 2.5 cm thick, can be seen to be clearly separated from the core (fig. 2).

The tremendous weight, the presence of a metal core, the separated exterior surface, and other peculiarities indicate an unusual casting procedure. However, scholars have been unable to provide an accurate description of the casting process and have failed to explain the extraordinary weight of the statue.

The original report by the excavator states that the object was hollow-cast and then filled with metal in a second casting procedure.[3] E. Porada doubts the accuracy of this description but does not offer a clear alternative.[4] P. Amiet and J. Spycket separately claim that the statue was cast in two halves and then assembled or soldered around a metal core.[5] In the most recent publication of this statue, F. Tallon writes, "A copper outer shell seems to have been cast in the lost-wax method over a bronze core." She also mentions that elemental analysis has shown the core to be bronze, a copper-tin alloy, with an average of 11% tin, while the exterior surface contains approximately 1% tin.[6] For practical purposes, the exterior surface will be referred to as made of copper, the core of bronze.

The casting process

The author was able to examine the statue of Napir-Asu when it was exhibited at the Met-

3 De Morgan, *Histoire et travaux* (supra n.1) 121.

4 E. Porada, *The art of ancient Iran: pre-Islamic cultures* (New York 1965) 61.

5 P. Amiet, *Elam* (Auvers-sur-Oise 1966) 340, 372; A. Spycket, *La statuaire du Proche-Orient ancien* (Leiden–Cologne 1981) 313-14.

6 Harper *et al.*, *Susa* (supra n.2) 134-35.

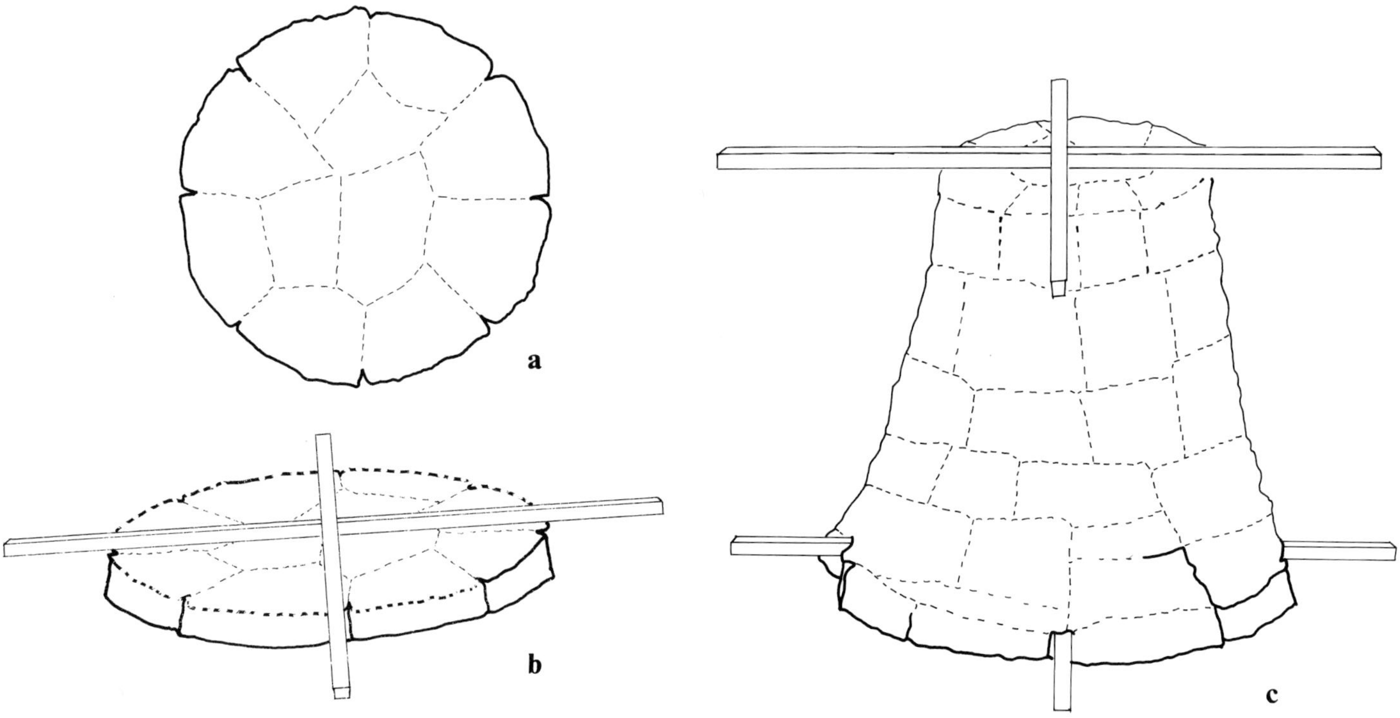

Fig. 3. Sketches of the proposed construction of the clay core. 3a. Top view of the bottom layer of clay bricks. 3b. Bottom layer of clay core bricks with two metal bars. 3c. Clay core completed halfway with two additional metal bars. 3d (overleaf) The completed core. Solid lines are based upon divisions observed on the statue's bronze core. Dotted lines are schematic, not based upon observations. (Drawings: author.)

ropolitan Museum of Art, New York (November 1992–March 1993) and to observe and document a series of technical characteristics. Together these allowed a detailed reconstruction of the casting process. Unusual as it may seem, the proposed casting procedure will be shown to be entirely consistent with the statue's function and with the words of the inscription.

Rather than listing and describing the characteristics of the statue, the proposed casting procedure will be described, with mention of the observed characteristics that support or indicate specific procedures.

The first part of the proposed procedure is a variation of the standard direct lost-wax casting process. It starts with the construction of the clay core. As a first step, a layer of clay bricks, *c.*8 cm high, was placed on a level floor (fig. 3a). On top of this, two copper or bronze bars were laid down, each square, *c.*3 x 3 cm in cross section. One was placed front to back, the other side to side (fig. 3b). Additional clay blocks were added to build up the core to a height of *c.*55 cm, when two more copper or bronze bars were added (fig. 3c). Again, they run more or less front to back and side by side: the former dips slightly from 59 cm high in front to 53 cm high in the back; the latter is off center and runs behind an imaginary left-to-right central line, from 4.5 cm on the proper right side to 13.0 cm on the proper left side. The core in the upper torso was then completed by adding more clay bricks (fig. 3d). Additional clay may have been added to fill large gaps and to smooth the core surface. Evidence for this part of the procedure is found in the outline of the ends of the four metal bars on the surface of the statue and in the brick-like structure of the bronze core as seen in the exposed sections (figs. 4-5).

The completed clay core needed to be dried and possibly fired to remove as much water as possible, as remaining moisture could cause problems in the actual casting procedure. The dried clay core was covered with wax, and the statue of Napir-Asu was modeled in wax, including the arms and hands, but without the head (see below). The thickness of the wax, typically 2.0-2.5 cm, increased to more than 10 cm for hands and feet.

Copper or bronze chaplets, 0.6 x 0.6 cm in cross section, were pushed through the wax into the clay core. Even though there are only 9 chaplets clearly visible in the sculpture, as well as two holes where chaplets were lost or removed, there must have been over 100 chaplets in order to

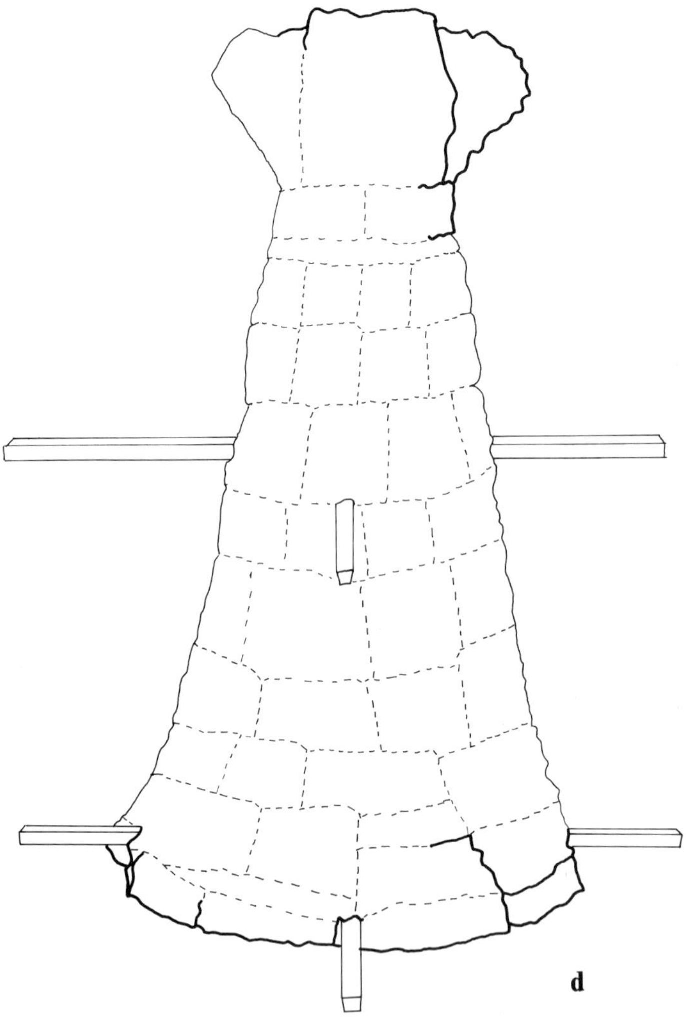

d

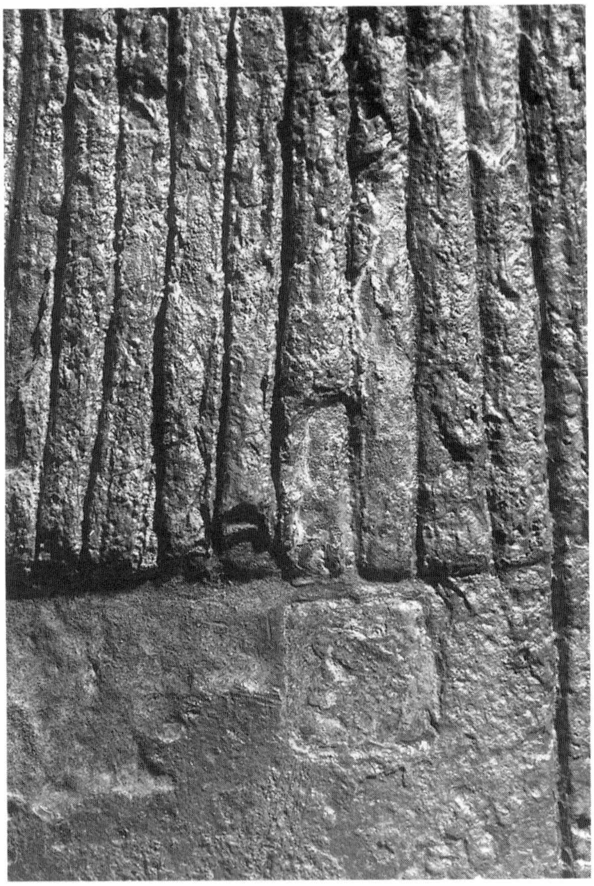

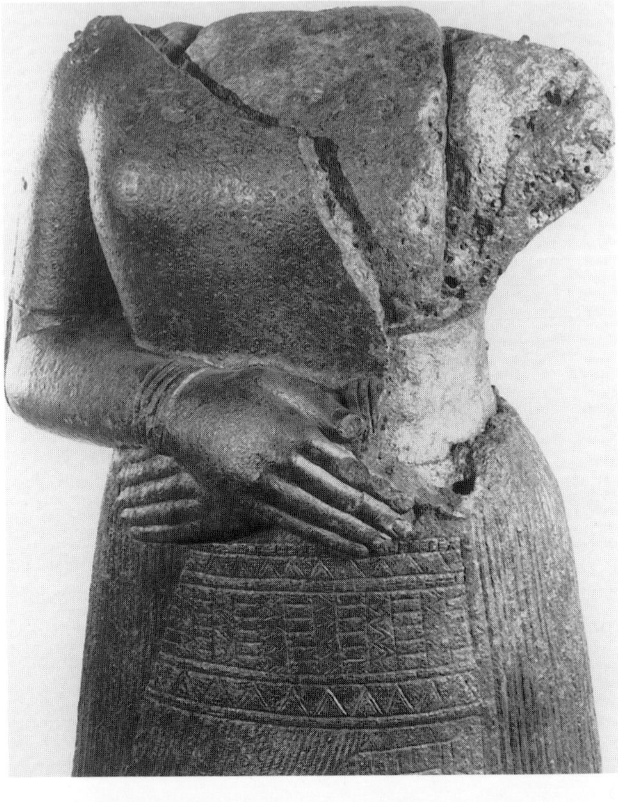

Fig. 3d (above). The completed core (see previous page).

Fig. 4 (top right). View of exposed cross section of metal bar, *c.*3.2 x 3.2 cm, on right hip.

Fig. 5 (lower right). View of exposed bronze core with three of the sections (front chest, left shoulder, and lower left side of torso) that show brick-like structure. (Photos figs. 4-5: Metropolitan Museum of Art.)

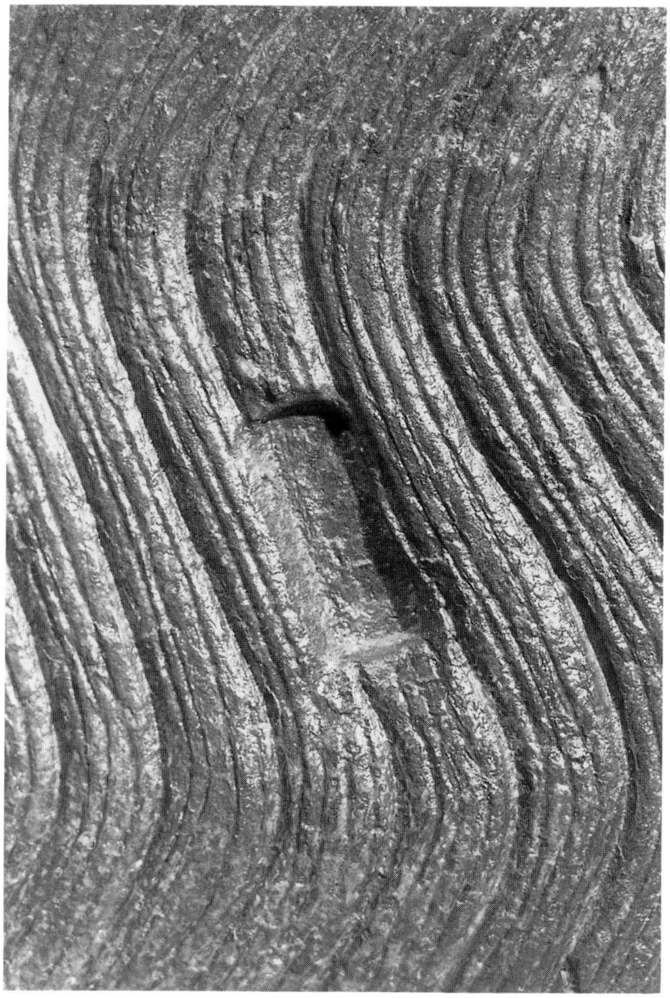

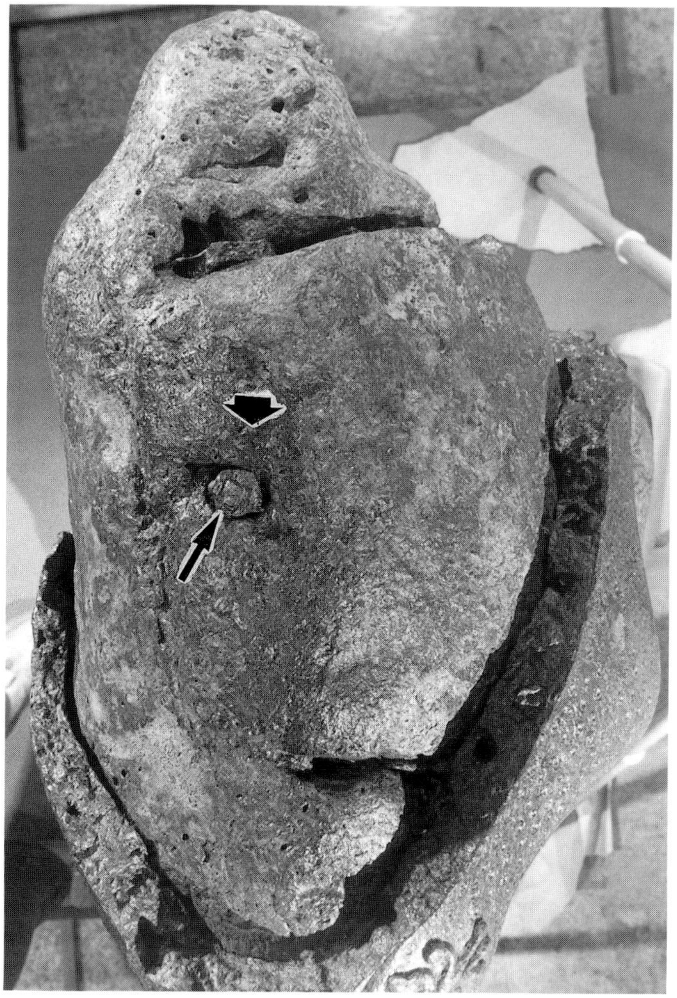

Fig. 6 (left). View of lower part of skirt on the back, showing rectangular cavity, 3.2 x 1.4 cm and 0.3 cm deep, that once held a repair patch.
Fig. 7 (right). View looking down on the top of the statue. In the center is a metal plug (arrow) with a chaplet (core pin) embedded in it (thin arrow). This configuration indicates that the head of Queen Napir-Asu was not cast integrally with the statue and suggests that a separately made head was fitted to the body before the actual casting. (Photos figs. 6-7: The Metropolitan Museum of Art.)

fix the space between core and outer investment and to hold the core in place during casting. A clay investment was built around the wax figure, and the entire assembly was placed in an oven or furnace. The molten wax was drained and/or burned, and molten copper was poured in the casting space. Since no divisions are visible, it is assumed that the casting was executed in one pouring operation or, more likely, quick consecutive pourings of molten copper.

After cooling, the usual post-casting procedures were followed, i.e., removal of the outer investment, removal of sprues and gates, cleaning, polishing of the metal surface, cutting or removal of chaplets, sharpening of details, additional decoration, and adding the inscription. Casting flaws were repaired by enlarging them to square or rectangular shapes and hammering pre-formed metal patches in the recesses (fig. 6).

At some time, either during or after the surface detailing, an unusual action was taken. The clay core was removed, the statue was turned upside-down, and the entire statue was filled with molten bronze (copper-tin alloy), probably in consecutive pourings from large crucibles. After the pouring was complete and after the bronze core had solidified and cooled, the now extremely heavy statue was set upright and moved to its place on the temple site. The 4 projecting metal bars undoubtedly facilitated the handling and movement of the statue at this point, as they had done during previous stages of its production.

Final procedures included the removal of excess metal bars and positioning and securing a separately made head of Napir-Asu (see below). Most likely, the addition of gold or silver foil and completion of surface details were also executed at this stage.

Observations and discussion

The following observations and discussion support the proposed casting procedures:

1. *Melting temperatures.* Pure copper melts at 1083° C; bronze containing 11% tin melts in the range of 810-1000° C. By pouring the lower melting bronze into the exterior copper surface, the temperature would almost certainly not go high enough to cause the two metals to fuse. Moreover, upon solidification and cooling, the bronze would shrink and separate from the exterior copper shell. This is exactly what can be observed: there is in many places a separation of up to several millimeters between the exterior copper shell and the bronze core (figs. 2 and 7).

In the alternative method, suggested by Tallon,[7] whereby the exterior copper surface would have been cast around an existing bronze core, considerable problems could be expected. The bronze core would provide a very effective heat sink for the molten copper, which would almost certainly solidify prematurely, causing major casting defects. The core would need to be heated considerably, but too high a temperature would cause partial melting of the core and result in the fusing of the exterior copper surface and the bronze core. To provide and control temperature conditions in antiquity so that a higher melting copper metal could successfully be cast around a massive bronze core would seem to be a nearly impossible task.

2. *Contour details of the bronze core.* Even though corrosion has obscured much surface detail of the bronze core, its surface contours provide a clear indication of the casting procedure. Where the core is exposed, as at the neck, shoulders, and the bottom of the skirt, the contours indicate the use of individually molded units, or bricks (figs. 5 and 7). The bronze core seems to have preserved the contours of the original clay casting core. This becomes evident when it is realized that the contours of the bronze core are defined by the interior surface of the exterior copper casting, which in turn duplicates the interior surface of the wax. Since the wax was modeled directly on the clay core, it follows that the contours of the bronze core reflect the surface structure of the clay core. The presumed use of clay bricks in the building of the core appears therefore to be well justified.

The alternative method of casting around a bronze core appears to include no reasonable explanation for the bronze core contours.

3. *Chaplets (core pins).* The use of chaplets, now firmly anchored in the bronze core, is entirely consistent with the proposed casting procedure (fig. 2). The presence of the chaplets cannot reasonably be explained by the alternative method, in which the bronze core was cast first. Moreover, they would probably not have provided sufficient support to keep the massive core in place during casting of the statue around it.

The head, as well as the area of the exterior copper surface where it would have been attached, is now missing. Nevertheless, close examination of the bronze core, just below the position of the head, provides two clues to a possible reconstruction of the manufacture or attachment method of the head. In the center of the top surface of the core, right under the location of the head, is a metal plug or rod, extending a few millimeters out of the bronze core (fig. 7). The plug is square in cross section, 1.5 x 1.5 cm, with rounded corners. In the center of the plug is what appears to be a chaplet, 0.8 x 0.6 cm. If this piece of metal is indeed a chaplet,

---

7 Ibid.

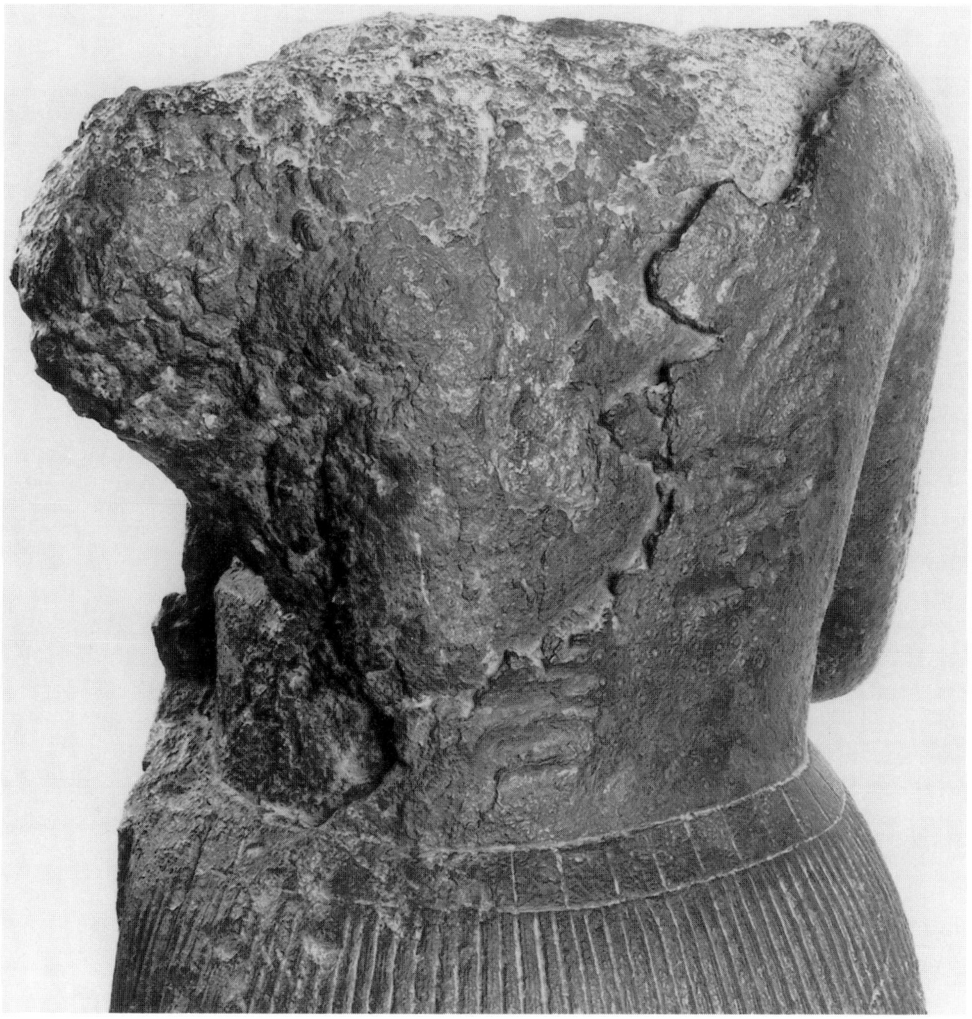

Fig. 8. View of back. Jagged upturned edges and impressions of slashes and blows may indicate vandalism, possibly associated with the forceful separation of head from body. (Photo: Metropolitan Museum of Art.)

then the statue must have been cast without a head, because the presence of a head cast integrally with the statue would not have allowed the use of a chaplet in this position.

The presence of the metal plug with an imbedded chaplet is peculiar but could be explained by the following proposed procedure. A wax model of the head, meant to be cast separately and mounted on a stick, possibly wood, needed to be placed on the wax model of the statue so that its placement, dimensions, etc., could be checked, measured, and/or adjusted. To accomplish this, a hole was made in the wax and also partially in the clay core; the head was placed on top of the body by inserting the stick in this hole. After modeling was complete and any necessary adjustments were made, the head with the stick was removed, the hole in the core filled with a clay plug, the area covered with wax, and a chaplet pushed through the wax into the clay plug. In the subsequent casting process, the wax would have been replaced by copper, and the clay core and clay plug by bronze.

Napir-Asu's head, in all likelihood, was made separately; but nothing can be said about the material from which it was made or details of its shape. The head must have been attached to the exterior copper surface at the neck and shoulders, at areas that are now missing. Since there are no marks of any kind, the method of attachment apparently did not involve the bronze core.

On the back of the right shoulder are several slashes and blows, as well as some deformations at the edges of the break that may indicate vandalism, possibly associated with the forceful separation of the head from the body (fig. 8).

A 3-mm-wide groove runs from the top of the skirt down each side to the bottom of the skirt. These grooves apparently led some scholars to believe that these were seams where two sections of the statue were fused together.[8] However, the shape and nature of these grooves, and two similar grooves that extend from the right shoulder down the right arm, are inconsistent with this theory. They closely resemble the grooves found on a number of classical bronzes where they served to hold the edges of precious metal foil (gold or silver) that was used to cover the bronze surface.[9] No silver or gold foil remains, but it seems very likely that the statue in antiquity was covered, at least in part, with gold or silver foil.

Conclusion

In addition to its remarkable aesthetic qualities, this imposing sculpture provides a wealth of information on technological issues. It is an important product from a civilization that enjoyed a highly advanced level of bronzecasting technology.

Even though no comparable bronzes have survived from the Middle Elamite period and very few large bronzes are known until classical antiquity, there is no doubt that large numbers of bronze statues were produced. Their chances of survival were simply exceedingly small. Sooner or later, most large bronzes were destroyed so that the metal could be re-used. Only in China, where ceremonial bronzes were placed in tombs, have sufficient numbers of large bronzes survived to make systematic studies of bronze technology possible. In the ancient Near East and the Mediterranean areas, no such systematic studies of large bronzes are feasible until the 5th c. B.C. and later. Studying surviving examples in combination with literary evidence and pertinent depictions on vases has resulted in a reasonably accurate, albeit incomplete, understanding of bronzecasting technology in the classical period in Greece and Rome.

Study of the statue of Napir-Asu has allowed us a glimpse into the highly developed bronzecasting technology of the Middle Elamite period. Not only was hollow lost-wax casting fully developed for large bronzes, but high temperatures also could be reached and maintained for very large batches of copper and bronze and for the casting process of large statues. The use of a bronze core in a hollow copper casting may be unique, but at the same time it is a strong indication of advanced knowledge of melting temperatures as a function of alloy compositions. Decoration techniques and repair methods (such as the use of rectangular patches to repair casting flaws) are essentially identical to those observed in Greek and Roman bronzes. Of course, there are differences: there is, for example, no evidence before the Classical period of the use of indirect lost-wax casting, nor of the extensive use of joining and welding of separately made parts.

The statue of Napir-Asu appears to have survived in part because it was deliberately made too heavy for thieves to remove it from its temple site. The inscription provides an important clue to the excessive weight of the statue. The curse implies a problem of theft and vandalism, which is not surprising considering the significant intrinsic value of copper and bronze. The curse by itself may not have been sufficient to prevent the statue from disappearing, but deliberately increasing the weight of the statue so that it could not be easily moved may have kept the statue in place. Whether or not this was the only reason for pouring the large amount of bronze in the statue cannot be proven, but the fact that the statue remained for more than 3,200 years at its original site, even though the head disappeared, demonstrates that the combination of the curse and the weight may have been extremely effective.

Los Angeles County Museum of Art, Conservation Center, 5905 Wilshire Blvd, Los Angeles

---

8 Amiet, *Elam* (supra n.5) 340-72; Spycket, *Statuaire* (supra n.5) 313-14.

9 See Paterakis, below p. 173 ff. and Sharpe, below p. 250 ff.

Sources of metals at Olympia: the Geometric period

Tamsey K. Andrews

This paper proposes sources for the copper, lead, and tin that supplied bronzecasters at the Greek sanctuary of Olympia from the late 9th c. B.C. to the early 7th c. B.C.

During the first systematic excavations at Olympia, carried out by German scholars between 1875 and 1881, out of *c.*14,000 artifacts recovered, some 7,500 were bronzes from the Geometric period.[1] Excavators in the 20th c. have discovered more Geometric bronzes. Excavation reports and studies published between 1890 and 1992 suggest that between 9,000 and 10,000 additional Geometric bronzes have been recovered at Olympia altogether.[2] Although these numbers are very high, the excavators from 1875 to the present have been unanimous in their belief that this represents only a fraction of the original quantities of bronzes.

The two largest categories of Geometric bronze dedications at Olympia are figurines and tripods. The figurines are primarily cattle and horses, but they also include small numbers of deer, birds, male charioteers, chariots, and chariot parts such as yokes and wheels.[3] A few of the figurines have been analyzed, and these are made of copper or of tin bronze.[4] The earliest figurines date to the late 9th or early 8th c. B.C., and tin bronze first appears at the beginning of the 8th c. B.C. when chemical analysis found more than 4% tin in bull figurine Br 1069, attributed to the local Argive-Olympian workshop and dated by W.-D. Heilmeyer to the first quarter of the 8th c.[5]

Solid-cast tripods of leaded copper appear at Olympia by the end of the 9th c. B.C. and are soon joined by the relief-decorated type, attributed to Argive bronzecasters.[6] A third solid-cast type attributed to a Corinthian workshop first appears at Olympia in the mid 8th c.; evidence for its on-site manufacture is inconclusive. A fourth type appearing in the mid 8th c. has hammered sheet-metal legs and cast cauldrons and struts between the cauldron sides and the legs, as well as cast handles and handle attachments. This type is attributed to an Athenian workshop and is identified by its hammered elements.[7] The hammered sheet-metal tripods are made of tin bronze.[8] All four tripod types are also known in miniature models at Olympia.

A third major category of Geometric bronzes found at Olympia consists of personal jewelry and dress accessories.[9] This is a substantial collection, outstanding for its typological variety and sites of origin which include Macedonia, Balkan Europe, and Central Italy. Objects include pins and fibulae, finger-rings and armbands, pendants, and an assortment of clothing accessories such as sheet-metal belts and sheet-metal decorative applications for belts.[10]

---

1 A. Mallwitz, *Olympia und seine Bauten* (Munich 1972) 9; T. Andrews, *Bronzecasting at Geometric period Olympia and early Greek metals sources* (diss., Ann Arbor 1994) 54, n.55.

2 Andrews, ibid. 54-57.

3 A. Furtwängler, *Die Bronzen und die übrigen kleineren Funde von Olympia* (Berlin 1890); W.-D. Heilmeyer, *Frühe Olympische Bronzefiguren. Die Tiervotive* (Berlin 1979). Heilmeyer (p. 14) counted 65 human figurines *versus* 4,042 bronze animal statuettes.

4 Furtwängler, *Bronzen* (supra n.3) 29; Heilmeyer, *Tiervotive* (supra n.3) 276-83 for analytical results of 19 figurines.

5 Heilmeyer, *Tiervotive* (supra n.3) 277.

6 M. Maass, *Die geometrischen Dreifüsse von Olympia* (*OlF* 10, Berlin 1978).

7 Ibid., esp. 68, 94 ff.

8 G. Varufakis, "Vorbericht über metallurgische Untersuchungen," in ibid. 133-34.

9 I. Kilian-Dirlmeier, *Anhänger in Griechenland von der mykenischen bis zur spätgeometrischen Zeit* (Munich 1979); H. Philipp, *Bronzeschmuck aus Olympia* (Berlin 1981); I. Kilian-Dirlmeier, "Bronzeanhänger der geometrischen und archaischen Zeit," in Philipp, *Bronzeschmuck* 345-77.

10 B. Fellmann, *Frühe Olympische Gürtelschmuckscheiben aus Bronze* (Berlin 1984); Philipp, *Bronzeschmuck*

Studies by Heilmeyer of all the bronze animals at Olympia[11] and by J.-L. Zimmermann of the bronze horses[12] have established that the majority of these figurines were made at Olympia by the local sanctuary workshop and by resident branch workshops from other Peloponnesian sanctuary foundries. Heilmeyer identified bronzes made at Olympia by resident Argive and Laconian workshops. Zimmermann redefined Heilmeyer's local Olympian workshop as 'Elean' and subdivided it into workshops from Triphylia, Pisatis, and Elis.[13] He also expanded Heilmeyer's list of resident branch workshops to include Messenia, Arcadia, and Athens, and identified a number of stylistically mixed workshop groups such as Argive-Arcadian, Arcadian-Elean, and Laconian-Olympian.

F. Willemsen[14] and M. Maass[15] concluded that the bronze tripods, like the figurines, were cast mainly on site by Olympian and Argive craftsmen.[16] Evidence cited by Zimmermann for on-site casting of bronze figurines by a resident Athenian workshop implies that an undetermined percentage of the Athenian-style hammered sheet-metal tripods found at Olympia, with their ornamental figurine attachments, were made on site as well.[17]

In summary, Geometric Olympia was a vast repository of lead-copper and tin-bronze votive figurines and tripods whose original numbers probably greatly exceeded the extant collection of between 9,000 and 10,000 items. The majority of them were made on site by Elean craftsmen and by masters of resident branch workshops from every major and most minor Peloponnesian sites who came to Olympia specifically to cast bronze at the sanctuary. What were the sources of copper, lead, and tin that supplied Olympia's foundries?

I propose that processed copper, lead, and tin were imported by Olympia's sanctuary officials and stockpiled for use at the sanctuary. If a Geometric sanctuary was an *oikos* of the gods, then it was as self-sufficient as its more mundane counterparts described in Homer. In the *oikos*, any specialized craftwork requiring skill beyond the ordinary was carried out by itinerant journeymen who furnished tools and knowledge but not raw materials.[18] It is not likely that the craftsmen who worked at Olympia's branch workshops brought their metal with them, given the Homeric model for journeymen and also taking into account the considerable weight of ready-made bronze or its components and the quantities required at Olympia.[19]

Olympia, however, is not close to sources of copper or lead even within the Peloponnesos, and in any case tin would have had to be imported.[20] The theory that copper from Cyprus, lead from Laurion, and tin from the Near East supported all Geometric Greek bronzemaking does not work well for Olympia. Olympia is part of a northwest Greek and Adriatic *koiné* with few Eastern connections until the Late Geometric period.[21] Contact with Athens begins in the mid 8th c., fifty years after the onset of lead-copper tripod casting at Olympia. Contact with Cyprus is not well attested among Olympia's Geometric artifacts. There is nothing in the published evidence to indicate that Cyprus supplied the copious amounts of copper that were the

---

(supra n.9); W. Kaspar, *Die Buckelverzierten Bleche Olympias* (Ludwig-Maximilians-Universität zu München 1972).

11 Heilmeyer, *Tiervotive* (supra n.3); id., "Giessereibetriebe in Olympia," *JdI* 84 (1969) 1-28.

12 J.-L. Zimmermann, *Les chevaux de bronze dans l'art géométrique grec* (Mainz 1989).

13 Ibid. 63, n.4; 65, n.13; 88.

14 F. Willemsen, *Dreifusskessel von Olympia* (Berlin 1957).

15 Maass, *Dreifüsse* (supra n.6).

16 Arguments summarized in Andrews, *Bronzecasting* (supra n.1) chapt. 3 passim.

17 Zimmermann, *Chevaux* (supra n.12) 88, 289 ff.

18 Homer's *demioergoi* of *Od.* 17.382-85 include journeymen carpenters whom we have no reason to suppose carried their wood around with them.

19 Andrews, *Bronzecasting* (supra n.1) 155-57, for an attempt to calculate amounts of bronze at Geometric Olympia.

20 Arguments summarized in Andrews, *Bronzecasting* (supra n.1) chapt. 5 passim.

21 H.-V. Herrmann, *Die Kessel der Orientalisierenden Zeit.* vol. I (Berlin 1966); 2 (Berlin 1979).

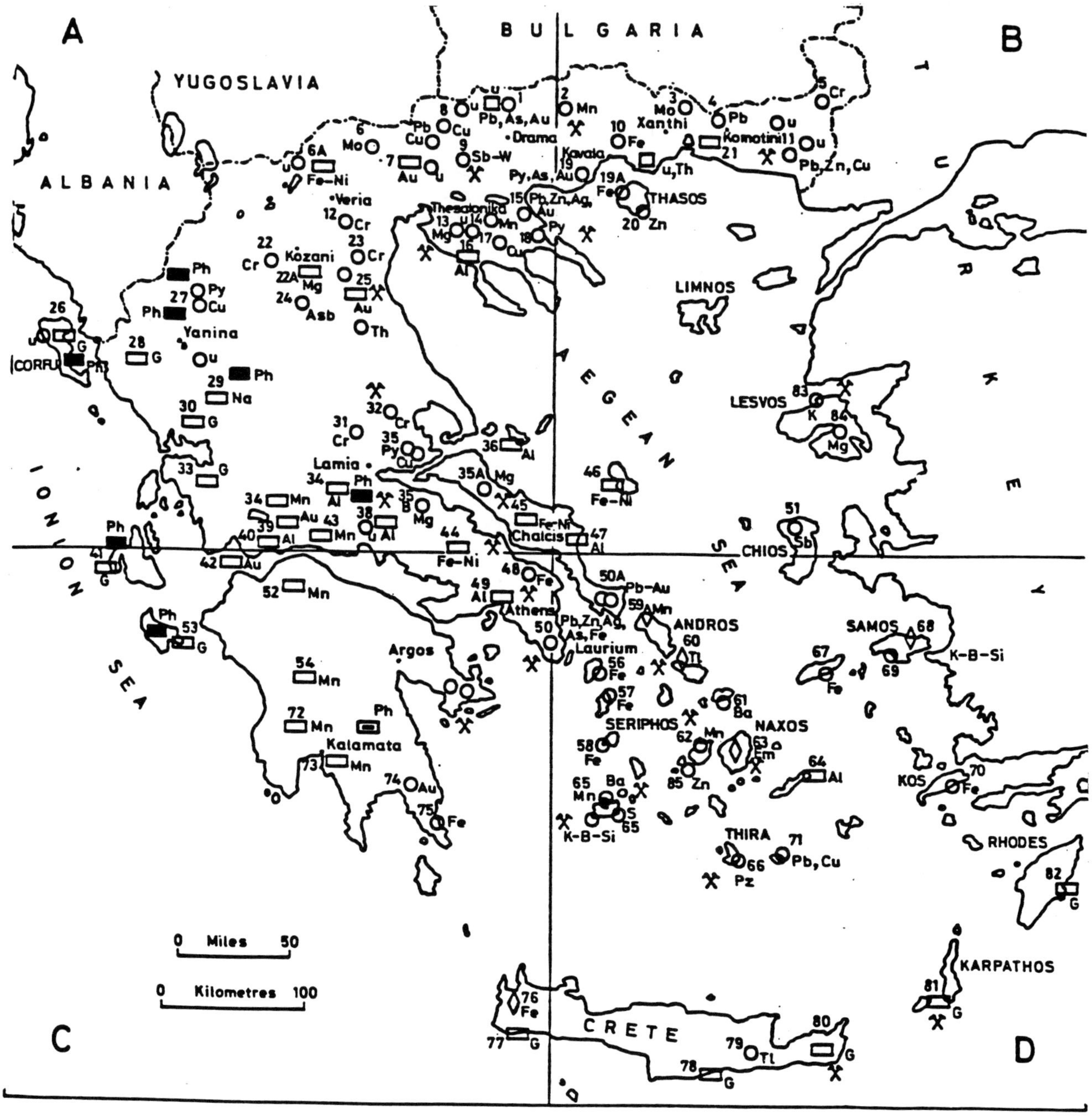

The principal mineral deposits of Greece. Al, aluminium; As, arsenic; Asb, asbestos; Au, gold; B, bentonite; Ba, barytes; Cr, chromite; Cu, copper; Em, emery; Fe, iron; G, gypsum; K, potash; Mg, magnesite; Mn, manganese; Mo, molybdenum; Na, salt; Ni, nickel; Pb, lead; Ph, phosphate; Py, pyrite; Pz, pozzuolana; Sb, antimony; Si, amorphous silica; Th, thorium; Tl, talc; U, uranium; W, tungsten; Zn, zinc

- ○ Deposits genetically connected with igneous rocks or with igneous activity
- ▭ Sedimentary, detrital, residual, weathering and placer deposits
- ◊ Metamorphic deposits
- ⚒ Operating mine
- ■ Phosphate—low grade
- ▣ Phosphate—high grade
- ○ □ (u, Th) Uraniferous rocks

Fig. 1. Principal mineral deposits of Greece. (Map: reproduced by permission from G. Marinos, "Greece," in F. W. Dunning *et al.* [edd.], *Mineral deposits of Europe. 2. Southeast Europe* [London 1982] 237.)

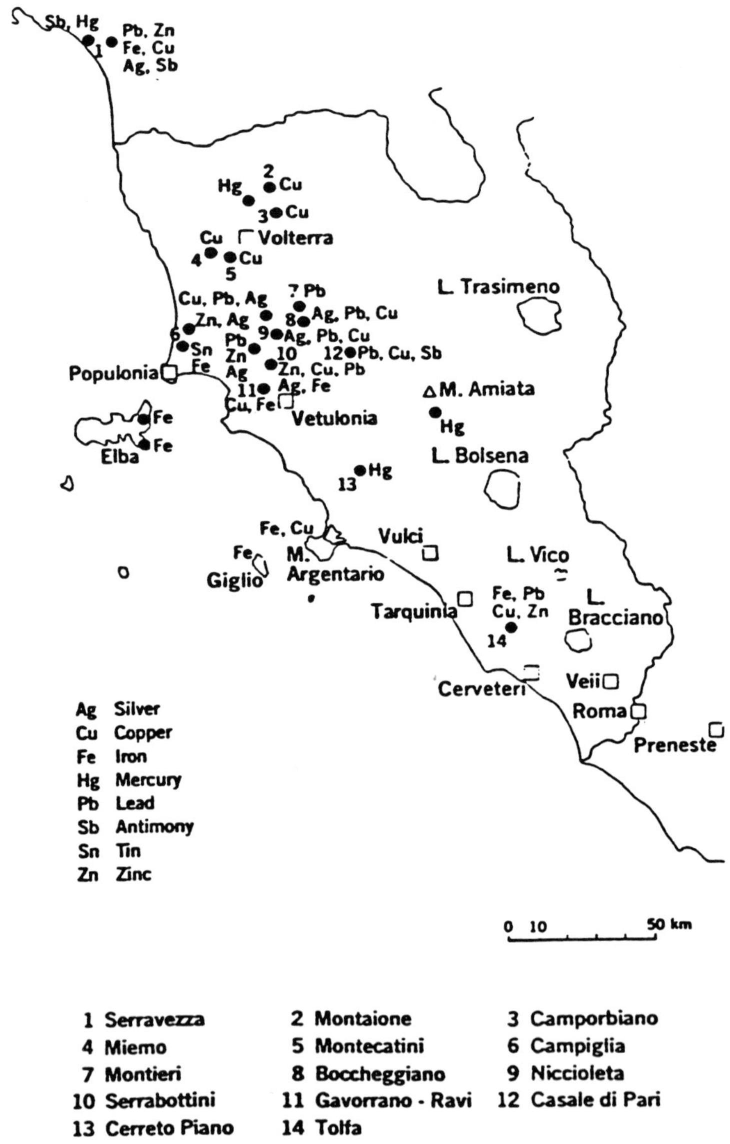

Fig. 2. Distribution of mineral deposits in Etruria. (Map: reproduced by permission of G. Markoe, Cincinnati Art Museum, from G. Markoe, "In pursuit of metal: Phoenicians and Greeks in Italy," in G. Kopcke and I. Tokumaru [edd.], *Greece between East and West: 10th-8th c. B.C.* [Mainz 1992] 71.)

mainstay of Olympia's bronze industry from the late 9th c. onward. Finally, the theory that tin was imported to Olympia from somewhere in the Near East contradicts Olympia's clearly western orientation and is not supported by any significant, published artifactual evidence at any time in Olympia's Geometric period.[22]

There are significant deposits of copper and lead in northern Greece and Balkan Europe (fig. 1), and of copper, lead, and tin in Etruria (fig. 2). I propose that these sources supplied early Olympia, certainly until the Late Geometric period when contacts with Athens and the Eastern Mediterranean were secure, and probably even later as part of an array of sources supplying the increasingly pan-Hellenic sanctuary. The evidence is the presence at Olympia of exceptional numbers of imported bronze personal adornments whose sites of origin overlap the sources of copper and lead — and tin to a lesser extent — in these regions.

The Olympia collection of bronze personal adornments and dress accessories consists almost entirely of objects not made on site.[23] Olympia leads all other Geometric sanctuaries in

22 Andrews, *Bronzecasting* (supra n.1) chapt. 5 passim, esp. 168-71.

23 Philipp, *Bronzeschmuck* (supra n.9); Kilian-Dirlmeier 1981 (supra n.9) 345-77; Andrews, *Bronzecasting*

imported items of this class which originate from Balkan Europe, northern Greece, and central Italy. These appeared at Olympia throughout the Geometric period, beginning in the early part.[24] The northern personal jewelry, including more than 100 votive belt discs, has been well documented.[25] The principal sites of origin are Thessaly, Chalcidice, and the culturally contiguous regions of northern Macedonia and the southern Balkans, particularly Bulgaria and the former Yugoslavia. These are regions rich in deposits of copper and lead (fig. 1)[26] and cassiterite tin.[27] I propose that this overlap is not coincidental, and that it indicates ongoing relations between Olympia and its northern suppliers of metals.[28]

Less well known are the bronze personal dedications of Italian style and origin that occur at Olympia in the Geometric period more frequently than at any other Greek sanctuary, beginning in the 9th c. B.C.[29] Among these are armor and weapons, mostly unique to Olympia, dating to the first and second quarters of the 8th c. These include a ridged, conical helmet with a pointed crest dated Villanovan Ib;[30] the bronze blade of a central Italian thrusting lance, 0.98 m long, of the first half of the 8th c.;[31] and part of a greave, of the type with rings for thongs along the edges, dated to the early 8th c.[32] Both Kilian and Herrmann see these and other early Italian finds at Olympia as evidence of an aggressive push by Greeks into Etruscan territory, prior to colonization, in a contest for access to the metal sources in the *colline metallifere* of central Tuscany.[33]

Italian bronze jewelry, armor, and weapons, therefore, begin appearing at Olympia simultaneously with the production of solid-cast lead-copper tripods by sanctuary craftsmen in the early 8th c. At the same time, or very soon after, on-site production of bronze figurines by the sanctuary workshop and the Argive branch workshop began. I propose that the concurrence of these events is not coincidental and that Olympia was benefiting directly from Greek success in obtaining access to central Tuscan metal sources. I conclude, then, that central Italy, northern Greece, and the southern Balkans were the most likely areas of origin for the copper, lead, and tin used for bronzecasting at Olympia, certainly in the first half of the 8th c. B.C. and probably together with Eastern Mediterranean sources in the second half of that century. I hope that future analytical studies of Olympia bronzes will specifically test this hypothesis through lead isotope analyses that include within their research designs questions concerning these sites of origin for Olympia's metals.

Ferris State University, Big Rapids, Michigan 49307

(supra n.1) 173 ff.

24 Philipp, *Bronzeschmuck* (supra n.9) 14-15; Kilian-Dirlmeier, *Anhänger* (supra n.9) 3.

25 Kilian-Dirlmeier, *Anhänger* (supra n.9); Philipp, *Bronzeschmuck* (supra n.9); Fellmann, *Gürtelschmuckscheiben* (supra n.10); K. Kilian, *Trachtzubehör der Eisenzeit zwischen Ägäis und Adria* (Munich 1975); K. Kilian, "Bosnisch-Herzegowinische Bronzen der Eisenzeit II aus Griechenland," *Gdisnjak Akademija Nauka i Umjetnosti Bosne i Hercegovine* 13 (1976) 163-71.

26 F. Dunning *et al.* (edd.), *Mineral deposits of Europe. 2: Southeast Europe* (London 1982) 144, fig. 1; 217, fig. 2.

27 Nine sites in Romania and the former Yugoslavia: V. McGeehan-Liritzis and J. Taylor, "Yugoslavian tin deposits and the Early Bronze Age industries of the Aegean region," *OJA* 6.3 (1987) 287-300; P. Glumac, *The advent of metallurgy in prehistoric southeast Europe* (Ann Arbor 1991) 65 ff.; Andrews, *Bronzecasting* (supra n.1) 167 ff.

28 Andrews, *Bronzecasting* (supra n.1) chapt. 5.

29 Philipp, *Bronzeschmuck* (supra n.9) 15, 286; K. Kilian, "Zum italischen und griechischen Fibelhandwerk des 8. und 7. Jahrhunderts," *HBA* 3.1 (1973) 1-33.

30 H.-V. Herrmann, "Altitalisches und Etruskisches in Olympia," *Atti del Convegno Internazionale Grecia, Italia e Sicilia nell' VIII e VII secolo a.C., Atene 15-20 ottobre* 1979, vol. 3 (1983) 271-94; K. Kilian, "Zwei italische Kammhelme aus Griechenland," *BCH* suppl. 4 (1977) 429-42.

31 Herrmann 1983 (supra n.27) 282-83 n.15; Kilian 1977 (supra n.30) fig. 4a; H. Weber, "Angriffswaffen," *OlF* 1 (1944) 146-65.

32 Kaspar, *Buckelverzierten* (supra n.10) no. 213, 94 ff.; Herrmann 1983 (supra n.30) 279-82.

33 Herrmann 1983 (supra n.30) 288; Kilian 1977 (supra n.30) 438.

Female figurines on Greek Geometric bronze tripods

Susan Langdon

The bronze tripod is the quintessential symbol of the Greek Geometric period, a transcendent image of competition, ostentatious wealth, and divine favor. Its ancestry in Mycenaean cooking pots suggests a uniquely Greek phenomenon in an age that appears increasingly orientalizing when viewed through the lens of recent scholarship. The tripod's heroic horse-and-warrior decoration and sheer monumentality, in some cases reaching 2 m tall, made it the most conspicuous votive offering seen in sanctuaries and, in a nearly image-free society, certainly the most memorable object 8th-c. worshippers ever laid eyes on. Proof of the tripod's visual and iconic power lies in its enduring symbolic rôle in Greek life through Hellenistic times, long after the original function of the object was forgotten and actual tripods of Geometric type had ceased to be manufactured.[1]

The horseleaders and spearbearers who grace handles and rims are inseparable from the tripod's meaning, even though their identities remain enigmatic. Scholars have claimed them to be Zeus, Pelops, unnamed heroes, mortal victors of chariot races, and aristocratic 'knights' with their horses.[2] These attachments have been instrumental in defining Geometric tripods wholly within the parameters of a competitive male world. My point of departure here is a group of female handle attachments that, although part of the archaeological record for as long as the male figures, have been excluded from previous discussions of the meaning and function of early Greek tripods. Some of the figures have, in fact, been noted as possible attachments, but their significance in comprising a female element in the larger system of tripod iconography has gone unremarked. A review of their historiography reveals past biases and approaches that led to their exclusion from assessments of tripods and, hence, from the canon of major Geometric works.[3] I shall attempt to redress the situation by examining the Geometric tripod cauldrons in light of this overlooked clue to their cultural significance.

Five female bronze figurines can be assigned to 5 tripods from 4 sanctuaries and can be listed in approximately chronological order as follows:

1. From the Apollo sanctuary at Delphi, an abstract nude with polos, hands against thighs (fig. 1).[4] Delphi Museum inv. 7730. Excavated 1939 on the Sacred Way between the base of the Boeotians and the opposite exedra; found with Corinthian pottery datable to 750-725 B.C. H. 16.5 cm; base 2 x 2.5 cm. Apparently complete but with corroded surface. Standing nude figure with small breasts; flat uptilted face with projecting nose and ears; chin-length hair; flat-topped headgear. Rectangular plaque under feet.

---

1 On the later life of the Geometric tripod form, see P. Amandry, "Sièges mycéniens tripodes et trépied pythique," *Φίλια ἔπη εἰς Γεώργιον Ε. Μυλωνᾶν* (Athens 1986) 167-84.

2 E. Kunze, "Zeusbilder in Olympia," *AuA* 2 (1946) 95-107; H.-V. Herrmann, "Pelops in Olympia," in *ΣΤΗΛΗ. Τόμος εἰς μνήμην τοῦ Νικολάου Κοντολέοντος* (Athens 1980) 59-74, esp. 70-74; M. Byrne, *The Greek Geometric warrior figurine: interpretation and origin* (Archaeologia Transatlantica X, Louvain-la-Neuve 1991) 40-47.

3 S. Langdon, "Significant others: the male-female pair in Greek Geometric art," *AJA* 102 (1998) 251-70.

4 P. Amandry, "Petits objets de Delphes," *BCH* 68-69 (1944-45) 36-74 at 38-39, pl. I; H.-V. Herrmann, "Werkstätten geometrischer Bronzeplastik," *JdI* 79 (1964) 17-71 at 48, figs. 33-35; N. Himmelmann-Wildschütz, *Bemerkungen zur geometrischen Plastik* (Berlin 1964) figs. 31-33; B. Schweitzer, *Greek geometric art* (London 1969) pls. 130-31; C. Rolley, *Monuments figurés, les statuettes de bronze* (*FdD* V.1, Paris 1969) 17, 19-26, no. 1; and review by P. Kranz, in *Gnomon* 45 (1973) 474-83 at 479; J. N. Coldstream, *Geometric Greece* (London 1977) 176, fig. 58c; M. Maass, *Die geometrischen Dreifüsse von Olympia* (*OlF* 10, Berlin 1978) 101; J. Floren, *Die geometrische und archaische Plastik* (Munich 1987) 48; S. Böhm, *Die 'Nackte Göttin'* (Mainz 1990) 151, B3, pl. 10b; Byrne 1991 (supra n.2) 49, 53, 231 no. 1.

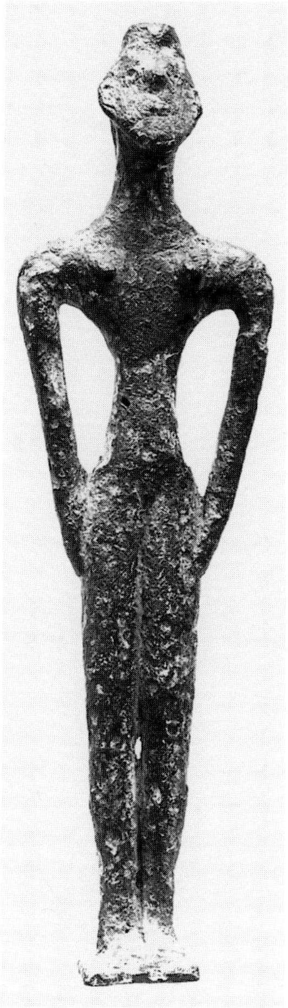

Fig. 1. Bronze figure from Delphi. Delphi Museum inv. 7730. (Photo: courtesy École française d'archéologie.)

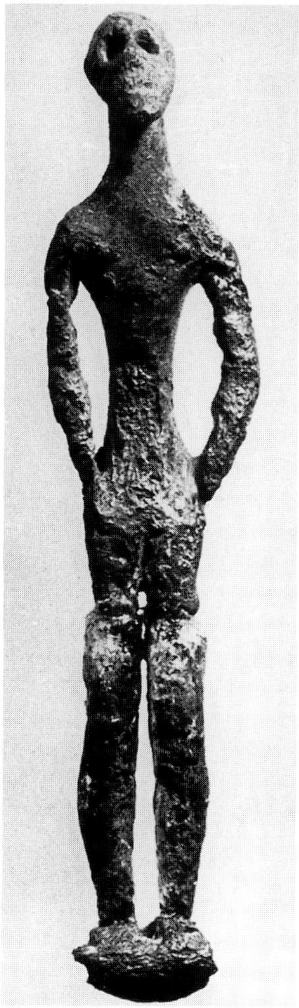

Fig. 2. Bronze figure from the Polis Cave, Ithaca. Stavros Museum. (Photo: courtesy Marburg Archäologisches Seminar.)

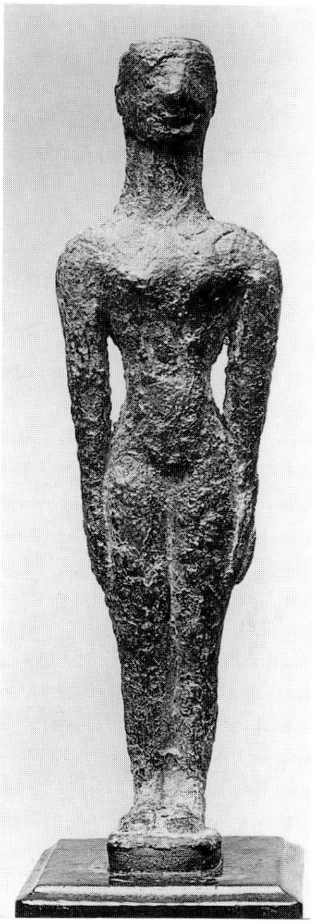

Fig. 3. Bronze figure from the Athenian Acropolis. Athens NM 6503. (Photo: courtesy DAI Athens, Neg. N.M. 3412.)

2. From the Polis Cave on Ithaca, a round-shouldered version in the same pose (fig. 2).[5] Ithaca, Stavros Museum. Excavated in 1932 in Polis area C-3. Legs broken above the knees, feet broken at ankles. H. 13 cm. Standing nude figure with hands against thighs; small breasts; uptilted face with pointed chin, hollowed eyes. Attachment plaque under feet.[6]

3. From the Athenian Acropolis, a third figure in the hands-against-thighs pose, with a more fully modeled body (fig. 3).[7] Athens, National Museum inv. 6503. From excavations of 1885-89. H. 15.8 cm; w. at shoulders

5 S. Benton, "Excavations in Ithaca III," *BSA* 35 (1934-35) 45-73 at 61 fig. 12, 62-63 no. 15, pl. 16; id., "The evolution of the tripod-lebes," *BSA* 35 (1934-35) 74-130 at 86; Herrmann 1964 (supra n.4) 48, 49 n.132; Himmelmann-Wildschütz, *Bermerkungen* (supra n.4) figs. 28-30; Schweitzer, *Geometric* (supra n.4) pls. 128-29; Rolley, *Monuments* (supra n.4) 19 n.5; id., *Les trépieds à cuve clouée* (*FdD* V.3, Paris 1977) 64 n.2; Coldstream, *Geometric* (supra n.4) 176; Floren, *Plastik* (supra n.4) 66 n.331; Böhm, *'Nackte Göttin'* (supra n.4) 152, B11, pl. 10d; Byrne 1991 (supra n.2) 141, 246 no. 13.

6 Some scholars have maintained that the legs, which are significantly thicker than the rest of the body, belong to a second figure: N. Himmelmann-Wildschütz, "Die Lanzenschwinger-Bronzen Olympia B 1701 und 1999," *AA* (1974) 538-44 at 540 n.16; Floren, *Plastik* (supra n.4) 66 n.331; Böhm 1990 (supra n.4) n.152. However, a photo of the figure taken before cleaning reveals evenly proportioned upper and lower parts and parallel breaks: see Benton, "Excavations" 1934-35 (supra n.5) 61 fig. 12.

7 A. de Ridder, *Catalogue des bronzes trouvés sur l'Acropole d'Athènes* (Paris 1896) iv-v, 293 no. 771, 294 fig. 279; Herrmann 1964 (supra n.4) 49-50, figs. 36-38; Himmelmann-Wildschütz, *Bemerkungen* (supra n.4) 16, figs. 34-36; M. Weber, "Zu frühen attischen Gerätfiguren," *AthMitt* 89 (1974) 27-46 at 43;

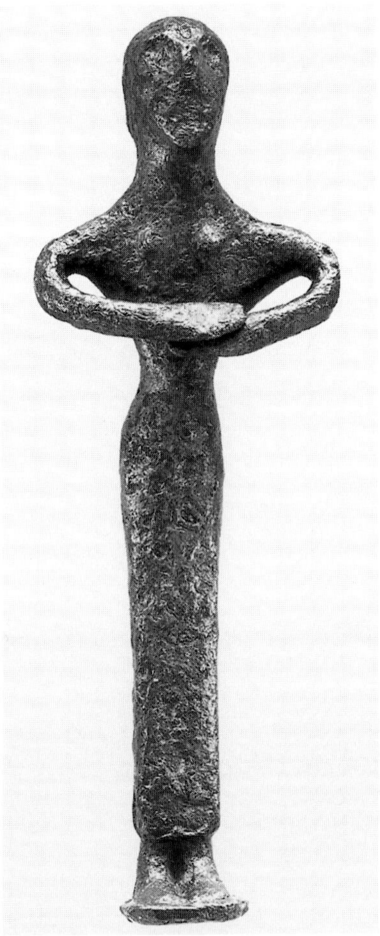

Fig. 4. Bronze figure from Delphi. Delphi Museum Inv. 3144. (Photo: courtesy École française d'archéologie.)

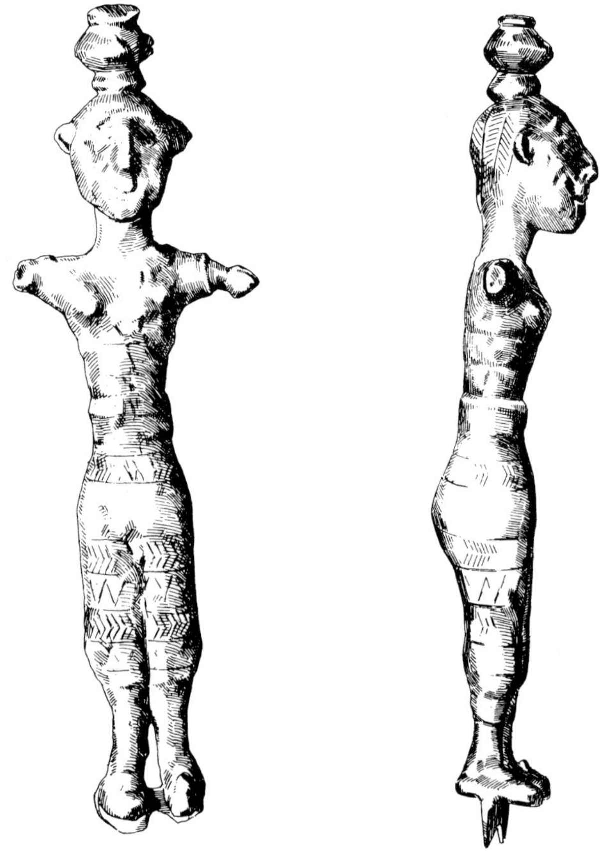

Fig. 5. Bronze figure from Olympia. Olympia Br 12607, Athens NM 6218. (Photo: after *Olympia Ergebnisse* IV [Berlin 1890] pl. 15 no. 266.)

4.45 cm; base 2.4 x 2.1 cm. Complete, but surface heavily corroded. Standing nude figure with arms and hands against thighs; modeled body with swelling breasts and abdomen; modeled lips, ears, nose; shoulder-length hair. Rectangular plaque under feet.

4. From the Apollo sanctuary at Delphi, a figure in an ankle-length robe with hands clasped together (fig. 4).[8] Delphi Museum inv. 3144. Excavated 1895 near the baths. H. 19.6 cm. Apparently complete, surface pitted. Standing figure with arms curved to front and hands riveted together at waist height; small breasts; face with long chin, indented eyes, nose curving in single line from brow; hair hangs to nape of neck; undecorated robe. Rectangular plaque under feet.

5. From Olympia, figure clad in a decorated robe and bearing a vessel-like object on head (fig. 5).[9] Olympia Br 12607; Athens, National Museum inv. 6218. From the 1875-81 excavations in the black layer north of the Prytaneion. H. 12.9 cm; w. at arms 3.9 cm; w. at feet 1.75 cm. Wiry arms broken at shoulders, apparently with right arm raised, left turned down; large head with modeled ears, nose, eyes, brows, hairline, and incised

---

Rolley 1977 (supra n.5) 101 n.3; Floren, *Plastik* (supra n.4) 42, pl. 3, 7; Böhm, *'Nackte Göttin'* (supra n.4) 151, B1, pl. 10a.

8 P. Perdrizet, *Monuments figurés, petits bronzes, terracuites, antiquités diverses* (*FdD* V, Paris 1908) no. 2; Herrmann 1964 (supra n.4) 49; Schweitzer, *Geometric* (supra n.4) fig. 124; Rolley, *Monuments* (supra n.4) 28-29, no. 8; Kranz 1973 (supra n.4) 479; Weber 1974 (supra n.7) 43; Coldstream, *Geometric* (supra n.4) 127 fig. 40, 128; Floren, *Plastik* (supra n.4) 54; Byrne, *Figurine* (supra n.2) 232 no. 35.

9 A. Furtwängler, *Die Bronzen* (*Olympia Ergebnisse* IV, Berlin 1890) no. 266, pl. 15; V. Müller, *Frühe Plastik in Griechenland und Kleinasien* (Augsburg 1929) 71, 86, 168, pl. 24, 300-1; U. Gehrig, *Die geometrischen Bronzen aus dem Heraion von Samos* (Hamburg 1964) 22 n.3; Herrmann 1964 (supra n.4) 43 n.118; Byrne, *Figurine* (supra n.2) 24-25, 229 no. 65.

mouth; biconical object on top of head; herringbone-incised hair hangs to shoulders in back; robe decorated below breasts with 10 bands of incised zigzags, dots, and hatches. Vertical tab under feet.

The key to recognizing these 5 figures as tripod ornaments is their clear means of attachment by horizontal (nos. 1, 2, 3, 4) and vertical (no. 5) plaques, which correspond precisely with those of male figures long established as tripod fixtures.[10] Figures were either soldered or riveted to the ring handles. Those that stood atop the rings were usually fixed by means of a vertical tab with one or two rivets beneath the figure's heels, which were necessarily set side by side. Smaller and earlier figures could be soldered directly to the handle. Alternatively, the figure could stand with greater freedom of foot placement on a flat plaque that was riveted or soldered to the vertical strap that attached handle to cauldron rim. This interior placement seems to have precluded a horse-and-groom pairing and may have led instead to the variant spearbearer type with a shield on his left arm. As Rolley noted, the female with arms down at her sides is ideally suited to this position on the tripod. There seems to be no direct correlation between traditionally recognized bronzeworking centers and figural placement on tripods; methods of attachment transcend stylistic boundaries.

Method, dates, and attributions

Chronology and provenance are the 'Scylla and Charybdis' of the study of Geometric bronze sculpture, and the issues are unlikely to be resolved by incontrovertible stratigraphic evidence. Geometric bronzes come almost without exception from mixed sanctuary deposits, while archaeological and ethnographic evidence supports a picture of on-site bronze votive production by both itinerant and local craftsmen. A general relative chronology in which smaller, more 'primitive' figures develop into highly stylized works raises little opposition, but the issue of workshops finds a wider range of views. Although Herrmann's landmark 1964 study has been widely accepted, his classification covers only 4 major styles — Laconian, Corinthian, Attic, and Argive — and the difficulties of practical application become clear when one turns to extra-canonical figures. Specialists constantly tinker with, refine, and even bypass altogether these conventional workshop designations, casting doubt on the basic premise that major artistic styles must reflect the leading *poleis*.

In trying to establish dates and sources for the female figurine attachments, one immediately encounters the limits of a strictly positivist approach. It is possible to enhance the limited archaeological testimony of the figurines by relocating them within a larger historical, metallurgical, and iconographical framework. Concerning provenance, I use the conventional terms 'Attic', 'Corinthian', and 'Argive' not only as useful metaphors for clusters of stylistic and technical characteristics but also because the polity connections implied by these terms may not be far off the mark. The evidence suggests locus-supported activities of larger scope than a model of sanctuary-based workshops and of a nature that has distinct socio-political overtones.

Dating the female tripod attachments depends directly on the association of the first three nudes (nos. 1-3) with an oriental nude goddess type with arms clasped against thighs, which is known throughout Egypt and the Near East in various media and through imports into Greece of ivory, terracotta, and other materials. The most famous Greek incarnation is the ivory Dipylon Goddess and her four companions found in Kerameikos grave 13.[11] By remarkable good fortune for the problem of chronology, in two instances Greek versions of this goddess type were excavated in deposits that included Geometric pottery. The ivory figures in grave 13 were

---

10 For methods of attachment, see F. Willemsen, *Dreifusskessel von Olympia* (*OlF* 3 Berlin 1957) 155-56; Rolley, *Monuments* (supra n.4) 19; Maass, *Dreifüsse* (supra n.4) 94-104.

11 Ivory figures from Kerameikos grave 13: G. Perrot, "Figurines d'ivoire trouvées dans une tombe du Céramique à Athènes," *BCH* 19 (1895) 273-95; E. Kunze, "Zu den Anfängen der griechischen Plastik," *AthMitt* 55 (1930) 141-62 at pls. V-VIII, beil. XL-XLI; for the date, J. N. Coldstream, *Greek Geometric pottery* (London 1968) 361.

accompanied by Attic LGIIa pottery datable to *c*.735-720 B.C. The same date-range for the Acropolis bronze 6503 (no. 3) may be assumed from the similarities of its swelling volumes and general proportions to those of the Dipylon ivories. Their close stylistic relationship, in particular their distinct swelling forms, has earned for both Acropolis 6503 and the Dipylon Goddess unchallenged attributions to Athenian workshops.

The Delphi bronze 7730 (no. 1) was found in a deposit buried on the Sacred Way containing other Geometric objects and numerous fragments of Corinthian Late Geometric pottery of 750-725 B.C.[12] While the situation of the Athenian closed grave deposit seems clear-cut,[13] that of the Delphi context, apparently a deposit of votives collected over time, is less secure, and many have sought an independent date for the bronze on stylistic grounds. The figure's spareness of form and geometricized head and torso recall the earlier stages of figural vase-painting (although not applicable to Corinth, the supposed home of this bronze). More convincingly, its abstraction marks the figure as early, although not the earliest, in a bronze sculpture tradition that gradually relaxes structure and softens outline. Most scholars agree on a relatively early date for Delphi 7730, preceding the Dipylon ivories and possibly prior to mid-century. The Delphi figure's proportions, calligraphic outline, lozenge-shaped torso, and flattened face bear familial resemblance to several male figures from Delphi that Herrmann established as Corinthian. The strong presence of Corinthian metalwork at Delphi is therefore comparable to that of the pottery.

Found in the Polis Cave strata with tripod fragments and Corinthian pottery ranging from Protogeometric to Late Geometric, the Ithaca bronze female figure (no. 2) is dated and attributed on the basis of its general similarities to the Corinthian figures: spareness of modeling and reduction of details, an uptilted face, and reflection of a similar prototype to that of Delphi 7730. The Ithaca figure lacks the architectonic structure of its counterpart from Delphi, which has caused it to be dated both later and (more often) earlier than the Delphi bronze.[14] Like many of the Polis Cave tripods, it can be understood as a local work produced under Corinthian influence.[15] This date and attribution accord well with what is otherwise known of the material remains on Ithaca, where the preponderance of Corinthian pottery indicates that a probable Corinthian trading station was established as early as 780. In fact, pottery imports until 730 are exclusively Corinthian.[16] The discovery of two oriental goddess types at both Delphi and Ithaca corresponds with known external relations of the two sites, which were linked by a similar cultural dependence on Corinthian pottery and bronzework.

The second Delphi tripod figure (no. 4) reveals another source of votives at that sanctuary. The low rounded cranium, bipart facial profile, and lozenge-shaped torso of the robed female establish her Attic pedigree, with correspondences in a male tripod figure from the Athenian Acropolis (NM 6616). Weber relates its head construction with that of Acropolis NM 6503 (no. 3) as well.[17] Although the Acropolis male NM 6616 has been dated as early as 750, the female

---

12 Amandry 1944-45 (supra n.4); Coldstream, *Pottery* (supra n.11) 366 n.2.

13 The objections of M. Robertson, *A history of Greek art* (Cambridge 1975) 44, seem unnecessary. The Dipylon Goddess has been shown to be based on a model of the Syrian Loftus Group, whose lower limits can be fixed by the Assyrian conquest of the Syrian cities completed in 720 B.C.: R. D. Barnett, *Ancient ivories in the Middle East* (Qedem 14, Jerusalem 1982) 46.

14 Coldstream, *Geometric* (supra n.4) 176, MGII, "one of the earliest of all handle figures"; S. Benton, "Further excavations at Aetos," *BSA* 48 (1953) 255-358 at 343 n.570, first half of 8th c.; Herrmann 1964 (supra n.4) 48, 49 n.132, first half of 8th c.; Floren, *Plastik* (supra n.4) 66 n.331, later than Delphi 7730.

15 J.-L. Zimmermann, *Les chevaux de bronze dans l'art géométrique grec* (Mainz 1989) 59-62, 177-78; Weber 1974 (supra n.7) 30.

16 Coldstream, *Pottery* (supra n.11) 353, 366. For recent work at Ithaca, see S. Symeonoglou, "᾿Ανασκαφὴ Ιθάκης," *Prakt* 1992 (1995) 200-10.

17 For Attic origins, see Rolley, *Monuments* (supra n.4) 28-29; Weber 1974 (supra n.7) 43; Coldstream, *Geometric* (supra n.4) 127; Herrmann 1964 (supra n.4) 50.

figure more plausibly belongs in the second half of the 8th c., in part because of her attire. Bonfante has noted that Greek conventions of censorship for the female figure begin in the Late Geometric period, when nude figures lack the sexual details found in their oriental models, and by the end of the century yield to dressed images.[18] Lacking external parallels for the pose of Delphi 3144, we may assume that she was a local invention, perhaps inspired by her nude predecessors on tripods.

The final female tripod figure, Olympia Br 12607 (no. 5), presents numerous difficulties in establishing date and source. The frequent use of incision to decorate robe and hair suggests a date well into the second half of the 8th c., while the large head and wiry limbs keep it from entering the 7th c. Herrmann drew attention to the bullet-shaped head with pointed chin and large eyes, connecting it with the Laconian centaur fighting group and the Samian lion group.[19] However, this attribution is difficult to maintain now that three decades of studies have found no evidence of a Laconian tradition of tripod manufacture. Moreover, Laconian sculpture of the 8th and 7th c. reveals a distinctive approach to construction that is characterized by sharp, angular features and well-articulated figure construction. Other aspects of the Olympia figure, including the vessel-carrying pose and pot's form, suggest both Peloponnesian and external influences, including Italic, in this probably local work.

In sum, the first three figures, all adapted from an oriental nude goddess type, are stylistically associated with the workshops of Corinth and Athens in the decades around 750 B.C., while the two later robed figures can be traced to Athens (no. 4) and perhaps a local Elian source (no. 5).

Iconographic observations

The iconographic variety apparent even among these few female figurines suggests both the import of forms based directly upon an oriental prototype (nos. 1-3) and local adaptations (nos. 4-5). Böhm's recent comprehensive study of the nude goddess demonstrates that of the variations circulating in Greece, only the type with arms clasped along her sides (Böhm's Type A) lacks local Bronze Age antecedents. This figure alone can be considered purely oriental in origin and newly introduced to Greece in the Iron Age. By contrast, three other and much rarer nude female types (Böhm's Types B-D) could have evolved locally from Bronze Age predecessors.

The three nude female tripod figures and the Dipylon ivories, all mainland products, constitute the earliest and the finest examples of this type in Late Geometric Greece, but they are not alone. A second bronze nude figure of the later 8th c. from Delphi is stockier and more rounded than her sister at the site and has deeply hollowed eyes.[20] Three examples from Rhodes include small bronze figures from Lindos and Kameiros as well as a very fine terracotta from Kameiros, all possibly late 8th c. in date.[21] To these examples can be added two related bronze images from Ialysos and Samos, in which each figure carries a vessel on her head.[22] Birds,

18 L. Bonfante, review of Böhm,*'Nackte Göttin'* (supra n.4) in *AJA* 99 (1995) 741-42. For the 'Homeric' character of dressed figures, see V. Jarosch, *Samische Tonfiguren des 10. bis 7. Jahrhunderts v. Chr. aus dem Heraion von Samos* (Samos XVIII, Mainz 1994) 87; for the 'unhomeric' character of nude figures see Böhm, *'Nackte Göttin'* (supra n.4) 125-26.

19 Herrmann 1964 (supra n.4) 43 n.118.

20 Delphi Museum inv. 3938; Perdrizet, *Monuments* (supra n.8) no. 1; Rolley, *Monuments* (supra n.4) no. 33, pl. 10; Böhm, *'Nackte Göttin'* (supra n.4) 151, B4.

21 For Lindos, see C. Blinkenberg, *Lindos, fouilles de l'acropole 1902-1914.* I: *Les petits objets* (Berlin 1931) 399 no. 1575; Böhm, *'Nackte Göttin'* (supra n.4) 156, B32. For Kameiros inv. 14388, see *ClRh* 6-7 (1932-33) 345, fig. 80.9. The Lindos example, like that from Kameiros, is possibly 7th c.; it cannot be as early as 9th c. (*pace* Böhm). For the Kameiros terracotta, see R. Higgins, *Greek terracottas* (London 1967) 19-20, pl. 6D; Böhm, *'Nackte Göttin'* (supra n.4) 150, T19.

22 For Ialysos, see M. Martelli, "La stipe votiva dell'Athenaion di Jalysos: un primo bilancio," in S. Dietz and I. Papachristodoulou (edd.), *Archaeology in the Dodecanese* (Copenhagen 1988) 104-20 at 107 fig. 4.

goats, and a Tree of Life accompany these nude *hydrophoroi* and underscore their derivation from Near Eastern, particularly North Syrian, art. In a Greek context their vessels may have carried connotations that distinguished them from unadorned figures of this type. A scrawny, poorly worked example of the nude standing female now in Athens is of unknown origin.[23] All the above are of smaller scale and clearly not from tripods.

A striking note in this limited early distribution is the type's near-absence on Samos and Crete until the early 7th c. Although Böhm and others have assigned certain terracottas from Samos to an 8th c. nude goddess type, more recent study of the material fails to support this view. Of the two Samian female nudes Böhm lists as Late Geometric, one has been redated to the 7th c. and the other seems similarly late in its rounded modeling compared with Late Geometric examples.[24] As Jarosch notes, the Samian Geometric terracotta females in oriental pose are depicted wearing a long dress, which is rendered in a solid dark wash or a pattern.[25] The rare Geometric nude females are only vaguely posed with arms against the body, slightly curved to the front rather than held vertically along the sides. In fact, all of the Heraion's earliest nude figures posed in the rigid gesture of hands clasped along the sides seem to be male, which further weakens the argument for a special familiarity with the oriental goddess type on Samos at this time.[26] Similarly, the type is surprisingly rare on Crete before its proliferation in Daedalic style. Böhm cautiously accepts as Late Geometric only a single example (unfortunately without illustration), an unpublished painted terracotta from the Itanos cave.[27]

Despite the notable popularity of this type in early Crete, Rhodes, and Samos, the tripod females predate by perhaps a generation any examples from datable contexts in those islands. Moreover, they apparently predate most of the foreign imports of the type into Greece, as can be gleaned from Böhm's survey of Egyptian and Syrian Type A figures of bronze and ivory in Greece. Of her 11 cited examples, eight Egyptian and three Syrian, all come from Samos, Rhodes, and Crete, and none can be securely dated to a pre-7th c. context. In some cases this is due to missing contextual information or the mixed nature of the deposits, in others to the lateness of contextual material. Despite the persistent chronological uncertainties surrounding much of the relevant material, the circumstantial evidence seems to indicate a distinct pattern by which we may further refine Böhm's picture and observe two paths of transmission. By the mid 8th c., the oriental Type A figure was being imitated on the Greek mainland in the workshops of Corinth and Athens, where it was used for tripod figures and the extraordinary set of Dipylon ivories. These were inspired not by a wave of imports coming through Crete and the Dodecanese but perhaps by more direct contacts between Greek and Near Eastern craftsmen. The stylistic similarities to North Syrian work of ivories, the Athenian bronze, and the later bronze Delphi inv. 3938 suggest the immediate source of this first wave of imitation. By the late 8th c., the type had produced spin-offs — smaller, independent bronzes produced as poorer reflections of monumental tripod votives — and the nude standing goddess enjoyed a certain vogue in bronze votive offerings on Rhodes (4 examples) and Samos (1 example).[28] Terracotta

An incomplete female figurine from Kameiros, inv. 14387, is probably of the same type: *ClRh* 6-7 (1932-33) 345, fig. 80.8. For Samos, see Gehrig, *Bronzen* (supra n.9) 3, 22-25 no. 2; remarkably, Floren, *Plastik* (supra n.4) 70 n.373, calls the Samian figures men.

23 Unpublished, Athens National Museum inv. 15150: Benton, "Evolution" 1934-35 (supra n.5) 62 n.5, confused this with Acropolis figure NM 6503.

24 Böhm, *'Nackte Göttin'* (supra n.4) 150, T15, T16, pl. 11c, d; Jarosch, *Tonfiguren* (supra n.18) pl. 54, no. 835.

25 Jarosch, *Tonfiguren* (supra n.18) 87, e.g., pl. 37, nos. 530-32, pl. 41, nos. 719-21; see also p. 79 on the lack of this nude goddess type in Geometric Samos.

26 E.g., Geometric nude female: Jarosch, *Tonfiguren* (supra n.18) pl. 44, no. 821; Geometric nude male: pl. 42, nos. 860, 863; pl. 55, nos. 696, 879, 882.

27 Böhm, *'Nackte Göttin'* (supra n.4) 149, T12.

28 On this relationship between tripod attachments and independent figurines, see C. Rolley, *Greek bronzes* (London 1986) 70.

examples include one Geometric figure from Kameiros and possibly a second from the Cretan Itanos Cave. By the 7th c., sites on Crete, particularly Gortyn, and on Rhodes, particularly Kameiros, had become increasingly interested in the image.[29] This spread of the type in the late 8th/beginning of the 7th c. may be seen as a secondary wave of imitation, perhaps inspired by the Egyptian and Syrian imports that Böhm tracks through Crete and the Dodecanese.

Although this survey of imports and imitations of the nude goddess in Greece may appear overly sceptical of early dates, it is important not to lump together all 8th c. representations as though they reflect a unified phenomenon. Rather, by distinguishing wherever possible earlier from later transmissions of the type and qualifying the different natures of these events, we can begin to understand why Greek bronzeworkers grafted an oriental female onto a well-established tradition of tripod decoration. Significantly, the nude goddess first arrives in Greek art not alone, as in the later phase, but in the company of warriors.

The Geometric tripods and their production centers

The possibility that the oriental nude standing goddess entered Geometric Greek art through bronze- and ivory-working centers at Corinth and Athens receives independent support from a series of metallurgical studies recently conducted by Rolley and colleagues.[30] Their compositional analyses of tripod parts from Delphi, Olympia, the Argive Heraion, Ithaca, and Athens upheld the traditional classifications, originally formulated by Maass and Rolley, of tripods into 4 categories based on style, technique, and chronology. Briefly, these correspond with early massive cast Argive tripods (Classes 1 and 2), Corinthian works with cast ribbed legs and handles (Class 3), and Attic hammered tripods (Class 4).

Compositional study showed that samples corresponding with the 4 groups contain differing quantities of tin, iron, and lead. Rolley found that, in contrast to the Argive groups which contained very minor amounts of tin (usually less than 2%), the third (Corinthian) and fourth (Attic) groups have significantly higher percentages, over 4% in the Corinthian subset of Group 3, between 5 and 9% in Group 4. This fits the generally accepted picture that Groups 1 and 2 represent the conservative output of Argive production active from the 9th to the mid 8th c., to which any tin content is accidental and results from the re-use of Mycenaean bronze. As early as the second quarter of the 8th c. in Corinth and toward mid-century in Athens, new bronzeworking centers created variations on the tripod form (i.e., different types of handles and legs) and added tin under the tutelage of Near Eastern artisans who may have been installed in Greece and maintained contact, at least for a time, with their customary tin sources.[31] It is plausible that these new Greek workshops picked up artistic forms along with the metallurgical innovations. The slender Delphi 7730 figure (no. 1), dated by many to before the mid 8th c., and the Corinthian-influenced if not manufactured Ithaca figure (no. 2) represent the first Greek imitations of Böhm's oriental Type A goddess. Coldstream has noted the resemblance of the early Corinthian tripod figures to North Syrian works, with their uptilted faces.[32] Attic works in bronze (no. 3) and ivory appeared soon after.

29 E.g., ivories from the Kameiros well: L. Schofield, "The influence of eastern religions on the iconography of ivory and bone objects in the Kameiros well," in J. L. Fitton (ed.), *Ivory in Greece and the eastern Mediterranean from the Bronze Age to the Hellenistic period* (London 1992) 173-80.

30 C. Rolley, "Bronzes grecs et orientaux: influences et apprentissages," *BCH* 107 (1983) 111-32; E. Mangou, S. Philippakis, and C. Rolley, "Trépieds géométriques de bronze: analyses complémentaires," *BCH* 110 (1986) 121-36; E. Mangou, M. Pernot, and C. Rolley, "Bronzes orientaux et orientalisants: analyses complémentaires," *BCH* 115 (1991) 561-77; C. Rolley, "Argos, Corinthe, Athènes: identité culturelle et modes de développement (IXe-VIIIe s.)," *Polydipsion Argos* (*BCH* Suppl. 22, 1992) 37-49.

31 Rolley 1983 (supra n.30) 127-30; Rolley 1992 (supra n.30) esp. 41 where he extends the date of Corinthian tripods back to the earlier 8th c. See also Guralnick, below pp. 35 ff

32 Coldstream, *Geometric* (supra n.4) 176.

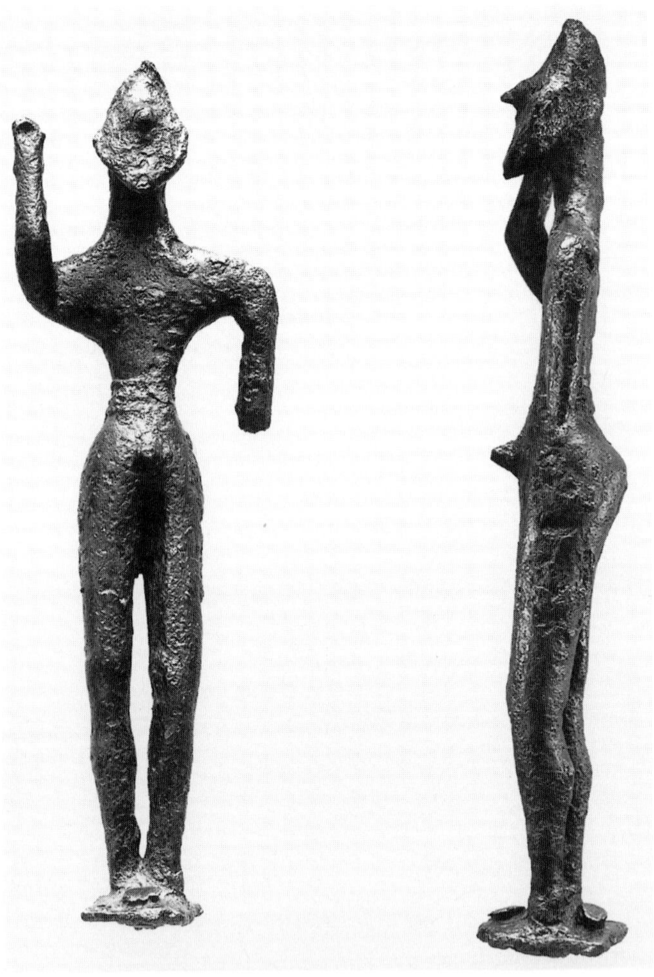

Fig. 6. Bronze figure from Delphi. Delphi Museum 2947. (Photo: courtesy École française d'archéologie.)

Support also comes from the male tripod figures. Argos seems to have originated the concept of horse and groom as tripod decoration, just as it was the source of the first horse attachments.[33] The idea of adding a groom to the tripod horses arose naturally in the Argive cultural milieu, without foreign influence. Where and how the groom was transformed into a spearbearing warrior bearing more than a passing resemblance to oriental smiting gods remains unclear. Byrne derived the mainland Geometric bronze warriors from Crete, a view with which there is much to agree in reference to the stylistic features and poses of the earliest figures at Olympia and Delphi.[34] These arguments are less convincing for the Late Geometric warriors, where the lack of a specific Cretan tradition of warrior figurines requires him to propose a development of mainland figures based ultimately on the Minoan salute and "receptivity to the motif" of imported Late Bronze Age oriental smiting figurines. On the mainland these transmissions then coalesced into warriors that resembled Near Eastern smiting gods. Byrne did not consider the evidence of the Greek Geometric standing nude females which, as we have seen, do not support Cretan intermediaries for their imagery. I suggest that the warrior figures, like the female tripod attachments, reflect direct contact with the Near East in the mid 8th c.

Increasingly formalized types began more or less simultaneously: right arms are raised and left arms lowered parallel with the body, and the hands are normally pierced to hold spear and horse rein or shield. Bronze tripod warriors Olympia B 4600, Athens NM 7415 from Delphi, and Athenian Acropolis NM 6616, representing the traditions of Argos, Corinth, and Athens respectively, all date *c.*750 B.C. or slightly earlier.[35] The essential difference among these figures is their gear. While the Argive group and the earliest Attic examples are bareheaded, the Corinthian series is apparently helmeted upon its introduction, with distinctive, if generalized, forward-curving pointed headgear (fig. 6).[36] In these highly stylized figures

33 For Argos first putting horses on tripods, see Zimmermann, *Chevaux* (supra n.15). For the two earliest human figures on tripods, Argive horse-and-man pair Olympia B4567, see Maass, *Dreifüsse* (supra n.4) 168-69, 228, cat. 154, pl. 40; Herrmann 1964 (supra n.4) 45 fig. 30; and male figure from the Argive Heraion, Willemsen, *Dreifusskessel* (supra n.10) pl. 43; Herrmann 1964 (supra n.4) 44, figs. 28-29.

34 Byrne, *Figurine* (supra n.2) esp. 109-57.

35 For Olympia B 4600 see E. Kunze, "Kleinplastik aus Bronze," *OlBer* VII (Berlin 1961) 138-75 at 145-51, pl. 60. For Athens NM 7415, see Rolley, *Monuments* (supra n.4) cat. 14. For Athens NM 6616, see Herrmann 1964 (supra n.4) 54 figs. 45-46.

36 Although few workshop attributions for the bronze figures find universal consensus, the following are widely accepted. For Argive workshops: Delphi 1785 and Munich SL1, Schweitzer, *Geometric* (supra n.4) pls. 140-43. For Corinthian: Delphi 2947, 1346, 3495, Rolley, *Monuments* (supra n.4) pls. I-II. For Attic: Athens NM 6620, Herrmann 1964 (supra n.4) 63 figs. 58-59; NM 6612, 6613, Schweitzer,

the elliptical head form terminates in a pointed chin and cranium, which in profile takes a forward curve. This particular form occurs mainly on tripod figures, rarely among the numerous independent bronze warrior figures, and in only a single case, to my knowledge, in vase-painting.[37] The abstract figural style frustrates attempts to identify precisely the helmet or headgear. The helmets have been drawn into the group of early examples of the Greek *Raupenhelme*, where high forward-curving crests are clearly delineated in such later bronzes as the early 7th c. 'Steiner' warriors.[38] The tripod warriors' helmets might be less schematized than their abstract figural style suggests, however, and correspond directly with the simpler, conical Urartian or Assyrian predecessors of the 9th and 8th c.[39] The important point is that the first figures connected with Corinthian style have helmets paralleled not in Greece but in the Near East, while Attic figures acquire headgear slightly later, and Argive horseleaders remain bareheaded for a significantly longer time. These new workshops thus extended tripod iconography by adding strong female figures at about the same time that they turned the horseleaders into helmeted warriors.

Expanding the meaning of the Geometric tripod

The presence of both nude and dressed female figures on tripods made in more than one bronzecasting center and dedicated in at least 4 cults in Greece suggests that these figures had become potent images within 8th c. Greek society. Their identity and meaning remain elusive, but the available artistic and archaeological evidence clarifies the way in which they were displayed. As tripod decorations the females were at least indirectly associated with warriors, but there are good reasons to believe that they were actually paired with males, facing each other across the cauldron on opposite ring handles. All representations of tripods with handle attachments depicted in miniature bronze specimens and painted pottery show symmetrically paired figures.[40] None of these shows human figure attachments, but extant pairs of identical male tripod figures may have come from the same tripods.[41] As to the female figurines, they correspond closely with males in size and style, and being numerically fewer than males are less likely to have been paired with other females. Perhaps not coincidentally, the Near Eastern prototypes of the nude standing females and the helmeted spearbearers were often created as pairs, smiting warrior with companion fertility goddess, types that continued

---

Geometric (supra n.4) pls. 159-61, 164-65. The Corinthian series, with its pointed headgear, is soon imitated at Olympia by the probably Elian group, including Olympia B 24 and Louvre 82: Schweitzer, *Geometric* (supra n.4) pls. 126, 127.

37 For the tripod pithos from Knossos, see H. Payne, "Early Greek vases from Knossos," *BSA* 29 (1927-28) 224-98 at 240 no. 38, pl. XI.10-11, XII.

38 For examples of the Geometric Raupenhelme, 'Steiner warriors,' see *OlBer* IV (Berlin 1944) pls. 38-46; tripod relief with two figures confronted over a tripod, Olympia B 1730, Willemsen, *Dreifusskessel* (supra n.10) pl. 63; two-figure war chariot (Olympia B 1671), lion-fighting group from Samos (Inv. B 190), and helmet maker (Metropolitan Museum of Art 42.11.42), see Schweitzer, *Geometric* (supra n.4) pls. 178, 186, and 200, respectively.

39 A. M. Snodgrass, *Early Greek armor and weapons* (Edinburgh 1964) 9-10, 12, 35; J. Borchhardt, *Homerische Helme* (Mainz 1972) esp. 68-70, 97-100, pls. 30, 34, 35; H. Pflug in A. Bottini *et al.*, *Antike Helme* (Mainz 1988) 11-26, esp. 22-26; J. Borchhardt in H.-G. Buchholz *et al.*, *Kriegswesen* 1 (*ArchHom* I, E1; Göttingen 1977) 68-72.

40 Miniature tripods with paired attachments, of bronze: Maass 1978 (supra n.4) pl. 58, nos. 391, 396, pl. 59, no. 397; of terracotta: E. Brann, *Late Geometric and Protoattic pottery* (Agora VIII, Princeton 1962) pl. 19, no. 338. Painted representations: Benton, "Evolution" 1934-35 (supra n.5) 103 no. 4, 105 no. 13, pl. 26.2.

41 Identical tripod figures: E. Kunze, "Bronzestatuetten," *OlBer* IV (Berlin 1944) 105-42, pls. 43-46; Kunze 1961 (supra n.35) 148 figs. 85-89, pls. 62-67; id., "Kleinplastik aus Bronze," *OlBer* VIII (Berlin 1967) 213-50, pls. 110-13.

from the Middle and Late Bronze Ages to the early first millennium.[42] These paired divinities expressed a holistic social prosperity, the female fertility principle of life to balance warrior-borne death. Long associated in Near Eastern tradition, male smiter and nude female were readily adapted to the physical requirements of tripod decoration through contact with and perhaps the mediation of foreign bronzeworkers. What was needed to introduce this imagery into the well-established realm of tripods was a similar adaptability to the interests of the 8th c. Greek patrons.

In answering this final question it is helpful to recall the remarkable changes that took place in central Greece during a single generation around 750 B.C. The earliest female figures, patterned after the oriental nude goddess, appeared on tripods of Corinthian and Attic style. Corinthian and Attic bronze workshops were established together with probably eastern-inspired innovations in tripod manufacturing techniques. The horseleaders of the new Corinthian tripods were given helmets of oriental type. Finally, in an isolated flurry of activity, eastern goods and artistic ideas, as exemplified by monumental Dipylon vases and orientalia in Athenian graves, were adopted by the élite as statements of class identity and status.[43] I propose that changes to quintessentially élite tripod were driven by the same motives. Even more forceful than a bareheaded horseleader was a helmeted warrior for heroic self-identification by the élite. Perhaps created in response to rising challenges to the established order, this new icon of the heroic warrior with female fertility companion offered a socially stabilizing message. In scale and in imagery the nude female tripod figure standing with arms against sides presents the strongest, even heroic, female image found in Geometric art. Standing on cauldrons in the company of warriors and horses, this aristocratic imagery evoked in Greek terms the dual foundations of society's survival: heroic valor and the sanctity of the *oikos*.

Department of Art History and Archaeology, University of Missouri-Columbia, MO 65211

---

42 H. Seeden, *The standing armed figurines in the Levant* (PBF I.1, Munich 1980); id., "Peace figurines from the Levant," in *Archéologie au Levant: Recueil R. Saidah* (Lyon 1982) 107-21; O. Negbi, *Canaanite gods in metal* (Tel Aviv 1976); A. Spycket, *La statuaire du Proche-Orient ancien* (Leiden 1981).

43 See also I. Morris, "The art of citizenship," in S. Langdon (ed.), *New light on a dark age* (Columbia, MO 1997) 9-43 for more on the mid 8th c. orientalizing phenomenon. M. Shanks, "Art and an archaeology of embodiment: some aspects of Archaic Greece," *CAJ* 5 (1995) 207-44, explores a "new expressive aesthetic" in 8th-7th c. Corinth that deploys warrior imagery within the self-referential world of the aristocrat.

Near Eastern and Egyptian bronzes in Greece

Eleanor Guralnick

Bronze Age Greeks evolved some very complex and technically challenging ways of working and decorating bronze. The inlaid swords and daggers from grave circle A at Mycenae are among the best examples of this work.[1] They date *c.*1600-1480 B.C. There is no evidence for the continued practice of these metalworking skills following the Late Bronze Age. Proto-Geometric solid-cast figurines, dating from the middle of the 10th to the middle of the 9th c.,[2] are the products of the simplest bronzeworking skills.

Beginning in the late 10th c., however, sophisticated bronze imports began to appear in Greece, from Egypt and the Near East. The earliest of these imports, elaborate repoussé hammered and tooled bowls from Cyprus or North Syria, have been found in graves at Athens (fig. 1), Lefkandi on Euboia, and Fortetsa and Arkades on Crete.[3] Some later bowls from the same

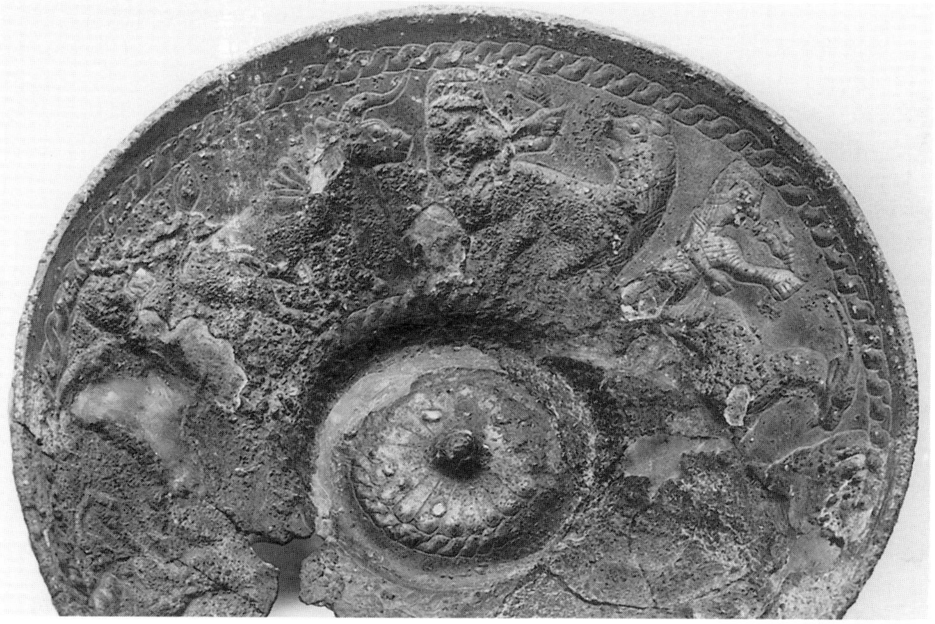

Fig. 1. Bowl. From Cyprus or North Syria. Found at Athens, Kerameikos grave 42. Bronze, diam. 17.0 cm. Athens, Kerameikos Museum Inv. No. M5. (Photo: courtesy G. Markoe; German Archaeological Institute, Athens, neg. KER 4847.

1 P. Demargne, *The birth of Greek art* (New York 1964) 192-93, figs. 263-66. For Mycenaean inlays and gold repoussé work, see R. Hampe and E. Simon, *The birth of Greek art* (New York 1981) figs. 172-78, 266, 268-70, 276-82, 287-88, 299, 310-16; S. Marinatos, *Kreta, Thera und das mykenische Hellas* (Munich 1973) pls. XLIX-LIII, figs. 192-94, 198, 200-7, 209-27; F. Matz, *The art of Crete and early Greece* (New York 1962) pls. 32, 41, 44-46.

2 Rolley, *Les bronzes grecs* 52, fig. 28.

3 For a catalog of all the bowls known before 1983, see G. Markoe, *Phoenician bronze and silver bowls from Cyprus and the Mediterranean* (California Classical Studies 26, Los Angeles 1983) 162-69, 203-9, 214, 233-41, 312-31, 339, nos. Cr1-13, G1-11, and R1. Excavation context and style led Markoe to assign bowls Cr1, G1, G9, and G10 to Period 1, the third quarter of the 9th c. or *c.*850-750 B.C. For recent finds of similar bowls at Lefkandi, see E. B. French, "Lefkandi: Toumba," *AR* 39 (1993) 40, fig. 33; M. R. Popham, P. G. Calligas, and L. H. Sackett, "Further excavations of the Toumba cemetery at Lefkandi, 1984 and 1986," *AR* 35 (1989) 118-19, 121, 123-24, figs. 5, 7, and 9; and H. W. Catling, "Archaeology in Greece, Lefkandi," *AR* 31 (1985) 15-16, figs. 20-21; M. Popham, "An engraved Near Eastern bowl from Lefkandi," *Oxford Journal of Archaeology* 14.1 (1995) 103-7, fig. 2.

workshop, dating from the late 9th through the 8th c., have been found at sanctuaries such as the Idaean cave on Crete, at Delphi, Olympia, Perachora, and Sparta, and on Rheneia and Rhodes.[4] By the 9th c. Egyptian lotus-handled jugs were being imported to Greece. They have been found in some numbers in graves at Lefkandi on Euboia, and at Fortetsa and Amnissos on Crete, but the largest number is from the Idaean cave.[5] These jugs combine hammered bodies with cast handles attached by rivets. The imported bowls and jugs provided Greeks with examples of several techniques used by foreign contemporaries in the manufacture of bronze artifacts.

The elegant decorative qualities of the imports were a strong contrast to the simple solid-cast products of contemporary Greek bronzeworkers. Over time, Greece became an increasingly good market for foreign bronze luxury products. It has been suggested that by early in the 8th c. a few North Syrian, Phoenician, and/or Cypriote bronzeworkers settled in Crete. Assyrian cuneiform records tell of repeated invasions to the Mediterranean coastal regions, plundering of valuables, and forced resettlement of populations during the reign of Assurnasirpal II in the 9th c. and especially during the reign of Sargon II in the last quarter of the 8th c.[6] A sculptured and inscribed stele erected by Sargon II on Cyprus, now in the Vorderasiatisches Museum, Berlin, testifies to his conquest of that island.[7] The hypothesis offered here is that a few skilled craftsmen immigrated to Crete to avoid forced resettlement in the land of the conquerors. The earliest products of these immigrants were purely Near Eastern in design and motifs. But soon they limited themselves to motifs and decorations that appealed to their exclusively Greek customers. Surely the resettled craftsmen or their descendants must have intermarried with local Greeks. Subsequent generations of these families can be thought of as Greeks, who as members of families with superior craft skills learned the full range of their fathers' and forefathers' technical skills. Ultimately, these workshops, initiated by immigrants, are the Greek workshops producing the earliest Orientalizing artifacts. The craft skills introduced to other Greeks by these workshops include hammering, repoussé, engraving, tracing, stamping, and joining bronze.

Egyptians have a long and continuous tradition of elaborately working and decorating bronze. By Dynasty 22 in the 9th c. B.C., Egyptians had developed the technique of making hollow-cast bronze statues of nearly life-size, often inlaid with gold, silver, electrum, carnelian, faience, frit, paste, glass, and other materials.[8] Hundreds of Egyptian bronzes have been excavated at the Heraion on Samos and elsewhere in Greece.[9] Many of the finest are hollow-

---

4 Ibid. Bowls Cr1-Cr2, G2-G8, and R1 are assigned to Period 2, the second half of the 8th c., *c.*750-700, particularly to the time of Sargon II, 722-705 B.C.

5 Excavated at Lefkandi: French 1993 (supra n.3) 40, fig. 33; Catling, "Lefkandi: Toumba" *AR* 28 (1982) 15-16; M. R. Popham, L. H. Sackett, and P. G. Themelis (edd.), *Lefkandi* 1: *The Iron Age* (London 1980); L. H. Sackett and M. R. Popham, "Lefkandi," *Archaeology* 25.1 (1972) 8-19, fig. on p. 18. Excavated on Crete: F. Halbherr and P. Orsi, "Antichità dell'antro di Zeus Ideo in Creta," *Museo italiano di antiquità classica* 2 (Florence 1888) 725, 855-56, pls. VI.1, XI.1, 10, and *Atalante* pls. XII.9-10, 12-13; J. K. Brock, *Fortetsa* (Cambridge 1957) 136, nos. 1571 and 1572, pl. 113; H. W. Catling, "Archaeology in Greece. Crete: Idaean Cave," *AR* 31 (1985) 61; id., "Archaeology in Greece. Crete: the Knossos area, 1974-76," *AR* 23 (1976-77) 12-14, fig. 27; F. Poulsen, *Der Orient und der frühgriechische Kunst* (Leipzig 1912) 22-24, nos. 9-10, 12, fig. 11; E. Kunze, *Kretische Bronzereliefs* (Stuttgart 1931) 159, no. 35; A. J. Evans, *Prehistoric tombs of Knossos* (London 1906) 54, fig. 54, pls. F, 66-69. For examples excavated in Egypt, see A. Radwan, *Die Kupfer- und Bronzegefässe Ägyptens, Prähistorische Bronzefunde*, II.2 (Munich 1983) 133-36, nos. 369-84; G. Roeder, *Ägyptische Bronzewerke* (Gluckstadt 1937) 70 n.4.

6 D. D. Luckenbill, *Ancient records of Assyria and Babylonia* (Chicago 1926) I-II; J. A. Brinkman, "The Akkadian words for 'Ionia' and 'Ionian'," in R. Sutton (ed.), *Daidalikon: Studies in memory of Raymond V. Schoder, S. J.* (Wauconda, IL 1989) 53-71.

7 E. Schrader, *Die Sargonsstele des Berliner Museum* (Berlin 1882) 1-36, pls. 1-2.

8 B. Bianchi, "Egyptian metal statuary of the Third Intermediate Period (circa 1070-656 B.C.) from its Egyptian antecedents to its Samian examples," in *Small bronze sculpture* 61-84.

9 U. Jantzen, *Samos VIII: Ägyptische und orientalische Bronzen aus dem Heraion von Samos* (Bonn 1972) 5-

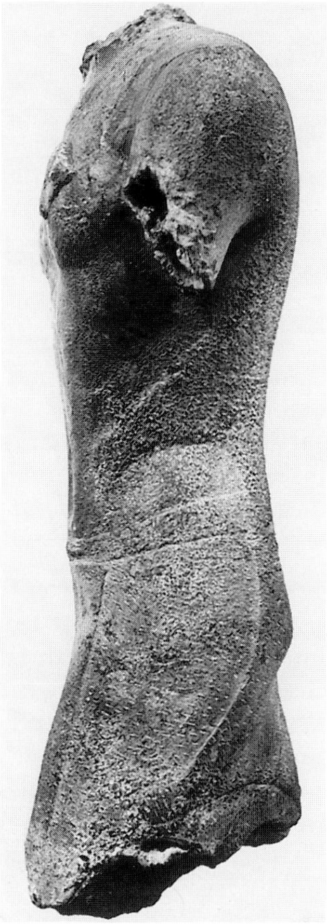

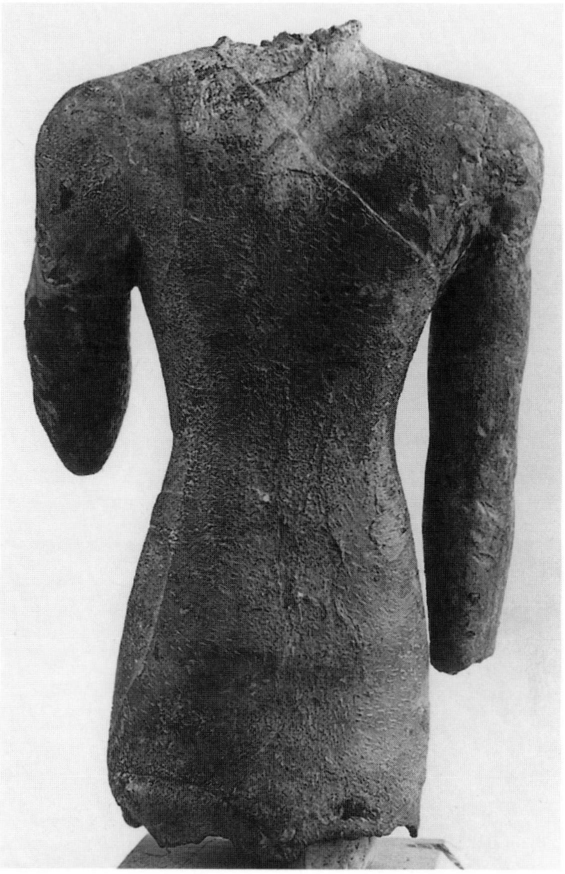

Fig. 2 (left). Statuette of a priest; unrestored side view, showing hollow arm and kilt. Egyptian, Dynasty 25. Found in the Heraion of Samos, B1312. Bronze, h. 26.6 cm. (Photo: German Archaeological Institute, Athens, Samos neg. 5503.)

Fig. 3 (right). Back of fig. 2, showing remains of gilding. (Photo: German Archaeological Institute, Athens, Samos neg. 5827.)

cast and inlaid statuettes that must be dated to Dynasty 25 and were buried in contexts dating to no later than the first third of the 7th c. A large, hollow-cast statuette of a priest has remains of gilding (figs. 2-3).[10] A hollow-cast statuette of a woman is prepared to receive several lost inlays (fig. 4).[11] A fine hollow-cast bronze statuette of Neith has an inlaid gold Horus in her back (fig. 5).[12] Like many other imported statuettes, the Neith is cast in several sections, arms fitted to shoulders by means of tenons and sockets. Other statuettes are held together with dowels or pegs. An Egyptian furniture fitting with a square tenon, now in the Pergamon Museum, Berlin, has the remains of gold foil or leaf inlays enhancing the papyrus capital.[13]

In contrast to the variety of techniques exhibited by the imports, 8th c. and earlier Greek artifacts are technically simple, solid one-piece castings, such as the Geometric statuettes of men and horses.[14] The earliest examples of Greek hollow casting are the bodies of a few Late Geometric bronze birds, with tail, head, and neck separately solid-cast and attached.[15] The

---

37, pls. 1-36; J. Sliwa, "Egyptian bronzes from Samos in the Staatliche Museum (Antikensammlung) Berlin," *Et&Trav* 13 (1983) 380-92. At the Getty symposium on *Small bronze sculpture* (1989), Kyrieleis mentioned that approximately a hundred Egyptian bronze statuettes had been excavated on Samos since Jantzen's 1972 catalogue was completed.

10 Jantzen, *Samos* VIII (supra n.9) 7, B1312, pls. 1-3.

11 Jantzen, *Samos* VIII (supra n.9) 13, B1216, pl. 15.

12 Jantzen, *Samos* VIII (supra n.9) 23, B354, pls. 27-28.

13 Jantzen, *Samos* VIII (supra n.9) 32, BB758, pl. 34.

14 *Master bronzes* 2-33, 35-41, nos. 14-24.

15 H. Lechtman and A. Steinberg, "Bronze joining: a study in ancient technology," in S. Doeringer *et al.*

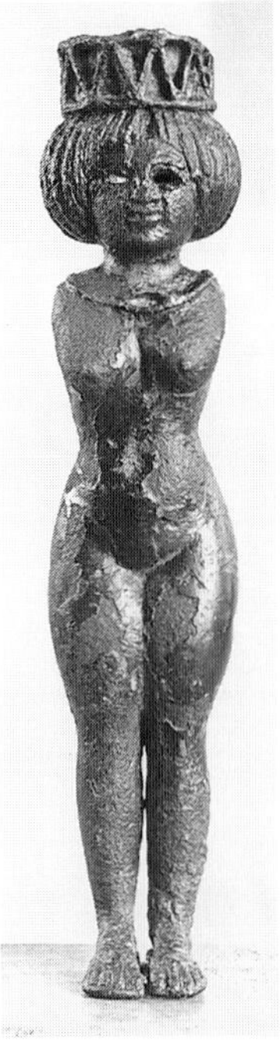

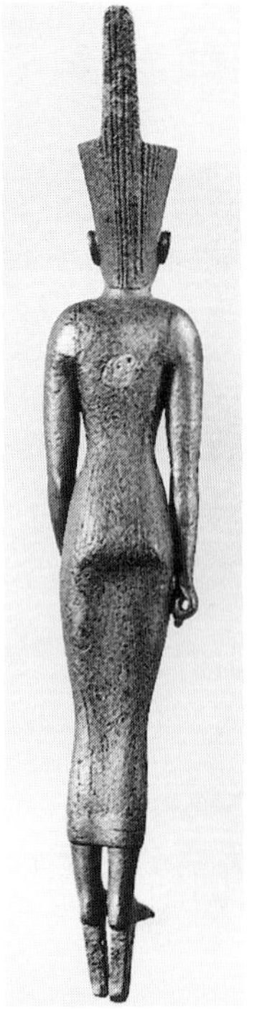

Fig. 4 (left). Statuette of a woman, prepared for lost inlays. Egyptian, Dynasty 25. Found on Samos, B1216. Bronze, h. 17.3 cm. (Photo: German Archaeological Institute, Athens, Samos neg. 5281.)

Fig. 5 (right). Back of a statuette of the goddess Neith, showing inlaid gold head of Horus in her back and the separately cast arms attached at the shoulder by tangs in sockets. Egyptian, Dynasty 25. Found on Samos, B354. Bronze, h. 0.225 m. (Photo: German Archaeological Institute, Athens, neg. 69/775.)

birds are probably from the very end of the 8th c. but most likely after the import of the hollow-cast Egyptian bronzes. At the very end of the 8th c., after long exposure to foreign imports using a variety of elaborate metalworking techniques, Samian metalworkers began to use such Near Eastern and Egyptian techniques as repoussé-shaped metal, folded joins, and riveting for the first time for the creation of griffin-head attachments on cauldrons. In the 7th c. other Greek metalworkers used these techniques for *sphyrelaton* bronze skin over solid-core statues.[16]

Beginning perhaps as early as the end of the 8th c. B.C., the Near Eastern technique of repoussé hammering to shape bronze was used by Samian Greeks to manufacture bronze cauldrons with separate rivet-attached hammered griffin heads with necks. The second quarter of the century saw a Samian innovation. Griffin heads were made of several, individually cast pieces, subsequently joined, and attached to hammered necks.[17] By the middle of the century some Samian griffin-head attachments were entirely hollow-cast bronze, made using piece molds.[18] The extraordinary quality of the Samian castings, composed of individual parts joined with exceptional skill, and of the earliest hollow castings, argues for serious training. There does not appear to be a period of experimentation, which would be likely if Greeks developed the art of bronze joining and hollow casting independently. Only three miscastings from this formative period have been excavated and published.[19] There can be little doubt that the imported lost-wax hollow-cast Egyptian statuettes on Samos inspired the subsequent development of lost-wax hollow casting on Samos. It is possible that a few Samians actually learned the process of hollow casting in Egypt. After all, M. Venit's recent studies of the Greek pottery from Naucratis in Egyptian museums has led to a much earlier dating, to the beginning of Dynasty 26, just after 663 B.C., for Greeks resident at that site.[20] This date for Greek residence in Egypt coincides remarkably well with Herodotus's assertion (2.178) and with the long-accepted approximation for the date for the creation of the elegant and technically challenging Greek hollow-cast bronze griffin heads, *c.*650 B.C.

(edd.), *Art and technology* (Cambridge, MA 1970) 14-22, figs. 15-17; *Master bronzes* figs. 23 and 25; Rolley, *Les bronzes grecs* fig. 43.

16 Haynes, *Technique* 11-20, fig. 2; Demargne, *Birth* (supra n.1) figs. 452-55; G. M. A. Richter, *A handbook of Greek art* (New York 1970) figs. 12 and 13.

17 U. Jantzen, *Griechische Greifenkessel* (Berlin 1955) 57 f., pls. 17 and 18.1-2; Haynes, *Technique* 15.

18 Haynes, *Technique* 43-47.

19 Haynes, *Technique* 43-46, pl. 6; Jantzen, *Greifenkessel* (supra n.17) 57 ff., nos. 47 and 48, pls. 17, 18.1-2; G. Kopke, "Heraion von Samos. Die Kampagnen 1961/1965 im Sudtemenos," *AthMitt* 83 (1968) 285, no. 101, pl. 113.4-5; Rolley, *Les bronzes grecs* 16, fig. 2.

20 M. Venit, *Greek painted pottery from Naucratis in Egyptian Museums* (ARCE Catalogue 7, 1988).

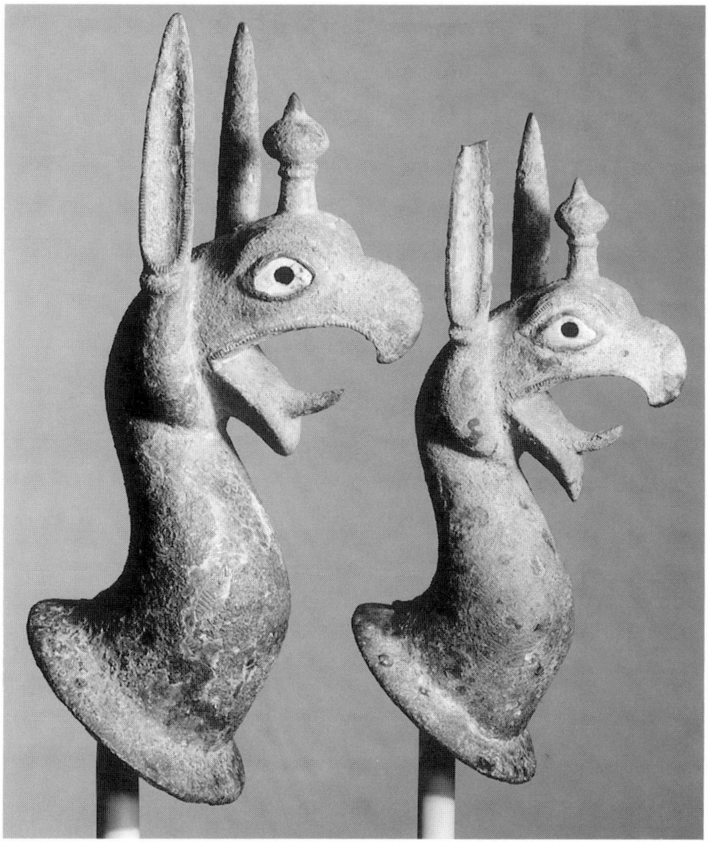

Fig. 6. Pair of griffin protomes with inlaid eyes. Bronze, h. 0.178 m. Chicago, Art Institute of Chicago, Katherine K. Adler Endowment 1994.38.1–2. (Photo: © 1996 Art Institute of Chicago, All Rights Reserved.)

The two fine Samian cast griffin heads in the Art Institute of Chicago (fig. 6) exhibit yet another Near Eastern and Egyptian connection.[21] The eyes are inlaid with stone, although the dark stone of the iris is now missing. The inlaid eyes rarely survive in either the 7th c. griffins or later bronze statues, but the openings for them should stimulate our imaginations to see bronzes as they once were. In a few rare cases, such as the bust of a winged goddess from Olympia, *c.*580 B.C.,[22] and the Delphi Charioteer, *c.*460 B.C.,[23] we can still appreciate Greek bronzes in all their glory. The inlays and gilding seen in classical Greek and Roman bronze statuary reflect use of technologies originating in Egypt and the Near East. The imports are the earliest examples of these techniques found in Greek lands.

Chicago, IL

---

21 Compare Jantzen, *Samos* VIII (supra n.9) B1690, B 1216, B1618, B342, and pls. 3, 15, 20, and 66, all of which are prepared for inlaid eyes, now lost.

22 Rolley, *Les bronzes grecs* 115, ill. 99.

23 Mattusch, *Greek bronze statuary* fig. 6.6; R. V. Schoeder, *Masterpieces of Greek art* (Greenwich, CT 1965) pls. 27-28; K. Papaioannou, *The art of Greece* (New York 1989) pl. 126.

The Dreros *sphyrelata*: a re-examination of their date and function

Irene Bald Romano

Introduction

The three *sphyrelaton* statuettes from Dreros on Crete (Heraklion Museum 2445, 2446, and 2447; figs. 1-7) are landmarks because of the rarity of Greek hammered sculpture, their conjectured early date, and their probable use in the cult of one of the earliest temples of the Greek Iron Age. Although the statuettes were uncovered at Dreros in 1935 and have since been included in nearly every handbook on Greek sculpture and in every discussion of the art and archaeology of Crete, there is surprisingly little unanimity concerning where these unique figures belong in the chronological framework of early sculpture.[1] Dates for the male and two female figures range from a high of *c.*750, contemporary with the date for the construction of the temple,[2] to a low of 650 B.C.[3] Concerning the function of the three statues, since Marinatos's publication of the temple and finds in 1936 the figures have been identified by most scholars as cult images: the male as Apollo, since there is later evidence (a 3rd c. B.C. inscription) that there was an important cult at Dreros dedicated to Apollo Delphinios; and the two females as Apollo's divine consorts, Leto and Artemis.[4] This paper is a re-examination and re-assessment of both the date and function of the three figures.

The context of the Dreros statuettes

The Dreros statuettes were accidentally uncovered by a farmer plowing his field. He cut through the back or south wall of the temple and, according to Marinatos, demolished the upper part of the 'Keraton' altar, breaking the statuettes, which were on the altar.[5] The Dreros temple plan is well known: a shallow pronaos leading to a cella which encloses a sunken rectangular hearth in the center, with columnar supports to the north and south. In the south-west corner is a stone bench (h. 0.95 m) on which were found a few sherds and terracottas, a 6th c. B.C. bronze Gorgoneion, bones, blackened earth, and ash. On the ground in front of the bench

---

1 The final publication of the Dreros *sphyrelata* is in preparation by G. Neumann, Tübingen University, and I acknowledge his publication rights. I have restricted my remarks in this paper to observations made from examining the statuettes in their display case and from published photographs and reports. S. Marinatos, "Le temple géometrique de Dreros," *BCH* 60 (1936) 214-56; id., "Ausgrabungen und Funde auf Kreta 1935-1936," *AA* (1936) 215-22. See further bibliography in C. Davaras, *Die Statue aus Astritsi* (*AntK* 8, 1972) 51-52 and I. B. Romano, *Early Greek cult images* (diss. Univ. of Pennsylvania 1980) 284-93.

2 For the high date, see I. Beyer, *Die Tempel von Dreros und Prinias A und die Chronologie der kretischen Kunst des 8. und 7. Jhs. v. Chr.* (Freiburg 1976) 13-20, no. 58: temple and bronzes date to the mid 8th c. B.C. A. Lembessi in *ΣΤΗΛΗ. Τόμος εἰς μνήμην τοῦ Νικόλαου Κοντολέοντος* (Athens 1980) 92, assigns the male figure a date "before the beginning of the last quarter of the 8th c."

3 Marinatos *BCH* 1936 (supra n.1) 255-56 and id., *AA* 1936 (supra n.1) 220. See below for explanation of date. J. Schäfer, review of G. Rizza and V. Santa-Maria Scrinari (below n.15), in *Gnomon* 44 (1972) 192, places all three statuettes in the Middle Daedalic period; M. Sturgeon, *Isthmia* IV: *Sculpture I: 1952-1967* (Princeton 1987) 33-34: early in the 2nd quarter of the 7th c. for the females by comparison with the caryatid figures on the Isthmia *perirrhanterion*; P. Blöme, *Die figürliche Bildwelt Kretas in der geometrischen und früharchäischen Periode* (Mainz 1982) 10-15, mid 7th c.

4 For the epigraphical evidence, see Marinatos, *BCH* 1936 (supra n.1) 253-55; H. van Effenterre, "Inscriptions archaïques crétoises," *BCH* 70 (1946) 588 f., no. 6; F. W. Blass, *SGDI*, no. 4952; *Inscr. Creticae* 84, no. 1. For a discussion of the Dreros statuettes as cult images, see Romano, *Images* (supra n.1). *Contra*, F. Brommer, "Gott oder Mensch," *JdI* 101 (1986) 37-53, rejects the statuettes as cult images and interprets them as single votives buried together.

5 Marinatos, *BCH* 1936 (supra n.1) 219-55; id., *AA* 1936 (supra n.1) 219-20.

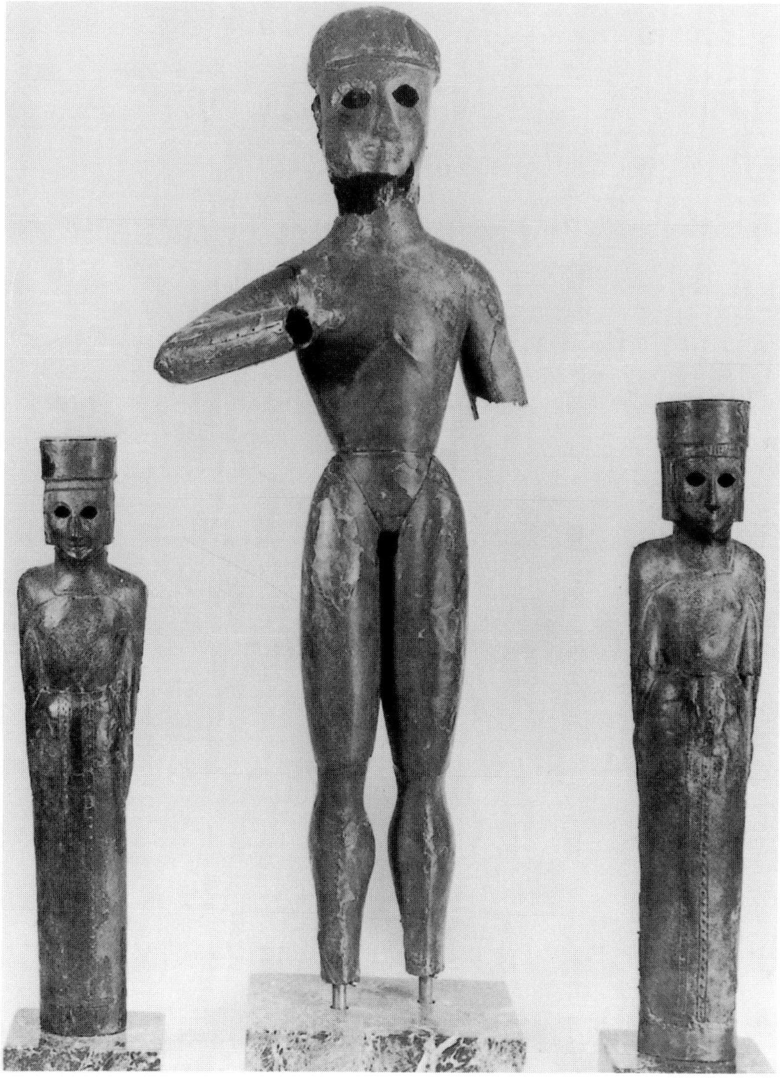

Fig. 1. Dreros *sphyrelaton* statuettes. Left to right: Heraklion Museum 2446, 2445, and 2447. The position of the male figure's right arm represents an earlier restoration. (Photo: courtesy Heraklion Museum.)

were more animal bones and carbonized earth. Just east of the bench along the same wall is a small stone box, Marinatos's 'Keraton' altar, 1.37 m long, built of three vertical slabs, with the fourth or west side formed by the east end of the bench. It was exactly at this spot, at a height of about 0.35-0.40 m, that Marinatos records the statuettes were found, two still standing on the altar and one slightly inclined. The box or altar was filled with earth, two iron knives, bones, and a great many goat horns. Marinatos postulated a wooden top for the altar with a hole cut through for the deposition of the bones and horns. In front of the altar were found more horns as well as a circular limestone offering-table. Marinatos dated the construction of the temple to the mid 8th c. B.C., based on the Geometric pottery inside and outside the building and on the construction technique and its slightly earlier features than those of Temple A at Prinias. He argued that the 'Keraton' was a construction later than the bench, since it used the east wall of the bench for its west wall. He dated the 'Keraton' to the mid 7th c. and assigned the statuettes to the same period.[6] Marinatos cited no pottery evidence to distinguish two interior arrangements at the south end of the temple. Yavis reports that there is evidence that some accumulation of deposition had built up before the stone slabs were laid to enclose the altar, showing that at least the stone enclosure walls were a later addition.[7]

---

6 Ibid.

7 C. G. Yavis, *Greek altars: origins and typology* (St. Louis 1949) 61.

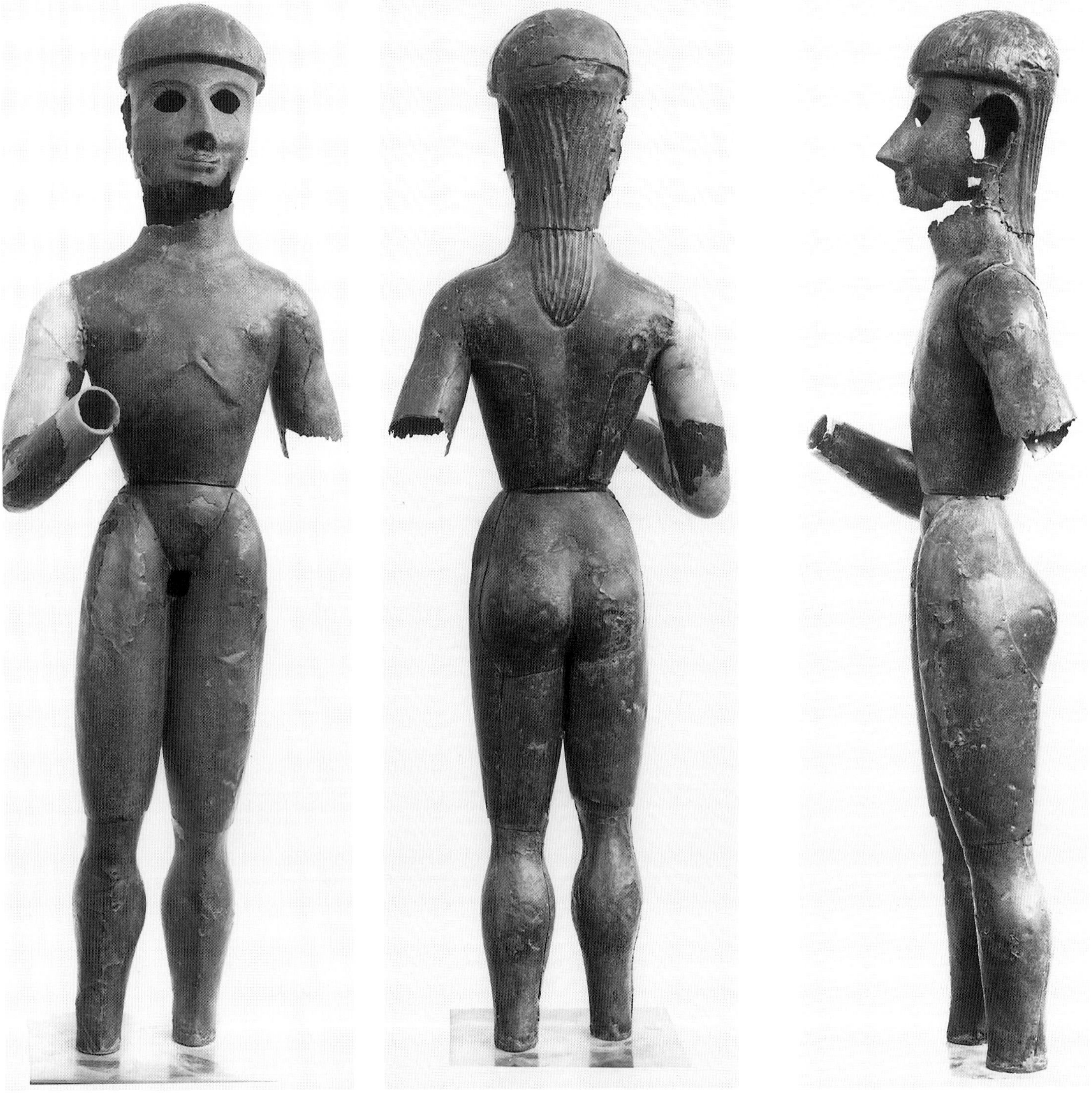

Figs. 2-4. Male figure from Dreros, front, back, and left side. Bronze, p.h. 0.80 m. Heraklion Museum 2445. (Photos: courtesy A. Frantz.)

The statuettes: description

It is important to bear in mind that the state of preservation of the statuettes when they were brought to the Heraklion Museum was very poor and that several different restorations of the figures have been attempted since 1936.[8] Their present heavy restoration makes description

8 For the fragments, see Marinatos, *AA* 1936 (supra n.1) 219-22, fig. 2. For a detailed study of the manufacturing technique, see the drawings by P. Cellini in J. Papadopoulos, *Xoana e sphyrelata* (*Studia archeo-*

of the restored *versus* original parts of the figures difficult. Some critical parts of the male figure (figs. 2-4) are well preserved and thus without question: the bent right arm, the torso, the pubic area, and the legs to above the ankles. The left arm is preserved only to above the elbow. The male is restored with the right leg slightly in advance of the left, yet it is uncertain if this is correct. The preserved height of the male figure is 0.80 m. Since the feet are not preserved, it is open to conjecture how this figure was supported.

The skull of the male is composed of a domed cap made in two sheets, front and back. The front sheet is divided into repoussé vertical sections that end in spiral locks with central knobs, some with tiny holes in the centers. The face is made of one finely hammered sheet with large empty sockets for the insertion of the eyes and ears. The front torso is made of a single plate with a subtly modeled low collar bone. Both nipples are restorations. The lower boundary of the thorax is triangular, with a sharp point at the apex. The narrow waist is sharply delineated by a row of tiny bronze rivets, the attachment to the lower body. The pubic area is triangular, with a rectangular piece cut out for the insertion of the genitals. The thighs bulge like cigars from the waist to above the knees, which are not preserved. The thigh piece is riveted to the buttocks along an arch from the waist along the side but not visible from the front. The shin bones of the lower leg are delineated by sharp creases.

If one examines the male figure from the back, it is clear that it was intended to be seen only from the front. Almost all of the riveting is on the back or to the back of the sides (fig. 3). A long triangular mass of hair, composed of a single plate connected with the back skull plate, falls along the line of the upper spine. The strands of hair in back are defined by the repoussé technique. The ends of the plate for the torso are folded over and riveted to the rear plate at points just below the tops of the shoulders and below the shoulder blades. The central spinal furrow is delineated by a shallow groove. The buttocks are protruding and well modeled. The thigh plates are wrapped around the back and riveted toward the inner edge, with subsidiary pieces at the back inside edge above the knees. The front plates of the lower legs are folded over and riveted toward the back on the left and right sides.

Kenfield's thesis that an armorer must have had a rôle in envisioning and manufacturing this male figure in terms of a corselet, *mitre*, and greaves is undoubtedly correct.[9] The total number of bronze sheets used in this figure is over 30,[10] and the average thickness of the plates is 4 mm. There is no trace on the interior of this figure of any core material, and it is unlikely, as Haynes points out, that *sphyrelaton* statues were ever hammered over a wooden core.[11] It is probable that the figure held an attribute in his right hand.[12] The bent right elbow signifies, at a minimum, a gesture.

The two female figures (Heraklion Museum nos. 2446 and 2447) (figs. 1, 5-7) are about half the size of the male; their heights are reported as 0.40 m (no. 2446) and 0.45 m (no. 2447).[13] One of the female figures is made of 10 hammered plates, the other of 8.[14] Their bodies are more or less cylindrical with arms flat against their sides, long fingers delineated but no trace of anything held at the sides. Each figure wears a belted *peplos* with an *epiblema* over the shoulders and upper arms. On the head each wears a low cylindrical *polos* with a repoussé design on the upper edges. On the better preserved (no. 2447) (figs. 5-7), the design is a narrow band with a simple scallop or a wobbly zigzag. Both have hair coiffed with short bangs peek-

---

logica 24, 1980) App. II, pls. IV, V, IX.

9 J. F. Kenfield, "The sculptural significance of early Greek armor," *OpRom* 9 (1973) 149-56.

10 Haynes, *Technique* 17.

11 Ibid. 12-13

12 See below.

13 Marinatos, *AA* 1936 (supra n.1) 218.

14 Haynes, *Technique* 17; Marinatos, *AA* 1936 (supra n.1) 217: females made of between 10 and 15 sheets; male of over 30.

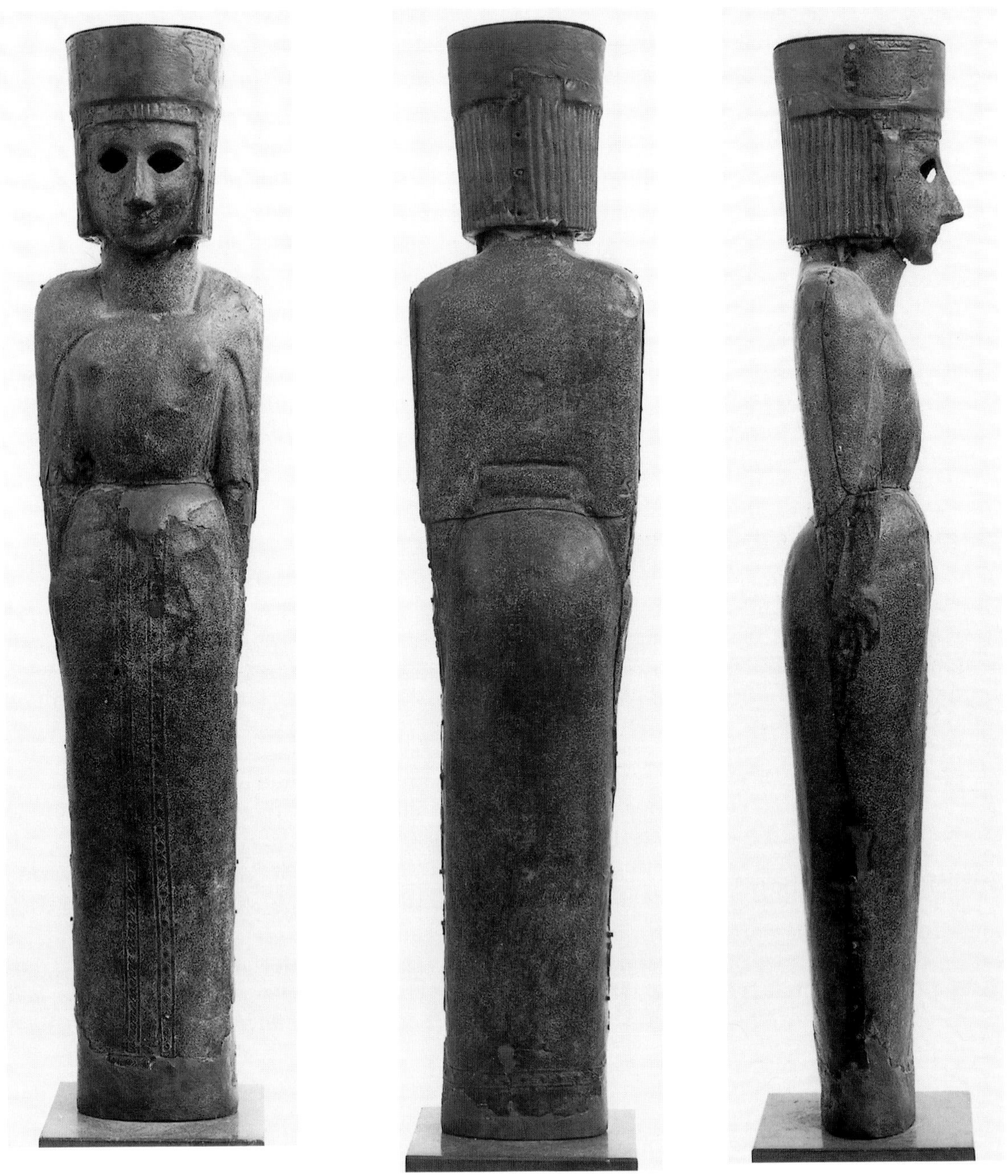

Figs. 5-7. Female figure from Dreros, front, back, and right side. Bronze, p.h. 0.45 m. Heraklion Museum 2447. (Photos: courtesy A. Frantz.)

ing out across the brow and a blunt cut at jaw length. Individual hairs are defined by repoussé work. Two *polos*-cum-hair plates are used for each figure. Both faces are ovoid and narrow with large oval eye sockets and arching eyebrows defined by a carination of the metal. The facial features are sharp and precise. On the larger figure (no. 2447) the tip of the nose and the chin are restored; on the smaller (no. 2446), the chin is mostly destroyed.

The skirts of the *peploi* are made of two plates each, front and back, and are riveted toward the back of the sides. As in the male figure, some attention has been paid to the positioning of the riveting so that the frontal view is the most acceptable. Both figures have protruding, arching buttocks. The skirt of the larger figure is better preserved, yet both have a similar repoussé pattern in panels down the front and along the lower horizontal border. On the larger figure (no. 2447) (figs. 5-7) the wide central panel is blank with narrow decorated bands to the right and left: on the right, a tightly wound, raised guilloche pattern with raised dots in the center of each braid; and on the left, joined tip to tip, is a pattern of diamond-shaped scales with raised dots at the center of each diamond. The design along the upper edge of the bottom seam is a diamond-shaped scale similar to the left vertical panel except running horizontally; the lower part of the border is not well-enough preserved to determine whether any pattern existed. Though the lower edges of the female figures are poorly preserved, it is likely that the skirts formed their supports.

The statuettes: style and chronology

The context helps only broadly in defining the chronology of these three statuettes. What remains is an examination of the stylistic and technical parallels for the figures. The first and most obvious observation is that none of the figures appears to exhibit the characteristics of the Cretan Daedalic style. The facial features and the body forms, of the male especially, are very plastic and full. The heads are not flat-topped and triangular with wedge-shaped faces, and the hair styles are clearly not typical of the wig-like coifs of the Daedalic style. Despite this, Rizza sees the elongated, triangular torso and the defined pubic area of the male as characteristics of the Early Daedalic style and assigns all three figures to his Early Daedalic phase (690-670 B.C.),[15] while Schäfer lowers their date and places them in the Middle Daedalic period (670-640).[16] The Dreros figures, however, bear little similarity to the other sculptures of the Cretan Daedalic style.

In relation to one another there are some very basic differences between the male and two female figures, e.g.:

— the scale (p.h. male 0.80 m versus p.h. females *c.*0.40 and 0.45 m) (fig. 1);

— the variation in the number of hammered plates (male: over 30 *versus* females: 8 and 10 or 10 to 15). The large discrepancy can be only partly explained by the differences between the open, nude male form and the draped female body form;

— the conception and execution of the male figure in terms of a suit of armor, while the females are conceived differently;

— the open, rather daringly executed form of the male with full bodily proportions *versus* the closed, columnar, controlled, static form of the females;

— differences in facial features, e.g., the male has full features with cheeks with some volume, low and rounded cheekbones, a relatively large horizontal mouth, and a broad nose, *versus* the rather pinched features of the females with long pointed noses, high sharp cheekbones, and tiny mouths. In profile the female faces are so narrow that there is barely any cheek or temple area, and the mouth and chin recede from the plane of the forehead. The one characteristic that makes them seem to look so very much alike, the open eye sockets, is, in fact, a characteristic of almost all bronze figures, both hammered and cast, larger than miniature scale.

Given the differences in appearance, it seems logical to approach the problem of chronology and the question of the function of the statues by considering the male figure separately from the two females, who are undeniably a pair, and to see what emerges.

Male statuette: parallels

For the male figure (figs. 1-4) Boardman has presented the most convincing parallels and argued for a late 8th c. B.C. date.[17] Two tiny (p.h. of better preserved one, 0.047 m) gold repoussé *kriophoros* figures from the burnt *dromos* deposit of the Khaniale Tekke Tomb 2 near Knossos bear a strong resemblance to the male from Dreros. The heads of the gold figures are domed and divided into sections by vertical lines that end in hook curls along the hairline. The backs of

---

15 G. Rizza and V. Santa-Maria Scrinari, *Il sanctuario sull'acropoli di Gortina* (Rome 1968) 224-25.

16 Schäfer 1972 (supra n.3) 192.

17 J. Boardman, "The Khaniale Tekke tombs II," *BSA* 62 (1967) 61.

the gold figures are largely destroyed. The burnt deposit is dated to the Late Geometric period, between 750 and the beginning of the 7th c. B.C.

Also of interest because of its closely dated context and features comparable to those of the Dreros male is a cast bronze statuette (h. 0.103 m) from Cretan Afrati, found in a level with pottery of the late 8th c. B.C.[18] The treatment of the hair is almost identical, both in front (the division of the hair into sections ending in curls at the forehead) and in back. The treatment of the hair on the back of the Dreros and Afrati statuettes is also curiously like the painted hair on the back of the Late Minoan IIIC terracotta goddesses with upraised hands from the Bench Sanctuary in the temple at Karphi (Heraklion Museum nos. 11042 and 11043) and, thus, may be regarded as a lingering Minoan feature.[19]

Finally, Kenfield's arguments that an armorer had a hand in the manufacture of the Dreros male statuette are also important for the chronology of the figure.[20] For the form of the corselet-like front of the Dreros male we can compare miniature votive corselets of the late 8th or early 7th c. from Cretan Praisas and Gortyn,[21] as well as the Late Geometric corselet from Argos.[22] It is probable that the general inspiration for much of Cretan metalworking, including the Dreros figure and Cretan armor, owes much to the Near East, yet the end products are uniquely Cretan, and it is within the Cretan realm that we find the parallels for the Dreros statuette.

Female statuettes: parallels

More problematic is the question of where the female statuettes fit into the picture (figs. 1, 5-7). The general type of the standing draped female with arms to her sides, wearing a *polos* and a *peplos* with an *epiblema* and a decorated front panel, can be documented on Crete from the first half of the 8th c., e.g., on the bronze belt from Tomb P at Fortetsa;[23] on the rectangular gold pendant with Phoenician-inspired elements from the Idaean Cave;[24] and the late 8th or early 7th c. limestone relief from Chania with a female figure in the doorway surrounded by archers defending against charioteers.[25] This figure type continues, however, into the 7th c. on Crete and elsewhere where there are well-known examples: the Daedalic Auxerre female,

---

18 J. Boardman, *Greek sculpture: the Archaic period* (London 1978) fig. 17, p. 11; Lembessi, *ΣΤΗΛΗ* (supra n.2) 87-95, pl. 25.

19 G. C. Gesell, *Town, palace and house cult in Minoan Crete* (Studies in Mediterranean Archaeology 67; Göteborg 1985) fig. 48a, b; Boardman 1967 (supra n.17) 61 also makes this point. Boardman, *The Cretan collection in Oxford: The Dictaean Cave and Iron Age Crete* (Oxford 1961) 86-88, no. 380, also cautiously offers a tantalizing bit of evidence from the Idaean Cave material in Oxford of a domed hammered bronze object (h. 0.053; diam. 0.097-0.085; th. *c*.0.001 m) that bears a striking resemblance to the domed head of the Dreros male. It has a constricted 'necking' that has vertical grooves (hair?) and two groups of three rivet holes. Boardman is careful to point out that there is nothing else from the Idaean Cave to indicate that there were bronze statuettes like those from Dreros. And we can add that there are no specific parallels between this male figure and the male figures on the Idaean Cave shields which are so Near Eastern in style and theme.

20 Kenfield 1973 (supra n.9).

21 Kenfield 1973 (supra n.9) 152-55; S. Benton, "Bronzes from Palaikastro and Praisos," *BSA* 40 (1939-40) 56-57, pl. 31.

22 Kenfield 1973 (supra n.9) 152-55; P. Courbin, "Une tombe géométrique d'Argos," *BCH* 81 (1957) 340-56.

23 J. K. Brock, *Fortetsa: Early Greek tombs near Knossos* (Cambridge 1957) 197-99, pls. 115 and 168: found in a pithos with two vases of PGB or EG date; N. Coldstream, *Geometric Greece* (London 1977) 100-1: 8th c. B.C.; Boardman 1967 (supra n.17) 59: *floruit* of style is end of 9th and first half of 8th c.

24 R. Higgins, *Greek and Roman jewellery* (2nd edn., Berkeley 1980) 109, pl. 17A: around 750 B.C.; Coldstream, *Geometric Greece* (supra n.23) 281: contemporary with the gold belt from Eleusis [8th c.]; Boardman 1967 (supra n.17) 60: early 8th c.

25 Davaras, *Astritsi* (supra n.1) 12, fig. 8.

though without the *polos*;[26] the female relief figures on the underside of the lintel on Temple A at Prinias;[27] and the korai wearing diagonal mantles on the *perirrhanteria* from Samos and Isthmia.[28] The draped type can be contrasted with the naked female, the Oriental-type goddess who appears, for example, in the mid 8th c., North Syrian-inspired and Athenian-manufactured, Astarte-like ivory female from the Athenian grave,[29] and on the two limestone plaques from Gortyn.[30]

The flat-topped, short *polos* derives originally from the Near East and is seen on Syrian and Egyptian imports to Greece[31] and on Eastern-inspired Greek artifacts. From Crete the parallels are of Near Eastern inspiration and begin in the 8th c.: the female heads on the penannular pendant from the Tekke tholos tomb,[32] and the females on the pendant from the Idaean Cave.[33] The form is the same but the decorative elements are different on the Geometric ivory female from the Athenian grave.[34] The short-cropped coif, once again, fits well in the Cretan milieu of the 8th and early 7th c. B.C., e.g., on the female on the Chania limestone relief; on the Tekke pendant; on the Idaean Cave pendant;[35] a female goddess(?) with upraised arms (a Minoan survival of the gesture) on an 8th or 7th c. plaque from Mathia Pediados (Heraklion Museum no. 6347);[36] in pottery, on a painted sphinx on a 7th c. North Syrian-inspired bowl from Arkades;[37] and on the two heads on an Orientalizing ivory pinhead from the Idaean Cave.[38]

For the repoussé details on the *polos* and *peplos* the parallels again put us in the Cretan sphere of the period of the 8th and early 7th c. B.C. Boardman cites a comparable pattern, the diamond-shaped scale, on the bronze greaves from the tholos tomb at Kavousi which, according to Boardman, contains nothing later than 700 B.C.,[39] although Coldstream assigns the tomb contents a date of 750-680 B.C.[40] This same pattern appears as a border motif on a bronze relief plaque from the same tomb at Kavousi.[41] The guilloche on the skirts of the Dreros females is a pattern that is relatively common in the Greek decorative repertoire of the Geometric, Orientalizing, and Archaic periods on pottery and bronze.[42]

---

26 Davaras ibid. 13, figs. 9-10; G. M. A. Richter, *Korai* (London 1968) no. 18, figs. 76-79.

27 Stewart, *Greek sculpture* fig. 29.

28 Sturgeon, *Isthmia IV* (supra n.3) 31-45: dated to the decade 660-650 B.C.

29 A. Snodgrass, *The dark age of Greece* (Edinburgh 1971) 344.

30 Rizza and Scrinari, *Gortina* (supra n.15) dates one plaque (with two females) to the Middle Daedalic phase, *c.*650 B.C., and the other (with male in the middle) to the Late Daedalic phase, while B. S. Ridgway (*The Archaic style in Greek sculpture* [Princeton 1977] 20-21) suggests they belong together and should perhaps be removed from the temple.

31 See references in Sturgeon, *Isthmia IV* (supra n.3) 31, n.69.

32 Higgins, *Jewellry* (supra n.24) 109, pl. 17E: *c.*800 B.C.

33 Ibid. pl. 17A.

34 Snodgrass, *Dark age* (supra n.29) and see also Sturgeon, *Isthmia* (supra n.3) 31, n.72 for other examples.

35 Chania relief: Davaras, *Astritsi* (supra n.1) 12, fig. 8; Tekke pendant: Higgins, *Jewellry* (supra n.24) 109, pl. 17E; Idaean Cave pendant: ibid. 109, pl. 17A.

36 S. Alexiou, "Η Μινοϊκὶ θεὰ μεθ'ὑψόμενον χειρόν," *CretChron* 12 (1958) 284, pl. ΙΓ', fig. 3: dated to end of the Orientalizing or beginning of the Daedalic period; Gesell, *Town* (supra n.19) 58 and 185, fig. 58.

37 J. Boardman, *The Greeks overseas* (2nd edn., New York 1973) fig. 30.

38 J. A. Sakellarakis, "The Idaean Cave ivories" in J. L. Fitton (ed.), *Ivory in Greece and the Eastern Mediterranean from the Bronze Age to the Hellenistic period* (British Museum Occ. Pap. 85, 1992) pl. 18b-d.

39 Boardman 1967 (supra n.17) 61.

40 Coldstream, *Geometric Greece* (supra n.23) 285. See drawing in D. Levi, "I bronzi di Axos," *ASAtene* 13-14 (1930-31) 87 and photograph of upside-down greaves on 99, fig. 31.

41 Coldstream, *Geometric Greece* (supra n.23) 285, fig. 92a. Boardman (1967 [supra n.17] 61) also identifies a pattern on the skirts of the Dreros females as a raised zigzag and cites the parallel pattern on the chest of the Tekke *kriophoros* and on the lion on a Fortetsa plaque, yet I do not see a zigzag pattern on the Dreros females.

42 E.g., Brock, *Fortetsa* (supra n.23) 179-80: Fortetsa pottery; E. Kunze, *Archäische Schildbände (OlF II, Ber-*

What is striking about the Dreros female heads, especially in comparison to the male head, is the extremely shallow profile, with barely any cheek or temple area, while the noses are very long and pointed (though restored at the tips) and the cheek bones are high and sharp. The chins on all three figures are at least partially damaged, so that it is hard to base anything on the small, forward-jutting restored chins of the females. Although Sturgeon points out the closeness of the facial features of the Isthmia *perirrhanterion* females to the Olympia B 28 cauldron attachment and to the profiles of the Dreros figures,[43] the divergence of the Cretan and Peloponnesian or Island styles seems to me to beg any really close comparison. The Dreros females do, however, as Sturgeon points out, seem to anticipate, in a general way, the developments of the second quarter of the 7th c. in the organization of the facial features, especially as seen in profile. The Dreros females must surely be placed prior to the Isthmia *perirrhanterion* and the comparable ones. The high cheek bones, pinched narrow features, and small mouths of the Dreros females are close to those of the *sphyrelaton* crowned female head from Olympia, dated to the second quarter of the 7th c. B.C.[44]

In body forms and proportions, the Dreros females with their slender bodies tapering to the bottom of the skirt, small breasts, narrow shoulders and hips, and gently arching buttocks are still some distance from works like the Daedalic Auxerre female with her broad shoulders, well-developed breasts, and larger hips. The slender Naxian Nikandre seems closer, yet her flat rectangular lower body is unlike the cylindrical form of the Dreros females. The slim Dreros females appear more like the mid 7th c. wooden goddess from the Samian Heraion.[45] The hands plastered to the sides of the body with exaggerated long fingers are very close to those of the fragmentary *sphyrelaton* females from Olympia, recently published posthumously by Kunze and dated to the third quarter of the 7th c. B.C.[46]

In summary, a precise date for the Dreros female figures is problematic. The comparative evidence for specific details puts the figures in the late 8th or first half of the 7th c. B.C. In the relative scheme they can be placed prior to the Auxerre and Nikandre korai, and also prior to the three fragmentary *sphyrelaton* females with Daedalic hair styles from Olympia and the crowned female head from Olympia. The female figures from Dreros, like the male, bear no characteristics of the Cretan Daedalic style and should be placed prior to the dominance of that style on Crete in the second or third quarters of the 7th c. In relation to the Dreros male, the female figures seem slightly more advanced in conception and stylistic details. Again the parallels for the female statuettes, as for the male, are mostly Cretan, and it can be convincingly argued that the females should be placed in the first quarter of the 7th c. B.C.

The statuettes: function

Although it is tempting to view the three hammered bronze images as a triad of deities,[47] like the male with flanking females on the Fortetsa bronze belt[48] or like the male with flanking naked females on the Gortyn limestone plaque,[49] the differences in the technical conception, scale, and details allow us to think instead of the origins of the male and the two females as independent of one another and to reassess the question of the identity of the figures.

---

lin 1950) Beilage 3 [1, 3, 5], 5 [1, 3, 5], 6 [3, 4, 6], 7 [1, 3, 5]: repoussé borders on shield bands of 7th and 6th c. B.C.

43 Sturgeon, *Isthmia* (supra n.3) 30-31, 34, pl. 83.

44 E. Kunze, "Sphyrelata," *OlBer* 9 (1994) 129-32, no. 11, pls. 53-56.

45 D. Ohly, "Neue Holzfunde aus dem Heraion von Samos," *AthMitt* 82 (1967) 89-99, Beil. 43-47.

46 Kunze 1994 (supra n.44) 102-13, esp. no. 5, pls. 39-40.

47 For an illustration of the Dreros *sphyrelata* as a triad of cult images on the altar, see Stewart, *Greek sculpture*, fig. 16.

48 Brock, *Fortetsa* (supra n.23) 134-35, no. 1568, pls. 115, 168.

49 Rizza and Santa-Maria Scrinari, *Gortina* (supra n.15) pl. IV.

The case for the Dreros male being an image of a god is relatively good: the figure is imposing and monumental in its appearance though, in actuality, less than a meter in height. The bent right arm suggests that the figure was gesturing and most probably held an attribute. Since the temple can be identified from later evidence as Apollo's, and since Apollo in the traditional guise we know him from Archaic and Classical iconography carries a bow in one hand,[50] we may with some confidence restore that same attribute here. In fact, a bow is a sufficiently large attribute to have been held in such a way as to obscure the rivets at the shoulder and on the outside of the arm, the only places on the front of the figure where the riveting is visible.[51]

For the female statues the case for their identification as deities seems not conclusive. In fact, they have much more in common with later korai figures for whom identity and meaning is a question but for whom correlation with specific divinities is open to dispute.[52] The lack of attributes and the lack of individualization of their features, dress, and manner to differentiate one from the other suggests that these females were not meant to represent specific divinities, like Leto and Artemis, as has been postulated, or any other. The iconography of Artemis seems well developed by this period, with early Iron Age representations of her as *Potnia Theron* with animals and branches,[53] although Artemis also appears in the 7th c. in 'hieratic form,' with *polos*, *peplos*, and arms to her sides, mostly in representations from the Laconian Orthia sanctuary.[54] It has been argued by Davaras that the *epiblema* is an element of attire reserved for divinities[55] and by others that the *polos* is a symbol of divinity.[56] Yet, that the *polos* and the *epiblema* are elements of attire restricted to the divine realm in Cretan iconography is speculative. If one looks within the context of Cretan art of the general period and examines possible images of Cretan divinities for gesture and attributes, we find the picture unclear. In one possible representation of a goddess (cult image?) from the same approximate time period, the female framed in the doorway on the limestone relief from Chania, it is worth noting that her right arm is bent and laid against her breast, in the manner of the Auxerre female.[57] What this gesture signifies is another question.[58] On the Fortetsa belt the male holds the wrists of the two identical, draped females, as on the 7th c. Gortyn plaque where the females are nude.[59] One element which is clear in Cretan triad representations is that the male and the females have in every instance the same approximate body height (discounting the height of the *polos*). In the case of the Dreros figures, the females are half the height of the male. Thus, we might question the identification of the three Dreros figures as a triad of divinities[60] and think instead of the female statuettes as independent, in some sense, of the male figure. The females might be votive images, dedicants in the service of the god, or

---

50 Romano, *Images* (supra n.1) 420-22.

51 Cellini, in Papadopoulos, *Xoana* (supra n.8) 99.

52 For the meaning of korai, see Ridgway, *Archaic style* (supra n.30) 108-12; Stewart, *Greek sculpture* 109-10; Richter, *Korai* (supra n.26) 3-4.

53 *LIMC* II, 624-29

54 *LIMC* II, 631-32.

55 Davaras, *Astritsi* (supra n.1) 59-65 with bibliography. See also E. Harrison, "Notes on Daedalic dress," *JWalt* 36 (1977) 37-48.

56 E.g., Ridgway, *Archaic style* (supra n.30) 108-12.

57 Chania relief: Davaras, *Astritsi* (supra n.1) 12, fig. 8; Auxerre female: Richter, *Korai* (supra n.26) no. 18, figs. 76-79.

58 Davaras, *Astritsi* (supra n.1) 12.

59 Fortetsa belt: Brock, *Fortetsa* (supra n.23); Gortyn plaques: Rizza and Scrinari, *Gortina* (supra n.15); and Davaras, *Astritsi* (supra n.1) 53-54, fig. 45 with bibliography.

60 P. Amandry (in *Guide de Delphes: Le musée* [Paris 1961] 218) has identifed three of the 6th c. chryselephantine statues from Delphi as a triad of Apollo, Leto, and Artemis, although he postulates that the females were made about 20 or 30 years later than the male and are stylistically different. I am grateful to K. DeVries for calling this reference to my attention.

priestesses, and it is not inconceivable that they served, like the 7th c. females of the Isthmia and Samos *perrirhanteria*, as supports, perhaps for a small wooden votive table or the like.[61]

Conclusion

In summary, I suggest, contrary to the currently accepted view that the three *sphyrelaton* statuettes were manufactured as a triad of deities for the temple, that the male statuette was manufactured first, in the later decades of the 8th c. B.C., as the cult image for the temple. Some years may have passed and an accumulation of bones and débris built up on the altar on which the statue stood. The altar may have been enclosed by three stone stabs and given a wooden top. The two female statues were made soon thereafter, in the first quarter of the 7th c., and added to the altar as votives, priestess figures, or table supports. All three Dreros *sphyrelata* stand firmly in the sphere of Cretan art of the Late Geometric–Early Orientalizing period and are representative of a general style, technology, and conception which combines Near Eastern (mostly North Syrian) elements with purely local Cretan ones to create uniquely Cretan images.

Mediterranean Section, The University of Pennsylvania Museum of Archaeology/Anthropology, Philadelphia, PA 19104

---

61 I am grateful to E. Harrison for this interesting suggestion. Because the upper edges of the *poloi* are not well preserved and it is unclear whether any part of the tops of the *poloi* are original, it is not possible to assess the technical evidence for the possibility that the females were used as supports.

Boeotian bow fibulae and the route of Helios

Michael J. Bennett

This article presents two late 8th–early 7th c. B.C. bow fibulae from Central Greece, one in the collection of the Department of Ancient Art, Harvard University[1] (figs. 1-2) and the other in the Shelby White and Leon Levy collection[2] (figs. 3-4). I propose that the iconography of each of these fibulae diagrams the route of Helios from dawn (*eos*) to dusk (*zophos*), as recounted in the Homeric Hymn to Helios and that this interpretation reveals important interconnections between pictures and oral poetry in early Greece.

The Harvard and Shelby White–Leon Levy bow fibulae

The Harvard fibula appears to map the arc of Helios across the sky by means of a sequence of environmental stages through which the sun passes from dawn to dusk (fig. 5). Incised lines on the crescent-shaped bow render Helios as a disk containing a complex composition of interlocking circles supported atop the connecting rein of a team of horses. The catchplate appears to be incised with a representation of a horse confronting a fish, perhaps together signifying the earthly zone — the horse standing for Gaia, dry land, and the fish for Pontus, tributaries over the land.[3]

The Homeric Hymn to Helios is, I submit, cognate with, and analogous to, the pictorial composition on the Harvard fibula.

> And now, O Muse Calliope, daughter of Zeus,
> begin to sing of glowing Helios whom mild-eyed
> Euryphaëssa, the far-shining one, bare to the Son of
> Earth and starry Heaven. For Hyperion wedded
> glorious Euryphaëssa, his own sister, who bare him
> lovely children, rosy armed Eos and rich tressed
> Selene and tireless Helios who is like the deathless
> gods. As he rides in his chariot, he shines upon men
> and deathless gods, and piercingly he gazes with his
> eyes from his golden helmet. Bright rays beam
> dazzlingly from him, and his bright locks streaming
> from the temples of his head gracefully enclose his
> far-seen face: a rich, fine-spun garment glows upon
> his body and flutters in the wind: and stallions carry
> him. Then, when he has stayed his golden-yoked
> chariot and horses, [he rests there upon the highest
> point of heaven], until he marvelously drives them
> down again through heaven to Ocean.
> Hail to you, lord! Freely bestow on me substance
> that cheers the heart. And now that I have begun
> with you, I will celebrate the race of mortal men
> half-divine whose deeds the Muses have showed to
> mankind.[4]

---

1 Arthur M. Sackler Museum, Harvard University Art Museums, Ancient Art Acquisition Fund through the generosity of Walter and Ursula Cliff, 1986.655. H. 0.17 m; w. 0.10 m. M. Bennett, "Engraved bow fibula," in S. Langdon (ed.), *From pasture to polis: Art in the age of Homer* (Columbia, MO 1993) 208-10, fig. 81, pl. 7.

2 Dimensions: h. 17.3 cm.; w. 9.7 cm. D. von Bothmer, *Glories of the past: Ancient art from the Shelby White and Leon Levy collection* (Exhib. cat., The Metropolitan Museum of Art, New York 1991) 97, no. 78.

3 For the horse and fish as representative of the elemental divisions Gaia and Okeanos on a contemporary plate fibula from Boeotia, see M. J. Bennett, "Engraved plate fibula," in Langdon, *From pasture to polis* (supra n.1) 78-80, fig. 18.

4 Hesiod (transl. H. Evelyn-White), *The Homeric hymns and homerica* (LCL, Cambridge, MA 1914) 459.

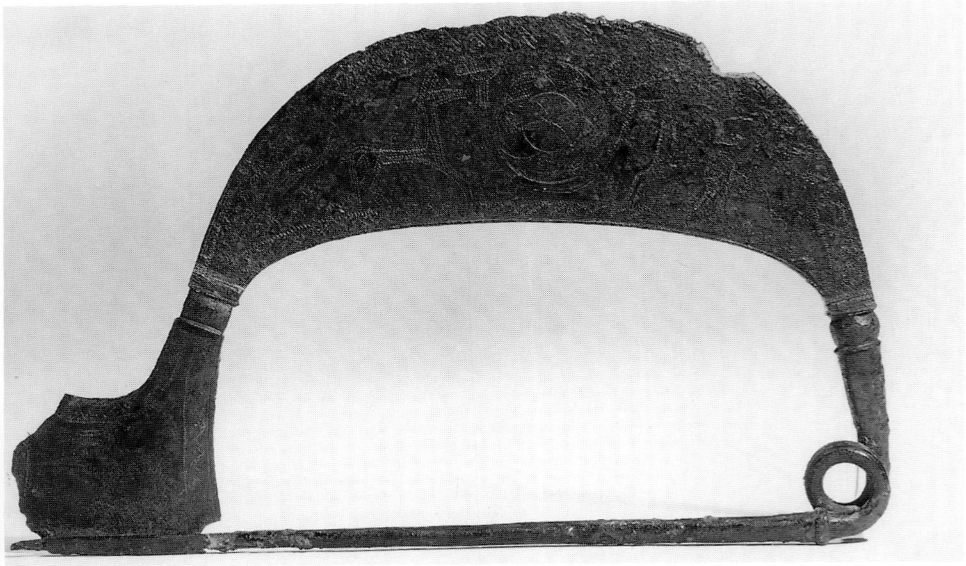

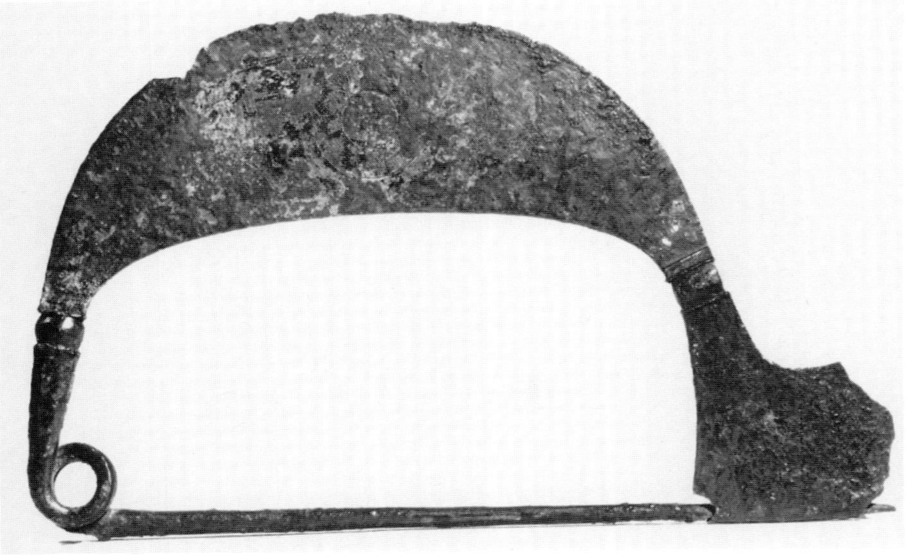

Figs. 1-2. Bow fibula, one side (top) and the other side (below). Boeotian or Attic. 750-700 B.C. Bronze, l. 0.17 m, h. 0.10 m. Cambridge, MA, Sackler Museum, Harvard University Art Museums, Ancient Art Acquisition Fund through the generosity of Walter and Ursula Cliff 1986.655. (Photos: courtesy of the Arthur M. Sackler Museum)

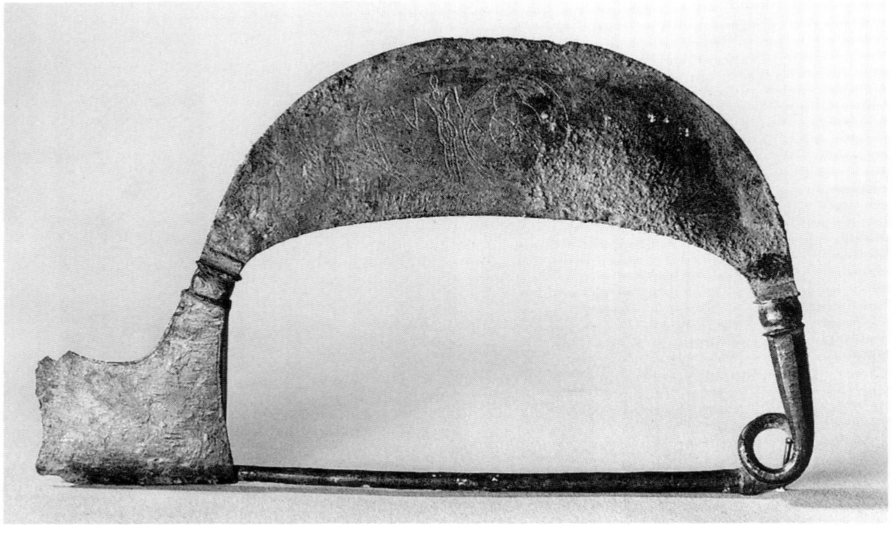

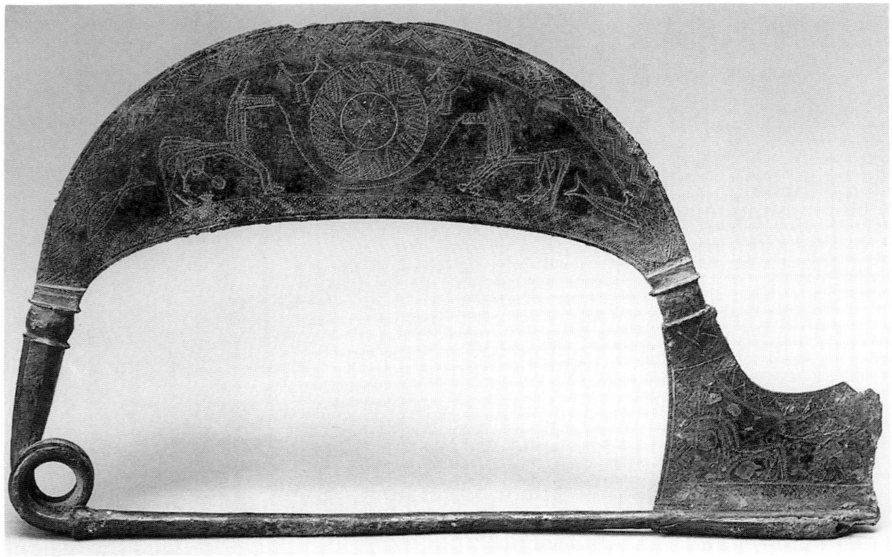

Figs. 3-4. Bow fibula, one side (top) and the other side (below). Boeotian or Attic. 750-700 B.C. Bronze, l. 0.173 m, h. 0.097 cm. New York, The Shelby White–Leon Levy collection. (Photos: O. Nelson, courtesy White-Levy collection.)

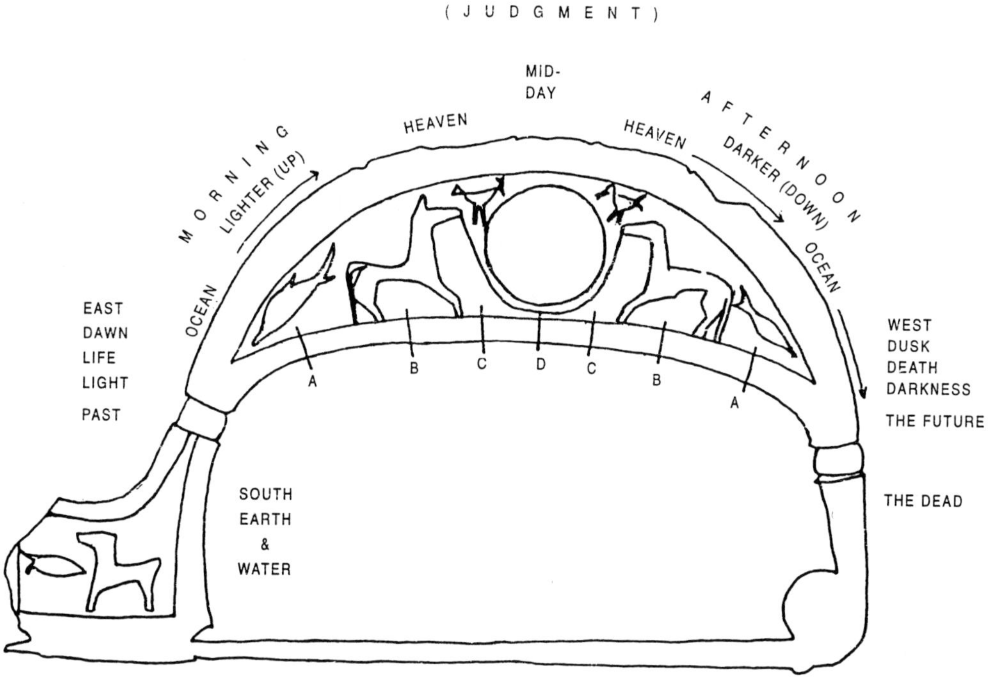

Fig. 5. Diagram of the front of the Harvard bow fibula (see figs. 1-2). (Drawing: author.)

Acknowledging the break in the hymn, it is still clear that Helios is visualized as a horse-drawn chariot that stops temporarily at mid-heaven, precisely the position of the disk on the fibula bow. Okeanos is represented by the pair of fish; Ouranos by the pair of birds, each bird placed above and in front of each horse. The symmetrical sequence: fish–bird–bird–fish predetermines the sun's course and is integrated into the discrete parts of the sun chariot, composing a linear ring: fish–horse–bird–disk–bird–horse–fish.

The Harvard fibula has one close parallel. It is in the Shelby White-Leon Levy collection in New York and is certainly by the same hand (figs. 3-4). It therefore may be used as commentary on the Harvard fibula. One side is nearly identical to the preserved side of the Harvard piece (compare figs. 3 and 1).[5] However, on the opposite side the craftsman has shown Helios himself standing to the left of the sun chariot, in the very act of unreining his horses, exactly as in the Hymn (fig. 4). Hence, we can be sure that the schema depicted on the two fibulae represents the route of Helios as a linear ring.

Linear rings: visual and verbal

This schema A-B-C-D-C-B-A is a visual expression of the poetic device known as ring composition[6] (fig. 5). Ring composition is fundamental to Greek epic poetry, manifested in speeches, scenes and, in the case of the *Iliad*, in the poem as a totality.[7] On the fibula bow, this compositional principle plots the cyclic route of the sun across the sky, a pattern that I have referred to as a time-signature.[8] The pattern is both balanced and dynamic. Furthermore,

---

5 A minor but notable difference: the left horse on the New York fibula is shown as ithyphallic, perhaps a reference to the horses of Eos, Phaethon, and Lampos: see G. Nagy, *The best of the Achaeans: concepts of the hero in Archaic Greek poetry* (Baltimore 1979) 197 ff.; also *Od*. 23.246.

6 See D. Lohmann, *Die Komposition der Reden in der Ilias* (Berlin 1970).

7 An incised Thessalian belt at Harvard (*c*.700 B.C.) outlines the plot of the *Iliad*, suggesting that an early oral version of the poem was imagined in visual terms as a linear ring. See M. J. Bennett, *Belted heroes and bound women: the myth of the Homeric warrior-king* (Lanham, MD 1997) chapt. 1: "The Harvard belt."

8 M. J. Bennett, "Geometric incised personal ornaments and the shape of epic time (abstract)," *AJA* 91 (1995) 13; id., *Belted heroes* (supra n.7) chapt. 2: "The Harvard Belt, the Harvard bow fibula and the

internal evidence in the *Iliad* shows that this linear ring, this time-signature, is strikingly central to the momentum of the plot.

The regular cycle of the rising and setting sun is a basic conceptual paradigm in Homeric epic. It calibrates time, defines space through illumination, and relates both to the sequence of events on the battlefield. This paradigm follows the pervasive tendency in early Greek thought to define the whole by pairs of opposition. Dawn is associated with the east, light, life, and the past; dusk is associated with the west, darkness, death, and the future.[9] The life cycle is thereby defined as a time-sequence, modulating degrees of illumination and progressive directional and environmental co-ordinates. An ideal state of equilibrium, a balance between the opposed polarities of dawn and dusk is reached when Helios momentarily stops at mid-heaven. At this moment, life literally hangs in the balance. In the *Iliad*, this moment is identified as one of divine judgment.

Solar cycles and epic battles

The route of Helios is the cosmic engine that drives heroic battle in the *Iliad*. In fact, the progressive action of the first major day of battle in the poem (the 'interrupted' battle) is explicitly linked to the route of Helios:

> So long as it was early morning and the sacred daylight increasing,
> so long the thrown weapons of both took hold and the men dropped under them.
> But when Helios stood bestriding the middle heaven,
> then the father balanced the golden scales, and in them he set
> two fateful portions of death, which lays men prostrate,
> for Trojans, breakers of horses, and bronze-armored Achaians,
> and balanced it by the middle. The Achaian death day was heaviest.
> There the fates of the Achaians settled down toward the bountiful earth,
> while those of the Trojans were lifted into the wide sky.[10]

The route of Helios is clearly the agent of ascending and descending fortunes on the battlefield, a cycle in which Zeus himself participates. With his golden scales, the father of the gods decides winner and loser at the very moment that Helios is suspended at mid-heaven.

The fundamental rôle of Helios in Iliadic warfare is seen again during the second major battle (the 'great' battle). Two more passages in the *Iliad* confirm the symbiotic relationship between solar movement and critical turning-points on the battlefield:

> So long as it was early morning and the sacred daylight increasing,
> so long the thrown weapons of both took hold and the men dropped under them.
> But at that time when the woodcutter makes ready his supper
> in the wooded glens of the mountains, when the arms and hands have grown weary
> from cutting down the tall trees, and his heart has had enough of it,
> and longing for food and sweet wine takes hold of his senses;
> at that time the Danaans by their manhood broke the battalions.[11]

Another important event later in the same day is also given a solar calibration:

> So long as the sun was climbing still to the middle heaven,
> so long the thrown weapons of both took hold, and the men dropped under them;
> but when the sun had gone to the time for the unyoking of cattle,
> then beyond their very destiny the Achaians were stronger
> and dragged the hero Kebriones from under the weapons
> and the clamor of the Trojans, and stripped the armor from his shoulders.[12]

---

shape of epic time".

9 See G. E. R. Lloyd, *Polarity and analogy: two types of argumentation in early Greek thought* (Bristol 1966) 15-85.

10 *Il.* 8.66-74. All translations of the *Iliad* are from R. Lattimore, *The Iliad of Homer* (New York 1951).

11 *Il.* 11.84-91.

12 *Il.* 16.777-80.

No Homeric battle is decided until after the moment of divine judgment at noon. The second appearance of the golden scales of Zeus shows that high noon marks the culminating moment in the poem, when Hektor turns to face Achilles, and his impending death:

> but when the fourth time they had come around to the well springs
> then the father balanced his golden scales, and in them
> he set two fateful portions of death, which lays men prostrate,
> one for Achilles, and one for Hektor, breaker of horses,
> and balanced it by the middle; and Hektor's death day was heavier
> and dragged downward toward death, and Phoibos Apollo forsook him.[13]

Bow fibulae: Homeric cosmographies

These two incised bow fibulae diagram the shape of epic time as a linear ring, the visual cognate of the poetic device of ring-composition. The cyclic pattern incised on them gives form to a circular conception of time behind the linear narrative of Homeric epic — a pattern derived from the route of Helios, the ultimate cyclic timekeeper. As the above passages demonstrate, the rhythm of epic battles is united with the repeating revolutions of Helios so that earthly events are actually imagined as being driven forward by the sun's tireless, regular, and circular journey.[14] Most tellingly, in the *Iliad* Nestor uses the positions of the sun (dawn, midday, night) to give his stories a time structure.[15]

A well-known group of large Boeotian bow fibulae dated to the early 7th c. B.C., clearly related to the two fibulae described here, features large, central, radiate disks as dominant emblems on their arched bows.[16] The Harvard and Shelby White–Leon Levy fibulae can provide the key to interpreting the iconography of their distinctive incised decoration. According to this model, all would represent Helios in the high-noon position of cosmic balance and divine judgment, presiding over and illuminating events in the earthly sphere. One fibula in this group shows specifically that the events pictured are heroic and Homeric (fig. 6).[17] Clearly depicted to the right of the Helios-disk is the wheeled Trojan horse, one of the earliest representations of the Trojan horse in Greek art and roughly contemporary with another wheeled Trojan horse featured on a terracotta pithos found on Mykonos.[18] To the lower left of the Helios-disk are Herakles and the Hydra.

This group of bow fibulae illustrates a wide variety of heroic activities. Warriors are shown stepping in a line,[19] sailing in ships,[20] and one rides a horse.[21] A man spears a lion.[22]

---

13 *Il.* 22.208-13.

14 The ἦμος clause in each of the passages cited above introduces a cyclical event to mark an unalterable event in the narrative with profound consequences. See A. P. Radin, "Sunrise, sunset: ἦμος in Homeric epic," *AJP* 109 (1988) 473-78. The day as a unit of time is fundamentally important to the structure of Homeric epic: see M. P. Nilsson, *Primitive time-reckoning: a study in the origins and first development of the art of counting time among the primitive and early culture people* (Lund 1920) 13 ff.; N. Austin, "The one and the many in the Homeric cosmos," *Arion* (1974) 219-74; N. Austin, *Archery at the dark of the moon: poetic problems in Homer's Odyssey* (Berkeley 1975) 67 ff.; G. P. Goold, "The nature of Homeric composition" *ICS* 2 (1977) 1-34; P. Vivante, "Rose-fingered dawn and the idea of time," *RAMUS* 8 (1979) 125-36; J. Van Sickle, "Dawn and dusk as motifs of opening or closure," in *Heroic and bucolic Epos (Homer, Apollonius, Theocritus, Virgil)* (Atti del convegno mondale scientifico di studi su Vergilio 1; Milan 1984) 125-47; O. Taplin, *Homeric soundings: the shaping of the Iliad* (Oxford 1992) 14-19.

15 *Il.* 11.670-761.

16 See R. Hampe, *Frühe Griechische Sagenbilder in Böotien* (Athens 1936) pls. 1-5.

17 B. Schweitzer (transl. P. and C. Usborne), *Greek Geometric art* (London 1971) 14, fig. 126, pl. 2.

18 See M. Ervin, "A relief pithos from Mykonos," *ADelt* 18 (1964) 37-75, pls. 17-30.

19 Hampe, *Sagenbilder* (supra n.16) pls. 3, 5.

20 Ibid. 4, 5.

21 Ibid. 1.12.

22 Ibid. pl. 1.

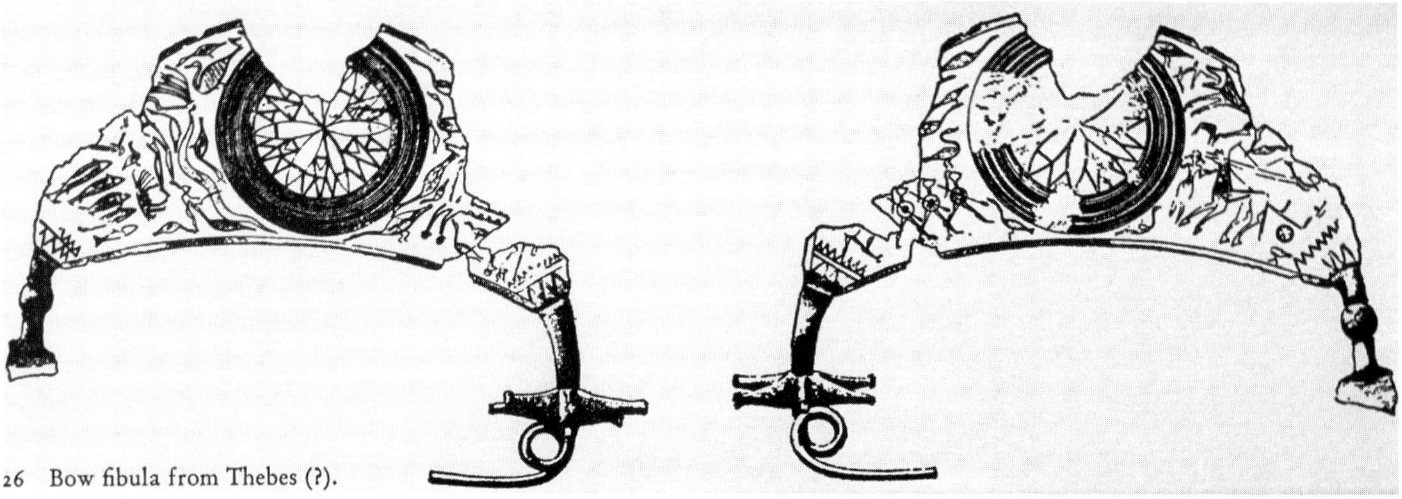

Fig. 6. Diagrams of bow fibulae. Reproduced from B. Schweitzer (transl. P. and C. Usborne), *Greek Geometric art* (London 1971) 14, fig. 126.

Two chariot groups flank one Helios-disk between fish below and birds above.[23] The fibulae feature cast rosettes and rosettes within the incised Helios-disks, all with 6 petals. For this reason, I suggest that the cast rosettes are a three-dimensional representation of the Helios-disk marking dusk (*zophos*), the end of the day and, more universally, the end of life. Held within the suspended judgment of Helios at midday, life in the human and natural spheres is shown full of vigor and activity. Heroes test their prowess. Fish ply the waters. Birds ride the air. Death, like the end of the day, brings a still darkness. These fibulae define mortality by representing its definitive moment — Helios at mid-heaven — but they also locate its deadline. The darkness of death will follow.

Odysseus: beyond the sun

While the route of the sun drives heroic battles in the *Iliad*, the travels of Odysseus in books 9-12 of the *Odyssey* are outside the tract of Helios and therefore outside the mortal sphere and the pulse of time. Given that the bow fibulae discussed in this article diagram the mortal world defined by the solar circuit, Odysseus's *Apologos* may be located outside this diagram, where the rules of the mortal world do not apply. The journey of Odysseus beyond the mortal time-zone, where he is offered immortality by Calypso,[24] illustrates the essential dilemma facing the hero: only a memorable death brings *kleos*, heroic renown — and memory is only possible in a timed world, within the orbit of Helios.

Odysseus recounts at the court of king Alkinoös the event that resulted in his displacement outside the mortal time-zone. He was carried south by the North Wind at a location near Cape Maleia, past Kythera.[25] The North Wind kept up for 9 days, pushing his ship outside the circuit of Helios. We know that Odysseus was beyond the sun, because from this moment the heavens betrayed no directional information and the mechanics of the cosmos, located outside the mortal sphere, were then encountered as personalities. Odysseus plainly assessed the situation:

---

23 Ibid. pl. 4.

24 *Od.* 5.208-9.

25 *Od.* 9.80 ff.

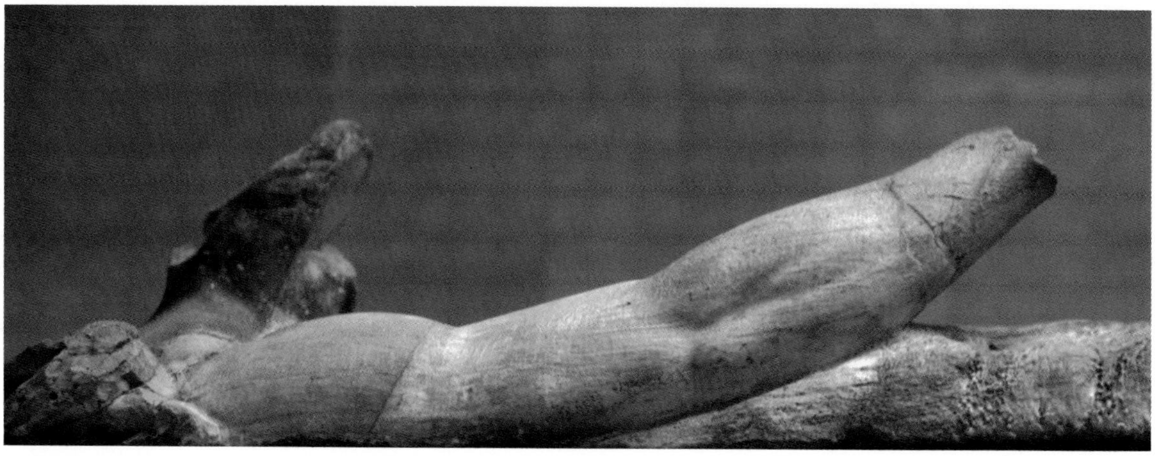

Fig. 7. Helios. From the east pediment on the Parthenon, Athens. London, British Museum. (Photo: author.)

> Dear friends, for we do not know where the darkness is nor the sunrise,
> nor where the Sun who shines upon people rises, nor where
> he sets, then let us hasten our minds and think, whether there is
> any course left open to us. But I think there is none.[26]

After this observation, Odysseus would encounter the Lotus Eaters, Polyphemos, the bag of winds on Aiolos's island, the Laistrygonians, Circe, the darkness of Hades, the Sirens, Skylla, Charybdis, the cattle of Helios and Kalypso — all entities beyond the sun, and thus unregulated by the rules of the timed world of mortals. Because Odysseus and his men are suspended in a timeless place, memory is dysfunctional and amnesia common. The fruit of the Lotus Eaters destroys memory.[27] So does Circe's drugged wine.[28] Ironically, although Odysseus does not drink Circe's wine, he still becomes forgetful and needs to be reminded of home by his men who had recovered from the wine-induced amnesia.[29] Odysseus heroically retains his memory in the years spent on Kalypso's island. In this sphere beyond the sun, only the Sirens have omniscient memory, including memory of the Trojan War.[30] But the Siren song is deadly.[31] This is because it is sung outside of the cycles of generational continuity, where it cannot be passed on by men caught in a timeless place with no past and no future.

This discontinuation of memory makes *kleos* impossible. In book 1 of the *Odyssey*, Telemachos perceptively states his father's situation:

> But now ingloriously (*akleos*) the storm winds have caught and carried him
> away, out of sight, out of knowledge and he
> left pain and lamentation to me.[32]

Telemachos describes Odysseus's disconnection with the solar cycles of mortality, where he is "out of sight" and "out of knowledge." Out of range of Helios, "the eye of heaven who knows everything because he sees everything," Odysseus is unseen, unheard, and unknown.[33] In such a circumstance, *kleos* cannot be recognized or transmitted. Helios is the agent of memory, in whose

26 All translations of the *Odyssey* are from Homer (transl. R. Lattimore), *The Odyssey of Homer* (Chicago 1967).

27 *Od*. 9.84 ff.

28 *Od*. 10.236.

29 *Od*. 10.472-74.

30 *Od*. 12.189 ff.

31 *Od*. 12.39-46.

32 *Od*. 1.241-43.

33 See C. Segal, "Bard and audience in Homer," in R. Lamberton and J. J. Keaney (edd.), *Homer's ancient readers: the hermeneutics of Greek epic's earliest exegetes* (Princeton 1992) 22.

absence, as in Hades, darkness descends like a stupor.[34] Odysseus therefore must achieve *nostos* to gain *kleos*. This is why heroic activities surround the central Helios-disks on late 8th–early 7th c. Greek bow fibulae. "Under the sun" is the only arena for heroic deeds that earn *kleos*.

The east pediment of the Parthenon

A 5th c. B.C. conception of Helios's governing influence, even on the Olympian gods, is given sculptural form on the Athenian Acropolis. In the east pediment of the Parthenon, the figure of Helios rises with two of his four horses in the left corner as Selene descends in the right corner (fig. 7).[35] With the above-mentioned Helios bow fibulae in mind, the east pediment of the Parthenon may now be understood to represent the birth of Athena, patron goddess of Athens, within a dynamic temporal frame affecting heroic events on earth.

Department of Greek and Roman Art, The Cleveland Museum of Art, Cleveland, OH

---

34 See E. Vermeule, *Aspects of death in early Greek art and poetry* (Berkeley 1979) 25.

35 See J. J. Pollitt, *Art and experience in classical Greece* (Cambridge 1972) 94.

Man or sphinx? An early Archaic bronze head in the Allard Pierson Museum

Patricia S. Lulof and Eric M. Moormann

The bronze head now in the Allard Pierson Museum (figs. 1-6)[1] was bought in 1974 from the widow of a Dutch amateur diver who discovered it in the 1960s in the sea off the Yugoslavian coast. The context of the find remains unknown, but it may have been a Greek or Roman vessel transporting the head as a work of art, as ballast, or as scrap metal.

Condition

The head is not well preserved. Many flaws and traces of scarring are visible. The left side appears to have been injured less and may have been protected by the sand of the seabed. The surface appears smooth today, however, because the holes, after having been cleaned with acid agents, were filled with a synthetic substance and the whole surface covered with a thick layer of varnish. Some of the following technical and iconographic observations, therefore, were based on photographs taken just after the acquisition of the head (fig. 7) and upon microscopic analysis.

Description

The head turns slightly to the right and has an asymmetrical appearance (fig. 1). The right tresses of hair hang free, while the left ones lie against cheek and neck. The left cheek is broader than the right cheek. The shape of the face is rather square, with a pointed chin and high cheekbones. Although barely preserved, the mouth apparently was small with straight, thin lips. The indentation below the lower lip can be distinguished, but the sulcus medianus is entirely lacking. There is a slight Archaic smile. All that remains of the nose is an irregular protrusion, but the nose was apparently small and straight.

The eyes, which are barely visible, are embedded in large sockets and must have been rather large. An old photograph (fig. 7) and examination under the microscope show that the eyeballs were originally filled with an unidentified black material. Only traces of the eyelids remain. Curved eyebrows are barely recognizable.

The hairstyle can no longer be distinguished clearly, but there probably was once a *taenia*, or fillet attached, judging from the old photograph (fig. 7), that has left a shallow horizontal depression just above the forehead. This depression has remnants of a black substance, probably a 'glue.' An indistinct series of flat, tongue-shaped scallops can be seen across the forehead, the remains of curls of hair.

The back of the head is no more than an unarticulated plane. The hair at the lower back (fig. 2) is divided into 5 braids; the two outer ones are the best preserved. The hanging tresses in front were worked entirely in the round on the left side: three braids are still recognizable (diam. 2.9 cm). The right braids are much thinner (1.3 cm). The left profile (fig. 4) shows the hair tresses at an angle of 30°. The left ear is barely visible, the hair on the head is corroded, but the scallops near the temples can still be seen. The right profile (fig. 3) shows a remarkably flattened face. The tresses of hair are at the same angle, but the tip of the outer braid on the back turns slightly outward.

---

1 Inv. no. 8946. H. 0.265 m; w. 0.195 m; d. 0.125 m; face 0.135 m; w. outer eye corners 0.10 cm; l. left tresses 0.065 m; l. right tresses 0.055 m; w. left cheek 0.045 cm; w. right cheek 0.049 m; weight 19 kg. Published: J. M. Hemelrijk, *Mededelingen van de Vrienden van het Allard Pierson Museum* [hereafter: *MededAPM*] 22 (1981) 3-4; J. M. Hemelrijk, *MededAPM* 24 (1982) 4, fig. 9; "Analyse van twee bronzenkoppen," *MededAPM* 43 (1988) 32-33; Rolley, *La sculpture grecque* 66, figs. 59-60.

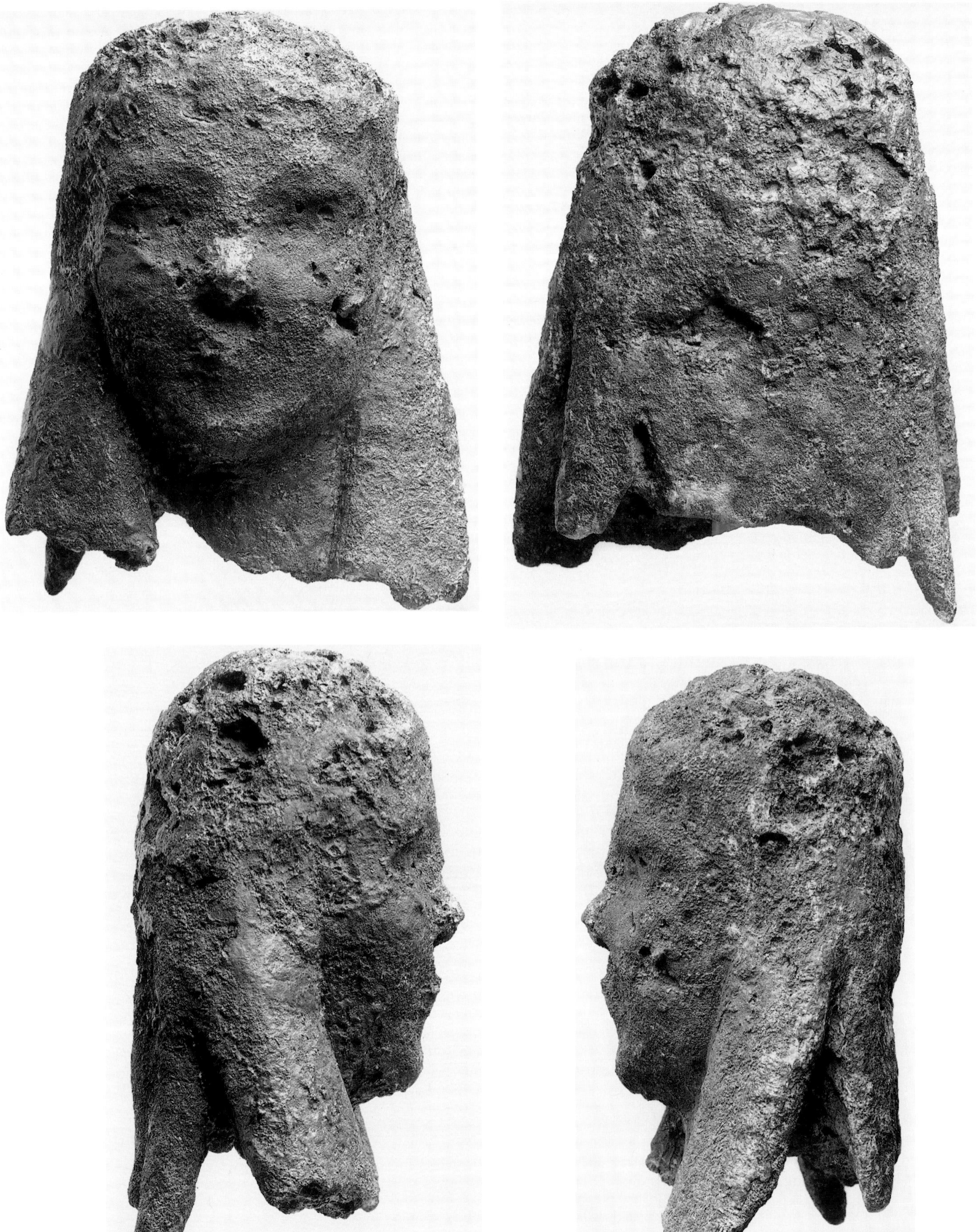

Figs. 1-4. Head of a sphinx, front (top left), back (top right), right profile (below left), left profile (below right). Bronze, h. 0.265 m. Amsterdam, Allard Pierson Museum 8946. (Photos: courtesy Allard Pierson Museum, M. Bootsman.)

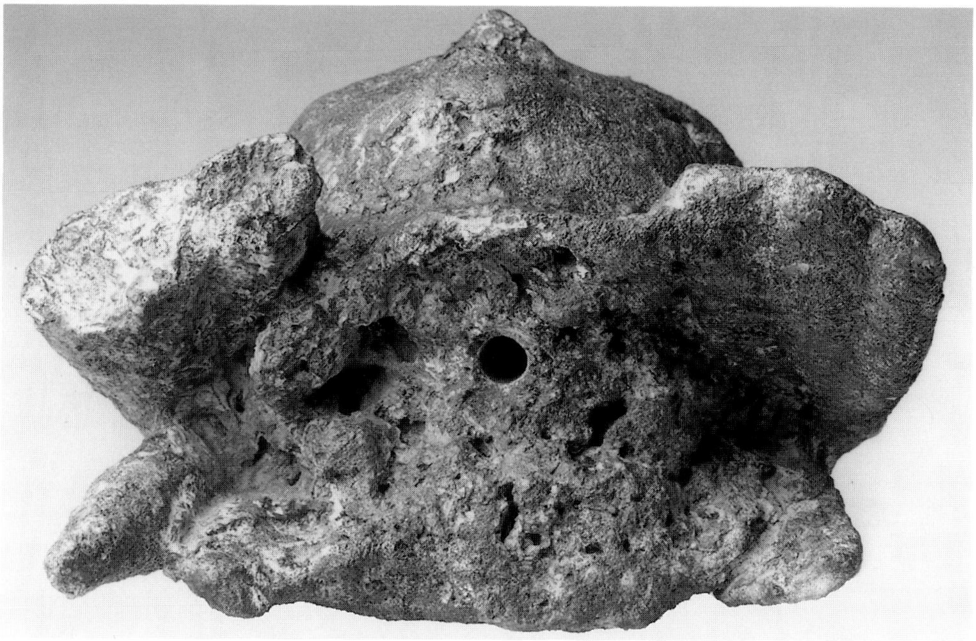

Fig. 5. Same, bottom. (Photo: courtesy Allard Pierson Museum, M. Bootsman.)

Today both ears are almost entirely worn off. However, the right ear is visible in old photographs as being set close to the head (fig. 7; cf. fig. 3). The outer helix is still preserved on both ears, but the tragus is visible only in the right ear. The ear shape resembles a stylized sickle, but, as the old photograph shows, helix, inner helix, and tragus were originally well shaped. There were small holes in the lobes, each containing a thin pin (today invisible); faint traces of gold are visible near the right ear.

Technical observations

The head is solid-cast, from an alloy of approximately 90% copper (Cu) and 10% tin (Sn).[2] The rather high proportion of tin could have created the effect of a silvery surface.

A pre-conservation photograph shows the end of a vent, almost square in section, on the right braid. Various holes in the surface are due not to corrosion in the sea but to problems in the casting. They are flaws that formed during the process of cooling. Two cracks in the center of the head can be explained in the same way. Since most of the air inclusions appear at the top of the skull, the head was probably cast upside down in a form dug into the earth.

X-ray photographs made recently reveal two deep holes between the braids and the neck, measuring 1.0 to 1.2 cm in diameter, reaching a depth of about 10.0 cm at an angle of 15° (see fig. 6). They can be explained as fixing points for pegs, used for connecting the head to the body. Microscopic analysis has shown traces of iron in these holes, from which we may conclude that the pegs were made of iron.

Reconstruction and interpretation

Neither the sex nor the nature of the head can be determined with certainty. The lack of symmetry has encouraged us to reconstruct the head as turned slightly toward its right shoulder. As this pose is not known for either kouroi or korai, we suggest associating the head with a seated sphinx, as shown in the reconstruction drawing (fig. 6).

---

2 The metallurgical analysis published in Hemelrijk 1987 (supra n.1) is incorrect. An accurate analysis, made in 1989 by J. Riederer in the laboratory of the Staatliche Museen Preußischer Kulturbesitz, Berlin, yielded the following percentages: Cu 89.11; Sn 9.55; Pb 0.12; Zn 0.01; Fe 0.29; Ni 0.18; Ag 0.05; Sb <0.01; As 0.09; Bi 0.05; Co 0.16; Au<0.01; Cd <0.001.

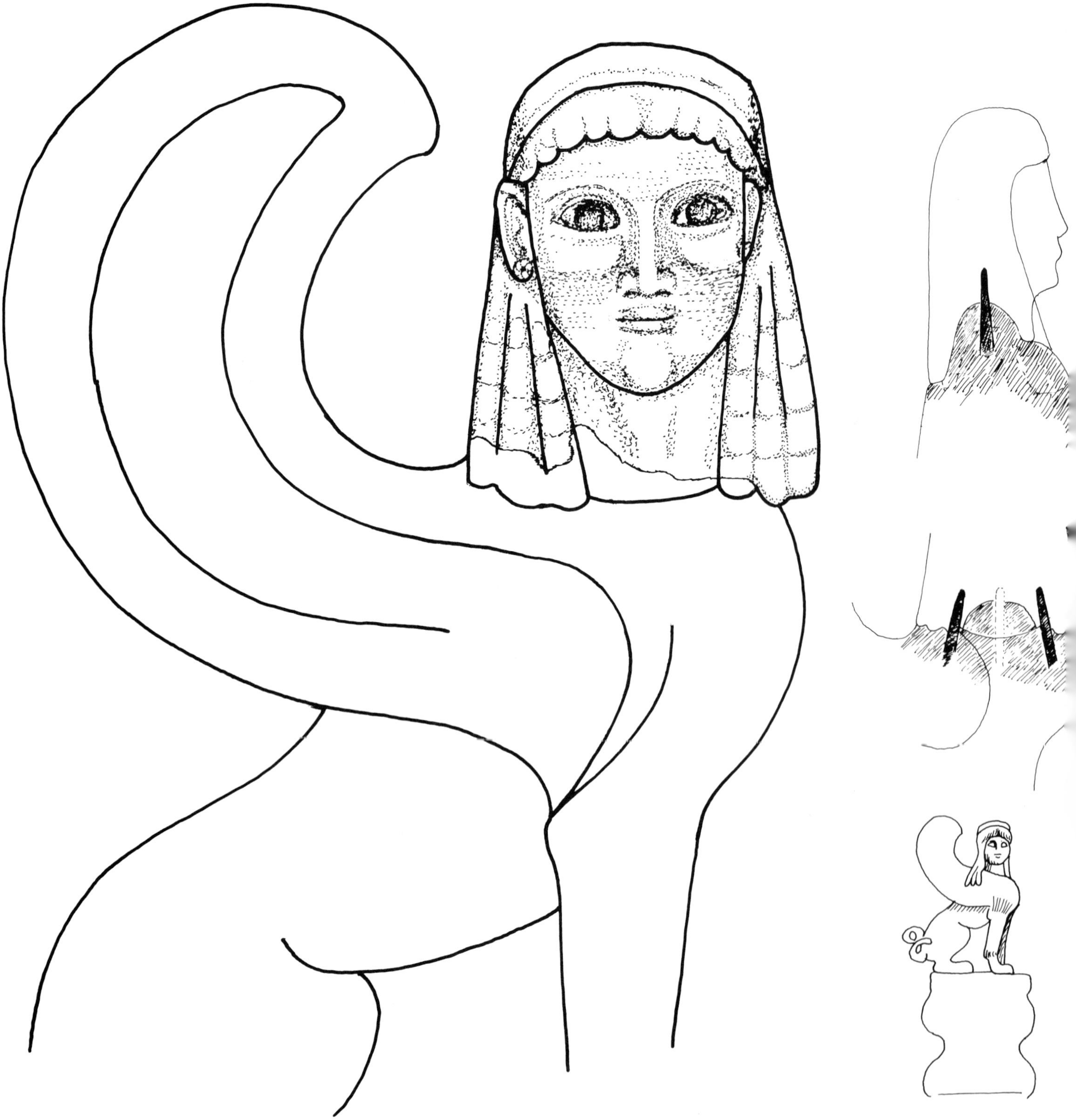

Fig. 6. Reconstruction of a statue with the Allard Pierson head. (Drawings: P. S. Lulof.)

The height of the figure can be calculated from the height of the face (0.13 m). Archaic standing figures usually have a proportion of 1 to 7, and sphinxes do not seem different: this would make the total height between 0.91 to 1.20 m, or about two-thirds life-size.

The enormous weight (19 kg) speaks against the probability of the head belonging to a solid-cast bronze statue, considering the cost of the material and the technical problems in producing such a monument. Moreover, to separate a solid-cast bronze head from a solid-cast bronze

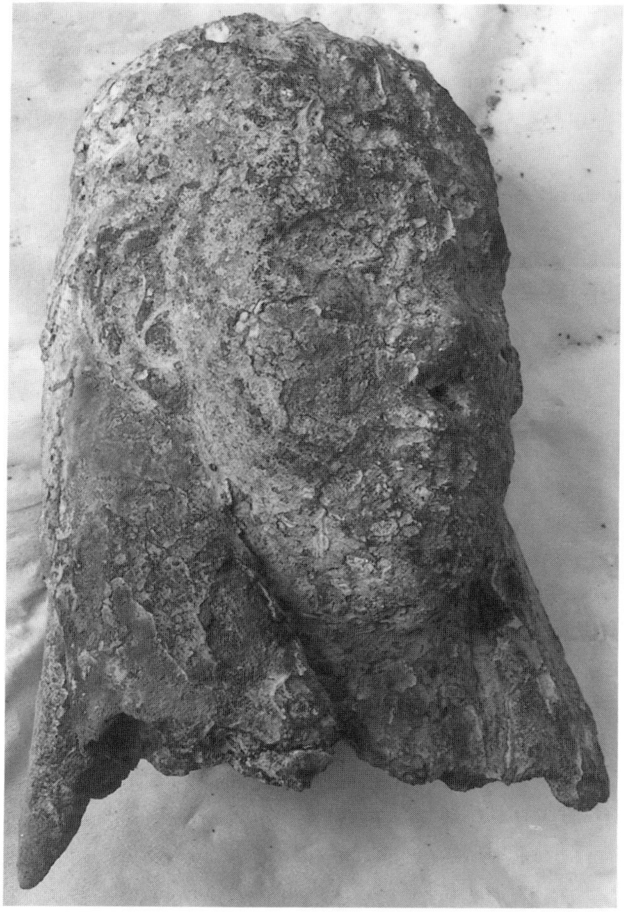

Fig. 7. Front, viewed from the left, before conservation. (Photo: courtesy Allard Pierson Museum.)

body would have required a pressure of at least 6 or 7 tons, according to information provided by J. A. F. Koens. The straight contour of the bottom of the neck (fig. 5) and, as noted above, the holes next to the neck, seen in x-rays, are also decisive factors in reconstructing the head as having been a separate casting. The bottom of the neck also has flanges that must have served to join the head to the upper part of the body. Therefore, it seems most likely that this head was intended to be placed on a limestone (or wooden) body: an *akrochalkos*, as it were, comparable to akrolithic and chryselephantine statues.

Such a precious statue probably served either as a votive offering in a temple precinct or as a guardian of a tomb. The sphinx would have crouched on a votive pillar or a stele, as the reconstruction indicates (fig. 6).[3] The tradition began around the middle of the 7th c. B.C. in various parts of the Greek world and remained in vogue until the last quarter of the 6th c.

Dating

J. M. Hemelrijk proposed three different dates for the sculpture. In his first short publication (1981), he dated the head about 550 B.C. and associated it with the early bronze-workers Rhoikos and Theodoros. His second publication (1982) suggested 580 B.C., while his third brief treatment (1988), related to a presentation of technical details, proposed 630-620 B.C. Recently, C. Rolley downdated the head to *c.*560 B.C. [4]

When analyzing the head's style we are misled by the poor state of preservation, which has caused the loss of nearly all the details of the facial features. The right ear, visible in the old photograph (fig. 7), is almost the only distinguishing feature to supplement the squarish shape of the head and the pointed chin. The lack of a fully worked earlobe may be explained by the presence of a rosette-like jewel (cf. fig. 6). Technical analysis yields no clues at all.

Initial contemplation of the head seems to confirm Hemelrijk's final dating proposal, and close examination of the head points to the early phase of Archaic art: the flatness of the face, the shape of the head, the tresses divided into three braids, as well as the presumably large eyes, are all encountered in early sculptures like the Lady of Auxerre — whose Daedalic forms, however, are far from similar to this head.[5]

A series of good comparisons can be found in sphinxes of Greek tomb monuments, beginning with the oldest monument known, now in the Metropolitan Museum of Art and dated by G. M. A.

---

3 See H. Demisch, *Die Sphinx. Geschichte ihrer Darstellung von den Anfängen bis zur Gegenwart* (Stuttgart 1979) 85-88; G. M. A. Richter, *The Archaic gravestones of Attica* (London 1961) 1-2, 6-7.

4 Rolley, *La sculpture grecque*.

5 Good discussions of Archaic sculpture: J. Floren, *Die griechische Plastik* 1: *Die geometrische und archaische Plastik* (*HdA* 5, Munich 1987); W. Martini, *Die archaische Plastik der Griechen* (Darmstadt 1990). They do not, however, include remarks that pertain to this monument.

Richter to 610-575 B.C.[6] The sphinx in the Ny Carlsberg Glyptotek, Copenhagen, dating to 560-550 B.C., shows the same features, but the outlines and surface are smoother, and the Archaic smile is broader.

If we consider korai and kouroi, we must conclude that no statue of the earliest groups is comparable. Both the ears and the general impression are different. As far as the korai are concerned, good comparisons can be made with monuments dated to the first half of the 6th c. B.C. Richter's Olympia Hera-Berlin Kore-Akropolis 593 Group, from about 600 to 570, has different ears, but the treatment of the hair is similar. A closer comparison is a sphinx in Delphi, from Richter's Cheramyes–Geneleos Group.[7] Some contemporary kouroi show the same features, but the only really similar figures are those in the large Tenea–Volomandra Group, with their jutting cheekbones.[8] The comparison provided by Rolley, a terracotta head of a sphinx in Agrigento, has most of the aforementioned characteristics, but its general presentation appears somewhat different.[9]

The stylistic elements that can be distinguished are too few to allow us to ascribe the head to one of the regional sculpture schools.

Conclusion

The solid-cast bronze head in the Allard Pierson Museum represents a sphinx. It must have been made during the second quarter of the 6th c. B.C. in a hitherto unidentified workshop of a daring bronze worker who may have been experimenting. His creation was an *akrochalkos*, to be compared with an *akrolithos*.

Instituut voor Mediterrane Archeologie, Universiteit van Amsterdam, 1012 GC Amsterdam

Acknowledgements

We owe many thanks to J. A. F. Koens, Amsterdam, who assisted with the technical research and pointed out many details that would otherwise have escaped our attention. X-ray photographs were made in the Röntgen Technische Dienst, Rotterdam. We are especially grateful to Ing. Klapwijk and Van der Meyden for their assistance. We are also indebted to R. van Beek of the Allard Pierson Museum and C. W. Neeft of the University of Amsterdam for helpful suggestions. R. Coates Stevens kindly corrected the English text.

---

6 Richter, *Archaic gravestones* (supra n.3) no. 1, fig. 7 for the ear.

7 Ead., *Korai: Archaic Greek maidens* (London 1968) 44-54, pl. 11f-h.

8 Ead., *Kouroi: Archaic Greek youths* (3rd edn., London 1970) 75-89, figs. 208-69.

9 Rolley, *La sculpture grecque* 305, fig. 313.

A newly discovered Archaic bronze statue from Metropolis (Thessaly)

Charalampos G. Intzesiloglou

In September 1994, during excavation of a Doric temple in the region of the ancient city of Metropolis in SW Thessaly (fig. 1), an Archaic hollow-cast bronze statue was discovered (figs. 2-5). The statue represents a hoplite wearing a helmet, cuirass, *peribrachionia* and *peripechia* (upper and lower arm guards), and greaves.

The statue is 0.802 m tall with its plinth. It is composed of two separate parts. The upper part includes the head with the neck, torso, and both arms, although the left arm was found separated from the body. The lower part consists of the lower body and the legs attached to a rectangular plinth, hollowed out underneath. The upper part was joined to the lower part by means of pins passing through four holes at the back, front, and sides of the cuirass, just above the flange.

The upper part of the head is covered by a conical helmet. On top of the helmet is a hole for the attachment of a crest, now lost. Part of the cylindrical pivot that supported the crest is preserved inside the helmet. A small hole at the back of the helmet might have been used for a strut to support the back of the crest. It is difficult to decide whether a small hole on the left side of the helmet served to attach another element of the helmet or resulted from a flaw in

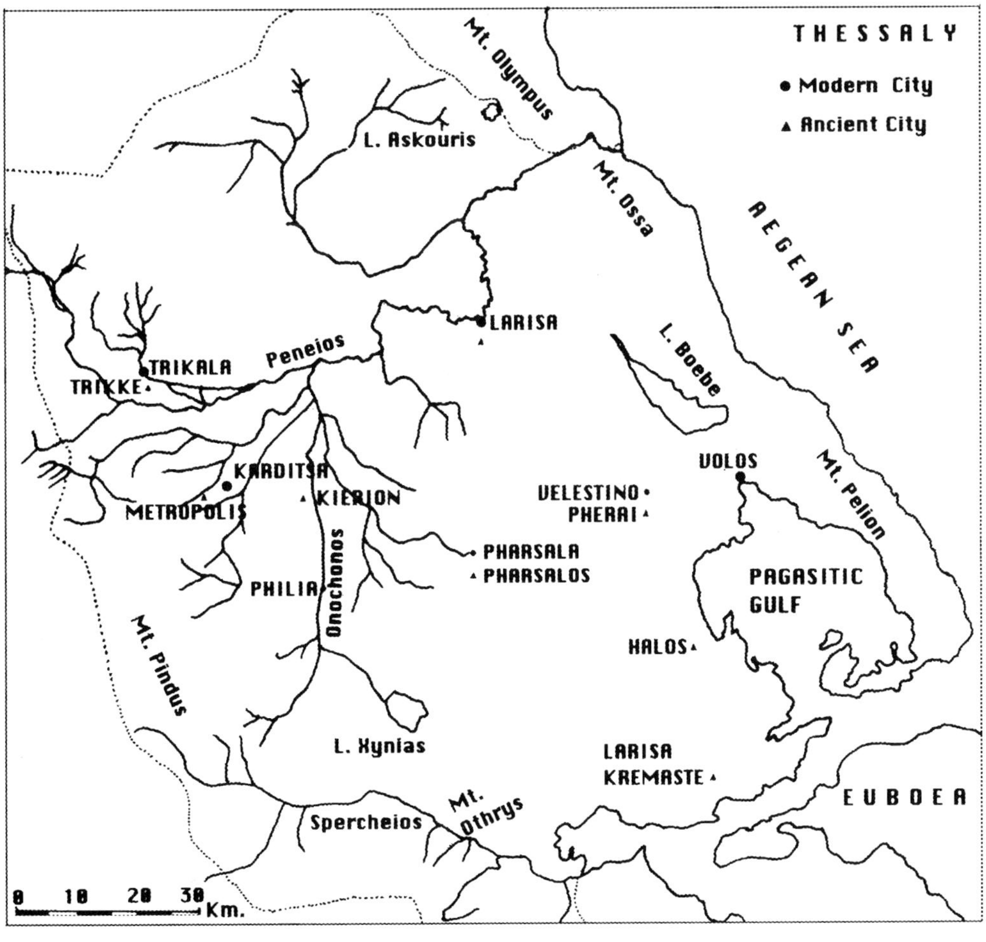

Fig. 1. Map of Thessaly.

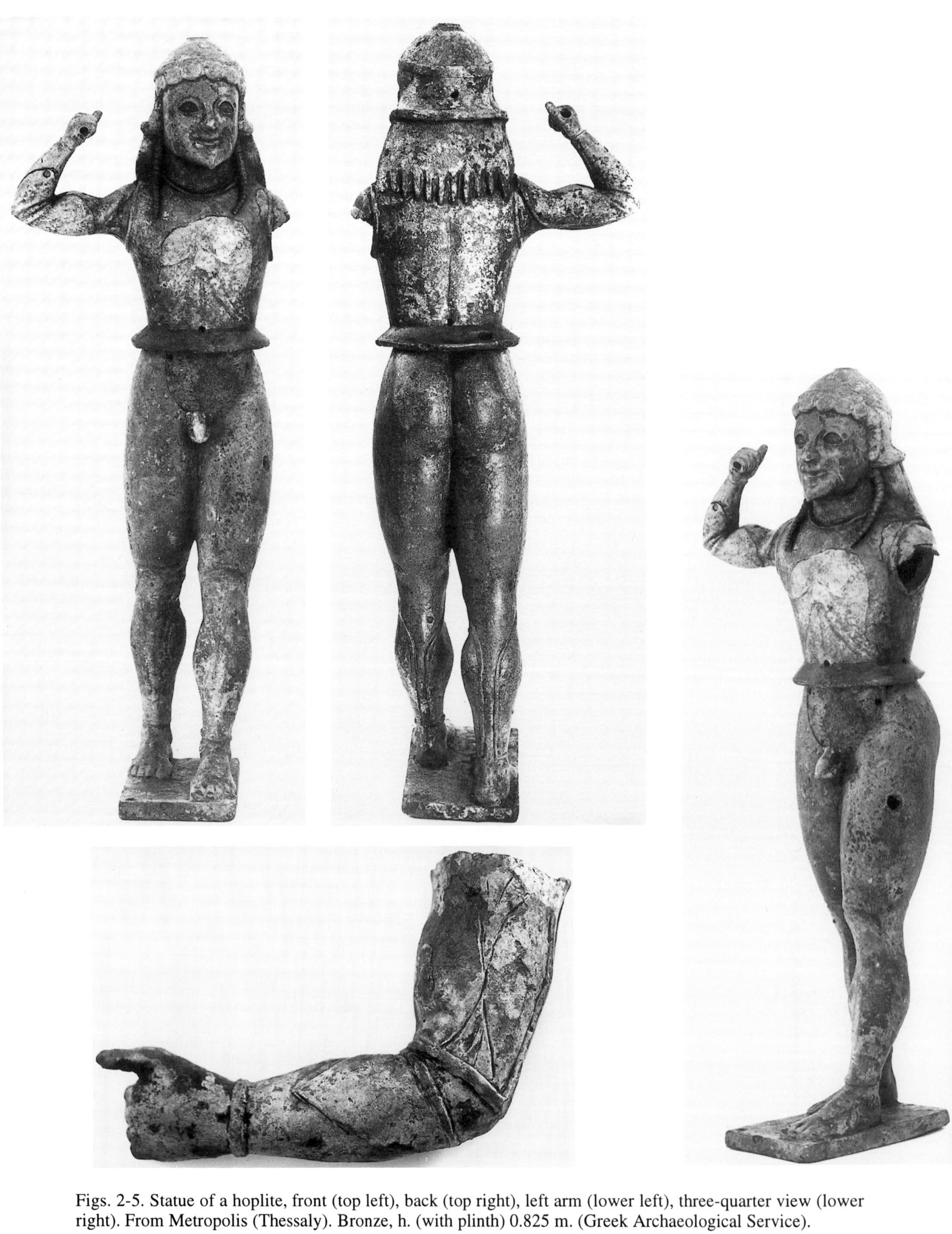

Figs. 2-5. Statue of a hoplite, front (top left), back (top right), left arm (lower left), three-quarter view (lower right). From Metropolis (Thessaly). Bronze, h. (with plinth) 0.825 m. (Greek Archaeological Service).

the casting. On the lower edge of the conical upper part of the helmet there is a narrow horizontal band. On the back of the helmet, above the hair, there is the slightly concave neckpiece, on the lower edge of which there is another, similar horizontal narrow band with 4 incised lines.

In the front view of the statue (fig. 2) we can see a row of 8 elaborate spiral curls lying across the broad forehead under the edge of the helmet. There are also two separately cast long locks, attached behind the ears and falling down on to the chest along each side of the neck. The thick, long hair is visible in the back view of statue (fig. 3). From under the lower edge of the helmet neckpiece springs the main mass of hair that falls down the back of the statue. The strands of hair are indicated as closely-spaced, wavy incised lines that end, on the back, in short, thin locks.

The oval, fairly narrow face ends in a pointed chin, indicating that the face was bearded, even though there is no incision indicating hair. The almond-shaped eyes are hollow, and it is possible that eyeballs in another material were made separately and inserted. The two flat ears are attached in front of the vertical edges of the neckpiece of the helmet, and they are not rendered in detail. The Archaic smile that characterizes statues of this time gives life and motion to the face. The head turns slightly to the left, and the result of this movement is the curve of the end of the left lock.

The chest is fully covered by a bell cuirass, with rolled edges at the openings for the arms and the neck and a lower edge that ends in a wide flange that flares out, giving the cuirass the shape of a bell. The two pectorals, the lower end of the ribs in front, and the shallow depression along the backbone are all rendered plastically. Two incised vertical lines in the middle of the lower part of the cuirass end at the flange below.

The right arm is raised and bent, and it is possible that the closed hand was holding a metal spear. Something resembling a fragment of spear was found some meters southeast of the temple. The right upper arm and forearm are protected by two separate pieces of armor, the upper arm guard and the forearm guard. The edges of these two upper and lower arm guards are indicated by rolled bands, so it is clear how they functioned when the arms were bent at the elbow. The forearm guard is plain, with no details sculpted in relief. In contrast, the front of the upper arm guard models the triceps muscle, and on each side is a semi-anthemion with three leaves in low relief. The right arm has a large patch, attached by means of three pins.

The left arm, which has not yet been re-attached (fig. 4), was lowered and bent. It also wears an upper arm guard and a forearm guard. The hand is closed with a hole in it to attach an attribute; there are no other traces on the arm for attaching an object. There are two main differences in the execution of the two arms. On the left arm, the upper arm guard's two semi-anthemia are indicated more sketchily by incised lines, and the forearm guard has a modeled, leaf-like ornament on the outer side near the elbow.

The top of the lower part of the statue is perfectly round, made to fit into the upper part. The semi-oval inset on the abdomen was made to receive a bronze sheet, now lost (fig. 2). We do not know if the sheet represented a *mitra* or if it was a patch on the abdomen. The sheet was attached by 4 bronze nails and two pins fitted into the two small holes preserved in the upper part of this area.

The left leg of the statue is advanced, as is usual in Archaic kouroi (fig. 5). The thighs are quite muscular, as can be seen in the front and side views. The circular hole in the left thigh may have served to support an object held in the left hand. The lower legs are fully covered by greaves that follow the forms of the leg. The edges of the greaves are indicated by a roll, and the knees are modeled. The feet are bare, and they are individually attached to the rectangular plinth, which is hollowed underneath. The plinth was attached to the stone pedestal on which it stood by means of pins that passed through two small holes, located in the two corners of the plinth not covered by the feet.

Stylistically, the statue can be dated to the third quarter of the 6th c. B.C. Judging from the place where it was erected, on the central stone pedestal inside the temple, it seems clear that it was the cult statue. According to an inscription, the temple was dedicated to Apollo, so it is possible that this bronze hoplite statue was a representation of that god. If this identification is correct, it is possible that the object held in the left hand was a bow, as was also the case with the Apollo at Amyklai.

Conservation of the bronze god is not yet finished, so we have only begun to study this statue. It offers many opportunities to increase our knowledge of the technique by which each part of the statue was produced in separate molds, the method used to join the parts, and the problem of the workshop. We will also study this type of cult image of Apollo as hoplite and the significance of the presence of this ἀρχαῖον ἄγαλμα in the temple in later centuries.

Archaeological Museum, 1, Athanasakis St., 38001 Volos

A lost bronze Athena signed by Kritios and Nesiotes (*DAA* 160)

Catherine M. Keesling

Among the 'biggest names' in Early Classical Athenian sculpture are Kritios and Nesiotes. They provide one of the few chronological fixed points for freestanding 5th c. B.C. sculpture, the date of 477/6 assigned to the Tyrannicides group by the Marmor Parium.[1] As far as we can tell, all of Kritios and Nesiotes's known statues were large-scale bronzes, and all have been lost; Roman marble versions of the Tyrannicides constitute the primary source employed in scholarly reconstructions of their sculptural style.[2] The study of lost bronze originals exclusively through marble sculptures of later periods, or *Kopienkritik*, for all its other dangers also tends to lose sight of the purposes for which the original sculptures were made. In the case of large-scale 5th c. bronzes, most were votive in purpose; context *does* matter, and 6 out of Kritios and Nesiotes's 7 known sculptural works were made to serve as votive offerings on the Athenian Acropolis. The sole exception is the Tyrannicides group in the Agora. In particular, the period of Kritios and Nesiotes's sculptural activity, between the Persian sack of 480 B.C. and the beginning of construction on the Parthenon, marked the transition from the Archaic to the Classical style on the Acropolis and also the transition from marble to bronze as the predominant material for votive sculptures. The history of this transition remains to be written, despite extensive study of the marble statues dedicated there, in particular the korai. In this paper I hope to demonstrate that, on the contemporary Acropolis, at least one sculptor in marble may have been inspired by Kritios and Nesiotes's work in bronze.

The evidence for Kritios and Nesiotes's sculptural work on the Acropolis consists of 6 signed statue bases included by A. E. Raubitschek in his 1949 catalogue *Dedications from the Athenian Akropolis* (= *DAA*).[3] Three of these bases (*DAA* nos. 120, 121, and 160) preserve foot-holes for the attachment of large-scale bronze statues, life-size or over life-size. One of these, inscribed with a dedicatory epigram followed by the artists' joint signature, gives valuable evidence for Kritios and Nesiotes's sculptural work that has been unjustly, and perplexingly, overlooked.

This is *DAA* no. 160, a round Pentelic marble base now on prominent display in the Acropolis Museum (fig. 1). It measures 0.44 m high and just under 1 m in diameter.[4] The inscription was damaged at some point after its discovery early in the 19th c., but luckily the now-missing portion of the artists' signature had been transcribed before that time.[5] What we have here without a doubt is the base for a life-size bronze original made by Kritios and Nesiotes. The date of 477/6 for the Tyrannicides, taken together with the re-dedication of two of Kritios and Nesiotes's Acropolis statues in the Roman period, suggests a date soon after the Persian sack of

---

1 J. Overbeck, *Die antiken Schriftquellen zur Geschichte der bildenden Künste bei den Griechen* (Leipzig 1868) no. 458. For discussions of Kritios and Nesiotes's work, see G. M. A. Richter, *The sculpture and sculptors of the Greeks* (New Haven 1970) 154-56 and Ridgway, *Severe style* 79-83.

2 C. Landwehr, *Die antiken Gipsabgüsse aus Baiae* (Berlin 1985) has recently argued, on the basis of fragmentary plaster casts of the Tyrannicides found in Baiae, that the marble versions we have may reflect Antenor's original statue group and not the replacement group made by Kritios and Nesiotes.

3 A. E. Raubitschek, *Dedications from the Athenian Akropolis* (Cambridge, MA 1949) nos. 120-23, 160, and 161. For line-drawings of all 6 inscribed bases, see A. Rumpf, "Zu den Tyrannenmördern," in E. Homann-Wedeking and B. Segall (edd.), *Festschrift Eugen von Mercklin* (Waldsassen–Bayern 1964) 142-43.

4 Diameter: 0.915 m; length of right and left feet: *c.*24 cm at the top of the cutting.

5 See Raubitschek, *DAA* (supra n.3) 177-78. For a full and more accurate transcription using the Attic alphabet, see *IG* I^3 848. The following is a restored Greek text of the inscription:
Ἀριστέας καὶ Ὄψσιος ἀνεθέτην/ τῇ Ἀθηναίᾳ ἀπαρχὴν Ὄαθεν./ Κριτίος καὶ Νησιώτης ἐποιησάτην (Aristeas and Opsios of the deme Oe dedicated this/to Athena as first-fruits./Kritios and Nesiotes made it).

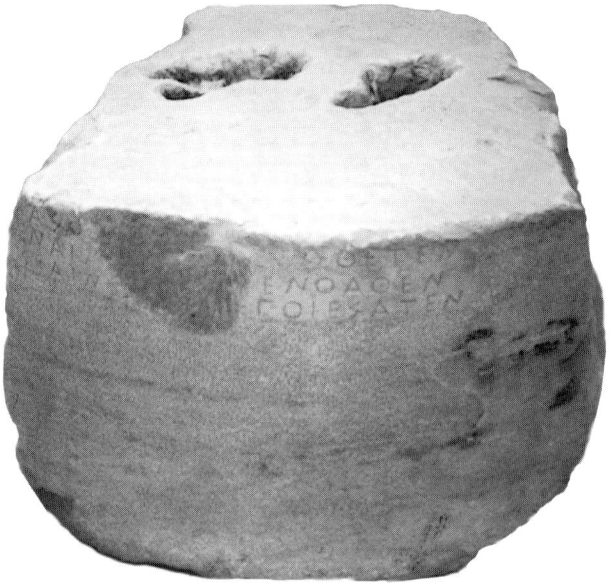

Fig. 1. Inscription. Base, *DAA* no. 160. Marble, h. 0.44 m, diam. 0.915 m. Athens, Acropolis Museum Akr. 13270. (Photo: author.)

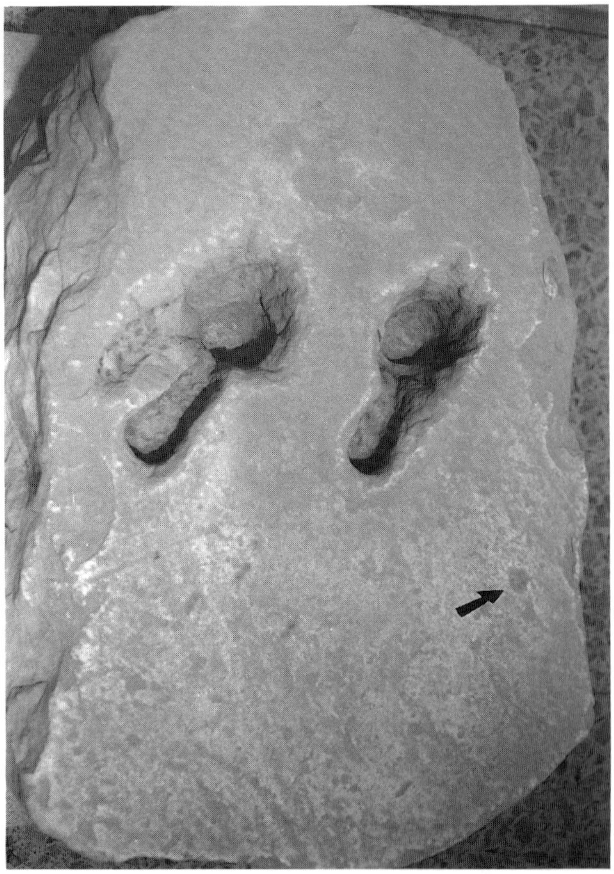

Fig. 2. Top of fig. 1. Arrow points to cutting for spear butt. (Photo: author.)

480 B.C. The two foot-shaped holes on the top of the base provide textbook examples of the dowel technique, in which lead was poured through holes in the legs of the statue in order to fasten the feet to the marble base. Here, deep sinkings under the balls of the feet allowed the lead to flow deep into the base under the feet, possibly around an iron core for added stability (fig. 2).[6]

At first glance, it appears that Kritios and Nesiotes' statue stood with its back to the inscribed side of the base, an impression created by the shape of the dowel holes beneath the feet. The primary objections to such a reconstruction are the rarity of statue bases inscribed on the back and the slight divergence of the feet when viewed from the inscribed side. Furthermore, we would normally expect the deeper sinkings within each dowel hole to correspond with the heel rather than the ball of the foot, though I should note that at least two other bases for 5th-c. bronze originals from the Acropolis (*DAA* nos. 111 and 166) feature larger and deeper dowel holes under the ball of the foot than under the heel. The feet stand roughly parallel to one another and close together, with the right foot advanced by about half a foot's length. Raubitschek's description in *DAA* suggests that the lost bronze statue represented Athena, but does not say why. My first-hand examination of the top of the base revealed that a dark spot which appears indistinctly in Raubitschek's photograph is the key that turns this statue from an anonymous standing figure into an Athena: this is a small cutting located in front of and to the right of the statue's left foot.[7] Jahn and Michaelis at the turn of the century published a drawing of the base in which the scale and position of the feet are not quite correct, but the cutting and the location of the inscription in relation to the feet are clear.[8] The cutting

6 For illustrations of the dowel technique, see Haynes, *Technique* fig. 8.

7 Raubitschek, *DAA* (supra n.3) 178.

8 O. Jahn and A. Michaelis, *Arx Athenarum a Pausania descripta* (Bonn 1901) pl. 38 fig. 5.

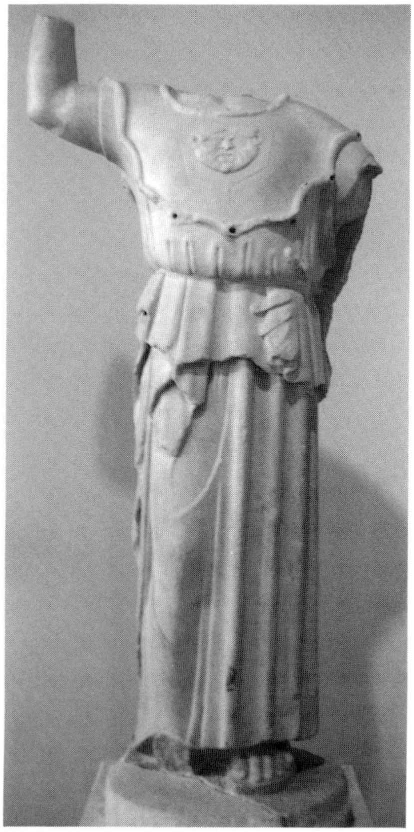

Fig. 3. Angelitos's Athena. Marble, p.h. 0.77 m. Athens, Acropolis Museum Akr. 140 (Photo: author.)

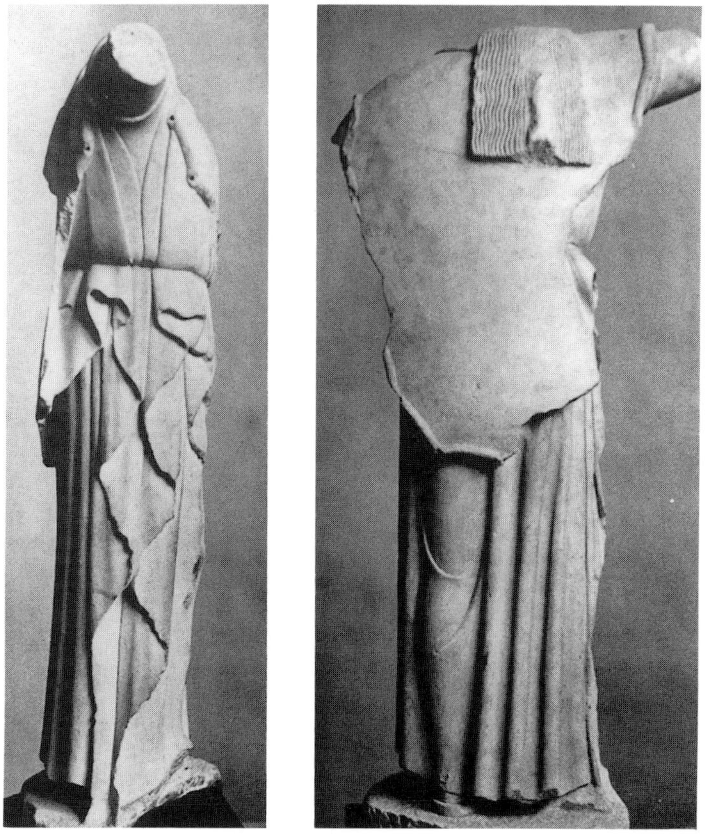

Fig. 4. Right side and back of fig. 3. (Photos: reproduced by permission from Langlotz 1939 [supra n.12]).

consists of a shallow circular depression about 2 cm in diameter surrounding a thin rectangular indentation 1.5 cm long. This indentation could have been made by a single stroke of a flat chisel, and the surrounding depression by two or three light strokes of a small point.[9] The depression can be explained as a spear hole, and the indentation within the cutting must have been intended to help secure the bronze butt of the spear, probably without melted lead.[10] Thus, the lost statue probably held a spear in its left hand, with the spear butt resting just in front of its feet.

But why Athena? To find a parallel for an Athena holding a spear, we do not have to look far. One of the most familiar Severe-style originals found on the Athenian Acropolis is the marble Athena dedicated by Angelitos, currently on display in the same room of the Acropolis Museum as *DAA* no. 160 (fig. 3).[11] Angelitos's Athena should really be called Euenor's, since he is the sculptor whose signature appears on the fluted column base shown together with the statue in a reconstruction drawing by Raubitschek.[12] Statue and base have been dated

9 Cf. Wade-Gery's classic analysis of the use of single flat chisel-strokes in the carving of Attic inscriptions: A. Wade-Gery, "Studies in Attic inscriptions of the 5th c. B.C.," *BSA* 33 (1935) 122-23.

10 Typical spear butts of the 5th c. were triangular in section and ended in a blunt, rounded point. For examples, see G. M. A. Richter, "Greek bronzes recently acquired by the Metropolitan Museum of Art," *AJA* 43 (1939) 194-201 and figs. 4 and 5; J. Camp, "A spear butt from the Lesbians," *Hesperia* 47 (1978) 192-95 and pl. 50. The rectangular indentation on the top surface of *DAA* no. 160 does not match the shape of a spear butt's point; the statuary spear butt might not have corresponded in shape with a real one.

11 E. Langlotz, "Die Koren," in H. Schrader (ed.), *Die archaische Marmorbildwerke der Akropolis* (Frankfurt am Main 1939) no. 5 and pls. 9-11.

12 A. E. Raubitschek, "Early Attic votive monuments," *BSA* 40 (1939-40) 32 fig. 41. See Ridgway, *Severe style* 31 and J. Hurwit, "The Kritios Boy: discovery, reconstruction, and date," *AJA* 93 (1989) 41-80.

stylistically to *c*.480. This marble Athena stands only half life-size but nevertheless displays conspicuous attention to detail and fine workmanship.[13] She too stands with feet parallel and right foot forward; because the front half of the right foot has broken off, the pose may best be seen from the back (fig. 4). From the back we also see the remains of a long helmet crest trailing down over Athena's hair and the displacement of her hair onto her right shoulder, revealing that her head, now lost, was turned toward her left. The most important detail for our purposes is the pose of the right arm, held outward from the body and bent 90° at the elbow (figs. 3-4).[14] The position of the arm makes the most sense if Euenor's Athena is restored leaning on a spear in a relaxed attitude.[15] Both the statue's plinth and the top of the base are broken just where we would expect the butt of this Athena's spear to rest, alongside the right edge of the right foot. The stance of Angelitos's Athena, with her right instead of her left foot forward, argues against her restoration in the so-called Promachos pose seen in several small bronze statuettes found on the Acropolis. These figures depict Athena attacking with a spear held in her right hand but always with her left foot forward to give vigor and momentum to the attack.[16]

What do we have thus far? Two statues with the same foot pose, both holding a spear. Can we really infer that Kritios and Nesiotes's statue looked anything like the marble Athena signed by Euenor? And, even if the statues did resemble one another, which came first? I wish to propose that Euenor based his marble statue upon the lost bronze original by Kritios and Nesiotes. My argument rests upon a series of points which, taken together, suggest that Euenor was familiar with the statue that stood on top of the base *DAA* no. 160.

The unusual viewing conditions created by the inscription on Kritios and Nesiotes' base provide a motive for Athena's head turn which is lacking in the marble statue made by Euenor. Angelitos's Athena stood atop a small column with a vertical inscription legible in its entirety by a viewer standing directly in front of the statue. The inscription on Kritios and Nesiotes's base is horizontal, making it necessary to walk one-quarter of the way around the base to read the inscription. Reading the inscription on the base was an important part of viewing any votive monument. If the statue turned its head either to its left, like the Athena dedicated by Angelitos, or to its right, the face would have been viewed in profile from the back, providing another incentive to walk all the way around the figure. The resulting statue would have looked very much like the Athenas represented on two Athenian red-figure oinochoai, one in the Metropolitan Museum of Art, the other in the British Museum, both from the second quarter of the 5th c.[17] Though these two vase representations have been seen as intentional references to Euenor's statue, we should note that the painted Athenas turn their heads in the opposite direction and hold their spears farther out from the body and behind their feet. The Athena on the Metropolitan oinochoe also stands on the wrong type of base, and the British Museum vase shows Athena not as a statue but as a living being turning to face a worshipper. I prefer to see both representations as vase painters' allusions to a type of figure that could be seen in more than one example on the Athenian Acropolis.

One detail of Angelitos's Athena that requires further explanation is the lappet of drapery falling over the right foot (fig. 4). This is the only point at which the drapery touches the top

---

13 The preserved height of Angelitos's Athena without her plinth is 0.77 m. The statue's head has been lost.

14 In Langlotz's photograph (here fig. 4), the statue is shown before the right elbow fragment had been identified and re-attached.

15 For a similar pose, see the marble double Athena relief in the National Museum, Athens (NM 82): K. Mylonas, "Ἀναθηματικὸν ἀνάγλυφον ἔξ Ἀττικῆς," *ArchEph* (1890) 1-5 and pl. 1.

16 For examples, see H. Niemeyer, "Attische Bronzestatuetten der spätarchaischen und frühklassischen Zeit," *AntP* 3 (1964) 7-31 and id., *Promachos: Untersuchungen zur Darstellung der bewaffneten Athena in archäischer Zeit* (Waldsassen–Bayern 1960).

17 G. M. A. Richter, *Red-figured Athenian vases in the Metropolitan Museum of Art* (New Haven 1936) 114-15 no. 84, pl. E88 fig. 84 (red-figure oinochoe near the Deepdene Painter, *c*.470-460); Raubitschek 1939-40 (supra n.12) pl. 12 fig. 42.

of the plinth, yet it coincides with the bent, free right leg and not with the straight left leg. Clearly Euenor wanted to emphasize the meeting of the edges of Athena's peplos in swallow-tail folds cascading down from a fastening on the right shoulder, but lengthening the drapery here is counter-intuitive, in that bending the leg as Athena does should pull the drapery up higher on the right side of the body. Looking back at Kritios and Nesiotes's base, it can be seen that the cutting for the right foot shows an extension along the outer edge of the foot (fig. 2). This cutting demonstrates first that Kritios and Nesiotes's lost bronze figure was draped, and therefore that the statue should be identified as Athena rather than as a male figure holding a spear, staff, or trident. Second, it shows that the bronze drapery of Kritios and Nesiotes's Athena touched the base at only one point, a small detail replicated exactly by Euenor.

The sculptural style of Angelitos's Athena has always raised more questions than it answers. Ridgway's comments stress its primacy as a "herald of the Severe Style," with the further observation that despite its small size "it has the stamp of monumentality characteristic of all major works."[18] The sculptor Euenor signed a total of 4 Acropolis statue bases, making him nearly as prolific as Kritios and Nesiotes. In contrast to them, he seems to have worked exclusively in marble.[19] Raubitschek perceived a contrast in style between the Severe, forward-looking Angelitos's Athena and the only other piece of sculpture we can associate with Euenor, namely the Archaic-looking feet of a kore (or Athena?) belonging to the base *DAA* no. 14. This contrast led Raubitschek to conclude that the two statues, though signed by the same sculptor, could not have been made by the same hand. He even went so far as to postulate a workshop connection between Euenor and Phidias, which would make it possible that the latter was the true sculptor of Angelitos's Athena.[20]

Both scholars' characterizations of Angelitos's Athena as incongruous respond to the sudden appearance of images of Athena in something akin to this pose in Athens after the Persian Wars. In addition to the two Athenian red-figure vases mentioned above, there is also the Mourning Athena relief from the Acropolis, in which the goddess appears in a freer mirror image of the pose used by Euenor, but still exhibiting the key elements of weight and free leg, spear, and head turn.[21] A small headless bronze statuette also found on the Acropolis depicts an Athena at rest, wearing an aegis over a peplos, and with right leg bent at the knee and right foot forward like Angelitos's Athena. From what remains of the arms, we can see that this Athena stretches her right arm out (perhaps holding a helmet or an owl) and appears to rest on a spear held in her left hand.[22]

Restoring Kritios and Nesiotes's statue as the origin of this new relaxed pose would help to explain the creation of a new popular image of Athena in the second quarter of the 5th c. This was the point in the history of the Acropolis when large-scale bronzes became the most popular dedications, overtaking both marble statues and small bronze statuettes. Since the dates of the Acropolis dedications remain far from precise, this shift can only be quantified in terms of overall statistics for the 6th and 5th c., using the material published by Raubitschek in *DAA* and new statue bases that have come to light since 1949 (fig. 5). The overall trend toward bronze statues over 1 m tall and away from marble statues and bronze statuettes does not mean that the

---

18 Ridgway, *Severe style* 29.

19 The Acropolis statue bases bearing Euenor's signature are the following: Raubitschek, *DAA* (supra n.3) nos. 14, 22 (the base for Angelitos's Athena), 23, and a new fragment published by C. Vlassopoulou, "Δύο αναθηματικές επιγραφές από την Αθηναική Ακρόπολη," *Horos* 8-9 (1990-91) 15-16 on which the name of Angelitos as dedicator may be restored.

20 Raubitschek 1939-40 (supra n.12) 35-36.

21 For the Mourning Athena relief, see most recently H. Jung, "Die sinnende Athena, Zur Deutung des Reliefs Athen, Akropolismuseum 695," *JdI* 110 (1995) 95-147. For a discussion of a Roman relief alluding to this Athena type, see B. Lichocka, "Une version romaine de l'Athéna Pensive" in *Πρακτικὰ του XII. Διεθνοὺς Συνεδρίου Κλασικὶς 'Αρχαιολογίας, Athens 4-10 September 1983* (Athens 1988) 161-64 and pl. 33 fig. 1.

22 Niemeyer 1964 (supra n.16) 22-23 and pls. 12 and 13 (NM no. 6454).

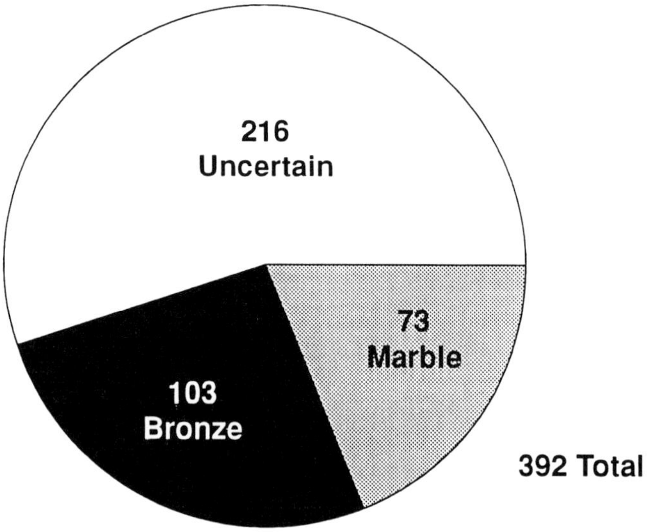

Fig. 5. Marble and bronze dedications on the Athenian Acropolis, *c.*600-400 B.C.

latter ceased to be dedicated on the Acropolis between the Persian Wars and the end of the 5th c. Nevertheless, Kritios and Nesiotes's lost statue could well have been the earliest large-scale bronze Athena dedicated on the Acropolis. When the extremely expensive and technically complex process of large-scale bronze casting became popular, dedicators of lesser means may well have sought to imitate prominent bronze statues offered by others and made by prestigious sculptors. The result would be a sequence of representations that, if not identical, were noticeably similar in pose and appearance. In a votive context, imitation makes sense because individuals who made dedications sought to achieve the highest possible prestige for their gifts to the gods. As a result, some of our 5th c. marble originals, among them Angelitos's Athena, may not be quite as original as they seem.

Classics Department, Georgetown University, Washington, DC 20057

Acknowledgements

I would like to thank J. G. Pedley and the staff of the Acropolis Museum for their help throughout my study of the Acropolis statue bases. Several participants in the 13th International Bronze Congress made suggestions that have improved this paper, in particular B. S. Ridgway and O. Palagia.

Who's who on the Berlin Foundry Cup

Jenifer Neils

Nearly every study of classical bronze statuary features the famous Attic red-figure kylix found in Vulci in 1835 and now in Berlin, which for J. D. Beazley served as the name-vase of his so-called Foundry Painter.[1] Its 8 (not counting inanimate statues) exterior figures constitute the most complete documentation of the personnel of an ancient Greek foundry, and it is therefore a key piece of evidence for any discussion of the bronze industry. Various scholars have identified the figures, inside and out, human and sculpted, in a number of different and sometimes conflicting ways, usually basing their identifications on what seems plausible in an Athenian foundry of the first half of the 5th c. B.C.

Literary references indicate that Athenian ateliers were relatively small, often staffed by metics and slaves, with citizens forming only about one-quarter of the labor force.[2] Industries were family-owned and operated, and skilled vocations were often passed on from father to son via apprenticeships rather than formal education.[3] Unlike today when artists enjoy a certain amount of prestige, the practice of *techne*, or craft, in ancient Greece carried no such connotaions; in fact, to be a laborer carried a social stigma. With this background in mind we can attempt to arrive at a more precise understanding of the rôles, relative status, and relationships of the figures on the Foundry Cup. By comparing them with other works of art, primarily Attic vase-paintings, it is possible to shed new light on these much-studied artisans.

To begin with the tondo (fig. 1), a standing, draped woman is presumably receiving a full bronze panoply from a seated armorer. There are no inscriptions to identify them as the smith god Hephaistos and the Nereid Thetis, but all scholars have accepted a mythological interpretation of the scene based on the text of *Iliad* 18.369-616, in which the mother of Achilles receives new armor for her son.[4] The woman has no attributes, but a hitherto-overlooked detail identifies Hephaistos beyond any doubt: there is a distinct disparity in the size of the armorer's feet. Although advanced, his left foot is considerably longer than his right. Visual clues to Hephaistos' lameness are more obvious in scenes of his return to Olympus, in which his lame foot can be either deformed or turned backward,[5] and seem not to occur in the rarer smithy

---

1 Berlin, Antikenmuseum F 2294. *ARV*² 400, 1. The most recent publication of the cup appears in *The fire of Hephaistos* 182-84, no. 1.

2 For discussion of Greek craftsmen, see R. J. Hopper, *Trade and industry in classical Greece* (London 1979) 126-46; A. Andrewes, *Greek society* (Harmondsworth 1967) 130-60; A. Burford, *Craftsmen in Greek and Roman society* (London 1972); H. Philipp, "Handwerker und bildende Künstler in der griechischen Gesellschaft," in H. Beck (ed.), *Polyklet* (Frankfurt 1990) 79-110, 512-18.

3 On the training of sculptors, see I. S. Mark, "The lure of philosophy: craft and higher learning in ancient Greece," in W. G. Moon (ed.), *Polykleitos, the Doryphoros, and tradition* (Madison 1995) 25-37.

4 See *LIMC* 4, s.v. Hephaistos, nos. 1-10 (A. Jacquemin). On the visit of Thetis to Hephaistos, see also F. Brommer, *Hephaistos* (Mainz 1978) 20-21, 207; K. Friis Johansen, *The Iliad in early Greek art* (Copenhagen 1967) 178-84. Friis Johansen noted that these representations of Hephaistos and Thetis all appear in the decade 490-480 and suggested that they might be politically motivated, i.e., a reference to the arming of the Greeks in their war against the Persians. If this is so, then it might make more sense to see the woman as Athena, goddess of battle, than as a passive Nereid. According to Apollodoros (3.14.6), Athena visited Hephaistos to obtain armor, and other female deities also needed armor for the Gigantomachy. The masks of Athena Ergane and Hephaistos on side A of the Berlin cup could be a deliberate reference to the deities in the tondo. The spear held by the woman would then be that of Athena, since Achilles never lost his and so needed no replacement. The only drawbacks to this suggestion are the fact that the woman does not wear an aegis and the addition of Athena to two of the four extant representations of the visit of Thetis to Hephaistos.

5 See Brommer 1978 (supra n.4) 10-17; R. Garland, *The eye of the beholder: deformity and disability in the Graeco-Roman world* (Ithaca 1995) 61-63, 113-14.

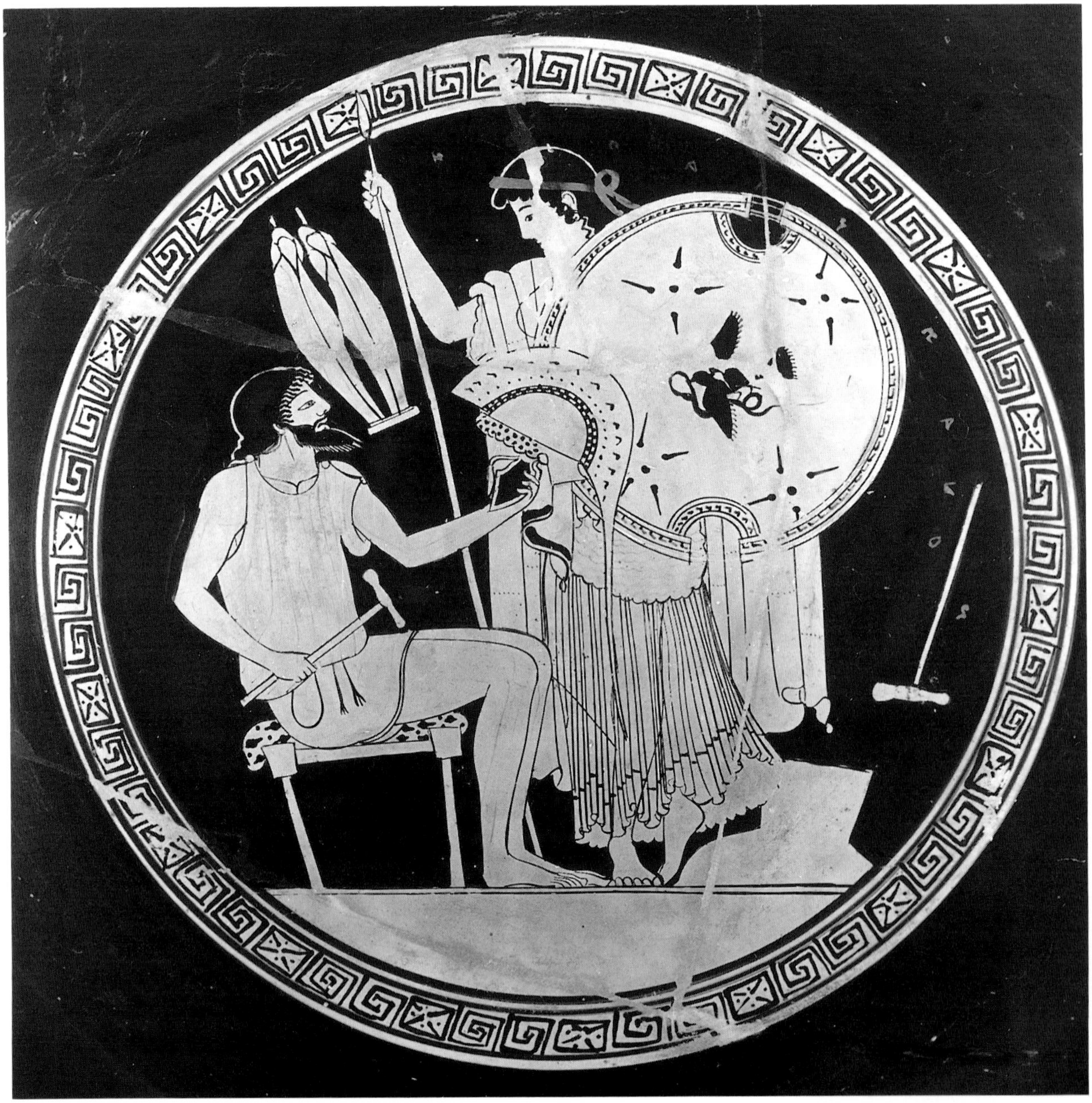

Fig. 1. Tondo, Berlin Foundry Cup by the Foundry Painter. Greek, made in Athens. 490-480 B.C. Earthenware, h. 0.12 m; diam. 0.305 m. Staatliche Museen zu Berlin–Preußischer Kulturbesitz, Antikensammlung F 2294. (Photo: Ingrid Geske; courtesy Antikensammlung.)

scenes. This subtle detail, characteristic of an artist whom Beazley dubbed "un realista greco,"[6] makes it absolutely certain that we are viewing the divine foundry.

On the exterior we are in a different realm. Here one can almost feel the heat of the furnace and empathize with the sweat and toil of the workers. Again the Foundry Painter uses subtle detail, here to distinguish the relative status of the figures in what can be read as one continuous scene. The workers of lowest status are appropriately closest to the ground and completely undressed; those of highest status are fully clothed and standing at leisure. In the finishing scene on side B (fig. 3), for example, the crouching nude scraper must be the assistant of his

6 J. D. Beazley, "Un realista greco," *Adunanze straordinarie per il conferimento dei premi della Fondazione A. Feltrinelli* 1.3 (1966) 53-60; id., "A Greek realist," transl. K. Huber and M. Robertson in D. Kurtz (ed.), *Greek vases: lectures by J. D. Beazley* (Oxford 1989) 78-83.

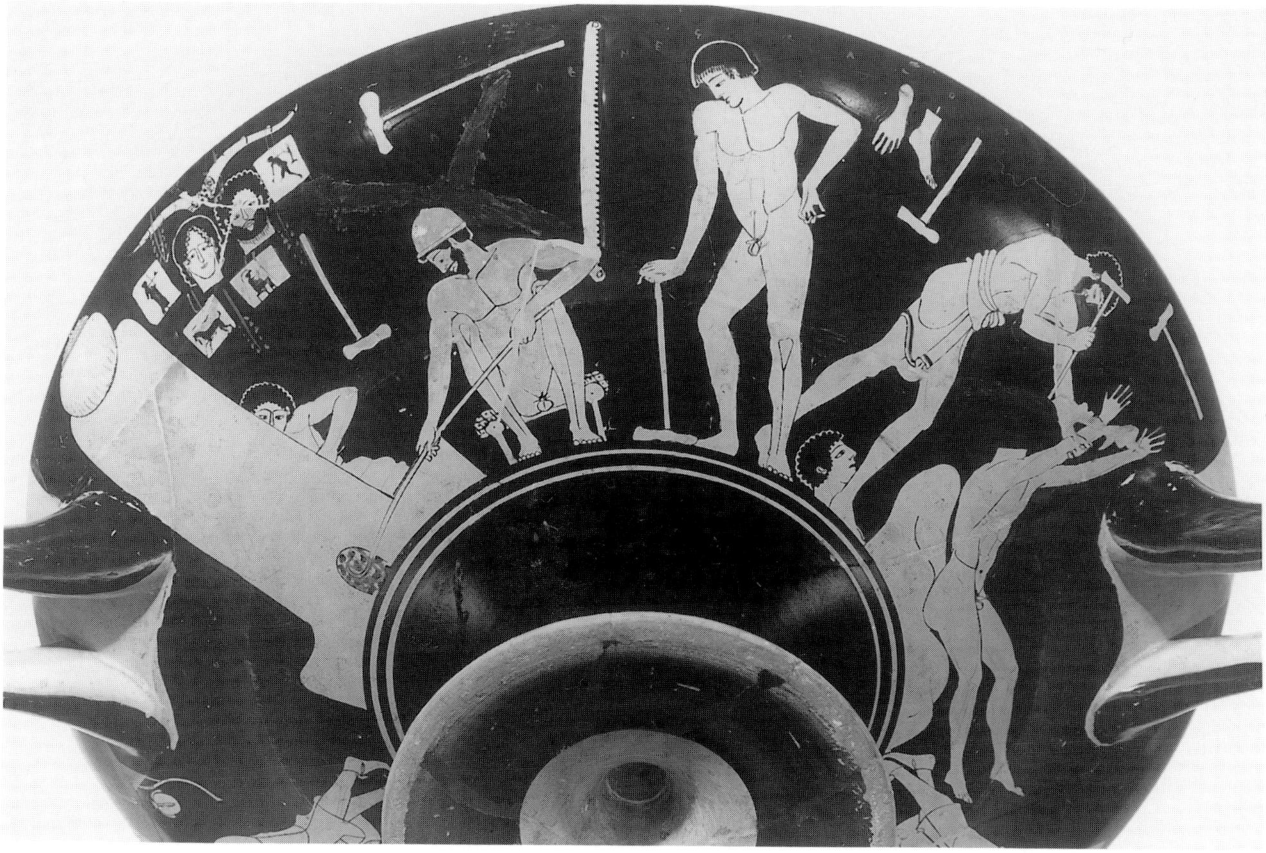

Fig. 2. Side A. (Photo: Ingrid Geske; courtesy Antikensammlung.)

standing, half-draped companion. His lower status is indicated not only by his nudity but also by an interesting detail, his snub nose.[7] Such unidealized, non-Greek profiles are often used in Attic vase-painting to indicate foreigners, particularly Blacks.[8] Many of the more skilled laborers in Attic workshops were from the East and Syria, and so the Foundry Painter may be attempting a realistic depiction of a foreign type, very possibly a slave, commonly seen in 5th-c. Athens.

The skull cap which he and his colleague on the other side wear seems to be typical of smiths, perhaps to protect their hair from flying sparks.[9] The nude figure on side A (fig. 2), seated on a very low stool, is adjusting the furnace, while his companion works the bellows. The latter's frontal face surely indicates his discomfort at the effort he is expending.[10] The stoker is also represented frontally, but in a distinctive position with his calves framing his torso and genitalia. That it might be another realistic touch is indicated by images of other craftsmen such as potters' assistants who crouch in this manner.[11] That it might also be a hum-

---

7 This aspect was noted by Greifenhagen in *CVA Berlin* 2, 25-26.

8 Cf. the Black groom of Onesimos (J. Boardman, *Athenian red figure vases: the Archaic period* [London 1975] fig. 229) or the Eastern archers (ibid. 134 detail 4). See F. M. Snowden, *Blacks in antiquity: Ethiopians in the Greco-Roman experience* (Cambridge, MA 1970). For barbarians in general, see W. Raeck, *Zum Barbarenbild in der Kunst Athens im 6. und 5. Jahrhundert v. Chr.* (Bonn 1981).

9 For a list of metalworkers wearing a *pilos*, see G. Zimmer, "Der Schmied in der Schale," *JBerlMus* 24 (1982) 8 n.9.

10 See Y. Korshak, *Frontal faces in Attic vase painting of the Archaic period* (Chicago 1987) 32, 69, no. 249, fig. 81.

11 Cf. also the smith on the fragmentary cup by the Euergides painter: *ARV*^{2} 92, 64; Boardman, *ARFV* (supra n.8) fig. 101.

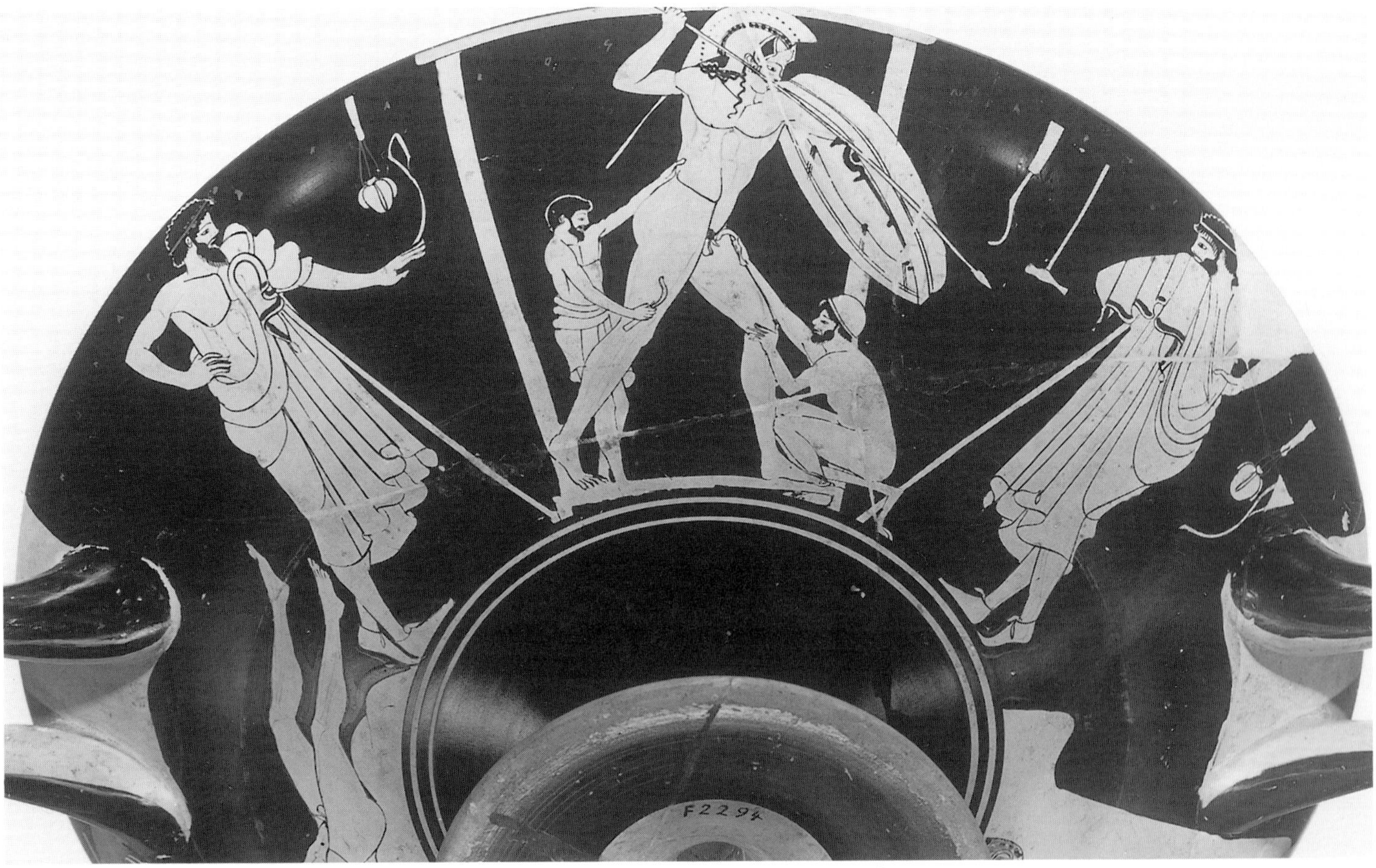

Fig. 3. Side B. (Photo: Ingrid Geske; courtesy Antikensammlung.)

orous touch is indicated by other forge scenes such as that by the Harrow Painter in Caltanisetta.[12] Here the frontal Hephaistos(?) is surrounded by satyrs, so the scene is meant to be comic. That the pose can also be considered somewhat obscene is indicated by the fact that it is normally reserved for satyrs, foreigners, symposium performers, and defecators.[13]

Thus it is clear that those working at the hot, dirty furnace have the lowliest tasks, while their comrades to the right are of higher status. They are artisans, piecing together an expensive life-size bronze statue. The younger is resting from his labors (is he the *Diogenes kalos* of the inscription?), while his half-draped elder is hammering away at the bronze. Their relationship is not unlike that of the two bronze workers on a black-figure oinochoe in London. The elder sits working at the furnace, while his co-worker looks on, hand on hip, mallet resting on the ground.[14] Might both of these pairs be father and son, since we know of such teams of sculptors from ancient literature? And is the younger boy gazing at the furnace or subtly directing our eyes to the comic pose of his inferior co-worker?

---

12 Caltanisetta CL 810. *Paralipomena* 354, 39*bis*; Boardman, *ARFV* (supra n.8) fig. 174.

13 Satyrs: see Korshak (supra n.10), figs. 74-79; M. L. Catoni, "Quando il ragazzo si fa satiro," *Prospettiva* 89-90 (1998) 74-84; I. Wehgartner, "Der Satyr des Sosias," in J. Oakley and O. Palagia (edd.), *Athenian potters and painters* (Oxford 1997) 203-12. Foreigners: bronze statuette in Boston, 01.7477; M. Comstock and C. Vermeule, *Greek, Etruscan and Roman bronzes in the Museum of Fine Arts, Boston* (Boston 1971) 33, no. 31. Symposium entertainers: *Paralipomena* 329, 14*bis*; Boardman, *ARFV* (supra n.8) fig. 68. Defecators: *ARV*^{2} 169, 7; Boardman, *ARFV* (supra n.8) fig. 84.

14 London, British Museum B 507. *ABV* 426, 9 (Keyside Class); J. Ziomecki, *Les représentations d'artisans sur les vases attiques* (Wroclaw 1975) 154, no. 29, fig. 19; G. Zimmer, *Antike Werkstattbilder* (Berlin 1982) fig. 11.

These questions are not possible to answer, so we turn now to the inanimate figure of the sculpture itself. Most scholars have identified this upright, nude youth as an athlete, and in particular a runner, even swift-footed Achilles.[15] Depictions of runners in this period typically show them leaning forward with one leg straight, one flexed, and one or both arms extended in front of the body. Well-known examples include the bronze statuette dedicated to Zeus at Olympia or the Ball-Player statue-base in Athens.[16] By rotating the Foundry Painter's statue into an upright position, we realize that his pose does not resemble that of a runner. He stands on his tiptoes and his arms are raised overhead.

Another suggestion is that he is a broad jumper, but he lacks the ubiquitous jumping weights and his legs should be bent at the knees and side-by-side.[17] The closest parallel for his pose is that of wrestlers and pankratists about to engage. They stand on tiptoe and raise one or both arms overhead, as seen on a 5th-c. grave stele of a wrestler from Attica[18] and on a red-figure mug in Cracow by the Penelope Painter.[19] In both the relief and the vase-painting the wrestlers are poised on tiptoes with their arms raised to the level of their heads. A Panathenaic prize amphora in Toledo by the Kleophrades Painter shows two pankratiasts thus posed, flanking a referee.[20]

Finally we turn to the most fully clad and shod men on the other side of the cup (fig. 3). They stand enveloped in their *himatia*, leaning on their walking sticks, right hands akimbo. Significantly, their strigils and aryballoi, symbols of the leisured palaestra-frequenting citizen class, hang in their vicinity. While it is often said that they might be the masters of the workshop,[21] it is hardly credible that sculptors would be shown dressed in voluminous *himatia*.[22] Both their garb and their relaxed attitude, in contrast to those of the workers, indicate that they must be aristocratic patrons, probably the men who have commissioned this great statue of a striding warrior. Their status is confirmed by their size in relation to the manual laborers who are finishing the bronze, a prominent deviation from 'reality' on the part of an artist known for his realism. That they are customers is corroborated by other vase-paintings that show similar standing males, usually elderly and so bearded, often in pairs in workshop scenes.[23] On a red-figure oinochoe in St. Petersburg, a draped man leaning on his walking stick and holding his aryballos and strigil stands before a seated cutler, clearly negotiating a sale.[24] It is obvious in all such scenes of craftsmen that we are meant to distinguish workers from patrons by dress, attributes, and pose.

---

15 H. A. Thompson, "A note on the Berlin Foundry Cup," *Essays in memory of Karl Lehmann* (New York 1964) 327.

16 Olympia B 26: O. Tzachou-Alexandri, *Mind and body: athletic contests in ancient Greece* (Exhib. cat., Athens 1989) 221-22, no. 113. Athens, National Museum 3476: ibid. 278-80, no. 167.

17 On the starting pose of jumpers, see J.-J. Maffre, "Deux pélikai attiques de Thasos," *BCH* 96 (1971) 339-58. See also J. D. Beazley, *Some Attic vases in the Cyprus Museum* (London 1948) 47-49.

18 Athens, National Archaeological Museum 2004. See Tzachou-Alexandri, *Mind and body* (supra n.16) 335-36, no. 225.

19 Cracow 1260: *ARV*^{2} 1302, 28.

20 The Toledo Museum of Art 61.24: *ARV*^{2} 1632; *CVA Toledo* 1 (*USA* 17) pl. 13.

21 For discussion of this hypothesis, see C. C. Mattusch, "The Berlin Foundry Cup: the casting of Greek bronze statuary in the early fifth century B.C.," *AJA* 84 (1980) 440-42.

22 On the luxurious dress of Athenian males, see A. G. Geddes, "Rags and riches: the costume of Athenian men in the fifth century," *CQ* 37 (1987) 307-31.

23 E.g., the black-figure amphora Boston 01.8035: Ziomecki, *Représentations d'artisans* (supra n.14) 149-50, no. 12, figs. 20 and 34; G. Zimmer, *Antike Werkstattbilder* (supra n.14) fig. 5.

24 Hermitage 2229: *ARV*^{2} 595, 72; Ziomecki, *Représentations d'artisans* (supra n.14) 153, no. 27, fig. 26; G. Zimmer, *Antike Werkstattbilder* (supra n.14) fig. 10.

While it is conceivable that these men are simply visitors to the workshop,[25] it seems more likely that they are customers. The presence of the patron seems to be a deliberate and necessary figure in earlier workshop scenes, perhaps as an indication of the success of the craftsmen. Two such patrons appear on another cup by the Foundry Painter, which shows a proud marble carver presenting his equestrian statue with the blessing of Athena Ergane.[26] The ultimate idealized workshop scene is that of the Leningrad Painter, in which Athena accompanied by two Nikai brings victory wreaths to three potters — divine patronage being even more desirable than human.[27] More of a realist, the Foundry Painter subtly places the image of Athena Ergane along with that of Hephaistos as votives next to the furnace. Just as Thetis is commissioning divine armor as protection for her son, so these patrons, whether public or private, are ordering a statue of a hero whose *kleos* will protect the state.[28] In the generation of the Persian Wars such protection was no doubt deemed desirable for the city.

In conclusion, the Foundry Painter's cup can be seen as a microcosm of Athenian society, from the lowly servile workers to the aristocratic patrons. On this kylix there is everything from an Olympian divinity, albeit deformed, to snub-nosed metics or slaves. The painter demonstrates a sense of humor, not inappropriate on a vase used at the symposium.[29] And perhaps most importantly in the 'banausic' world of the Kerameikos,[30] the imagery features the rôle of the craftsman, and recognizes the importance of both divine and human patronage.

Case Western Reserve University, Cleveland, Ohio

---

25 As suggested by P. Cloché, *Les classes, les métiers, le trafic* (Paris 1931) 58. See also D. B. Thompson, "The house of Simon the shoemaker," *Archaeology* 13 (1960) 234-40.

26 Munich 2650: *ARV*² 401, 2. Ziomecki, *Représentations d'artisans* (supra n.14) 155, no. 34, fig. 33.

27 Milan, private coll.: *ARV*² 571, no. 73; Ziomecki, *Représentations d'artisans* (supra n.14) 154, no. 32, fig. 13.

28 On the inherent power of victor statues, see L. Kurke, "The economy of *kudos*," in C. Dougherty and L. Kurke (edd.), *Cultural poetics in archaic Greece* (Cambridge 1993) 131-63.

29 At the risk of reading too much humor into this vase, I posit two further allusions. First, the headless bronze statue lying on a rough clay ground recalls Prokrustes, the opponent of Theseus, who is often depicted on a low rocky bed, and the sculptor, hammer in hand, suggests the Attic hero who turned the tables on his victim. For these images in Attic vase-painting, see J. Neils, *The youthful deeds of Theseus* (Rome 1987) passim. Second, the artisans involved in the coldwork on the warrior statue suggest slaves strigiling their master; given the position of one of the strigils, there may even be homoerotic connotations.

30 See N. Himmelmann, *Realistische Themen in der griechischen Kunst der archaischen und klassischen Zeit* (Berlin 1994); H. A. Shapiro, "Correlating shape and subject: the case of the Archaic pelike," in J. Oakley and O. Palagia (edd.), *Athenian potters and painters* (Oxford 1997) 63-70

An old saw

Kenneth R. Cavalier

The Foundry Cup is the name piece of the Foundry Painter, who was a strong follower of the Brygos Painter.[1] On it are shown a furnace, various tools, workers, and statues in different stages of completion. Of particular interest is a large saw depicted on the rear wall (fig. 1). Poor reproduction of this tool over the years has made discussion of the use of the saw nearly impossible, but it appears to indicate the use of wood in the foundry. It will be argued here that this saw supports the use of wooden models in early Greek bronzecasting.

One reason examination of the saw has been cursory is that mistakes were made in the illustrations and descriptions of the cup in several major scholarly works dealing with Greek sculpture. In the early editions of *Sculpture and sculptors of the Greeks,* G. M. A. Richter's drawing of the cup shows the saw with only one hole at the bottom (presumably for insertion of the handle) and with the blade made rather narrow and its teeth inaccurately depicted as jagged points on the side of the blade,[2] so that the saw almost appears serrated on both sides. This drawing apparently came from T. Schreiber's *Atlas of classical antiquities.*[3] It was reprinted in such works as R. J. Forbes's *Technology in ancient Greece*, C. Singer's *History of technology,* and G. Savage's *Concise history of bronzes.*[4] H. Blümner's *Home life of the ancient Greeks* reproduces a different drawing: the saw is shown with a narrow blade and the handle drawn in, and its position is moved from behind the fire tender's elbow toward the man with the axe; no holes are visible.[5]

In L. Casson's *Technique of early Greek sculpture,* there is a photograph of the kylix, and it is clear that the teeth of the blade are rectangular in shape and only on one side. However, only the bottom portion of the blade, showing a hole for a handle, is visible.[6] Casson, however, must have known the other drawings, as he writes that there is only one hole for a handle.[7] In J. Charbonneaux's *Greek bronzes,* the drawing shows the correct two holes, but the teeth are rendered as triangular rather than rectangular.[8] This is the modern convention for depicting saw teeth.[9] In R. Carpenter's *Greek sculpture,* there are two holes and the teeth are more rectilinear,[10] but in the 1964 Argonaut edition of A. Furtwängler's *Masterpieces of Greek sculpture,*[11] the saw disappears altogether, as it does in D. Haynes's drawing published in 1992.[12] The erroneous drawings were replaced by a better version much like Carpenter's in recent editions of

---

1 C. C. Mattusch, "The Berlin Foundry Cup: the casting of Greek bronze statuary in the early 5th c. B.C.," *AJA* 84 (1980) 435-44; ead. in *The fire of Hephaistos* 182-84, no. 1. See also Neils, above p. 75.

2 G. M. A. Richter, *The sculpture and sculptors of the Greeks* (rev. ed., New Haven 1950) 495, fig. 430.

3 T. Schreiber, *Atlas of classical antiquities* (London 1895) pl. 8, fig. 6.

4 The drawing appears in R. J. Forbes, *Studies in ancient technology* 8 (Leiden 1964) 35, fig. 10, and at id., "Metallurgy" in C. J. Singer *et al.* (edd.), *A history of technology* 1 (Oxford 1956) 51. It also appears in G. Savage, *A concise history of bronzes* (London 1968) 48, ill. 26, where the caption acknowledges Schreiber.

5 H. Blümner (transl. A. Zimmern), *The home life of the ancient Greeks* (London 1895; New York 1966) 508, fig. 202. The drawing first appears in H. Blumner, *Leben und Sitten der Griechen* (Leiden 1887) 162, fig. 54.

6 L. Casson, *The technique of early Greek sculpture* (Oxford 1933; New York 1970) 159-60.

7 Ibid. 224.

8 J. Charbonneaux (transl. K. Watson), *Greek bronzes* (London 1958; New York 1962) 27.

9 Careful examination of the one-man bow saw on Boston 01.8035, with its depiction of a smith's shop, reveals incised triangular teeth in this very convention.

10 R. Carpenter, *Greek sculpture* (Chicago 1960) 78, figs. 2-3.

11 A. Furtwängler, *Masterpieces of Greek sculpture* (London 1895; rev. edn. Chicago 1964) 111, fig. 14. Interestingly, the cup does not appear, drawn or otherwise, in the 1985 edition of Furtwängler.

12 Haynes, *Technique* 78, fig. 5. This may, of course, merely be a result of the editing of the area shown in the drawing, but it does remove this important tool from consideration.

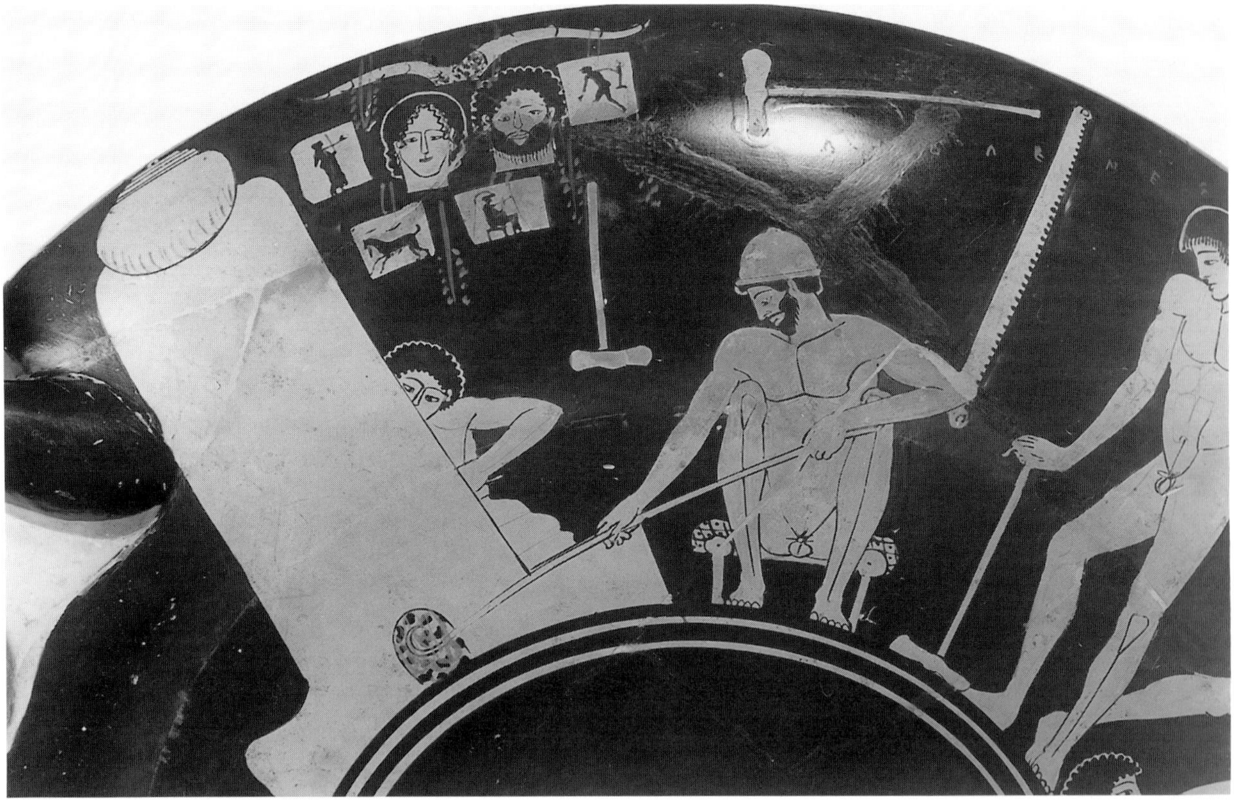

Fig. 1. Detail of Berlin Foundry Cup, by the Foundry Painter. Greek, made in Athens. 490-480 B.C. Earthenware, h. 0.12 m; diam. 0.305 m. Berlin, Staatliche Museen zu Berlin–Preußischer Kulturbesitz, Antikensammlung F 2294. (Photo: I. Geske; courtesy Antikensammlung.)

Richter's book (1974), but the problems of inaccurate drawings have interfered with the proper study of the cup[13] and affected descriptions of the saw. Even C. Mattusch, after personal examination of the cup, describes "A long saw, of uncertain use ..." and then compares it with the short saw depicted on a fragmentary kylix in Florence where "an armorer appears to be using a short saw, perhaps as a form of hacksaw, to work on a greave ...".[14]

Casson states that the saw was "carefully depicted with large teeth" and that the precise use of such a large saw (he reckoned it *c*.4 feet long) was difficult to determine. First, he suggests that the saw might be needed only "... when ends of separately cast limbs had to be fitted to a separately cast torso." Then he adds, "The size of this saw, however, seems too great for so minor a task and something in the nature of actual amputation of a bronze limb seems indicated." He says this would only happen in the event of a serious miscasting, and in a footnote wonders, "It may be, of course, that this is merely the saw used in sawing the logs for the furnace."[15] It seems more likely to me that the size of the blade and the nature of the teeth indicate that the saw was used neither to trim separately cast pieces nor to amputate. In piece casting, why would one attach a miscast piece only to have to amputate it later?

A good view of the saw hanging on the wall (fig. 1) clearly shows the rectangular teeth along one side of the blade and the two handle holes. The teeth are like those on two-handled crosscut saws used by modern lumberjacks (fig. 2). Such teeth are totally unsuitable for metal use, as comparison with a hacksaw blade readily shows. These saws are used for woodcutting. The deep gaps between the teeth are for removing sawdust from the kerf, the groove or notch

13 The difficulties of transferring the drawing from the curved surface of the kylix to a two-dimensional surface can be seen in the souvenir mug designed for *The Fire of Hephaistos* exhibition, where the upper handle hole is much less clearly defined, obscuring the indication that this is a two-person saw.

14 Mattusch 1980 (supra n.1) 437, n.14.

15 Casson 1970 (supra n.6) 224.

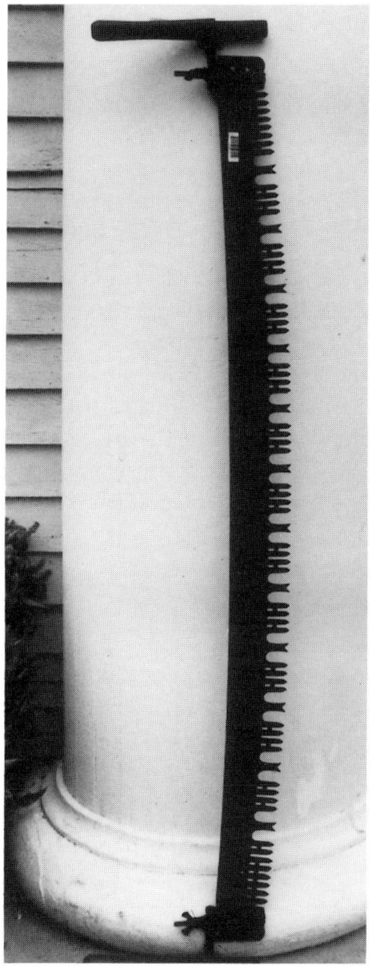

Fig. 2. Two-handled crosscut saw. (Photo: author.)

made by a saw or axe. Such a blade is used for crosscutting the grain of the wood. A comparison with a similar-sized modern saw (fig. 2) indicates that it was used by two men to cut large logs.

It might be argued that this is a conventional method of representing a saw with triangular teeth (as in Charbonneaux's drawing), but the careful depiction of the more difficult to draw four-stroke rectilinear teeth, rather than two-stroke triangular ones, makes this unlikely. The saw on the Foundry Cup is too large and with the wrong type of teeth to be used on metal. It must have been used for woodcutting. There must have been a need for wood in the foundry. What might that need have been?

Casson's explanation of the saw's use for firewood is given some support by the position of the tool behind the seated fire-tender's elbow. However, the cap of Hephaistos worn by this figure leads me to see him as of major importance and to wonder if it would be his job to get the fuel. Olson has indicated that "... the charcoal burner was a marginal individual with no proper place in the city,"[16] arguing that urban residents most probably purchased their firewood and charcoal from a market called τὰ ξύλα.[17] He points out that "even in the countryside the gathering and carrying of wood was regarded as extremely heavy, undesirable labor, more suitable for slaves than free citizens."[18] Given the prominence of this saw, the likelihood that it was to cut firewood which would then have had to be made into lighter, more transportable charcoal in a lengthy process (most often done far outside the city in the mountains where the large heavy trees requiring a two-person saw grew) seems dubious. Should we expect to find so obscure a reference to the source of charcoal prominently displayed within the depiction of a foundry? It seems unlikely that the smith was responsible for the manufacture of charcoal.

---

16 S. Douglas Olson, "Firewood and charcoal in Classical Athens," *Hesperia* 60.3 (1991) 417-18. Olson cites "the difficult life of the old peasant misanthrope Knemon in Menander's *Dyskolos*, who "... does this work for himself," quoting ζῇ μόνος ... ξυλοφορῶν σκάπτων τ', ἀεὶ πονῶν (Menander, *Dys.* 30-32) and talks about the servant who "... mentions the man ᾧ ξυλοφορῶ" from *Her.* 52, p. 415-16. He also points to Aristophanes' depiction of Dikaiopolis in *Acharnians* 272, passages *Ach.* 34, 36 and *Wasps* 301 f., as examples of urban dependence on others for fuel. He links the inability to buy enough fuel to a "basic sign of poverty," citing Aristophanes, *Pl.* 535; 951-54 (Olson, 416). Quoting Aristophanes, *Ach.* 212 to discuss the charcoal carriers and *Ach.* 609 which names one of the chorus Εὐφορίδης, "Son of Good at Carrying," Olson suggest this task of transporting charcoal from the countryside to the city was a way for poor peasants to "... earn hard money to buy goods they needed but could not produce on their own." Further evidence that charcoal was probably produced in the countryside and then imported into the city to the central market for sale can be found in the quote of Andokides which "... says that one of the ultimate low points of war is the moment at which 'we see the charcoal burners coming from the mountains into the city'," fr. 4 Blass (Olson 418).

17 Olson also cites Aristophanes fr. 403 K-A as possible evidence for a central wood market τὰ ξύλα, 418-19. Mentioning fr. 13 K-A of the late 5th c. comic poet Philyllios as quoted at Pollux, 7.110, Olson shows the urban tradesman of charcoal seller (ἀνθρακοπώλης) had certainly been identified. He says "Urban residents of Athens with no other resources, as well as representatives of various industries, would have come to this central market to purchase their fuel, which they, their servants, or hired porters known as ξυλόφοροι would then have carried off to their homes or places of business. Carrying wood for hire must have been backbreaking labor with no job security whatsoever and was recognized as one of the lowest occupations available for a free man" (Olson 419).

18 Ibid. 415, 419 n.41.

The position of the saw may suggest its use. Its depiction behind the master worker near the hanging models and spare heads seems to indicate a tool of major importance, perhaps one used in the casting process. The use of such saws implies finer cutting tasks, such as squaring ends or making large beams. Since the production of charcoal involves a yield estimated by Olson at no more than 15-20% of the wood pyrolized,[19] the fine cutting implied by this tool is not required to make charcoal fuel.

What about depictions of kilns and iron foundries where the saw is not present? In other bronzeworking scenes, there are representations of woodcutting saws, although usually of the one-man bow saw. Curiously, if the saw is for firewood, there are few saws and none so large or prominent in other foundry scenes, even when the furnace is shown and where fuel was needed.[20] It would be convenient to say that in bronzeworking depictions there are saws and in iron-working depictions there are none, but certain armorer vases seem to belie this. Some bronzeworking scenes have saws and others do not, but saws are present on at least four important bronzeworking representations, three without furnaces[21] and on the Foundry Cup with them. Does it not seem that the saw is connected more firmly with bronzeworking than with the firewood of the furnace? I am unaware of any pottery kiln scenes where saws are depicted, despite the potter's similar need for fuel.

Carpenter's discussion of the area of the Foundry Cup workshop near the saw notes that the presence of the spare foot and hand hung on the wall by a nail indicates that they are wooden models.[22] This theory was a revision of one Kluge had proposed for the use of wooden models in 1929.[23] Both Mattusch[24] and Haynes[25] have discredited Kluge's theory and Carpenter's revis-

---

19 Ibid. 412, discusses the transport of charcoal from the countryside to the city as a means for the poor to raise cash. Clearly, if the charcoal represented between one-fifth and one-quarter of the weight and volume of unprocessed logs, the incentive was for charcoal producers to process the material before transport to the city. The difficulty of transporting logs (of a diameter requiring this large two-person crosscut saw) into the city from sites undoubtedly far away on mountainsides, only to *then* transform them into a material (one-fifth of the weight and volume) mitigates against the manufacture of the fuel in the city.

20 Boston 01.8035, a black-figure amphora with a smith's shop, depicts an ironworking, not bronzeworking, scene and may be the one example of a saw in the presence of a working furnace, but there are surprisingly few furnaces linked with saws. If we look at the red-figure column krater from the necropolis of Sabucina, Caltanisetta 20371, illustrated in R. D. Gempeler, "Die Schmiede des Hephast — Eine Satyrspielszene des Harrow-Malers," *AntK* 12 (1969) 16-21 and London B 507 oinochoe we see a working forge but no saw. The red-figure oinochoe sometimes called "Smith Takes a Holiday," Athenian Agora P 15210, also shows a furnace but no saw, and Berlin F 1980.7 also has a smith with neither saw nor furnace (see Mattusch, *Greek bronze statuary* 233, A.20; 239, A.32, respectively).

21 Saws appear on the Nolan amphora (Boston 13.188), Athena modeling a horse (Berlin F 2415 oinochoe), and the fragmentary Florence kylix cited in Mattusch 1980 (supra n.1) 437, n.14.

22 Carpenter 1960 (supra n.10) 69-80.

23 K. Kluge, in K. Kluge and K. Lehmann-Hartleben (edd.), *Die antike Erzgestaltung und ihre technischen Grundlagen*, 1. *Die antiken Grossbronzen* (Berlin 1927) 82-90, first asserted that both sand casting and lost-wax casting had been used in antiquity.

24 Mattusch, *Greek bronze statuary* 22-26 discusses the influence of Kluge and his theory and then discusses "a second and divergent trend of thought about technique that has developed in recent years" (p. 26), listing R. J. Forbes and H. Maryon as opponents of Kluge's sand-casting idea. She goes on to cite U. Jantzen and F. Chamoux and state "... scholars have at last rejected sand casting as a technique known during antiquity" (p. 28). See esp. n.51 for a list of recent works concerned with ancient bronze technology.

25 Haynes, *Technique* 57-64 discusses the glyptic or plastic nature of the model and states (57-58) that Kluge and Carpenter's wooden "... cores ... are almost certainly an archaeological myth", although he does go on to say (58) "... it remains an undeniable fact that wood played an important part in archaic Greek sculpture ..." and that "... the possibility that archaic Greek bronze-casters sometimes carved their models from wood, cannot be excluded ...". Haynes expresses "... doubts about Kluge's glorification

ion for lack of evidence, and Mattusch denies there is any reason to see as made of wood the models hanging on the same wall as the saw.[26]

But let us return to the woodcutting saw on the wall of the Foundry Cup. Was it a crosscut saw for providing modeling material? Are the foot and hand on the wall made of wood? What about the spare heads hanging to the left of the furnace? Considering the duplicate facial parts of the Agora kouros mold, might these be alternative heads, not replacements for miscasts or votives but rather alternative models available for the discerning customer? It may seem a horrible thought — mix and match statues with 'off-the-rack' bodies and custom designed visages. This sounds too much like mass production. Yet recent study of several bronzes in *The Fire of Hephaistos* exhibition revealed that this may not be quite the heresy it first appears.

The piecemeal construction of bronzes would lend itself to such a practice. Pliny says Lysippos was supposed to have created 1,500 bronze statues.[27] One wonders if a large percentage had the same two or three faces? However, before we speculate about an ancient equivalent of Henry Ford making production-line bronze statues, let us remember the expense of materials and inventory if those hanging heads are made of bronze. They must be made of wood or clay, and the saw urges their interpretation as wooden models. Considering the perishability of wood, the depiction of the saw remains our only archaeological evidence for such models.

School of Architecture, University of British Columbia, Vancouver V6T 1Z2

---

of the chisel ..." (61) and argues for the much greater use of more plastic modeling materials, especially by the classical period, in his chapt. 6.

26 Mattusch 1980 (supra n.1) 439, n.32.

27 Pliny, *NH* 34.37.

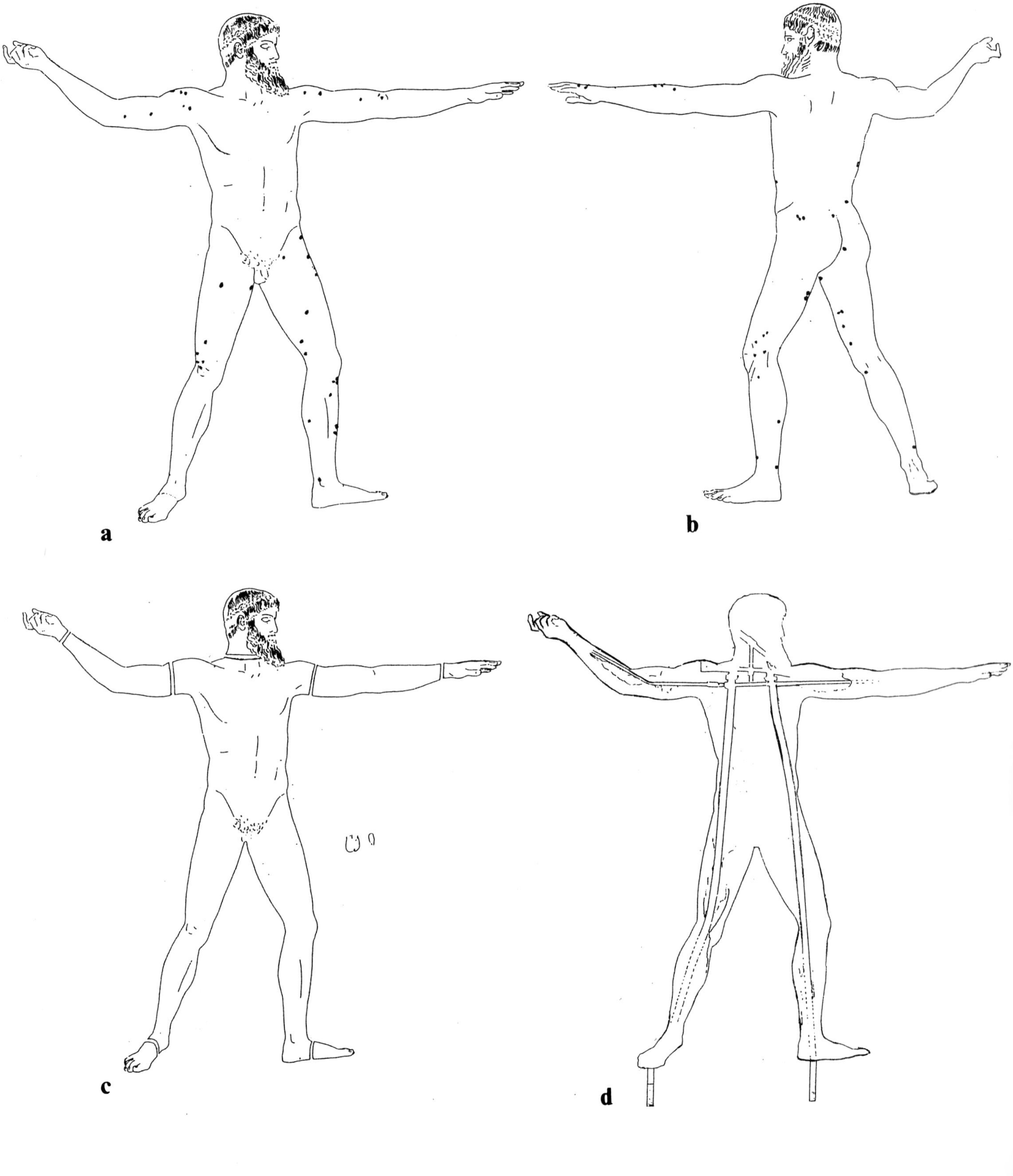

Fig. 1 a-b) Drawing showing patches and repairs; c) Drawing of the joins; d) drawing of the modern armature. (Drawings: A. Litti, 1996.)

to Semni Karouzou *in memoriam*

Some remarks on the bronze god of Artemision

Olga Tzachou-Alexandri

The magnificent bronze statue in the National Archaeological Museum, Athens, found in 1926 and 1928 in the sea off Cape Artemision in Euboia, has been the object of several thorough studies.[1] Scholars have been concerned with style and identification without, however, reaching any definitive conclusions. It is widely accepted that the statue was made during the decade 460-450 B.C. The type is the striding god, a reflection of an early two-dimensional type, represented by the Ugento God in the National Museum, Taranto,[2] and the Munich Zeus.[3] The bronze statuette from Dodona, now in the Archaeological Museum, Berlin,[4] dated to the Early Classical period, has the same pose and gesture as the Artemision God.

Famous sculptors who represent the main stylistic trends of the Early Classical period have been proposed as the creators of this noble piece of art. The names of Onatas,[5] Kalamis,[6] Myron,[7] and Hageladas[8] have been suggested, but the styling of the hair recalls that of the Omphalos Apollo,[9] usually assigned to Kalamis. This last attribution seems to me the most convincing since, as will be discussed below, the result of recent clay core analysis of the statue points to an Athenian provenance. As to the identity of the figure, a number of possibilities

---

1 Inv. no. 15161: h. 2.09 m: *Deltion* 10 (1926); Παράρτημα 86ff. *BCH* 52 (1928) 466; Γ. Οικονόμος, *PraktAkAth* 3 (1928) 750 ff., pls. 1-3; F. Noack, "Der neue Gott aus dem Meere," *Antike* 5 (1929) 219 ff.; id., *AA* 44 (1929) 162; Χ. Καρούζος, "Ο Ποσειδών του Αρτεμισίου," *Deltion* 13 (1930-31) 41-104; J. Jüthner, "Die Grossbronze vom Artemision," *AthMitt* 62 (1937) 136 ff.; A. E. Raubitschek, "Early Attic votive monuments," *BSA* 40 (1939-40) 34; E. Homann-Wedeking, "Zu Meisterwerken des strengen Stils," *RömMitt* 55 (1940) 200, 203, 206 ff.; V. H. Poulsen, "Myron: ein stilkritisches Versuch," *ActaArch* 11 (1940) 1 ff.; C. A. Robinson, Jr., "The Master of Olympia," *AJA* 46 (1942) 76; G. E. Mylonas, "The bronze statue from Artemision," *AJA* 48 (1944) 143 ff.; L. Curtius, *Interpretationen von sechs griechischen Bildwerken* (Bern 1947) 69-82; K. Schefold, "Archaische Plastik," *WürzJbA* 2 (1947) 45; J. Dörig in J. Boardman *et al.*, *Die Griechische Kunst* (Munich 1966) 127 f.; E. Simon, *Die Götter der Griechen* (Munich 1969) 89 f.; B. S. Ridgway, *Severe* 62; J. Kleine, "Zur Datierung des Poseidon vom Kap Artemision," in *Festschrift G. Kleiner* (Tübingen 1976) 49-59; J. Dörig, *Onatas of Aegina* (Leiden 1977) 7-8, ills. 5, 26, 28; R. Wünsche, "Der Gott aus dem Meer," *JdI* 94 (1979) 77 ff.; D. Finn and C. Houser, *Greek monumental bronze sculpture* (Leiden 1983) 78-85; Mattusch, *Greek bronze statuary* 5-6, 99, 137, 150, 151-54, 184 n.114, 186, 212; G. Hafner, "Zu Kalamis," *Rivista di Archeologia* 15 (1991) 61 ff.

2 Inv. no. 12137: N. Degrassi, *Lo Zeus Stilita di Ugento* (Rome 1981); C. Rolley, "Les bronzes grecs: recherches récents, pt. 5, "Écoles et styles archaïques," *RA* 1986, 389-91; Mattusch, *Greek bronze statuary* 7, 14-15, 60, 64-66, 67-71, 79-80, 98-99, 103, 110-14, 135, 138, 150, 184, 206, 212; Haynes, *Technique* 85, 88, 117 n.17; R. Thomas, *Bronzestatuetten* (Darmstadt 1992) 70, fig. 54.

3 Inv. no. Br. 4339: G. Kopcke, "Eine Bronzestatuette des Zeus in der Münchener Glyptothek," *MüJb* 27 (1976) 7-28; M. Maass, *Griechische und römische Bronzewerke der Antikensammlungen* (Munich 1979) 17-19; Mattusch, *Greek bronze statuary* 68-69, 114, 150; R. Thomas, *Bronzestatuetten* 69, fig. 53.

4 Inv. no. 10561: K. Neugebauer, *Antike Bronzestatuetten* (Berlin 1921) 50, fig. 28; E. Langlotz, *Frühgriechi-sche Bildhauerschulen* (Nüremberg 1927) pl. 37; E. Walter-Karydi, "Bronzen aus Dodona: Eine Epirotische Erzbilderschule," *JbBerlMus* 23 (1981) 11 ff., fig. 38, and pp. 38 f.; Thomas, *Bronze statuettes* (supra n.2) 92, fig. 38; W. Schiering, *Die Bronzestatuetten des Zeus von Dodona* (Reclams Werkmono-graphien no. 134; Stuttgart 1969) 22.

5 R. Lullies and M. Hirmer, *Greek sculpture* (London 1960) 75; J. Boardman *et al.*, *The art and architecture of ancient Greece* (London 1967) 278; Homann-Wedeking, (1940) (supra n.1) 200, 203 f., 206 ff; Dörig, in Boardman *et al.*, *Die griechische Kunst* (supra n.1) 127 f.

6 Καρούζος 1930-31 (supra n.1) 93f; Curtius, *Interpretationen* (supra n.1) p. 73; Raubitschek 1939-40 (supra n.1) 34; G. Hafner 1991 (supra n.1) 64.

7 Poulsen 1940 (supra n.1) 1ff.

8 Mylonas 1944 (supra n.1) 160; Robinson 1942 (supra n.1) 76.

9 *LIMC* II (1984) s.v. Apollo, no. 599, with bibl. (B. Lambrinudakis *et al.*); Hafner 1991 (supra n.1) 61 ff.

have been suggested, such as Zeus[10] or Poseidon[11] or even an athlete.[12] Nevertheless, the pose and the gesture of the statue are more typical of Zeus, while a trident is not normally held like a throwing weapon. Furthermore, it would be practically impossible for an over-lifesize statue, standing in the open air, to hold a trident, since prevailing weather conditions would cause the long weapon to waver, resulting in the loss of stability of the statue and in its breaking. The possibility that this is a cult statue has also been discussed.[13] However, a cult statue in action is unusual for the early 5th c. B.C. For the time being, the lack of an attribute or an inscription renders identification of the statue problematic. Furthermore, the circumstances of the discovery of the artifact, as well as the lack of evidence concerning the origin or destination of the ship that transported the bronze god and the other pieces of art, do not offer any basis for further discussion of the identification of the statue.[14]

The purpose of this paper is to give technical information on the method of manufacture of the statue. Some useful remarks have already been made by P. Bol,[15] C. Mattusch,[16] and D. Haynes.[17] Photographs taken at the period of the statue's restoration and x-radiographs taken recently help to illuminate details of the process by which the statue was cast.[18] They can also provide information about the modern installation of this sculpture in the museum. Of high importance for the identification of the sculptor are the chemical analyses of the samples taken from the clay core and from the bronze.

After the most recent technical studies[19] of the existing material, it is generally agreed that life-size or larger statues were already being produced by the lost-wax process by the end of the 6th c. B.C. There were two main methods of the same process: the direct[20] and the indirect.[21]

---

10 *BCH* 52 (1928) 466; Οικονόμος 1928 (supra n.1) 750; Noack, *Antike* 1929 (supra n.1) 219 ff.; Noack, *AA* 1929 (supra n.1) 162; G. M. Young, "Six original photographs of the bronze Zeus from Artemision," *BSA* 37 (1936-37) pls. 26-30; Wünsche 1979 (supra n.1) 77 ff.; Mylonas 1944 (supra n.1) 143 ff.; W. Schwabacher, "The Olympian Zeus before Pheidias," *Archaeology* 14 (1961) 104-9; C. A. Robinson, Jr., "The Zeus Ithomatas of Ageladas," *AJA* 49 (1945) 121-27.

11 Καρούζος 1930-31 (supra n.1) 41-104; Kleine 1976 (supra n.1) 51; Raubitschek 1939-40 (supra n.1) 34; Homann-Wedeking 1940 (supra n.1) 206; Simon, *Götter* (supra n.1) 86-90; K. Schefold, "Archaische Plastik," *WürzJbAltWiss* 2 (1947) 45; *LIMC* VII (1994) s.v. Poseidon, no. 28 (E. Simon).

12 Jüthner 1937 (supra n.1) 136 ff.

13 Cult statue: V. H. Poulsen, "Der Strenge Stil: Studien zur Geschichte der griechischen Plastik 480-50 v. Chr.," *ActaArch* 8 (1937) 140. Not a cult statue: Ridgway, *Severe* 62.

14 Ν. Μπέρτος, "'Άγαλμα του 'Αρτεμισίου ... 'Έκθεσις περὶ τῆς ἐξερευνήσεως τοῦ βυθόυ της θαλάσσης 'Αρτεμισίου," *Deltion* 10 (1926); Παράρτημα 86 ff.; R. Herbig, *Gnomon* 5 (1929) 637; Wünsche 1979 (supra n.1) 106 n.80.

15 Bol, *Bronzetechnik* 151, fig. 109, and 153 n.94.

16 Mattusch, *Greek bronze statuary* 137, 153.

17 Haynes, *Technique* 59, 108, 117 n.25.

18 Twenty-five x-radiographs were taken by a Demokritos team supervised by H. Andreopoulou-Mangou, chemist at the National Archaeological Museum.

19 E. Formigli, "La tecnica di costruzione delle statue di Riace," in *Due bronzi* 104ff. See also E. Paribeni, "Le statue bronze di Porticello," *BdA* 69 (1984) 1 ff.; Bol, *Bronzetechnik*; C. Houser, *Greek monumental bronze sculpture of the fifth and fourth centuries B.C.* (New York 1987); C. Mattusch, "The earliest Greek bronze statues and the lost wax process," in *Griechische und Römische Statuetten und Grossbronzen* (Akten der 9 int. Tagung über antike Bronzen, Wien 1986; Vienna 1988) 191 ff.; G. Zimmer, "Das Mädchen von Kyzikos," ibid. 66ff; D. Williams, "Knight rider: the Piot bronze," *AA* 1989, 529 ff.; C. Mattusch, "The casting of Greek bronzes: variation and repetition," in *Small bronze sculptures* 125 ff.; Zimmer, *Bronzegußwerkstätten*; Haynes, *Technique*; Mattusch, *Classical bronzes*.

20 See Mattusch, *Greek bronze statuary* 16-19. See also Haynes, *Technique* 24 ff.; the writer claims (34 f.) that this technique was practically never used for life-size statues.

21 The invention of the method is ascribed by D. Haynes to Rhoecus and Theodorus: "The technique of the Erbach griffin-protomai," *JHS* 101 (1981) 137; Formigli, in *Due bronzi* 107 ff. See also Mattusch, *Greek bronze statuary* 194.

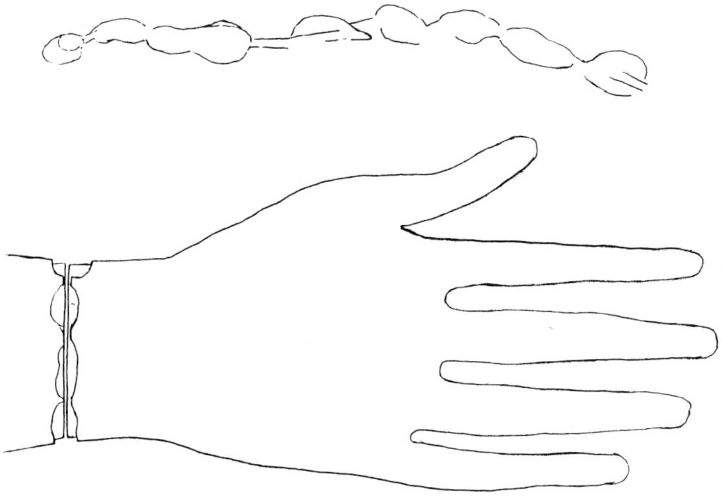

Fig. 2. Drawing of the left hand join, showing the oval "basins" method of attaching the hand to the arm. (Drawings: A. Litti, 1996.)

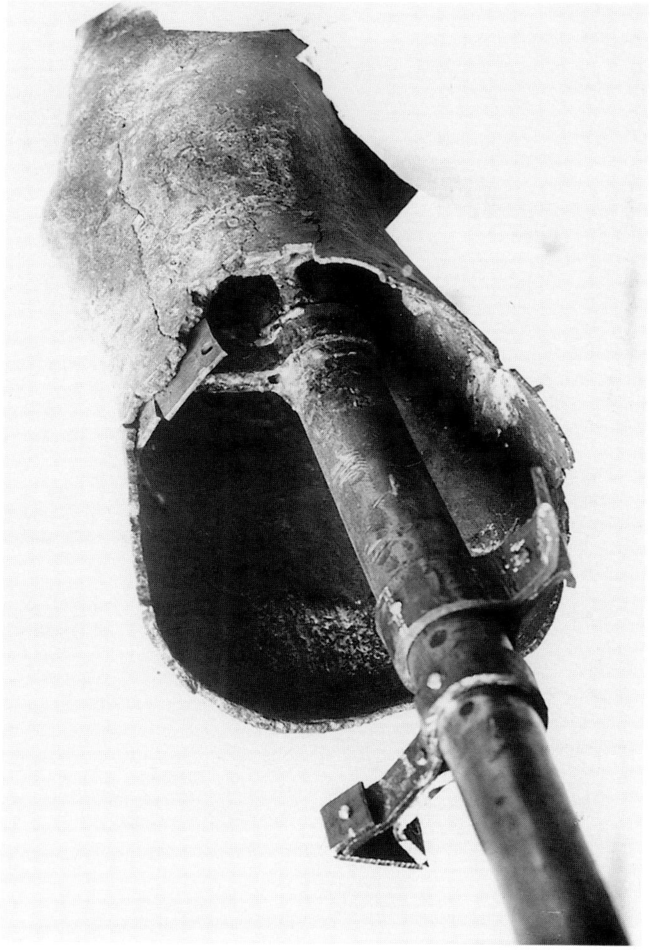

Fig. 3. Right leg of the God from Artemision. The walls of the bronze are thin and of uniform thickness. (Photo: Museum archives.)

Since the original model is destroyed during the process of direct casting, bronzecasters invented a safer way of creating a statue — the indirect lost-wax process. This new method differs from the direct method in that the wax model, which is melted out of the mold and so 'lost', is not the bronzecaster's original model but rather a mechanically produced replica, an 'intermodel' or wax working model.[22] The basic characteristics of indirect lost-wax casting are: a) the walls of the bronze are thin and of uniform thickness, following the exterior contours of the statue, and b) the statue is hollow and cast in sections.[23] The earliest known example of large-scale statuary in Greece cast by this method is the Apollo from Piraeus, dated about 530-520 B.C.[24]

---

22 For the use of the term, see Haynes, *Technique* 27 n.18.

23 As described by Mattusch, *Greek bronze statuary* 19 f. However, Haynes (*Technique*, 34, 38) believes that the roughness of the interior is not always the result of the use of the direct lost-wax process: uneven walls might equally be the result of molding or casting the core in a piece-mold fitted with a temporary lining of wax or clay, since it would be difficult to fit this evenly into all the small and narrower recesses of the mold.

24 E. Homann-Wedeking, *Archaic Greece* (London 1968) 143; Ridgway, *Severe* 20; C. Mattusch, *Casting techniques of Greek bronze sculpture* (Diss., Univ. of North Carolina 1975) 212 f.; *LIMC* II (1982) s.v. Apollo, no. 432 (B. Lambrinudakis *et al.*); Γ. Δοντάς, "Ὁ χάλκινος Ἀπόλλων τοῦ Πειραῖα," in H. Kyrieleis (ed.), *Archaische und klassische griechische Plastik* (Mainz 1986) 181-92; Mattusch, *Greek bronze statuary* 74-82; Haynes, *Technique* 52 n.42.

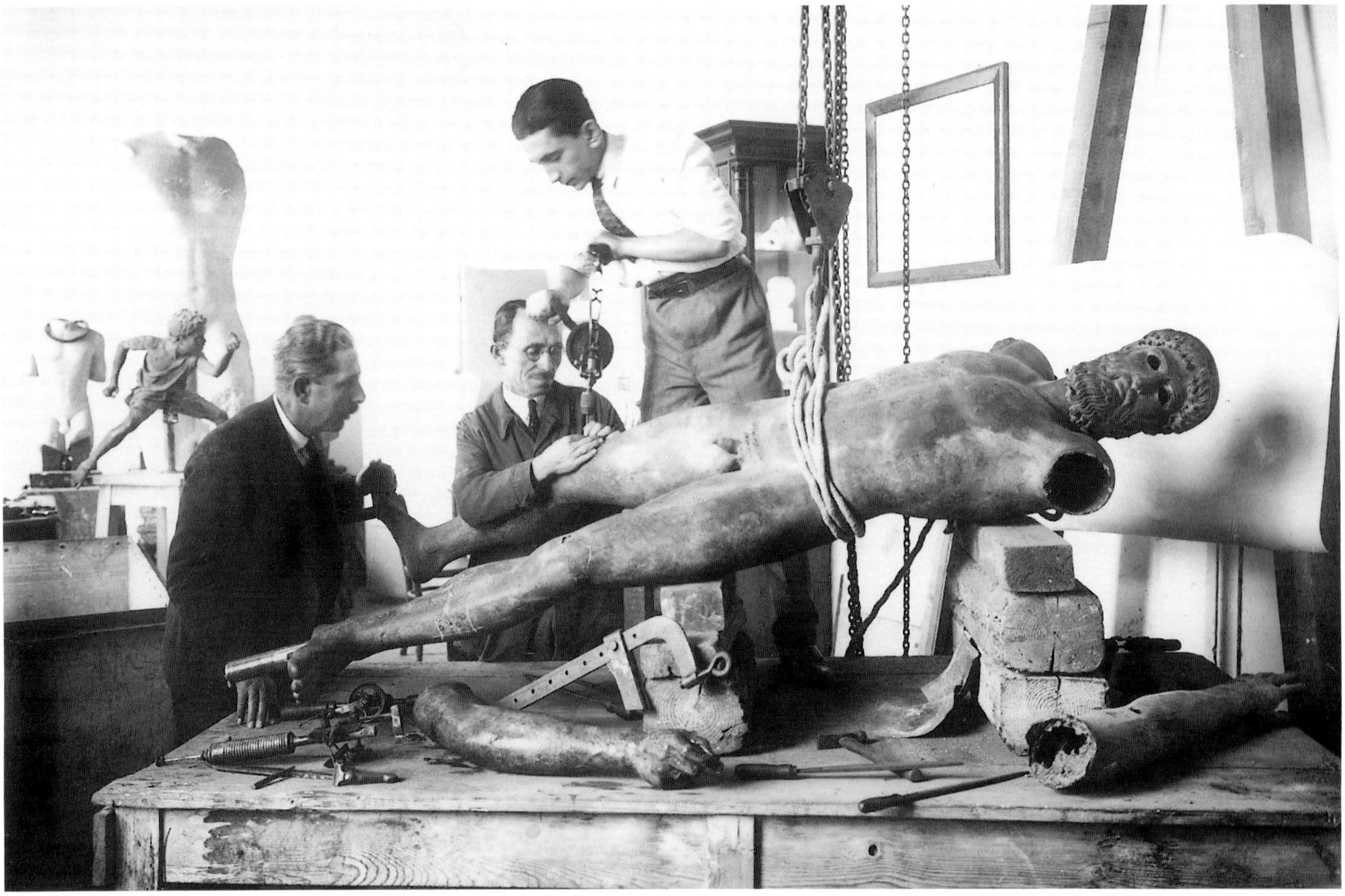

Fig. 4. Photograph taken during early restoration, showing the clay core still inside the left arm. (Photo: Museum archives.)

The early date of the discovery of the Artemision God resulted in the lack of any technical description of its interior, but there is reasonable evidence to suggest that the statue was cast in sections by the indirect lost-wax process. The detailed study conducted by E. Formigli on the production of the Riace Bronzes is of great help in understanding the method used for the Artemision God. Photographs of the right leg (fig. 3), the right arm, and the torso of the statue, taken during its restoration, show that the walls of the bronze are thin and of uniform thickness. The inner surface seems to be smooth and regular. Therefore, it can be safely assumed that the statue was cast by the indirect lost-wax process. Furthermore, close inspection of the surface of the statue has helped to identify the number of sections in which the sculpture was cast and the manner in which these were joined.

The statue was cast in one large section, consisting of the torso and legs, and several smaller sections, including the head, arms, hands, genitals, and the front halves of the feet (fig. 1c). Each section[25] was probably produced from its own working model for which a self-contained piece-mold was made.[26] An x-radiograph shows the join of the neck. Although, with the exception of a small piece in the skull, the core of the statue is no longer preserved, we can infer from the smooth and uniform interior surface that the working models were constructed by lining the mold-pieces with wax, then pressing the core material into them layer by layer.[27]

25 Formigli (supra n.19) 121 ff.

26 See Haynes, *Technique* 65.

27 For the different possibilities concerning the construction of the 'intermodel', see Haynes, *Technique* 65 ff. According to Haynes's description, the intermodel of the Artemision God should have followed meth-

The working model of the torso would have been the only section that, for support reasons, would have required an armature; and we must conclude that it was placed in position at the end of the procedure, before closing the molds.[28] A photograph of the statue taken during restoration shows the left arm and the clay core still inside it, and there are no signs of an armature used for connecting it to the body (fig. 4).

Samples taken from the remains of the clay core in the head and analysed at the Chemical Laboratory of the National Archaeological Museum[29] prove that the clay had an Attic provenance (Appendix: Table 1). This indicates that the statue was produced in Athens. Analysis of the bronze alloy was then undertaken for comparative purposes.[30] Samples were taken from 6 parts of the statue, corresponding to the separately cast sections (Appendix: Table 1). A comparison of the statue's chemical composition with that of other bronze sculptures shows that the alloy used is typical of the unleaded bronze and low-leaded bronze used for the production of Classical Greek statues, in particular the Piraeus Apollo, the Riace Bronzes, and the Marathon Youth.[31]

Since piece-casting is attested from the end of the Archaic period,[32] Greek bronzecasters of the middle of the 5th c. B.C. had acquired considerable experience in making strong and invisible joints, as is the case with this statue. All the joins of the Artemision God are metallurgical.[33] Mechanical joining was used during the modern articulation of the statue, as proven by the photograph of the right leg (fig. 3). Old photographs of the right arm and the right leg show that at the interior edges there is no excess weld-metal, indicating that the weld-metal had solidified before reaching the bottom of the gap between the edges of the joint. Therefore, in this case we must exclude the technique known as flow-welding.[34] The interior of the Chatsworth Head[35] in the British Museum illustrates the difference between the two methods.

To strengthen the joins of the separately cast sections, such as those of the head, the arms,[36] and the left hand, the bronzecaster of the Artemision God used the method of the oval basins[37] (fig. 2), also seen on the Riace statues[38] and the youths of Antikythera[39] and Marathon.[40] The bronzecaster cut shallow half-ovals in the outer surface of the bronze on either side of the joint, thus forming oval basins; then he filled each basin with welding metal, increasing in this manner the strength of the join. It is interesting to note that the joins of the head to the torso

---

od III or IV, as is the case with the Riace statues.

28 Haynes, *Technique* 65.

29 The sampling was done by a team from the National Archaeological Museum, consisting of P. Papastamatis and G. Skandalos under the supervision of H. Andreopoulou-Mangou.

30 Ibid.

31 See the comparative data published by Haynes, *Technique* 87, table 2.

32 See above n.24.

33 For the methods of joining, see H. Lechtmann and A. Steinberg, "Bronze joining; a study in ancient technology," in S. Doeringer *et al.* (edd.), *Art and technology: a symposium on classical bronzes* (Cambridge, MA 1970); E. Formigli, "Tradizioni e innovazioni nella metallotecnica etrusca," in *Etruria mineraria: Atti del XII Convegno di Studi Etruschi e Italici, 1979* (Florence 1981) 65 ff.; Formigli (supra n.19) 121 ff.

34 For the method of flow welding, see H. Maryon, "Metal working in the ancient world," *AJA* 53 (1949) 105 f.; H. Drescher, *Der Überfangguss* (Mainz 1958) 153; Lechtman and Steinberg ibid. 14.

35 Haynes, *Technique* 94 pl. 8; id., "The technique of the Chatsworth head," *RA* 1968, 101-12.

36 Both arms of the statue were broken off, very probably at the same points where they had originally been joined. An old photograph shows the statue without the arms: *Deltion* 10, 1926, Παράρτημα (supra n.1) 86 fig. 1; Noack 1929 (supra n.1) pl. 19.

37 For this method, see Formigli 1979 (supra n.33) 65 ff.; Haynes, *Technique* 95 f., 96 fig. 6.

38 Formigli 1984 (supra n.19) 124 f., figs. 23, 24.

39 Join at left instep and both thigh joins.

40 Neck join and left arm join.

and of the hands to the arms are nearly invisible.

The front halves of the feet are joined to the statue with a metallurgical join (fig. 1c), as is the right hand; the molten metal between the joined sections is 1 mm wide. There has been no additional strengthening of these joints. The front of the foot was cast separately in other bronze statues, such as the Selinus Youth,[41] the Livadhostro Poseidon from Kreusis,[42] and the Riace Bronzes.[43]

A careful examination of the God's head reveals no vestiges of later additions and castings, such as those seen on the Chatsworth Head,[44] where the welded joins attaching free-hanging curls are visible, and on Riace A for some of the curls.[45] The x-radiographs of the top part of the head are opaque, revealing that the head of the Artemision God is thick and of irregular casting.[46] In addition, we now know that some of the original clay core has been preserved in that area. Irregularities in the thickness of the walls indicate that here the bronze is thick due to the additions. Direct wax additions for the ears, the nose, the hair across the forehead, and the beard would have been placed on the wax working model of the head. When this was ready, the bronzecaster would have cast all the pieces together. This process has been described by Formigli[47] and is generally accepted. Details treated in this way are the small shell-curls of the Zeus from Olympia,[48] the beards of the Riace Bronzes,[49] and the tousled locks of the Antikythera Youth[50] and the Olympia Boxer.[51]

The mouth of the God[52] was cast separately, as a single unit, by the direct lost-wax process and attached to the head mechanically. Other examples of the use of this technique are the two Riace Bronzes,[53] the Berber from Cyrene,[54] the Antikythera Youth,[55] the Olympia Boxer,[56] the Piraeus "Muse",[57] and the Arundel Sophocles.[58] Another anatomical detail that was made separately in a copper-rich alloy and inset are the nipples of the statue.[59] It seems that, for the mouth and the nipples, the shapes were cut out of the wax working model and inserted in the corresponding cavities after casting.[60]

All the linear details on the hair and the beard were completed on the model and worked over with the tracer after casting.[61] The brows of the God[62] show grooves that indicate that

---

41 Mattusch, *Greek bronze statuary* 137; P. Marconi, "Palermo. Restauro della statua bronzea d'arte greca detta l'Efebo di Selinunte," *BdA* 8 ser. 2 (1928-29) 233-34.

42 Δ. Φίλιος, "Χαλκούν Ἄγαλμα Ποσειδώνος εκ Βοιωτίας," *Arch Eph* 1899, pl. 6; *LIMC* VII (1994) s.v. Poseidon, no. 23 (E. Simon). The seams are visible only by close inspection of the statue.

43 Formigli 1984 (supra n.19) 121 ff., 122 fig. 19, 123 fig. 20.

44 Haynes, *Technique* 112, figs. 2-4.

45 Formigli 1984 (supra n.19) 129 f., fig. 27.

46 Mattusch, *Classical bronzes* 79.

47 Formigli 1984 (supra n.19) 130.

48 P. Bol, *Grossplastik aus Bronze in Olympia* (OlForsch IX; Berlin 1978) pls. 3-5.

49 *Due bronzi* II pls. 9-14, 16-17.

50 R. Lullies and M. Hirmer, *Griechische Plastik*[4] (Munich 1979) pl. 217.

51 Bol, *Grossplastik* (supra n.48) pls. 30-32.

52 Καρούζος 1930-31 (supra n.1) pl. 5.

53 *Due bronzi* I, pls. 16, 27 c, d; figs. 29, 30.

54 Lullies and Hirmer (supra n.50) pls. 196-7.

55 Lullies and Hirmer (supra n.50) pl. 216.

56 Lullies and Hirmer (supra n.50) pl. 229.

57 S. Karouzou, "Sur la grande statue féminine en bronze trouvée au Pirée," in *Actes du Ve Colloque int. sur les bronzes antiques* (Lausanne 1979) pl. 22.

58 H. Walters, *British Museum Bronzes* pl. 64.

59 Καρούζος 1930-31 (supra n.1) pl. 3.

60 For the process, see Formigli 1984 (supra n.19) 135. See also Haynes, *Technique* 110, 111 pl. 13.

61 See Καρούζος1930-31 (supra n.1) pl. 4-5. For the tools and the method used, see E. Formigli and W. D. Heilmeyer, "Praenestiner Cisten in Berlin," *AA* 1986, 128.

62 See Καρούζος 1930-31 (supra n.1) pl. 5.

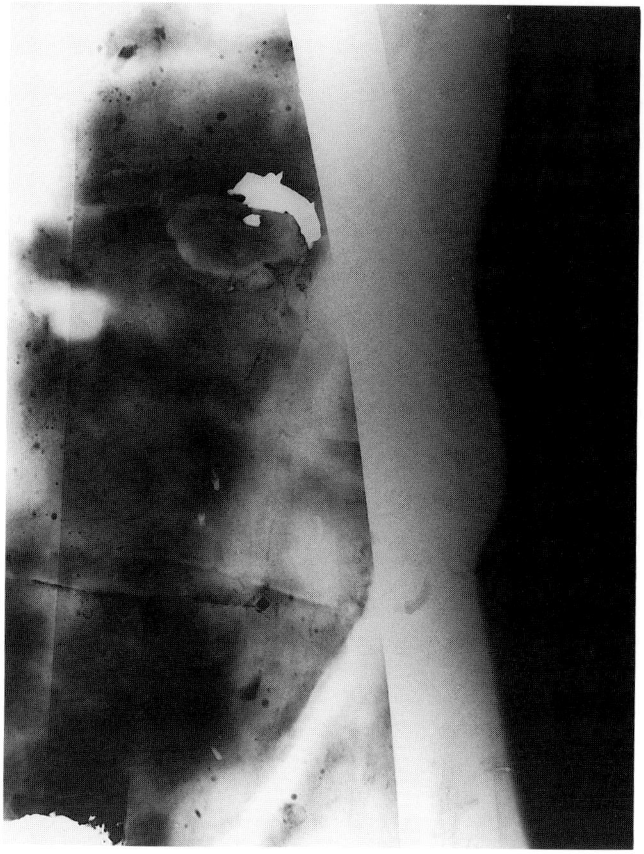

Fig. 5. X-ray of the abdomen and left side of the torso. An inner seam is clearly visible. (Photo: Demokritos.)

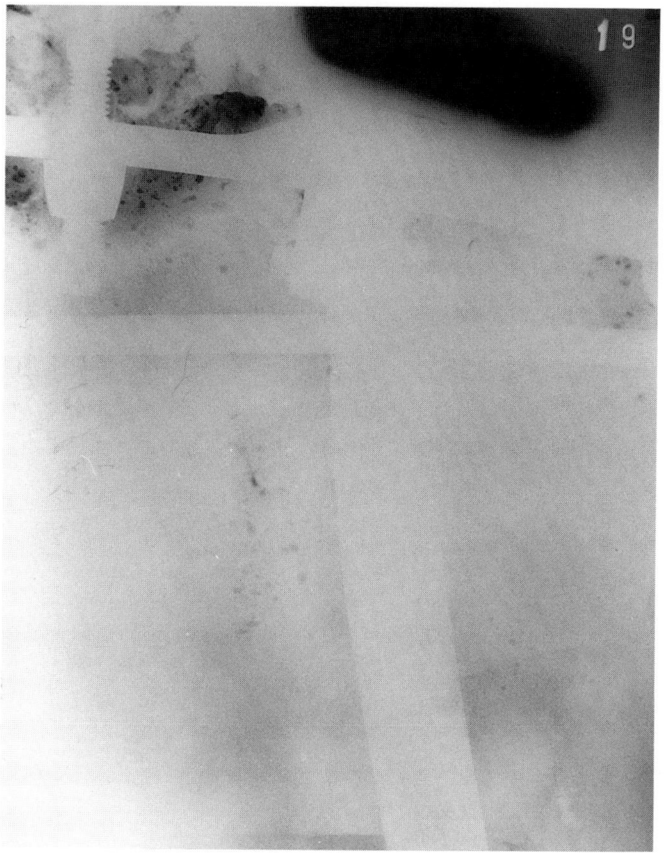

Fig. 6. X-ray of the pectorals and left side of the torso, showing the modern armature. (Photo: Demokritos.)

they were cut in the bronze and the edges covered with silver or copper foil, in order to add color.[63] Parallels can be seen on other small-scale statues of the same period.[64]

The eyes of the God are now lost; they were probably inserted from the outside, as on many Greek statues. Only some eye lashes are still in place. A pair of eyes from an Archaic statue, a recent acquisition of the Metropolitan Museum of Art,[65] offers the best example of the kind.

In preparing the wax working model for casting, the bronzecaster would have removed any blemishes caused by the piece-molding and concealed the joins; but we may perhaps recognize in an x-ray photograph (pl. 5) the trace of one join in a long horizontal furrow running across the lower abdomen, reproducing the inner surface of the wax.[66]

A number of round, square, or rectangular patches are detectable on the surface of the statue (figs 1a-b).[67] They cover holes left by gates, chaplets, or defects and cavities caused by gas bubbles during pouring. Some of these patches have fallen off, and the cavities underneath show slightly undercut sides. As we have already noted, in order to cover the cavity the

63 For the method of gilding, see Haynes, *Technique* 112-13 with nn.

64 See the following examples: the Poseidon from Kreusis in the National Archaeological Museum, Athens 11761: see above n.42; the Zeus from Ugento: Degrassi 1981 (supra n.2) 139, pls. 8-10; the head of a youth from the Athenian Acropolis in the National Archaeological Museum, Athens X6590: J. Boardman *et al.* 1966 (supra n.1) pl. 166; O. Tzachou-Alexandri, *Mind and body: athletic contests in ancient Greece* (Athens 1989) 176 no. 67; the youth from Selinunte: Finn and Houser 1983 (supra n.1) 147, pl. 6.3.

65 Inv. no. 1991.11.3a,b: *MetMusArtBull* 8 (summer 1981); Mattusch, *Classical bronzes* pl.1. See also Haynes, *Technique* 107 pl. 10, and 106 for the technique.

66 Haynes cites other examples too: *Technique* 35.

67 For the use of patches, see Haynes, *Technique* 98.

bronzecaster inserted in the hole a thicker patch, which expanded through hammering. The x-ray photographs show a good number of patches of varying dimensions; some are very well fitted in their holes and are nearly invisible.

Traces of tools, such as the round-headed hammer and the scraper, used for finishing the surface of the statue, are not easy to recognise; modern mechanical cleaning and coating with nitro-cellulose lacquer make their detection nearly impossible.

In antiquity Greek bronze statues were usually mounted on stone bases to which they were attached by their feet, using lead tenons.[68] The modern mount for the left foot of the Artemision God is connected to the modern structural armature of the entire statue (fig. 1d). This is constructed of horizontal and vertical metal bars and rods. A flat horizontal bar (fig. 1d) is connected to two rods extending vertically down to the feet, while a third vertical rod supports the head. A second horizontal bar is used to secure the arms in place through lock nuts (fig. 6). X-radiographs show the armature at the level of the breasts (fig. 1d). The rods inside the lower legs and the hands are held in place with lead. Both of the statue's feet are attached to the base with screws. An old photograph, taken when the statue was removed to the museum basements during World War II, illustrates the modern technique. The statue's original mounting probably consisted of lead tenons through the same holes in its feet. It is also possible that the left foot was held in place by the rod of the armature passing through the leg and was additionally secured with a lead tenon. However, this method is only hypothetical and is not attested from other known examples.[69]

Future investigation in the area of the shipwreck off Cape Artemision may reveal important information concerning the statue's provenance. Furthermore, the progress of modern technology, especially in relation to the examination of ancient bronze statues, could provide us with useful information and enhance our knowledge of the technique of the bronze God of Artemision.

26 Athinas Street, Voula-Attica, GR-16673

Acknowledgements

To Dr. K. Demakopoulou, present Director of the National Archaeological Museum, I express my warmest thanks for facilitating my research in the museum. I would also like to thank Dr. H. Andreopoulou-Mangou, chemist at the same museum, for preparing the x-ray photographs and for undertaking the analysis of the clay and copper samples. Thanks are also due to Mrs. A. Litti-Lapa, sculptress at the museum, who prepared the sketches presented here. My warmest thanks also go to Dr. A. Alexandri who checked the English and typed the manuscript.

68 Formigli 1984 (supra n.19) 137, fig. 36 b, c.
69 Formigli 1984 (supra n.19) 136 and 137 fig. 36 a.

Appendix

Helen Andreopoulou-Mangou

TABLE 1: CHEMICAL ANALYSIS OF THE BRONZE GOD FROM ARTEMISION IN THE NATIONAL ARCHAEOLOGICAL MUSEUM, NO. 15161

A. % Chemical Composition of the copper alloy

No	Sampling sites	Cu	Sn	Pb	Zn	As	Sb	Ag	Fe	Ni	Co	Au	Bi
1	Head (above left eye)	86.65	11.42	0.06	0.01	0.47	0.05	0.02	0.09	0.01	0.03	N.D.	N.D.
2	Right hand (palm)	85.99	12.62	0.04	0.02	0.38	0.11	0.01	0.18	0.01	0.02	N.D.	N.D.
3	Periphery (left part)	86.93	11.10	0.06	0.01	0.25	0.07	0.01	0.13	N.D.	0.02	N.D.	N.D.
4	Left foot (ring toe)	87.06	10.68	0.04	N.D.	0.45	0.12	0.01	0.07	N.D.	0.01	N.D.	N.D.
5	Right foot (little toe)	87.75	9.87	0.04	N.D.	0.41	0.08	0.04	0.08	N.D.	0.02	N.D.	N.D.
6	Right sole	87.42	10.55	0.04	0.02	0.42	0.11	0.04	0.28	0.01	0.02	N.D.	N.D.
	Mean value x	86.97	11.04	0.05	0.02	0.40	0.09	0.02	0.14	0.01	0.02		

N.D.=Not Detected

B. % Chemical Composition in oxides of the clay core

No		SiO2	Al2O3	CaO	MgO	Fe2O3	K2O	Na2O	MnO	NiO	Cr2O3	TiO2	Cu	Sn
1	Clay core from head	63.45	8.52	11.51	3.81	6.45	1.36	0.78	0.12	0.04	0.08	0.65	3.17	N.D.

Analysis of the 6 samples shows that all 6 parts of the statue were made from unleaded bronzes (alloys of copper and tin) with tin contents ranging from 9.87% to 12.62% (mean value of tin content 11%). Comparison of the chemical composition of the alloy of the Artemision God with the composition of other statues[70] shows that the unleaded bronze composition was mainly used for Archaic and Classical (pre-Hellenistic) statues. On the other hand, leaded bronze was widely used for statuettes of the Archaic and Classical periods.[71] From the end of the 4th c., statues of leaded bronze appeared in mainland Greece, and leaded bronze was the rule during the Roman Empire.

Analysis of the clay core shows that it is a fine textured calcareous clay with 11.51% CaO. Analyses of core clays of other bronze statues are presented by Schneider[72] and by Formigli and Schneider.[73] Based on the elements Mg, Cr, Ni, used as fingerprints elements of a clay origin,[74] the clay core could be of Attic origin.

Chemistry Laboratory, National Archaeological Museum, Athens (1996)

---

70 Haynes, *Technique* 87.

71 P. Craddock, "The composition of copper alloys used by the Greek, Etruscan and Roman civilizations: 2. the Archaic, Classical and Hellenistic Greeks," *JArchSci* 4 (1977) 103-23.

72 G. Schneider, "Investigation of crucibles and moulds from bronze foundries in Olympia and Athens and determination of provenances of bronze statues," in Y. Maniatis (ed.), *Proceedings of the 25th International Symposium on Archaeometry, Athens 1986* (London 1989) 305-10.

73 E. Formigli and G. Schneider, "Antiche terre di fusione," in E. Formigli (ed.), *Antiche officine del bronzo, Seminario at Murlo, 26-31 luglio 1991* (Rome 1995) 69-102.

74 R. Jones, *The Greek and Cypriot pottery* (Fitch Laboratory, British School at Athens 1986) App. 1, 896.

Another Early Classical Apollo from Athens?
The numismatic evidence for the prototype of Stephanos' Athlete

John H. Kroll

This paper explores a suggestion made by this author in *The Athenian Agora* XXVI: *The Greek coins* (Princeton 1993) 125, n.70, pl. 18.270, that the statue of a nude male deity represented on some bronze coins of 2nd c. A.D. Athens does not depict Theseus or Hermes, as stated in published catalogues, but is instead an Early Classical statue of Apollo. Since the pose is very similar to that of the young male statue-type best known from the Villa Albani athlete signed by Stephanos, pupil of Pasiteles, it was further suggested that the Apollo statue in Athens was in fact the prototype of the Stephanos Athlete, and that the Orestes–Electra group in Naples, which incorporates the Stephanos figure, should accordingly be identified as a group of Apollo with Leto.

The more this suggestion is pursued, however, the more untenable it becomes. In *Klassizistische Statuen* (Mainz 1974) pls. 42.4 and 44.1, P. Zanker illustrates two reproductions of the Stephanos figure with attributes belonging to Hermes, while the two-figure group in Paris and Adolphseck involving the Stephanos figure and another youth (ibid. pl. 42.5) does not admit a mythological interpretation for identifying the Stephanos figure with Apollo either.

Further difficulties emerge from a re-examination of the coins. Although the 6 surviving specimens depicting the Athenian statue were struck from the same reverse die, wear or imperfect striking have obscured the rare, crucial attributes of the figure on all. In the right hand, held down at his side, is a crook-like object with the curved end forward. The specimen in Berlin has a second, fainter curved line above the hand, suggesting that the figure held a double-curved bow and arrow — hence the *quondam* Apollonian identification. Casts collected of the other specimens, however, indicate that the critical second curved line results from a hairline crack in the die and is not part of the original design, with the result that the thick, tapering object held up in the left hand can no longer be plausibly considered an arrow. The evidence for Apollo collapses, and the figure returns to its earlier, enigmatic status. It is still unclear what the figure is holding. The object in the right hand is probably not a strigil, nor the object in the left a club, since neither strigils nor clubs were held in the way these objects are held on the coins. Nor is it really certain from these badly preserved coins whether the figure is beardless or bearded. Without a perfectly clear image to go on, we may never know who this deity is supposed to be.

Color signature

page 2: color plates for J. Riederer (see p. 282)

pages 3-6: color plates for M. Ratka and P. R. Sahm (see p. 197)

pages 7-8: color plates for A. M. McCann (see p. 97)

Chart 1. Concentration of nickel

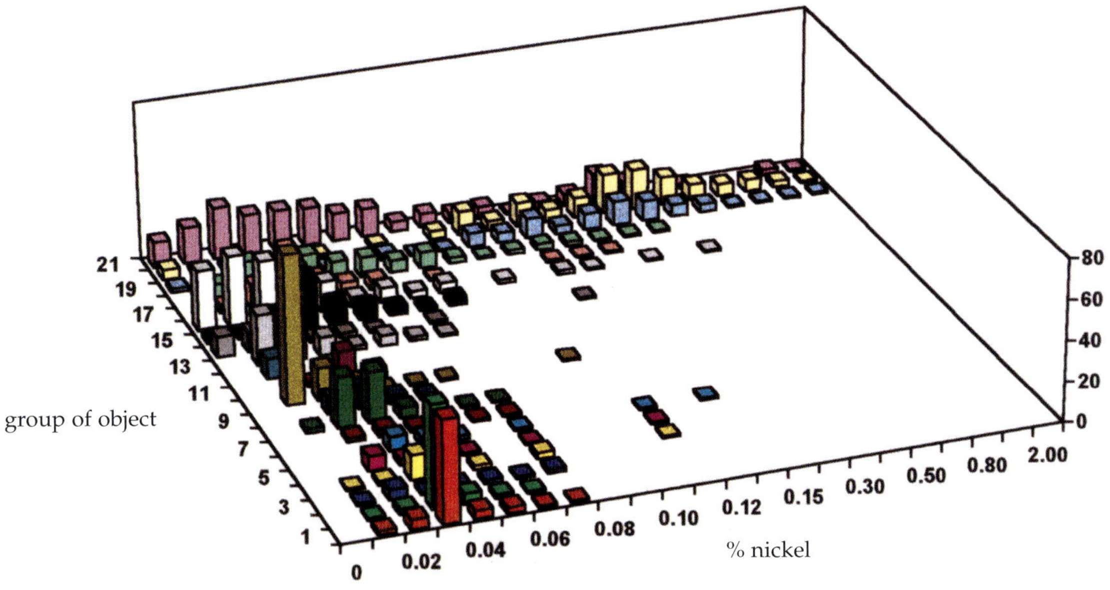

Chart 2: concentration of arsenic

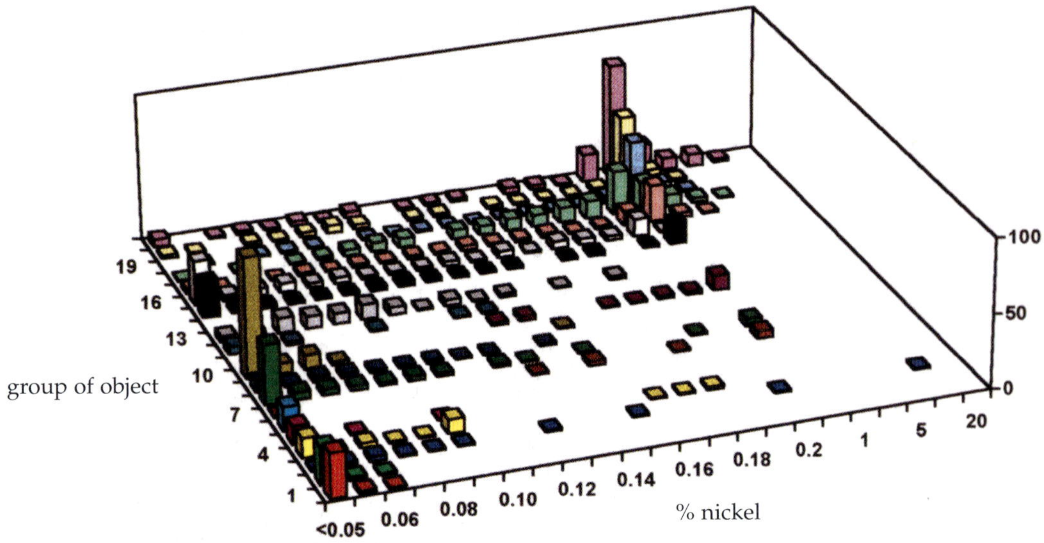

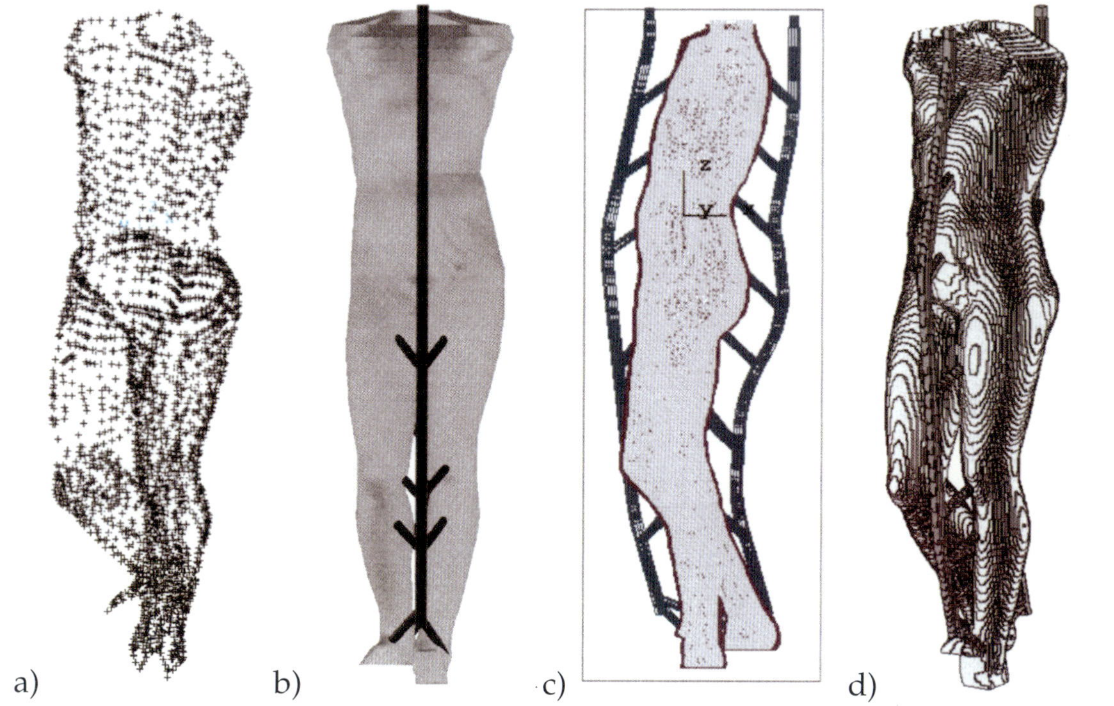

Fig. 1a. Measurement data reconstituted by computer. 1b. Surface constructed by CAD. 1c. CAD data in MAGMAsoft. Gray = core, black = casting. The figure clearly shows the thin-walled geometry of the statue. 1d. The subsequent enmeshment of the casting.

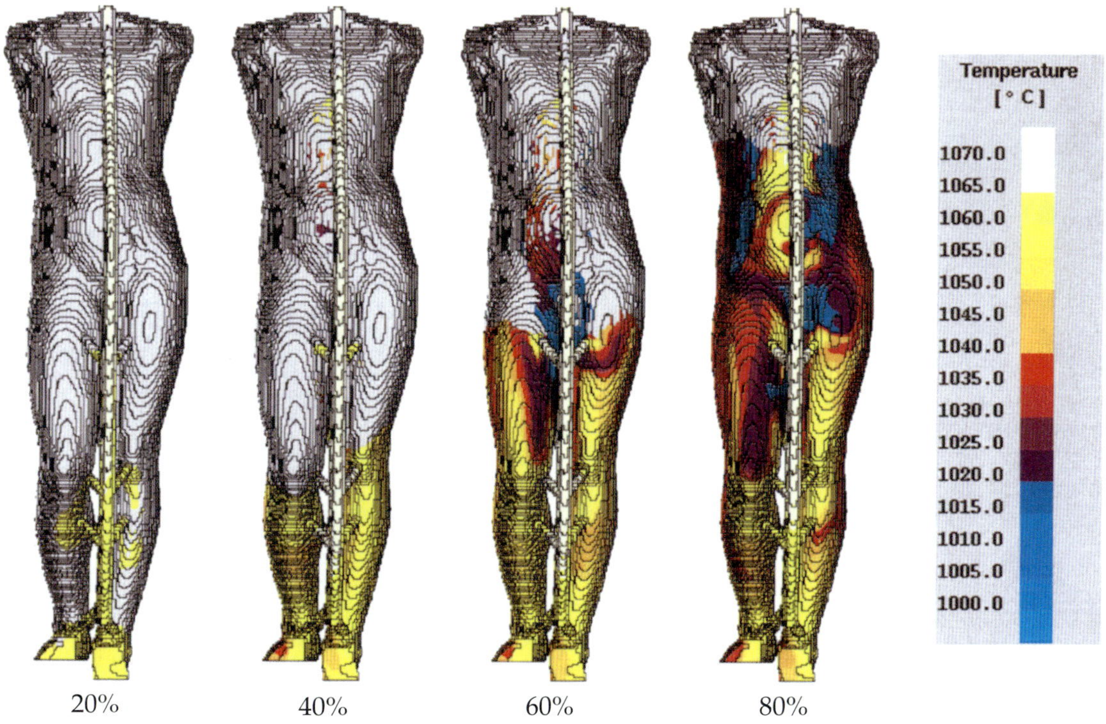

Fig. 2. Mold filling simulation. The pictures show the front view of the casting. The temperature scale illustrates the range between casting and melting temperatures.

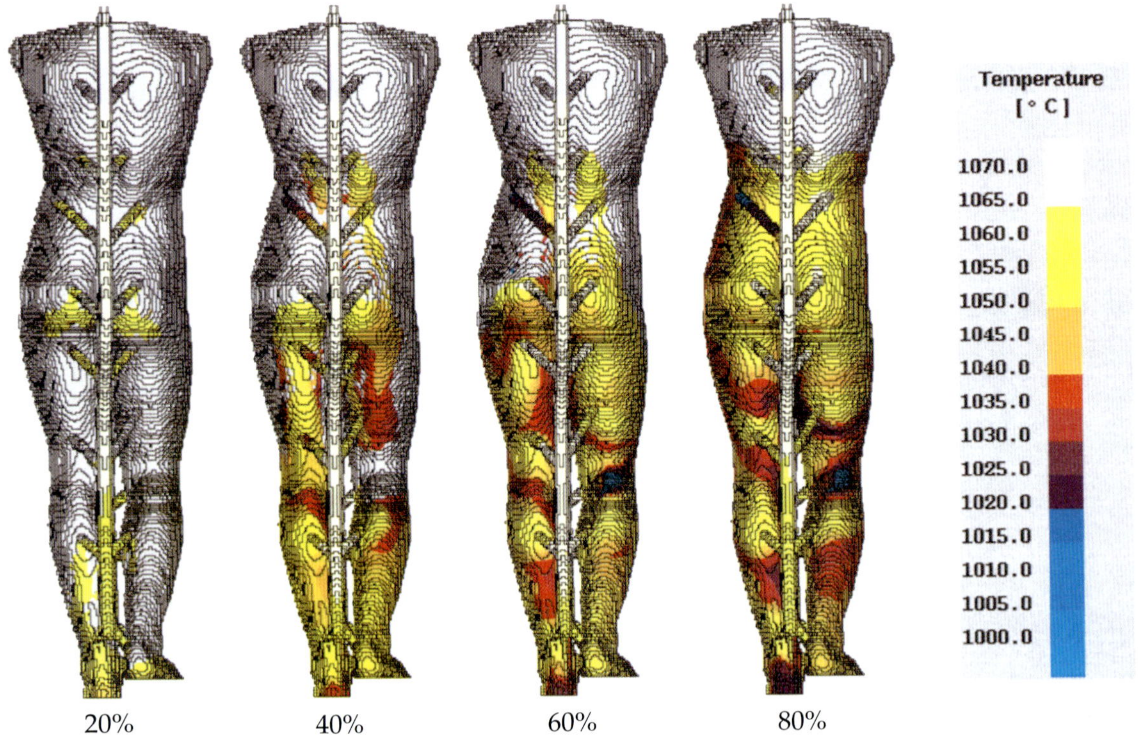

Fig. 3. Mold filling simulation. The pictures show the back view of the casting. The casting material is a bronze with 10% tin and 2% lead; the mold material is a clay mixture like an ancient mold material.

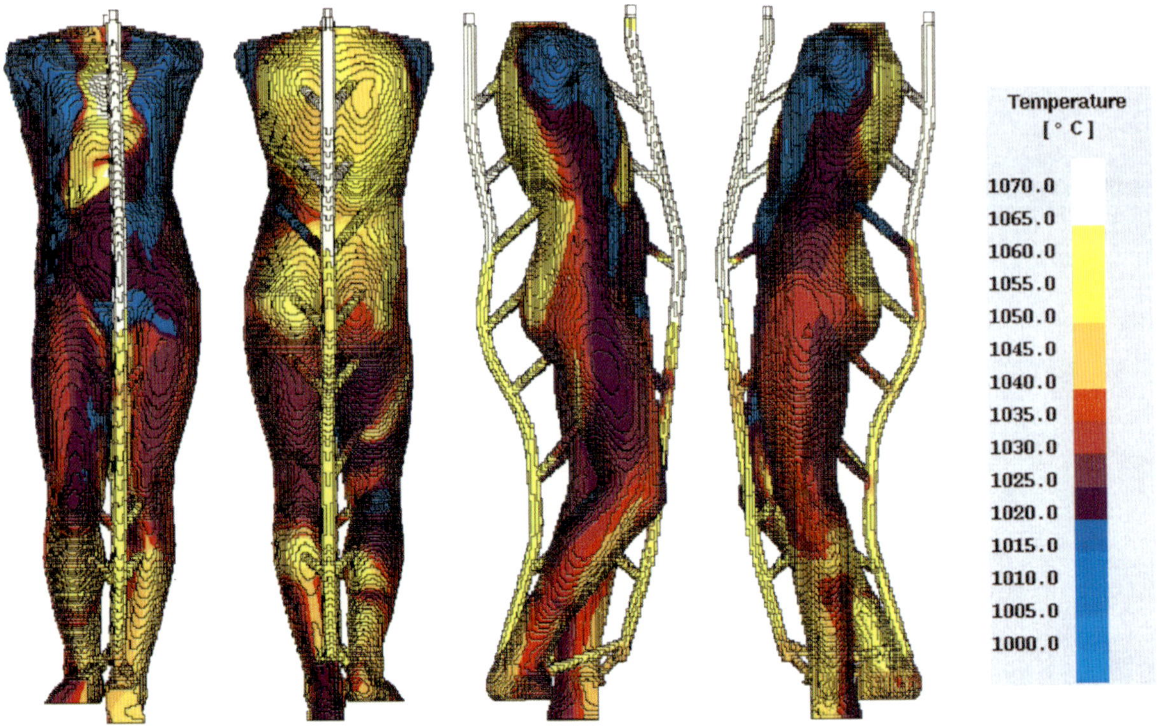

Fig. 4. Temperature distribution at the end of the filling process.

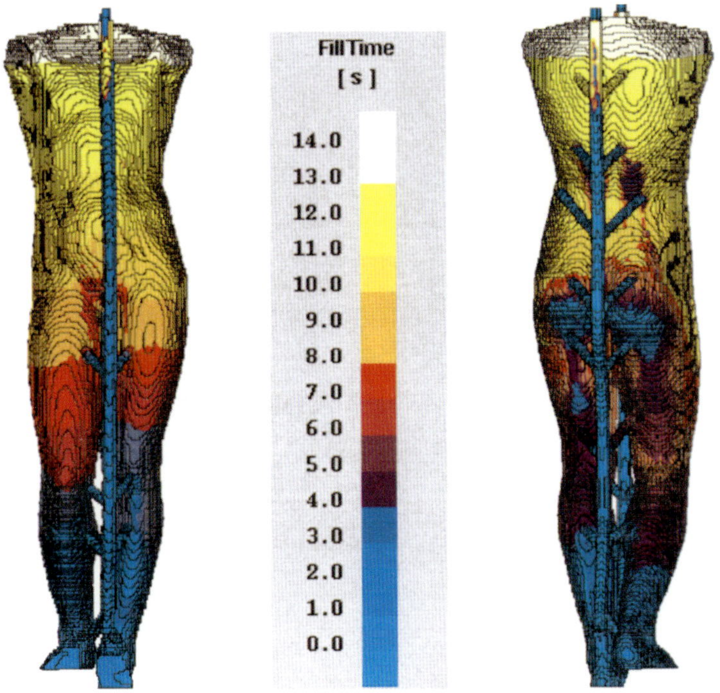

Fig. 5. Time sequence of the filling process. The color of the volume elements show when these were filled with melt. The color scale has been adjusted to reflect the filling time.

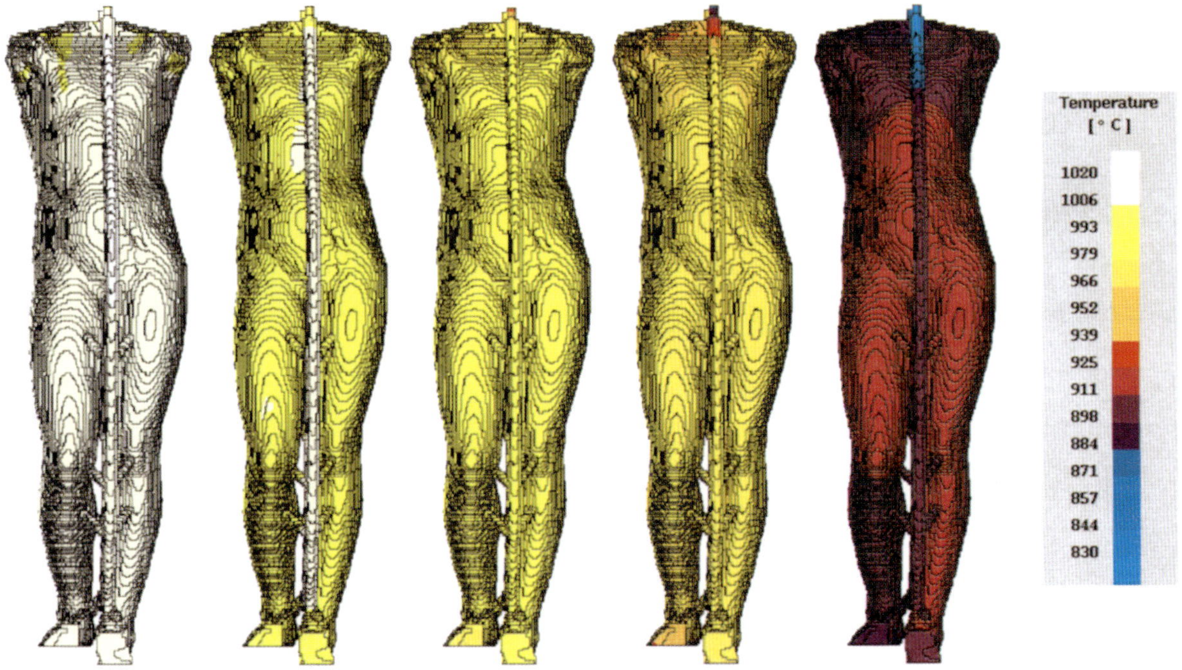

10%	30%	50%	70%	90%
0:32 min	1:17 min	2:39 min	4:56 min	11:16 min

Fig. 6. Temperature distribution in the casting during solidification. The temperature scale illustrates the solidification interval.

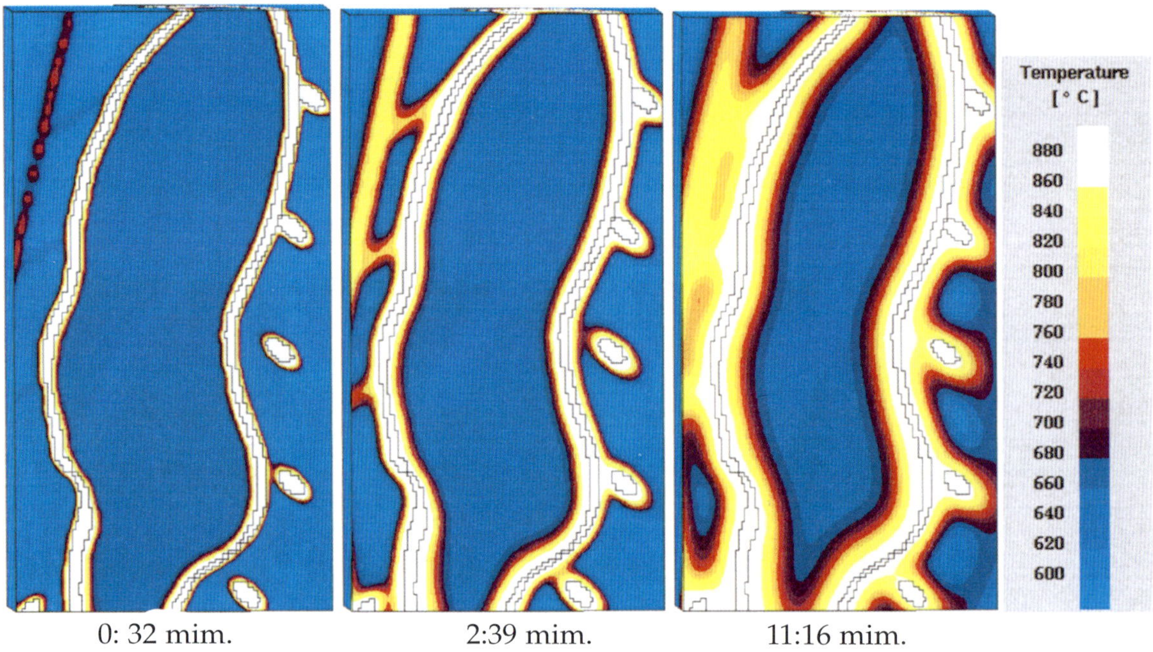

Fig. 7. Temperature distribution in the mold during solidification. The pictures show a longitudinal side cross section. The casting has a black border. Because of the temperature scale selected, the casting appears completely white.

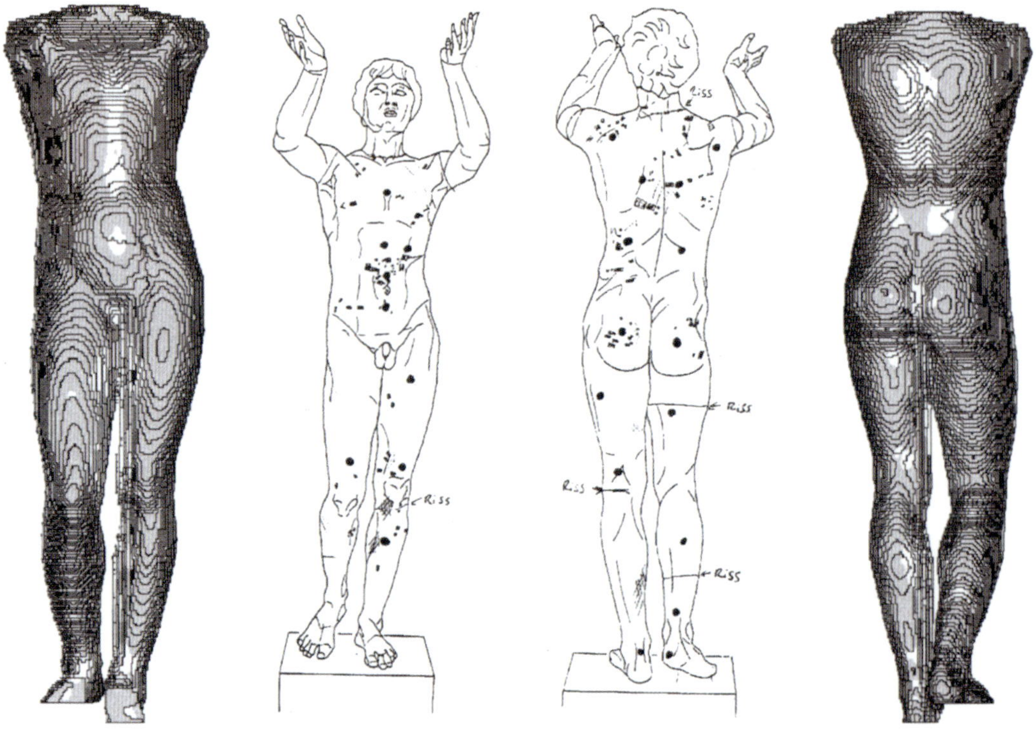

Fig. 8: Application of a post-processing criterion function. Consistent with the examination of the surface of the bronze, the simulation shows increased porosity in the area of the gates.

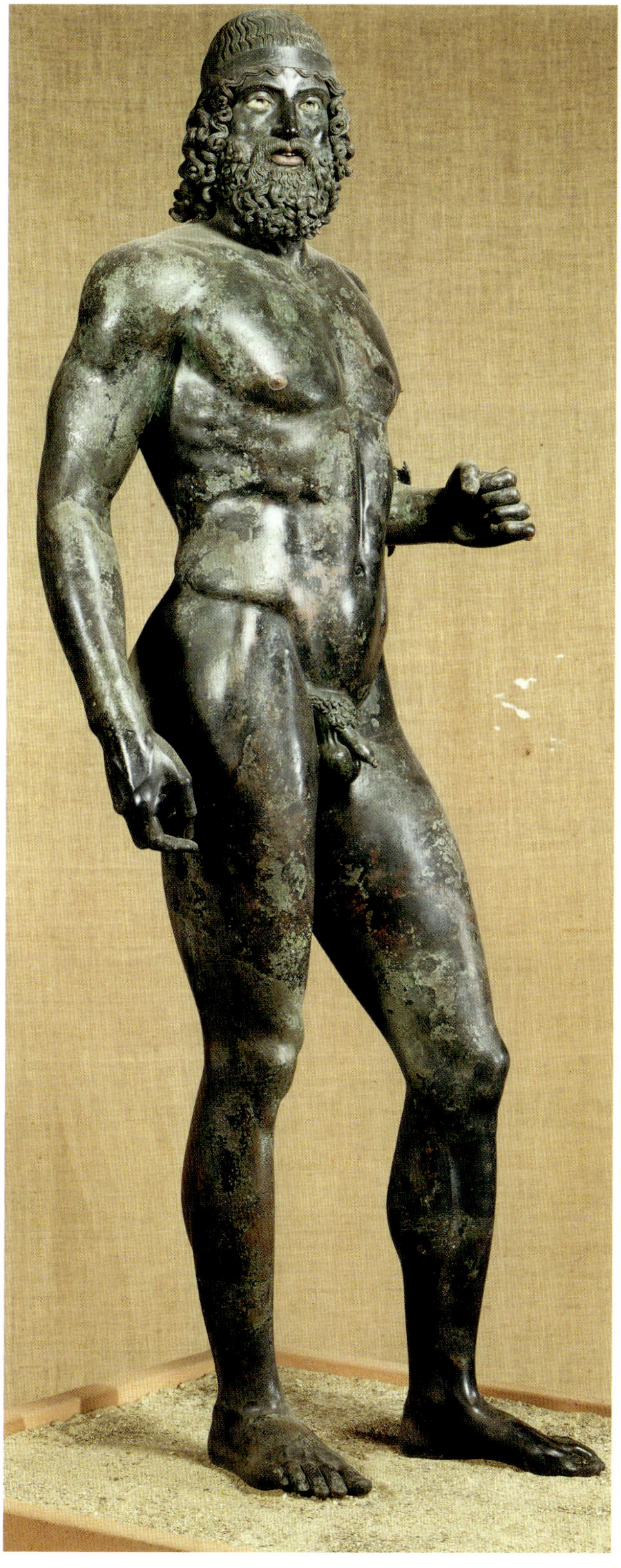

McCann fig. 1 (color). Riace A. Bronze, h. 1.98 m. Reggio Calabria, Museo archeologico. (Photo: Scala/Art Resource, NY.)

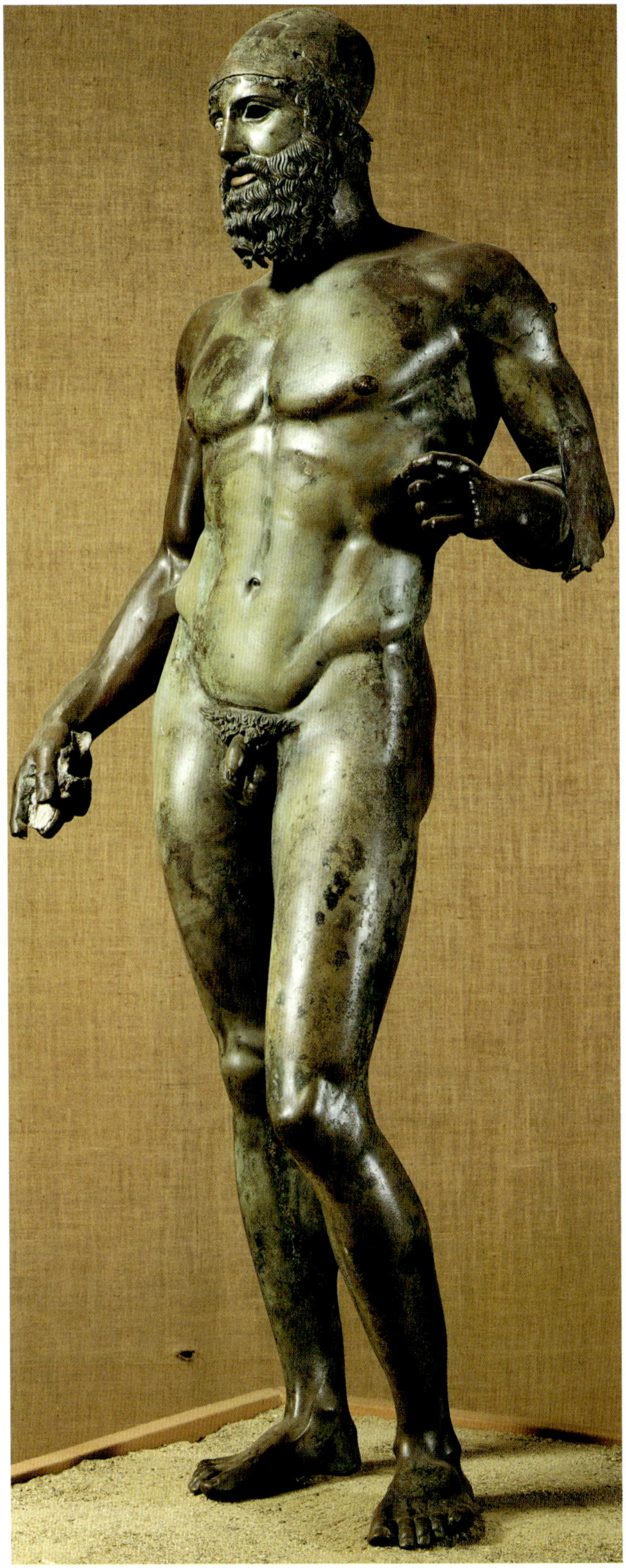

McCann fig. 2 (color). Riace B. Bronze, h. 1.97 m. Reggio Calabria, Museo archeologico. (Photo: Scala/Art Resource, NY.)

The Riace bronzes: Gelon and Hieron I of Syracuse?

Anna Marguerite McCann

Introduction

The recent restoration and additional technical studies undertaken by the Istituto Centrale del Restauro in Rome on the two bronze, nude, male, over life-size statues found off the marina of Riace in Calabria in 1972 give the opportunity for a fresh stylistic evaluation of these magnificent works of art (figs. 1-2 in color, and 7).[1] The question of whether the Riace bronzes, designated Statue A and Statue B, were made by the direct or indirect casting method I leave to the technical experts who have studied the interiors of the statues.[2] The focus of this study is on their exteriors and what the eye can see.

An important result of the recent restoration work is the mineralogical analyses of their clay cores by G. Lombardi of the University of Rome.[3] He identified only three areas in Greece as geologically compatible with the mineral composition of the cores: Argos, Delphi, and central Euboea. In Magna Graecia, Lombardi compared only one site — Sybaris in Calabria, the region where the statues were found. But geologically Sybaris was also found compatible and cited as a possible place of origin for the workshop that produced the statues.[4] The majority of scholars to date have placed the original home of the statues in Greece.[5] I would like here to

---

1 See Melucco Vaccaro, below p. 124; ead., "The Riace bronzes: recent advances from the 1992 intervention," *13th Br. Cong.* 95. Also: F. F. Martin, "Due anni di microscavo dentro i bronzi di Riace," *Corriere della sera*, February 25, 1996, 23; G. Lattanzi, unpublished report of congress in Rome, November 29-30, 1996, for *Archaeology*. We eagerly await the scientific publication of these analyses. For the report of the earlier restoration work done in Florence from 1975-79, see E. Formigli, "La tecnica di costruzione delle statue di Riace" in *Due bronzi* 1, 107-42.

For a summary of recent scholarship to date, see Mattusch, *Greek bronze statuary* 200-11 and esp. 207 n.98. Also: B. Cohen, "Perikles' portrait and the Riace bronzes," *AJA* 60 (1991) 465-502, pls. 113-16; F. Giudice, "Il bronzo A di Riace ed una lekythos del pittore di Achille," *13th Br. Cong.* 21; J. R. Hale, "Phormio, Hermolycus, and the Riace Warriors: two Athenian naval heroes from the Acropolis," American Philological Association Annual Meeting 1994 (abstract); E. B. Harrison, "Early classical sculpture, the bold style," in C. G. Boulter (ed.), *Greek art, archaic into classical* (Cincinnati Classical Studies 5, 1985) 40-65, pls. 37-50; R. R. Holloway, *The archaeology of ancient Sicily* (London 1991) 109-12 [henceforth *AAS*]; id., "The severe style, new evidence and old problems," *QuadTicinesi* 17 (1988) 55-79; C. Houser, *Greek monumental bronze sculpture of the fifth and fourth centuries B.C.* (New York 1987) 119-25; L. M. Lombardi Satriani and M. Paoletti (edd.), *Gli eroi venuti dal mare* (Rome 1986); Rolley, *La sculpture grecque 1*, 347-50; C. de Grazia Vanderpool, below p. 106; ead., "Serial twins: Riace B and some Roman relatives," *13th Br. Cong.* 99.

2 Melucco Vaccaro (supra n.1). Cf. Mattusch, *Greek bronze statuary* and Mattusch, *AJA* 84 (1980) 435-44. The similarity of measurements, statuary type, technique, and bronze alloy supports Mattusch's conclusions for the indirect lost-wax casting technique. Also, the recent studies of both F. Giudice and C. de Grazia Vanderpool (supra n.1) on the close relationship of both Riace A and B to a common statuary model are further evidence for the popular use of master molds from which many wax working models could be made. Differences were introduced in the finishing of the wax models.

For a recent clear description of lost-wax casting in antiquity, see C. C. Mattusch, "The preferred medium: the many lives of classical bronzes," in *The fire of Hephaistos* 15-43.

3 See Lattanzi 1996 (supra n.1).

4 Cf. G. Schneider and E. Formigli, "Untersuchungen von Gusskernen griechischer und römischer Grossbronzen" in *Akten des XIII int. Kongress für klassiche Archäologie* (Berlin 1988) 618-19, who suggest, on the basis of other analyses of the clay cores, that statue A is probably from Athens and statue B from Corinth. I have not, however, seen a full scientific report and believe that at this point in time we do not have enough comparative information from either Greece or Italy to identify securely the provenance of ancient statues on the basis of clay analyses alone.

5 Summary in Mattusch, *Greek bronze statuary*, and J. Marcadé, "Rapports techniques et publications arch-

explore the suggestion of their possible origin in Magna Graecia,[6] keeping in mind that artists and their copy books traveled in the ancient world and that the statues could have been made in Magna Graecia by Greek-trained artists.[7]

Discovery

First, several things about the circumstances of the statues' discovery are significant. Their find-spot at the southern and eastern side of the toe of Calabria does not prove that the original ship was coming from Greece. These are among the most treacherous currents of the whole Mediterranean, as counter currents meet and are drawn up through the narrow Straits of Messina. Ships can be blown off course for a wide distance. Also, it is clear from the schematic map of the find site, made two years later by the late N. Lamboglia on information supplied by their discoverer, S. Mariottini, that this was not an ancient wreck site.[8] The figures were found in shallow water at a depth of only 5 m. They were lined up side by side in the curve of a reef about 200 m from shore. It seems likely that they were originally found in deeper water, perhaps by local fishermen dragging the ocean depths, and removed to this temporary hiding place in anticipation of being smuggled away to be sold abroad. C. Panella mentions that 6 pottery sherds, probably from late Hellenistic or Roman amphorae, were found in the concretions adhering to the statues;[9] one of these appears under the right arm of Statue A in contemporary newspaper photos,[10] but the sherds could not be found on my visit to the museum in 1990.

Style and date

These now famous and much published statues are familiar to all students of Greek sculpture. Their larger-than-life size and nudity indicate that they are warrior-heroes or kings. They are very similar in pose, divisions of the anatomy, and size, down to a centimeter (A: 1.98 m; B: 1.97 m). They both held shields on the left arms, probably spears in the right hands, and both were originally helmeted.[11] They also share strong technical similarities. Both are made of a similar tin-bronze alloy with only traces of lead, except for the left hand and right arm of B, which have lead content of 9.8 to 14.5%.[12] They clearly belonged together as a pair, made

---

éologiques: à propos des bronzes de Riace," *RA* 1986, 89-100.

6 Holloway, *AAS* (supra n.1) 109-12, has also suggested that the figures are from Magna Graecia and identifies them as a pair of Sicilian *oikists*. He dates them both about 450 B.C. and attributes them to a common monument although by different artists. Cf. E. Paribeni, "I bronzi di Riace," *Due bronzi* 2, 307-12, who also suggests that they come from Magna Graecia but that A, identified as Ajax of Locris, was made by a follower of Pythagoras of Regium about 460 B.C. Statue B he interprets as a *strategos* made about 400 B.C. as a later companion.

7 Scholars have also suggested the presence of Greek mainland artists in Magna Graecia or artists from this region who studied in Athens. M. Bell has convincingly argued that the recently discovered marble charioteer from Motya was made by an Attic artist who came to Selinus: "The Motya Charioteer and Pindar's Isthmian 2," *MAAR* 40 (1995) 1-42. He suggests that the charioteer came to Motya as booty when the Carthaginians sacked Selinus in 409 B.C. The beaded curls of the hair and the rounded modeling of the idealized features of the face with its restrained expression, however, are very different in style from either of the heads of the Riace bronzes.

8 P. A. Gianfrotta, "Il naufragio," in Satriani and Paoletti, *Gli eroi* (supra n.1) 25-37, with plan on p. 31 from N. Lamboglia 1974; Holloway 1988 (supra n. 1) 109-11.

9 "Frammenti ceramici: analisi tipologica e ipotesi di provenienza," in *Due bronzi* 1, 31-35; cf. Holloway 1988 (supra n. 1) 64, n.1.

10 A. Pearce, "Heroic bronzes of fifth century B.C. regain old splendor," *Smithsonian* 12 no. 8 (Nov. 1981) fig. on p. 125.

11 I accept B. Cohen's identification of a lost, pushed-up Chalcidian helmet for A, and a Corinthian one for B: see Cohen 1991 (supra n.1) esp. 480, 484.

12 Formigli in *Due bronzi* 1, 120-22; Mattusch, *Greek bronze statuary* 206. It has been assumed that the right forearm and hand of B are later repairs. However, high lead content appears more often in bronzes from

from a common model if not from the same working model, and were meant to be viewed together on a common monument.

But the differences in both style and mood clearly indicate the hands of two different artists who have deliberately contrasted two different hero types. Do these differences also indicate a difference in date? Some scholars have said so, and would date statue A earlier, by as much as 30 years.[13] The differences are, however, best understood as the result of two artistic temperaments rather than differences in time. Statue A has a wider stance, sharper twist of the head to the right, and his left arm pulled more sharply back. The parts of his thinner torso are more strongly delineated, giving a sense of tension to the aggressively masculine figure. Statue B, in contrast, is posed in a softened S-curve, using chiastic positioning of the limbs that reveals the influence of Polykleitos and his Doryphoros, as many have noted.[14] The separate parts of B's heavier torso flow together, the right shoulder drops slightly, and the right hip is curved outward. His lower right arm is freer from the body. The result is a more relaxed and passive figure.

The heads are particularly different in spirit, although they share a similar structure with sharpened planes and hard edges of the linear eyebrows typical of the Early Classical style.[15] Statue A, the more youthful, has a slightly opened mouth revealing silver teeth. The individual locks of his curly hair and beard are separately attached and the heavy-lidded eyes give an individual look to the alert and authoritative figure. The larger eyes of Statue B, in contrast, are wide open, and his straighter beard is treated as a solid mass. The more frontal position of the head with its slight inclination and the broader classicizing features portray a more placid and older man. J. Boardman summarizes, "The main difference between them lies in what the sculptors sought to express — the arrogant self-confidence of a young leader: the mature strength and stolidity, now a little slack and tired it may be, of an older warrior."[16]

In fact, their differences have been used by pornographic comic book artists to illustrate a contrast in sexual appeal.[17] A's tense masculinity arouses women viewers, while B's softer curves and passive expression attracts the homosexual male. However this may be, all agree that A is distinctly more assertive and masculine, while B is the softer, more passive, feminine figure. Ancient viewers must have also been aware of these differences. Their eyes were trained to see the world in contrasts of opposites. A common theme of classical myth or drama is the struggle between man and woman. The statues are contemporaries of the struggling figures from the metopes of Temple E at Selinus[18] or the heroes and heroines of Aeschylus's tragedies performed in the theater at Syracuse. Or they may be seen in the light of the popular dualist philosophy

---

Etruria and Magna Graecia, i.e., the Ugento god, id., 70-71. More analyses are needed, but it is clear that artists could calculate alloys to satisfy particular needs. Differently alloyed batches of bronze could well have been used in the same workshop. See Holloway 1988 (supra n.1) 63 n.30.

13 P. E. Arias, "Lettura delle statue bronze di Riace," in *Due bronzi* 2, 243-50. Most recently, see Rolley, *La sculpture grecque* 347-50.

14 i.e., Harrison 1985 (supra n.1) 53. See W. G. Moon (ed.), *Polykleitos, the Doryphoros and tradition* (Madison 1995).

15 See Harrison 1985 (supra n.1) 47. She believes that both statues are contemporary, from a common monument dating before 450 B.C., and are products of the Early Classical or, to use her term, the 'Bold Style.' She suggests that the statues come from one of the groups of Homeric heroes dedicated at Olympia, and specifically the dedication of the Achaeans that stood in front of the Temple of Zeus.

16 J. Boardman, *Greek sculpture: the classical period* (London 1985) 54; id. (ed.), *The Oxford history of classical art* (Oxford 1997) no. 87, pp. 97-99. Boardman also believes that the statues are contemporary and possibly from a single group but by different artists.

17 O. Taplin, *Greek fire* (New York 1990) 86-89, who cites the Milanese porno-comic strip magazine *Sukia*, 1981. The popularity of the bronzes and their sexual impact upon the public is more fully discussed by L. M. Lombardi Satriani, "Il successo dei bronzi," in Satriani and Paoletti, *Gli eroi* (supra n.1) 121-44.

18 Holloway, *AAS* (supra n.6) 104, figs. 127-30; V. Tusa, *La scultura in pietra di Selinunte* (Palermo 1984) 119-23, pls. 12-21.

of Empedocles of Acragas (*c*.493-433 B.C.) as expressions of the contrary impulses of Love and Strife. The Riace warrior heroes are presented deliberately as a contrasting pair of opposites.

I see the Riace bronzes as contemporary masterpieces of the international Greek Early Classical or Severe style, belonging to a common monument, but works by two different artists. They are not as advanced in the easy chiastic positioning of the arms and legs as the Doryphoros of Polykleitos,[19] but neither do they belong to the beautiful idealized world of Pheidias and the mature Classical style of the Parthenon pediments. Thus, I would agree with those who date the statues before 450 B.C. but after the sculptures of the east pediment of the Temple of Aphaia at Aegina (*c*.475 B.C.).[20] They are closer in time to the bronze Zeus from Cape Artemision[21] or the sculptures from Olympia (470-457 B.C.).[22] But they differ in style from Aeginetan, Argive, or Athenian works of art that we know, although the artist of Statue B was particularly familiar with the early works of Polykleitos.

Magna Graecia

Ancient sources

It is in the western Greek world, where these magnificent works of art by master sculptors were discovered, that the mixture of stylistic and technical features discussed above can be found. Only one bronzecaster from this region and time is known from the ancient sources — Pythagoras of Rhegium, who is one of five mentioned by Pliny.[23] He specialized in athletes in motion, and his statues of victors could be seen at Olympia in Roman times. Pliny praised him as surpassing Myron in skill and because "he was the first to represent sinews and veins and was more exact in modeling hair."[24] He is also cited as the first sculptor "to aim at compositional rhythms and commensurability of parts."[25] Other subjects were nudes and "a lame man at Syracuse which makes people who look at it actually feel the pain of its sore."[26] Pythagoras is seen as a great innovator, with his bold style bridging the transition from Archaic to Classical art. Unfortunately, no sure attributions to him have been secured, although one can safely assume that he had pupils and a large and influential workshop. Whether the Riace bronzes could be products of Pythagoras or his school must remain in the realm of speculation. There must have been many other sculptors in western Greece, but unless they exhibited in one of the Panhellenic sanctuaries their names and works have escaped the historical record.

Sculpture[27]

We know that the tyrants of Sicily liked to glorify themselves and their cities by victories in the great Greek sanctuaries, but they preferred to give commissions to famous artists of the mother country to increase their prestige. We know of a number of victories of the Deinomenid brothers of Gela and Syracuse at Olympia and Delphi, but their preference was for Aeginetan artists. The most famous of their dedications is the Delphi bronze Charioteer, commissioned by

---

19 Harrison 1985 (supra n.1) 53, who writes that Polykleitos "must count as the pioneer of the Beautiful Style, and his Doryphoros may well date as early as 450 B.C."

20 For discussion of date of pediments and style, see Ridgway, *Severe style* 13-17.

21 Ead. 62-64. See also Tzachou-Alexandri, above pp. 86 ff.

22 Ridgway, *Severe style* chapt. 2: Boardman (supra n.16) chapt. 4, with earlier bibliography. For a stylistic link between the Zeus and the sculptures at Olympia, see Holloway 1988 (supra n. 1), who suggests that both are the works of Ageladas of Argos.

23 Pliny, *NH* 35.49-52. See Stewart, *Greek sculpture* 138-39, 237-38, 254-55, who places his work between 480 and 450 B.C. Originally from Samos, Pythagoras is believed to have migrated to Italy in 494 B.C.

24 Pliny, *NH* 34.59.

25 Diogenes Laertius 8.47.

26 Pliny, *NH* 34.59.

27 For a recent (1996) exhibition of western Greek art in the Palazzo Grassi, Venice, see the catalogue, G. P. Carratelli (ed.), *The Western Greeks*; note particularly the excellent discussion by C. Rolley, "Sculpture in Magna Graecia," 369-98.

Polyzalos of Gela after his victory probably in 474 B.C.[28] While close in time to the Riace bronzes, the calm figure with his bold columnar drapery and flattened curls is very different in style and mood.

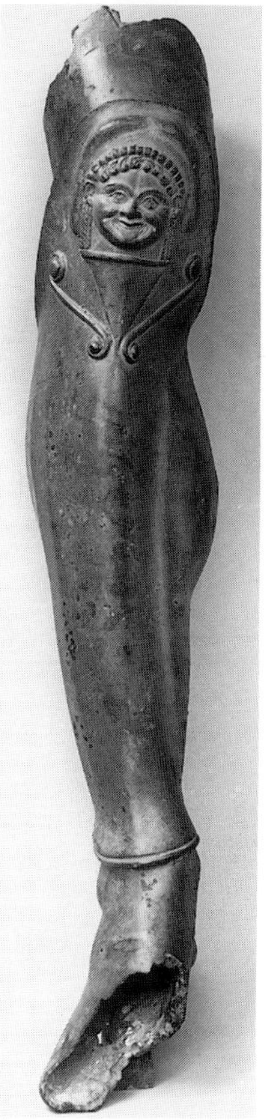

Fig. 3. Leg of a horseman. From Taras Bronze, h. 0.82 m. London, British Museum GR 1886.3-24.1. (Photo: courtesy of the Trustees of the British Museum.)

What evidence do we have, then, of large-scale bronze statues made by local artists of Magna Graecia? Unfortunately, there are only a few examples left to give a tantalizing glimmer of the riches that once must have decorated the western Greek cities. From the Archaic period the bronze Zeus from Ugento, while only 0.71 m tall, is a stunning example of the high quality of western Greek bronzes. He has been identified with a Tarantine workshop and dated *c.*530 B.C.[29] The style and statuary pose closely reflect monumental Greek art. Rolley points out both Laconian and Corinthian influence and cites the piece as an example of "the eclecticism of Italiote works."[30] Through the mixing and synthesis of different features artists often created new forms with an original style that was only possible in the artistic climate of Magna Graecia. We are still dealing with Greek art but not with artists who copy but rather use "inventive eclecticism" to produce works of art that often have a vibrant and spontaneous power that is lacking in contemporary Greek art. Rolley concludes, "The balance, restraint, and sense of proportion that characterize some of the schools of Mainland Greece are only some of the many aspects of Greek art; Italiote sculpture manifests another. But it is not necessary to hypothesize native influences in order to explain the development of this art: it is just as Greek as that of Athens or Samos."[31]

From the 5th c. B.C., D. Williams recently re-published the remains of a splendid bronze leg in the British Museum of heroic scale, together with fragments of drapery. He reconfirmed the provenance as Taras (fig. 3).[32] He convincingly identifies the fragments (known as the Piot bronze) as belonging to a seated warrior on horseback. He estimates the figure was 2.35 m tall, or one and one-third times life-size. The leg is greaved with a humanizing Medusa head as decoration. Williams compares the style of the finely modeled leg and ankle to that of Riace A. They share long, slim proportions with exaggerated calf muscles set high up the lower leg. He further notes the high lead content of the bronze, a feature shared with the Ugento bronze as well as other bronzes from Magna Graecia and Etruria in contrast to pieces from the Greek mainland.[33] Williams suggests that the original monument commemorated Taras's victory over its northern Italic neighbors the Peucetians and Iapygians. It was set up in Delphi between 470 and 450 B.C. and was described by Pausanias as a work of Onatas the Aeginetan and Klynthos. The Piot bronze he believes may be a copy or quotation of the Delphi group set up at home and made by a local artist. Such dual dedications were not unusual. The British Museum warrior horseman may be the hero Taras or Phalanthos of Lakedaimon rearing over the dead body of the fallen king Opis of the Iapygians.

---

28 For bibliography and discussion, see Ridgway, *Severe style* 33, 34, 42; Harrison 1985 (supra n.1) 56 n.4; Holloway 1988 (supra n.1) 59, 60 n.20.

29 Mattusch, *Greek bronze statuary* 65-71 and n.41 for bibliography.

30 Rolley, *La sculpture grecque* 373, 385, 384 and 551 for color plates.

31 Ibid. 380.

32 British Museum GR 1886.3-24.1: "Knight rider: the Piot bronze," *AA* (1989) 529-51.

33 See above n.12.

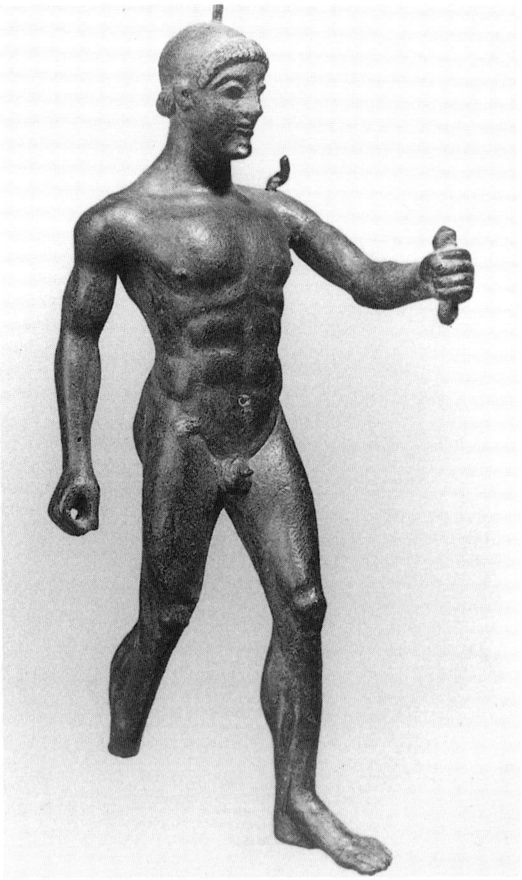

Fig. 4. Statuette of Apollo. Bronze, h. 0.25 m. Bari, Museo archeologico. (Photo: Carratelli, *Western Greeks*, p. 379.)

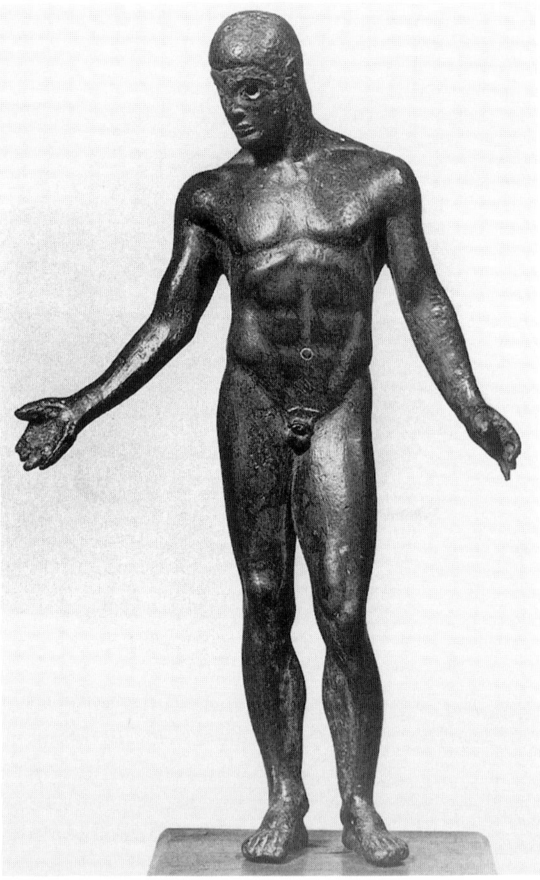

Fig. 5. Statuette from Adrano. Bronze, h. 0.195 m. Syracuse, Museo archeologico regionale, Paolo Orsi. (Photo: Langlotz and Hirmer, pl. X.)

We are on firmer stylistic ground when we turn to some small bronzes of high quality from Magna Graecia that appear to reflect monumental art.[34] One is a statuette from Bari of a striding Apollo holding a bow in his outstretched left hand with probably arrows or a laurel branch in his left (fig. 4).[35] The figure, cast in solid bronze, is 0.25 m high. On his left shoulder and head are remains of bronze projections probably connected with the casting of the figure. But also they might be explained if the statuette was a working model for a larger sculpture, so the artist did not feel the need to finish the statuette. The figure is Early Classical in style, although the rigid severity of the stance and the clear, separate divisions of the muscles of the torso suggest an early date within the period between 480 and 450 B.C. The expressive posture and open forms, with the feet planted firmly on the ground, are features we have noted particularly in Riace A. An emphasis on movement, open forms, and animation over formal balance and structure are characteristics that Rolley also cites as distinguishing features of the art of western Greece in comparison with mainland Greece.[36] Like Riace A, it is in three-quarter view that the Bari figure is best seen and communicates to the viewer the power of a larger, lost work of art.

---

34 The complete, half life-size bronze youth from the area of Selinus acquired by the city of Castelvetrano, stolen in 1962 and recovered in 1968, and now in the Museo Nazionale, Palermo, is not discussed here because of its poor quality and condition. Except for the exaggerated length of the thighs that bear a relationship to the proportions of Riace A, there is little to compare in style. See E. Langlotz and M. Hirmer, *Magna Graecia* (Rome 1968) 273, fig. 81; Mattusch, *Greek bronze statuary* 135-38, fig. 6.7, with earlier bibliography; Holloway, *AAS* (supra n.6) 103-4; *The western Greeks* cat. 180, dated 480-460 B.C., h. 0.847 m.

35 Bari, Museo Archeologico 4396: *The western Greeks* cat. 160, color pl. p. 379, dated 490-460 B.C.; Langlotz and Hirmer, *Magna Graecia* (supra n. 34) 273-4, figs. 82-83.

36 Rolley, *La sculpture grecque* 380.

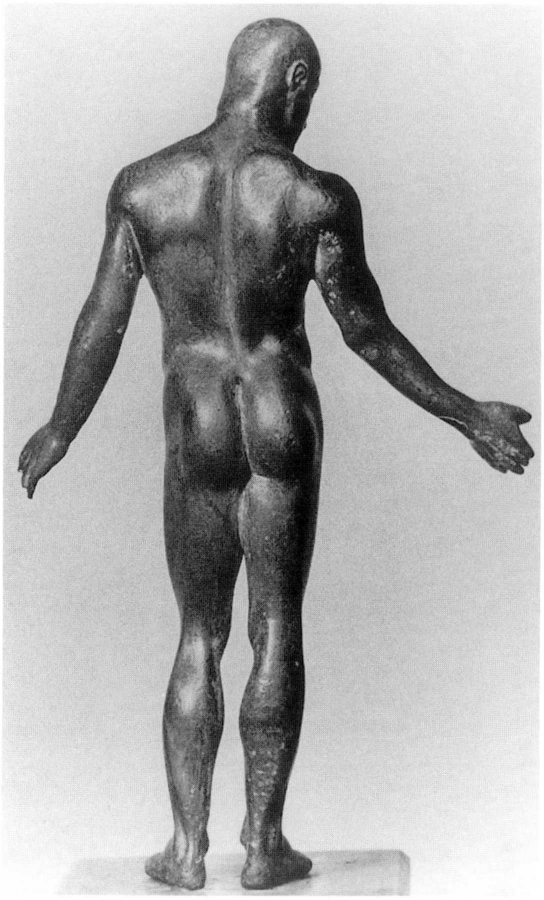

Fig. 6. Statuette from Adrano, back. (Photo: Langlotz and Hirmer, fig. 84.)

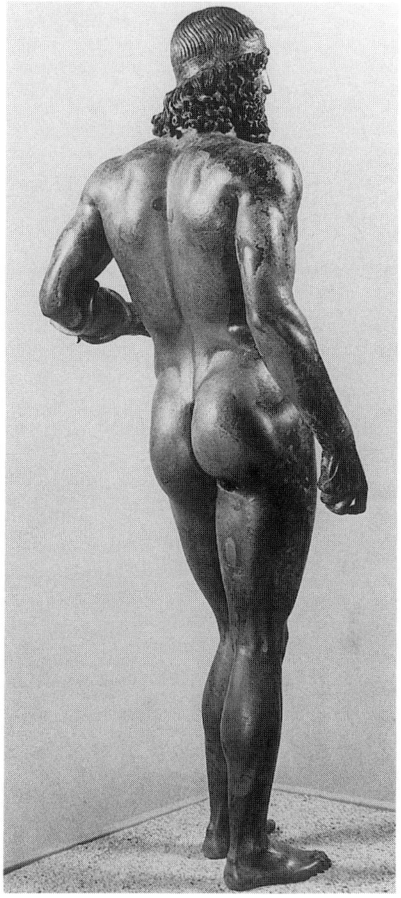

Fig. 7. Riace A, back. (Photo: *Due bronzi* 2, pl. 38; courtesy of Soprintendenza Archeologica di Toscana e Calabria.)

A bronze statuette, from Adrano on the southwest slope of Mt. Aetna, of an athlete pouring a libation, brings us closer in time to the Riace figures (fig. 5).[37] The easy rhythm of the contrapposto, the organic unity of the anatomical parts, and the expressive posture of the outstretched arms with the slightly inclined head place the statuette probably close to 460 B.C. The open movement of the arms gives animation to the frontal figure as well as the turn of his head to the right. Both the Adrano bronze and Riace A share long-legged proportions that differ from the more compact forms of Polykleitos's athletes. Comparing the back views of the two bronzes (figs. 6-7), the unifying rhythm of the parts of the body through the dominating curve of the spine is similar and anticipates Polykleitos in the concern for a unified whole. The Adrano boy surely reflects a lost monumental work of art of the quality of the Riace A master.

Location and identity

If the style of the Riace bronzes can be linked to Magna Graecia, where might they come from and whom do they represent? The fate of the Greek cities of southern Italy and Sicily in the 5th c. B.C. is well known. In Sicily, the cities not sacked by the Carthaginians were destroyed by the Greeks. When the Romans fought the First and Second Punic Wars, there was little left of 5th c. art to carry away. Only the great port city of Syracuse with its twin harbors remained a key center for the western Greek world until Roman times, when it was finally con-

---

37 Langlotz and Hirmer, *Magna Graecia* (supra n.34) 246, pl. X; Holloway, *AAS* (supra n.6) 109, fig. 135; Stewart, *Greek sculpture* 139, fig. 255, h. 0.195 m.

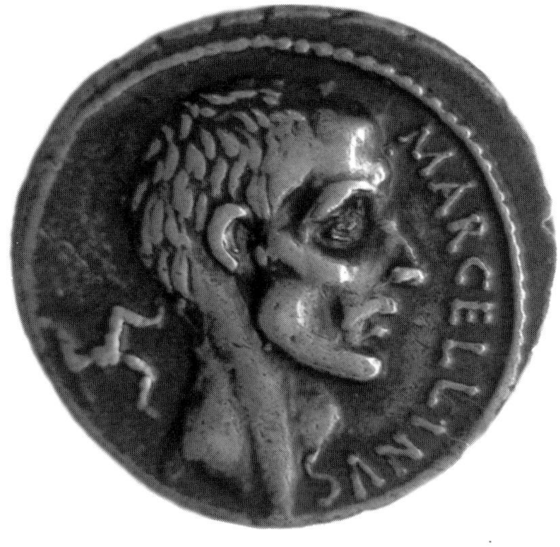

Fig. 8. Denarius of Marcellinus, Rome, 50 B.C. Obv.: M. Claudius Marcellus, r.; behind, *triskeles*, referring to capture of Syracuse; before, MARCELLINUS. London, British Museum. (Photo: author.)

Fig. 9. Rev. of fig. 8. M. Claudius Marcellus carrying a trophy into the temple, indicating his *spolia opima* from his sack of Syracuse; on r., MARCELLUS; on l., COS. QVINQ. London, British Museum. (Photo: author.)

quered by Marcellus, the 'sword of Rome,' in 211 B.C. (figs. 8-9). Plutarch writes of the countless works of Greek art that Marcellus shipped back to Rome, arousing criticism among some who saw Greek art as a threat to traditional Roman values.[38]

Gelon of Gela (491–478 B.C.)

Syracuse, founded by the Corinthians in 733 B.C., was re-founded by the tyrant Gelon of Gela in 491 B.C. He moved half of the population of Gela to Syracuse and restored the aristocrats (*gamoroi*) to power under his military monarchy. With his defeat of the Carthaginians at the battle of Himera in 480, Gelon became a great hero praised by Pindar for "gathering back Hellas from the weight of slavery."[39] He greatly enriched the city with temples, a new agora, and docks. When Gelon died in 478, he was mourned by all of Syracuse and entombed in a 9-story structure.

Hieron I (478–467 B.C.)

Gelon was succeeded by his brother Hieron I, who continued the aggressive policies of his brother but was viewed as a cruel despot. His great victory was the defeat of the Etruscans in a naval battle off Cumae in 474 B.C. He dedicated at Olympia a bronze Etruscan helmet to honor this event, also commemorated by Pindar. Hieron, too, was a founder of cities (*oikistes*), but he was hated for his ruthless deportation and killing of the inhabitants of Catane to found the new city of Aetna with citizens from Syracuse. To celebrate the event he invited Aeschylus to Syracuse, who wrote a play, now lost, called *The Women of Aetna*, probably produced in Syracuse during his visit *c.*470 B.C. Pindar was also invited by Hieron to honor the founding of Aetna in poetry. Like his brother, Hieron competed in games at Olympia and Delphi and was a great patron of the arts, but he was never heroized like his brother.[40] Hieron died in 467 and was buried in his city of Aetna.

---

38 Plutarch, *Marcellus* 21; M. Santirocco, "Syracuse and Roman philhellenism," in B. D. Wescoat (ed.), *Syracuse, the fairest Greek city* (Rome–Atlanta 1989) 45-48. For the *denarius* of moneyer P. Cornelius Lentulus Marcellinus minted in Rome in 50 B.C., showing on obverse the portrait head of his ancestor M. Claudius Marcellus with the *triskeles* referring to the capture of Syracuse and on the reverse Marcellus carrying a trophy into the temple commemorating this event, see M. H. Crawford, *Roman Republican coinage* (Cambridge 1974) no. 439, pl. 52; E. A. Sydenham, *The coinage of the Roman Republic* (London 1952) 187, no. 1147, pl. 29.

39 Pindar, *Pythian* 1.

40 B. D. Wescoat, "Introduction: 'Syracuse, richest and fairest of all cities'," in Wescoat, *Syracuse* (supra

Conclusions

Can we see Riace A and B as two Sicilian *oikists*, the first pair of tyrant-heroes of Syracuse, Gelon and his brother Hieron I?[41] Perhaps the statues were commissioned by Hieron I as part of his artistic commemoration of the founding of Aetna in 474 B.C., establishing himself on equal terms with his famous brother as a founder-hero. Could the proud but hated Hieron I, the great patron of the arts, be Riace A, while Riace B represents his older beloved brother Gelon? They would be seen by the inhabitants of Syracuse as a contrasting pair of *oikists* and brothers, a pair of opposites in keeping with the dualist cosmology of the famous philosopher of the period, Empedocles of Acragas. To the people of Syracuse, accustomed to the tragedies of Aeschylus, they would be viewed as dramatic protagonists, male and female, love and strife — two opposite personalities, the one active, the other passive.[42] Two contemporary artists were deliberately chosen to portray these differing personalities. The artist of Riace A was chosen for his vigorous enthusiasm for the Severe style suitable to the rendering of the arrogant Hieron. The artist of Riace B, more advanced in style and familiar with the early work of Polykleitos, was selected for the softer and more rhythmic treatment of forms to interpret the dead, heroized, older brother.

Over two millennia have passed between our eyes and theirs, and we are attuned to view life in more complicated terms. But the mixture of stylistic currents represented by the two Riace statues seems to fit best the artistic climate of western Greek art.[43] Perhaps the Riace bronzes are precious documents of a lost bronze workshop in the great port city of Syracuse. We may never securely solve the mystery of the Riace bronzes. But with the recent opening up of the deep sea for exploration using the new technology,[44] there is hope of discovering other ancient bronzes in the sea to fill in the gaps of our understanding of Greek art as it evolved in both the eastern and western Mediterranean.

Department of Archaeology, Boston University

---

n.38) 19, 20; C. Patterson, "Tyranny in colony and mother-city," ibid. 25-28; R. Rehm, "Aeschylus in Syracuse: the commerce of tragedy and politics," ibid. 31-34.

41 See above n.6. Holloway, *AAS* (supra n.6) 112, has already suggested that the statues represent a pair of *oikists* from Sicily but would connect them with Acragas, Gela, or Camarina. They would then have been carried off as spoils of war by the Phoenicians after their destruction of these cities in 406-405 B.C. He would date them both about 450, made by different artists for a common monument. On the importance of *oikists* for Sicilian colonies, see Wescoat, *Syracuse* (supra n.38) 17, 18.

42 On the role of antithesis in the interpretation of Greek art, see Stewart, *Greek sculpture* 139.

43 If the Riace bronzes are from Syracuse, an artistic tie to the mother city of Corinth would be expected. Such a tie would explain the close use of Riace B for a model for the statues of Gaius and Lucius Caesar at Corinth discussed by Vanderpool below.

44 See the results of the first archaeological exploration of the deep sea with a remotely operated vehicle in 1989 and the discovery of a Roman trade route and late Roman merchant ship in A. M. McCann and J. Freed, *Deep water archaeology* (JRA Suppl. 13, 1994).

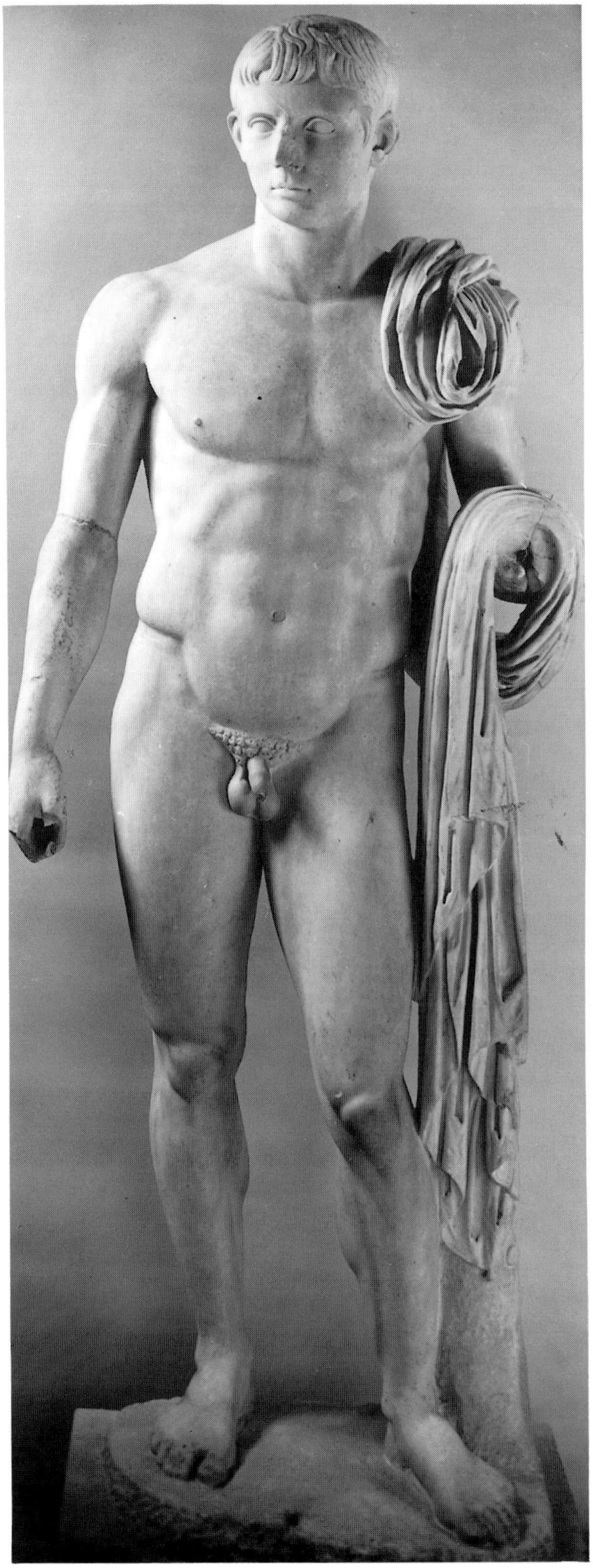

Fig. 1. Gaius Caesar, from the so-called Julian Basilica, Corinth. Marble, h. (with ancient plinth) 2.04 m. Corinth, Archaeological Museum S1065. (Photo: I. Ioannidou and L. Bartzioti; courtesy of the Corinth Excavations, American School of Classical Studies at Athens.)

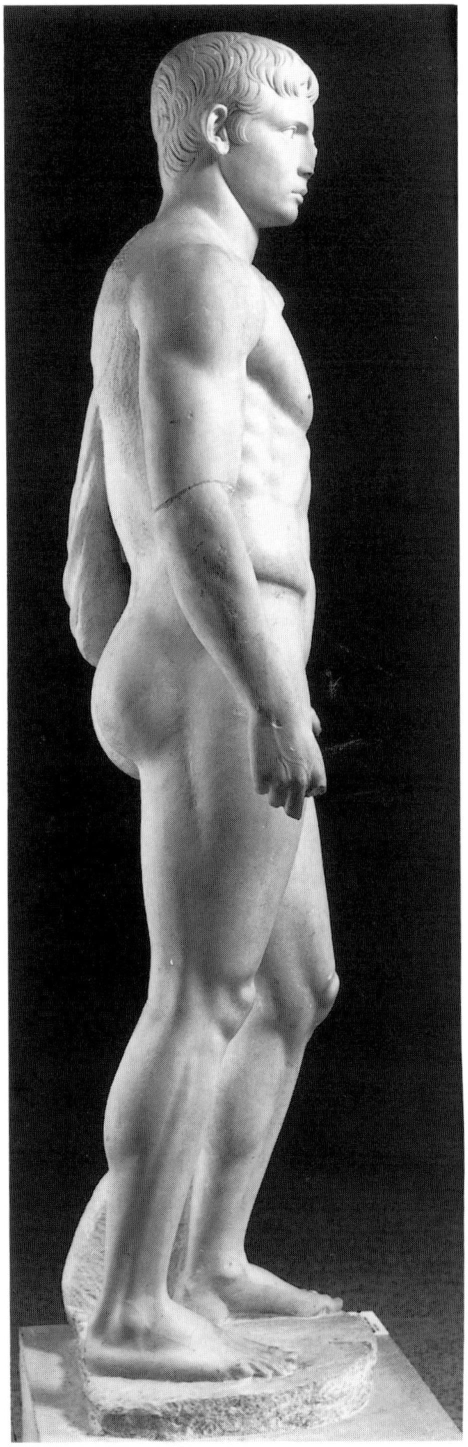

Fig. 2. Gaius Caesar, right profile. (Photo: I. Ioannidou and L. Bartzioti; courtesy of the Corinth Excavations, American School of Classical Studies at Athens.)

Serial twins: Riace B and some Roman relatives

Catherine de Grazia Vanderpool

Once, when we looked at a Roman statue that closely resembled what we knew (or thought we knew) was a Greek original, we labeled the Roman sculpture a *copy*. Now we know that there are many ways in which Romans reacted to Greek originals. The Greeks too imitated, adapted, and replicated the work of others as well as their own. Thus, the primary model for other works becomes an original *concept* or *model* or *prototype*, a grouping of proportions and measurements that could be adapted or adopted by the originator himself for a series of works, or by one of his colleagues or contemporaries, or perhaps by later related or unrelated artisans.

It is the purpose of this paper to examine the family tree of one of the very few monumental bronzes of ancient Greece which has survived, the figure known as Riace B, found with an equally monumental figure known as Riace A off the southern coast of Italy. At the same time, the paper considers the theory of serial production of monumental bronzes as presented by C. Mattusch.[1] In her view, Riace B forms part of a series going back to one original model, which produced a family sharing the same basic form in outline, in proportion, and in measurement, differing only in finished details and in attributes. This theory of masterpieces in multiples may not fit our notion of the importance of originality and uniqueness, nor A. Furtwängler's concept of "Meisterwerke," but it may be a more accurate notion of how Greek workshops functioned.

Evidence from the world of Roman sculpture may shed new light on the origins of Riace B and may offer new evidence for Mattusch's theories. The evidence also helps us understand how Roman adaptations of Greek originals were affected by underlying ideologies. The nearly identical statues of two young men (figs. 1 and 3), found with a togate figure of Augustus (fig. 4) in the so-called Julian Basilica in the Forum of Corinth, have long been discussed with respect to their identification.[2] Early in their modern history, they were identified as Gaius and Lucius Caesar, adopted sons of Augustus. The identifications flip-flopped over the years: the earliest publications suggested the complete figure as Lucius, and the partial figure as his older brother Gaius.[3] I and others — now most recently J. Pollini in his publication on their portraiture — have concluded that the complete statue represents Gaius, and the fragmentary work represents his younger brother Lucius.[4]

---

1 C. C. Mattusch, "The casting of Greek bronzes: variation and repetition," in *Small bronze sculpture* 135-38; ead., *Classical bronzes* esp. 64, 65, 221.

2 Corinth nos. S1065 and S1080, found in the so-called Julian Basilica during excavations in 1914, along with a statue of Augustus, inv. S1116, found the following year. Although the statues are now displayed in the Corinth Museum as a group, they were not discovered together. The statue of Augustus was found lying in the southwest corner of the building (May 14, 1915, notebook 75, pp. 333-37). S1065 was found in the cryptoporticus to the north of the central niche in the east wall (October 30, 1914, notebook 72, pp. 137-38), and S1080 was found to the south of the niche, but built into a late wall, where the statue had obviously been re-used as building material after the destruction of the basilica in the late 4th c. A.D. (November 20, 1914, notebook 72, p. 189). However, the close similarities in marble, workmanship, and style suggest that they were originally set up as a group and only later in their history scattered within the same building.

3 E. H. Swift, "Imperial portraits at Corinth, II. Gaius and Lucius Caesar," *AJA* 25 (1921) 142-59; F. P. Johnson, *Corinth* IX: *The sculpture 1896-1923* (Cambridge, MA 1931) nos. 134 (Augustus), 135 (Gaius), 136 (Lucius), 70-76; id., "Gaius and Lucius Caesar?" *AJA* 45 (1941) 603-9.

4 J. Pollini, *The portraiture of Gaius and Lucius Caesar* (New York 1987) nos. 14 (Gaius), 38 (Lucius), 56-59, 83-87, 99, 107. He summarizes in detail all the preceding scholarship and concurs on the identification of S1065 as Gaius Caesar, the older son of Julia and Agrippa, and S1080 as Lucius Caesar, his younger (by two years) brother. In my *Excavations of the American School of Classical Studies at Corinth: the Roman portrait sculpture* (Diss. Columbia Univ. 1973) S1065 and S1080 are cat. nos. 12 and 14 respectively, and identified as Gaius and Lucius in that order.

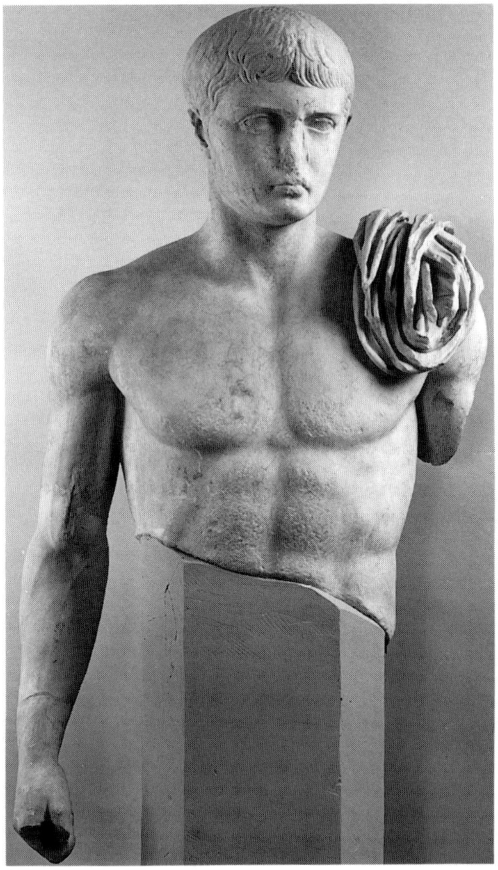

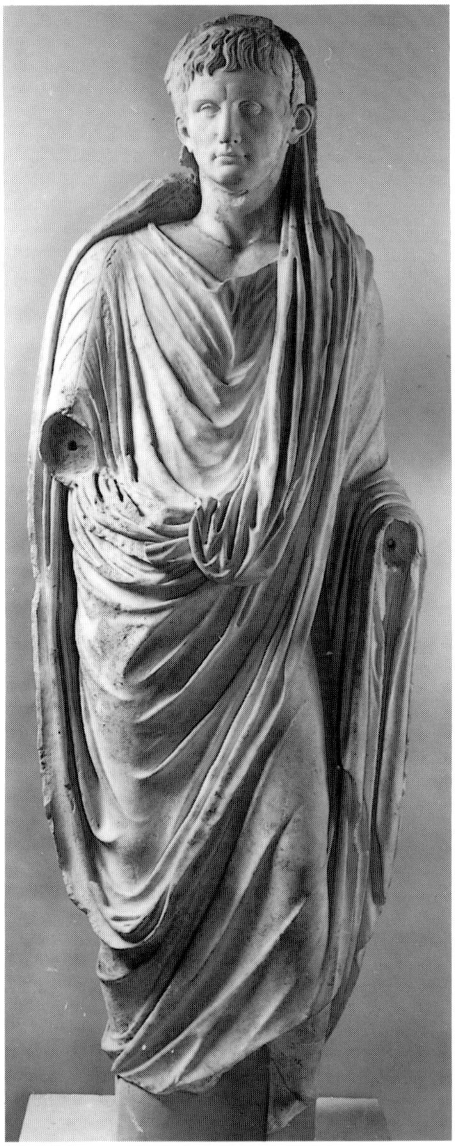

Fig. 3. Lucius Caesar, from the so-called Julian Basilica, Corinth. Marble, ph. 0.88 m. Corinth, Archaeological Museum S1080.

Fig. 4. Augustus, from the so-called Julian Basilica, Corinth. Marble, h. 2.05 m. Corinth S1116. (Both photos: I. Ioannidou and L. Bartzioti; courtesy of the Corinth Excavations, American School of Classical Studies at Athens.)

The portrait types of both boys are assimilated to that of Augustus, although the sharp planes and prominent modeling of Augustus's features have been modified. These modifications befit their youth, particularly evident in the soft, pouting mouths and full, rounded chins. Technically, the Corinthian Augustus and the portrait of Gaius are particularly close, especially in the hard chiseling of the eyelids, brow, and hair. The portrait of Lucius is softer, perhaps by a different hand, and perhaps as an indication of his youth in relation to his older brother.

The material and technique of all three statues point to Attica, which probably provided the newly founded Corinth with much of its figural and architectural sculpture in the early Empire. Each was carved from a single block of marble which shows all the characteristics of Pentelic: lightly weathered to an eggshell white, the stone has fine crystals but is seamed and flawed with large streaks of mica.

The Julian Basilica group most likely was conceived and executed at the very end of the 1st c. B.C., when the young men were still alive and when there was good reason, in Corinth, to set up statues celebrating the age of Augustus.[5] The year 2 B.C. is key to this picture. In Rome itself,

5 Pollini, *Portraiture* (supra n.4) places S1080 in his Type IV grouping, as late Augustan, coinciding with

Augustus celebrated the completion of the Forum of Augustus and the Temple of Mars Ultor.[6] The architectural complex celebrated not only Rome but also the Julian family, more clearly identified with Rome than ever before. That same year, and probably not coincidentally, the 18-year-old Gaius set out on his maiden campaign to the East. His route almost undoubtedly took him through Corinth, although there survives no explicit reference to his visit; however, his presence may be reflected in the Corinthian duoviral coinage of *c.*2 B.C., which portrayed Gaius and Lucius facing each other on the reverse, with Augustus himself on the obverse.[7] In Athens, Gaius was celebrated as the "new Ares", perhaps at the same time, and these were also the years which saw an entire Temple of Ares moved into the center of the ancient Athenian Agora.[8] Not only did Augustan Rome draw heavily on imagery from old Greece in creating monuments central to its public presentations, but these images were also absorbed by, or inflicted on, Greece itself, as illustrated most extensively in Athens. This would have been a highly auspicious time in which to honor Augustus and the imperial succession with a sculptural group in Corinth. Augustus himself appeared as first citizen, his togate figure embodying those qualities spelled out so clearly in word and images on Augustan coinage: *pax, pietas, concordia, iustitia,* and, in 2 B.C., *pater patriae.* In Corinth, the figure may have had additional meanings: *patronus*, adopted son of, and heir to, the founder of the colony and father not only of his country but of the heirs-by-adoption.[9]

As for the heirs, although the statue of Gaius is almost completely preserved, as is half that of Lucius, studies of these works have focused almost exclusively on the heads. Yet the body too would have carried a set of meanings, as did the Polykeitan Doryphoros, pinnacle of manly virtues, which was used over and over again, in copies or in modified creations, for portrait statues of the Roman period. The multiple occurrences of the Doryphoros, crowned by a variety of portraits — imperial and private — over a broad chronological span, might suggest that the meaning is generic, a broad reference to classical form identified with classical ideals, but this notion has been considerably refined by the work of P. Zanker, J. Pollini, and others.[10]

Gaius's assumption of the consulship in A.D. 1. This grouping would be just three years later than a type which he associates with Gaius's journey east in 2 B.C. He acknowledges, however, the similarity of Type IV to the figure on the Uffizi altar. In fact, these fine divisions among groupings, which still show some internal variations, may be hazardous, particularly when moving into a provincial context where information may be outdated or transformed in transmission and adaptation. For historical and stylistic reasons, including the close similarity of both Augustus and Gaius to the dated Uffizi relief, I prefer to place the Corinthian Gaius in 2 B.C., as part of a Julian family monument created on the occasion of his *profectio*. The statue portrays the 18-year-old Gaius, still beardless, with the rounded chin and full curving mouth of late adolescence, the same person we see in the statue from Otricoli and in the Uffizi relief. Pollini's last grouping, Type V, indeed shows the same person but with a leaner face and the softly curling, longer sideburns, lower facial hair, and moustache associated with a first beard — perhaps, as Pollini suggests, a type created when Augustus's heir had assumed his first military command.

6 P. Zanker, *The power of images in the age of Augustus* (Ann Arbor 1990) 192-227; id., *Forum Augustum* (Tübingen 1968).

7 M. Amandry, *Le monnayage des duovirs corinthiens* (BCH Suppl. 15, 1988) 46-47, 50-51, pls. X-XI.

8 T. L. Shear, Jr., "Athens: from city-state to provincial town," *Hesperia* 50 (1981) 356-77, esp. 362; M. and E. Levensohn, "Inscription on the south slope of the Acropolis," *Hesperia* 16 (1947) 68-69 on *IG* II^2 3250, referring to Gaius as the 'new Ares' probably dated A.D. 2 or later; M. Hoff, *The Roman Agora in Athens* (Diss., Boston Univ. 1988) 52-54 on the Temple of Ares, and 259-77 on the imperial cult in Athens in the Augustan period.

9 That the Corinth type may be related to a statue type actually created in Rome, perhaps toward the end of the 1st c. B.C., and then transmitted to the colonies, is suggested by the remarkable similarity between it and the altar from the Vicus Sandalarius, now in Florence, dated securely to 2 B.C.: Uffizi inv. 972. Zanker, *Power* (supra n.6) 125, fig. 101; B. Rose, *Dynastic commemoration and imperial portraiture in the Julio-Claudian period* (Cambridge 1997) 104-6, cat. no. 33, pl. 111.

10 J. Pollini, "The Augustus from Prima Porta and the transformation of the Polykleitan heroic idea: the rhe-

A closer look at the statues of Gaius and Lucius confirms that here, too, the choice of portrait statue embodied highly specific content, incorporating a precise set of meanings appropriate to the message which the patrons wished to convey.

There is enough left of Lucius's torso to show that the body type selected for both figures is identical: only their heads are in mirror position. The youths are shown unclothed, with cloaks balanced on their shoulders, then looped over their left arms, their right hands lowered and loosely clasped around a now-missing object. If it were not for the position of the left leg, planted firmly on the ground, the pose would be close to that of the Polykleitan Doryphoros. The familiar chiastic motif of Polykleitos's canon, which opposes working leg to working arm and trailing leg to trailing extended arm, is varied in the Corinth statues by planting the left foot firmly on the ground. However, they are similar in other respects: the uplifted head turns right, in the direction of the right, weight-bearing leg; the tipped angle of the pelvis is echoed by a line carried through the pectorals and the shoulders. The sturdy volumes of the muscles, the full curve of the back and buttocks, the well-rounded highly defined pectorals, the curve of the epigastric arch, the segmentation of the abdomen, the prominent *linea alba*, and the proportions, these are also typical of the environment of Polykleitos. In profile, the well-muscled bodies described a characteristic S-curve, although much of the back shoulder area of Gaius is missing due to a broad micaceous streak which flawed the marble at this point, forcing the sculptor to a rough-point finish (fig. 2).

Thus, the schema of the statue of Gaius is very close to that of the most familiar of classical Greek works, with the significant exception of the left leg, which is at rest, and thus differs from the forward impetus of the Doryphoros. A search for parallels to the pose among surviving works ascribed to Polykleitos and his followers finds several that also exhibit a static rather than active position but none shows precisely the same combination of body type and gesture. The type has been characterized as a Roman adaptation of a Polykleitan figure, and while there are similarities to a Hermes type best represented by the so-called Mercure Richelieu in the Louvre, there are also significant differences.[11] While the draping of the cloak is similar, as is the stasis of the pose, the body positions are almost completely reversed.

The dissimilarities could be attributed to the creativity of Roman-period workshops if it were not for the fact that there exists a work that is strikingly similar in pose and scale to the Corinth statues: Riace B.[12] In almost every detail the basic poses are the same: the static chiastic pattern, the position of the arms, the ponderation, the lift of the head. Think away the heads and attributes, and drop a possible prejudice against cold Roman imitations of classical forms, and we see that the statues in outline are identical. When a schematic drawing of Gaius flanks one of Riace B (figs. 5-6), the similarity is striking: the major difference is in the distance between the feet, with Gaius's left foot pushed slightly farther to the left than Riace B's. In profile too the outline is virtually identical, except for the position of the right arm, which is farther forward in Riace B, closer to the side in Gaius. As for the distinctive rounded upper back on Riace B, the marble of the same area in Gaius was seriously flawed, and the sculptor was forced to leave this area flat. I will return to these differences below.

In surface details, there are some remarkable similarities, for example the distinctive pattern of veins over ankle and foot, the prominent line of the calf muscle, which is modeled in

---

toric of art," in W. Moon (ed.), "Polykleitos, the Doryphoros, and tradition," *Wisconsin studies in the classics* (Madison 1995) 262-82; Zanker, *Power* (supra n.6) esp. 245-52; C. Maderna-Lauter, "Polyklet in Rom," in H. Beck, P. C. Bol, and M. Buckling (edd.), *Polyklet: Der Bildhauer der griechischen Klassik* (Mainz am Rhein 1990) 376-85; G. Lahusen, "Polyklet und Augustus," ibid. 393-96.

11 B. S. Ridgway, "Sculpture from Corinth," *Hesperia* 50 (1981) 432, characterizes the statues of Gaius and Lucius as "stock bodies in the Polykleitan tradition"; ead., *Roman copies of Greek sculpture: the problems of the originals* (Ann Arbor 1984) 102, where she describes Gaius and Lucius as adaptations of a Polykleitan type, with the addition of drapery.

12 *Due bronzi.*

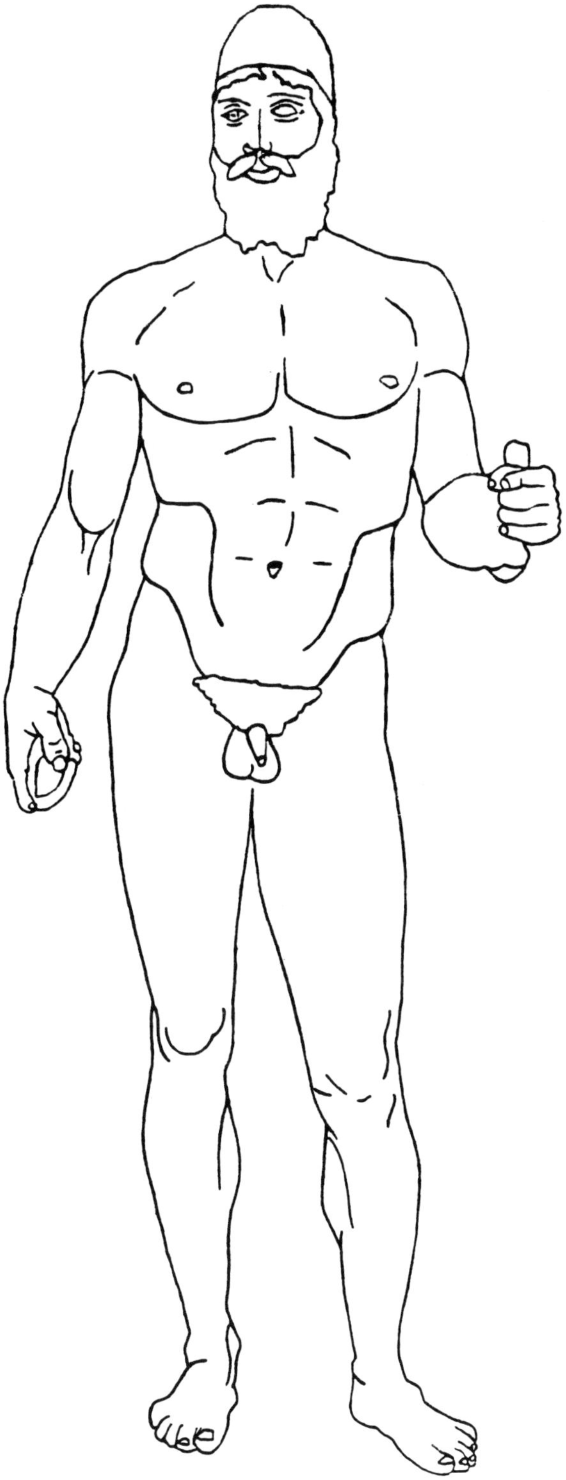

Fig. 5. Line drawing of Riace B.

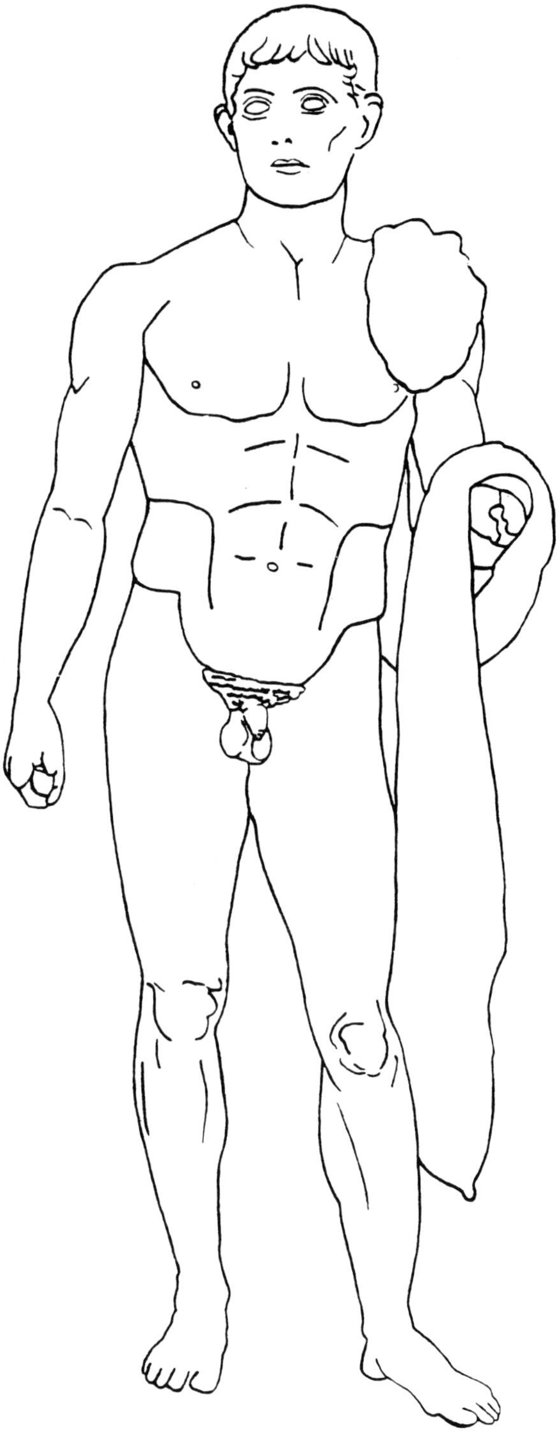

Fig. 6. Line drawing of Gaius. (both drawings: S. Potavin.)

Riace B but sharply chiseled in the Corinthian work, and the bunched muscle over the right kneecaps in both statues. The statues are also remarkably close in size. In their principal publication, the Riace statues were measured over several hundred points:[13] wherever possible, the Corinthian statues were measured in the same locations. In all, the two works were compared

13 C. Sabbione, "Tavole delle misure," in *Due bronzi* 221-25, App. 2.

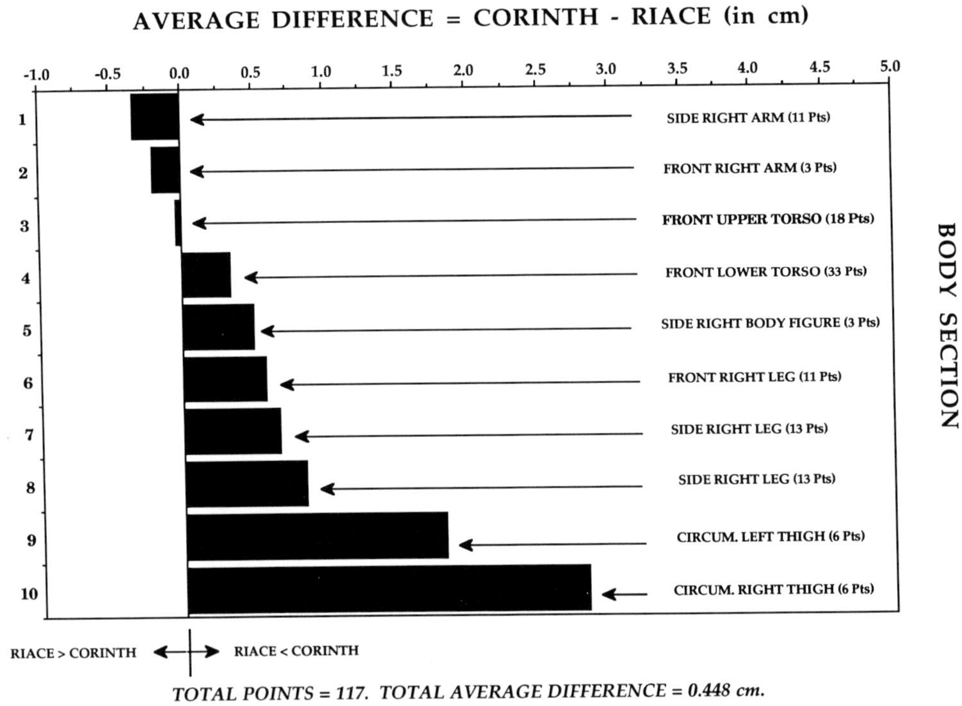

Fig. 7. Table comparing measurements of Gaius and Riace B.

at 118 different points; the overall average difference between the two statues was 4.5 mm (fig. 7). The largest number of measurements was taken over the torso; there, the average difference was even less, 1.8 mm. Except for the upper torso and right arm, Gaius is slightly larger than Riace, averaging 4.5 mm on the front lower torso, where 33 points were measured, and from 5.6 mm to 2.8 cm over the legs. The greatest difference is in the circumference of the thighs, which range from 1.75 cm to 2.75 cm larger. While the feet and ankles are also identical in measurement, Gaius's left foot is placed *c.*2 cm more to his left than that of Riace B. The only areas where Gaius is smaller than Riace B are the front upper torso, where measurements over 18 points show an average 1 mm smaller than Riace B, and the right arm, averaging 3 mm less than Riace B. The surface treatment of the two statues is noticeably different: Gaius's muscles and skin are smoother, more youthful, while B's are those of a more mature, adult male.

While it might seem that there would be many more examples preserved of this rather simple schema, there are actually very few, if adhering to the outlines described already. It might appear a coincidence that Gaius is so close to Riace B if it were not for the fact that there is another pair of statues with precisely the same schema and same measurements, from the Theater of Lepcis Magna.[14] These statues are clearly identified by their attributes as the Dioskouroi: next to the right legs are horse protomes, and both youths wear the *pilos*. The statue with right arm preserved carries an inverted, sheathed sword. Given the quirks of preservation, and the fact that there is a relatively small corpus of sculpture left from the Roman world, it is fortunate indeed to have this pair from Lepcis.[15] They seem to confirm what

---

14 G. Caputo, *Le sculture del teatro di Leptis Magna* (Rome 1976) 27-29 no. 7, pl. 6; no. 8, pls. 7-8. Pentelic marble; total h. no. 7 including plinth 2.15 m; no. 8 including plinth 2.20 m, head from chin to apex of *pilos* 38 cm. Found in the area of the proscenium of the theater. Caputo dates the original to a Polykleitan circle with Pheidian influence, of the second half of the 5th c. B.C.

15 There are also two other examples, which are, however, related by motif but not scale. One is from Baiae, now in Naples, and one is from Carthage, now in the Louvre. They appear to be less precise renditions of the same pattern, except for the facts that their left arms are held slightly lower than on the Corinth and Lepcis works and that the Baiae figure holds an inverted sword in his left hand: T. Lorenz, "Die Dioskuren in der römischen Plastik," *Meded* n.s. 3, 38 (1976) 19, figs. 14-15. He calls these free renditions of the Doryphoros. He also gathers together other Dioskouroi types, none of which are as close to the group under discussion as are those in Naples and the Louvre.

one might have suspected, given the duality, the 'twinness,' of the statues in Corinth: that the latter probably invoke a flattering comparison of Gaius and Lucius to Castor and Pollux.[16]

It was under Augustus that the principal ritual related to the Dioskouroi, the annual parade known as the *transvectio equitum,* was restored, a ceremony which celebrated the Roman victory over the cities of the Latin League at Lake Regillus in the early 5th c. B.C., where the Dioskouroi supposedly joined the Romans in fighting the Latins.[17] According to legend, after the battle they materialized in the Forum itself, where they announced the victory and watered their horses at the Lacus Iuturnae. Thus, Castor and Pollux were adopted as a symbol of Rome victorious, and from earliest times they also served as patrons of the equestrian order. In Augustus's *transvectio equitum,* the procession was led by the *principes iuventutis,* as Gaius was styled in 5 B.C. and Lucius in 2 B.C. In the description by Dionysius of Halikarnassos, *Ant.Rom.* 6.13.4, they presented a heroic picture: on white horses, dressed in purple robes, bearing shields and spears made of silver. That this simile likening the boys to the Dioskouroi spread to the provinces is suggested by an inscription from Cyprus (*IG* III 997), dated 7/6 B.C.-A.D. 2, in which they are styled twin sons and Augustus is characterized as Zeus. Thus, it would not be unreasonable to identify the statues in Corinth, in type so close to the Lepcis Dioskouroi, as a sculptural simile equivalent to the Cyprus inscription. The horse protome and *pilos* are missing, but a knowledgeable patron or viewer would have understood the simile — and I will return to this point later when discussing the possible origins of the Dioskouroi type represented by the Lepcis/Corinth figures.

The repetition of this type in no less than four Roman statues suggests that all four derive from a common and significant ancestor. Where might this have stood and who might have made it? What would be an appropriate original for honoring the imperial heirs assimilated to Dioskouroi? Perhaps the most famous Dioskouroi in Classical Greece were the bronze statues created by Antiphanes of Argos for the Spartan victory monument of Lysander in Delphi. It was dedicated soon after Lysander crushed the Athenians at Aigospotamoi in 405/4 B.C. and dominated the sanctuary's main entrance, eclipsing, appropriately, the smaller Athenian monument flanking it on the west.[18] Pausanias 10.9.7-10 gives a detailed description, confirmed in many points by archaeological and epigraphical evidence. In pride of place in the front row, west end, stood Antiphanes' Dioskouroi, symmetrical and perhaps in mirror image, as in many representations of the Dioskouroi, with Zeus-born Pollux to the viewer's right and the mortal Castor to the left.[19] According to Pausanias's description, the Dioskouroi are followed by Zeus, Apollo, Artemis, Poseidon, Lysander, Agias, and Hermon, in front of a crowd of statues representing the Spartans and their allies. He enumerates 37 figures, 9 in the first row and 28 in the second. According to archaeological and epigraphic evidence, there may have been more: 29 or 30 in the back row and 10 in the front. The traces of footprints on bases associated with the

---

16 Others have noted the possibility that the Corinth representations evoke the Dioskouroi: B. S. Ridgway, *Fifth century styles in Greek sculpture* (Princeton 1981): "It is tempting to suggest that the two statues were erected to recall not so much the Julian princes themselves but the Dioskouroi, as Gaius and Lucius were called." Also Pollini, *Portraiture* (supra n.4) 19: "The statues ... recall classical figures like the Dioskouroi."

17 B. Poulsen has summarized arguments for the association of Gaius and Lucius with the Dioskouroi: "The Dioscuri and ruler ideology," *SymbOsl* 66 (1991) 119-46. She discusses the possibility of Augustan precedents for Tiberius's action in re-dedicating, in A.D. 6, the Temple of Castor in his own name and that of his late brother Drusus, postulating a prior intention to consecrate the Temple in honor of Gaius and Lucius.

18 On the monument at Delphi, the original publication of the inscriptions is in *Fouilles de Delphes* III: *Epigraphie,* fasc. 1, 24-40. Later, principal sources include J. Pouilloux and G. Roux, *Enigmes à Delphes* (Paris 1963) 55-60 (with earlier bibliography); J.-F. Bommelaer, "Note sur les navarques et les successeurs de Polyclète à Delphes," *BCH* 59 (1971) 43 ff.; id., *Lysandre de Sparte: histoire et traditions* (Paris 1981) 14-16.

19 On the positions: Bommelaer, *Lysandre* (supra n.18) 15-16.

figures of Castor and Pollux suggest standing figures, with no trace of horses or protomes. The remaining footprints on the fragmentary statue bases in the front row suggest all were in the range of 1.90 m in height, close to the actual measurements of the Corinth and Lepcis statues, while those in the back row were shorter.[20]

The monument celebrated a great moment in history not only for the Spartans but also for a pan-Peloponnesian host that included Corinthians, Sikyonians, and others, all of whose leaders were celebrated in bronze.[21] While Corinth eventually became a Roman colony proud of its ties to Rome itself, it was also Peloponnesian and Greek.[22] We should not forget that among Corinth's chief benefactors was the Spartan G. Iulius Eurycles who, with other Spartan nobles, traced his descent from Castor and Pollux. In this and other ways they made much of their noble Hellenic ancestry, while at the same time honoring their Roman *patrones:* Eurycles may have founded the cult of Caesar and Augustus in Sparta.[23]

It may have been a Euryclid who, at the time of Gaius's voyage east, commissioned the group in Corinth honoring the Augustan family and succession. The Euryclids rose to prominence in the last half of the 1st c. B.C. and were influential throughout the Peloponnese, especially in Sparta and Corinth, until the middle of the 2nd c. A.D. According to an inscription found at Corinth, one of them, a Eurycles Herculanus (perhaps to be associated with the Gaius Julius Eurycles Herculanus who was adopted by C. Julius Eurycles at some point between 18 and 12 B.C.) was responsible for some kind of building activity in the area of the Julian Basilica during the Augustan period.[24] Perhaps it was he or a member of his family who commissioned the group honoring Augustus and his offspring. While Augustus himself was shown togate, as a Roman citizen, the young men appeared as twin heroes, future *soteres,* protectors of their country, a rôle well expressed through the simile of the Dioskouroi. The simile also could have made veiled reference to the patrons themselves, Spartans and therefore descendants themselves of the Dioskouroi.[25] By adopting one of Antiphanes's Dioskouroi as the model for the statues of Gaius and Lucius, the sponsors of the Augustan statue group flattered the imperial family and, at the same time, paid tribute to local pride.

To return to the theme of serial statues: what might this connection of Gaius and Lucius with the Delphi Dioskouroi tell us about Riace B? I believe Riace B and the original bronze Dioskouros derived from the same original model or prototype developed in an Argive workshop, perhaps even that of Antiphanes. The original model, which might even have

---

20 Bommelaer, *Lysandre* (supra n.18) 15, n.40.

21 Paus. 10.9.4 lists men from Sparta, Boeotia, Chios, Rhodes, Knidos, Ephesos, Miletos, Myndos, Euboia, Corinth, Troezen, Epidauros, Pellene, Hermione, Phokis, Megara, Sikyon, Ambrakia, and Leukas.

22 There is evidence that some Greeks, at least, regarded Corinth with scorn: it was a foreign growth in their midst, a once-noble Greek city given now to "scoundrel slaves." For the attitude of truly Greek towns to the upstart Corinth, see A. J. S. Spawforth, "Corinth, Argos, and the imperial cult: Pseudo-Julian, Letter 198," *Hesperia* 63 (1994) 211-32, esp. 227-28; in the epigram by the Augustan poet Krinagoras of Mytilene, the colonists are described as "shopsoiled slaves," expressing Greek scorn at what they chose to view as the servile origins of Corinth's new population. In Spawforth's interpretation, *Letter* 198 reveals that Argos shares in the disdain of Corinth's *romanitas.*

23 On the Euryclids in Corinth: A. B. West, *Corinth* VIII. 2: *Latin inscriptions: 1896-1926* (Cambridge, MA 1931) 46-53, nos. 67 and 68; J. H. Kent, *Corinth* VIII. 3 *The inscriptions: 1926-1950* (Princeton 1966) 124-25, no. 314; G. W. Bowersock, "Eurykles of Sparta," *JRS* 51 (1961) 111-18. Eurycles built a bath for Corinth, and he and descendants held a number of major magistracies in the first century of the city's life.

24 Kent, *Inscriptions* (supra n.23) no. 314.

25 On the importance and typology of the Dioskouroi in the iconography of Roman Sparta: J. Sanders, "The Dioscuri in post-classical Sparta," in O. Palagia and W. Coulson (edd.), *Sculpture from Arcadia and Laconia: proceedings of an international conference* (Oxford 1993) 217-24; and, in the same volume, G. Steinhauer, "Iconography of the Dioskouroi in Roman Sparta," 225-35 [in Greek]. The boys are represented on numerous votive reliefs, chiefly of Augustan date.

predated the Lacedaemonian monument, was pressed into use as the victorious Spartans mustered at least 9 sculptors to produce 39 or more monumental bronzes in the late 5th c. B.C. From the original model were taken master molds. These in turn gave birth to working models, where craftsmen introduced those changes which made, on the one hand, the statue of a mature, bearded warrior and, on the other, a youthful ephebic Dioskouros.

However, there are, as I mentioned earlier, differences. Some can be explained as solutions to the technical problem of translating a bronze original into marble, but others are not so easily explained. As already noted, Riace B's right arm is held farther forward than that of Gaius, and it is some 3 mm larger in circumference. A technical analysis of the bronze has shown that Riace's entire right arm was repaired in antiquity, perhaps even in the Roman period, judging by the composition of the metal.[26] Thus, Gaius's arm, held closer to the body, may actually replicate the position of the original, prior to the repair. In addition, Gaius's feet are *c*.2 cm further apart than those of Riace B, and his thighs roughly 2 cm larger in circumference. The slight spreading of the feet and the thickening of the legs may have been adjustments to increase the tensile strength of the marble, as was the addition of the tree trunk support.

There are other differences. Riace B clearly depicts a more mature man: he wears a heavy beard, and his body is physically more developed, although some of the latter may be due to the greater skill of the 5th c. sculptor and the greater flexibility of the medium of bronze. However, this difference in the musculature could easily have been introduced in the working model, to distinguish the bodies of young men from the knotted, matured body of a seasoned soldier.

The attributes, too, differ. The Lepcis statues are clearly identified as Dioskouroi through the addition of horse protomes and *piloi*, while the Corinth statues have an implied association with the Divine Twins. All four statues share the attributes of cloak and probably sword: the hands of Gaius and Lucius are loosely clasped, the opening thus formed having a rectangular profile with rounded corners. One could easily restore the hilt of a sheath or sword. The position of Riace B's right hand suggests he held an object with a rounded profile, although the nature of this object is hotly disputed. On his left arm he held a shield, unlike the Corinth and Lepcis statues. Although their left hands are now missing, their left shoulders and forearms were draped with the rich folds of a cloak, pushed almost casually to one side. For the Roman-period statues, the question is whether the attributes were derived from the original or were introduced by the Roman sculptors. The answer may be, both: the drapery from the original, and the sword from the Roman sculptors.

Although the motif of precarious drapery has often been described as a Roman addition, it is common in late 5th and 4th c. B.C. art, whether vase-painting or sculpture, usually associated with representations of boys and youths as well as youthful heroes and deities, among them the Dioskouroi and Hermes. Numerous Attic grave reliefs, both elegant and humble, show some slight variant on the motif of the quietly standing frontal, nude boy or youth with drapery looped over the left shoulder and arm.[27] The other attributes of the various grave reliefs may provide further clues to the meaning of this drapery: they include pets or implements such as the strigil associated with the gymnasium. No warrior's equipment is associated with these figures, suggesting that these boys and youths were not yet full-fledged soldiers. Instead, the representations imply either a child still at home, in the case of the pets, or a youth undergoing athletic training, with the gymnasium implements. The casualness of the garment, pushed to one side, as if about to be divested in preparation for sport, gives an air of youthful spontaneity and energy to the figures.

Thus, I would suggest that the drapery motif on the Corinth–Lepcis figures may derive from the Greek original. Furthermore, the significance is quite specific: it identifies the Dioskouroi

26 C. C. Mattusch, *Greek bronze statuary* 206.

27 C. W. Clairmont, *Classical Attic tombstones* (Kilchberg 1993).

as very young men, on the verge of manhood, and groups them with other extremely youthful heroes, such as Theseus and Peirithous. These are youths barely out of school, so to speak, and at the very beginning of their careers as full-fledged soldier-citizens. The drapery motif, with its links to the gymnasium, also recalls that, according to legend, the Dioskouroi were skilled athletes: both had been Olympic victors, Castor at boxing and Pollux at the footrace. They were exemplars of youthful *arete*, ideal ephebes.

It is less certain that the sword derives from a Greek original. While pre-Roman representations of the Dioskouroi show a certain preference for the spear over the sword, in the Roman period the sword is more common, with a meaning that may be particularly appropriate to Roman representations.[28] The dedicatory inscription of the Lepcis Magna Theater refers to Annobal Rufus as *ornator patriae amator concordiae*. The inverted sword, common to all four of the Roman statues, and which occurs in many other contexts as well, conveys clearly the notion of victory and *concordia*. An interesting parallel is provided by one of the central figures on the breastplate of the Augustus Prima Porta: a military figure of uncertain identity carries in his left hand an inverted sword, while he extends his right in a gesture of apparent *rapprochement*, or *concordia*, to the Parthian figure holding a Roman standard.[29] Thus, the appearance of the lowered, or cradled, sword in the hands of the Dioskouroi conveys the notion of battle completed, concord or peace achieved — concepts central to Augustan imagery. Perhaps then the sword was actually a Roman addition to the original Greek motif.

In the foregoing, I have attempted to show that Riace B and the original of the Corinth Dioskouros type derived from the same ancestral model, whose offspring were individualized by the variations on the final surfaces and the addition of attributes. Hair and beard styles could be changed, muscles could be knotted or smooth, cloaks could be added or not, but the underlying scheme and measurements would be the same, since all were derived from the same original. The possibility that the Corinth statue portraits of Gaius and Lucius were born from the Dioskouroi by Antiphanes of Argos suggests that their bronze classical relative Riace B is also the product of a 5th c. B.C. Argive workshop.[30] The next, logical question concerns where Riace B stood in antiquity: was it made for the same monument? This does not necessarily follow, since sequences of statues descending from the same model could be created over a number of years and for many different purposes. For the moment, I will be content with attaching it to the workshop of Antiphanes, and leave open the question of its original use.[31] This original model gave birth to a series of bronzes. Centuries later, one of them was used by unknown Attic or Corinthian sculptors to create the statues of the sons of Augustus.

The American School of Classical Studies at Athens

Acknowledgements

I would like to thank warmly the Director of the Corinth Excavations of the American School of Classical Studies, C. K. Williams, II, for permission to work on the portrait sculpture at Corinth, and the excavation's Assistant Director, N. Bookides, for her assistance in obtaining the photographs in figs. 1-4, by I. Ioannidou and L. Bartzioti.

---

28 Lorenz 1976 (supra n.15) 17-27.

29 D. E. E. Kleiner, *Roman sculpture* (New Haven 1992) 63-65, fig. 42, with references to bibliography of the statue and discussion of the identity of the breastplate figures.

30 This theory may find some confirmation in the analysis of its clay core, which closely matches the profile of Argive clay: A. Melucco Vaccaro, "The Riace bronzes. Recent Advances from the 1992-95 intervention," *13th Br. Cong.* In her oral presentation, Melucco Vaccaro also noted substantial technical differences in the construction of the cores for Riace A and B, a further indication that they may be from different workshops. See Melucco Vaccaro, below p p. 124 ff..

31 So far I have not mentioned Riace A. This is because I believe its genealogy may differ from Riace B. Apart from obvious differences in outline and style, the measurements vary — not by much, to be sure, but by more than the difference between Riace B and Gaius — and I believe we have to take these apparently miniscule numbers very seriously. In this, I differ from Mattusch, who believes that both A and B derive from the same original model: Mattusch, *Classical bronzes* 63-64.

Il bronzo A di Riace, una lekythos del Pittore di Achille, ed il problema degli "state burials"

Filippo Giudice

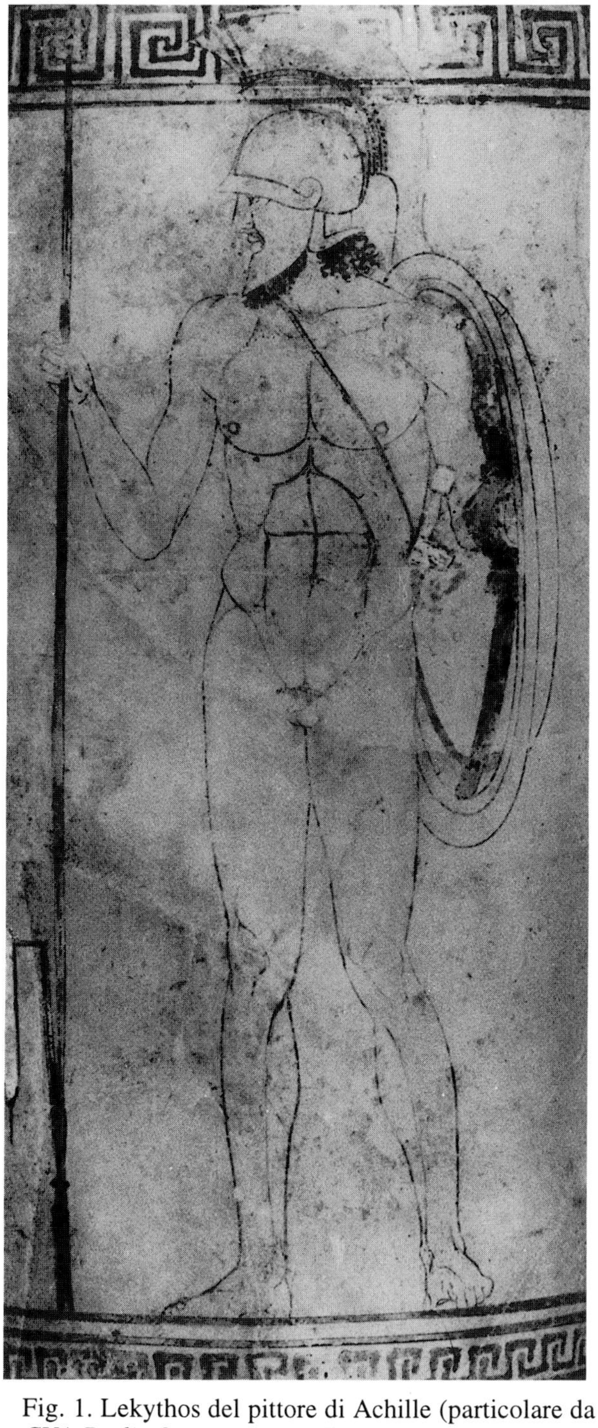

Fig. 1. Lekythos del pittore di Achille (particolare da *CVA Berlin* 8, tav. 14). Berlino, Antikenmuseum.

L'acquisizione recente da parte del museo di Berlino di un vaso attico,[1] proveniente da una collezione privata svizzera (fig. 1), ha finora sottratto alla dovuta attenzione degli studiosi dei bronzi di Riace, rinvenuti nel 1972, un elemento prezioso per l'analisi stilistica ed il loro inquadramento cronologico.[2] Questo "originale" di pittura vascolare del V sec. a.C. suggerisce, in realtà, una serie di spunti e consente di ritornare su alcuni problemi: dalla cronologia, al significato, alla destinazione dei due capolavori. Il dibattito sui due bronzi ha, infatti, utilizzato a confronto in special modo opere di scultura e, conseguentemente , studi ed ipotesi si sono fondati, per la maggior parte, su copie di epoca romana.

Il vaso in questione è una lekythos attica a fondo bianco, attribuita al pittore di Achille, il più giovane allievo del pittore di Berlino.[3]

---

1 *CVA Berlin* 8, 27-28, f. 3055, tavv. 12-14 (qui bibliografia precedente). V. comunque I. Wehgartner, *Ein Grabbild des Achilleusmalers* (Berlin 1985).

2 Per una breve anticipazione, cfr. F. Giudice in *Magna Graecia* 27.5/6 (maggio-giugno 1992) 3-4; id. in *AViva* 12.37 n.s. (1993) 80.

3 Sul pittore di Achille, J. D. Beazley, *Attic red-figure vase-painters* (Oxford 1962) 986-1010, 1661, 1676-77, 1708; id., *Paralipomena* (Oxford 1971) 177, 345, 437-39, 448, 516; G. M. A. Richter, *Attic red-figured vases* (New Haven 1946) 117 ss.; M. Cagiano De Azevedo, s.v., in *EAA* I (1958) 34; E. Paribeni, "Attici vasi," in *EAA Suppl.* 1970 (1973) 114; P. E. Arias, "Attici vasi," in *EAA* II *Suppl. 1971-1994* (1994) 550, fig. 616; R. Olmos Romera, "Contribución al estudio del Pintor de Aquiles en Madrid," *ArchEspA* 49 (1976) 9-29; D. C. Kurtz, *Athenian white lekythoi. Patterns and painters* (Oxford 1975) passim, figg. a pp. 34-37; ead., "Vases for the dead. An Attic selection 750-400 B.C.," in *Ancient Greek and related pottery* (Symposium, Amsterdam 1984; Amsterdam 1985) 314 sgg.; ead., "Mistress and maid," in *La parola, l'immagine, la tomba. Atti del colloquio int. di Capri* (*AnnAStorAnt* 10, 1988) 141-49; ead., "The Achilles Painter's white lekythoi" in *EYMOYSIA. Ceramic and iconographic studies in honour of*

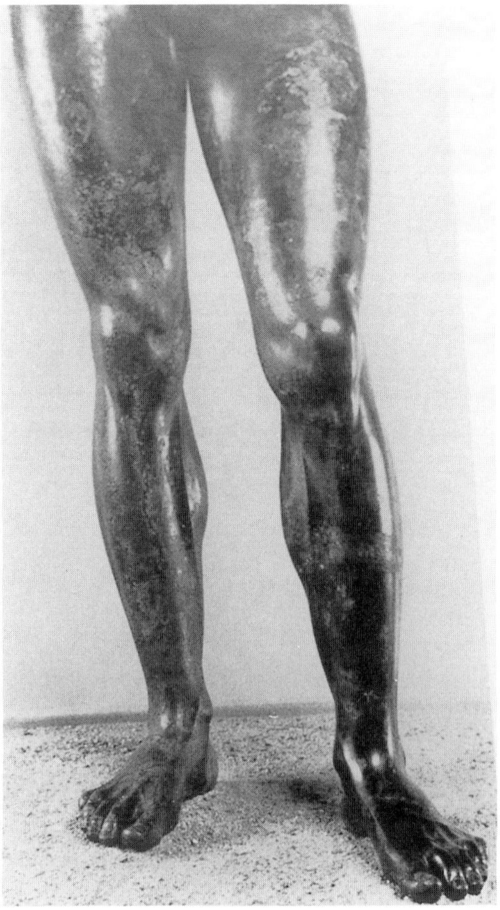

Fig. 2a. Bronzo A da Riace, particolare delle gambe. Reggio Calabria, Museo Nazionale. (da *Due Bronzi* tav. A, 1.)

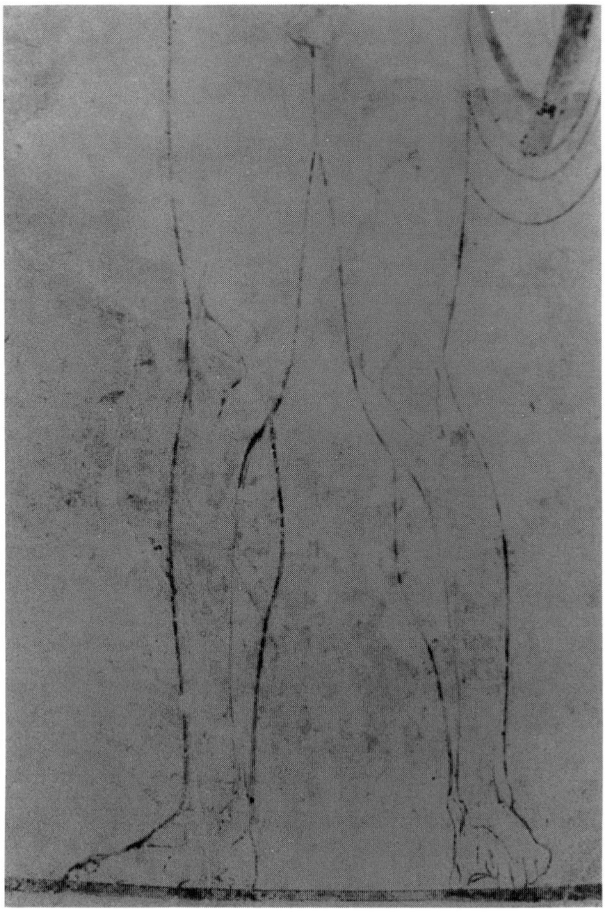

Fig. 2b. Lekythos del pittore di Achille: particolare delle gambe del guerriero. Berlino, Antikenmuseum. (da *CVA Berlin* 8, tav. 14.)

In esso è rappresentata, a lato di una stele, una figura nuda di guerriero stante, il quale calca l'elmo sulla testa, ha una spada al fianco, regge col braccio sinistro un grande scudo e si appoggia con la mano destra ad una lunga asta. La testa è resa di profilo verso destra, il torso è di prospetto, la gamba destra è di profilo, la sinistra è di prospetto. Fatte salve le peculiarità del disegno nei confronti di una scultura a tutto tondo, la figura richiama in maniera sorprendente, tranne che per la posizione del braccio destro, la statua A dei bronzi di Riace, della quale ripete in maniera assolutamente fedele l'anatomia corporea. Alcuni dettagli possono meglio illustrare la vicinanza delle due opere: è possibile confrontare il modo di reggere lo scudo (fig. 5 a-b), che, come è noto, nella statua A è andato perduto, ma che il pittore della nostra lekythos ha probabilmente visto ancora a posto; o, ancora, il rendimento dei muscoli pettorali e addominali (fig. 3 a-b); o la testa (fig. 4 a-b) (ormai senza elmo nel bronzo, con esso nel vaso); o, infine, le gambe della statua modellate leggermente di scorcio, e le stesse appiattite dal nostro pittore sul fondo del vaso, con un piede di profilo e l'altro di prospetto (fig. 2 a-b) (cfr. comunque il rendimento dei polpacci). Un unico elemento differisce nei due "originali": nel bronzo A il guerriero porta in basso il braccio destro, mentre nel vaso egli porta in alto l'avambraccio, reggendo una lancia.

Quali valutazioni, preliminarmente, è possibile dare dell'impressionante somiglianza tra il bronzo A di Riace ed il guerriero berlinese?

È fuori di dubbio che il ceramografo abbia voluto riprodurre sul suo vaso un'opera di scultura. G. M. A. Richter annota:[4]

Alexander Cambitoglou (Sydney 1990) 105-12; v. bibliografia citata in *CVA Berlin* 8, 28 (supra n.1).

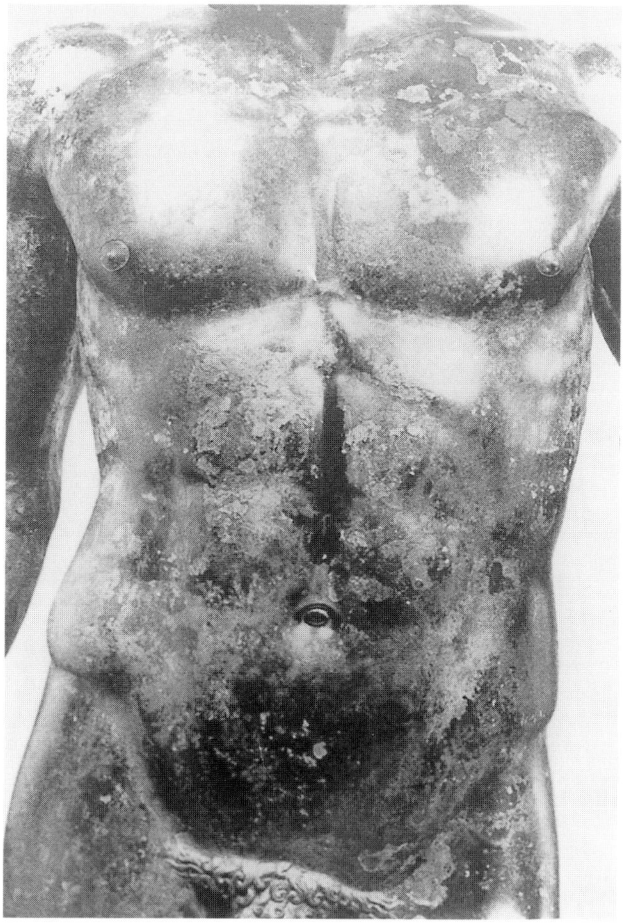

Fig. 3a. Bronzo A da Riace, particolare del torso. Reggio Calabria, Museo Nazionale. (da *Due Bronzi,* tav. A, 1.)

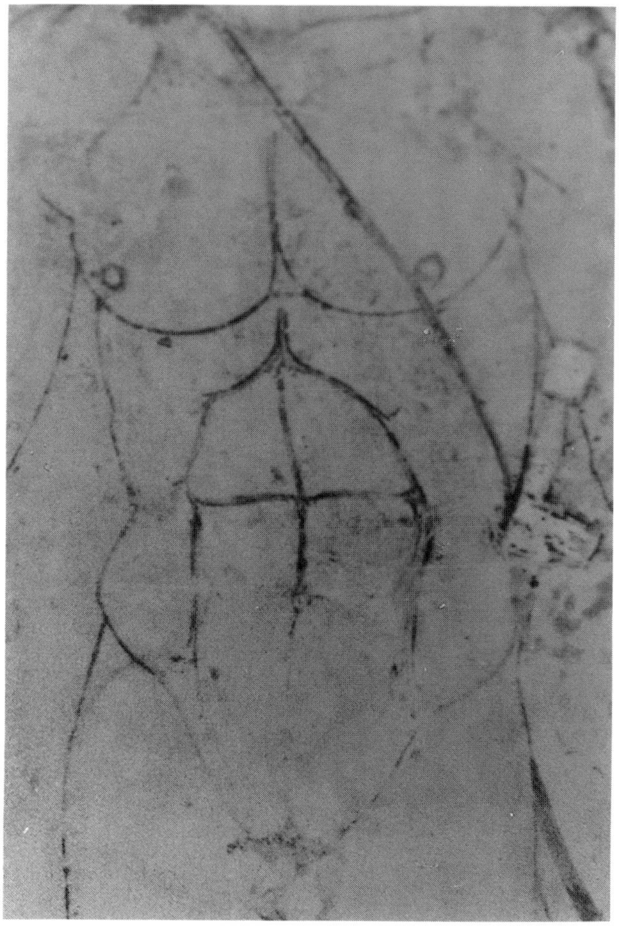

Fig. 3b. Lekythos del pittore di Achille: particolare del torso del guerriero. Berlino, Antikenmuseum. (da *CVA Berlin* 8, tav. 14.)

> In a few instances scenes on vases seem to have been copied from specific figures. Thus the youth mounting his horse, on a pelike in Berlin, strikingly resembles a group on the west side of the Parthenon frieze; and the two youths with a bull, on an oinochoe in Baltimore, may be an adaptation from figures on the south side of the frieze. That sculptures were copied on vases during this period and later is definitely shown by the representations, for instance, of the Tyrannicides on a fragment in Boston ... and of Myron's Athena on an oinochoe in Berlin.

E gli esempi, com'è ampiamente noto, si possono facilmente moltiplicare. Il problema nel caso specifico sta nello stabilire se il pittore di Achille abbia voluto concedersi una "licenza" nel rendimento del braccio destro: avrebbe appeso al fianco sinistro la spada e, all'opposto, avrebbe spostato nel destro la lancia, per una migliore leggibilità del disegno; o, se egli abbia riprodotto una statua "gemella" del bronzo A, non ancora ritrovata. Il dubbio tira in ballo l'altro problema della sede originaria del bronzo prima del trasporto in nave e del successivo naufragio. È noto che tra le ipotesi più accreditate, pur con i vari problemi cronologici connessi, vi sono quelle di una provenienza dei bronzi di Riace dal donario degli Achei ad Olimpia, o da quello di Maratona a Delfi, o dal gruppo degli eroi eponimi nell'Agorà di Atene.[5] Nella lekythos (fig. 1) il guerriero è vicino ad una stele[6] e fa parte chiaramente di un gruppo funerario

---

4 G. M. A. Richter, *Attic red-figured vases* (supra n.3) 117; cf. pure G. Neumann, *Einwirkung der Grossplastik in der Vasenmalerei* (1979).

5 La bibliografia è numerosa. V. specialmente A. Busignani, *Gli eroi di Riace. Daimon e techne* (Firenze 1981); G. Foti e C. Sabbione, *I bronzi di Riace* (Novara 1981); G. Foti e F. Nicosia, *I bronzi di Riace* (Firenze 1981); A. Giuliano, "I grandi bronzi di Riace," *Xenia* 2 (1981) 55-62; id., "I grandi bronzi di Riace. II," *Xenia* 3 (1982) 41-46; id., "I grandi bronzi di Riace. III," *Xenia* 5 (1983) 5-6; v. pure W. Fuchs,

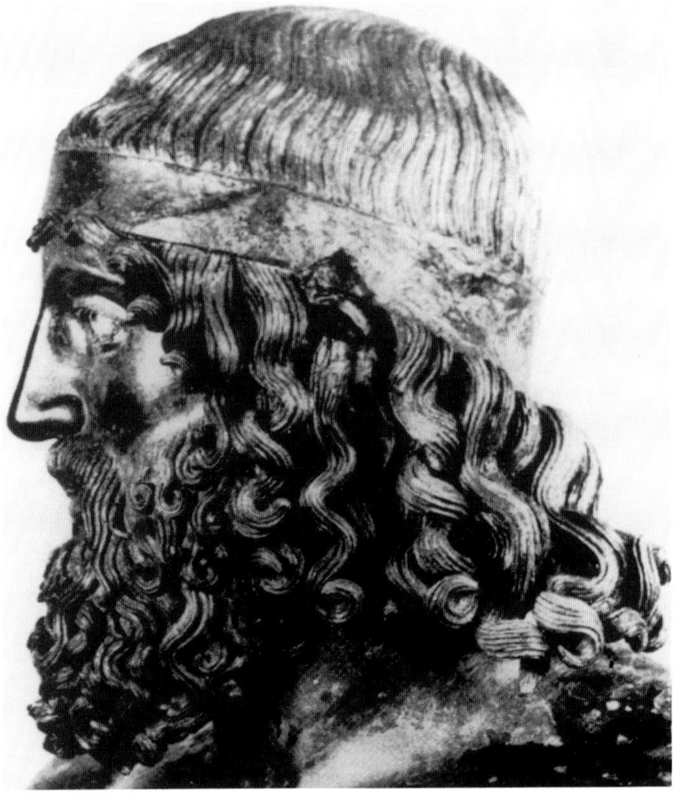

Fig. 4a. Bronzo A da Riace , particolare della testa. Reggio Calabria, Museo Nazionale. (da *Due Bronzi* tav. A, 2.)

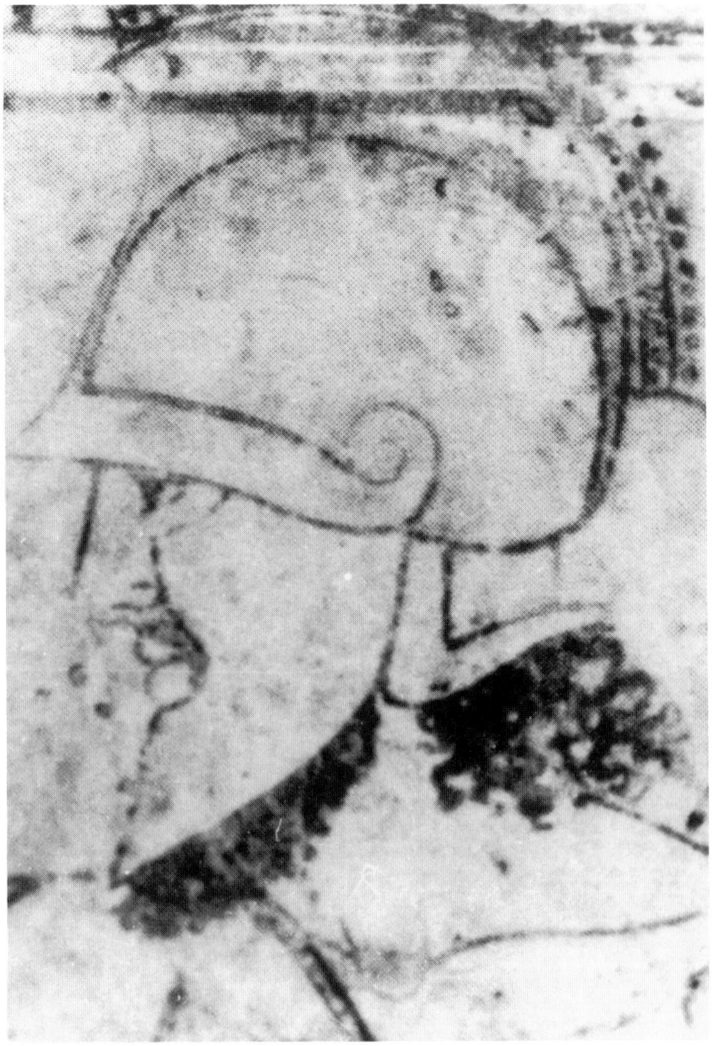

Fig. 4b. Lekythos del pittore di Achille: particolare della testa del guerriero. Berlino, Antikenmuseum. (da *CVA Berlin* 8, tav. 14.)

(a destra della stessa è un vecchio): ci si chiede, allora, fino a che punto il pittore abbia innovato e variato rispetto a quello che ha visto. La risposta evidentemente non è facile e bisogna rivedere tutta la questione. Un elemento tuttavia mi sembra definitivamente accertato: un "originale" del pittore di Achille, chiaramente ispirato al bronzo A, pone questo prima del 450 a.C. e liquida ogni ipotesi di una datazione successiva alla metà del V sec. a.C.[7]

"Zu den Großbronzen von Riace," *Boreas* 4 (1981) 25-28; id., "Zu den Großbronzen von Riace," in *Praestant Interna. Festschrift für U. Hausmann* (Tübingen 1982) 34 ss.; E. B. Harrison, "Early Classical sculpture: the bold style," in C. G. Boulter (ed.), *Greek art. Archaic into Classical* (Leiden 1985) 40 ss. (spec. p. 50 ss.); C. O. Pavese, "Interpretazione dei bronzi di Riace," *StClOr* 32 (1982) 13-58; H. P. Isler, "Die Bronzekrieger von Riace," *AW* 14 (1983) 3-6 (qui altra bibliografia); L. M. Lombardi Satriani e M. Paoletti (a cura di), *Gli eroi venuti dal mare* (Roma–Reggio Calabria 1986); AA.VV., *Due bronzi* (qui rassegna bibliografica a cura di L. De Lachenal e M. A. Rizzo); Rolley, *Die griechischen Bronzen* 36 ss.; O. R. Deubner, "Die Bronzen von Riace. Versuch einer Deutung und Kunsthistorischen Zuordnung," in *Πρακτικα του XII Διεθνους Συνεδριου Κλασσικης Αρχαιολογιας, Αθηναι 4-10 Sept. 1983* (Athens 1988) 74-78; G. Dontas, "Some remarks on the bronze statues of Riace Marina," ibid. 89-96; W. Fuchs, "Thesen zu den Riace-Statuen," ibid. 97-98; Mattusch, *Greek bronze statuary* passim.

6 Sulle stele nelle lekythoi a fondo bianco, v. I. Baldassarre, "Tomba e stele nelle lekythoi a fondo bianco," in *La parola, l'immagine, la tomba* (supra n.3) 107-15.

7 Per i bronzi di Riace ritenuti "classicizing creations" cf. specialmente B. S. Ridgway, *Fifth century styles*

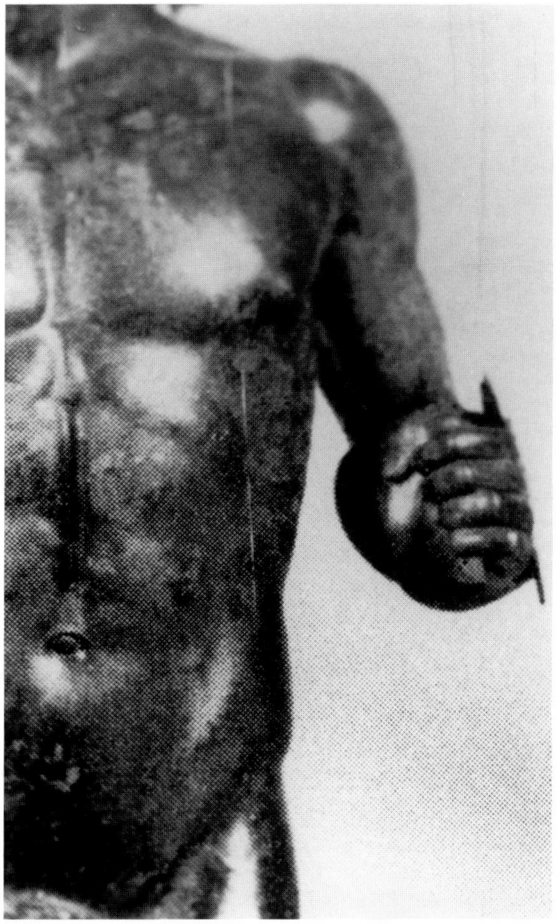

Fig. 5a. Bronzo A da Riace, particolare del torso e del braccio sinistro. Reggio Calabria, Museo Nazionale. (da *Due Bronzi*, tav. A, 1.)

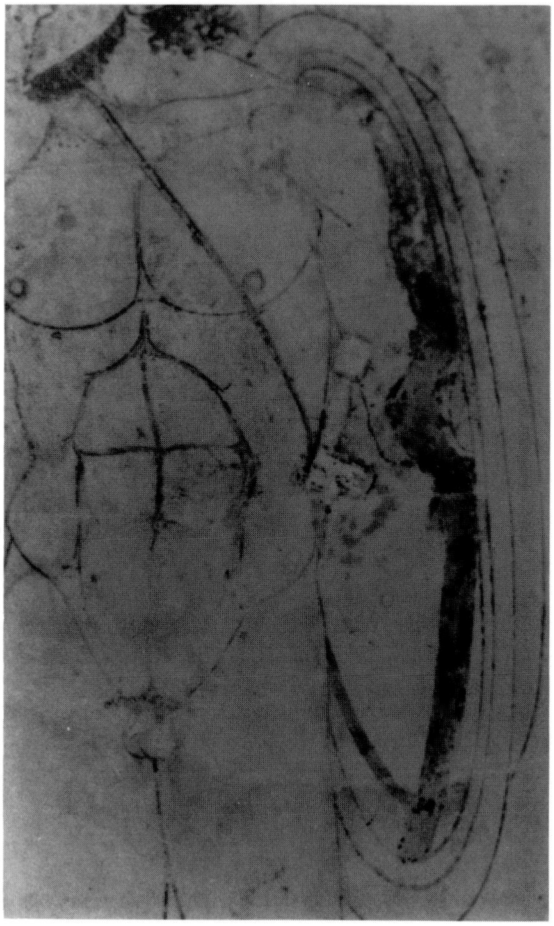

Fig. 5b. Lekythos del pittore di Achille: particolare del torso e del braccio sinistro del guerriero. Berlino, Antikenmuseum. (da *CVA Berlin* 8, tav. 14.)

A questo punto, per una comprensione migliore del problema del rapporto pittore di Achille-Bronzo A di Riace, vale la pena di riflettere sulla produzione di questo ceramografo.[8] Egli è definito dal Beazley "pupil of the Berlin Painter towards the end of the older artist's career" e, ancora

> he is the great master of white lekythos. His red-figure vases nearly always have a sober beauty, but few of them — like the pointed amphora in the Cabinet of Médailles — reach the height of his best white lekythoi, which are among the masterpieces of ancient drawing.

Un pittore di lekythoi di alta qualità, quindi, la cui produzione può essere inquadrata con le parole di D. C. Kurtz:

> More than 200 of his vases have been preserved; half are red-figure and half white-ground. The shapes of the former are varied but the white-ground are all cylindrical lekythoi. The earliest were made around 460, the latest not long after 440. All but a few of the very latest use lustrous golden paint for the outlines of the patterns and figures.

E , ancora,

> 76% of them have feminine scenes ... On 7% a male is substituted for one of the females, in the same environment, and on the remaining 17% a tombstone is introduced, usually between two persons of the same sex, who are often female and look as if they have been lifted from the domestic scene

---

in Greek sculpture (Princeton 1981) 237-38; v. pure C. Houser, "The Riace Marine bronze statues, Classical or classicizing" in *Source notes in the history of art* I, n.3, 5-11.

8 Cfr. J. D. Beazley, ARV^2 (supra n.3), 986-1010, 1661, 1676-77, 1708; id., *Paralipomena* 177, 345, 347-49, 448, 516; *Beazley addenda. Additional references to ABV,* ARV^2, and *Paralipomena* (2nd edn. compiled by T. H. Carpenter; Oxford 1989) 106, 311.

> without change. The lekythoi with tombstones are mature to late works by the painter, and their iconography has been influenced by the fashion, already well established among other lekythos painters, for iconography appropriate to the funerary function of the vase.[9]

Tralasciando tutti i vasi senza la figura del guerriero, non possiamo non segnalare che finora in tutte le lekythoi a fondo bianco il guerriero si accompagna ad una figura femminile, mentre nel nostro vaso egli è visitato dal vecchio padre, come se il ceramografo avesse voluto sottolineare una sua diversa collocazione nel contesto sociale, essendo morto ancor prima del matrimonio. Ma l'elemento che stupisce e pone un interessante interrogativo è quello della "posizione statuaria del guerriero" che presuppone un modello scultoreo e non una figura vivente, diversamente dagli altri guerrieri dipinti dal pittore. Una spiegazione può essere trovata nella particolare situazione della società del tempo alla ricerca di nuovi modelli iconografici, nel momento in cui le leggi suntuarie sembrano avere proibito l'erezione di statue. Bisognerebbe dire, parafrasando J. Bažant:

> C'est ansi que, dans le deuxième quart du Ve s. av. J.-C., une tradition iconographique fut créé, tradition qui devait connaître un développement prodigieux dans la seconde moitié de ce même siècle. ... Mais [aggiunge Bažant] il fallait que le défunt fut représenté sous tous ses aspects, et non pas seulement comme héros immortel. Le public athénien voulait que l'identité du mort reste ambiguë ... Néanmoins, les peintres parvinrent à un compromis: le défunt est tantôt un héros, tantôt un revenant qui se lamente sur son sort (ou tous les deux à la fois).[10]

Percorrendo questa intuizione di J. Bažant, la nostra lekythos svela il messaggio che vuole esprimere: nel momento in cui le leggi suntuarie proibiscono agli Ateniesi di innalzare statue, e di interrompere quindi la serie della statuaria privata a tutto tondo, e nel momento in cui la lekythos dipinta a fondo bianco con la stele al centro del corpo si afferma come il messaggio più immediato per affermare la nuova ideologia funeraria, il pittore vascolare — o la committenza più avveduta che per la prima volta deve inventarsi una "nuova iconografia" — rivolge la propria attenzione alla statuaria esistente, realizzando in questa maniera una nuova sintesi tra ideologia aristocratica, legata alla statuaria, e legge democratica che ne impediva la realizzazione nel bronzo o nel marmo: sulla persistenza di questa ideologia trova spiegazione il frammento di Boston con la rappresentazione dei Tirannicidi trovato nel recinto funerario di Dexileos! [11]

Ma — ed è questo l'altro problema — dobbiamo immaginare il vuoto assoluto nella scultura funeraria, per cui i ceramografi potevano ispirarsi solo a statue non funerarie? È questo il pensiero di R. Stupperich[12] per il quale "all the evidence points to the fact that state burials, until the time when private grave stelai were reintroduced, were left as simple as the private burial precincts." Oppure, al contrario, dobbiamo pensare che le leggi suntuarie risparmiassero le tombe di stato — necessariamente non numerose e per questo pervenute a noi in scarso numero

---

9 D. C. Kurtz, *Mistress and maid* (supra n.3) 145. V. pure ead., *Athenian white lekythoi* (supra n.3) 51; R. Garland, *The Greek way of death* (Ithaca 1985) 108, 166.

10 J. Bažant, "Entre la croyance et l'expérience: la mort sur les lécythes à fond blanc," *in Iconographie classique et identités régionales, Paris 26 et 27 mai 1983* (BCH suppl. 14) 42.

11 Cf. G. M. A. Richter, *Attic red-figured vases* (supra n.4) 117, 141 ss.

12 R. Stupperich, "The iconography of Athenian state burial in the Classical period," in *The archaeology of Athens and Attica under the democracy* (Proceedings of an International Conference, December 4-6, Athens 1992) 100; v. pure id., *Staatsbegräbnis und Privatgrabmal im klassischen Athen* (Diss. Münster 1977); e, ancora, M. Collignon, *Les statues funéraires dans l'art grec* (Paris 1911); D. C. Kurtz e J. Boardman, *Greek burial customs* (London 1971) 135 ("We have no clear material evidence for the funerary use of free-standing statues of men. There is, however, reason to believe that there were such memorials; indeed Pausanias describes them"); C. W. Clairmont, *Patrios nomos* (BAR Int. Ser. 161, Oxford 1983) (v. specialmente p. 62 ss; 74 ss.); v. pure U. Koehler, "Eine griechisches Gesetz über Todtenbestattung," *AthMitt* 1 (1876) 139 ss.; K. Kübler, "Der attische Grabbau," *AthMitt* 22 (1949) 7-22; A. D. Nock, "The cult of heroes" in *Essays on religion and the ancient world* 2 (Oxford 1972) 593 ss.; E. Pottier, *Etude sur les lékythes blancs attiques à représentations funéraires* (Paris 1963).

— per il cui ornamento continuarono ad essere prodotte statue o gruppi a tutto tondo?: lo stesso Pausania (1.29) ne cita lungo la via verso l'Accademia; o possono pur anche avallare questa ipotesi i frammenti di statue a tutto tondo rinvenute nel Ceramico e databili durante il periodo dello stile severo e protoclassico?

In realtà, la lekythos di Berlino con una statua di guerriero a fianco di una stele riapre il problema dell'esistenza di statue funerarie pubbliche innalzate in onore degli eroi caduti, e questo in parallelo con le statue dedicate nei donari come quello di Maratona a Delfi, o nella stessa Agorà di Atene. I bronzi di Riace potrebbero far parte dei gruppi destinati ad ornare questi "State burials", ed i ceramografi poterono riprodurre sui vasi questi gruppi funerari, riuscendo in tale modo a conciliare il vecchio ideale eroico aristocratico e la nuova dura legge democratica.[13]

Istituto di Archeologia, Università di Catania

---

13 Per il problema generale v. J.-P. Vernant, "L'idéologie de la mort héroïque," in G. Gnoli and J.-P. Vernant (edd.), *L'idéologie funéraire. La mort, les morts dans les sociétés anciennes* (Cambridge 1982) 14-15; S. C. Humphreys, "*Patrios nomos*: state burial in Athens and the public cemetery in the Kerameikos," *JHS* 64 (1944) 37-66; S. Humphreys, "Family tombs and tomb cult in ancient Athens: tradition or traditionalism," *JHS* 110 (1980) 96 ss.; A. M. D'Onofrio, "Aspetti e problemi del monumento funerario attico arcaico," in *La parola, l'immagine, la tomba* (supra n.3) 83 ss.

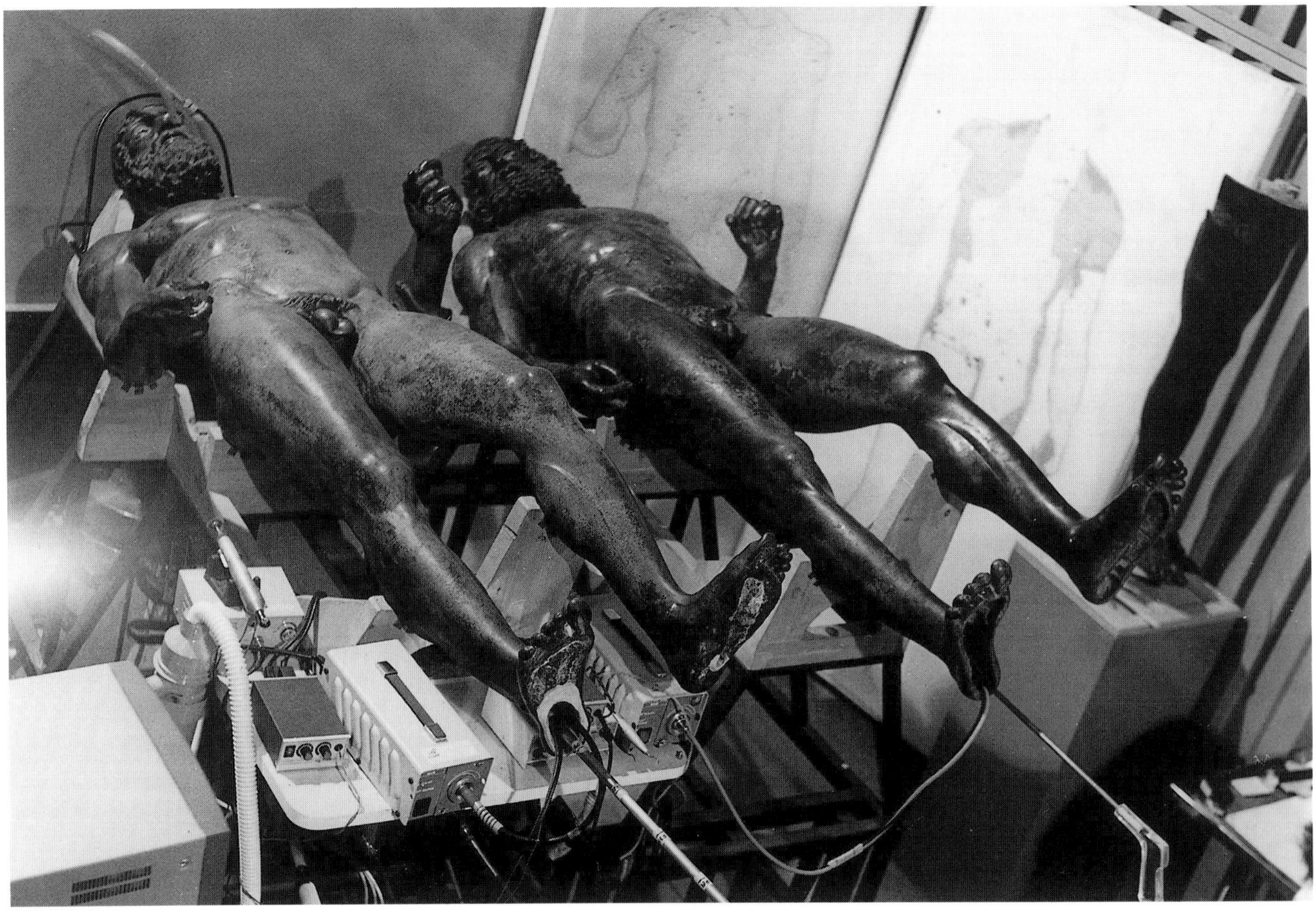

Fig. 1. View of the laboratory in the Reggio Calabria National Museum during the 1992–95 intervention.

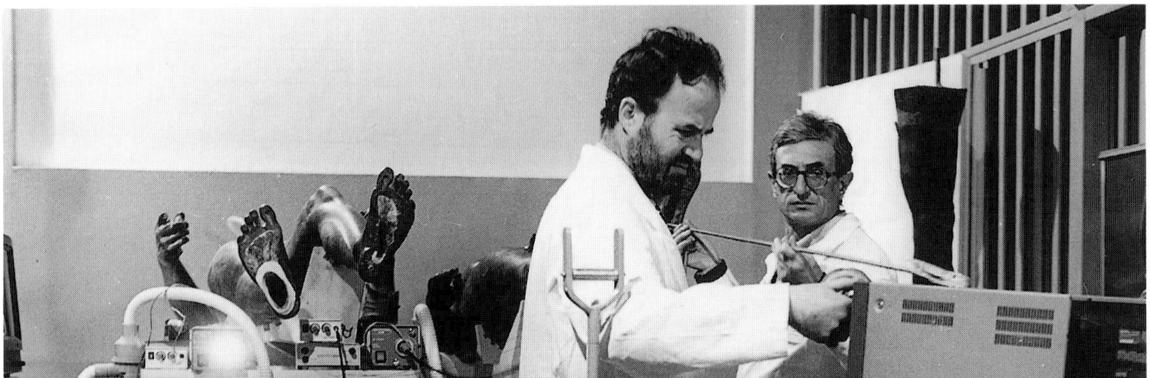

Fig. 2. View of the laboratory in the Reggio Calabria National Museum during the 1992–95 intervention. (Both photos: FINMECCANICA.)

The Riace bronzes 20 years later: recent advances after the 1992-95 intervention

Alessandra Melucco Vaccaro

The two famous bronze statues were found in 1972 in the Ionian Sea off the coast of Calabria, sent to the Center for Restoration of the Soprintendenza Archeologica located in Florence, and then displayed to the public in 1981.[1] Since then, the statues have been on view in the Museo Nazionale in Reggio Calabria. In the period from 1992 to 1995, the statues underwent a complete new treatment, carried out in full view of the public, by M. Micheli, M. Vidale, and the staff of the Istituto Centrale del Restauro of Rome and of the Soprintendenza Archeologica di Reggio Calabria, guided by the author and G. De Palma.[2]

The starting point of the intervention was the problem that was not solved in the laboratories of Florence: the statues had not been emptied, and inside them was still a great amount of clay core material that was impregnated with salts since the statues had been in the water for many centuries. The clay had to be removed because salt is highly damaging to the conservation of bronze. However, in consideration of the exceptionally fine condition of the two bronzes and the absence of lacunae, the mechanical and chemical instruments used to drain them in the course of the first restoration had not removed all of the clay.[3]

The Istituto Centrale del Restauro instituted a new study in 1992, using endoscopes for the first time to examine the interior of each body. Having surveyed the interiors of the statues, a project was designed for removing the clay cores by means of equipment used in laparoscopic surgery. At the end of an articulated arm that can go all the way inside the interior was attached a microcamera,[4] for viewing and recording images, and the instruments necessary not only to remove the clay nucleus but also to perform all the remaining operations — sampling, mechanical cleaning of the interiors, and application of anti-corrosion treatments.

This report will deal generally with the technical and conservation aspects of the intervention but in particular with the evidence for casting procedures. In fact, a discovery was made that suggests a new approach to the study of classical bronze statuary production.

While observing the images of the interior, we noticed that the core was not a shapeless and undifferentiated mass. It was formed in thin layers, whose thickness and particle size decreased from the interior to the exterior (figs. 3-10). The presence of such layers of core, and the opportunity for the first time to carry out a thorough examination of the interiors of the statues, all required a strategy different from the one originally planned. Because the cores of ancient bronze statues have generally been destroyed or disregarded during restoration, the idea of simply removing the core mechanically was immediately abandoned. The project was reshaped and a stratigraphic micro-excavation inside the statues was carried out, operating as far as possible, in this unusual situation, like an archaeological field excavation. Evidence about the inside walls and casting clays was charted and recorded by means of cross sections, and stratigraphic charts were plotted. These charts, together with video documentation, allowed us to locate precisely every element taken from the interior.

The quantity and the speed of removal of materials and the images recorded by microcamera required the creation of an excavation logbook, the main features of which can be summarized by some figures: 60 kg of clay core were extracted from B, and a little less from A; 1,200

1 *Due bronzi*; review by J. Marcadé, *RA* 1986.1, 89-99; A. Giuliano, *L'arte greca* 2 (Milan 1987) 677-78; Rolley, *Die griechischen Bronzen* 37-40.

2 The intervention was possible thanks to the financial and technological support of FINMECCANICA.

3 E. Formigli, in *Due bronzi* figs. 52-55.

4 This was a Toshiba Microcamera.

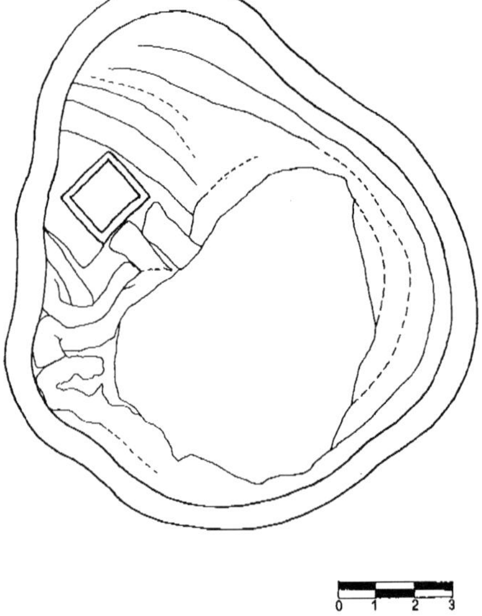

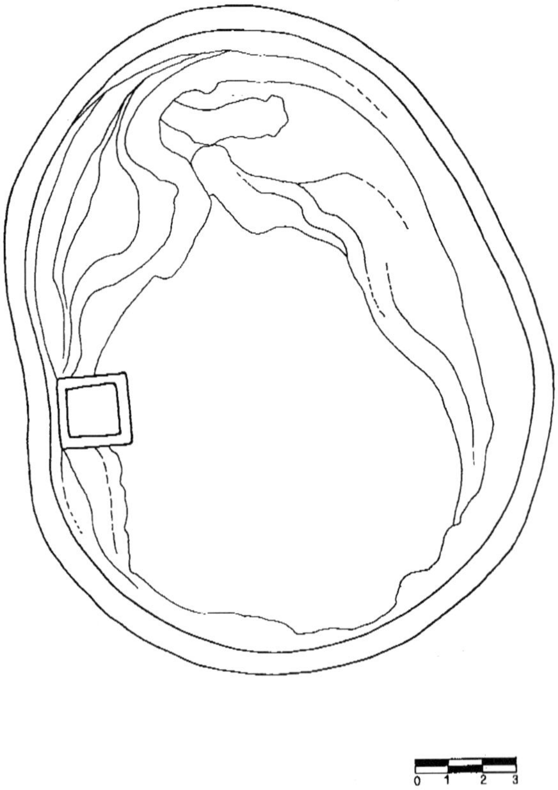

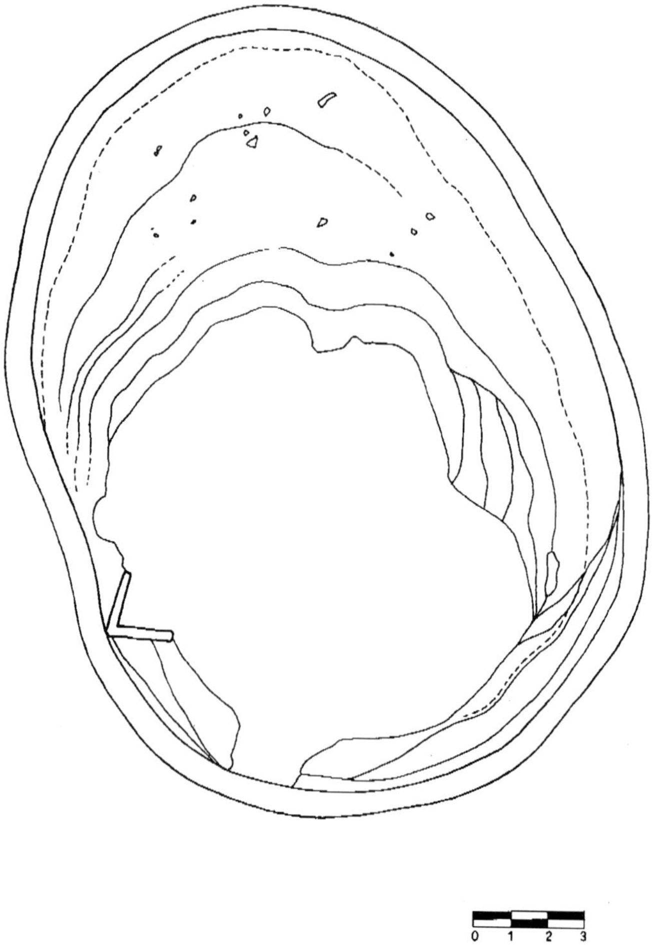

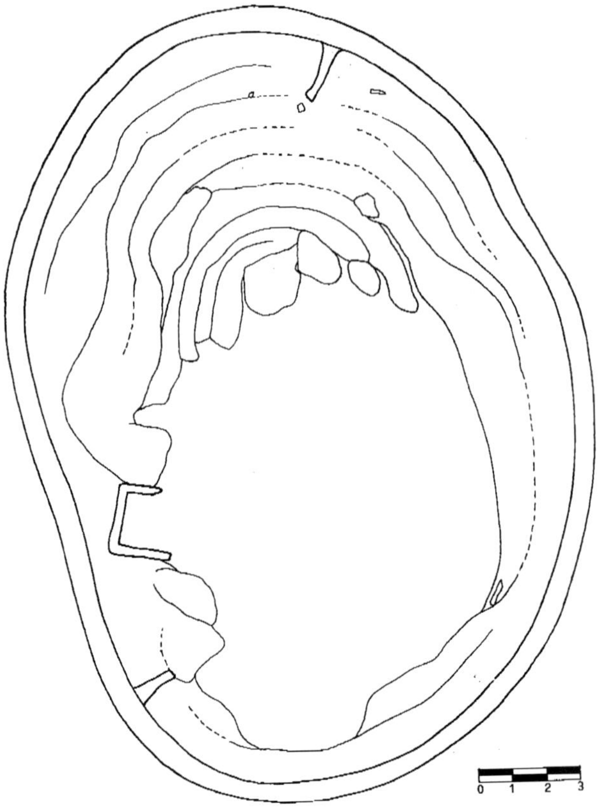

Fig. 3 (top left). Riace A, right leg, cross section 55 cm above the heel. Fig. 4 (top right). Riace A, right leg, cross section 70 cm above the heel. Fig. 5 (lower left). Riace A, right leg, cross section 75 cm above the heel. Fig. 6 (lower right). Riace A, right leg, cross section 80 cm above the heel. (All photos: Istituto Centrale del Restauro.)

stratigraphical units, data points from 80 cross sections, and 1,400 digital images charted all activities and the evidence collected during micro-excavation.

So far, great differences have emerged in the core clays from the two statues, confirming previous remarks mainly from German scholars,[5] and providing further support to the thesis of different chronology, different style, and different workshop for the two bronzes. Bronze B's construction (figs. 7-10) was considerably more elaborate compared to A (figs. 3-6), and is characterized by a great number of thin, strongly separated layers, reinforced by animal hair. This leads us to postulate rather long drying periods between one step and the next. In addition, particle size tends to decrease from inside to outside, and the outermost layer consists of a fine clay slip, like a sort of 'skin,' an extremely refined and accurate finishing surface. In comparison, the layers in A are less evident and not so clearly separated, as if between the spreading of one layer and the next not so much time had elapsed.[6]

On the basis of this exceptional documentation, we put forward the hypothesis that the Riace bronzes were produced by the direct instead of the indirect process.

To date, scholarly opinion has held that great Classical bronze statuary was at first produced by the so-called direct process,[7] which consists in applying wax directly to a freehand-shaped model. A significant change is supposed to have taken place during the first quarter of the 5th c. B.C., when this process was replaced by the indirect lost-wax casting process. This used a negative intermediate or master mold, taken from the original artist's model and then lined with wax. After that, the casting clays were poured into the wax-lined mold in a semi-liquid state ("sciacquo") by agitating, or spread in a solid state, applying it in the separate, hollow wax-lined molds that later were joined. The introduction of iron supports through the clay was considered, according to the current interpretation, to be one of the last operations.[8] This important technical improvement, the indirect method, aimed at preventing the original freehand model by the sculptor from being destroyed by accidents during casting procedures, was argued to be at the basis of the rise in the social rôle of bronzecasters, clearly attested by historical and figurative sources in Late Archaic times.[9]

The main argument in favor of this reconstruction of casting sequences was the supposition that the core was shapeless, the result of pouring and agitating.

The structure of the Riace bronzes' cores, as our exploration and excavation of the interiors can demonstrate, is characterized by a surprisingly careful stratification of great sophistication. In the legs of both statues the structure consists of clearly concentric components built up around the iron support. This is a squared sheet of metal with a wooden core, very like the *kanabos* mentioned by Pollux, *Onomastikon* 10.189, providing the support around which the model was hand-shaped.[10] In the remaining parts of the core, mostly in the chest, which had already been removed by ancient bronzecasters, there are traces of the same complex stratification. "Sciacquo" is out of the question in the Riace statues, and there are no traces of joints.[11] It is

---

5 E. Formigli and G. Schneider, "Antiche terre di fusione," *Officine* 1993, 69-102.

6 As for the contribution that archaeometric characterization of casting clays can give to the question of the place of origin of our bronzes, G. Lombardi has stressed that Sicily, Calabria, and the Cycladic Islands are out of the question; see forthcoming.

7 For a recent summary, see E. Formigli, s.v. "Bronzo," in *EAA, II Suppl.* (1971-94) 738-44. For a view radically opposed to the one here discussed, see Haynes, *Technique*. For a more nuanced attitude, see Bol, *Bronzetechnik* (and review by C. Rolley, *RA* 1988.2, 340-43; W.-D. Heilmeyer, "Il progresso tecnico nella fusione dei bronzi di età classica," *Officine* (1993) 13-26.

8 The following stages, identical in the two processes, consist in creating the exterior refractory shell or mantle and in placing vents for wax and gases and gates for molten metal. For a summary with careful graphic reconstruction, see Mattusch, *Greek bronze statuary* 22-23.

9 Heilmeyer 1993 (supra n. 7) 25.

10 Zimmer, *Bronzegußwerkstätten* 129-31.

11 For joints in the Samian Youth, see W.-D. Heilmeyer, "Neue Untersuchungen am Jungling von Salamis," *Archäologische Bronzen* 137-38.

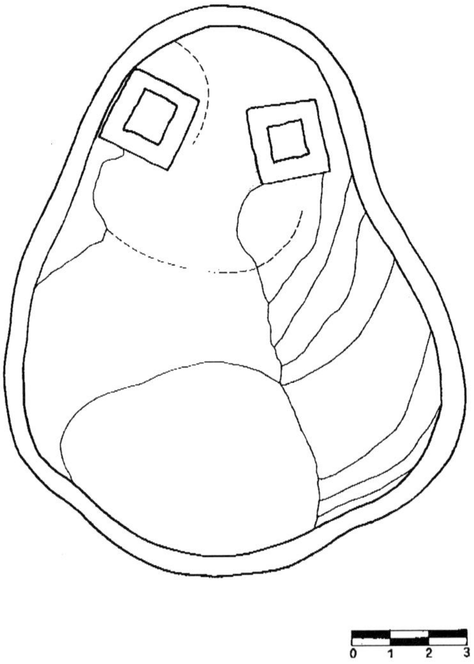

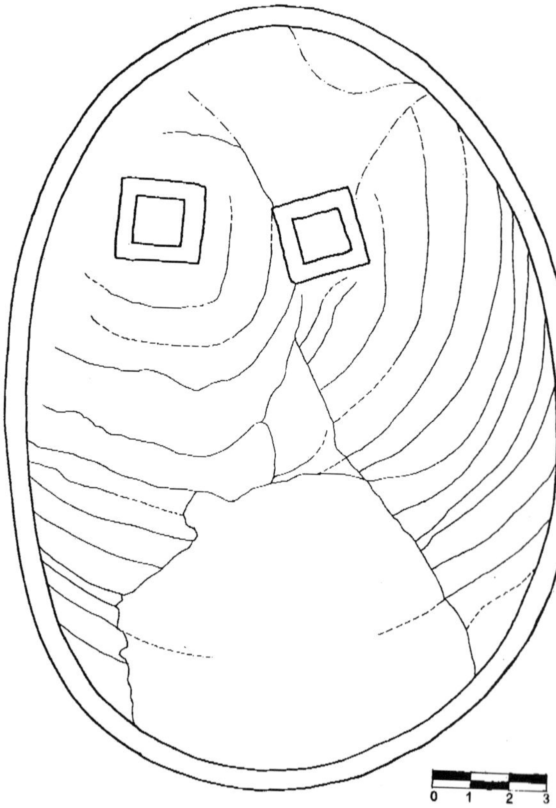

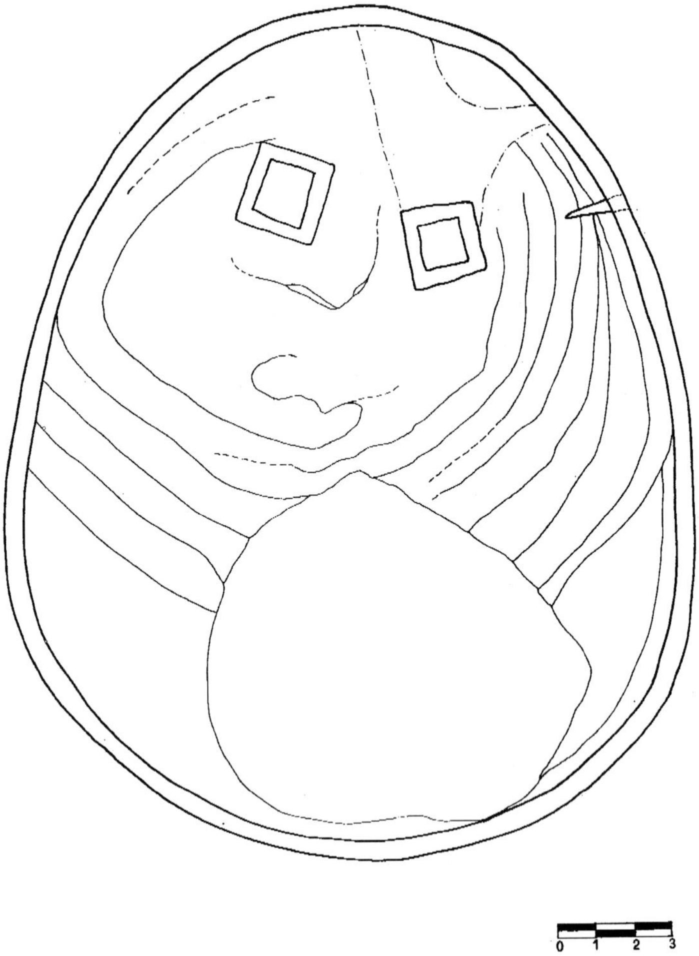

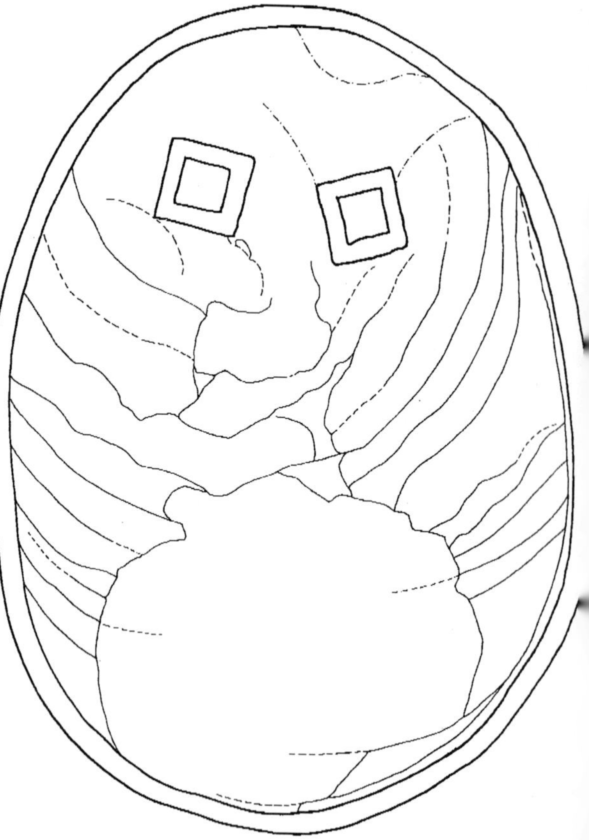

Fig. 7 (top left). Riace B, right leg, cross section 55 cm above the heel. Fig. 8 (top right). Riace B, right leg, cross section 70 cm above the heel. Fig. 9 (lower right). Riace B, right leg, cross section 75 cm above the heel. Fig. 10 (lower left). Riace B, right leg, cross section 80 cm above the heel. (All photos: Istituto Centrale del Restauro.)

impossible that the iron support was inserted in the core later: on the contrary, it was ascertained during micro-excavation that the clay layers wind themselves around the support; hence, it provides initial support, just as bone supports muscle.

This organic construction corresponds well with the classical conception of art as *techné*.[12] It is a unified process, characterised by a harmony between aesthetic result and handworking skills, the reason, we believe, that Pliny said, *sed aemulatio et in materia fuit* (*NH* 34.9), referring to the well-known rivalry between Myron and Polyclitus.[13] It explains why Plutarch, referring to the great bronze artist Polyclitus, said that the pivotal moment of the artistic work is "when clay is in the fingernail" (*Quaest. Conv.* 2.3.2), a passage to be understood in a quite literal sense. [14]

In our laboratory we have simulated the construction stages of a leg, by wrapping clay slabs of decreasing thicknesses — 'lasagne' according to the culinary terminology of Benvenuto Cellini — around an iron support. This clay model does not have the same dimensions and texture as the final bronze: we called it the 'thin model' because it would not reach its final dimensions until the wax panels were added, creating every detail of the surface.[15]

We can now refute Haynes's belief that the direct process was never used to fashion the main parts of statues in Classical Greece, because it was impossible that the clay model, already covered by wax, could be cut into as many sections as were needed for casting.[16] On the contrary, it is possible that different parts of the freehand-shaped model were executed separately. Inside Bronzes A and B we found evidence of reinforcement points, corresponding to the structure's critical sections, particularly the pelvis. We also found traces of systems for attaching, or detaching, the limbs. This raises the possibility that the construction of the statues did not take place in a single step, but rather that the statues were assembled and disassembled several times and that the different portions were cast in pieces. In the case of the Athena Promachos, for instance, which was 9 m high, we wonder whether the clay model (however created) was ever wholly assembled and erected.[17]

Here we focus on the difference between the two processes — the direct and the indirect —that is not simply a technical improvement because it concerns the relationship (a very complex one) between the sculptor and the bronzecaster and is based on the rôle of the model. The clay model[18] was so important that an oinochoe in Berlin (dating to 470 B.C., the same cultural period as Bronze A) shows Athena Ergane herself shaping a horse in clay.[19] This also demonstrates the important role that was played by clay sculpture, the mother of all artistic skills and techniques.[20]

The beginning of the 5th c. seems too early for the change from the direct to the indirect process.[21] A way to reproduce the original model mechanically with an intermediate wax

---

12 R. Bianchi Bandinelli, *Storicità dell'arte classica* (Firenze, 2nd edn. 1950) 5.

13 For commentary, see G. Zimmer, "Die Quellen," *Archäologische Bronzen* 38-39.

14 Ibid. 43-44. The first to approach this passage archaeologically was E. Pernice, "Untersuchungen zur antiken Toreutik," *ÖJh* 1904, 179.

15 Our experimentation thus asserts that the relationship between thin and regular bronze walls and the indirect method in classical times is pure prejudice, *contra* Heilmeyer 1993 (supra n.7) 20 ff.; Haynes, *Technique* 34; Mattusch, *Greek bronze statuary* 158.

16 Haynes, *Technique* 24-33, 34-38.

17 Zimmer, *Bronzegußwerkstätten* 129-30.

18 The use of sand and plaster is not proved by the archaeological evidence: Zimmer, *Bronzeguß-werkstätten* 127-28.

19 Zimmer acknowledges the horse as a model for casting (ibid.).

20 The freehand-shaped model embodies this link; Pasiteles in particular said *plasticen matrem caelaturae et statuariae scalpturaeque* (Pliny, *NH* 35.156).

21 M. Torelli, "Roman arts, 43 B.C. to 69 A.D," in *CAH* 10 (1996) 940-42. It serves no purpose to support the current hypothesis to recall that molding was a technical advance in use as early as the 7th c. B.C.

working model does not fit the cultural climate of the Late Severe and High Classical periods. This important innovation seems much more suited to satisfy the need — typical of later periods — for quick molding and re-molding of a cast. We suppose that this important change could have taken place in the 4th c. Therefore, it is not a mere coincidence that Pliny (*NH* 35.153-54), referring to Lysimachus, Lysippus's brother, recalls his *inventio*: a manner of portraying that, in order to achieve maximum realism, availed itself of wax casts — molded on the model's face — which were then re-molded. Pliny adds, in a very controversial passage, that this invention (i.e., the use of casting) had become so widespread that no statue was made without the use of clay (whether a clay mould, or the clay of the three-dimensional model, remains the question).

Particularly in the Neo-Attic age, and throughout the Roman Imperial period, the rôle played by clay molding increased both in clay sculpture and in bronzecasting, as is proven by ancient authors.[22] This had the purpose of developing and reproducing original works chosen from lists of selected masterpieces, as is clearly shown by the plaster molds from Baiae.[23]

Ancient sources do not provide us with full descriptions of the process of ancient bronze-casting, as has been underlined by G. Zimmer to whom we are indebted for an excellent commentary on the few passages concerning this technique. Therefore, most of the technical steps proposed, which postulate use of the indirect technique, have not been deduced from ancient texts but from post-classical authors. The latter range from Biringuccio to the well-known "The casting of Perseus" by B. Cellini, not to mention the brief introductory pages preceding G. Vasari's *Lives*, and current casting techniques.[24]

Archaeological evidence about casting techniques is far from conclusive, as C. C. Mattusch has underlined,[25] and the relationship between the study of ancient techniques and archaeology has very seldom been set in correct terms, being too often permeated by the spirit of the engineer rather than by history, as Zimmer has rightly stressed.[26] The scientific excavation and study of casting pits is a recent development, but fragments yielded by such excavations are generally parts off the clay mantle (outer refractory shell), which was broken and discarded on the spot, at the end of the casting process. The finds recovered from a casting pit in the Agora, which included not only the outer shell but also two series of negative imprints of an Archaic kouros's head, have been interpreted by Mattusch as testifying to the indirect process, whereas P. C. Bol has seen them as proof of the direct process.[27]

While on the outer surfaces of ancient bronzes earlier technical steps have been erased by extremely refined polishing and finishing, data concerning the important internal surface have

---

for griffin protomes or other serial objects, as is stressed by C. C. Mattusch, "The production of bronze statuary in the Greek world," in *Das Wrack* 2, 789-800, 801-7. For a commentary on the very improbable opinion that the two Riace bronzes were obtained by elaborating the same rough model (Mattusch, *Greek bronze statuary* 208), see C. Rolley, *RA* 1990.2, 407.

22 It is not a matter of chance that, after the invention of coroplastic in high Archaic times, and the invention, in that context, of molding and replicas attributed to Boutades from Sikyon, the pivotal passage is placed by Pliny (*NH* 35.153-55) in the period of Lysippus and later in Arkesilaos's and Pasiteles's Neo-Attic milieu.

23 See A. Melucco Vaccaro, "Originale e copia: storia di un rapporto," in R. Paris (ed.), *Dono Hartwig: originali ricongiunti e copie tra Roma e Ann Arbor; ipotesi per il Templum Gentis Flaviae* (Exhib. cat., Palazzo Massimo alle Terme, Rome 1994) 119-42.

24 Zimmer, "Die Quellen," in *Archäologische Bronzen* 38-40; id., *Bronzegußwerkstätten* 128-29; *The treatises of Benvenuto Cellini on goldsmithing and sculpture* (transl. C. R. Ashbee) (New York 1967) esp. 790-800; V. Biringuccio, *De pirotechnia* (ed. A. Carugo; Milano 1959) esp. 228-32; R. Bettarini and P. Barocchi (edd.), *Giorgio Vasari: le vite .. nelle redazioni del 1550 e 1568* (Florence 1966-87).

25 Mattusch, *Greek bronze statuary* 15-30.

26 Zimmer, *Bronzegußwerkstätten* passim; reviewed by C. Rolley, *RA* 1992.2, 382-85 (as well for criticism against "l'antiquité conçue comme une vague entité sans histoire").

27 Mattusch, *Greek bronze statuary* 55-58; Bol, *Antike Bronzetechnik* 37.

been largely disregarded or lost.[28] Until now the core was never correctly examined or preserved.[29] Possible research on the Delphi Charioteer, on the so-called Artemision God, and on the Antikythera bronzes has probably been rendered impossible by old-fashioned restoration. However, clays are still present and ought to be thoroughly examined in the Ugento Zeus, which underwent restoration at the Istituto Centrale del Restauro but whose interior was not examined, and in the Livadostro Kouros in the National Museum of Athens. It is a happy circumstance that in the case of the Piraeus Kouros restorers kept the inner core clays (which have been described by Dontas and Mattusch), so they may be available for further research.[30]

Our German colleagues, and W.-D. Heilmeyer in particular, using another medical technology, Computerized Axial Tomography (or CAT scan) adapted to this purpose, have conducted very interesting non-destructive surveys of the internal structure of certain bronzes. The Kythera head (end of the 6th c. or beginning of the 5th c. B.C.)[31] in particular revealed concentric layers very similar to those we found, in which the outermost and thinnest layer replicates the bronze's inner features. The so-called Getty Youth, the athlete wearing the crown, has also been examined,[32] and a new survey is presented below (Podany and Scott, pp. 178-91).

Our experience of micro-excavation, so far unique, will be better understood in the light of similar studies once they have been conducted. Further analyses, which can only be achieved through wide-ranging international co-operation and research, will enable us to determine if the crucial innovation, from direct to indirect casting technology, really took place in the 4th c. B.C., as we suggest, or later.

Ministero per i Beni e le Attività Culturali, Piazza del Popolo 18, 00186 Roma

28 Interpretation of tool- or fingermarks on inside walls is controversial (in particular in cases of fragmentary bronzes) and equivocal, being very difficult to trace back either to the clay model or to the wax lining of the working model. The only sure argument in favor of indirect casting is that of dripmarks (see Haynes, *Technique* 34-41), which are absolutely absent in the Riace bronzes.

29 See Tzachou-Alexandri above, p. 91.

30 Mattusch, *Greek bronze statuary* 65-68, 70, 74-82, 128-35.

31 *Archäologische Bronzen* 126-31.

32 J. Frel, *The Getty Bronze* (2nd edn., Malibu, 1982). More recently see C. C. Mattusch, *The victorious youth* (Getty Museum Studies on Art, Los Angeles 1997).

A Greek choral singer from Rome

Malcolm Bell, III

In 1643 the bronze sculpture of a boy (figs. 1-2) came to light on the Janiculum Hill in Rome. Restored as a genius with cornucopia, the work entered the Barberini Collection. In the early 19th c. the bronze was inherited by the Sciarra family, and in 1892 it passed by sale to the Ny Carlsberg Glyptotek. In the 1960s the 17th c. additions were removed. The Copenhagen bronze is the subject of a recent, detailed study by the author.[1]

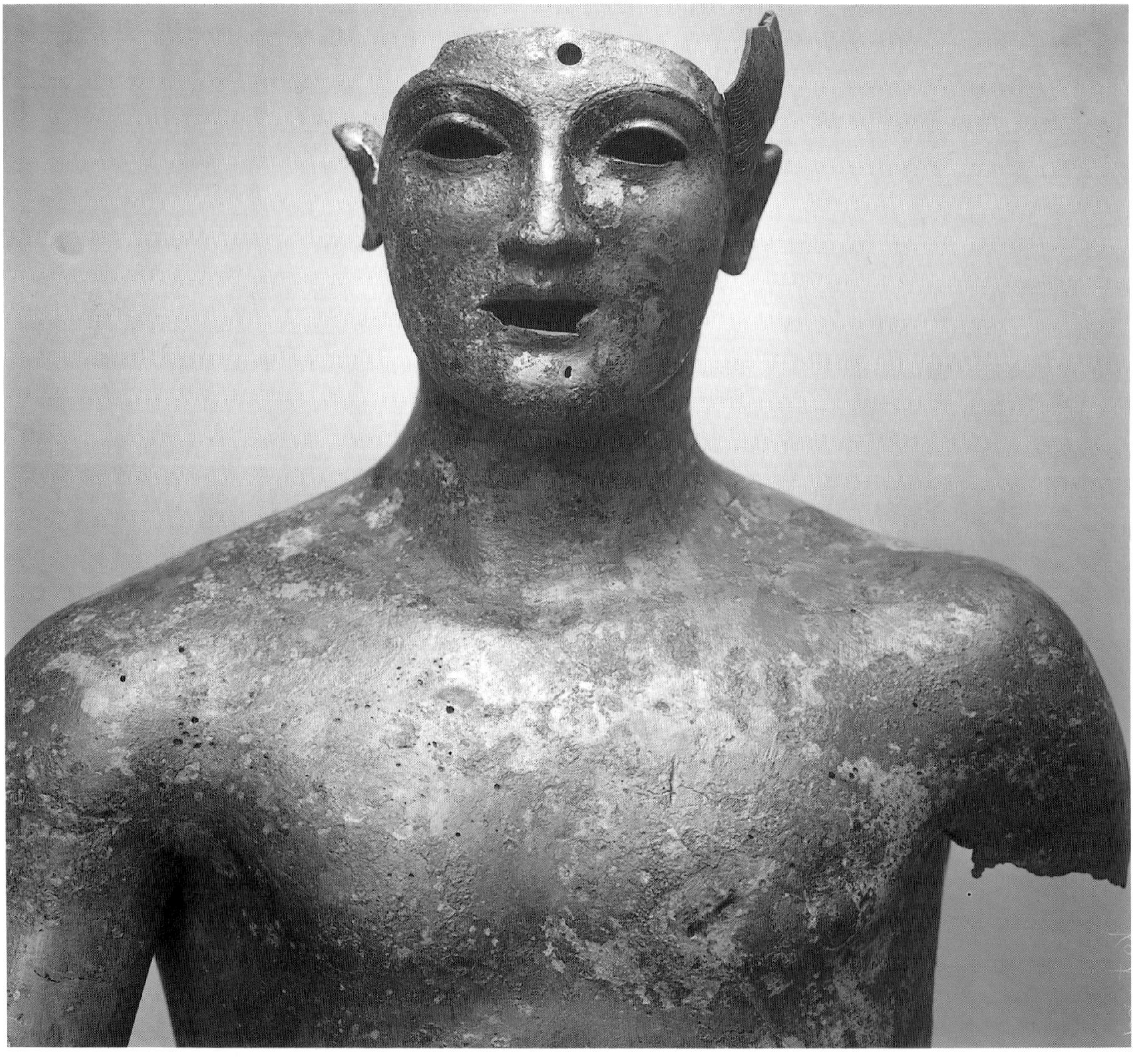

Fig. 1. Youth, detail of face and upper torso. Bronze, p.h. 1.02 m. Copenhagen, Ny Carlsberg Glyptotek 2235. (Photo: courtesy Ny Carlsberg Glyptotek.)

1 "Il canto del choreutes. Un bronzo greco dal Gianicolo," *Ianiculum-Gianicolo (Acta Inst.Rom. Finlandiae* 16 [1996]) 77-99. I am grateful to J. Neils for reading my paper at the 13th Bronze Congress.

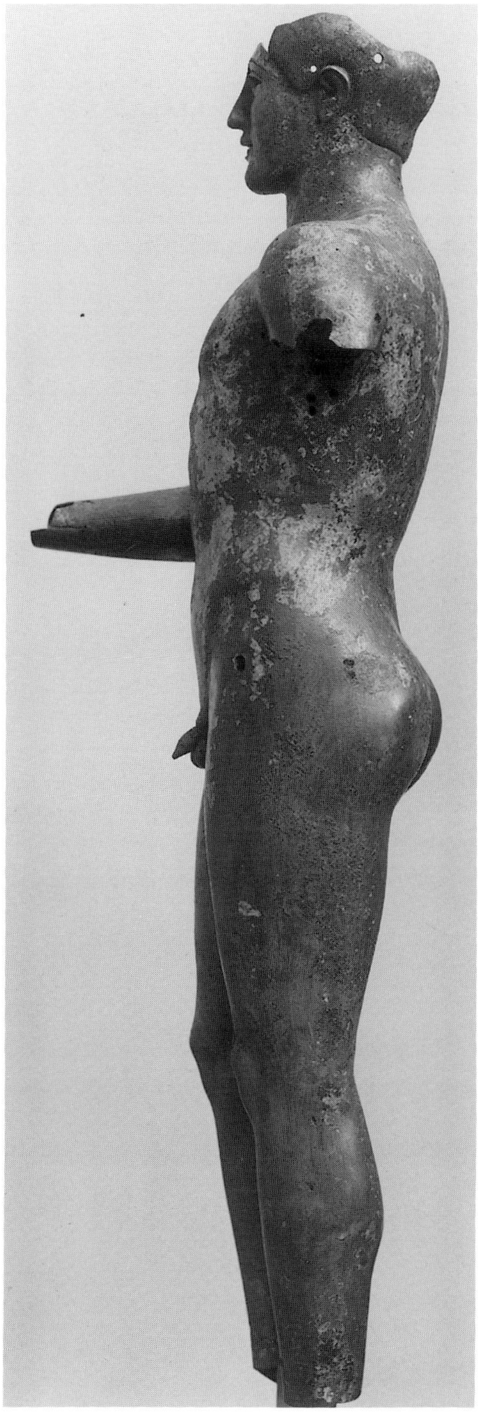

Fig. 2. Youth, left profile. (Photo courtesy Ny Carlsberg Glyptotek.)

Although J. J. Winckelmann and others believed the bronze to be Etruscan, a consensus now holds that it is a Greek work of the early 5th c. B.C. Scale (original h. *c.*1.20 m), subject (pre-adolescent *pais*), technique (copper inlay of eyebrows, lips, and nipples), and style (tentative naturalism of the early 5th c.) support such an attribution. Although some have suggested a South Italian or Sicilian origin, the lack of parallels makes a provenience on the Greek mainland more likely.

Clues for the identification of the subject are the boy's open mouth and the incised, feather-like markings visible around his left ear. The latter should be recognized as representing the lower part of a cap of feathers. Headdresses called *psilinoi* were worn by youthful choral singers competing in the *Gymnopaidiai* at Sparta, and it is thought that these were originally made of feathers. If, as seems likely, the boy is such a *choreutes*, or choral singer, his open mouth can readily be explained by proposing that he is singing.

A group of small bronzes of Peloponnesian provenience was shown by H. T. Wade-Gery to represent Spartan *choreutai.*[2] The only previously known large-scale choral singers were described by Pausanias (5.25.2-4) as having stood in front of the Temple of Zeus at Olympia. Consisting of 35 *paides* accompanied by teacher and flautist, the group was dedicated by the Messenian population of the Sicilian city of Messina early in the 5th c. B.C. to commemorate a youthful chorus that had drowned in the straits on the occasion of a festival in Rhegion. The sculptor was Kallon of Elis. (Pausanias also saw nearby a second group of *paides*, the work of Kalamis, dedicated by the city of Akragas in Sicily; and these may also have been *choreutai.*) It seems likely that the drowned chorus of the *Messenoi* would have been shown in the act of performing: that is, singing with open mouths.

The bronze from the Janiculum appears to belong to the decade 480-470 B.C. The boy's identification as a choral singer suggests that he originally belonged to a dedication like the one at Olympia, and it seems at least possible that he could originally have been part of the Messenian dedication itself, brought to Rome at some later time. Date, style, and subject do not rule out such an origin for the Copenhagen boy. We can note that most choruses consisted of even numbers of singers, allowing division into hemi-choruses; Pausanias mentions 35 singers in the Messenian dedication, and another singer would give the requisite even number.

When and why the sculpture should have been brought to Rome are unanswerable questions. 19th c. oral tradition held that the boy was found outside the Porta San Pancrazio along the Via Aurelia, where dedication in a sanctuary seems the most probable form of re-use. The boy would then be one of the many works of sculpture brought to Rome from Greek cities and sanctuaries. Were our guess about his origins correct, the boy from the Janiculum would also become one of the very few surviving large-scale bronzes from Olympia.

Univ. of Virginia

2 H. T. Wade-Gery, "A note on the origin of the Spartan *gymnopaidiai*," *CQ* 43 (1949) 79-81.

Bronzecasting and ivory-bending: technical affinities in Classical Greek sculpture

Kenneth D. S. Lapatin

Ancient Greek sculptors mastered various media. Pheidias, the most renowned, fashioned images not only of bronze but also of marble and wood as well as of gold and ivory. As work in one medium is unlikely to have proceeded wholly independently of that in another, I have explored connections between the production of large-scale hollow-cast bronzes and chryselephantine statues.

Chryselephantine images prior to Pheidias were constructed of individually carved ivory faces, hands, and feet attached to wooden cores that were subsequently gilded. The colossal scale of the Athena Parthenos and Zeus Olympios, however, was unprecedented and constituted considerable technical difficulties, for the exposed flesh of these statues surpassed the size of any tusk. Greek and Latin authors suggest that by the 5th c. B.C. age-old techniques of furniture production had been developed to such a degree that tusks could be 'unscrolled' into thin sheets of ivory with substantially larger dimensions than sectioned pieces; classical and mediaeval writers, moreover, preserve recipes for chemically softening ivory to shape it as desired. The feasibility of such processes is confirmed not only by modern patents filed by 19th and early 20th c. craftsmen, but also by practical experiments carried out by the author (fig. 1). These experiments and literary sources both suggest that ivory softened to the consistency of wax could be pressed into and formed by molds, procedures remarkably akin to those employed in indirect lost-wax bronzecasting. If this reconstruction of monumental chryselephantine production approximates actual practice, Pheidias and his successors appear to have ingeniously adapted their experience in fashioning large-scale bronzes to the creation of their most celebrated statues in gold and ivory. See my full text, "Pheidias ἐλεφαντουργός," *AJA* 101 (1997) 663-82.

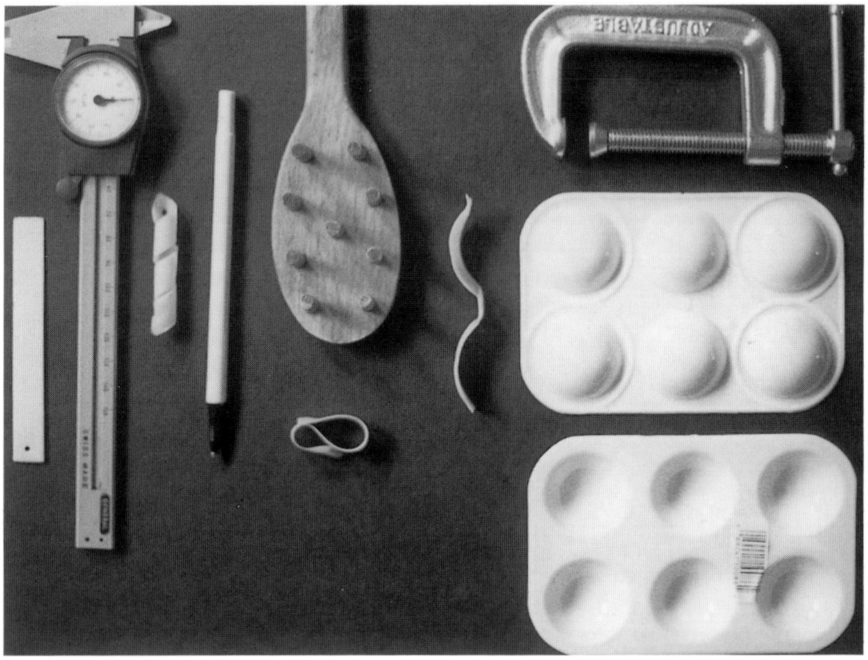

Fig. 1. Ivory veneers for piano keys before and after bending. Right to left: untreated veneer; calipers; twisted veneer and pen around which it was twisted; bent veneer and pasta fork through whose teeth it was bent; molded veneer and nesting paint trays between which it was clamped. The three curved veneers were softened by immersion in commercially available distilled white wine vinegar for 24 hours (one of the many methods recommended by ancient and mediaeval authors); they were then rinsed in water and molded to shape under pressure for an additional 24 hours. (Photo: author.)

Broken statues, shattered illusions: *mimesis* and bronze body parts on the Akropolis

Diane Harris-Cline

Of all the large-scale bronze statues dedicated on the Athenian Akropolis during the 5th and 4th c. B.C., the heads of only two have been recovered in archaeological excavations. One is the so-called Akropolis Youth, discovered in 1866 while digging foundations for the Akropolis Museum.[1] The date of between 470 and 460 B.C. places it after the Persian sack. The head's similarity to the Kritios Boy and the Blond Boy is apparent in the hairstyle, rolled with a fillet around the head, and the Severe style facial features such as the puffy eyelids and the rounded cheeks. The second is the Akropolis Warrior, found near the Propylaia in 1886, and dated to the early 5th c. B.C. by comparison to the dying warrior (or Laomedon) on the East pediment at Aigina.[2] We only have his head, without helmet. This bronze statue was probably damaged during the Persian Wars.[3] These two heads, and the stone statue-bases with cuttings for feet, are all the archaeological evidence that survives for large-scale bronze statues on the 5th c. Akropolis. For the 4th c., there is nothing.

Pausanias, who with Pliny the Elder supplies the most information about ancient sculptors and their works, described 60 bronze statues standing in Athens in his day, including the Athena Promachos on the Akropolis. Pausanias, however, was reporting long after the sack of Sulla in 86 B.C., which was followed by large-scale looting of statuary from Greece for export to Italy.[4] How can we find out anything more about bronze statues on the 4th c. Akropolis? The answer may be sought in the field of epigraphy.

The common theme in my research over the past decade or so has been the recovery of the lost material culture on the Akropolis in the 5th and 4th c. B.C., to restore to our memories the vases, musical instruments, armor and tools, furniture, and statues not only in ivory and wood but also in gold, silver, and bronze.[5] This is not possible through archaeological excavation, since they were in perishable and precious materials, nor through survey techniques, valuable as they might be. The question of what we can know about the works of art and precious treasures once kept on the Akropolis in the period after the Persian Wars, can be answered through excavating the basements of the British Museum, London, and the National Museum, Athens: from reading inscriptions. All that can be seen now on the Akropolis is the architectural remains. Some dedications, bronzes, marbles, and ceramics from the Archaic Akropolis are housed in the museums, thanks to the Persian destruction. But what can we learn about the dedications and treasures kept on the Akropolis after this, in the Classical period? Archaeological excavation cannot recover them, while literary sources mention only a selection of

---

1 Mattusch, *Greek bronze statuary* 92; Mattusch, *Classical bronzes* 101-2. From all Greece, fewer than 30 bronze statues are preserved dating to the Archaic and Classical periods combined. Of these, only 11 retain their extremities, and only 2 are still attached to their original bronze plinths.

2 Stewart, *Greek sculpture* pls. 247-50.

3 The Warrior may have been a votive offering or a statue representing a legendary hero; see Mattusch, *Greek bronze statuary* 92.

4 Paus. 1.22.4-28.4.

5 D. Harris, *The treasures of the Parthenon and the Erechtheion* (Oxford Monographs on Classical Archaeology 1995); ead., "Freedom of information and accountability: the inventory lists of the Parthenon," in R. Osborne and S. Hornblower (edd.), *Rituals, finance, politics, Athenian democratic accounts presented to David Lewis* (Oxford 1994) 213-25; ead., "Bronze statues on the Athenian Acropolis: the evidence of a Lycurgan inventory," *AJA* 96 (1992) 637-52; ead., "Thucydides 2.13.4 and the inventory lists," *Horos* 8 (1991) 75-82; ead., *The inventory lists of the Parthenon treasures* (Diss., Princeton Univ. 1991); ead., "Nikokrates of Kolonos: metal-worker for the Parthenon treasurers," *Hesperia* 57 (1988) 329-37, pl. 88.

objects and tend not to be contemporary eye-witness accounts but passages written several hundred years after the Classical period. The epigraphical sources have proven to be the most fruitful avenue for recovering the material culture of the Akropolis which cannot be investigated through the traditional archaeological methods.

For the restoration of bronze statues on the Akropolis in the 4th c., we have an inscribed marble stele, an inventory list made by the treasurers of Athena, which describes in some detail over 25 bronze statues.[6] The contents of this inventory are of interest to many in the fields of archaeology and art history, since it lists statues that are now lost. I would like to explore several questions: first, what did the statues look like? second, why are they in various states of disrepair? and, finally, what did it mean to an ancient viewer to look at a broken statue? This leads to the further questions of what was the function of Greek votive sculpture? and did a statue still satisfy that function if it was broken? This in turn leads, I believe, to the reason these particular broken statues were destined for the melting pot and recorded on stone.

In the inventory, statues of children, youths, and bearded and beardless men are described. A few of the figures held animals or objects in their hands. The statues are listed by gender and age. This is significant in that it provides an idea of what the Greeks themselves called their statues. In modern times we have artificially assigned certain types of statues Greek names: *kouroi* and *korai* are the obvious examples. From the inventory list, we learn what the 4th c. Athenians called their statues. Of the 25 statues listed, three are children (παις), and two are small children (παιδίσκος).[7] Six are nudes (γυμνός) without further modification. Four are males (ἀνδριάς) without stating whether they had beards or not, while four others are explicitly called beardless (ἀνδριάς ἀγενεῖον) and another three were bearded (ἀνδριάς γενεῖος). In addition, three statues were Palladia, bringing the total to 25.

The use of the term ἀνδριάς is an important iconographic marker, since it signals that the statues did not represent deities. While the terms ἀνδριάς and ἄγαλμα are interchangeable for a statue of a human subject, only ἄγαλμα may be used for a god.[8]

The descriptions of these statues can be very detailed, noting missing features such as fingers, toes, and the attributes or offerings the statues used to hold. The general condition of the statue is often mentioned, sometimes using the phrase 'not healthy' (οὐκ ὑγιής), or 'not in good shape'. Many of the statues were in some state of disrepair, which implies that they were manufactured considerably earlier than the date of the inventory list, *c.*330 B.C., and were both old and falling apart.

Large bronze statues were manufactured in pieces, then soldered and jointed together. Scientific examination of ancient life-size bronze statues reveals that often the feet, hands, head, long shoulder locks, and attributes were cast separately, using the indirect lost-wax process, and that an interior armature helped support the pieces after soldering.[9] There are many ancient references to the process of manufacture, such as Philo of Byzantion, who in *De Septem Miraculis* 4 says, "first the craftsmen model the statues, and then, after cutting them up into their natural parts, they cast them, and in the end they put the pieces together and stand the statue up."[10] Both ceramic and bronze evidence supports the statement that statues were made

---

6 IG II^2, 1498-1501A. IG II^2, 1500 and 1501 are in the Epigraphical Museum, Athens. IG II^2, 1499 is in the British Museum. See Harris 1992 (supra n.5) 637-52.

7 The difference between a *pais* and a *paidiskos* may have been the size of the statue, rather than the relative age of the figure.

8 H. Philipp, *Tektonon daidala* (Berlin 1968) App. 1, pp. 103 ff. Cf. Thuc. 1.134; Gorgias, *VitSoph* 82 B 11, 18; Eur., *Hekabe* 560; Pindar, N. 5.1 ff. *Agalma* is the standard Archaic Greek word for 'dedication'; see Stewart, *Greek sculpture* 75.

9 See H. Bluemner, *Technologie und Terminologie der Gewerbe und Kunste bei Griechen und Römern*; Mattusch, *Greek bronze statuary* 104; Haynes, *Technique.*

10 Mattusch, *Greek bronze statuary* 104.

in pieces. The inventory list mentions the state of disrepair of each statue, and the absence of feet in a number of cases suggests that they were lying on the ground like piles of corpses. Without feet, they could no longer have been attached to their bases at the time of the inventory. The ankles and feet seem to have been particularly vulnerable areas on bronze statues. The Getty bronze, a nude victor of late 4th or early 3rd c. date, is missing its lower legs and feet, a parallel to the state of disrepair of the statues on the Akropolis.[11]

In large-scale bronzecasting, body parts could be subdivided into manageable sections and soldered together at the latest stage of production. In total, 21 of the 25 statues are described as in some state of disrepair by the inventory; and because of the poor preservation of the inventory itself, I find it probable that all of them were listed as missing some body part or attribute.

This indicates two things: first, that the statues listed were large, life-size or over, not figurines. Figurines of bronze do not have missing fingers or eyes; the method of manufacture is often not pieced together but cast as a solid unit. And second, the state of disrepair suggests that the statues were older than the inscription. The inscription serves as the *terminus ante quem*, the date prior to which all the statues listed must have been manufactured, but the disrepair indicates that they were perhaps considerably older. I think that these statues had been dedicated on the Akropolis quite a few years before the inventory was made in the late 330s.

The statues in the inventory were all votive offerings or dedications, as evidenced by the names of dedicants attached to some of them. Why did these individuals leave bronze statues on the Akropolis? What were their motivations for making an offering of a statue? Often they were presented to redeem a vow previously made in a prayer. Inscribed stone bases and columns include such phrases as, "Peikon the potter dedicated this as a tithe to Athena by a vow."[12] The equivalent Latin term is *ex voto*, which we use as a noun for such a votive offering. A Greek word used on inscribed bases of statues is ἄγαλμα — an ornament for the place of worship, something pleasing. A statue can be called εικων as well, meaning an image, a reflection of the real thing it mimics. Alternatively, a statue can fall into the broader category of ἀνάθημα — something left behind, set up, dedicated.

Temples and sanctuaries were crowded with dedications in the Classical period, and sometimes the shrines were so filled with statues that one could hardly walk. An inscription from Rhodes of the 3rd c. B.C. says, "No one is permitted to request that a statue be raised or some other votive offering set up in the lower part of the sanctuary ... or in any other spot where votive offerings prevent people from walking past."[13]

Why were descriptions of these particular statues inscribed on stone? Most commonly, inventories were made of precious objects for the annual audit of the boards of treasurers (ἱεροποῖοι) to certify that their duties were fulfilled. Inventories were occasionally made when there was a need for making records prior to a melting down of metal objects for coinage or consolidation to make new ritual vessels or dedications (called a καθαίρεσις, housecleaning). The Akropolis inscription appears to be the second type of inventory, made just prior to melting down the bronze statues.

The inventory was a first step toward organizing the Akropolis, commemorating the statues on stone before they were melted down for re-use. The appearance of the stele and the letter forms and heights suggests a date in the 330s B.C. These statues were probably inventoried as part of the reorganization of the sanctuary under the *epimelete* and orator Lykurgos. Lykurgos

---

11 J. Frel, *The Getty Bronze* (Malibu 1978); see now also C. Mattusch, *The victorious youth* (Malibu 1997).

12 *IG* I^3 633, inscribed on a column capital.

13 F. T. van Straten, "Religious history as the history of mentality: the believer as servant of the deity in the Greek world," in H. S. Versnel (ed.), *Faith, hope and worship: aspects of religious mentality in the ancient world* (Leiden 1981) 78-79.

was charged with reforming the Panathenaic festival and fashioning new ritual vases and utensils, or πομπεῖα, for the various sanctuaries of Attika. He was also responsible for commissioning new statues in addition to the *pompeia*. The most famous statue he commissioned was the portrait of Sokrates by Lysippos set up in the Pompeion, but he also had statues set up of the three great tragedians, Aeschylus, Sophocles, and Euripides.[14] That statues were important and significant to him may be seen in his opening lines of the oration against Leokrates: "Justice towards you, Athenians, and reverence for the gods, shall mark the opening of my speech against Leokrates, now here on trial; so may Athena and those other gods and heroes whose statues are erected in our city and the country round receive this prayer."[15] The speech dates to 330, probably just a year or two after the melting down of these bronzes. I find it likely that Lykurgos also commissioned artists to make new statues out of the melted bronze. He certainly commissioned several gold- and silversmiths at this time to make new ritual vessels from the many smaller gold and silver dedications in storage on the Akropolis.[16] Such meltdowns of dedicated objects to manufacture new ones were not thought to be impious acts. Authorized and supervised by the Boule, under the direct supervision of the treasurers of Athens, artists like Nikokrates melted down dedications to manufacture larger, consolidated, ritual vases. The act of melting down the votives was commemorated on stone by the inventories, and the treasurers of Athena carefully recorded on stone how much gold was given to each metalsmith and how much each new vessel weighed.

The bronze statues on the Akropolis were probably inscribed on stone to record the memory of the original dedications and their dedicants before they were melted down. Dedications were made in order to leave a lasting memento of the more ephemeral acts of sacrifice and prayer. If the statue were gone, the memory of the act would be gone, unless it was inscribed and set up in the sanctuary as a reminder.

Why were these particular bronze statues destined for the melting pot? It might be that once the statues were damaged or deteriorating, they were no longer deemed perfect enough or suitable enough for offering to the god. The realism of statues is what struck the eyes of Kokkale and Kynno in Herondas's Fourth Mime, and statues do not look like real human beings if the arms are broken off at the wrist like stumps or hobbled by the absence of a leg.[17] Perhaps a statue was no longer deemed a statue once it had missing body parts. From classical discourse on the subject, it is apparent that the ancient sculptors sought to replicate or imitate life, and their greatest achievement was considered to be the illusion of reality, that a statue seemed so life-like it could breathe. The term *mimesis* has two aspects, likeness and life-likeness.[18] In the case of Lysippos's portrait of Alexander, it was both its likeness, or similarity, to his physiognomical forms that would have been admired and also its life-like appearance and reflection of his character traits, thoughts, and feelings. From the beginning of Greek sculpture, statues were admired for their *mimesis* of life: Daidalos is said to have made such life-like figures that they had to be chained down to prevent them from walking away.[19]

The illusion of life would be shattered should a statue break. If it lost an eye, or a hand, or broke a leg, that would emphasize the material of the statue, and the statue would lose its ability to act as an εἰκών, a likeness, or as an ἄγαλμα, a wonder to behold, a delight. In other words, a statue with missing pieces is no longer a statue, it is merely a collection of body parts.

---

14 *OCD*, s.v. Lykurgos (G. L. Cawkwell). He also had official copies made of their works, which Ptolemy Philadelphos later borrowed for the Library of Alexandria and never returned.

15 Lykurgos wrote 15 speeches; this is the only one preserved.

16 See Harris 1998 (supra n.5) 329-37, pl. 88.

17 See discussion in T. Gelzer, "Mimus und Kunsttheorie bei Herondas, Mimiambus 4," in *Catalepton: Festschrift für Bernhard Wyss zum 80. Geburtstag* (Basel 1985) 96-116.

18 M. Steiber, "Aeschylus's *theoroi* and realism in Greek art," *TAPA* 124 (1994) 85-119.

19 Stewart, *Greek sculpture* 73.

Quintilian refers to the process of bronzecasting as a parallel to the craft of composing a speech, and says a speech is not a speech until it is put together from all its parts, just as a statue is not a statue unless all its parts are put together. "Whoever claims that these commonplaces do not pertain to the orator does not believe that a statue is begun when its parts are being cast ... In fact, although all of the parts have been cast, it is not a statue until it is put together."[20] There may have been a feeling that a statue is no longer a statue if it is not whole and is missing parts.

A statue in Greek is *agalma*, a delight to behold. A broken statue is no longer a delight to behold, just scrap metal. But surely these statues could have been repaired. Ancient patches are known in both marble sculpture and bronze, as is the case for the Marathon boy, found off the coast of Attica near Marathon, whose arms were reattached in antiquity.[21] Why weren't these statues on the Akropolis just given new fingers or feet or eyes or attributes? The reason may have to do with Lykurgos. He was an orator and appointed *epimelete* (or financial administrator) for the Akropolis, and, as previously mentioned, had commissioned Lysippos to make the portrait of Sokrates in the Pompeion.[22]

Sokrates certainly had opinions about the nature of sculpture and, indeed, about all the arts. The theory of *mimesis*, that art was an imitation of life, a shadowy reflection of reality and yet related to reality by being its image, a reproduction and re-enactment of its subject matter, is recorded in Plato.[23] Xenophon describes a conversation between Sokrates and a sculptor on the topic of *mimesis*.

> Once Sokrates visited Kleiton the sculptor and, during the conversation with him, he said, "That the runners, wrestlers, boxers, and pankratiasts you make, Kleiton, are beautiful I see and know. But how do you produce in your sculptures that which most strongly attracts the souls of people by the sight of it, namely the appearance of life?" When Kleiton was embarrassed and did not answer immediately, Sokrates said: "Well, do you make your sculptures to appear more alive (ζωτικώτερος) because you make your work from the shape of living beings?" "Yes just so," he answered.[24]

For the portrait of Sokrates, Lykurgos hired none other than Lysippos. Why? Pliny the Elder in the *Natural Histories* describes Lysippos's work as being fresh and new:

> He is said to have contributed much to the art of casting statues by representing the hair in detail, by making the head smaller than earlier sculptors had, and by making the bodies slenderer and more tightly knit, as a result of which the height of his statues seems greater. There is no Latin term for the Greek word *symmetria* which he observed with the utmost precision by a new and previously unattempted system which involved altering the square figures of earlier sculptors; and he used commonly to say that by them, that is, earlier sculptors, men were represented as they really were, but by him they were represented as they appeared.[25]

The Latin poet Propertius said, *gloria Lysippo est animosa effingere signa,* "the glory of Lysippos is to create statues with soul."[26] It was said that he made images that lived, missing only actual breathing and movement.[27] The discourse concerning older and newer ways of representing the human form was likely to have generated much discussion about *mimesis*, the reflection of reality in the arts.

In the 330s B.C., Lysippos's work was new and fresh when Lykurgos hired him to make the portrait of Sokrates. Surely Lykurgos chose him after an interview, after studying his body of

---

20 Mattusch, *Greek bronze statuary* 105.

21 Stewart, *Greek sculpture* fig. 497.

22 Diog. Laert. 2.43.

23 E.g., Plato, *Rep.* 10.595a-608b; *Ion* 530c; Aristotle, *Poetics* 1-5.

24 Xen., *Mem.* 3.10.6-8. Parrhasias the painter is interviewed in 3.10.1-6.

25 Cf. R. Carpenter, *The esthetic basis of Greek art* (rev. ed., Bloomington 1959) 96.

26 Prop. 3.9.9.

27 Kallistratos, *Descriptiones* 6, describing the Kairos of Lysippos; for text, see F. P. Johnson, *Lysippos* (Durham, NC 1927) 282-83; cf. Frel, *Bronze* (supra n.11) 19.

work, and deciding that his work was most pleasing and fashionable. As *epimelete* in charge of cleaning up the Akropolis, he must have also looked around, seen these old, broken statues, and thought they were not worth patching, better to melt them down, clean up the place, and hire new craftsmen to make more modern statues. His aesthetic senses probably also told him that the newer statues were being harmed by proximity to broken ones, since the broken bodies shattered the illusion of life in the well-preserved statues. And using a phrase from medical terminology, he judged the broken statues to be in poor condition, perhaps even contagious: οὐκ ὑγιής.

That Lykurgos hired metalsmiths at this time is attested—Nikokrates of Kolonos was one of them.[28] That silversmiths could make bronze statues is also attested: Pliny (*NH* 34.84), for example, writes, "Though Boethos of Chalkedon is more famous for his work in silver, he is the artist of the boy strangling a goose with all his might."[29] Perhaps another inventory or account will be discovered soon to confirm that these craftsmen made new statues from the melted bronze under the supervision of Lykurgos.

Even to ancient writers the work of Lysippos signaled a high point in style, and shortly thereafter art was thought to have rapidly declined, or, as Pliny wrote, after 296 B.C. *cessavit deinde ars,* "art thereafter ceased."[30] The stimulation for aesthetic development may have been spurred by such events as these, where a new innovative style catches on, making obsolete the older styles and works to the point where melting the older works down makes more sense than patching them up.

There is another element to consider: the idea ascribed to Demokritos that the ancient poet — and perhaps by extension, artist — was an instrument of the Muse.[31] In Plato's *Ion* (533e-534d) the poet is said to be out of his senses in an ecstatic trance as he is possessed by a Muse. In the *Phaedrus* (245a) Plato writes, "He who without the divine madness comes to the door of the Muses, confident that he will be a good poet by art, meets with no success, and the poetry of the same man vanishes into nothingness before that of the inspired madman." Artistic inspiration, such as a sculptor like Lysippos clearly possessed, was believed to be divinely inspired.[32] We might think of it as the aesthetic insight that provides the energy for the labor. Artists instinctively refer to this when they speak of being seized upon by an idea and of being caught up in the fury of aesthetic activity. It is as if someone outside of the artist inspires, forces, and compels him — the Muse.[33] In terms of offerings to a divinity, the divinely inspired new style of ἀγάλματα would be thought to be far more delightful to the divinity than patched-up, old statues. And certainly the defective bronze bodies, fallen off their bases or missing their arms and eyes, were not pleasing to the gods — or to the Athenians.

In the *Republic* (601d) Plato wrote, "the excellence or beauty or truth of every structure, animate or inanimate, and of every action of man, is relative to the use for which nature or the artist has intended them."[34] The use and function of these bronzes was to please the gods: if it

---

28 Harris 1988 (supra n.5)

29 Cf. "It is a cause for wonder that in the art of chasing gold, no one has become famous, while in the art of chasing silver, many have. The most highly praised, however, is Mentor ... Four pairs of silver vessels were all he made, and none of these is now extant ... Varro writes that he possessed a bronze statue by him": Pliny, *NH* 33.154-57.

30 *NH* 34.49. Cf. Carpenter, *Esthetic basis* (supra n.26) 98.

31 Demokritos was a polymath and as such had a deep interest in art; Diogenes 9.46-69 records that he wrote treatises on painting, on colors, on linear perspective, on rhythms and harmony; cf. E. Keuls, *Plato and Greek painting* (Leiden 1978) 128.

32 See Keuls, ibid. 134 for an opposing view; she does not think that "Plato or Democritus or any other thinker of the Hellenic age associated it with painting or sculpture."

33 Cf. K. Wall, *A classical philosophy of art: the nature of art in light of classical principles* (Washington, DC 1982) 37-39.

34 W. J. Verdenius, *Mimesis – Plato's doctrine of artistic inspiration and its meaning to us* (Leiden 1949) 28.

no longer satisfied that aim by being broken or old-fashioned, then it was no longer excellent or worthy. I would note that Plato is writing as a near contemporary of the Lykurgan inventory;[35] not that his ideas necessarily reflect those of the average Athenian, but rather reflect those of the intellectual élite, in which circle I would place Lykurgos, who may have been reflecting accepted or discussed ideas.

In conclusion, the inventory that was the starting point for this discussion was recorded in the 330s under the reforms of Lykurgos as part of straightening up the Akropolis and clearing it of damaged dedications.[36] Its significance lies in the information it provides to supplement the archaeological and literary evidence for some bronze statues that once stood on the Akropolis in the Classical period. The melting down of these statues suggests that the Greeks may have had an aversion to broken statues, a feeling that they were no longer convincing as *mimesis* of life, were ineffective as ἀγάλματα, and were not suitable for display. The change in art styles represented by the work of Lysippos may also have had an influence on Lykurgos's aesthetic sensibilities and could have been a reason that he ordered that the statues not be patched or repaired but melted down.

Since the original stele, as I have restored it, listed bronze statues on both front and back, it is fair to say that the 25 surviving descriptions represent only a small percentage of the total number of statues collected, stacked in piles, and inventoried in preparation for the melting pot. This destruction of scores of Classical bronze statues by the Athenians themselves was motivated by a desire to clear off the accumulation of votive statues that had begun to clutter the sanctuary but also by an aesthetic sense that the statues were broken and therefore no longer suitable for gifts to the gods and that, even if repaired, they would not be ἀγάλματα — wonders to behold — since they were of the older style of sculpture and not as real-looking as Lysippos's and the style of the younger generation of workers. The broken statues on the Akropolis shattered the illusion of realism in adjacent statues in good repair. This was not aesthetically pleasing, and Lykurgos had them melted down in a veritable holocaust of bronze body parts in the fires of Hephaistos.

Department of Classics, University of Cincinnati, OH 45221

---

35 The *Republic* was written *c*.360.

36 *IG* II^2, 1498-1501.

Studying the core material of ancient bronzes

Cees D. van den Bergh

Large bronze objects must be cast hollow, not only for economic reasons but also for technical ones. It is also obvious that these bronze objects have to be made hollow before casting, that is to say as wax models. Before casting, the hollow wax model has to be filled with core material or the final bronze object will be solid. The core must be of a refractory material that does not deform or change chemically at high temperatures.

The rôle of the core material may seem a subsidiary detail of the casting. And in a certain way it even seems logical to remove the core material after casting a bronze object. For centuries the core material has usually been removed and has remained underestimated. It is a pity that very few researchers have realized that core material is fundamentally changed by the different stages of bronzecasting and registers everything as a kind of mirror of the process. It can provide many details, for instance, of the heating of the casting, not only about the specific casting temperature but also about the whole heating process. In particular, the layers of core material closest to the inner and outer bronze surfaces can give a very detailed indication of the heating of the mold before casting in order to expel the thin working wax model. If this operation is not completed in the correct way, the so-called casting skin will be very thick and difficult to remove from the cast bronze.

Another important detail is how the core material was applied to the inside of the hollow wax model. If possible, direct examination of the inner surface of the bronze object or x-ray pictures can provide information about this question (e.g., fig. 1). Another important issue is the retention of moisture by the core material. Much time should not elapse between the end of the heating of the mold and the filling of the mold with liquid bronze. To avoid damage from humidity on the mold, the temperature of the mold should not go lower than about 200° C.

Egyptian bronze statue EA 22784 in the British Museum, which conserves more core material than bronze and which can be easily studied inside, is providing a splendid opportunity to study its core material in an exhaustive manner.[1]

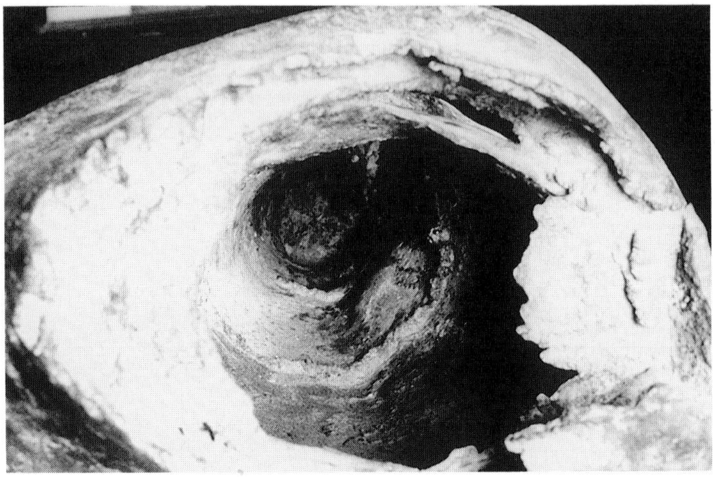

Fig. 1. View inside Roman arm. Bronze. Rome, Museo Nazionale Romano Inv. 1501. (Photo: author).

1 See J. Taylor, P. Craddock, and F. Shearman, "Egyptian hollow–cast bronze statues of the early first millennium B.C.: the development of a new technology," *Apollo* (July 1998) 9-14 (EA 22784 appears as figs. 4 and 8, and the alloy is published as "arsenical copper containing *c*.3.5% of arsenic and *c*.25% of lead, with only traces of tin"). P. Craddock considers the article in *Apollo* to be a short note; questions about the core material were not studied.

Nachklänge berühmter Meisterwerke auf griechischen Klappspiegeln

Agnes Schwarzmaier

Noch in der 1. Hälfte unseres Jahrhunderts galt es in der Tradition der Meisterforschung als eine selbstverständliche Tatsache, daß die Kleinkunst in den meisten Fällen von als vorbildhaft angesehenen Schöpfungen der "großen Meister" — Bildhauer wie Tafelmaler — abhängig sei. So benutzte man Darstellungen der Kleinkunst, um verlorene großplastische Meisterwerke zu rekonstruieren, die man nur aus literarischen Nachrichten kennt. Heute steht man dieser Ansicht zunehmend skeptischer gegenüber und wird am Einzelfall genau prüfen wollen, ob eine Darstellung in der Kleinkunst wirklich von einer Großplastik "kopiert" ist oder nicht. Das soll im Folgenden an zwei Beispielen geschehen.

1) Auf dem Relief eines Klappspiegels in Baltimore[1] (Abb. 1) steht Herakles einer bekleideten Frau gegenüber, die man aufgrund von Parallelen als Hesperide interpretiert hat. Ein Baum und ein ungelenk dastehendes Eroskind, das zu dem Helden aufschaut, füllen die Mitte der Komposition. Das Heraklesfigürchen erinnert sofort an den Herakles Farnese, denn es stützte ursprünglich seinen linken Arm auf eine Keule.

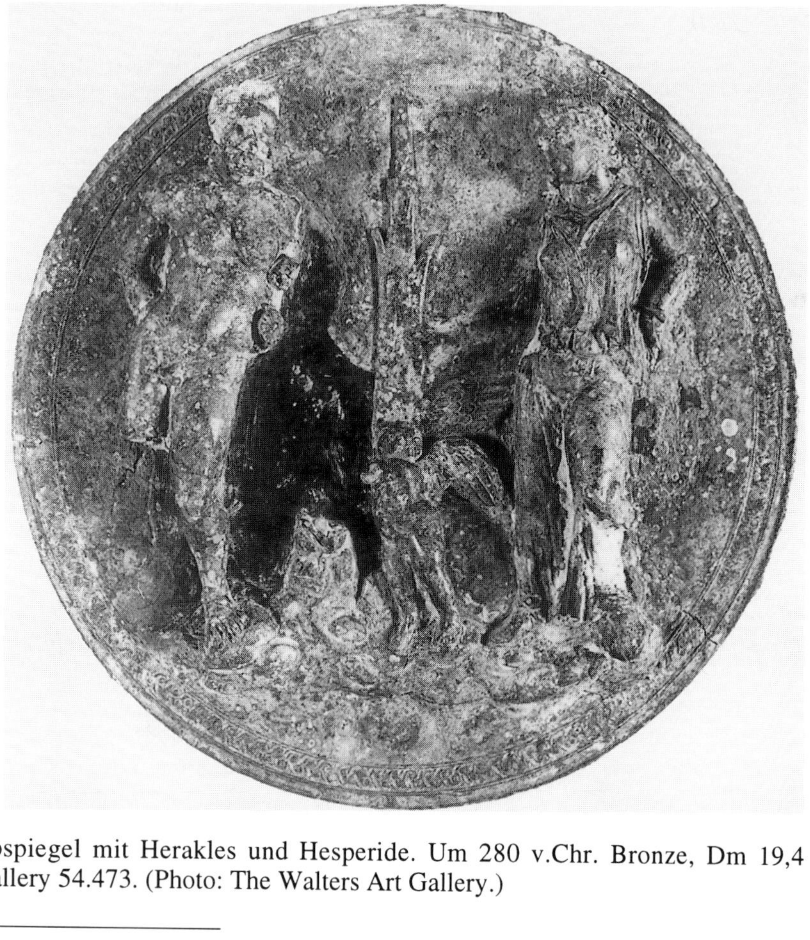

Abb. 1. Klappspiegel mit Herakles und Hesperide. Um 280 v.Chr. Bronze, Dm 19,4 cm. Baltimore, Walters Art Gallery 54.473. (Photo: The Walters Art Gallery.)

Zusätzlich zu den Abkürzungen gemäß *AJA* 96 (1991) 4 ff. und der *ArchBib* 1992 gelten folgende:

Sichtermann, *Ganymed* — H. Sichtermann, *Ganymed. Mythos und Gestalt in der antiken Kunst* (Berlin 1953)

Züchner — W. Züchner, *Griechische Klappspiegel* (JdI-Erg. Heft 14, 1942)

1 Baltimore, Walters Art Gallery 54.743: E. D. Reeder, *Hellenistic art in the Walters Art Gallery* (Baltimore 1988) 128 f., Nr. 45 mit Abb.

Vergleicht man den großplastischen Typus Farnese in seiner Neapeler Kopie, die von D. Krull als beste Überlieferung des Originals angesehen wird,[2] mit dem Figürchen des Klappspiegelreliefs, fallen trotz dessen fragmentarischen Zustandes neben einer überwiegenden Zahl von Gemeinsamkeiten auch einige Unterschiede auf, die von der Umsetzung der dreidimensionalen Figur ins Relief herzurühren scheinen. Dazu gehören das seitlich gestellte Spielbein, durch das das Standmotiv seine Labilität verliert, und die stärkere Kopfwendung über die linke Schulter, mit der der Held Kontakt zur Hesperide aufnimmt.

Über das Abhängigkeitsverhältnis der Kleinplastik von der großplastischen Schöpfung kann schon aus chronologischen Gründen kein Zweifel bestehen, da die Lysipp zugeschriebene Großbronze wohl um 320 v. Chr., das Spiegelrelief dagegen erst im frühen 3. Jh. geschaffen wurde.[3]

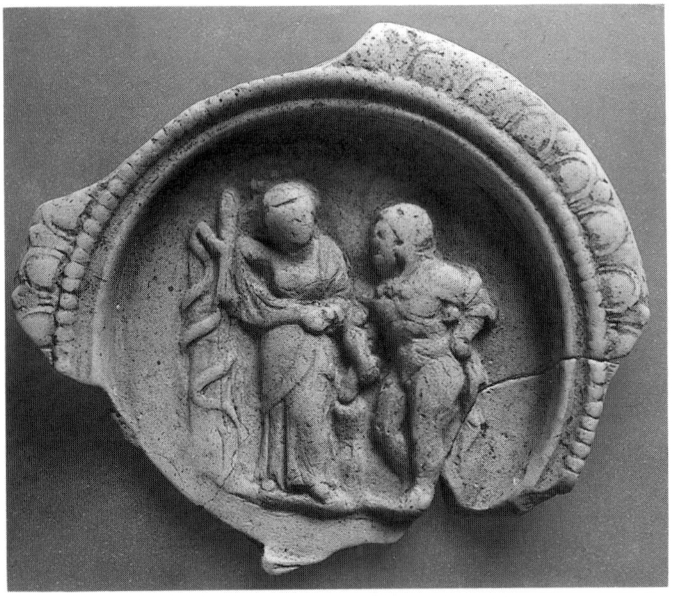

Abb. 2. Reliefschälchen mit Herakles und Hesperide. 3 Jh. v.Chr., Ton, Dm 9,6 cm. Olympia T 199. (Photo: Athen Inst Neg. Ol 3754.)

Die Deutung der Szene sichert ein Reliefschälchen in Olympia (Abb. 2),[4] dessen Relief wohl von einer Metallarbeit abhängig ist. Wiederum stehen sich Herakles und eine Frau gegenüber. Die Schlange, die sich um den Baumstamm in der Bildmitte windet, kennzeichnet diesen als Apfelbaum im Hesperidengarten. Für den Herakles stand offenbar wiederum der Herakles Farnese Pate, jedoch mit wesentlich größeren Veränderungen, da die Figur mit vertauschten Seiten ins Profil gewendet wurde. Das Löwenfell fällt nicht über die Keule, sondern hängt wie ein Kapuzenmantel im Rücken und ist um den Ellenbogen gewickelt.

Diese Abweichungen, einerseits zwischen dem Herakles des Spiegelreliefs und dem des Reliefschälchens und andererseits dem Herakles Farnese gegenüber, passen gut zu dem, was man über die Arbeitsweise der Toreuten in ihren Werkstätten weiß.[5] Die Künstler setzten unter Zuhilfenahme von Tonmodeln und deren Gipsausformungen die Figuren aus frei kombinierbaren Teilformen für die einzelnen Körperteile und -haltungen zusammen und trieben nach diesen Vorbildern die neuen Arbeiten freihand — also ohne eine Matrize. Ebenso existierten Modelle für Tiere oder Bäume. Diese Vorgehensweise erlaubte eine Fülle von Variationsmöglichkeiten in der Körperhaltung, Bekleidung etc., und ersparte jedesmal einen neuen Entwurf, denn die Modelle waren für ganz unterschiedliche Figuren und Szenen versatzstückhaft verwendbar.

Diese Technik läßt sich an einer Serie sehr ähnlicher Klappspiegelreliefs beispielhaft nachweisen[6] und wird bestätigt durch eine ganze Anzahl von Tonmodelfunden von der Athener Agora und aus Korinth oder den Gipsabgüssen aus Memphis in Hildesheim, die oft nur wahllose

---

2 D. Krull, *Der Herakles vom Typ Farnese* (Frankfurt–Bern 1985) 10-22, 336, Taf. 1-4.

3 Krull ibid. 352-56; Reeder (supra n.1) 129.

4 Olympia Inv. T 199: U. Hausmann, "Reliefmedaillon Herakles und Hesperide," *X. OlBer* (1981) 211 Abb. 77; id., *OlForsch* 27 (1996) 5 ff., Nr. 3, 9, Taf. 1.

5 Verf., *Griechische Klappspiegel, Untersuchungen zu Typologie und Stil* (AthMitt Beiheft 18, 1997) 35-42.

6 z. B. Athen NM 12074 und 14480 (Züchner 18 KS 21 Taf. 13, 42 KS 52 Abb. 18), wo motivisch ganz ähnlich angelegte Figuren in Armhaltung, Kleidung und Attributen variiert sind.

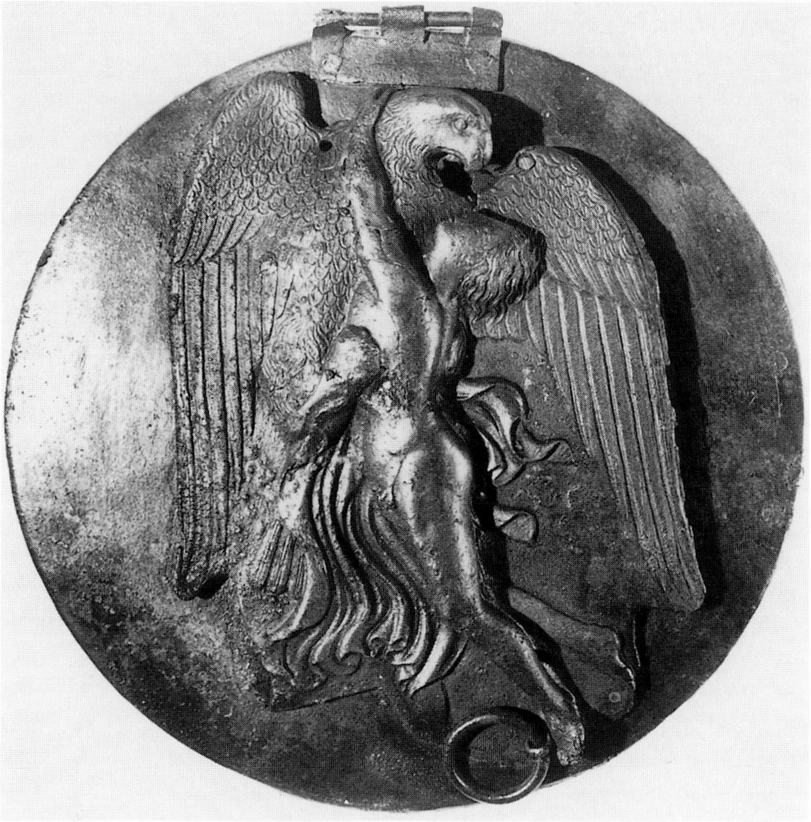

Abb. 3. Klappspiegel mit dem Raub des Ganymed. Um 340 v. Chr. Bronze, Dm 15,5 cm. Berlin, Staatliche Museen M.I. 7928. (Photo: Antikensammlung, Staatliche Museen zu Berlin - Preußischer Kulturbesitz Ant. 8794.)

Ausschnitte der Gesamtkomposition wiedergeben.[7] Sie wurden in der Regel von besonders gelungenen Metallarbeiten abgenommen.

Man muß sich für den oben genannten Fall des Herakles Farnese also vorstellen, daß ein Toreut die Anregung der lysippischen Großbronze aufnahm und für sein Relief und den konkreten Erzählzusammenhang anpaßte. Damit wurde das Motiv zu einem festen Bestandteil im Formenvorrat der Toreutenwerkstatt und konnte genauso umgewandelt, kombiniert und mit neuen Attributen zur Bekleidung o. ä. versehen werden wie der übrige Mustervorrat der Werkstatt.

Mit diesem Beispiel im Hinterkopf soll nun ein zweiter Fall betrachtet werden: Plinius erwähnt[8] unter den Werken des Künstlers eine bronzene Gruppe, in der der Adler den Knaben Ganymed durch die Lüfte entführte. Besonders betont Plinius, wie vorsichtig der Adler mit seiner Beute umging, damit seine Krallen den Körper des Knaben nicht verletzten.

In großplastischen römischen Kopien scheint die berühmte Gruppe des Leochares nicht überliefert zu sein, will man den Begriff "Kopie" nicht für den im Vatikan aufbewahrten Tischfuß gebrauchen.[9] Andererseits gibt es seit der 2. Hälfte des 4. Jhs. eine ganze Reihe von Entführungsdarstellungen des Ganymed durch den Adler — ein Thema, das im 4. Jh. neu auftaucht — die man mit der Schöpfung des Leochares in Verbindung zu bringen versuchte.[10] Eine Schlüssel-

---

7 E. Reeder Williams, "Ancient clay impressions from Greek metalwork," *Hesperia* 45 (1976) 41-66; D. B. Thompson, "Mater caelaturae," *Hesperia* 8 (1939) 285-316; ead., "Ostrakina toreumata," *Commemorative studies in honor of T. L. Shear* (Hesperia Suppl. VIII, 1949) 365-72; C. Reinsberg, *Studien zur hellenistischen Toreutik* (Hildesheim 1980).

8 Pliny, *NH* 34.79.

9 s. u.

10 Sichtermann, *Ganymed* 39-62; *LIMC* IV (1988) s.v. Ganymedes Nr. 195-200, 202, 203 (Sichtermann).

rolle nahm hier immer das Relief auf einem Klappspiegel der Berliner Sammlung ein (Abb. 3),[11] einerseits seiner hohen künstlerischen Qualität wegen, andererseits weil darauf der Hinweis des Plinius zutrifft, der Adler habe seine Krallen im Gewand des Ganymed verborgen. Besonders M. Bieber,[12] in abgeschwächter Form auch G. Richter[13] und H. Sichtermann,[14] traten dafür ein, daß der Berliner Spiegel die beste Vorstellung vom Werk des Leochares gebe und man bei dessen Rekonstruktion deshalb von ihm ausgehen müsse. So ist — gerade auch unter methodischem Gesichtspunkt — zu fragen, ob die Verbindung des Spiegels mit der großplastischen Gruppe zulässig ist. Dazu sind zwei Schritte der Untersuchung notwendig: Zum einen muß das Spiegelrelief innerhalb seiner Gattung und im Verhältnis zu den von ihm abhängigen Tonreliefs betrachtet werden. Zum anderen muß man die übrige archäologische Überlieferung zum Ganymedraub, soweit sie sich auf das 4. Jh. zurückführen läßt, mit dem Spiegelrelief vergleichen, um festzustellen, ob es von ihr in wichtigen Punkten abweicht.

Zunächst zu dem Spiegelrelief innerhalb seiner Gattung:

Das Relief zeigt den Adler frontal zum Betrachter mit auseinandergeklappten, jedoch gesenkten Flügeln. Sein zur linken Seite gewandter Kopf ist fast freiplastisch herausgearbeitet, um die Illusion zu erhöhen, daß Ganymed — ganz von der Seite gesehen — mit den Armen an seinem Hals hängt. Seinen Körper durchzieht eine starke Spannung, der Kopf ist weit in den Nacken zurückgeworfen, während Ganymeds Mantel wie eine Folie die Konturen seines nackten Körpers umspielt. Die vom Mantel verdeckten Klauen des Adlers, mit denen er Brust und Rücken des Knaben umfaßt, scheinen dagegen im Kräftespiel kaum Bedeutung zu haben.

Nach stilistischen Kriterien kann man das Relief durch die Gegenüberstellung mit dem Herakles-Auge-Spiegel der Sammlung Stathatos im Athener Nationalmuseum[15] oder dem Spiegel mit der Darstellung von Aphrodite und Eros aus der Großen Blisniza[16] um 340 v. Chr. datieren, also später als Furtwängler, Züchner u. a.[17] bisher dachten.

Offenkundig von ihm abhängig ist das Relief auf einer Tonplakette aus Capua,[18] mit 16 cm Höhe nur wenig größer als das Berliner Spiegelrelief, das mittels einer Matrix von einer Metallarbeit abgeformt wurde.[19] Gegenüber dem Berliner Spiegel fallen allerdings trotz ähnlicher Grundkomposition auch einige Unterschiede ins Auge. Der Adlerkopf ist zur anderen Seite gedreht, und Ganymed hängt nur noch mit dem rechten Arm an seinem Hals, während der gesenkte linke in die Falten seines Mantels faßt. Die gelängten Proportionen des Ganymed, besonders die überlangen Beine, sprechen zudem für eine etwas spätere Datierung der zugrundeliegenden Metallarbeit.

Die Abweichungen zwischen Spiegelrelief und Tonplakette lassen sich — wie beim oben geschilderten Fall des Herakles Farnese — leicht aus der Arbeitsweise der Toreuten erklären. An anderen Beispielen ist nachweisbar, daß die Vorlagen in den Ateliers z. T. über sehr lange Zeiträume aufbewahrt, bei erneuter Verwendung der neuen stilistischen Mode angepaßt und auch über weite Strecken verhandelt wurden.[20]

---

11 Berlin, Staatliche Museen M.I. 7928: Züchner 62 KS 86, Taf. 7; Sichtermann, *Ganymed* 46 f., 84 K 140, Taf. 7.3.

12 Thieme-Becker 23 (1929) s. v. Leochares I, 66 f. (Bieber).

13 G. M. A. Richter, *Sculpture and sculptors of the Greeks* (4th edn., New Haven 1965) 286.

14 Sichtermann, *Ganymed* 46 f., 61.

15 Athen, NM St. 312: G. P. Oikonomos in P. Amandry, *Collection H. Stathatos* III (Strasbourg 1963) 73-80, 89, Taf. 10, Nr. 19; *LIMC* III (1986) s.v. Auge Nr. 9 mit Abb.

16 St. Petersburg, Ermitage BB 68: Züchner 12 KS 11, 215, Abb. 121; Schwarzmaier, *JdI* 111 (1996) 131, Abb. 19.

17 A. Furtwängler, *Die Sammlung Sabouroff* II (Berlin 1887) Text zu Taf. 147; Züchner 62 KS 86, Taf. 7.

18 Capua, Museo Campano Inv. 985: M. Bonghi-Jovino, "Una tabella capuana con ratto di Ganimede ed i suoi rapporti con l'arte tarentina," in J. Bibauw (ed.), *Hommages à M. Renard* III (CollLatomus 103, 1969) 66-78, Taf. 27.

19 Bonghi-Jovino ibid. 67.

20 Reinsberg (supra n.7) 245 f., 260-69, 272, 276; Schwarzmaier (supra n.5).

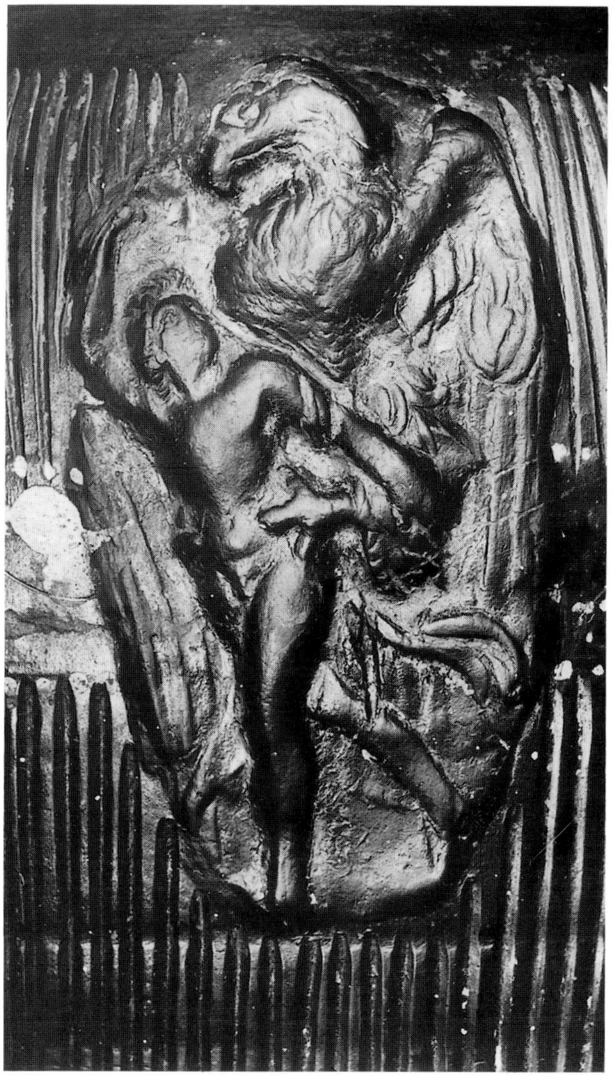

Abb. 4. Detail aus der Plakettenamphora. Um 300 v.Chr. Ehemals Berlin, Staatliche Museen V.I. 5901. (Photo: Antikensammlung, Staatliche Museen zu Berlin - Preußischer Kulturbesitz Ant. 7263.)

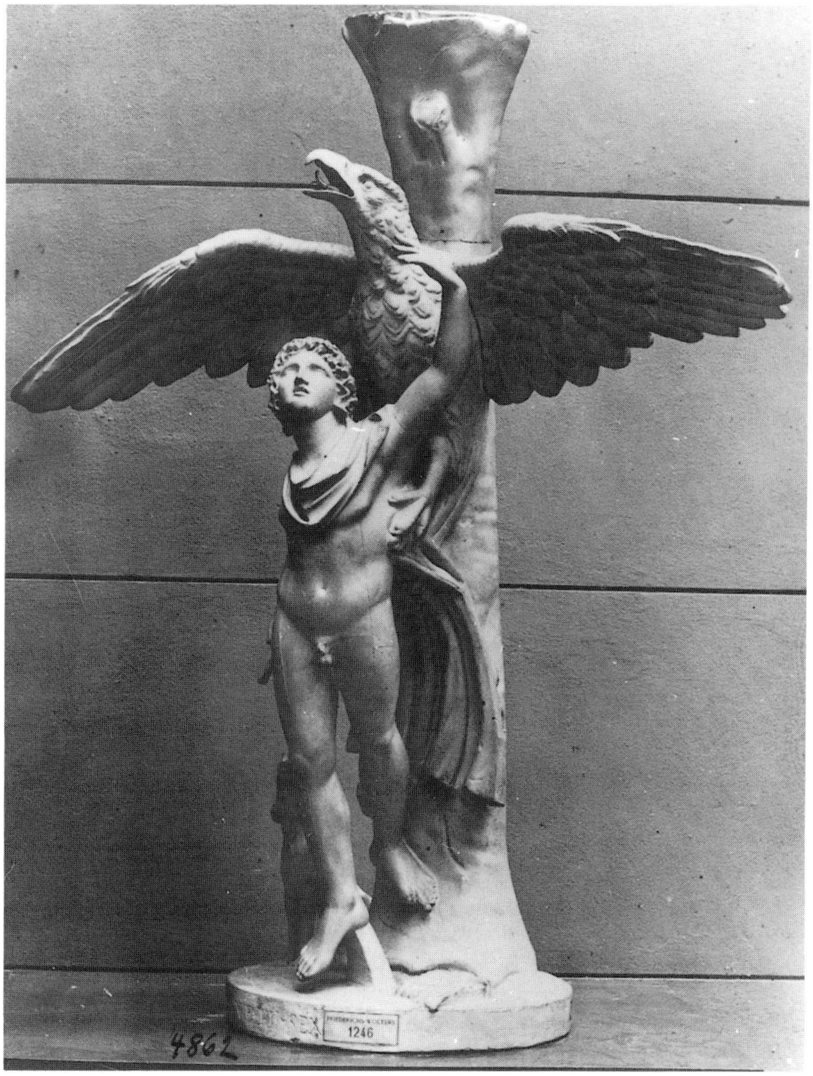

Abb. 5. Tischfuß. 2 Jh. n.Chr. Vatikan, Galleria dei Candelabri 118, nach dem ehemals in Berlin befindlichen Gipsabguß. (Photo: Rom Inst. Neg. 4862.)

Auch die Reliefs der schwarzgefirnißten Plakettenvasen sind normalerweise von Treibarbeiten abgeformt. Eine Fassung des Ganymedraubes kennt man von mindestens drei verschiedenen Gefäßen.[21] Die beste und vollständigste fand sich auf einer Strickhenkelamphora in Berlin, einem Kriegsverlust (Abb. 4),[22] auf der sie — anscheinend zusammenhanglos — mit zwei Heraklesdarstellungen verbunden war. Die Vase wird allgemein um 300 oder in den frühen Hellenismus datiert,[23] doch bedeutet dies für die abgeformten Metallreliefs nur einen *Terminus ante quem*. Das Ganymedrelief paßt m.E. aufgrund seines Aufbaus, der Proportionen, der Körperdrehung und des Bewegungsablaufs besser in die Mitte des 4. Jhs. als an dessen Ende.

---

21 Ph. Bruneau, "Ganymède et l'aigle," *BCH* 86 (1962) 194-200, Abb. 1-2bis.

22 Ehemals Berlin, Staatliche Museen V.I. 5901: Bruneau ibid. 198 f., Abb. 2; Sichtermann, *Ganymed* 51 K 142, Taf. 5.1.

23 Bruneau ibid. 197; *LIMC* IV.1 (1988) s.v. Ganymedes Nr. 198 (Sichtermann).

Sein Zusammenhang mit den beiden eben betrachteten Reliefs ist lockerer. Zwar stimmt der Adler etwa mit der Capuaner Fassung überein, doch wirkt der Ganymed durch seine Körperdrehung ungleich bewegter. Sein Rumpf und das vorgestreckte linke Bein sind fast frontal zu sehen, während das rechte im Hintergrund von der Seite abgebildet ist. Der erhobene rechte Arm hält sich am Adlerflügel fest, dazu chiastisch ist der linke gesenkt, ohne jedoch ins Gewand zu greifen. Und der Kopf dreht sich weit zur linken Schulter. Damit erinnert der Ganymed an laufende oder schwebende Gestalten wie den Eros der Berliner Bronzehydria[24] aus dem mittleren 4. Jh. Stimmt dies, verträte die Plakettenamphora die früheste erhaltene Fassung des Themas.

Hätte man nicht die Frage nach dem Ganymed des Leochares im Hinterkopf, würde man zunächst einmal alle drei Darstellungen als Werke der Flächenkunst verstanden haben, die für das zweidimensionale Medium konzipiert waren.[25] Sie zeigen, daß die Toreuten hier genauso mit einem Motiv umgingen wie beim Herakles Farnese. Ob ein solches Motiv dann von einem berühmten Werk wie dem Ganymed des Leochares beeinflußt oder unabhängig ist, soll dahingestellt bleiben.

In einem zweiten Schritt soll nun die archäologische Überlieferung gesichtet werden, die immer auf die Bronze des Leochares bezogen wird:

Das wichtigste Stück ist ein etwas über 1 m hoher römischer Tischfuß aus Marmor in der Galleria dei Candelabri im Vatikan (Abb. 5),[26] der wohl in Rom gefunden wurde. Er wurde 1786 von Vincenzo Pacetti stark ergänzt. Unter anderem sind große Teile der Arme und Beine des Ganymed, Adlerkopf und -flügel sowie der Hund auf der Plinthe (von dem aber Reste vorhanden waren) Ergänzungen des 18. Jhs. Sie riefen teilweise starke Kritik hervor.[27] Da aus dem 4. Jh. v.Chr. bisher keine Ganymeddarstellung mit seitlich ausgebreiteten Adlerschwingen bekannt ist, spricht vieles dafür, daß die Flügel gesenkt waren. Auch die Kopfwendung des Adlers nach oben wird mangels Parallelen zurecht angezweifelt. Im Bezug auf die Armhaltung sprechen die antiken Ansätze sowie die Muskulatur im Schulter- und Brustbereich dafür, Pacettis Ergänzung etwas zu modifizieren. Der zurückgeführte rechte Arm war wohl seitlich näher an den Körper gerückt, ebenso der erhobene linke, der zusätzlich wohl steiler nach oben ausgestreckt war in Richtung auf Adlerhals oder Flügel, ähnlich wie dies zwei Kleinbronzen in Paris und Berlin zeigen, von denen später noch die Rede sein soll. Auch ob Ganymed ein Pedum in der Hand hatte, ist unklar.

Nun stellt sich die Frage, wie man sich das Bronzeoriginal des Leochares vorstellen muß, wenn der Tischfuß wirklich auf diese Bronze zurückgeht, zumal auch deren genaue Datierung innerhalb der Lebenszeit des Künstlers nicht bekannt ist.[28] Die Tischstütze in Form eines Baumstammes gilt generell als Zufügung des römischen Kopisten.[29] Bei Hund und Syrinx herrscht dagegen in der Forschung keine einheitliche Meinung.[30] Das größte Problem bereitet es aber, sich vorzustellen, wie die Statue aufgestellt war bzw. wie ihre Statik funktionierte, wenn

---

24 Berlin, Staatliche Museen M.I. 8068: G. M. A. Richter, "A fourth-century bronze hydria in New York," *AJA* 50 (1946) 363, Taf. 24.4.

25 E. Künzl, *Frühhellenistische Gruppen* (Köln 1968) 29 f.

26 Sichtermann, *Ganymed* 40-46, 81 f. K 106, Taf. 3, 4.1-2, 6.1; G. Lippold, *Die Skulpturen des Vatikanischen Museums* III.2 (Berlin-Leipzig 1956) 216-19, Nr. 83, Taf. 103-4.

27 Sichtermann, *Ganymed* 41-44; Künzl (supra n.25) 28.

28 Der Ganymed wird — meist aus stilistischen Gründen ausgehend vom vatikanischen Tischfuß oder nach der bei Plinius überlieferten Akme des Künstlers — zwischen 370 v. Chr und der Alexanderzeit angesetzt: Sichtermann, *Ganymed* 61 f.; Künzl ibid. 30. Der Ansatz von G. Donnay, "La chronologie de Léochares," *REA* 61 (1959) 300-9, bes. 307, um die Mitte des 4. Jhs. beruht auf der hypothetischen Aufstellung des Originals in Troja.

29 Künzl ibid. 28 mit Anm. 50; F. Winter, "Die Komposition der Ganymedgruppe des Leochares," *JdI* 32 (1917) 226-28, Abb. 1-2.

30 Winter ibid.; Sichtermann, *Ganymed* 59.

man die Stütze in ihrem Rücken wegzudenken hat.[31] Eine sichere methodische Handhabe, um diese Fragen zu entscheiden, fehlt bisher, da es keine Parallelüberlieferung gibt. Nur wenige Darstellungen des Ganymedraubes in der Kleinkunst sind dem Tischfuß motivisch so ähnlich, daß man eine Abhängigkeit von demselben Original wahrscheinlich machen könnte.

Zwei sehr summarisch gearbeitete bronzene Gerätfüße — in der Pariser Bibliothèque Nationale und in der Berliner Antikensammlung[32] — sind vom Aufbau her dem Tischfuß vergleichbar, da eine Löwenklaue die Funktion des Baumstammes als Stütze für Adler und schwebenden Ganymed übernimmt. Letzterer bietet jeweils dem Betrachter den nackten Oberkörper frontal dar und hält sich mit dem linken Arm am Hals des Adlers fest, während der rechte ohne Attribut herabhängt. Der Adler — mit ausgebreiteten, aber gesenkten Flügeln — umgreift mit seinen Krallen die Taille des Jünglings. Ein Gewandstück scheint im Rücken herabzufallen und führt über den Oberschenkel des linken zurückgestreckten Beines. Der gesenkte Kopf des Adlers und der nach oben gewendete Blick des Ganymed begegnen sich. Die motivischen Unterschiede zum vatikanischen Tischfuß betreffen nur Partien, die dort ergänzt sind.

Mehrere Goldohrringpaare — z.B. in New York aus der Sammlung Bachstitz,[33] im Neapeler Nationalmuseum,[34] oder in Berlin[35] — aus dem späten 4. oder der 1. Hälfte des 3. Jhs. v. Chr., die den vom Adler entführten, schwebenden Ganymed zum Thema haben, geben für die Haltungsmotive von Armen und Beinen weniger her, da sie als Paare zwei zueinander symmetrisch angelegte Gruppen abbilden. Bei den Exemplaren des 3. Jhs. wird Ganymed zudem, entsprechend einer Mode, die auch an den gleichzeitigen Erotenohrringen abzulesen ist, mit kindlichen Körperformen ausgestattet.

Andere Darstellungen des Ganymedraubes in der Kleinkunst weichen noch weiter von den bisher betrachteten und auch voneinander ab, so daß sie zur Klärung der Frage nichts Neues beitragen können. Fassen wir also diesen Überblick über die Entführungsdarstellungen zusammen: Genaue Übereinstimmungen in der Haltung von Armen und Beinen etc. weisen nur die beiden bronzenen Gerätfüße und der Tischfuß auf, vorausgesetzt man erkennt an, daß letzterer falsch rekonstruiert ist. Alle anderen Stücke wirken wie freie Variationen einer zugrundeliegenden Idee, ähnlich wie dies schon für die Reliefdarstellungen aus Metall und Ton geschildert wurde. Damit bleibt die Materialbasis für die Rekonstruktion der von Plinius beschriebenen Bronzegruppe relativ brüchig. Doch zeichnet sich klar ab, daß sich der Ganymed des Berliner Klappspiegelreliefs in zumindest einem Zug von den anderen Darstellungen unterscheidet — und mit ihm das Capuaner Tonrelief. Beide Male ist Ganymed im Profil mit dem frontalen Adler verbunden, im Gegensatz zur sonst vorherrschenden Frontalität. Außerdem wurde ja schon dargelegt, daß das Spiegelrelief als zweidimensionales Werk komponiert ist und wie das Capuaner Relief den handwerklichen Gesetzmäßigkeiten der Toreutik unterliegt. Aus diesen Gründen halte ich es für methodisch unzulässig, den Ganymed des Leochares mit Hilfe des Berliner Klappspiegelreliefs rekonstruieren zu wollen.

Seminar für Klassische Archäologie der Freien Universität, Kiebitzweg 11, D-14195 Berlin

Mein Dank für vielfältige Hilfe bei der Abfassung dieser Arbeit gilt H. R. Goette, U. Kästner, G. Platz, E. D. Reeder und Chr. Schaefer.

---

31 Winter ibid. 227f.; Lippold (supra n. 26) 217.

32 Sichtermann, *Ganymed* 48, 80 K 91, Taf. 6.2 (Berlin); 81 K 102, Taf. 5.2 (Paris).

33 New York, MMA 37.11.9, Harris Brisbane Dick Fund 1937: B. Deppert-Lippitz, *Griechischer Goldschmuck* (Mainz 1985) 227, Abb. 163; Sichtermann, *Ganymed* 49 f., Taf. 7.1-2.

34 Neapel, NM 126423 und 126428: *LIMC* IV (1988) s.v. Ganymedes Nr. 203 mit Abb. (Sichtermann).

35 Berlin, Staatliche Museen: Sichtermann, *Ganymed* 80 K 89-90, Taf. 6.4-5.

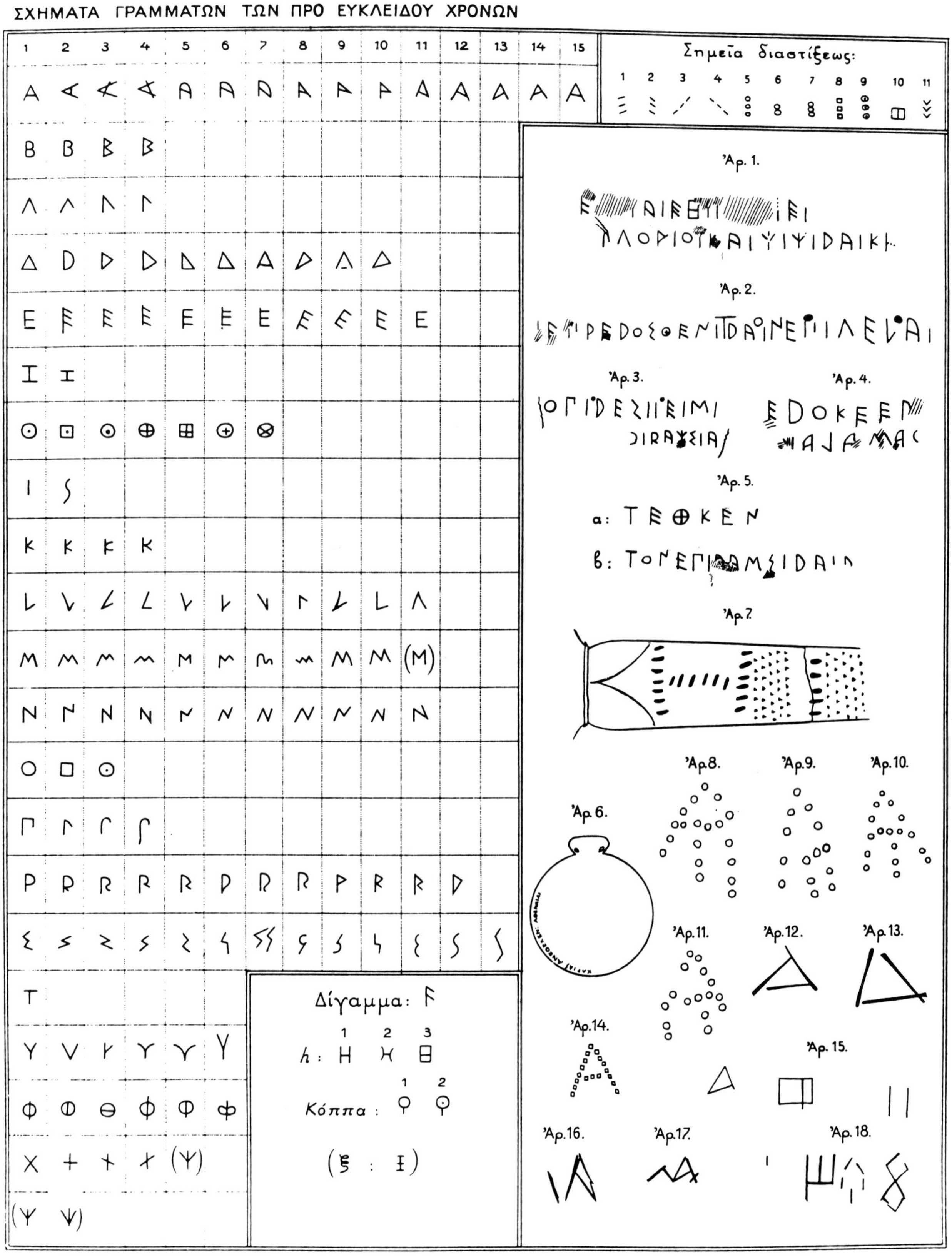

Fig. 1. Plate 1 of the Lolling-Wolters *Κατάλογος*. (Reproduced by kind permission of the Archaeological Etairia of Athens.)

Early publications of bronze inscriptions from the Akropolis

Patricia A. Butz

This paper is concerned with historiography, specifically the early historical writings documenting the bronze inscriptions found on the Athenian Akropolis. My interest in the recording of these bronze inscriptions grew out of a symposium held in September of 1994 at the German Archaeological Institute in Athens to honor the epigraphical and topographical achievements of H. G. Lolling, Director of the Epigraphical Museum, Athens, from 1888 until his death in 1894. My investigation of Lolling's various publications relating to the *editio princeps* of *IG* I^3 4, the "Hekatompedon Inscription", included his *Κατάλογος τοῦ ἐν Ἀθήναις Ἐπιγραφικοῦ Μουσείου*. Bronze is one of two major materials covered in the *Κατάλογος*, and it is clear that any study of these dedicatory inscriptions from the Athenian Akropolis must depend on Lolling's early work, published posthumously in 1899. It was edited and completed by P. Wolters, who was chosen by the Archaeological Etairia of Athens for his expertise and as a countryman of Lolling's,[1] hence the proper designation Lolling-Wolters in the epigraphical literature. While most of the bronzes from the *Κατάλογος* have been incorporated into *IG* I^3,[2] there has never been a re-publication or photographic treatment of the bronze inscriptions from the Akropolis as a whole. Other, more recent finds, notably Akropolis 6474 (*IG* I^3 48bis), published by D. Peppas-Delmousou in 1971 as the single extant example of an Attic decree on bronze,[3] would certainly be a major addition to such a corpus, showing the important use of bronze for inscriptions other than dedications on the Akropolis.

Lolling's preface to the *Κατάλογος* outlines the hierarchy of goals for publishing the collection of the Epigraphical Museum.[4] The portion ultimately completed by Wolters was to have been the first part of the first volume of inscriptions whose provenance was the Akropolis; a second volume was to have been devoted to inscriptions in the lower city, outside Attika, and in other provinces of Greece. The actual contents of the single extant volume of the *Κατάλογος* are thus limited to dedications from the Akropolis and are divided according to the major media: Ἐπιγραφαὶ ἐπὶ χαλκωμάτων and Ἐπιγραφαὶ ἐπὶ λίθων. Wolters mentions that Lolling left half of the 129 bronze inscriptions unfinished, as opposed to his near completion of the 398 entries of inscriptions on stone.[5] Perhaps for this reason, the bronzes are simply treated as a homogeneous group of dedications and are not further divided by specifics, such as type of object carrying the inscription or nature of the dedication, as are the stone entries. Since it is not subdivided, the bronze section may, therefore, have a better chance of exemplifying the overall chronological development of Greek inscriptions idealistically referred to by Lolling in his own preface.[6]

---

1 H. G. Lolling (ed. P. Wolters), *Κατάλογος τοῦ ἐν Ἀθήναις Ἐπιγραφικοῦ Μουσείου* (Athens 1899) ε′ and ζ′.

2 Appendix I of my article, "H. G. Lolling and the *editio princeps* of the 'Hekatompedon Inscription'," written for the aforementioned DAI symposium, offers a concordance between the work of Lolling and *IG* I^3.

3 Πέππα-Δελμούζου, Ντ. "Χαλκῆ ἐπιγραφὴ τοῦ Μουσείου Ἀκροπόλεως," *AE* 1971.137-45.

4 Lolling-Wolters, *Κατάλογος* ε′-ζ′. Note that the format of the title page, with the subdivisions Τόμος Πρῶτος and Τεῦχος Πρῶτον, implies the greater intention of the project, although it was never realized.

5 Ibid. η′.

6 "Διὰ τῶν περὶ τοῦ σχήματος τῶν γραμμάτων καὶ τῶν ἄλλων γενικῶν εἰσαγωγικῶν εἰς ἑκάστην ἐπιγραφὴν παρατηρήσεων ἅμα δὲ διὰ τῶν παρ′ αὐτα τὰ κείμενα παρατεθειμένων χρονολογικῶν σημειώσεων καὶ δι′ αὐτῆς τῆς ὅσον ἔνεστι χρονολοθικῆς κατατάξεως τῶν ἐπιγραφῶν ἐκτυλίσσεται ἐξ ἑαυτῆς οὕτως εἰπεῖν ἡ γενικὴ ἱστορία τῆς ἀττικῆς καὶ ἰωνικῆς γραφῆς." (Ibid. ς -ζ′).

Lolling puts great emphasis on the shape of letter-forms, exemplified in the single plate of pre-Eukleidian letter-forms that illustrates the *Κατάλογος* (fig. 1). Notes specifying individual letter-forms designated on the chart accompany the epigraphic text of each catalogue entry; the chart is to be referred to constantly as a means of visualizing the inscription. It is therefore possible to construct as individual a picture of the inscription as far as the details of the chart allow while printing the texts uniformly, a practice that is similar to that used in *IG*. In this way, as Lolling himself explains, the great expense of facsimile reproductions or the use of upper case epigraphical typefaces, where a mixture of forms can create a confused effect, is avoided.[7] Furthermore, for each entry the *Κατάλογος* always gives references to additional texts or visual renderings of the inscription, including upper case transcriptions. This bibliographic data is offered immediately after the physical description of the inscription and the material on which it is carried — also a practice followed in later corpora. It is significant that Lolling's chart of letter-forms contains 18 line-drawings, all for bronze inscriptions, fitted into a column alongside the tabular divisions for letter-form development.[8] Line-drawings of some of the inscriptions on stone occur within the text, but the isolation of this group of bronze inscriptions on the plate privileges the class in a very particular way.

Two cross references occur constantly throughout the individual bibliographies for the various bronze entries in the *Κατάλογος*. The earlier and more epigraphical is the article by A. G. Bather, "The bronze fragments of the Acropolis," containing 65 entries for bronze inscriptions found on the Acropolis during the 1885-89 excavation seasons;[9] all 65 entries are cross-referenced in the *Κατάλογος*.[10] The body of Bather's article is a brief checklist, which immediately shows the simplicity of these dedications and the fact that the majority are to Athena. Two very useful plates provide line-drawings of the inscribed portion of each fragment. Furthermore, objects are listed as to type: vessel fragments, spearhead and helmet fragments, an ornament, a knob, a weight, a statuette, a shield, and a number of fragments uncertain as to function. Bather notes outstanding palaeographic features: for example, the dotted delta[11] (considered by H. Immerwahr to be an original bronze form)[12] or the occurrence of upside-down alphas when the remainder of an inscription has upright letter-forms.[13] Bather seems to offer a blanket *terminus ante quem* for the entire group of Attic and non-Attic bronze

---

7 Ibid. ζʹ.

8 These drawings are labeled consecutively ('Αρ. = ἀριθμός); these numbers, however, do not correspond with catalogue entries for the respective bronze inscriptions, which are given in Roman numerals. The equivalents are as follows:

'Αρ. 1 = I	'Αρ. 10 = CXV
'Αρ. 2 = II	'Αρ. 11 = CXVI
'Αρ. 3 = III	'Αρ. 12 = CXVIII
'Αρ. 4 = V	'Αρ. 13 = CXX
'Αρ. 5 = VII (a and b)	'Αρ. 14 = CXXI
'Αρ. 6 = XLV	'Αρ. 15 = CXXVI
'Αρ. 7 = XCI	'Αρ. 16 = CXXVII
'Αρ. 8 = CXIII	'Αρ. 17 = CXXVII (same as above)
'Αρ. 9 = CXIV	'Αρ. 18 = CXXVIII

9 A. G. Bather, "The bronze fragments of the Acropolis," *JHS* 13 (1892-93). Note that only the first part of the Bather article (pp. 124-30) is epigraphical; it carries no subtitle or indication that a second part, subtitled "II. Ornamented bands and small objects" (pp. 232-71), follows later.

10 Lolling-Wolters, *Κατάλογος* (supra n.1) 29-33.

11 Bather 1892-93 (supra n.9) 126, no. 6.

12 Referring to the dotted delta, see H. Immerwahr, *Attic script: a survey* (Oxford 1990) 137: "Although I left the question of origin open in *Classical Studies Ullman*, I am still inclined to assume a bronze origin." See pp. 136-37 for his full discussion of the delta letter-form.

13 Bather 1892-93 (supra n.9) 125, no. 3.

inscriptions, namely the Persian destruction, with those pieces inscribed in the Attic dialect dating as early as the end of the 7th c. B.C.[14]

Only 50 of the 129 *Κατάλογος* bronze inscriptions are included in A. De Ridder's classic of 1896, *Catalogue des bronzes trouvés sur l'Acropole d'Athènes;* yet unquestionably the De Ridder catalogue is a more ambitious and influential reference tool, particularly for its sculptural component, than the Bather article. The publication has 835 entries and 340 illustrations with an additional 8 full plates and is printed using a variety of upper case fonts attempting to simulate the inscriptions when they occur, juxtaposed to the lower case rendering of the text. Unfortunately, the capital fonts are mixed and/or employed indiscriminately in many cases.[15] What De Ridder does provide are invaluable photographic illustrations for numerous objects that are inscribed. While the inscription invariably suffers to some degree with the heliographic technique employed in the publication, these illustrations provide very valuable evidence for the placement of the inscription when it can be seen.[16] De Ridder divides his work into 3 major parts. The first is labelled *instruments* and includes vessels, toilet articles, military equipment, trade, and miscellaneous articles. The second and third are animal figurines and human statuettes, respectively. The highest concentration of inscribed material is almost equal for the following areas: vases, military equipment, and male and female statuettes.[17] Representing the last group, the striding Athena Promachos with her inscribed platform base is probably the most well-known of any object in the catalogue. Interestingly, De Ridder illustrates the statuette but not the inscription (fig. 2), which has rarely been reproduced in any visual format despite the pre-eminence of the bronze figurine.[18]

---

14 Ibid. 130.

15 For example, see A. De Ridder, *Catalogue des bronzes trouvés sur l'Acropole d'Athènes* (Paris 1896) 73-74, no. 219, where the mix of Archaic and Classical forms for epsilon and nu is particularly noticeable. In addition, De Ridder prints a weighted *h*eta, upright mu, and weighted alpha for the inscription; the "Classical" nu is also weighted. Compare with Bather 1892-93 (supra n.9) pl. 6, no. 9, and Lolling-Wolters, *Κατάλογος* (supra n.1) no. XVII. Despite the discrepancies, however, there is the sense in De Ridder of the desire for accuracy in the shifting of fonts and especially in those entries rendered in the pointillist technique (for example, nos. 281, 282, 283, 287); also the desire for completeness. He closes his introduction with these words:

> Je terminerai en signalant un certain nombre d'inscriptions sur bronze que j'ai dû simplement indiquer. M. Lolling a en effet laissé une étude complète de ces documents, et je n'aurais pas voulu empiéter sur ses droits. Du moins, aurais-je souhaité de pouvoir renvoyer à son travail. Je regrette que, malgré les efforts de M. Cavvadias, cette permission m'ait été refusée (p. 3).

Interestingly, Wolters seems to imply a sequel to the *Catalogue* by the following remark, although there is no such indication on De Ridder's title page or in his preface or introduction:
". . . ὁ ὑπὸ De Ridder κατάλογος (Catalogue des bronzes trouvés sur l'Acropole d'Athènes) οὗτινος ἄρτι ἐξδόθη ὁ πρῶτος τόμος" (*Κατάλογος* 1-2).

16 The De Ridder publication employs 8 heliogravures for its major plates; the 340 figures appear to be heliographs printed as line-drawings and occur throughout the text. Not every object, let alone every inscription, is illustrated. One of the most successful is fig. 191 illustrating no. 601, a stepped rectangular base of bronze measuring 17.7 cm long, 5.8 cm wide, and 4.4 cm high according to the entry. The inscription runs around three sides of the base, but only one side is actually shown. So clear is the illustration of these last 11 letters, however, that De Ridder chooses not to print the full transcription. The base, in fact, is equivalent to Lolling-Wolters, *Κατάλογος* no. IX, where fortunately the full text is cited (with 3-point interpuncts) as follows:

> Αἰσχίνες · Χαρίας · ἀνεθέlτεν · τἀθεlναία(ι) · ἀπαρχέν.

17 The actual count in De Ridder is as follows: 15 entries in the subcategory of vases; 14 entries in the military subcategory (including helmets, shields, spears, swords, and battle axes); and 15 in the division of human statuettes (including inscribed bases as well as inscribed figures). By contrast, De Ridder lists only 3 inscribed animal statuettes (nos. 515, 527, and 529).

18 *IG* I^3 540 (= Lolling-Wolters, *Κατάλογος* no. XXVIII = De Ridder, *Catalogue* no. 796, fig. 302) lists only two drawings of the inscription, one in the Ἀρχ. Ἐφ. 1887 (p. 142, fig. 5) and the other in A.

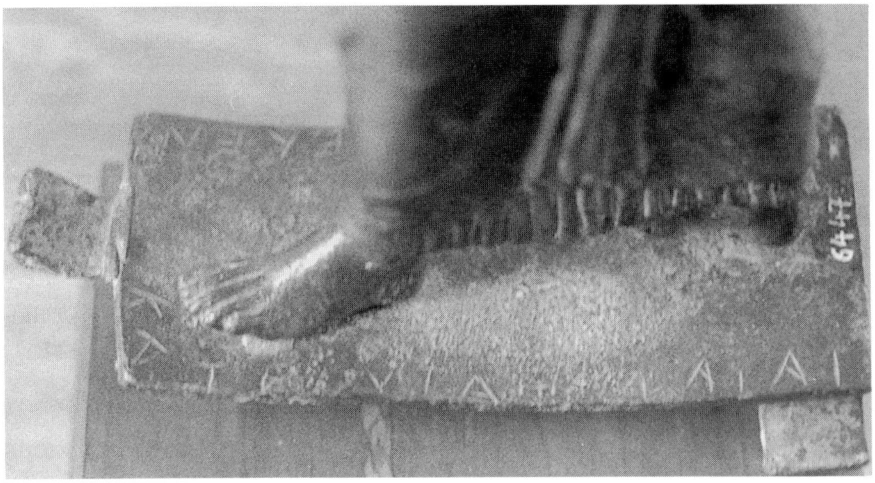

Fig. 2. *IG* I^3 540. Inscribed base of the Athena Promachos from the Akropolis. Bronze, length of base .118 m. Athens, National Museum X.6447. (Photo: author.)

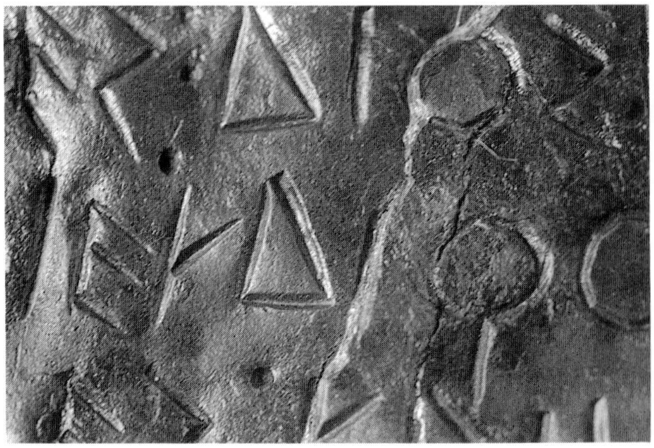

Fig. 4. Detail of *IG* I^3 510, showing ductus of the inscription in portions of lines 2, 3, and 4. Range of H of letters 0.013-0.020 (Photo: author.)

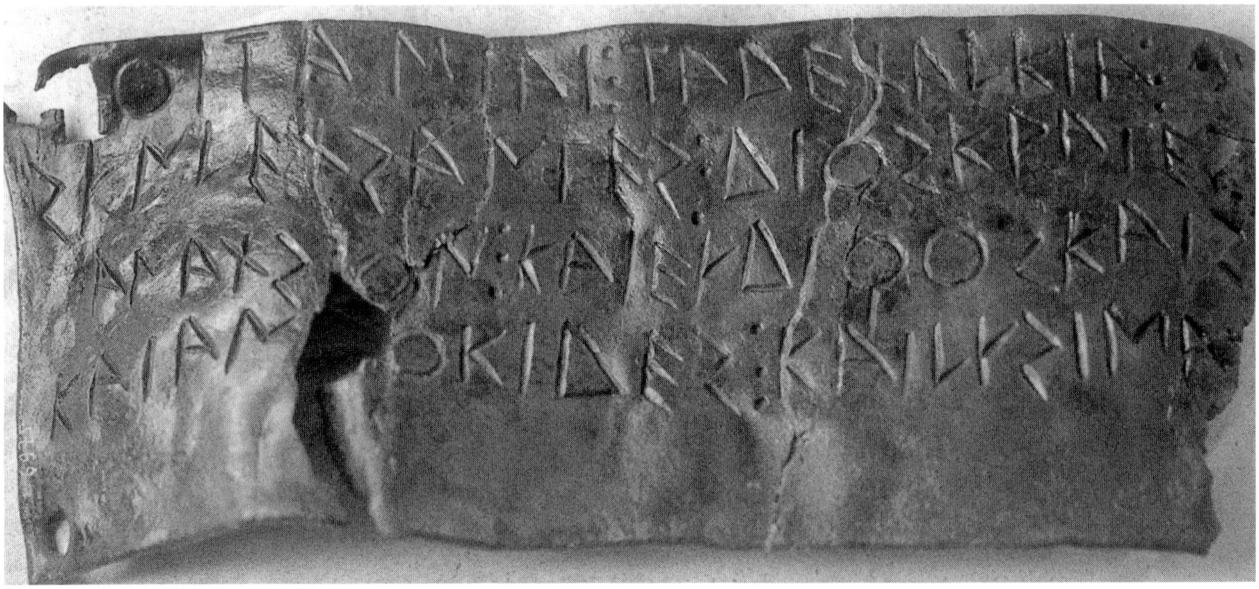

Fig. 3. *IG* I^3 510. Dedication by the Treasurers of Athena from the Akropolis. Bronze, pres. length *c.* .25 m. Athens, National Museum X.6975. (Photo: author.)

Among this remarkable assortment of dedications on bronze that has survived from the Akropolis, the foremost example for bronze epigraphy must be *IG* I^3 510 (fig. 3), recording a dedication: made by the Treasurers of Athena.[19] It is considered the only surviving bronze plaque of early date from Attica by L. Jeffery, who dates the text *c.*550(?) B.C.[20] Lolling-Wolters describes the object carrying the inscription "Ἔλασμα χαλκοῦν"[21] and prints the text (with 3-point interpuncts) as follows:

Arbanitopoulos, *Ἐπιγραφική* I (p. 95, fig. 66). The corpus dates the dedication *c.*480-470?, which reads the same as Lolling-Wolters:

Μελεσò ἀνέθεκεν | δεκάlτεν τἀθεναίαι.

For the Athena Promachos statuette, see especially the plates (two views, one in color) and the catalogue entry in A. Delivorrias (ed.), *Greece and the sea* (Athens 1987) no. 96.

19 Lolling-Wolters, *Κατάλογος* no. XI; De Ridder, *Catalogue* no. 428.

20 L. H. Jeffery, *The local scripts of Archaic Greece* (rev. edn., Oxford 1990) 72 and 77, no. 21.

21 Lolling-Wolters, *Κατάλογος* no. XI. In commenting more fully on this *lamella aenea,* the corpus suggests the possibility of the plaque being part of a στήλη χαλκῆ as described by A. E. Raubitschek in

Hοι ταμίαι · τάδε χαλκία · - -
συνλέχσαντες · Διὸς κρατερ[όφρονι ϙόρει - -
'Αναχσίον · καὶ Εὔδιϙος καὶ Σ - -
καὶ 'Ανδοκίδες · καὶ Λυσιμαχ - -

The antiquity of the inscription as an Attic document in the public sphere[22] and its relationship to an inventory[23] are aspects that have attracted scholarly attention. But I would suggest that its significance also lies in the self-referential form of the inscription: that is to say, this is an inscription on bronze about bronze used as the medium of dedication: τάδε χαλκία.[24] It is instructive to compare Lolling's entry with the other two sources examined here. Because of his disposition of categories, De Ridder is reduced to putting the plaque under

---

Dedications from the Athenian Akropolis (Cambridge, MA 1949) 352: " ... consisting of a wooden or stone stele on which bronze plaques were fastened with nails." There is clear evidence of one nail hole in the lower left corner of the plaque; the broken rectangle in the upper left corner must also have been a nail hole. The corpus lists a third hole preserved after the interpunct in line 1, just before the break on the right side, and marking the middle of the plaque. The damage along the right side is considerable, however, and there are other breaks, including internal ones. Compare my fig. 3 with Jeffery ibid., pl. 3, no. 21, where the latter appears to have holes or indentations in all four corners. The plaque was clearly restored at the time of the Jeffery photograph and shows the filling of the large break in lines 3-4 and the 3 or 4 corner holes or depressions, as well as repair work along the right side. My examination of the inscription in September 1996 showed that these restorations have now been removed. The positive determination of the third nail hole in the first line is an important factor for any restoration, as well as the question of display. For further discussion of the evidence for bronze stelai and how they were displayed, see R. Stroud, "A fragment of an inscribed bronze stele from Athens," *Hesperia* 32 (1963) 138-43, especially 138, n.1 for literary references; also 139-40 for the possible format of a fully bronze stele based on evidence provided by the unique fragment receiving its *editio princeps* in the article.

22 L. Threatte, *The grammar of Attic inscriptions. I: Phonology* (Berlin 1980) 2: "The mid-sixth-century bronze plaque inscribed by a group of *tamiai*, I^2 393 (= *LSAG*, p. 77, no. 21), is without parallel at Athens, but as there are no contemporary public texts in this early period it is impossible to say such plaques were rarer at Athens than elsewhere, where they are sometimes well attested, as e.g., at Elis ... ."

23 D. Harris, *The treasures of the Parthenon and the Erechtheion* (Oxford 1995) 14, more for the rôle of the treasurers making the dedication than the bronzes themselves. Harris makes the point, "Strictly speaking, the inscription is a dedicatory plaque, not an inventory." Indeed, the treasurers are listed by name, albeit brokenly, whereas the objects being dedicated are not. The restoration of the broken lines is conservative in Lolling-Wolters compared with the corpus, where space is allotted for 8 treasurers' names, reflecting the belief that 2 treasurers were named representing each tribe (only 3 of the supposed 8 names are, however, intact). I would suggest that the plaque is far from complete, and it is possible that the objects could still have been listed in inventory fashion following the break after τάδε χαλκία, or conceivably after the names of the treasurers, if the items were short and the spacing could accommodate them. Spacing in this inscription is not sure, especially if one re-evaluates the center nail hole. For a later dedication recording items in such an inventory-like fashion, see *IG* II^2 4511; also *SEG* 33 (1983), no. 196 for bibliography on *IG* II^2 4511, supporting its identification as a dedication despite its fragmentary nature. I am grateful to S. Aleshire for drawing my attention to *IG* II^2 4511 as a possible parallel.

24 The question arises as to the meaning of χαλκία for this inscription. Harris, ibid., now translates the word as "metals" (cf., D. Harris, "The inventory lists of the Parthenon treasures" [Diss., Princeton Univ. 1991] 20, where her translation reads "bronzes"), explaining that χαλκία as a term "was not exclusive to bronze or copper until relatively late (1st *c.* B.C.) but was a generic term." There is, however, a very specific definition given in *LSJ*, for which *IG* I^3 510 is cited as important support (s.v., χαλκίον: copper vessel, cauldron, or kettle). To repeat, if there were need for further amplification or even enumeration of such vessels in *IG* I^3 510, I believe that there would be ample room for such a restoration in the broken portions mentioned above. It is also important to remember that copper is the principal and defining substance of bronze, despite other additives that critically establish its identity and behavior as an alloy; hence bronze legitimately comes under the non-generic rubric of copper, χαλκός. I would unhesitatingly translate τάδε χαλκία as "these bronze vessels."

"miscellaneous objects" as the single "inscription," *per se*, in his catalogue, and does not offer an illustration. Instead, he prints the inscription in an upper case font that is particularly problematic in terms of attempting a facsimile.[25] Lolling's notations directing the reader, letter-form by letter-form, to his chart[26] are far more accurate, as may be judged from the inscription proper (fig. 4). Bather does not include the inscription in his checklist. Yet the finding of this inscription was clearly considered a highlight of the 1887-88 season,[27] and received its *editio princeps*[28] precisely during the excavation period that Bather covers in his article.

Τάδε χαλκία, referring to the dedicated bronzes, probably cauldrons, by the Treasurers of Athena in *IG* I[3] 510, recalls the restoration [[Τὰ χαλκία τὰ ἐ]μ πόλει, which opens the B-metope of the "Hekatompedon Inscription". If the restoration is correct, the first 4 lines of the metope, down to the 9-point interpunct, are concerned with the treatment of these metal objects. Such epigraphic evidence confirms that bronze prompted a protocol of behavior for the ancient Greeks that went far beyond its intrinsic value as a metal. The attitude manifests itself in such acts as inscribing directly on the bronze object or its base in the form of a dedication; also in the very identification and recording of the object or objects involved. The act is intensified and made more self-reflexive when both the dedicating and the recording are done together on the same piece of metal, as with the dedication by the Treasurers of Athena. The early publications recording the inscribed bronzes from the Akropolis in simple catalogue format, most successfully by Lolling-Wolters, are themselves representatives of the last stage in this same tradition.

3755 Greenhill Road, Pasadena, CA 91107

Acknowledgements

I wish to thank the organizers for the opportunity to present this aspect of H. G. Lolling's work at the 13th International Bronze Congress. I am indebted to I. Zervoudaki and the National Archaeological Museum, Athens, for permission to study the technique and palaeography of several of the bronze inscriptions discussed by Lolling, Bather, and De Ridder; and to A.-I. Trianti and the Akropolis Museum for permission to study *IG* 1[3] 48bis. My deep appreciation also goes to B. Petrakos, Secretary General of the Archaeological Etairia of Athens, for permission to use plate I from the Lolling-Wolters *Κατάλογος*; and to S. Aleshire, who generously consented to read an earlier draft of the paper. Needless to say, the views and any errors that remain are entirely my own.

---

25 De Ridder, *Catalogue* 142.

26 Lolling-Wolters, *Κατάλογος* no. XI, where the letter-forms according to the chart are given as follows: α12, δ6, ε10, h3, κ1, κ2 (only in line 1), μ6, ν5, ϙ1, ρ9, σ5, υ3, χ3.

27 J. E. Harrison, "Archaeology in Greece, 1887-1888," *JHS* 9 (1888) 118-33, esp. 125 for the inscription, together with a line-drawing indicating 4 nail holes in the corners of the extant plaque.

28 *CIA* IV, 1, no. 373[238] (= *IG* I s, no. 373[238]+), the first citation given for the inscription in Lolling-Wolters, *Κατάλογος* no. XI, indicating precedence over the *Δελτίον ἀρχ.* (1888) 55. *IG* I s offers the further explanation: *Imaginem tituli ed.* Kavvadias, *Deltíon* 1888 p. 55 (cf. *Journal of the Hellenic studies* IX (1888) p. 125). *Nos damus e delineatione, quam transmisit* Lolling." Note that both the drawing and Lolling's explanation as printed in *IG* I s show three holes in the plaque, one after the interpunct in line 1. The physical properties, restoration, and palaeography of this inscription and other selected examples in Lolling-Wolters are elements that I intend to return to in a future publication.

A fine example of toreutic art from Epirus

Eliana Raftopoulou

An important seal ring comes from a cist grave discovered by chance in 1959 in the village of Kerason, in Epirus.[1] The double-sided seal, of gilded silver,[2] has an oval bezel and a swivel ring.[3] Both the unique engraved representation on the obverse and the exceptional quality of the workmanship classify it as a rare example of its art.[4]

On the obverse, a standing youth is shown attacking a seated woman (fig. 1). The youth, who wears a *chlamys* and a *petasos*, moves toward his left, holding a sword upright in his right hand, while with his left hand he grasps the woman by her raised left arm. Dressed in a rich Ionic *chiton* and seated on an altar, she attempts to resist, although she is already wounded in the breast. On the left side of the bezel, traces of letters have been restored as the names of Orestes and Clytemnestra.[5] Thus the seal depicts the murder of Clytemnestra by her son.

There is a wealth of detail in the decorative motifs, for example, the large palmettes and scroll patterns that represent embroidery or textile designs on Clytemnestra's *chiton*; the stippling of tiny dots on Orestes's *chlamys*; Clytemnestra's finely woven veil (with its dotted band and fringe along the length of the border); the sandals with their complex laces; the spiral bracelets; and the decorated altar.

The figures are rendered with full, sturdy body shapes and relatively large heads. Orestes's muscular torso is accentuated by the motion of attack and the diagonal formed by his shoulder strap, while his *chlamys*, fastened at the breast, flows freely behind his back. Clytemnestra, who is seated in a rather loose, off-balance pose, holds the palm of her left hand open, in a barely rendered, rather formless gesture of supplication. Her wide *chiton* is rendered with a sometimes wavy, sometimes antithetical line of the folds. The emphasis on the floral motifs of the garment, as well as the fine veil, are characteristic of the rich style at the close of the 5th c. B.C.,[6] a dating also supported by the head types and the linear folds of the drapery.

On the basis of this brief description, traces can be discerned of Ionic influence, both in terms of the human figures and the decorative elements, as well as in the artistic technique and the Attic motifs. These are most clearly seen in the seated woman, whose basic attitude derives from an earlier type, that of the seated Aphrodite from the Circle of Pheidias,[7] where for the

---

1 Nome of Preveza, at the 48th km on the road between Ioannina and Arta: G. Daux, *BCH* 84 (1960); *Chronique* (1959) 745, fig. 2; S. Dakaris, *Οι Γενεαλογικοί μύθοι των Μολοσσών* (Athens 1964) 91, pl. 3; I. P. Vokotopoulou, Οδηγός Μουσείου Ιωαννίνων (Athens 1973) 47 (Room A, Case 11) inv. 4279, pl. 14; *Κατάλογος Εκθέσεως, Εθν. Αρχ. Μουσείο (20 March - 10 September 1995)* 62, no. 31.

2 The hair, clothing, accessories, and the altar are gilded. The technique of gilding silver is common: D. Musti *et al.*, *L'oro dei Greci* (Rome 1992) for example no. 137, silver kylix, Plovdiv, Museo Archeologico 1516; B. Filow and I. Welkow, *JdI* 45 (1930) 294.3, pl. 9: "Selene ... Ende des 5 Jhr." With regard to finger rings in this technique: T. Homolle, *BCH* 6 (1882) 122: ὑπόχρυσος ... ὑποκεχρυσωμένος.

3 Diam. bezel: 0.039 x 0.032 m; th. bezel: 0.004 m; h. ring: 0.033 m; th. ring: 0.005 m. The ring has a nearly circular body, decorated with an engraved, schematic scroll pattern repeated 4 times (fig. 2). On the reverse of the seal, central engraved motif: a pumpkin flower which rises on spiral tendrils. On the border is a crown of myrtle leaf encircling a floral wreath with palmettes pointing alternatively up and down. Excellent state of preservation.

4 Cf. J. Boardman, *Greek gems and finger rings* (London 1970) 224 ff., fig. 230: "its style and complexity go far beyond anything in this or any other 4th c. group."

5 Cf. P. R. Franke, *Die antiken Münzen von Epirus* 1 (Wiesbaden 1961) 86 n.5; *LIMC* VI.1 (1992) s.v. Klytaimestra, 77, no. 32.

6 Cf. Franke (supra n.5): "aus der Zeit um 400 v. Chr."; N. G. L. Hammond, *Epirus* (Oxford 1967) 156, 510: "silver seal of the late 5th c."

7 Cf. Helbig[4] IV (1972) no. 3229 (W. Fuchs), Villa Albani: "sogenannte Olympias"; Helbig[4] II (1966) 1326

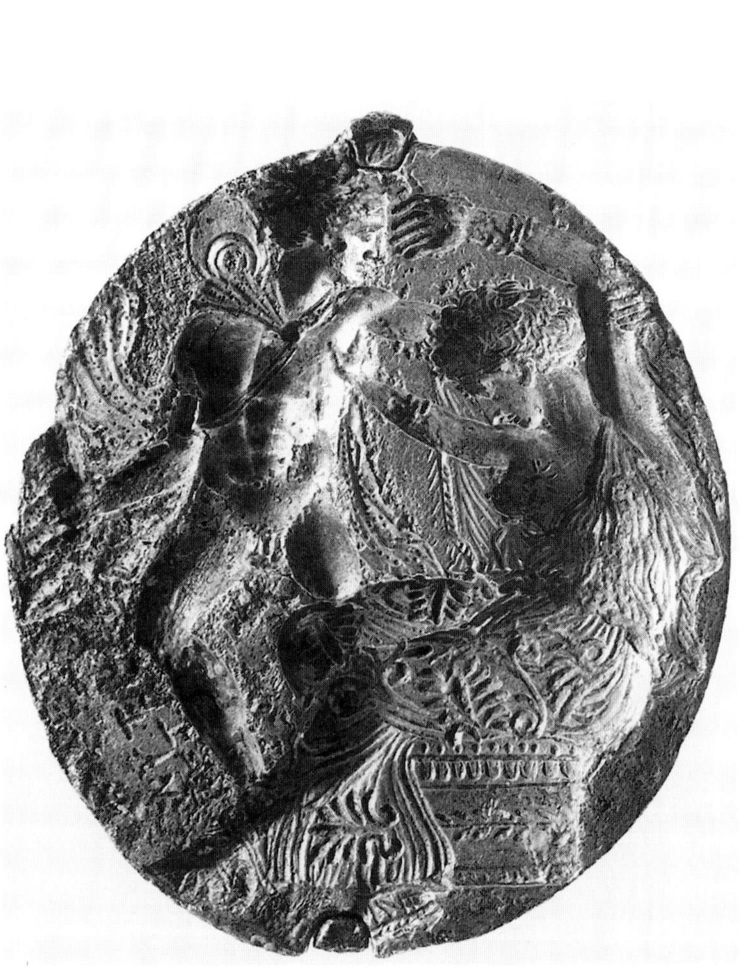

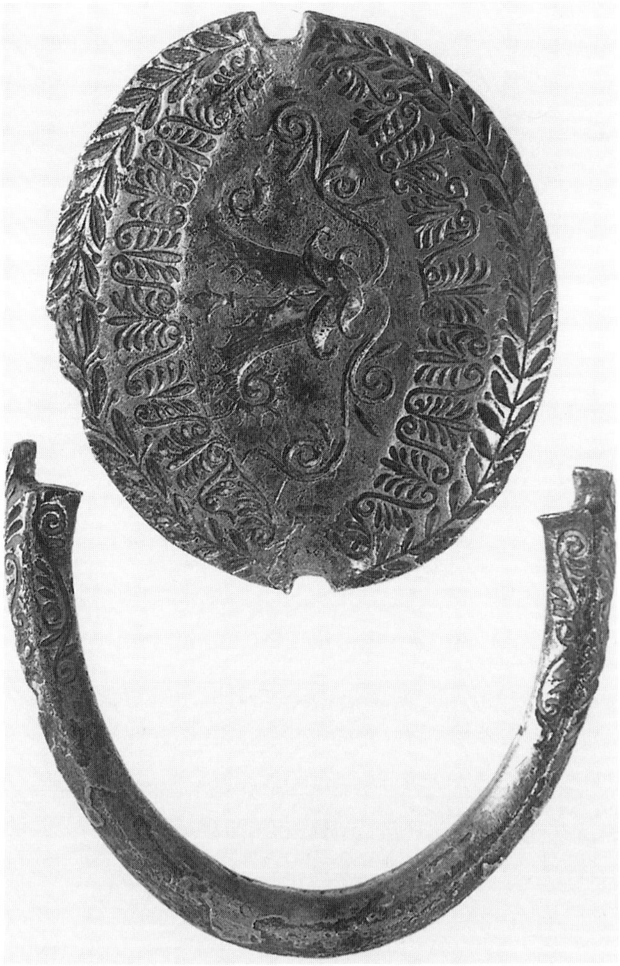

Fig. 1. Obverse of seal ring from Kerason, Epirus. Greek, *c.* late 5th c. B.C. Gilt silver, diam. of bezel 0.039 x 0.032 m. Ioannina, Museum 4279. (Photo: author.) Fig. 2. Reverse. (Photo: author.)

first time in sculpture the three-quarter view is presented as the principal view. An important characteristic of this statue, the exceptionally rich drapery whose folds form a dense linear texture, is distantly echoed in the ribbon-like folds of Clytemnestra's *chiton*. Her pose is also related to that of the Barberini Suppliant, particularly in the slackness of her pose and the nakedness of her breast, as well as in the design of the *chiton* and her snaky locks, which reflect the precision which one associates with the art of metalwork.

The pair in conflict in art of the advanced 5th c. B.C. (as well as related, antithetical groups consisting of two figures) can be seen, with variations, in the Amazonomachy Frieze from the Temple of Apollo at Bassae, Phigaleia. There is an obvious iconographic correlation with slab no. 535 in the British Museum[8] from the west frieze of this temple, in terms of the opposed forces of the bodies and the similarity in poses. On this slab the altar on which the Amazon sits seeking asylum is also depicted. On slab no. 532 in the British Museum[9] from the east frieze of the temple, we can also observe similarities in the depiction of movement, although here it is in the opposite direction. Both the frieze and the seal representation date to approximately the same time, and the seal must have been based on the Peloponnesian relief.

(H. v. Heintze) Capitoline Museum; W. Fuchs, *Die Skulptur der Griechen* (Munich 1993) 265, fig. 293 "Werk des phidiasischen Kreises," "um 430/420"; G. Becatti, *Problemi Fidiaci* (Rome 1951) fig. 294, pl. 96.

8 Cf. C. Hofkes-Brukker and A. Mallwitz, *Der Bassai-Fries* in *der ursprünglich geplanten Anordnung* (Munich 1975) 77 f.: pl. H16-535 (left group).

9 Ibid. 83 f., pl. H20-532 (left group); the representation on this slab is completed at the left lower corner by the representation of an altar, so that here as well the scene is related to a violation of asylum.

Thus, by comparing our motif to the types of sculpture in the round and architectural relief work, the influence of contemporary large-scale sculpture on the art of metalwork is confirmed once more: the iconographic motifs were converted and adapted in small-scale renderings, utilizing a different material and technique. On the other hand, as D. B. Thompson observes,[10] metalwork also influenced marble sculpture in the techniques of rendering — the depiction of drapery, the exceptionally fine workmanship, etc.

Aside from the dual composition, the significance of this seal centers on its subject matter, the murder of Clytemnestra by Orestes. If we should choose to investigate the iconographic sources of the scene, which are independent of the literary tradition, a primary example would be the disk seal of steatite from Crete in the Metropolitan Museum of Art, New York.[11] The engraved representation, which has been called "an unusually fine example of engraved art from the very late 8th or early 7th c. B.C.,"[12] is of a standing, clothed woman in the act of attacking a seated, nude man. In regard to M. I. Davies's interpretation of the scene as the murder of Agamemmnon by Clytemnestra, various opinions have been given. However, even though the chronological gap between the two is very large, the correspondences between the Cretan seal and this seal are quite striking. The composition is arranged in the same way within a circular frame: a) a standing figure on the left and a figure sitting upon a low seat on the right, b) heads facing each other in profile, and c) similar movements of the arms, crossing one another. Thus, the Cretan seal could be the archetype of this kind of representation, within a general process of iconographic development of the theme, which Davies calls the "death of a seated figure." Furthermore, the rendering of the theme on the Metropolitan Museum seal, with its intense depiction of momentary violence, as portrayed by the motion-filled linear shapes of the bodies and the antithetical diagonals of their limbs, is similar to the scene on the seal from Kerason. During the development of this theme over time, we can observe, at about the middle of the 7th c. B.C., a related mythological scene on an Ionic relief pithos from Boeotia (Thebes)[13]. In the center of the representation, a seated figure, facing left, is being attacked from the left by a standing nude youth. The youth brandishes a sword in his right hand and grasps the right wrist of the seated figure with his left hand, while to the right a clothed woman stands watching. We are here confronted with a murder scene involving three individuals: they are either Neoptolemos–Priam–Hecuba[14] or Orestes–Aegisthus–Clytemnestra.[15] In these representations, it is the consistency of the types that is of interest: a standing youth and a seated figure in an attitude of supplication — all in accordance with the typical arrangement of the scene.

More immediately connected with the scene on our seal is the representation of the murder of Clytemnestra (as it is usually identified) on a bronze belly-guard from Crete in the Olympia Museum, which dates to around the middle of the 7th c. B.C.[16] The scene appears to take place in an interior space, as could also be the case in the representation on the Kerason seal, because of the presence of the altar — a significant iconographic element that already appears in

---

10 Cf. D. B. Thompson, *Hesperia* 8 (1939) 309 f.

11 MMA 42.11.1, diam. 19 mm: cf. M. I. Davies, *BCH* 93 (1969) 224 ff. n.1, figs. 6-8; G. M. A. Richter, *Catalogue of engraved gems: Greek, Etruscan, and Roman* (Rome 1956) no. 3, pl. I: "VIII c. B.C."

12 Cf. Davies 1969 (supra n.11).

13 Cf. R. Hampe, *Frühe griechische Sagenbilder in Böotien* (Athens 1936) 56, R4, pls. 36, 38, 39 (Boston 528, cat. pl. 52).

14 Cf. ibid. 71: "drei Figuren und einen Gegenstand, auf dem die mittlere Figur anscheinend sitzt."

15 Cf. K. Schefold (trans. A. Hicks), *Myth and legend in early Greek art* (New York 1964) 48, pl. 36.b: "Death of Aegisthus," "second quarter of the 7th c. B.C."

16 Olympia Museum 4900: A. Mallwitz and H.-V. Hermann, *Die Funde aus Olympia: Ergebnisse hundertjähriger Ausgrabungstätigkeit* (Athens 1980) 99, no. 61, fig. 11: Stadion - Nordwall, "2 Hälfte 7 Jh.v.Chr."; Rolley, *Greek bronzes* no. 232: "Half of a belly-guard"; "Orestes and Clytemnestra, or Menelaus and Helen." Cf. K. Fittschen, *Untersuchungen zum Beginn der Sagendarstellungen bei den Griechen* (Berlin 1969) 187 f., SB107, fig. 17.

similar scenes on bronze reliefs from Olympia[17] that date to the 6th c. B.C. The appearance of the same basic thematic elements on the belly-guard, as well as the certain meaning of the scene depicted on our seal, lend support to an interpretation of the scene portrayed on the belly-guard as one of matricide (Orestes-Clytemnestra).

In addition to the examples of metalwork and ceramics I have just mentioned, which date from the end of the 8th to the beginning of the 6th c. B.C., another antecedent, a painted rendering of the matricide on a red-figure hydria in the Nauplion Museum,[18] dating to around 440 B.C., is chronologically closer to our seal. The presentation of the motif around the body of the vase conforms, although more loosely composed, to the well-known type. The scene, which contains three figures, is by an artist of the group of Polygnotos and is considered to be a direct portrayal of a scene from the *Choephoroi* of Aeschylus,[19] just as our seal was, apparently, inspired by Sophocles's *Electra*.[20] The presence of the altar on the scene from the hydria, which is not mentioned in the literary tradition (as we have seen), has presented difficulties for scholars.

The seal's relationship to vase-painting of the rich style of the late 5th c. can also be seen in thematic correspondences, such as the motif of the seated Clytemnestra and similar figures from the circle of the Meidias Painter.[21]

What should be stressed, however, is the aesthetic independence of our artist in relation to the painstaking sophistication and frequently arbitrary rendering of the movement of the folds and the excessive decorative tendency of the rich style. We have here, in contrast, the sense of classical restraint, the simplicity of the drapery, along with the marked plasticity of the outlines of the human figures. The aesthetic tone approaches that of the painter of the amphora in the Museo Civico in Arezzo[22] (abduction of Hippodamia), a work dating to the beginning of the period of the rich style, around 410 B.C.

The chronological context of our seal is more specifically fixed according to Boardman's classification in the Salting Group, which dates to the early 4th c. B.C., although I can discern kindred elements in the chronologically earlier Cassandra Group[23] of *c.*400 B.C., which is named by the gold finger ring in the Metropolitan Museum.[24] This seal ring, which has a bezel

---

17 E.g., the bronze relief, Olympia Museum M77; cf. Mallwitz-Hermann, *Funde aus Olympia* (supra n.16) 85, no. 48, pl. 48: "der Stufenbau ist als Altar zu verstehen"; *Greek art of the Aegean Islands* (Exh. cat., The Metropolitan Museum of Art, New York 1979) 185, no. 148: "Greek (Samian?), about 570." Also cf. Schefold, *Myth and legend* (supra n.15) 93, fig. 40: "Shield-relief. *c.*570-560 B.C. – Olympia."

18 Inv. 11609 (no. 180 in the Glymenopoulos Collection): Beazley, *ARV*[2] 1061.154; cf. L. B. Ghali-Kahil, *BCH* 75 (1951) 316 ff., pls. 30-31, figs. 1, 2; E. Vermeule, *AJA* 70 (1966) 18, no. 34, n. 69; J. P. Small, *RömMitt* 83 (1976) 127 nn.50-52; *LIMC* VI.1 (1992) s.v. Klytaimestra, p. 77, no. 36; lastly, cf. *Απο τη Μήδεια στή Σαπφώ, Κατάλογος Εκθέσεως, Εθνικό Αρχαιολ. Μουσείο (March 20-10 September, 1995)* 62 ff., no. 32.

19 Cf. ibid.; *EAA* V (1963) s.v. Oreste, 741 ff.

20 Cf. Dakaris, *Γενεαλογικοί* (supra n.1) 91 n.2: "The metalworker has been inspired by the scene from Sophocles's *Electra*": verse 1415: παῖσον εἰ σθένεις διπλῆν.

21 E.g., New York, MMA pelike 37.11.23; cf. G. M. A. Richter, *AJA* 43 (1939) 1 ff., fig. 3; here, the broad curves of the bodies, the comfortable low seat, the crossed legs, and large feet all coincide.

22 Inv. 1460; cf. J. Charbonneaux *et al.*, *Grèce classique* (Paris 1969) 320: Casalta, Atelier du "Peintre du Dinos" "vers 410" and p. 281; E. Simon, *Die griechischen Vasen* (Berlin 1976) 224/225; (Beazley, *ARV*[2] 1157, 25): "Der Vorderseite kommt nach Beazley dem Meidiasstil nähe."

23 Cf. Boardman, *Greek gems* (supra n.4) 224 f., fig. 230; 222, pl. 709; 298, New York 80, pl. 14: "around 400 B.C. or little later." Similar elements are bodies in three-quarter view, head in profile, the large style of the design, and the supple rendering of the figures.

24 MMA 53.11.2: cf. Richter, *Engraved gems* (supra n.11) 22, no. 80, pl. XIV: "about 400-380 B.C."; ead., *Engraved gems of the Greeks, Etruscans, and Romans* (London 1968-71) 92 ff., no. 294: "early 4th c. B.C." Broad oval; the ring element, triangular in section, is similar in design to that of our seal ring. Cf.

shaped like ours, has similar iconographic details (figures with similar body types and drapery) and the same intense depiction of movement. What is more, the connection of the figure of Cassandra with the figures on the Bassae frieze, noted by Richter, is also an important point of reference for our seal, as we have already seen. The narrative force of the image of Cassandra, who kneels at the feet of the statue of Athena, combined with the high quality of its rendering, makes it a remarkable example of the art of metalwork, although the artistic quality of our seal from Kerason is, I think, even more exceptional.

The composition on the circular bezel is characterized by the closely linked figures, by the partial overlapping of the bodies, and by the intersecting movements of the arms in this pathos-filled depiction of violence. In this regard, the rendering of the scene follows the principle of the close-knit unit, which depends on earlier scenes of this sort of Pheidian inspiration. The axes of the bodies intersect, expressing an antithetical outward flow of movement. This movement, in turn, is balanced by the confrontation of the heads, which are turned in the direction of an imagined central axis. In vase-painting one can already discern — in the work of the Penthesilea Painter[25] (*c.*460 B.C.) — an attempt to incorporate the figures into a circular ground. In our seal, because of the arrangement of the bodies, the scene is in total harmony with its circular setting. The opposition between the naked body of Orestes and the wavy foldings of the background give the feeling of depth, while the traces of perspective in, for example, the foreshortening of the limbs (right thigh and right forearm of Orestes, right arm of Clytemnestra) give the impression of movement within the field.

Therefore, the circular, miniature representation we are here examining possesses affinities with (*mutatis mutandis*) the compositional conception of large-scale sculpture, as can be seen in the Attic relief from the Villa Albani in Rome[26] where one can discern the traces of a circular composition.

This find from Kerason is considered by S. Dakaris[27] to be a product of a Tarentine workshop, and the close relationship of this artistic center with northern Greece is well known. However, the precise identification of local toreutic workshops is made difficult by the shared technical and stylistic elements and influences and the use of the same themes. With regard to the choice of subject matter, two well-known Neo-Attic examples[28] (said to be from South Italy) are of particular importance: the relief of Ajax and Cassandra from the Villa Borghese,[29] and the much more closely related relief of the Murder of Priam in the Museum of Fine Arts, Boston (fig. 3).[30] The composition of the former exhibits a number of similarities with our

---

D. Williams and J. Ogden, *Greek gold: jewelry of the classical world (*Exhib. cat., The Metropolitan Museum of Art, New York 1994) 62 f., no. 16.

25 Cf. Charbonneaux *et al.*, *Grèce classique* (supra n.22) 244, fig. 275: Attic art, from Vulci, "about 460," Munich, Staatliche Antikensammlungen 2688. Cf. also E. Pfuhl, *Malerei und Zeichnung der Griechen* 2 (Munich 1923) 468 § 503, fig. 445; M. Robertson, *Greek painting* (Geneva 1959) 115 f., 120.

26 Helbig[4] IV (1972) no. 3257 (W. Fuchs); Villa Albani, Rome, no. 985; cf. B. Lullies and M. Hirmer, *Greek sculpture* (New York 1957) 81 ff., pls. 179-81: "all movements are subordinated to a circle that begins at the right hand of the rider."

27 Cf. Dakaris, *Γενεαλογικοί* (supra n.1) 91; *LIMC* VI.1, s.v. Klytaimestra, p. 77, no. 32, "sceau en argent ... (art tarentin?)."

28 Cf. W. Fuchs, *Die Vorbilder der neuattischen Reliefs* (Berlin 1959) 149, nn. 204-5; 174 nos. 16-17.

29 Of unknown provenance: Helbig[4] II (1966) 717, Villa Borghese no. 1956, LXIV: "1 Jht. vor Chr." (W. Fuchs); various dates have been assigned to the relief: P. Wuilleumier, *Tarente des origines à la conquête romaine* (Paris 1939) 290 ff.: "influence de l'art péloponnésien"; G. Schneider-Hermann, *BABesch* 41 (1966) 28 ff., fig. 1: "attische Einflüsse" ... "nachklassische Kunst Süditaliens" ... "von ungefähr 400 v.Chr."

30 Cf. L. D. Caskey, *Catalogue of Greek and Roman sculpture, Museum of Fine Arts, Boston* (Cambridge, MA 1925) 176 f., no. 99: "fine grained Greek marble," "Neo-Attic School," "the prototype may have been a relief, or perhaps a painting of the late 5th c. B.C." The iconographic parallels are obvious; Comstock-Vermeule, *Sculpture in stone* 145-46, no. 234: "*c.* 50 B.C.-A.D. 50."

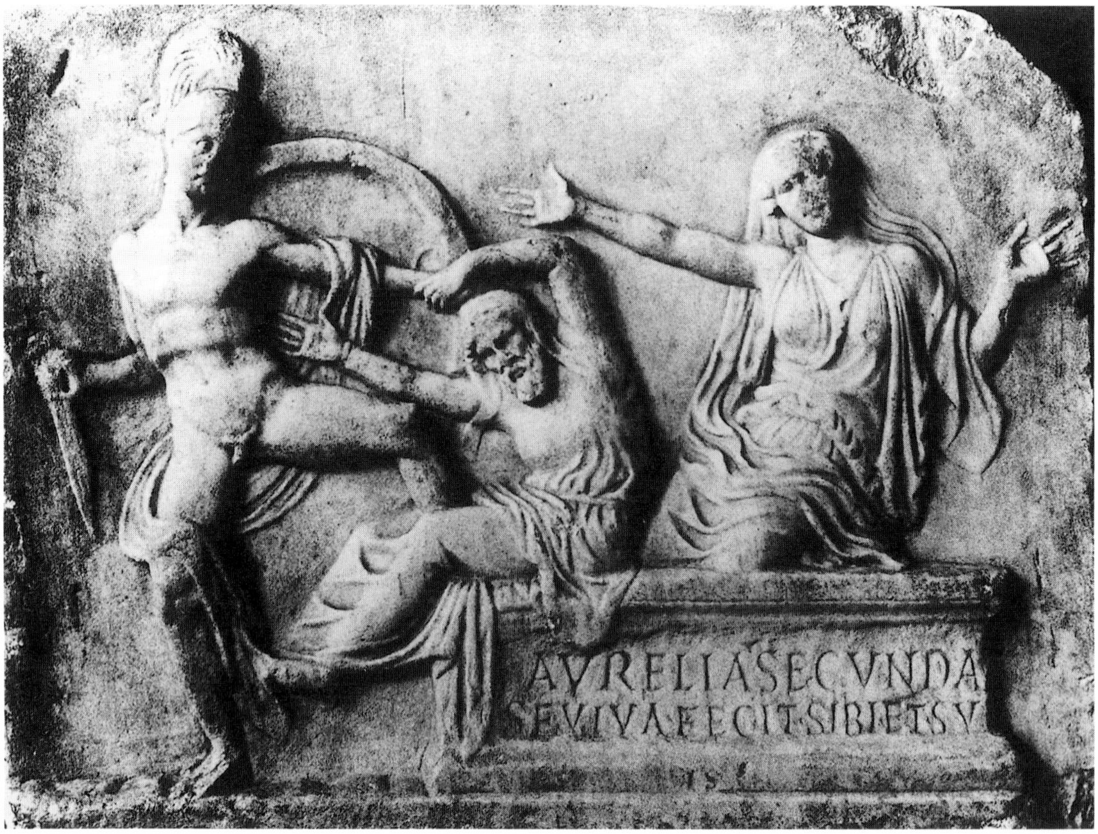

Fig. 3. Relief with the Death of Priam. Greco-Roman, *c.*50 B.C. – A.D. 50. Marble, h. 0.38 m, w. 0.49 m. Boston, Museum of Fine Arts, 04.15. (Photo: courtesy Museum of Fine Arts.)

work in the way the figures and their movement are rendered, while the latter can be placed in the same iconographic tradition as the representation on our seal. It is probable that this relief derives from a Classical prototype of about the end of the 5th c. B.C. Thus, it should be viewed as an additional example which can be ultimately traced back to the ancient archetype of "the death of the seated figure" to which we have referred.

On this seal, the influence of large-scale sculpture is strongly felt even through the refinement of the engraver's art, and the seal is clearly within the Attic artistic tradition. In regard to this monumental quality, we should mention the remark of the great 19th c. Danish sculptor A. B. Thorwaldsen, noted by H. B. Walters[31] about the Siris bronzes: "The grandiose does not consist in mere mass, since these diminutive works are truly great."

30, Karneadou Str., 10675 Athens

31 H. B. Walters, *Select bronzes, Greek, Roman, and Etruscan in the British Museum* (London 1915) pl. 31 (285).

In memoriam prof. Ivani Venedikov (10.01.1916-19.08.1997) et Bogdani Nikolov (16.08.1926-25.08.1997)

The bronze vessels from tomb 2 in the Mogilanska Mogila tumulus at Vratsa (NW Bulgaria)

Evgeni I. Paunov and Narcis T. Torbov

This paper presents a group of 5 bronze vessels of Greek origin, a complete wine set excavated in tomb no. 2 of the Mogilanska Mogila tumulus in Vratsa. Although the vessels were found in 1965, they have remained unpublished. The set comprises a hydria, an exquisite oinochoe, two richly decorated situlae, and a shallow *podanypter*. The set must have been used during the feasts of the buried ruler. The aim of this paper is their detailed description, technological and stylistic analysis, comparison with similar finds, dating, and incorporation into the context of active Greek trade with Thrace during the Classical and Early Hellenistic periods.

The archaeological context

The dazzling finds from the Mogilanska Mogila tumulus — the silver-gilt greave (*knemis*), the gold wreath and earrings, and the many gold and silver vessels and appliqués — have been included in every recent exhibition and catalogue of Thracian art.[1] Without them, it would be impossible to imagine the archaeological and ethnic map of Thrace in the 4th c. B.C.

The archaeological rescue excavations of the Mogilanska Mogila tumulus in the center of the town of Vratsa were conducted in November 1965 for only 12 days and under extremely difficult working conditions under the supervision of I.Venedikov and B. Nikolov.[2] The vessels were found in the western (main) chamber of tomb 2 (dimensions 12 x 6 m). I. Venedikov wrote in his preliminary publication in 1966 that the vessels were found about 1.5 to 2 m to the north and on the right of the skeleton of the so-called princess.[3] However, the burial was probably that of an adolescent or young man. The bronze vessels were arranged together with an iron candelabrum, while the silver phialae, the pine cone-shaped jug, and other objects (including a smashed bronze helmet of Chalcidian type, a wooden quiver with many bronze arrowheads, a few iron spearheads) were placed in another group more to the side.[4]

Because large stone fragments had collapsed from the walls of the tomb, the vessels were damaged and deformed to various degrees. In the 1970s they were partly restored by V. Vassilev of the National Archaeological Museum, Sofia. Today all of them (except the *podanypter*) are exhibited in one of the halls of the District Museum of History, Vratsa. They were registered in the inventory of the Archaeology Department by B. Nikolov on March 9, 1966, as inv. nos. B 233 to B 237.

---

1 I. Venedikov and T. Gerassimov, *Thracian art treasures* (London 1975); A. Fol and I. Marazov, *Thrace & the Thracians* (New York 1977); I. Venedikov, *Thracian treasures from Bulgaria* (Exhib. cat., The Metropolitan Museum of Art, New York 1977); R. F. Hodinott, *The Thracians* (London 1981); G. von Bülow, *Treasures of Thrace* (New York 1987); *Gold of the Thracian horsemen: treasures from Bulgaria* (Exhib. cat., Palais de la civilisation, Montreal 1989); *Traci: arte e cultura nelle terre di Bulgaria dalle origini alla tarda romanità* (Exhib. cat., Palazzo Ducale, Venice, 1989); *The riches of the Thracian rulers* (Exhib. cat [Tokyo 1994]); *Ancient gold: the wealth of the Thracians: treasures from the Republic of Bulgaria* (Exhib. cat., Museum of Fine Arts, Boston 1998).

2 I. Venedikov, "Un nouveau découverte: tombeau tumulaire thrace à Vraca" [Bulgarian, French summary], *Archeologija* (Sofia) 8.1 (1966) 7-15; id., "Le tumulus de Vraca," *Etudes Balkaniques* 5 (Sofia 1966) 243-38; id., *The Vratsa treasure* [Bulgarian, English summary] (Sofia 1975); B. Nikolov, "Die Mogilanisch-Hügel im Vratza" [Bulgarian, German summary], *Musées et monuments de la culture* 1 (Sofia 1988) 28-34; B. Nikolov, *Four Thracian treasures* (Sofia 1988).

3 I. Venedikov 1966 (supra n.2) 12.

4 I. Venedikov, *Vratsa treasure* (supra n.2) 35; B. Nikolov, *Four Thracian treasures* (supra n.2) 21.

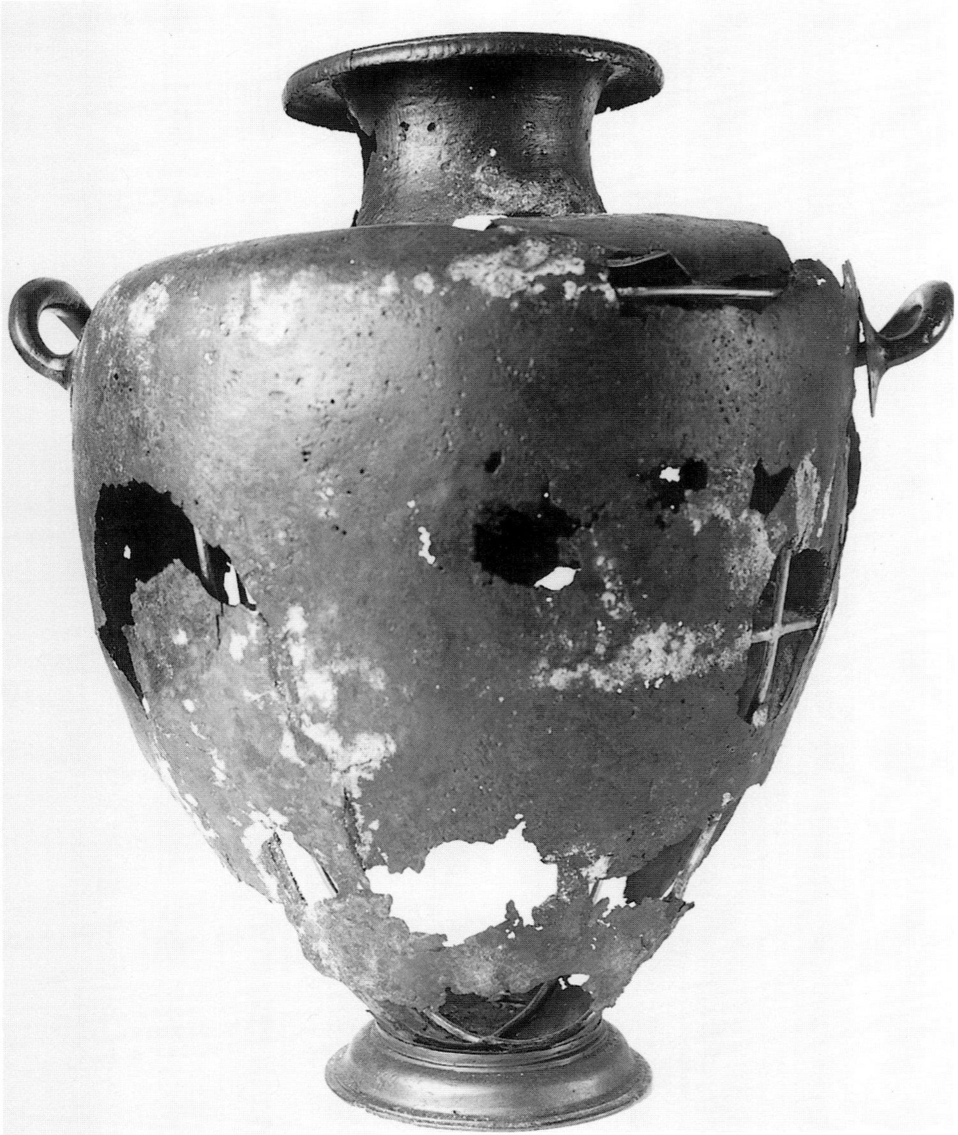

Fig. 1a. Bronze hydria from the Mogilanska Mogila tumulus. Vratsa, Museum of History, no. B 233. (Courtesy Museum of History, Vratsa; Photo: © 1996 Krassimir Georgiev, Sofia.)

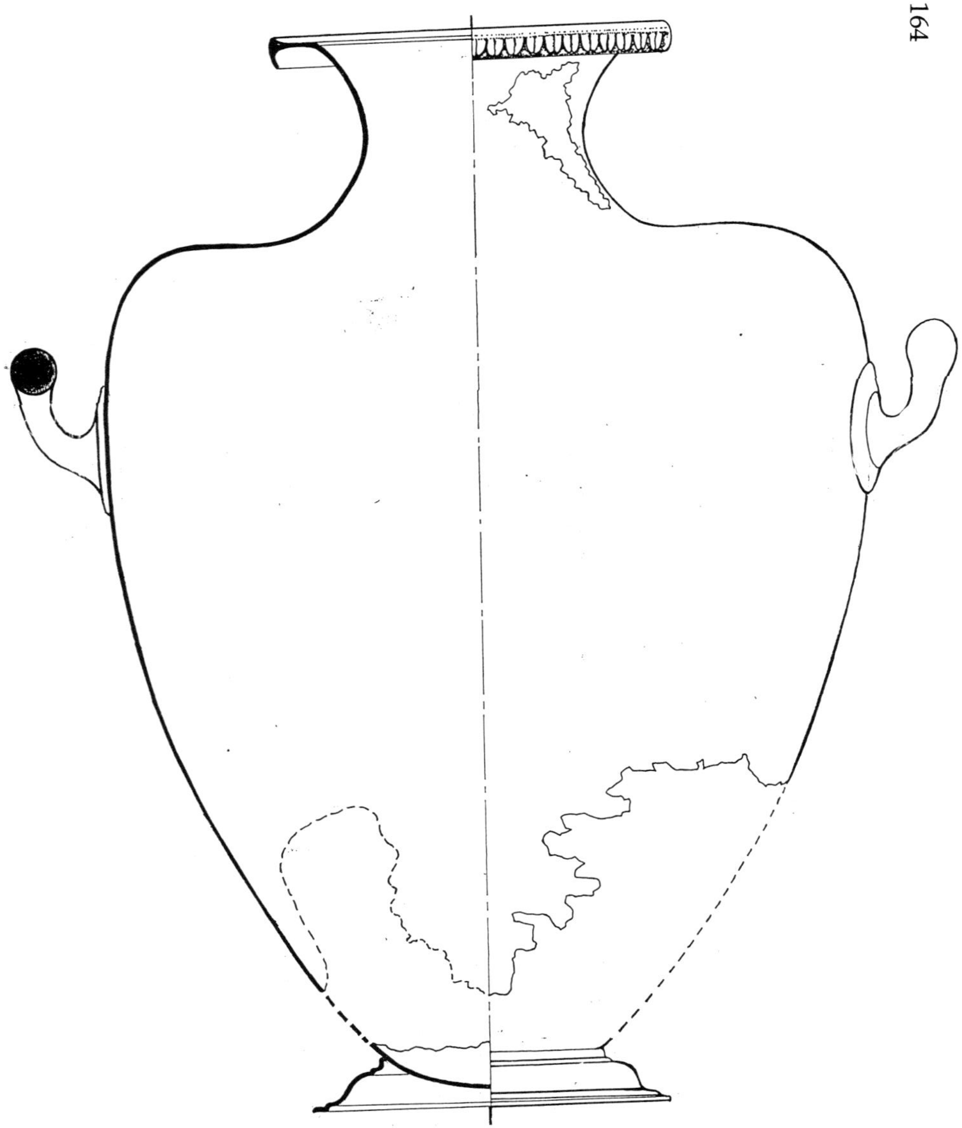

Fig. 1b. Drawing. (Drawing: © 1996 Nikolay Tomov, Vratsa.)

Description and analysis

The hydria is the largest vessel and it is the natural center of the entire set (figs. 1a-b). It is of the classical ovoid type.[5] The two horizontal handles and the tall ring-shaped foot were cast separately and soldered to the vessel's body. The height of the hydria in its present restored form is 0.415 m, its maximum diameter is 0.32 m, and the diameter of the mouth rim 0.16 m. The only decorative element is a frieze of Ionic kymation around the mouth rim, barely discernible as a result of the heavy corrosion. This type of hydria — undecorated and without a vertical handle on the body — was standard throughout the 4th c. B.C. Among numerous parallels, it is possible to cite the hydriae from Amphipolis (grave find)[6] and from Veroia[7] (grave no. 12 on Siderou Stathmou street), dated to the first half of the century and to 370-350 B.C. respectively. We believe that the hydria from the Mogilanska Mogila tumulus can be dated to the same period.

The oinochoe has a sophisticated bipartite form: a cylindrical body and an intricate funnel-shaped slender neck flaring into a beaked trefoil mouth (figs. 2 a-c). It is richly decorated and in an excellent state of preservation. A narrow band along the mouth with everted rim is presented as an Ionic kymation. The lower part of the handle resembles an acanthus shoot with a double volute and a palmette-like base. The height of the oinochoe is 0.245 m, its maximum diameter is 0.15 m, and the diameter of the bottom 0.115 m. The closest parallels come from Thrace and Macedonia. From Thrace they are the tumulus finds from Alexandrovo near Lovech, from Leshnikova Mogila near the village of Shipka in the Kazanluk plain, and from a tumulus find in Mezek. The specimen discovered in Alexandrovo,[8] with a silver phiale bearing the inscription ΚΟΤΥΟΣ ΕΓΓΗΙΣΤΩΝ, is without a handle and its workmanship is much cruder; but the vessel from Shipka[9] demonstrates excellent workmanship and was, moreover, discovered with a silver jug and phiale bearing a barely distinguishable inscription. The jug from Mezek has no handle and only a vague drawing has been preserved of it.[10] All three specimens are very accurately dated with the help of the other cited vessels to the first half of the 4th c. B.C. or even to its second quarter, during the reign of Kotys I (*c.*383-359 B.C.). The northernmost example of this small but elegant vessel for pouring wine can be discerned in the oinochoe from the Zelenskiy Kurgan tumulus on the Taman Peninsula in Ukraine, found in a rich grave with a complete set of silver and bronze vessels for feasts and dated by a posthumous *stater* of Alexander III the Great and a Panathenaic amphora to about 320 B.C.[11]

Four similar vessels come from ancient Macedonia. The first is from a grave tumulus near Arzos, in the lower Hebros valley, i.e., from southern Thrace, dated to the end of the 4th c.[12]

---

5 On the hydriae shapes, see E. Diehl, *Die Hydria. Formgeschichte und Verwendung im Kult des Altertums* (Mainz 1964); Rolley, *Griechischen Bronzen*; O. D. Ganina, *Antichni bronzi iz Pishchanogo* (Kiev 1970) [Ukrainian, English summary]. Compare also A. de Ridder, *Les bronzes antiques. Musée national du Louvre* II (Paris 1915).

6 *Archaia Makedonia = Ancient Macedonia* (Exhib. cat., Museum of Victoria, Melbourne, Australia [Athens 1988]).

7 K. Ninou (ed.), *Treasures of ancient Macedonia* (Exhib. cat., Archaeological Museum of Thessalonike; Athens 1979) no. 68, pl. 13.

8 B. Filow, *Die Grabhügelnekropole bei Duvanliy in Südbulgarien* (Sofia 1934) 184-85, fig. 205, now in the National Archaeological Museum, Sofia, inv. no. A 2240.

9 G. Kitov, "Les tumuli royaux dans 'La vallée des rois thraces,'" *Orpheus: Journal of Indo-European and Thracian studies* 5 (Sofia 1995) 18-19, fig. 10; id., "The Thracian valley of the kings in the region of Kazanluk," *Balkan studies* 37.1 (Thessaloniki 1996) 5-34, esp. 27, perhaps quite a bit earlier than the Vratsa oinochoe.

10 I. Welkow, "Die Ausgrabungen bei Mezek und Svilengrad," *Bulletin de l'Institut archéologique Bulgare* 11 (1937) 136, fig. 129 (drawing only) [Bulgarian, German summary],

11 B. Pharmakowsky, "Rußland," *AA* 1913, 182, fig. 19.

12 Archaeological Museum of Komotini, no. 1888, h. 0.265 m: D. Triandaphyllos, *Deltion Chronika* 30 B'2 (1975) 101; *Treasures of ancient Macedonia* (supra n.6) no. 460, pl. 61; N. Yalouris *et al.*, *The search for*

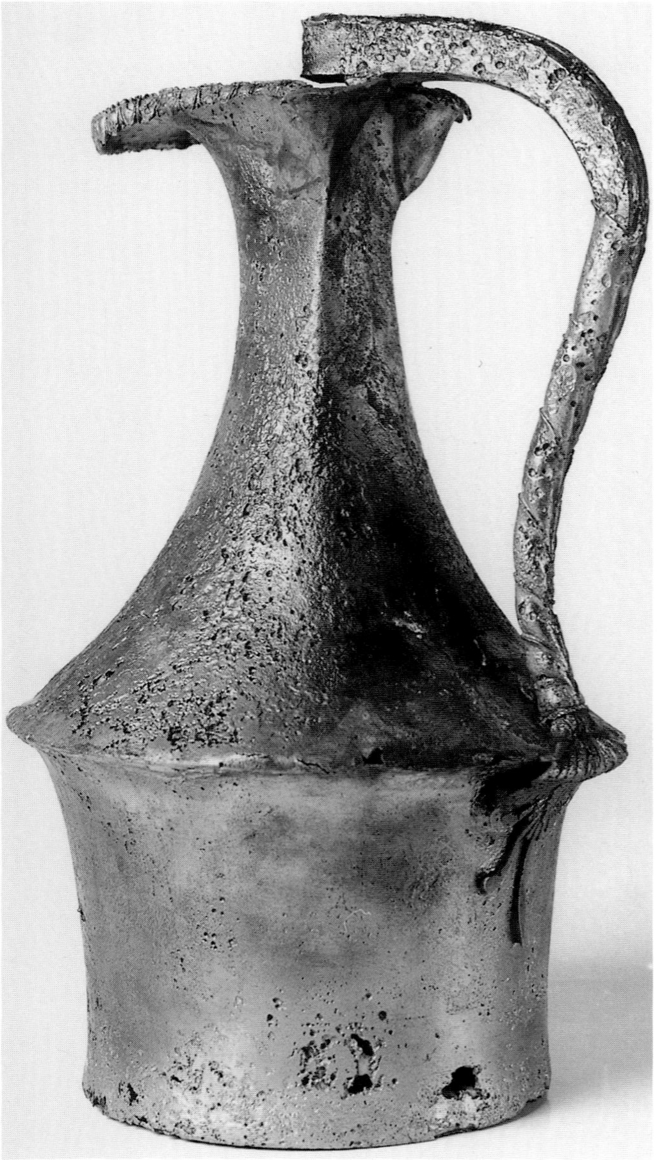

Fig. 2a. Bronze oinochoe from Mogilanska Mogila tumulus. Vratsa, Museum of History, no. B 234. (Courtesy Museum of History, Vratsa; Photo: © 1996 Krassimir Georgiev, Sofia.)

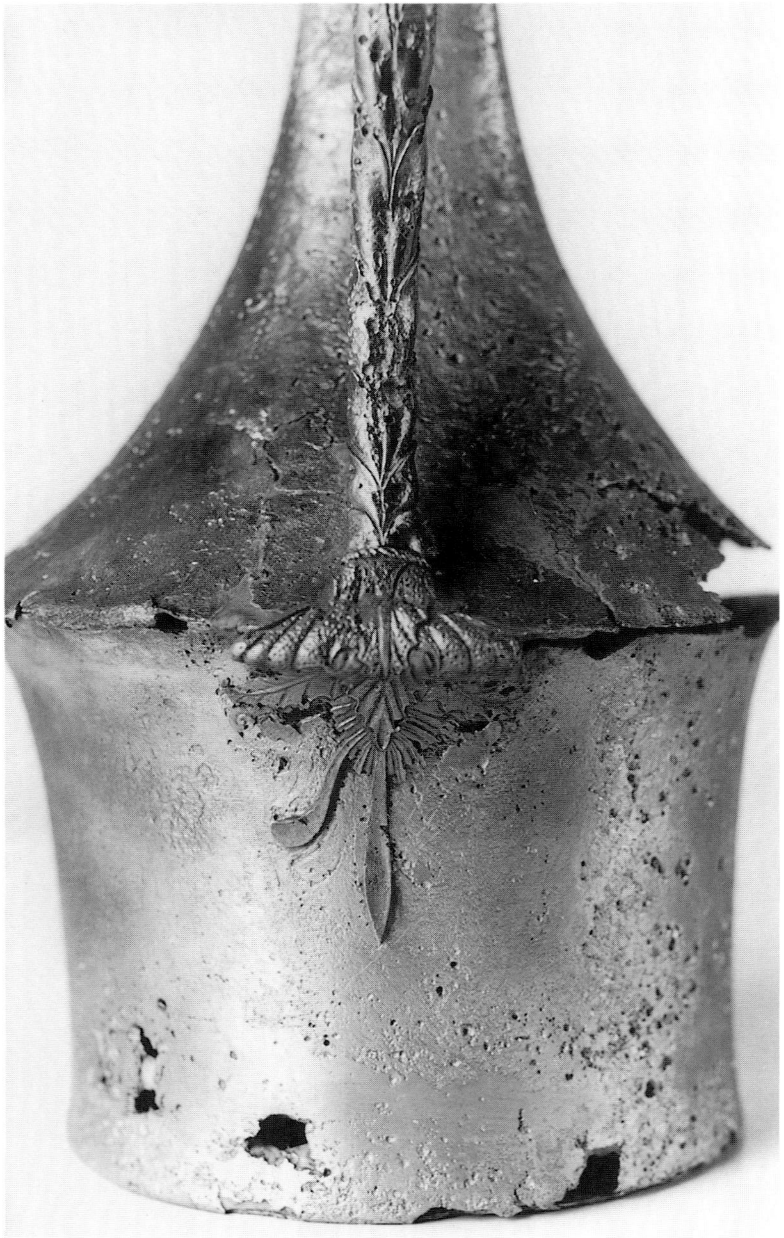

Fig. 2b. Detail with the handle ornaments. (Photo: © 1996 Krassimir Georgiev, Sofia.)

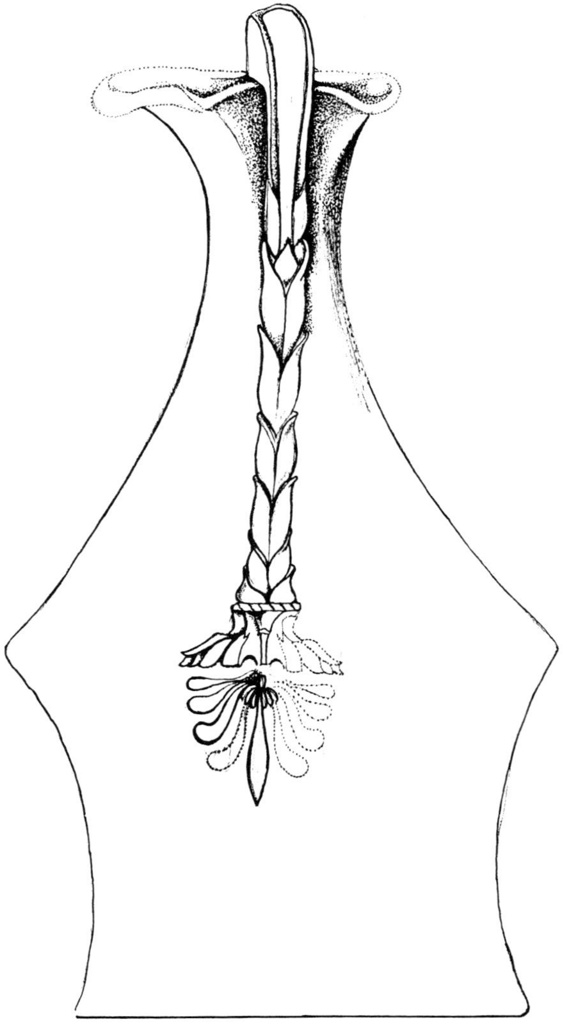

Fig. 2c. Drawing. (Drawing: © 1996 Nikolay Tomov, Vratsa.)

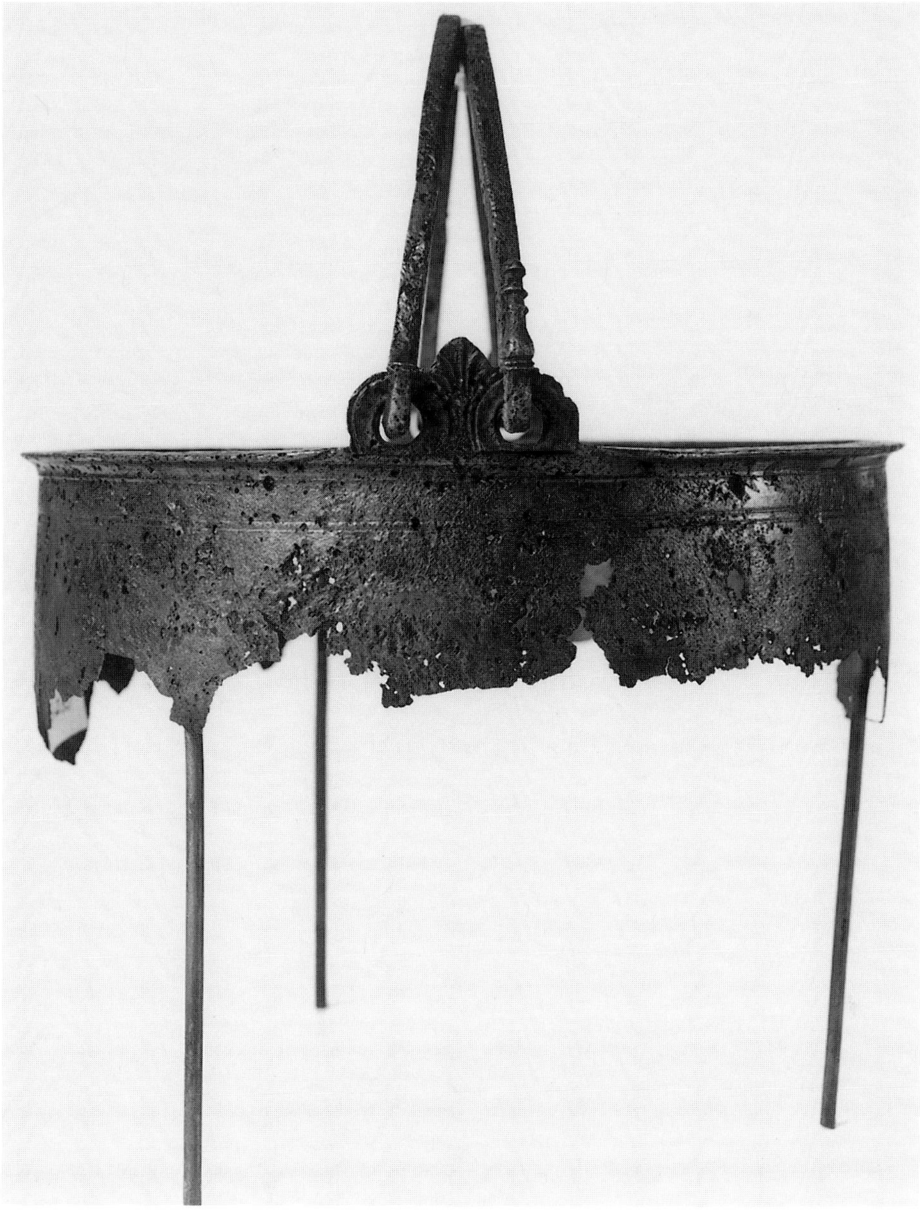

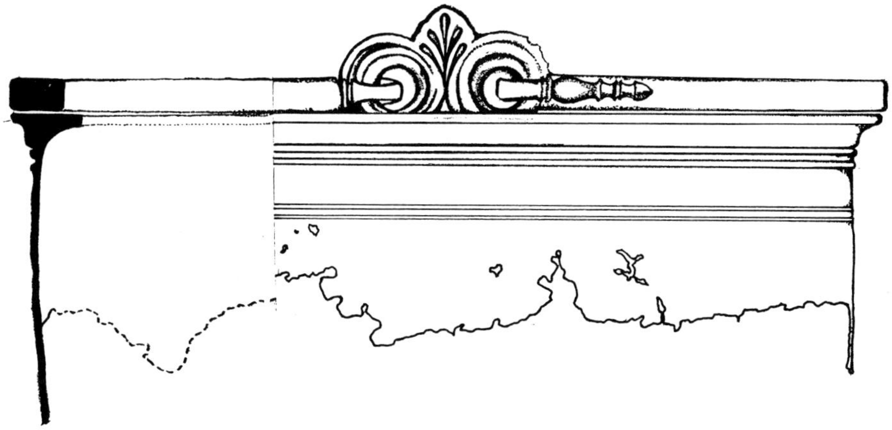

Fig. 3a (top). Bronze situla no. 1 from Mogilanska Mogila tumulus. Vratsa, Museum of History, no. B 235. (Courtesy Museum of History, Vratsa; Photo: © 1996 Krassimir Georgiev, Sofia.)
Fig. 3b (bottom). Drawing. (Drawing: © 1996 Nikolay Tomov, Vratsa.)

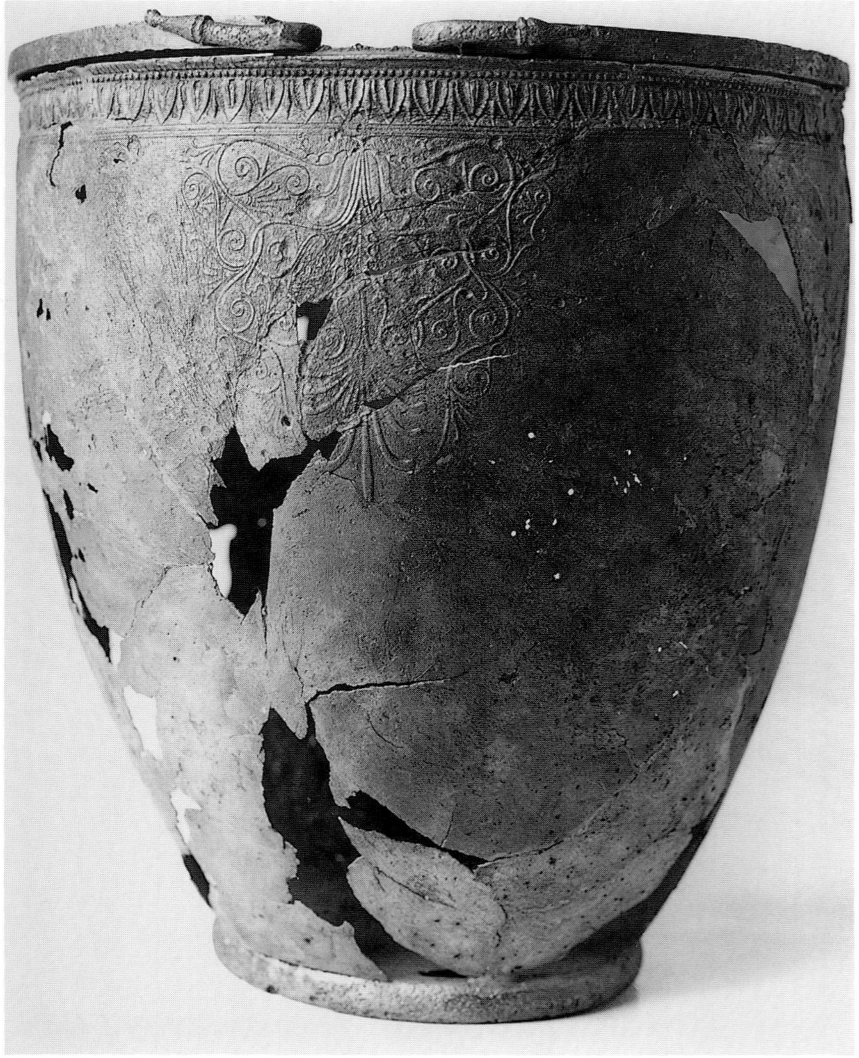

Fig. 4a. Bronze situla no. 2 from Mogilanska Mogila tumulus. Vratsa, Museum of History, no. B 236. (Courtesy Museum of History, Vratsa; Photo: © 1996 Krassimir Georgiev, Sofia.)

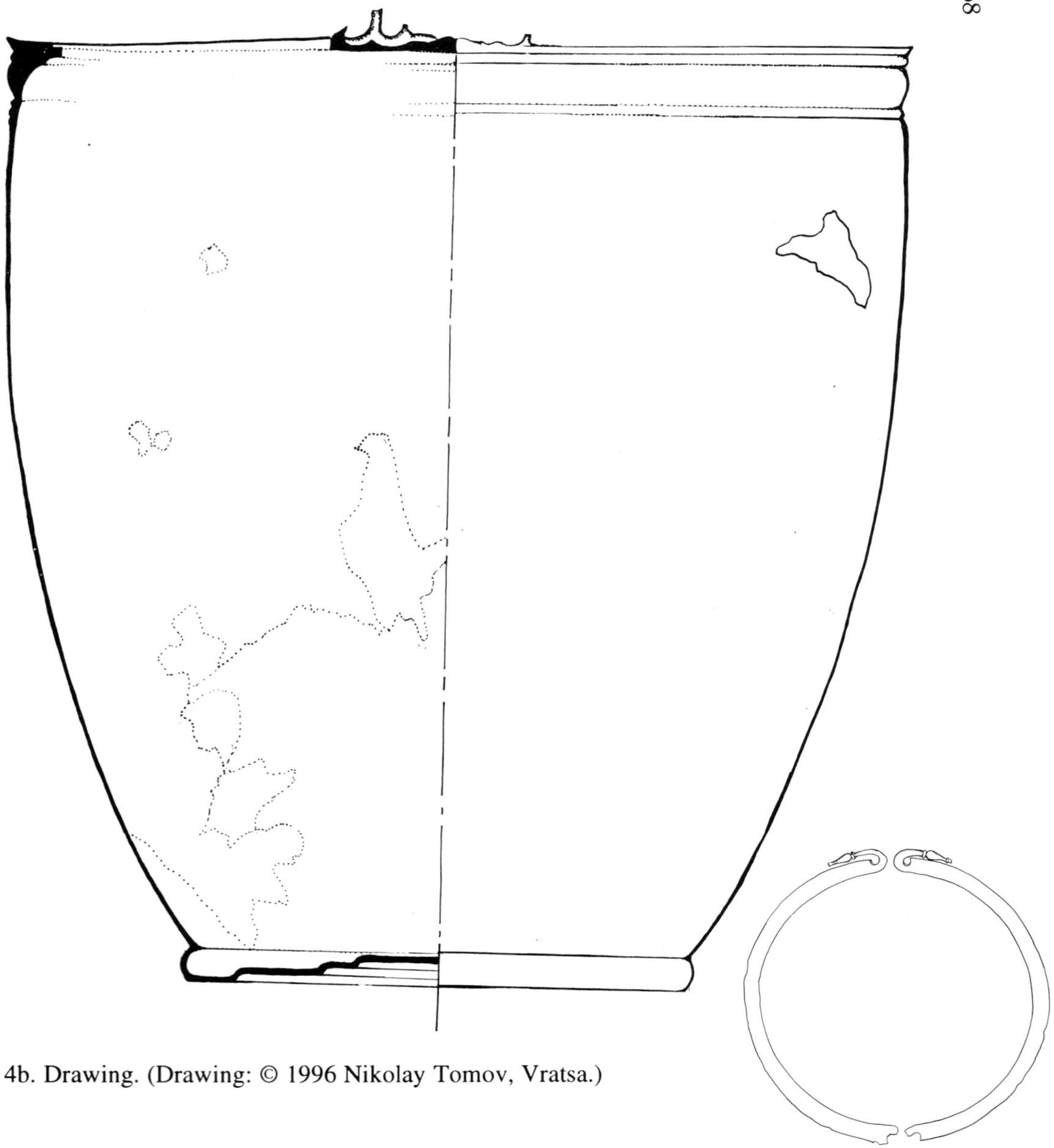

Fig. 4b. Drawing. (Drawing: © 1996 Nikolay Tomov, Vratsa.)

The other three vessels were discovered in and around Thessaloniki: 1) in Stavropolis, a district of Thessaloniki, in a grave excavated in 1964, dated *c.*350-320 B.C.;[13] 2) in Derveni, from grave A of the necropolis, together with the known hydria and papyrus, dated generally to the last quarter of the 4th c.;[14] and 3) a silver oinochoe from Vergina, Tomb II — the so-called prince's tomb — with proposed dating *c.*325 B.C.[15] A similar example of this type of vessel was sold at Sotheby's, New York, in 1992. It is a splendid silver oinochoe, perhaps the most beautiful of all, dated by analogy with the Vergina oinochoe in the third quarter of the 4th c.[16]

The vessels of this group, which are of a limited quantity but of exquisite quality, are regular components of the sets of vessels used on festive occasions throughout the entire 4th c. The oinochoai were used to pour the wine into cups and phialai during symposia.

The next two vessels from Mogilanska Mogila are situlae.[17] Their ornamentation differs, but both are bell-shaped. The first situla is very poorly preserved (fig. 3). The middle part of its body is missing, and its original height cannot be determined at present. The diameter of the rim is 0.215 m, of the base 0.11 m; the preserved height is 0.085 cm. The two bucket handles of the vessel are attached by means of ears, shaped in the middle like stylized palmettes in low relief. Immediately below the rim is a frieze framed by two incised lines. This situla is most similar in terms of its type and ornamentation to that of the Mramor tumulus near the town of Panagyurishte and is dated to the same time — the middle or the third quarter of the 4th c. B.C.[18] The situla from Vratsa was included in I. Venedikov's study of this type of bronze vessel in Thrace[19] and he has dated it to the first half of the 4th c., but it was even more difficult to define any date before conservation.

The second ceremonial situla is better preserved (figs. 4 a-b). A few fragments of its wall were missing because of corrosion, and it has been restored, but this is compensated by its magnificent decoration. It has a total height of 0.243 m, mouth diameter 0.24 m, and base diameter 0.124 m. The loops are broken and now missing, only their bases are discernible. The ends of the handles are twisted at an angle of 180° and end in shapes resembling bottles. Two delicate moldings form the ornamentation — one frieze of Ionic kymation runs below the molded rim and an intricate floral pattern appears just below the loops: an elaborate palmette, a mass of volute scrolls, and blossoms at the upper corners. The ornamental design emerges from an open growth of acanthus. This is an extremely refined and complex metalwork technique of integrating the decoration into the thin walls of the vessel. This operation is compared by some scholars with applying the relief line in Attic red-figure vase-painting. Vratsa situla no. 2 has also been briefly described by I. Venedikov in the group of "Situlae with ornamentation below the handles."[20] However, he erroneously described it as coming from the village of Poudriya in the Vratsa area. These vessels seem to have been very popular in mainland Greece as well as in

---

13 M. Siganidou, *Deltion Chronika* 20 B'2 (1965) 411; *Treasures of ancient Macedonia* (supra n.6) no. 271, pl. 40; *Archaia Makedonia* (supra n.6) no. 341.

14 C. Makaronas, *Deltion Chronika* 18 B'2 (1963) 194, pl. 225a; *Treasures of ancient Macedonia* (supra n.6) no. 159, pl. 24; *Search for Alexander* (supra n.12) no. 135; *Archaia Makedonia* (supra n.6) no. 231.

15 M. Andronicos, *Vergina: the royal tombs and the ancient city* (2nd edn., Athens 1988) 209, fig. 172.

16 *Sotheby's important antiquities*, cat. no. 6383 (New York, December 17, 1992) no. 134 (h. 0.229 m).

17 For Greek situlae, their origin, style, and decoration, see P. J. Riis, "The Danish bronze vessels of Greek, early Campanian, and Etruscan manufacture," *Acta Arch* 30 (1959) 18-26; L. Byvanck-Quarles van Ufford, "Remarques sur les relations entre l'Ionie grecque, la Thrace, et l'Italie," *BABesch* 41 (1966) 34-49; M. Candela, "Situli metalliche e ceramiche a beccuccio nel IV e III secolo a. C. Origine e diffusione," *BABesch* 60 (Leiden 1985) 24-59. For Celtic imitations of Greek situlae, see J. Kastelic, *Situla art: ceremonial bronzes of ancient Europe* (New York 1965).

18 B. Filow, "Denkmäler der thrakischen Kunst," *RömMitt* 32 (1917) no. 32, 45-48, fig. 37. Originally dated by B. Filow to the late 4th or early 3rd c. B.C.

19 I. Venedikov, "Les situles de bronze en Thrace," *Thracia* 4 (Sofia 1977) 59-103, cat. no. 41.

20 Ibid. 101-2, no. 27, fig. 47 (incorrect caption).

Magna Graecia and among the Thracians in the 4th c. Obviously the taste for such metal buckets spread to Classical and Early Hellenistic Thrace and Macedonia. Some later pieces from Pompeii and Apulia date to the Late Hellenistic period.

The ornament below the handles resembling a palmette occurs on situlae from the village of Chernozem near Plovdiv,[21] as well as on situlae from the Mal Tepe tomb near Mezek[22] (but with handles cast separately and soldered onto the body); from the Waldalgesheim find (now in the Landesmuseum, Bonn);[23] and some Late Hellenistic examples.[24] However, two other vessels are the closest comparisons. The first is the bronze situla from a grave in the Kalamaria area of Thessaloniki, dated to the end of the 5th c. B.C.[25] About this vessel B. Barr-Sharrar wrote, "the graceful contour of the body, together with the palmette and scroll design cast into the wall under the handle, immediately betrays classical traditions, which did not originate in Macedonia."[26] Such traditions did not originate in Thrace either. Barr-Sharrar assumes that the situla from Kalamaria came from an Athenian bronzecasting workshop or that it was produced by skilled craftsmen who had been trained in that fine style somewhere in Attica. It seems perfectly justifiable to identify in the same way the second situla from the Mogilanska Mogila tumulus in Vratsa.

The second comparison is a splendid bronze situla from the so-called Prusias find — a complete drinking set of silver vessels found in Prusias (mod. Bursa, Turkey), now in the Metropolitan Museum, New York.[27] The palmette of this situla is more austere and Classical in form than that from Vratsa, which is elaborate, splendid, and even extravagant.

Finally, it is possible to cite a small fragment from a similar situla from Budva on the Illyrian coast of the Adriatic (Montenegro), strangely dated by L. Popoviç to the 3rd c. B.C.[28]

In our opinion, it has become clear that the second Mogilanska Mogila situla was imported from the south. Perhaps the situla, together with some other objects of a Greek character in the

---

21 P. Detev, "Fouilles de la nécropole tumulaire presque village Chernozem, arrondissement Plovdiv," *Annuaire de Musée national archéologique à Plovdiv* 7 (1971) 43, figs. 9-10 (photograph not clear) [Bulgarian, French summary].

22 B. Filow, "Die Kuppelgräber von Mezek," *Bulletin de l'Institut archéologique Bulgare* 11 (1937) 57-59, no. 22, fig. 60, esp. detail fig. 61 [Bulgarian, German summary]; also B. Filov, "The beehive tombs of Mezek," *Antiquity* 11 (1937) 300-4; and I. Venedikov 1977 (supra n.19) 88, fig. 44; 101, cat. no. 26.

23 B. Schröder, *Griechische Bronzeeimer im Berliner Antiquarium* (= 74. Winckelmanns Program; Berlin 1914) 10 ff., fig. 6, no. 4; E. Pernice, *Gefässe und Geräte aus Bronze* (= *Die hellenistische Kunst in Pompei* IV; Berlin 1925) 26-28, fig. 39; P. Jacobsthal, *Early Celtic art* (Oxford 1944) 87, 141-43, pl. 100, fig. 156h. See also G. Zahlhaas, "Der Bronzeeimer von Waldalgesheim," *HBA* 1 (1971) 115 ff., and W. Schiering, "Zeitstellung und Herkunft der Bronzesitula von Waldalgesheim," ibid. 5 (1975) 77 ff.

24 For the Pompeii examples, see E. Pernice, *Gefässe und Geräte* (supra n.23) 14 ff., fig. 19 ff. See also a splendid bell-shaped situla from the Museum of Fine Arts, Boston, dredged from the Tiber river: MFA 65.394, h. 0.375 m; Comstock-Vermeule, *Bronzes* 338-39, no. 477.

25 *Treasures of ancient Macedonia* (supra n.7) no. 332, pl. 47. For the entire grave group, see K. Rhomiopoulou, in *Festschrift G. Mylonas* (Athens 1989) 194 ff., pl. 45-46.1 [Greek, English summary].

26 B. Barr-Sharrar, "Macedonian metal vases in perspective: some observations and tradition," in *Macedonia and Greece in Late Classical and Early Hellenistic times* (Studies in the history of art 10; Baltimore 1982) 127-29, fig. 8.

27 MMA 1972.118.88, Bequest of Walter C. Baker, 1971; dated in the second half of the 4th c. B.C.; h. 0.249 m; diam. mouth 0.194 m; ex-coll. W. Fabricius: K. A. Neugebauer, *Antiken in deutschem Privatbesitz* (Berlin 1938) 47, pl. 91, no. 214; G. M. A. Hanfmann, *Ancient art in American private collections* (Exhib. cat., New York 1954) 37, pls. 86, 88, no. 307; D. von Bothmer, *The search for Alexander: supplement I to the catalogue* (New York 1982) 8-9, no. S 28; id., *A Greek and Roman treasury* (= *MMA Bulletin* 42.1 summer 1984) 46-47, no. 74.

28 L. B. Popoviç *et al.*, *Greek, Roman and Early Christian bronzes in Jugoslavia* (Belgrade 1969) no. 59, fig. 59.

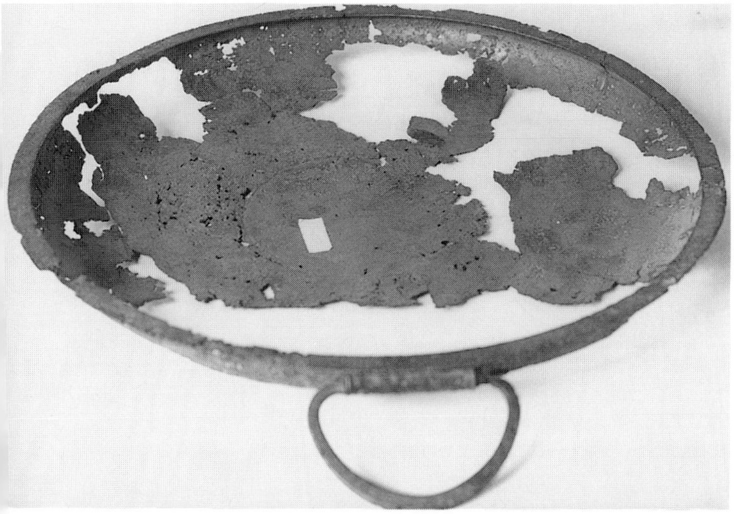

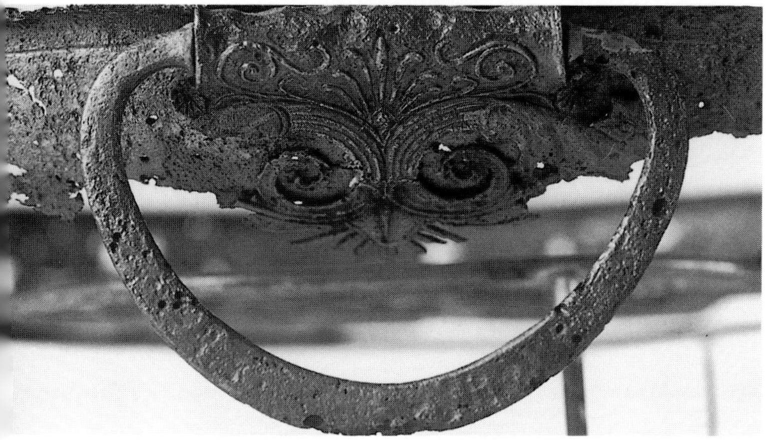

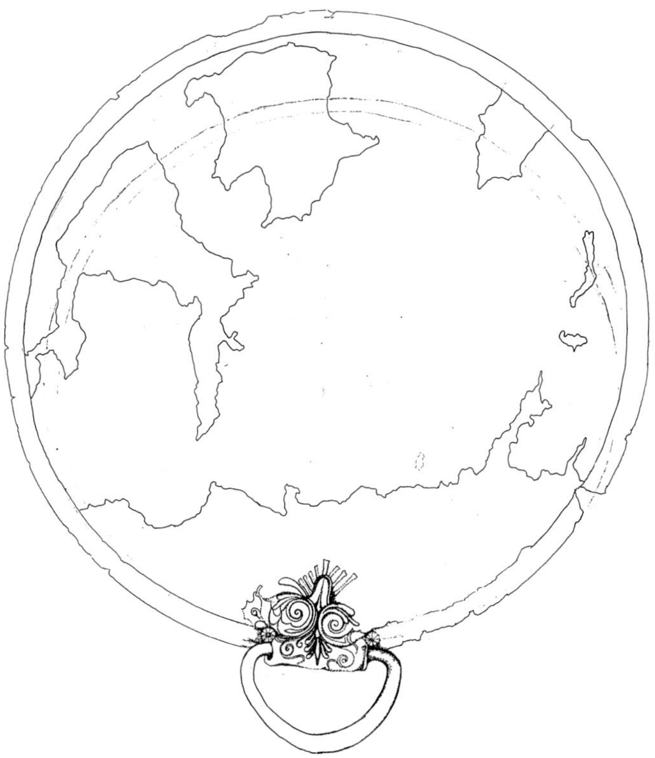

Fig. 5a (top left). Bronze podanypter from Mogilanska mogila tumulus. Vratsa, Museum of History, no. B 237. (Courtesy Museum of History, Vratsa; Photo: © 1996 Krassimir Georgiev, Sofia.). Fig. 5b (below). Detail. (Photo: © 1996 Krassimir Georgiev, Sofia.). Fig. 5c. Drawing.

find from Vratsa, had been a part of the booty of the Triballi during their march against Abdera in 376/5 B.C.[29]

The last vessel in the Mogilanska Mogila tumulus set is a *podanypter,* or washbasin (figs. 5 a, b), a low shallow vessel. It is well preserved with the exception of small parts of the walls, one of the handles, and the foot. The diameter of the rim is 0.335 m, the height 0.085 m, and the diameter of the base 0.115 m. Two handles and a low ring-shaped foot were cast separately and soldered onto the body. The handles resemble the Greek letter Ω, while their bases are decoratively shaped like elongated, open-work double palmettes.

An attempt at dating the vessels

All the vessels from the set for feasts placed in tomb 2 of the Mogilanska Mogila tumulus in Vratsa were clearly imported, undoubtedly from Greece. Although there are small differences in their various dates, between the late 5th and the middle or third quarter of the 4th c. B.C.,

29 Diod. Sic. 15.36.1-4; *Scholia in Aristid. Panath.*, 172.7. On the Thracian tribe of Triballi and their location, see generally A. Fol, *Thrace and the Balkans in the Early Hellenistic epoch* (Sofia 1975) [Bulgarian, English summary] ; A. Fol and T. Spiridonov, *Historical geography of the Thracian tribes til the 3rd c. B.C.* (Sofia 1983) [Bulgarian, German summary] ; and N. Theodossiev, "The Tryballi: some problems of their historical development," *Bulgarian Historical Review* 1-2 (1992) 78 ff. [Bulgarian, English summary]. Recently, see N. Torbov and E. Paunov, "Thracian finds near the vicinity of Mezdra," *Annals* 2.3-4 (1995) 46-52 [Bulgarian, English summary]; and A. Fol, *History of the Bulgarian lands in antiquity to the 3rd c.* B.C. (2nd edn., Sofia 1997) [Bulgarian, English summary].

they undoubtedly constituted elements of a ceremonial drinking set that had been collected by the Thracian dynast. The imprecise dating is due, on the one hand, to the still inadequate chronology of works of toreutics and bronzecasting, due both to the now obsolete dating of tomb complexes and, on the other hand, to the simple fact that bronze vessels (similar to arms) were used for a long time, sometimes for more than a century, before they were placed in graves and tombs.[30] Nevertheless, the bronze vessels from the Mogilanska Mogila tumulus in Vratsa can be dated confidently to the decades in the middle of the 4th c. B.C.

Conclusion

In spite of this 'fluid' chronology of the bronze vessels from Vratsa, they form a homogeneous group of objects probably used during feasts in which the dynast buried in tomb no. 2 in Mogilanska Mogila participated when alive.

The bronze utensils produced in and imported from Greek *poleis* on the northern coast of the Aegean, in the Propontis, and in Western Asia Minor, dominate the inventory of the Thracian burials. The Vratsa group of vessels is yet another example of their frequent appearance in the burial complexes in Thrace. Vessels were made for real use, but in tombs they testified to the power of the buried ruler. However, in the lands of present-day NW Bulgaria, the ceremonial set of vessels from Vratsa remains the only one of its kind, three decades after its discovery.

We hope this modest paper, which we dedicate to the memory of both discoverers, will contribute to the study of one of the most important components of Greek imports in ancient Thrace — the bronze vessels.[31]

44, Aleko Konstantinov Street, Floor 1, BG-1505 Sofia (E.I.P.)
Department of Archaeology, District Museum of History, BG-3000 Vratsa (N.T.T.)

Acknowledgements

For their valuable assistance and help, the authors are very grateful to A. Fol and L. Getov (Univ. of Sofia) as well as to V. P. Vassilev (Bulgarian Institute of Archaeology, Sofia). We are also greatly indebted to C. A. Picon, B. Barr-Sharrar, C. C. Mattusch, and B. B. Shefton for their useful guidance, advice, and pertinent comments.

---

30 B. D. Filow (unter Mitwirkung von K. Schkorpil), *Die Archaische Nekropole von Trebenischte am Ochrida-See* (Berlin/Leipzig 1927) 81 ff.; V. P. Vassilev, *Bronzegefässe aus der Nekropole bei Trebenischte. Untersuchungen zur antiken Metallbearbeitung* (= Ausgrabungen und Forschungen 19; Sofia 1988) 7 n.5, 118 [Bulgarian, German summary].

31 After submitting this paper for publication, we read a new study of the palmette-ornamented type of bell situlae (like the better-preserved Vratsa vessel, see fig. 4a-c) by B. B. Shefton: "The Waldalgesheim situla: where was it made?" in C. Dobiat (ed.), *Marburger Studien zur Vor- und Frühgeschichte* 16 (= Festschrift für Otto-Herman Frey zum 65. Geburstag, Marburg 1994) 583-93, with discussion of all the extant specimens, their Aegean origin, their development, and the architectural prototypes of the decoration (mainly on the Erechtheum and the Belevi Mausoleum), as well as newly proposed dates. Shefton calls the situlae of Group A the Waldalgesheim Group and appends a working list of this group. He also names Group B the Vratsa Group (p. 586, nn. 13, 15), after a find of the same name. We can now add the Vratsa situla no. 2 to that list. Shefton addressed the same problems in "Magna Graecia, Macedonia, or neither? Some problems in 4th c. metalwork," in *Magna Grecia, Epiro e Macedonia. Atti del 24° convegno di studi sulla Magna Grecia, Taranto, 5-10 ottobre 1984* (Taranto 1985) esp. 403-7.

Athenian gilded bronzes from a conservation perspective

Alice Boccia Paterakis

Several fragments of a gilded bronze[1] equestrian statue dating to the late 4th c. B.C. were recovered from a well in the Athenian Agora in 1971 (figs. 1-2).[2] The fragments consist of a life-size leg, two drapery pieces, a sword, a Pegasus from the helmet, straps, a bit, and a palmette. The statue has been identified as a portrait of the Macedonian king Demetrios Poliorketes.[3] A gilded bronze female head dating to the 5th c. B.C. was found in another well in the Agora in 1932 (figs. 3-4).[4] This statue has been attributed to Nike, the winged goddess of victory.[5]

Technology

Bronze

The equestrian fragments and head were cast by the lost-wax method. Several samples of the bronzes were analyzed by Atomic Absorption Spectrometry (AAS) in the 1970s.[6] The equestrian statue fragments, except the sword, were found to be heavily leaded tin bronze with 28% to 35% lead. The sword is a tin bronze with a low lead content of 1.75%. Both compositions are known to have been used during the Hellenistic period.[7] The Nike head is a tin bronze of a composition found in other statues of this period.[8]

Cladding

The statues were gilded by the foil gilding method, with sheets of silver that had been gilded by diffusion bonding.[9] Both statues preserve grooves in the surface for the attachment of the gilded cladding. The sheets were hammered around the bronze and secured with a silver wire that was hammered into the grooves.[10] The sheets and wire are preserved in places. The cladding was analyzed with the Scanning Electron Microscope (SEM) in 1976, which determined the absence of copper in the gold and silver layers. The SEM examination showed interdiffusion, or diffusion bonding, of the gold and silver, which may have been achieved by hammering with or without annealing.[11] A mixture of calcium carbonate and bleached beeswax found inside the Nike head was identified by chemical analysis and infrared spectroscopy in 1960.[12] It may have been used as an adhesive for the attachment of the eyes in the sockets, a hairpiece on the head, or the cladding onto the statue.[13]

---

1 The terms 'bronze' and 'copper alloy' are used interchangeably.

2 T. L. Shear, "The Athenian Agora: excavations of 1971," *Hesperia* 42 (1973) 164-73.

3 C. Houser, "Alexander's influence on Greek sculpture as seen in a portrait in Athens," *Macedonia and Greece* (Studies in the History of Art 10, Washington, D.C. 1982) 229-38.

4 T. L. Shear, "Excavations in the Athenian Agora: the sculpture," *Hesperia* 2 (1933) 519-27.

5 H. A. Thompson, "A golden Nike from the Athenian Agora," *Harvard Studies in Classical Archaeology*, suppl. vol. 1 (1940) 183-210.

6 P. Craddock, "Report on the composition of eight fragments of bronze sculpture from the Athenian Agora," British Museum Research Laboratory (London 1977) unpublished.

7 Ibid.

8 Ibid.

9 A. B. Paterakis, "Gilded bronze sculpture from the Athenian Agora," *Gilded Metals Symposium, St. Paul, 1995* (forthcoming); W. A. Oddy, "Vergoldungen auf prähistorischen und klassischen Bronzen" in H. Born (ed.), *Archäologische Bronzen. Antike Kunst, moderne Technik* (Berlin 1985) 64-71.

10 Paterakis 1995 (supra n.9).

11 W. Sheridan, unpublished report, Agora Excavations.

12 M. Farnsworth and I. Simmons, "A unique cement from Athens," *Hesperia* 29 (1960) 118-22.

13 Ibid.

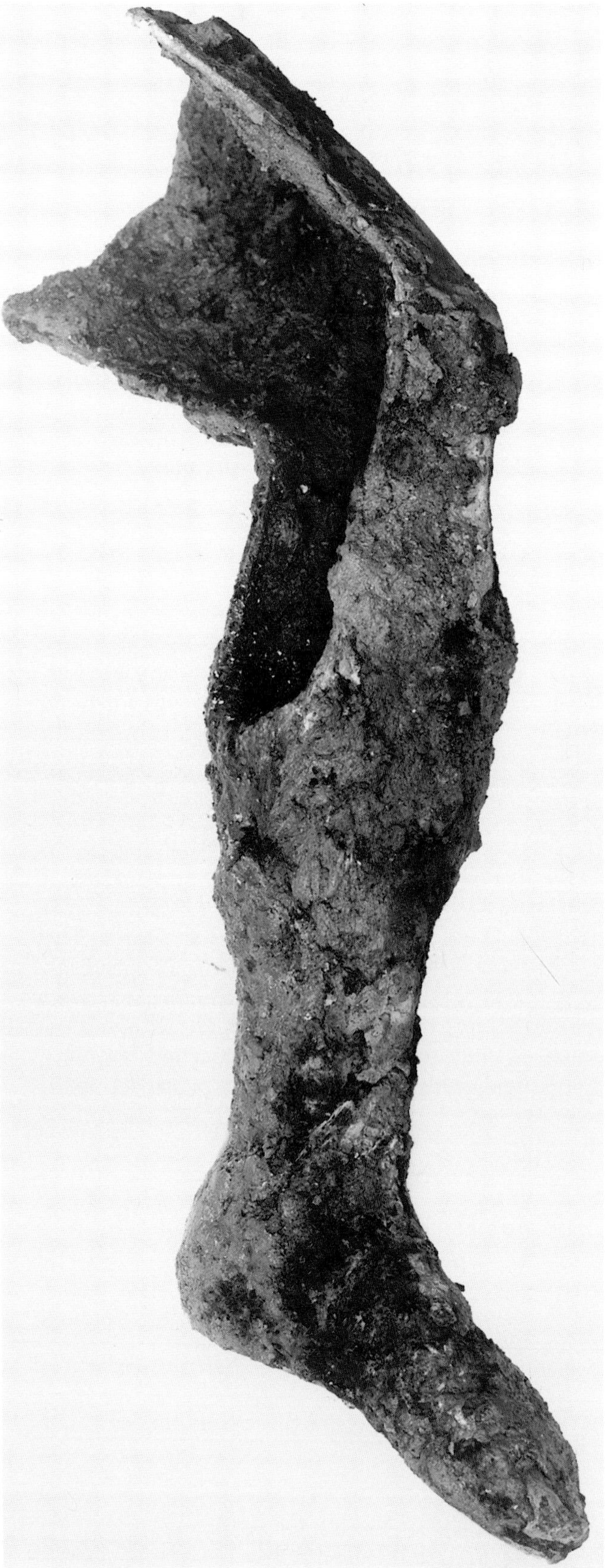

Fig. 1. Equestrian leg before cleaning. Gilded bronze, l. 0.87 m. Athenian Agora B 1384. (Photo: American School of Classical Studies at Athens: Agora Excavations.)

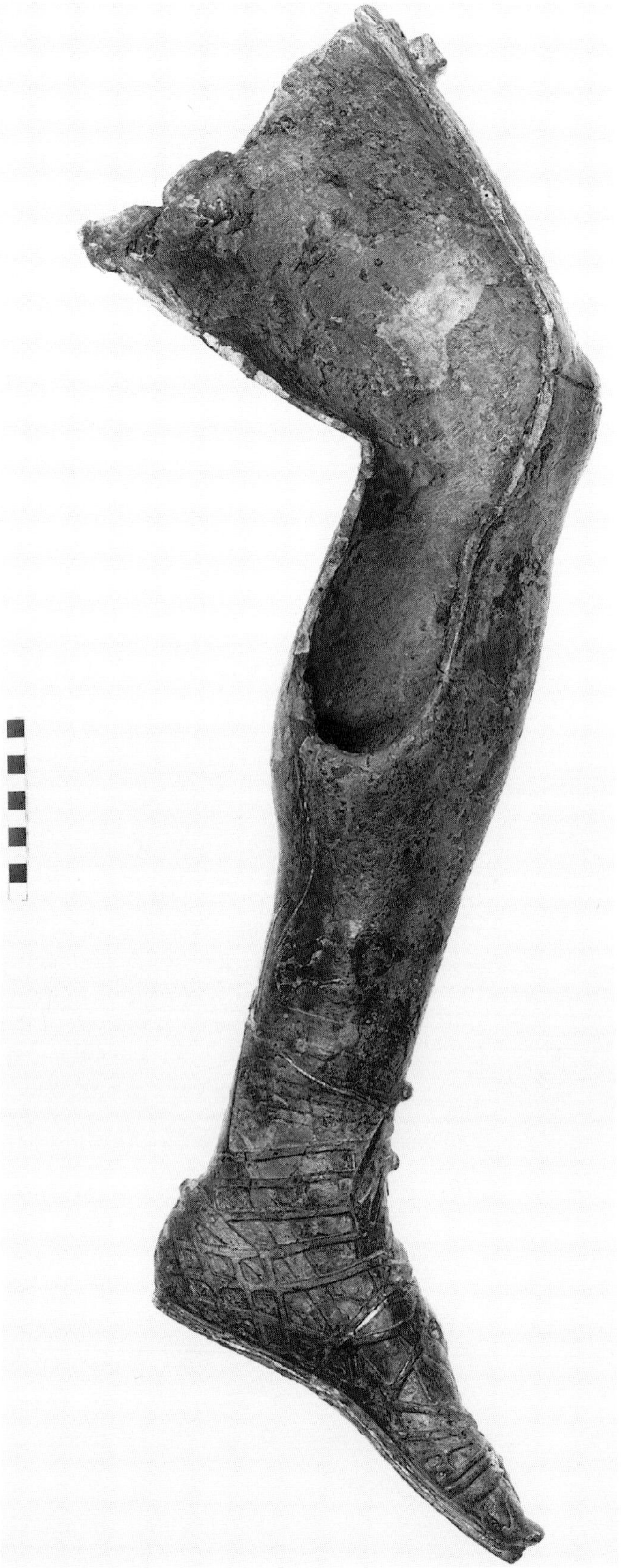

Fig. 2. Equestrian leg after cleaning. (Photo: American School of Classical Studies at Athens: Agora Excavations.)

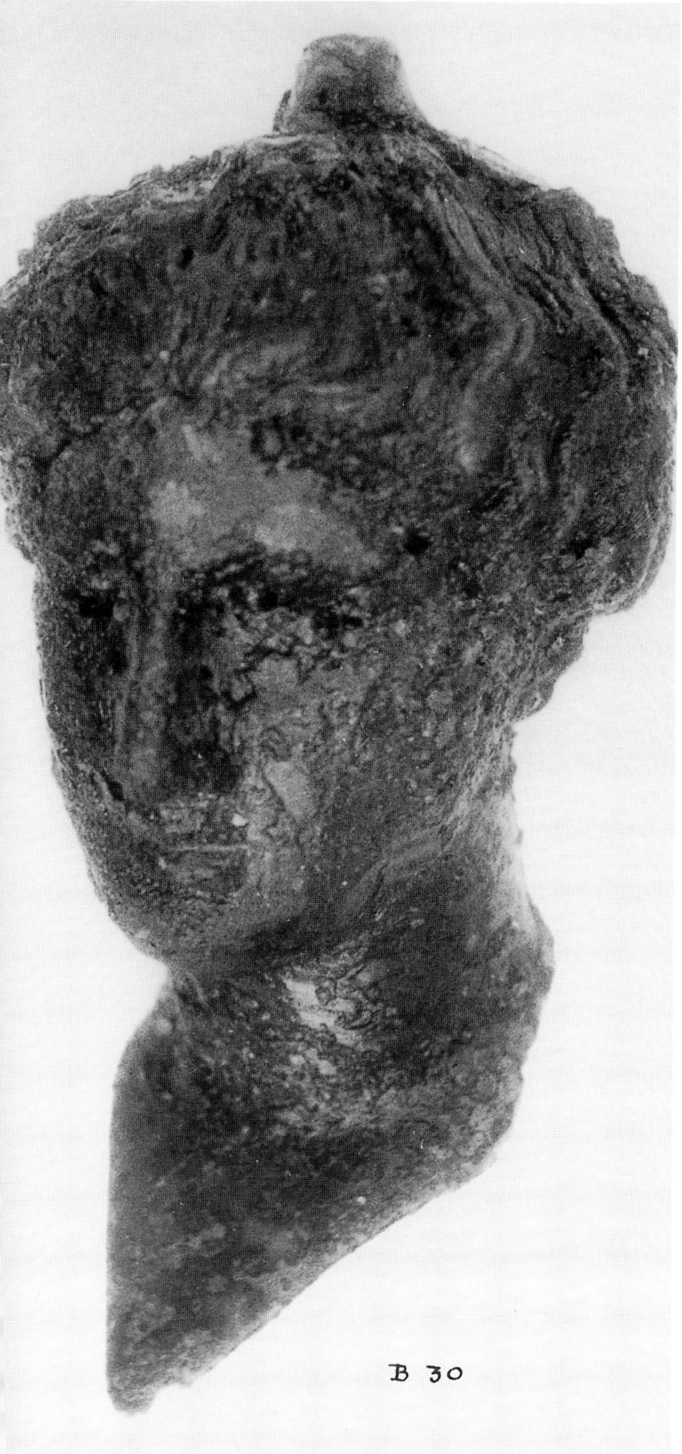

Fig. 3. Nike head before cleaning. Gilded bronze, h. 0.2 m. Athenian Agora B 30.

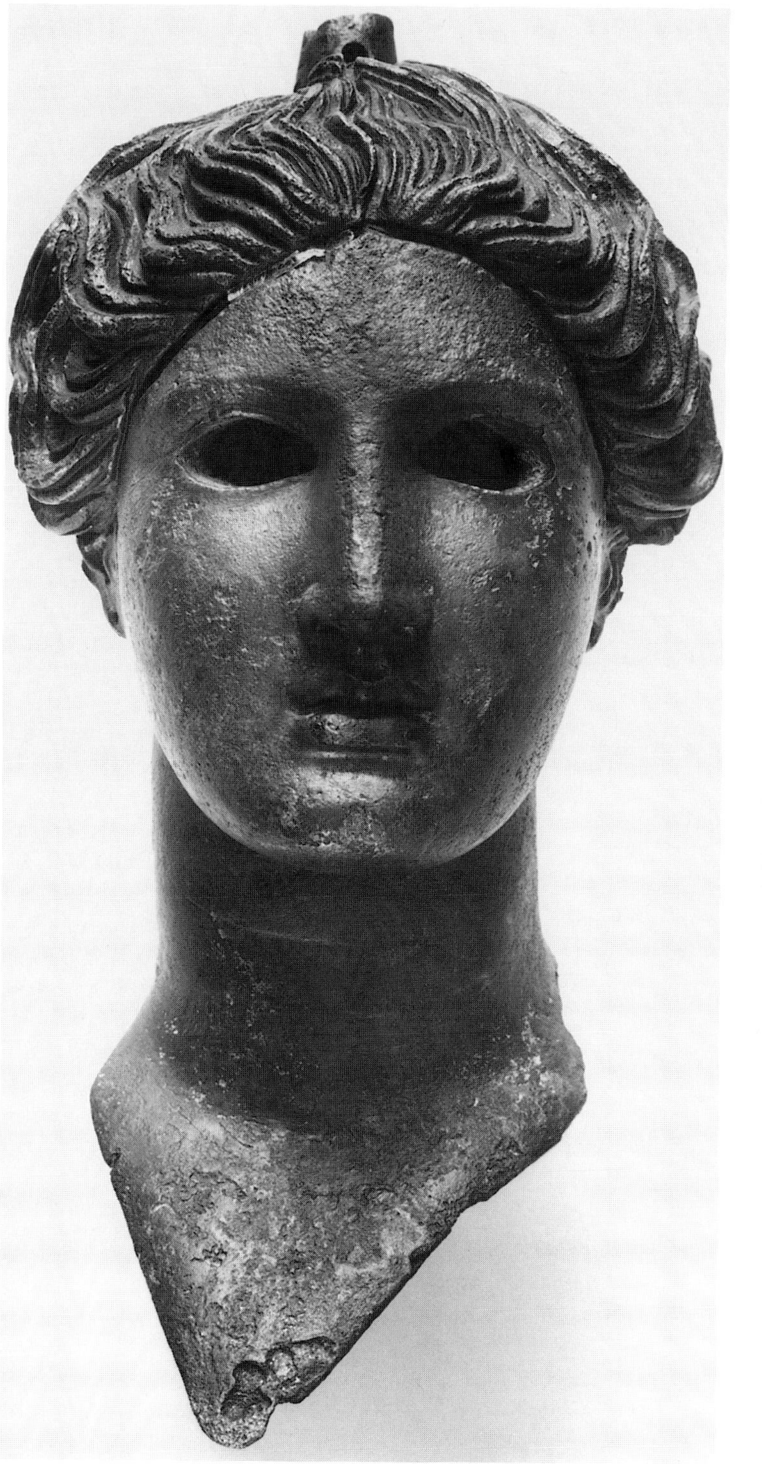

Fig. 4. Nike head after cleaning. (Photos: American School of Classical Studies at Athens: Agora Excavations.)

Corrosion

Examination sought evidence of deterioration and corrosion in the pre-burial, burial, and post-burial phases of the statues. Unfortunately, the corrosion products removed during cleaning were not reported. Recent examination revealed cuprite (copper oxide), malachite (basic copper carbonate), cerussite (white lead carbonate), nantokite (copper chloride), paratacamite/atacamite (basic copper chloride), and acanthite (silver sulfide).

Pre-burial

Once the statues were erected in ancient Athens, they were exposed to atmospheric elements such as rain. The cladding, if well sealed, may have protected the bronze. Corrosion of the copper alloy by atmospheric agents could have occurred wherever cracks in the cladding permitted their penetration. Examples of likely corrosion phenomena are cuprite from oxidation, and nantokite and paratacamite/atacamite from chlorides blown in from the sea. Bronchantite and antlerite (basic copper sulphates), found on outdoor bronze statues today, could have formed if sulfur had been present in the atmosphere. Wherever the silver cladding was in contact with the underlying bronze, galvanic corrosion of copper could have occurred since it is less noble than silver.[14] The copper corrosion products could have spread under the gilded silver wherever voids were present and protruded from cracks in the cladding onto the surface of the gold. Assuming diffusion bonding of silver and gold was achieved throughout the cladding, there should have been no corrosion at the gold-silver interface. Wherever atmospheric corrodants could reach the underlying silver through cracks in the gold or open seams, silver corrosion products could have formed. Chlorides and sulfur in the atmosphere could have caused the formation of chlorargyrite (silver chloride) and acanthite (silver sulfide).[15] Erosion of the gilded surface from wind-blown particulate matter could have exposed the underlying silver.

Burial

Most of the precious cladding was stripped from both statues before they were discarded, thereby exposing most of the copper alloy surface to corrosive attack. Wherever silver cladding remained in contact with the bronze substrate, galvanic corrosion could proceed. Oxygen during burial influenced corrosion formation; in aerobic conditions cuprite formed an inner corrosion layer and malachite formed the outer layer from dissolved carbon dioxide in ground water. Cerussite formed in pockets of the heavily leaded bronze in contact with malachite. Nantokite formed in the inner corrosion layer from chlorides dissolved in ground water. Nantokite with oxygen and moisture could have formed bronze disease (paratacamite, atacamite) while in the well. Hydrogen sulfide is produced by sulfate-reducing bacteria or by decaying organic matter and can contribute to the formation of chalcocite, geerite, and covellite (copper sulfides) and acanthite.[16] Silver sulfide was found on the silver; it can creep over the surrounding gold surface and adheres more strongly to gold than to silver.[17] Copper sulfides can creep over surrounding surfaces, including gold, without interacting chemically with those areas.[18]

Post-burial

Upon excavation the equilibrium which the objects had achieved with their burial environment was disrupted, and the changes in moisture, light, and oxygen levels initiated new corrosion. A discussion of post-burial corrosion follows.

Conservation treatment

Conservation treatments attempted to remove encrustation and corrosion formed during the pre-burial and burial phases which prevented the identification and study of the artifacts. Cleaning, however, can lead to new corrosion by the removal of corrosion products, which exposes underlying metal and alteration products to oxygen and moisture. An example is the removal of malachite exposing underlying nantokite to oxygen and moisture, which allows the formation of bronze disease. As a consequence, conservation necessitates stabilizing the object in its new environment.

---

14 L. Selwyn, "Corrosion chemistry of gilded silver and copper," *Gilded Metals Symposium, St. Paul 1995* (forthcoming).

15 Ibid.

16 S. J. Duncan and H. Ganiaris, "Some sulphide corrosion products on copper alloys and lead alloys from London waterfront sites," in *Recent advances in the conservation and analysis of artifacts* (London 1987) 109-18; Selwyn 1995 (supra n.14).

17 Selwyn 1995 (supra n.14).

18 Ibid.

In the 1930s the Nike head was soaked in boiling water, which may have leached organic matter from the carbonate/beeswax adhesive inside.[19] Electrochemical cleaning with zinc and a 2% solution of sodium hydroxide left traces of zinc that were detected by AAS (figs. 3-4).[20]

Conservation treatment of the equestrian statue may be divided into three phases. The first phase, for which there are no records, appears to have consisted of the mechanical removal of corrosion products from all objects and the chemical cleaning of some fragments (figs. 1-2). Palmette fragments, which may have been cleaned with zinc and sodium hydroxide, preserve a dark, powdery surface with copper plated onto the gold. Traces of zinc detected by AAS resulted from this chemical cleaning. Another palmette fragment preserves white crystals with a blue, powdery efflorescence.[21] These white crystals may be sodium acetate trihydrate, which are formed with sodium from sodium-based cleaning compounds such as Calgon (sodium hexametaphosphate) and acetic acid vapors from wooden storage drawers.[22] The sword was recovered in two pieces, which were doweled and filled with a polyester resin paste filler.

The second phase of conservation treatment consisted of the stabilization of active bronze disease on the leg, sword, and larger palmette fragment. Unsuccessful attempts with silver oxide were followed by a 3% solution in ethanol of benzotriazole ($C_6H_5 N_3$), which successfully stabilized the leg and palmette. Silver sulfide on the surface of the silver and gold cladding was removed with ammonium thiosulphate.[23]

In the third phase of treatment the original putty fill in the sword was found to shelter an extensive area of bronze disease which was stabilized with benzotriazole after removal of the putty. The gap was then filled with Chemical Metal polyester paste.[24] Lacquering with Incralac[25] completed treatment. Analysis of the corrosion products will verify their identification.

Corrosion after conservation, and long-term preservation

After conservation, the artifacts are exposed to indoor atmosphere in storage or display. The airborne sulfur-containing compounds, hydrogen sulfide and carbonyl sulfide, can react with copper and silver to form copper sulfide and silver sulfide. Nitrogen dioxide, chlorine, and ozone increase the corrosion rate by catalyzing the reaction.[26] Lacquering should offer some protection from atmospheric pollutants, moisture, and oxygen. The copper alloy objects may be kept in a low relative humidity (<35%) or in low oxygen levels to prevent bronze disease.[27] Silica gel or other desiccants, as well as an oxygen absorber such as Ageless, may be used.[28] A sulfur absorber may be used to protect the objects from the formation of silver and copper sulfide.[29]

American Academy in Rome

---

19 Farnsworth and Simmons 1960 (supra n.12).

20 The cleaning procedure is described in Shear 1933 (supra n.4)

21 K. Hall, unpublished report, Agora Excavations.

22 N. Tennent and T. Baird, "The identification of acetate efflorescence on bronze antiquities stored in wooden cabinets," *The Conservator* 16 (1992) 39-43, 47.

23 L. Weier, unpublished report, Agora Excavations.

24 Chemical Metal is manufactured by Plastic Padding Ltd., Wooburn Industrial Park, Wooburn, High Wycombe, Bucks., HP10 OPE, UK.

25 The Incralac used consists of Paraloid B44-S acrylic resin, toluene, ethyl alcohol, benzotriazole, and Paraplex G-60. It is manufactured by the CTS company, Via Monteverdi 53, 50019 Sesto Fiorentino (FI) Italy.

26 Selwyn 1995 (supra n.14).

27 D. Scott, "Bronze disease: a review of some chemical problems and the role of relative humidity," *JAIC* 29 (1990) 193-206; M. Gilberg and D. Grattan, "Oxygen-free storage using Ageless oxygen absorber," *Preventive conservation practice, theory and research* (Preprints of IIC Ottawa Congress 1994) 177-80.

28 Gilberg and Grattan 1994 (supra n.27).

29 W. A. Oddy, "Chemistry in the conservation of archaeological materials," *The science of the total environment* 143 (1994) 121-26.

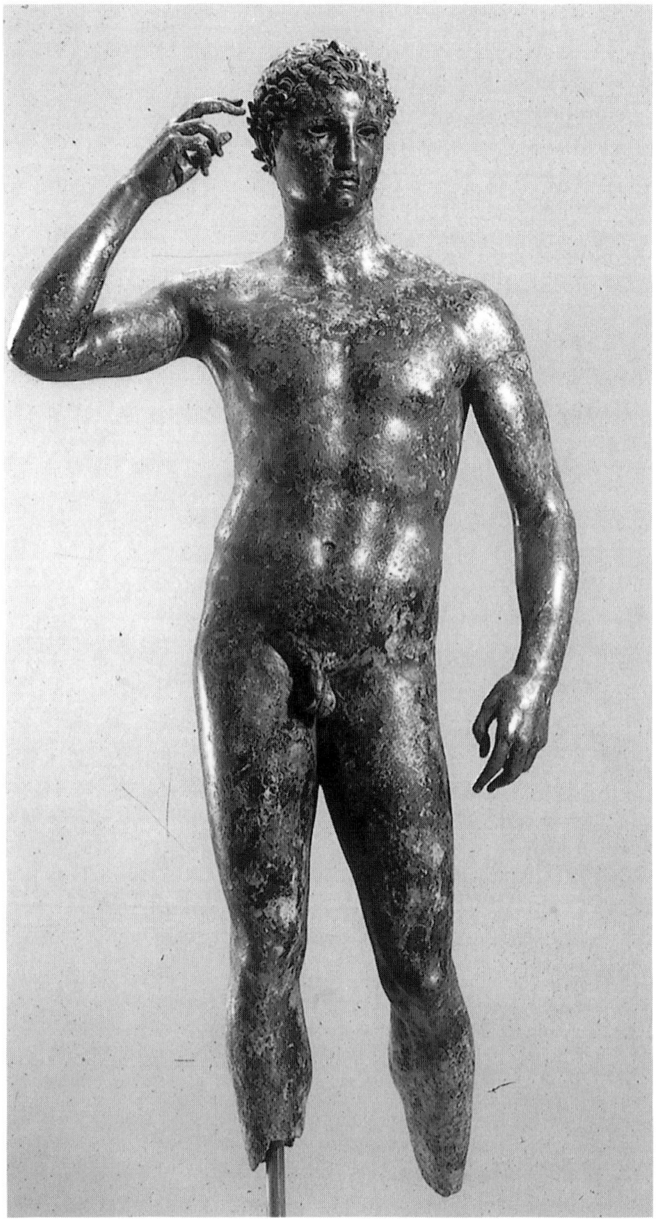

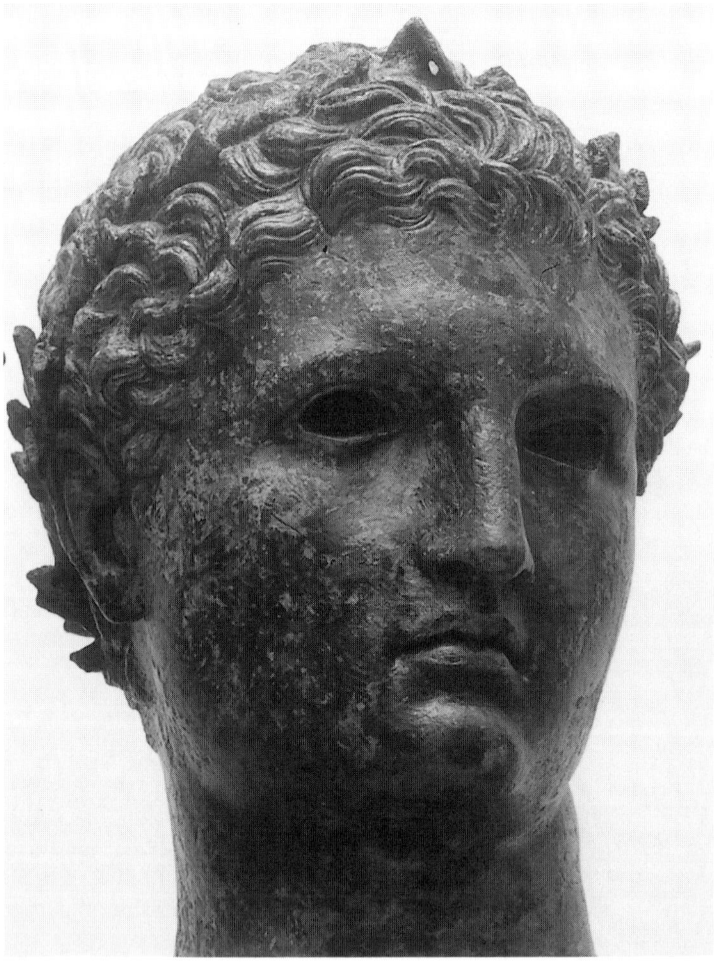

Fig. 1 (left). The Victorious Youth. Bronze with copper inlay, h. 1.51 m. Los Angeles, The J. Paul Getty Museum 77.AB.30. (Photo: The J. Paul Getty Museum.)

Fig. 2 (above). Detail of the head. Note the depth of the added curls, which are solid bronze but cast as a unit with the head. (Photo: The J. Paul Getty Museum.)

The Getty Victorious Youth reconsidered: initial report on the scientific and technical re-examination

Jerry Podany and David Scott

Since 1977 when the Getty Museum first exhibited the life-size bronze statue of a victorious youth, often referred to as the Getty Bronze, the statue has been recognized as one of the great large-scale casts to survive from antiquity (fig. 1). Thought on stylistic grounds to date from the late 4th c. B.C., the bronze was recovered in June 1963 by fishermen off the northeast coast of Italy. Except for the feet and eyes, the bronze has survived complete.

Since the discovery of the youth, there have been numerous scholarly articles about its date and attribution. Some propose that the bronze originated from within the 'school' of Lysippos, while others attribute the casting to Lysippos himself. Whether the bronze is indeed an athlete,[1,] or was meant to depict a youth of privileged class also remains a matter of discusion.[2] Despite these ongoing questions there have been only two full publications dedicated to the bronze, a monograph written by J. Frel in 1982 and one by C. Mattusch in 1998.[3] To date, however, no discussions regarding the bronze have benefited from a thorough technical and scientific study of the work, and many 'technical' observations are still based upon initial work carried out at the Doerner Institut[4] and by the restorer who undertook the cleaning of the bronze in 1972.[5]

Given the importance of the statue and the technical information remaining to be uncovered, the Department of Antiquities Conservation at the Getty Museum has launched a thorough re-investigation. The project has several major goals, including correcting previously mistaken conclusions regarding the manufacture of the bronze; supporting other conclusions; adding to our knowledge of ancient bronzecasting techniques; and providing more detailed information to further the study of ancient objects in general. It will come as no surprise that while some observations provide immediate explanations, others raise yet more questions. This paper presents some of the initial results of the study. These results focus on the casting technique used to manufacture the bronze; on an initial study of the core material; on recent alloy analysis; and on dating the organic remains found in the core material to establish more firmly a casting date.

Manufacture

Initial studies of the bronze statue reported evidence of direct lost-wax casting.[6] More recent investigation has observed the same evidence and come to a different conclusion, that is, that the bronze was predominantly manufactured using an indirect method.[7] More 'direct' modeling

---

1 Discussions with S. Rugg, physiologist at the University of Southern California, suggest that the casting does not exhibit any particular physical development which can be associated with a specific athletic event.

2 J. Frel, "Lysippe et son influence," in J. Chamay and J. L. Maier (edd.), *Hellas et Roma* V (Rome 1987) 89.

3 J. Frel, *The Getty Bronze* (Malibu 1982); C. C. Mattusch, *The victorious youth* (Los Angeles 1998).

4 J. Riederer, October 1971 analytical report, Doerner Institut, Munich (on file at the J. Paul Getty Museum).

5 H. Herzer and V. Kinnius, 1972 report, Munich (on file at the J. Paul Getty Museum).

6 Frel, *Bronze* (supra n.3) 11; Herzer (supra n.5). The direct method is rarely noted for large-scale bronzes. In the technique the core is modeled to an almost finished stage and then wax is added to the worked surface. The finished form and surface of the sculpture is modeled in this final layer of wax which is then directly invested for casting. The interior of the final casting takes on the negative impressions of the molded core (since the wax added over the molded core will have little influence on the textures of the outer core surface). In most instances the walls of the bronze are uneven and relatively thick. Appendages such as noses, ears, hair curls, etc., will be solid bronze since they had been added at a later point to the final wax model in solid wax.

7 The indirect method begins with the making of a mold from an initial sculpture or part. The wax is then

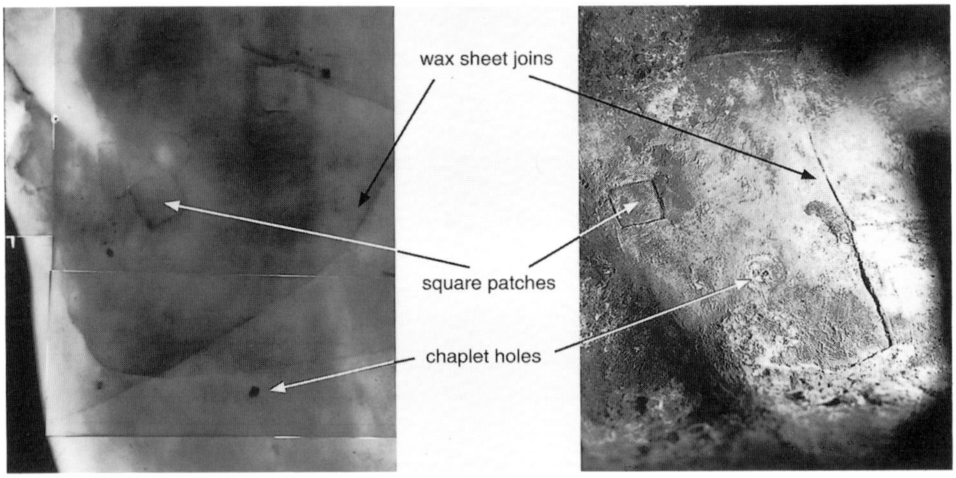

Fig. 3. Left: a radiograph. Right: interior view showing the edge-to-edge wax sheet joins, several of the large square patches, and numerous chaplet holes. (Photo: Department of Antiquities Conservation, The J. Paul Getty Museum.)

can be assumed in the area of the head, where added hair curls and sculpted features were surely completed by the addition of more wax to the basic form (fig. 2). The initial conclusion that the bronze was made by the direct method may well have been encouraged by the popular notion, often still put forward today, that the result of a direct casting is somehow a masterpiece of greater value than a bronze created by the indirect process. It must also be said, however, that now we more readily recognize the signs of indirect casting, since we have more information and a larger comparative data-base. It is also more widely recognized that large-scale bronzes of this period completed by the direct method are quite rare, if in fact they exist.

One of the most conclusive characteristics which points toward the indirect process is the ample evidence of the use of polygonal wax sheets to line the molds made for this casting. One early study concluded that the sheets were laid over a prepared core and then sculpted.[8] While this scenario is possible, it is not supported by the features of the inner surface of the bronze, which represents the accessible and worked inner surface of a wax working model. The joined edges of the wax sheets are preserved quite clearly and are visible in radiographs[9] and endoscopic photographs (fig. 3). The abutted edges, preserved in the casting, indicate that the wax joins were made with nothing resisting the deformation of the wax along the edge of the join as the sheets were pressed together. Should the wax sheets have been applied to an already existing core, which surely would have been dried and hardened in order to resist the pressure of applying the wax sheets, the wax would have taken the impression of the core surface and not retained the deformed detail of the soft wax join. In addition to this, we have observed areas where the wax was clearly smeared in the process of application and joining. These features support the notion that the wax sheets were applied to the interior of an open mold. It is likely that the craftsman first applied a thin layer of wax to the mold interior surface in order to assure fidelity to the wax model. This was followed by the production of wax sheets of a predetermined thickness. The sheets were then cut to specific interlocking shapes and pressed onto the interior of the mold.[10] Through experimentation we have found that by pouring molten beeswax over the surface of a cold polished marble slab covered with a wet

pressed, painted, or slurried into the mold. The resulting wax model is filled with core, which is pressed, packed, or poured into the interior cavity. The core material reproduces the texture of the wax surface with which it is in contact. This texture is transferred to the interior surface of the cast bronze. The thickness of the cast wall is normally quite consistent.

8 Herzer (supra n.5).

9 The authors would like to thank J. Maish, Associate Conservator of Antiquities, the Getty Museum, for his invaluable assistance in producing these radiographs.

10 Haynes, *Technique* 35, 70.

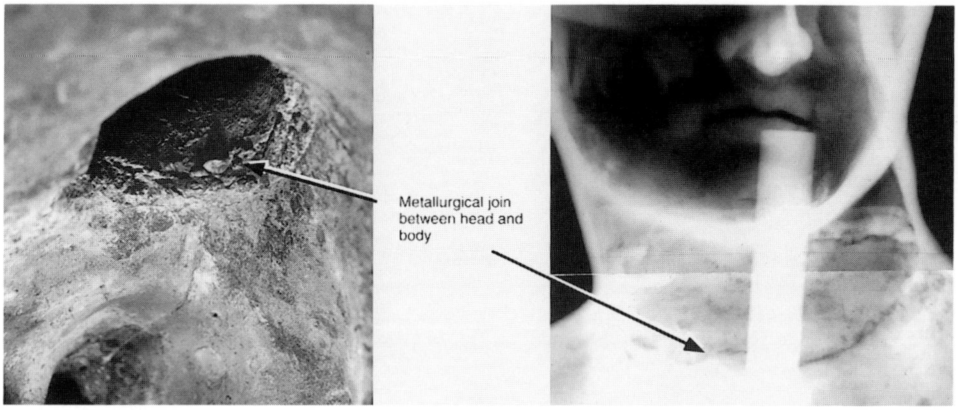

Fig. 4. Left: an interior view of the head-to-torso join (arrow), showing the bronze over-spill of a metallurgical join. Note also the seam along the upper area of the shoulder, running from the neck to the right arm hole. Right: radiograph showing the typical features of a metallurgical join between the head and torso. (Photo: Department of Antiquities Conservation, The J. Paul Getty Museum.)

cloth, the thickness of the cast wax sheet can be easily controlled using wooden or metal dams along the edge of the marble slab. These dams determine the thickness of the sheet by creating an open-faced mold which is simply filled and kept level during cooling.

The wax sheets produced in our experiments were *c.*4 mm thick and were joined together on top of a previously wax-coated plaster mold using several techniques of cutting and joining. The results were then molded, cast in plaster, and radiographed for comparison to the radiographs of the Getty youth. At least one of these techniques of cutting and joining produced results quite similar to the features observed in the radiographs of the torso area.

Using pre-cast wax sheets allowed the artisan to control both the casting thickness, which is relatively consistent throughout the figure, averaging 4 mm, as well as to take advantage of the economy of time this technique offered. Once the wax model or wax sections were unmolded, only minor effort was needed to finish the exterior of the wax. Observations of the internal features of the bronze indicate that the interior of the wax form was of little consequence to the craftsman, since seams are not fully pressed together, often leaving a thinner bronze wall at the seam, as can be seen clearly in the radiographs (fig. 3).

Radiographs also indicate that the legs, arms, and head were prepared for casting using a very different technique. There are no seams beyond where the left and the right arms are attached to the torso, nor are there any in the legs or in the head above the neck. It appears then that these parts of the figure were prepared using a different technique. The arms were cast separately and then connected to the torso metallurgically by welding or by hot flow joins. The head was also attached by means of a metallurgical join in the neck (fig. 4).[11] This type of join can be contrasted to the wax-to-wax join of the left leg (fig. 5).

Once the wax model was completed, rectangular iron chaplets were inserted. There is visible evidence for 23 iron chaplets (fig. 3), though more were probably used. The chaplets were pushed through the wax before filling the model with core material, and a flare of wax surrounding each chaplet hole is preserved in bronze, protruding toward the interior (fig. 6). This flared edge would not have been possible had the core already been in place and resisted the free deformation of the wax. It should also be noted that several chaplets penetrate quite near a wax sheet join, suggesting that there was no particular relationship between the sheets and the chaplet placement.

Although there have been some exceptions, the literature on ancient casting techniques has held that the presence of an interior armature indicates use of the direct casting technique. Ear-

11 We are grateful to C. Mattusch for her assistance in this observation.

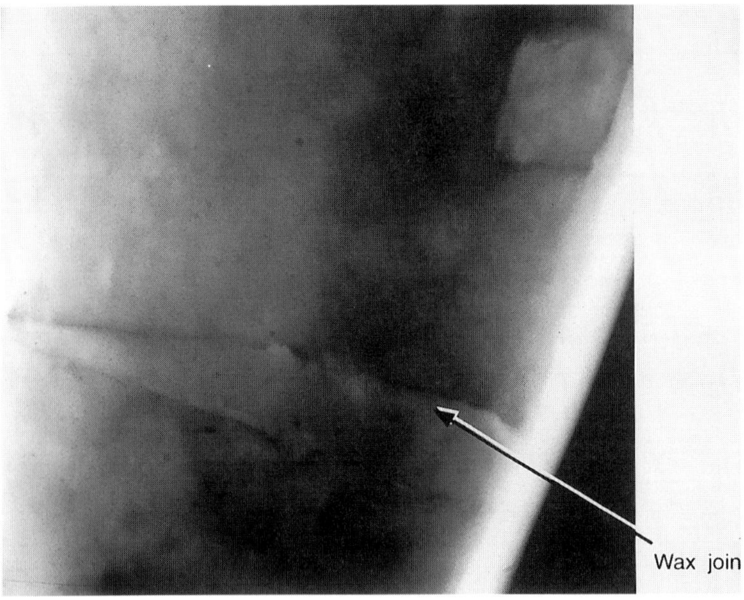

Fig. 5. Radiograph of the wax-to-wax join of the left leg. Note the clean appearance of the seam as compared to the metallurgical joins in fig. 4.

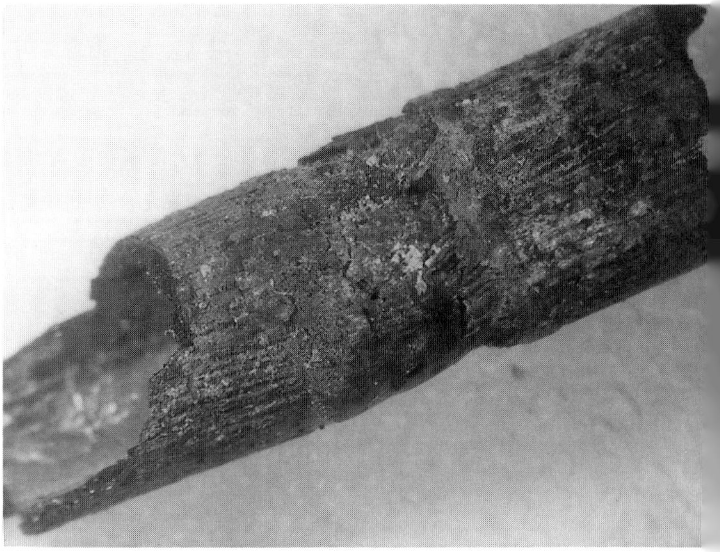

Fig. 7. Fragment of a reed stem found in the removed core material. (Both photos: Department of Antiquities Conservation, The J. Paul Getty Museum.)

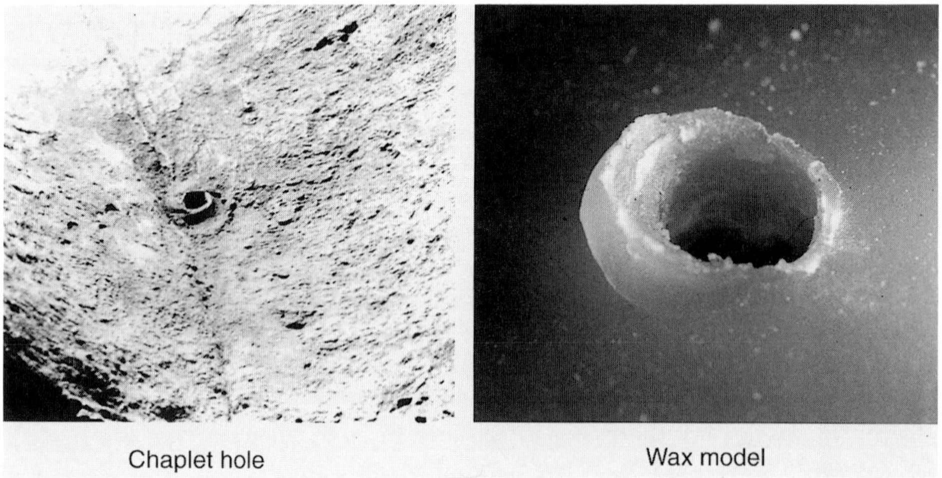

Fig. 6. Left: an interior view showing a chaplet hole. Right: a wax model of a chaplet hole made by pushing a similar size rod through a beeswax slab. Note the flaring wax edges along the outer circumference of both holes. (Photo: Department of Antiquities Conservation, The J. Paul Getty Museum.)

ly technical reports on the Getty statue refer to several reed armatures and to a wooden rod, all of which were found embedded in the core at various locations. Unfortunately no photographs of the reeds or wooden rod exist, and only small fragments of reed material (5-8 mm in diameter) were saved in the early efforts to remove the core (fig. 7). The presence of these rods was used to argue for direct casting, assuming that they formed an armature to support the core during its sculpting. However, the diameter of the existing reed fragment argues against that function. If the surviving fragments are representative of the reed 'armature' found by the restorer, they surely would have been too small and too weak to act as a supporting structure for the considerable weight of core to model a life-size figure. It is more likely that these rods served dual functions as gas vents, core stabilizers, and/or internal anchors for the assembly of the various major segments, either when assembled in the wax or later during metallurgical joining of the arms and head. Radiographs of the right arm reveal a void along the axial length of the arm where a reed was likely to have been (fig. 8). It is unclear if the reed was re-

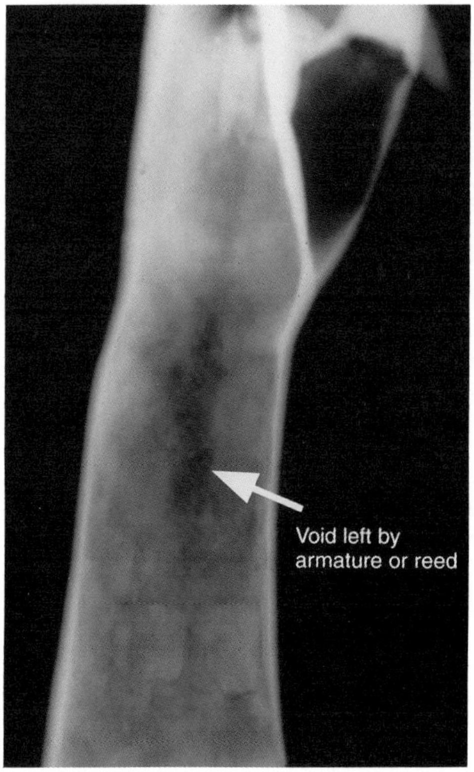

Fig. 8. Radiograph of the right arm, showing the hollow void along its axial length. This void may have been due to the presence of an armature or reed inserted into the core. (Photo: Department of Antiquities Conservation, The J. Paul Getty Museum.)

moved during the evacuation of the core, intentionally retrieved by the craftsman before or after casting, or burned away during casting. The latter is quite unlikely, since at least the charcoal remains would have been preserved and since a considerable amount of uncharred or only slightly charred organic material has been found in the core débris, indicating that temperatures did not reach much higher than 450° F in central locations of the core. The reed may have served a number of purposes, including one as a support for the core material to prevent dislocation due to impact, shrinkage, or sudden temperature change during casting. Its open structure, or indeed the void left by it after it was removed, may equally have served as a gas vent. Such use of voids left by rods is well attested in the historical literature on casting techniques.[12]

One of the most intriguing technical details found on the Getty youth is a number of roughly square patches whose function has yet to be fully understood. These squares are unlike the patched flaws common to most ancient bronzes, including this statue. The patches present show a metallurgical structure indicating that they were cast and then cold-worked without annealing. Examination of one of these small bronze patches from the upper proper left arm revealed a tin content of about 9%, very similar in composition to the body itself. The trace elements arrived at by ICP-MS[13] analysis suggests that the same copper was used for casting the patch as for casting the figure.

This small patch had become detached, and it was therefore possible to carry out a non-destructive metallographic examination by polishing one of the straight edges. Examination of the polished cross section (fig. 9) reveals a distorted cast structure. This is evident from the remaining, uncorroded, dendritic microstructure, which also reveals that the cast alloy has been cold-worked to shape from the cast condition. The resulting microstructure is therefore quite unusual in showing a heavily strained and cold-worked cast material with extensive slip planes visible both in the as-polished and etched sections. As a result of this metallographic study, the sequence of events for making these small surface patches can be suggested. First, an impression of the hole (normally a roughly rectangular area chiseled to a depth of a few millimeters) could be taken in wax or clay and a small mold prepared from the resulting impression. The cast patch could then be cold-hammered to a specific curvature or flatness, and hammered into position in the prepared surface of the bronze. Since the patch had been extensively cold-worked, it would be considerably harder than the bronze casting itself and therefore displaced metal will tend to represent movement of the bronze casting rather than producing further flattening of the patch with the danger of loss of shape. It is interesting to be able to confirm in this case that the small patches on the bronze surface were prepared as precast blank sheets, ready to be hammered into position, and that they were not simply cut from fragments of worked and annealed sheet metal, as might be supposed.

12 N. E. Spretson, *A practical treatise on casting and founding* (London 1880) 202-5.
13 Inductively Coupled Plasma Mass Spectrometry carried out by West Coast Analytical Services Inc., Santa Fe Springs, CA.

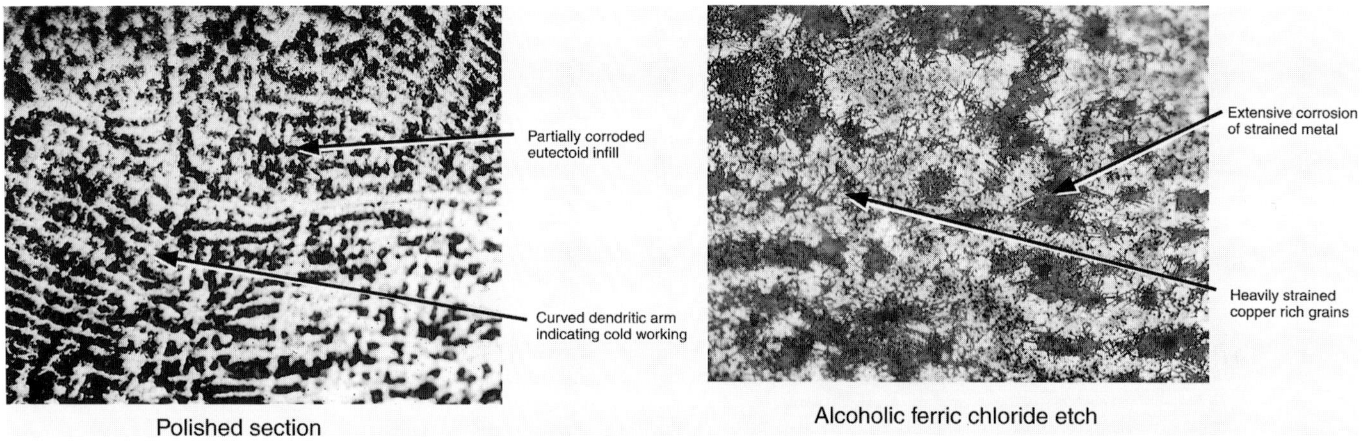

Fig. 9. Cross section of the repair patch. Left: polished, showing distorted dendritic structure with partially corroded eutectoid infill. The distortion shows that the cast structure was hammered without annealing. Mag. x60. Right: etched section of patch showing a heavily strained grain structure resulting from severe cold-working of the metal, perhaps to hammer it into position. Mag. x120. (Photo: Getty Conservation Institute, Museum Services.)

In addition to this type of patch, over 36 relatively large squares, all of them *c.*2.5 x 2.5 cm, present quite different characteristics. They are not only rather large but they also fill cut voids that penetrate all the way through the casting wall (fig. 3). The squares are mostly concentrated in the torso area, though several appear in each leg, arm, and hand (fig. 10). No evidence for them has been found in the head.

ICP-MS analyses of the square and adjacent body have indicated that the compositions are quite similar and most probably of the same batch of metal. A feasible explanation for the squares is that relatively standardized square holes were cut in the wax model in order to form bridges between the core and the outer investment. These bridges, as suggested by Haynes,[14] would have acted as core stabilizers. Contrary to the suggestion of Haynes, however, this study has not found any evidence that the square holes were patched using the so-called flow-in technique, but rather that they were cold-patched in the traditional method. The latter involves the casting of a small patch to shape, or cutting the patch from a larger pre-cast sheet, and then hammering the patch into place. We drew this conclusion from the radiographs, which show a clear decrease in density along the perimeter of each patch. Such a characteristic is more consistent with cold patching and not with a flow-in patch, since the latter process would surely have filled all voids with metal. Similar arguments can be made against the proposal that these squares were done in wax on the wax model.[15]

Metal analysis

Studies of the composition of the bronze go back to 1971,[16] when a report was issued from the Doerner Institute showing the results of an analysis carried out by Atomic Absorption Spectroscopy for 9 elements, whose results are shown in Table 1. There is a significant amount of tin present — 10.7%, and there are trace impurities of lead, iron, silver, nickel, cobalt, and antimony. As part of the new analytical study, clean metal drillings from a number of different parts of the bronze were analyzed. There are separately cast components, and different batches of metal were used to cast the bronze.

Element	%
Copper	89
Tin	10.7
Lead	0.05
Zinc	n.d.
Silver	0.04
Nickel	0.05
Cobalt	0.08
Antimony	0.10
Iron	0.04
Sum	100.04

Table 1. Composition of the Bronze, analyzed by the Doerner Institut in 1971.

14 Haynes, *Technique* 70.
15 See Mattusch, *Victorious youth* (supra n.3) 70-72.
16 Riederer 1971 (supra n.4)

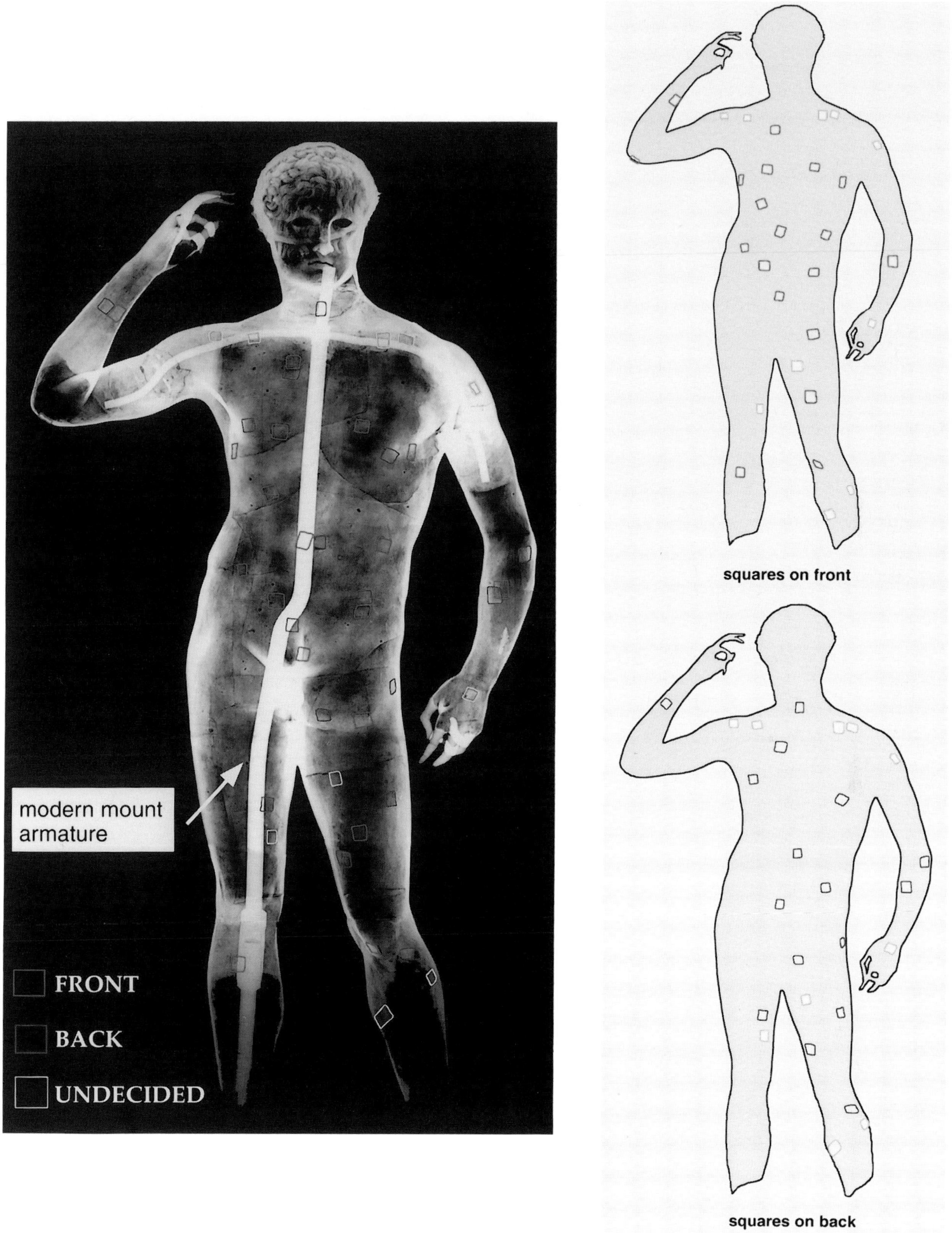

Fig. 10. Map of the large square patches and diagrams of those present on the front of the bronze (upper) and those on the back (lower). (Photo: Department of Antiquities Conservation, The J. Paul Getty Museum.)

Table 2

Sample: Getty Bronze from
Proper left broken leg, #77.AB.30

SemiQuantitative Report
Inductively Coupled Plasma – Mass Spectrometry

	ppm	Detection Limit		ppm	Detection Limit
Aluminum *	6	5	Mercury	ND<2	2
Antimony *	146	0.7	Molybdenum	ND<5	5
Arsenic *	1600	5	Neodymium	ND<0.7	0.7
Barium *	34	2	Nickel *	457	3
Beryllium	ND<0.7	0.7	Niobium	ND<0.7	0.7
Bismuth	2.3	0.7	Osmium	ND.0.7	0.7
Boron	ND<4	4	Palladium	ND<0.7	0.7
Bromine	ND<3000	3000	Platinum	ND<0.7	0.7
Cadmium *	0.9	0.8	Praseodymium	ND<0.7	0.7
Calcium	ND<5000	5000	Rhenium	ND<0.7	0.7
Cerium	1.4	0.7	Rhodium	1.4	0.7
Cesium	1.7	0.7	Rubidium	ND<0.7	0.7
Chromium	ND<900	900	Ruthenium	0.7	0.7
Cobalt *	1290	0.7	Samarium	ND<0.7	0.7
Copper	MATRIX		Selenium *	69	30
Dysprosium	ND<0.7	0.7	Silver *	365	0.7
Erbium	ND<0.7	0.7	Sodium	ND<10000	10000
Europium	1.7	0.7	Strontium *	4.4	0.9
Gadolinium	3.6	0.7	Tantalum	ND<0.7	0.7
Gallium	ND<10	10	Tellurium	3.1	0.7
Germanium	ND<30	30	Thallium	ND<0.7	0.7
Gold	20.9	0.8	Thorium	ND<0.7	0.7
Hafnium	ND<0.7	0.7	Thulium	ND<0.7	0.7
Holmium	ND<0.7	0.7	Tin *	99400	1
Iodine	ND<2	2	Titanium	ND<9	9
Iridium	ND<0.7	0.7	Tungsten	ND<5	5
Iron	ND<2000	2000	Uranium	ND<0.7	0.7
Lanthanum	ND<0.7	0.7	Vanadium	ND<10000	10000
Lead *	623	1	Ytterbium	ND<0.7	0.7
Lithium	ND<3	3	Yttrium	ND<0.7	0.7
Lutetium	ND<6	6	Zinc *	52	2
Magnesium	10	6	Zirconium	ND<0.7	0.7
Manganese	ND<50	50			

Date analyzed: 3-26-96
Elements not analyzed: All Gasses, C, P, S, K, Si, Sc, In, Tb
MATRIX = major element * = quantitative result

Table 3

SemiQuantitative Report
Inductively Coupled Plasma – Mass Spectrometry

	ppm	Detection Limit		ppm	Detection Limit
Aluminum	16	10	Manganese	ND<200	200
Antimony	80	3	Mercury	ND<8	2
Arsenic	ND<1000	1000	Molybdenum	30	10
Barium	83	5	Neodymium	ND<1	1
Beryllium	ND<7	7	Nickel	510	30
Bismuth	3	1	Niobium	ND<2	2
Boron	ND<30	30	Osmium	ND<2	2
Bromine	ND<1000	1000	Palladium	ND<4	4
Cadmium	ND<100	100	Platinum	ND<2	2
Calcium	ND<2000	20000	Praseodymium	ND<1	1
Cerium	ND<4	4	Rhenium	ND<1	1
Cesium	ND<1	1	Rhodium	ND<1	1
Chromium	ND<4000	4000	Rubidium	ND<4	4
Cobalt	1150	4	Ruthenium	ND<3	3
Copper	MATRIX	30	Samarium	ND<3	3
Dysprosium	ND<2	2	Selenium	ND<200	200
Erbium	ND<1	1	Silver	300	3
Europium	3	1	Sodium	ND	ND
Gadolinium	3	2	Strontium	ND<3	3
Gallium	ND<300	600	Tantalum	ND<1	1
Germanium	ND<600	200	Tellurium	ND<2	2
Gold	ND<200	1	Thallium	ND<2	2
Hafnium	ND<1	1	Thorium	ND<1	1
Holmium	ND<1	4	Thulium	ND<1	1
Iodine	107	1	Tin	128000	10
Iridium	ND<1	20000	Titanium	66	40
Iron	ND<20000	1	Tungsten	ND<2	2
Lanthanum	0	200	Uranium	ND<1	1
Lead	ND<1	8	Vanadium	ND<1000	1000
Lithium	870	10	Ytterbium	ND<2	2
Lutetium	ND<8		Yttrium	ND<2	2
Magnesium	ND<10		Zinc	50	20
	1100		Zirconium	ND<2	2

Date Analyzed: 1-15-96

Elements not analyzed: All gasses, C, B, Sc, In, Tb, K, Na, Si, P
MATRIX = Major element

Table 4

SemiQuantitative Report
Inductively Coupled Plasma – Mass Spectrometry

	ppm	Detection Limit		ppm	Detection Limit
Aluminum *	11	7	Mercury *	ND<1	1
Antimony *	123	0.9	Molybdenum *	ND<2	2
Arsenic *	1740	20	Neodymium	ND<0.9	0.9
Barium *	8	3	Nickel *	480	2
Beryllium *	ND<7	7	Niobium	ND<0.9	0.9
Bismuth *	7	0.9	Osmium	ND<0.9	0.9
Boron *	ND<200	200	Palladium	ND<0.9	0.9
Bromine	ND<300	300	Platinum	ND<0.9	0.9
Cadmium *	ND<1	1	Praseodymium	ND<0.9	0.9
Calcium *	ND<400	400	Rhenium	ND<0.9	0.9
Cerium	ND<0.9	0.9	Rhodium	4	0.9
Cesium	ND<0.9	0.9	Rubidium	ND<0.9	0.9
Chromium *	ND<40	40	Ruthenium	ND<0.9	0.9
Cobalt *	1250	0.9	Samarium	ND<0.9	0.9
Copper	MATRIX		Selenium *	ND<30	30
Dysprosium	ND<0.9	0.9	Silver *	410	0.9
Erbium	ND<0.9	0.9	Sodium *	ND<1000	1000
Europium	ND<0.9	0.9	Strontium *	2	0.9
Gadolinium	1	0.9	Tantalum	ND<0.9	0.9
Gallium	ND<1	1	Tellurium	3	0.9
Germanium	ND<2	2	Thallium *	ND<0.9	0.9
Gold *	18	2	Thorium	ND<0.9	0.9
Hafnium	ND<0.9	0.9	Thulium	ND<0.9	0.9
Holmium	ND<0.9	0.9	Tin *	115000	1
Iodine	ND<8	8	Titanium *	11	5
Iridium	ND<0.9	0.9	Tungsten	3	0.9
Iron *	580	600	Uranium	ND<2	0.9
Lanthanum	ND<0.9	0.9	Vanadium *	ND<0.9	400
Lead *	561	0.9	Ytterbium	ND<0.9	0.9
Lithium *	ND<20	20	Yttrium	ND<0.9	0.9
Lutetium	ND<6	6	Zinc *	ND<20	20
Magnesium *	37	5	Zirconium	ND<0.9	0.9
Manganese *	ND<4	4			

Date Analyzed: 9-9-96

MATRIX = Major Element * = quantitative results
Elements not analyzed: All gasses, C, P, S, K, Si, Sc, In, Tb

Table 5

SemiQuantitative Report
Inductively Coupled Plasma – Mass Spectrometry

	ppm	Detection Limit		ppm	Detection Limit
Aluminum *	ND<9	9	* Mercury	ND<1	1
Antimony *	101	9	* Molybdenum	ND<3	3
Arsenic *	1530	30	Neodymium	ND<1	1
Barium *	ND<4	4	* Nickel	470	2
Beryllium *	ND<8	8	Niobium	ND<1	1
Bismuth *	9	1	Osmium	ND<1	1
Boron *	ND<300	300	Palladium	ND<1	1
Bromine	ND<400	400	Platinum	ND<1	1
Cadmium *	ND<1	1	Praseodymium	ND<1	1
Calcium *	ND<400	400	Rhenium	ND<1	1
Cerium	ND<1	1	Rhodium	3	1
Cesium	ND<1	1	Rubidium	ND<1	1
Chromium *	ND<50	50	Ruthenium	ND<1	1
Cobalt *	1100	1	Samarium	ND<1	1
Copper	MATRIX		* Selenium	ND<40	40
Dysprosium	ND<1	1	* Silver	320	1
Erbium	ND<1	1	* Sodium	ND<1000	1000
Europium	ND<1	1	* Strontium	4	1
Gadolinium	ND<1	1	Tantalum	ND<1	1
Gallium	ND<2	2	Tellurium	2	1
Germanium	ND<3	3	* Thallium	ND<1	1
Gold *	18	2	Thorium	ND<1	1
Hafnium	ND<1	1	Thulium	ND<1	1
Holmium	ND<1	1	* Tin	121000	2
Iodine	ND<10	10	* Titanium	ND>5	5
Iridium	ND<1	1	Tungsten	3	1
Iron *	ND<700	700	Uranium	ND<1	1
Lanthanum	ND<1	1	* Vanadium	ND<900	900
Lead *	567	1	Ytterbium	ND<1	1
Lithium	ND<30	30	Yttrium	ND<1	1
Lutetium	ND<7	7	* Zinc	32	20
Magnesium *	33	6	Zirconium	ND<1	1
Manganese *	ND<5	5			

Date Analyzed: 9-9-96,
MATRIX = major element * = quantitative results
Elements not analyzed: All gasses, C.P,S, K, Si, Sc, In, Tb

Table 2 shows the ICP-MS data obtained from a drilling from the lower broken edge of the statue's left leg. The analytical method chosen, that of inductively coupled plasma-mass spectrometry, provides quantitative and semi-quantitative data over a range of some 65 elements at quite low detection limits, based on a sample size of about 20 mg of clean drillings. Elements marked with an asterisk in the Table have been determined in completely quantitative mode during the analysis, while the remaining elements are determined semi-quantitatively. Twenty-three elements were detected as being present. Notable features include the determination of 9.9% tin content; the very low bismuth content of 2.3 ppm's; the relatively large amount of cobalt at 1290 ppm's, and small but significant trace amounts of lead, zinc, nickel, silver, selenium, and tellurium.

Table 3 supplies an analysis from one of the separately cast components — clean drillings from the tip of an olive leaf broken from the wreath. Although the range of elements detected in this analysis was somewhat less than that shown in Table 2, similar analytical trends can be seen, such as the very low bismuth content, correspondingly high cobalt content, and similar elemental impurities such as lead, nickel, silver, and zinc. It is possible that the olive leaf, and therefore the head, were cast from a slightly different batch of metal, since the tin content is in the region of 12.8% for this analysis. There are, of course, fairly common variations in composition from different regions of the same bronze object, regardless of whether they have been separately cast or not. Given these variations, it cannot be certain that the tin content of 12.8% represents a casting made in a different bronze. Certainly the similarities in the impurities suggest that a very similar or identical batch of copper was used as the stock metal for manufacture of these parts.

To clarify this problem, clean metallic drillings were selected for two more ICP-MS studies: one from a large square patch on the proper right elbow, and another from the body itself adjacent to this large patch on the elbow. As can be seen from Tables 4 and 5, the tin content in the patch was found to be 11.5% and in the body 12.1%. The trace elements for both samples is, once again, so similar as to suggest that they must be made from the same batch of metal.

Final confirmation of this was shown in another set of analyses taken from a patch of the left leg above the knee, shown in Table 6, and drillings free of corrosion taken from the leg adjacent to the patch (Table 7). The tin content in both samples was estimated at 10.8%, and the trace element variation is again identical, confirming that probably all of the patches used to finish the statue were made from exactly the same metal stock as was employed for the casting of the various parts.

Core

As many authors who have written on the technical aspects of ancient bronzes have noted, the interior of a bronze is a rich source of information. The interior surface can provide information on casting technique, joining technique, and even later repair. A wealth of information can also be found in the retained core material. Properly examined, the core may provide information about the location of the workshop, the date of the casting, and the casting temperature, as well as indications of welded-on or cold-worked additions and repairs. Detailed technical studies of core material have only recently been undertaken, however, and the presence of core in either Greek or Roman bronzes is, at best, rare. Fortunately, the Getty statue was recovered with the majority of its core in place. Unfortunately, the material was removed, presumably to protect the figure from active salts introduced during the sea burial. Removal of the core destroyed much of the evidence of layering and compositional changes that may have provided evidence about joining techniques. For example, it is reported that the core material around certain joins in the Riace bronzes differed from the main body of the core. Early reports regarding the Getty Youth also indicate a difference in core texture, color, and composition around the neck and upper arms. This relates directly to the areas where metallurgical joins were made between the torso and the head, as well as between the torso and the arms. It is likely that the

Table 6

Sample: Bronze athlete: sample 8
Left leg patch above knee. Clean drillings

SemiQuantitative Report
Inductively Coupled Plasma – Mass Spectrometry

	ppm	Detection Limit		ppm	Detection Limit
Aluminum *	ND<70	70	* Mercury	ND<1	1
Antimony *	132	1	* Molybdenum	1	1
Arsenic *	1600	30	Neodymium	ND<1	1
Barium *	3	1	* Nickel	584	4
Beryllium *	ND<4	4	Niobium	ND<1	1
Bismuth *	8	1	Osmium	ND<1	1
Boron	ND<100	100	Palladium	ND<1	1
Bromine	ND<600	600	Platinum	ND<1	1
Cadmium *	ND<1	1	Praseodymium	ND<1	1
Calcium *	ND<200	200	Rhenium	ND<1	1
Cerium	ND<1	1	Rhodium	2	1
Cesium	ND<1	1	Rubidium	ND<1	1
Chromium *	ND<50	50	Ruthenium	ND<1	1
Cobalt *	1560	1	Samarium	ND<1	1
Copper	MATRIX		* Selenium	43	40
Dysprosium	ND<1	1	* Silver	295	1
Erbium	ND<1	1	* Sodium	ND<3000	3000
Europium	ND<1	1	* Strontium	2	1
Gadolinium	ND<1	1	Tantalum	ND<1	1
Gallium	ND<2	2	Tellurium	2	1
Germanium	ND<1	1	* Thallium	ND<1	1
Gold *	55	1	Thorium	ND<1	1
Hafnium	ND<1	1	Thulium	ND<1	1
Holmium	ND<1	1	* Tin	108000	1
Iodine	ND<5	5	* Titanium	ND>6	6
Iridium	ND<1	1	Tungsten	2	1
Iron *	490	400	Uranium	ND<1	1
Lanthanum	ND<1	1	* Vanadium	ND<300	300
Lead *	579	1	Ytterbium	ND<1	1
Lithium *	ND<100	100	Yttrium	ND<1	1
Lutetium	ND<6	6	* Zinc	57	2
Magnesium *	112	4	Zirconium	ND<1	1
Manganese *	6	2			

Date Analyzed: 9-13-96, and 9-18-96

MATRIX = major element * = quantitative results
Elements not analyzed: All Gasses, C,P,S, K, Si, Sc, In, Tb

Table 7

Sample: Bronze athlete: sample 11
Clean drillings from body adjacent to patch

SemiQuantitative Report
Inductively Coupled Plasma – Mass Spectrometry

	ppm	Detection Limit		ppm	Detection Limit
Aluminum *	ND<60	60	* Mercury	ND<1	1
Antimony *	121	1	* Molybdenum	ND<1	1
Arsenic *	1500	30	Neodymium	ND<1	1
Barium *	4.6	1	* Nickel	533	3
Beryllium *	ND<4	4	Niobium	ND<1	1
Bismuth *	8.6	1	Osmium	ND<1	1
Boron *	ND<100	100	Palladium	ND<1	1
Bromine	ND<600	600	Platinum	ND<1	1
Cadmium *	1.1	1	Praseodymium	ND<1	1
Calcium *	ND<200	200	Rhenium	ND<1	1
Cerium	ND<1	1	Rhodium	3.1	1
Cesium	ND<1	1	Rubidium	ND<1	1
Chromium *	ND<50	50	Ruthenium	ND<1	1
Cobalt *	1450	1	Samarium	ND<1	1
Copper	MATRIX		* Selenium	ND<30	30
Dysprosium	ND<1	1	* Silver	287	1
Erbium	ND<1	1	* Sodium	ND<2000	2000
Europium	ND<1	1	* Strontium	ND<1	1
Gadolinium	ND<1	1	Tantalum	ND<1	1
Gallium	ND<2	2	Tellurium	1.9	1
Germanium	1.6	1	* Thallium	ND<1	1
Gold *	50.2	1	Thorium	ND<1	1
Hafnium	ND<1	1	Thulium	ND<1	1
Holmium	ND<1	1	* Tin	108000	1
Iodine	ND<5	5	* Titanium	ND>6	6
Iridium	ND<1	1	Tungsten	ND<1	1
Iron *	560	400	Uranium	ND<1	1
Lanthanum	ND<1	1	* Vanadium	ND<400	400
Lead *	636	1	Ytterbium	ND<1	1
Lithium *	ND<100	100	Yttrium	ND<1	1
Lutetium	ND<5	5	* Zinc	56	2
Magnesium *	70	4	Zirconium	ND<1	1
Manganese *	ND<2	2			

Date Analyzed: 9-13-96, and 9-18-96

MATRIX = major element * = quantitative results
Elements not analyzed: All Gasses, C,P,S, K, Si, Sc, In, Tb

original casting core of these segments was carved away and an alternative core was introduced in order to undertake the joining. Unfortunately, the exact location of this change in core composition remains unknown, as does the possibility of fully characterizing this difference. It is nonetheless to the credit of the restorer that at least one third of the core material was saved and transferred to a variety of boxes, each marked with the general locations from which the core had been removed.[17]

In general the core material ranges in color from gray to buff.[18] Based upon a variety of analytical approaches, which included microscopy, x-ray diffraction, and x-ray fluorescence, the bulk of the core can be defined as a marl (calcareous paste of sea-bed origin).[19] There are large amounts of calcium carbonate, quartz, and feldspars throughout the core. The composition of the core is quite similar to the cores of several other Greek cores investigated.[20]

Although we have not found the degree of layering reported in the earlier studies, we have distinguished at least three layers in the larger segments of the core material, which have remained intact. This includes an almost total core cross section taken in 1971 from the broken joint of the left arm (fig. 11).

17 The authors wish to thank I. Calinescu for her invaluable assistance in sorting and properly packing the core material during her internship (1995) in the Department of Antiquities Conservation.

18 This contradicts the earlier report by Herzer and Kinnius in 1972 (supra n.5), which stated that the core consisted of loamy mixture with sand. In the chest and belly areas, the core was almost exclusively of yellowish loamy sand, comparatively loose in texture and surrounded by a denser yellow sand.

19 Identified by J. Twilley, Conservation Scientist for the Los Angeles County Museum of Art.

20 K. C. Lefferts, L. J. Majewski, E. V. Sayre, and P. Meyers, "Technical examination of the Classical bronze horse from the Met," *JAIC* 21 (1981) 18. A. Melluco-Vaccaro (pers. comm., 1996) indicates that the Riace bronzes also have a change in core composition near the metallurgical joins.

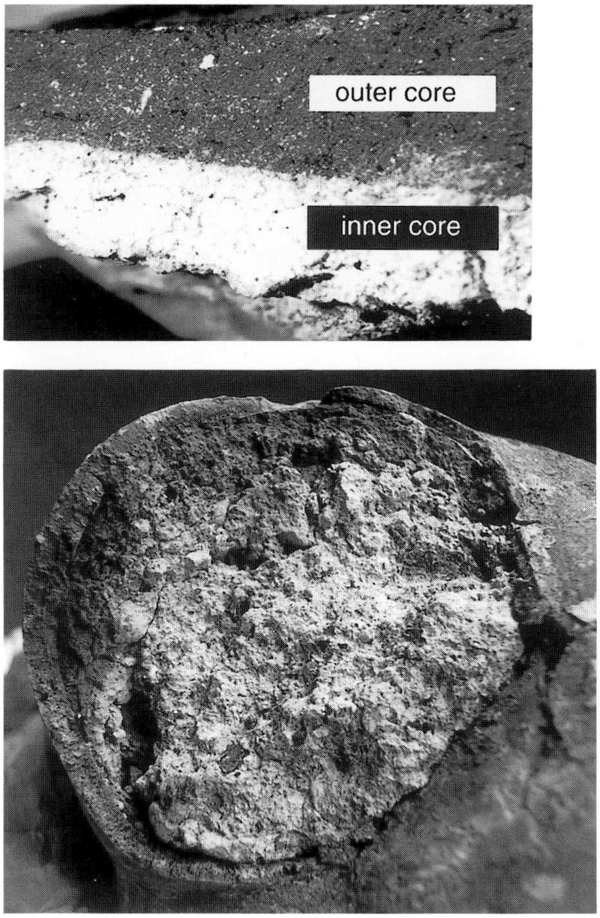

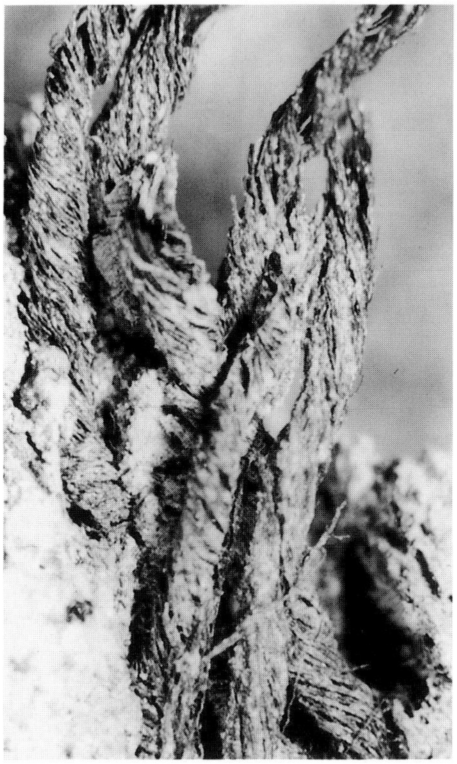

Fig. 11 (left). Cross section of the core before removal from the torso area. Note the double layering in the upper image. The dark and more dense layer would have been in direct contact with the molten bronze (or the inner surface of the wax model initially), and the lower, lighter colored bulk layer filled the remaining cavity of the bronze. (Photo: Department of Antiquities Conservation, The J. Paul Getty Museum.)
Fig. 12 (right). Some of the fiber embedded in the core material. (Photo: Department of Antiquities Conservation, The J. Paul Getty Museum.)

The layers of the core mostly differ in the percentages of the material used: sand, carbonaceous material, and small amounts of clay. The fine, compact, and gray-to-black layer nearest the bronze surface is a discrete and intentional layer measuring between 1.5 and 5 mm in thickness. It is distinguished from the interior layer by the high percentage of charcoal present (presumably added to increase porosity and contribute to a reducing atmosphere in order to assure that the casting process would proceed smoothly and with little oxidation). The presence of titanium was detected only in this layer, suggesting the possible addition of clay.[21] The next layer contains a rather dramatic increase in organic débris, some only slightly charred or not charred at all. This débris includes a wide range of material such as olive pits, stems, grape seeds, nut shells, remnants of leaves, twigs, charcoal, charred reeds, grass fibers, and, most interestingly, a large amount of bast fibers[22] that appear to have been cut from woven cloth (fig. 12). Publication of the latter component, the full characterization of which will add significantly to our understanding of bronze-casting technology in ancient times, is being prepared

---

21 The authors are grateful to J. Twilley for this analysis and observation.

22 Identified by W. McCrone of McCrone Research Institute, Chicago, in January 1996, and by K. Jakes, Dept. of Textiles and Clothing, Ohio State University, in March 1996.

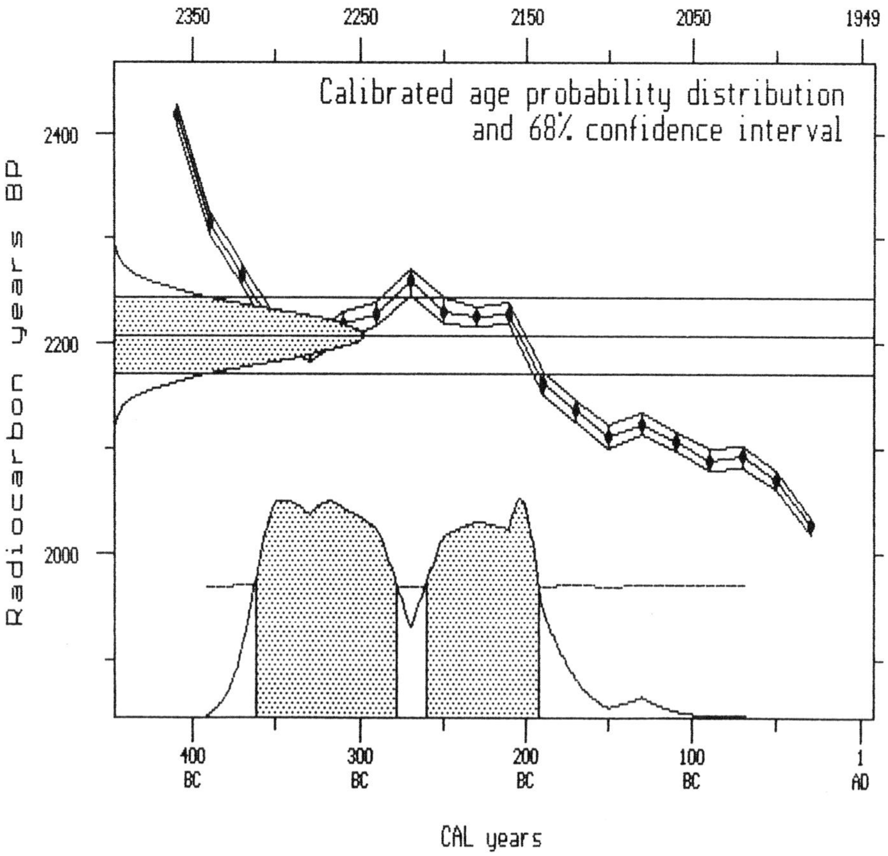

Fig. 13. Radiocarbon results showing the placement of the arrived-at radiocarbon date and the relationship to the calibration curve. (Chart provided by Rafter Radiocarbon Laboratory, Institute of Geological and Nuclear Sciences Limited, New Zealand.)

by M. Svoboda.[23] This layer also has a higher calcium carbonate constituent, much of it as foraminifera (micro fossils). Retention of the crystalline alignment of the foraminifera suggests that they were not part of a burned lime addition but perhaps part of the marl.

Dating

The full technical examination of any bronze, and perhaps especially this bronze, would not be complete if it did not apply the findings to the problem of dating. In the case of the Getty bronze, a date of the late 4th c. B.C. had been arrived at through two means: Frel's purely stylistic approach[24] and the thermoluminescence and carbon-14 dating of samples taken from the core. The latter analysis must, however, be brought into question since the two techniques resulted in quite different dates. Core material removed prior to the initial radiography of the bronze was TL-dated to 135 B.C. Carbon 14 gave an age of 670 B.C. These were added together and divided by two to get 400 B.C.[25] As a result, the date attributed to the bronze, when stylistic opinion was added to the consideration, was the late 4th c. B.C.

Given the rather unorthodox method of arriving at a date for the casting, one of the priorities of this re-examination was to provide a more dependable direct dating analysis. To

---

23 M. Svoboda, "A preliminary investigation of the casting core material from a bronze in the J. Paul Getty Museum collection: identification of fiber inclusions" (forthcoming).

24 Frel, *Bronze* (supra n.3)

25 Herzer 1972 (supra n.5).

this end new C^{-14} analysis was carried out.[26] The samples used were an olive pit supposedly from the upper left arm (providing 282 mg of sample) and an olive pit said to be from the neck or chest area (providing 379 mg sample), as well as organic débris from sifted core material (344 mg sample) and a charred reed segment from the upper left arm (102 mg sample). The average radiocarbon age from these samples is 2207 B.P. +/- 37 B.P. When this radiocarbon age is calibrated, it coincides with an irregular area of the calibration curve so that the shape of the curve dominates the final error (fig. 13). At the 68% confidence limits, the calibrated dates for the averaged samples are 362 B.C. to 278 B.C. *and* 260 B.C. to 192 B.C. Both ranges are equally likely on the basis of the measurement. The corresponding range at the 95% confidence level is 377 B.C. to 167 B.C. As a result, the casting dates from between the mid 4th c. B.C. and the early 2nd c. B.C., a relatively broad range.

Conclusion

In the relatively short time that this study has been underway a number of previously held assumptions about the Getty Victorious Youth have been either brought into sharp question or confirmed. The bronze has been shown to be an indirect cast, correcting the early reports that the casting was done by the direct method. Significant new information has been provided concerning the method of adding wax sheets to the mold. The composition of many different components of the bronze has been established and detailed. Studies of the core material have revealed important information about the characteristics and dating of materials used in the statue's construction, which in turn bears upon stylistic dates that have been proposed.

New questions have been raised about certain technical features. What drives this study is the desire to gather as much information as possible before stating any conclusions, taking into account the many interpretations of what is known about the sculpture, irrespective of their source or feasibility. Each of these interpretations is being tested against what can be observed, what is practical, and what improved analytical techniques can offer. It is hoped that at its completion the project will have provided a firm understanding of one of the great classical bronzes to have survived and new insights into the world of the ancient foundry.

Antiquities Conservation, J. Paul Getty Museum, Los Angeles, CA 90049

---

26 Rafter Radiocarbon Laboratory, Institute of Geological and Nuclear Sciences Limited, New Zealand, 1995.

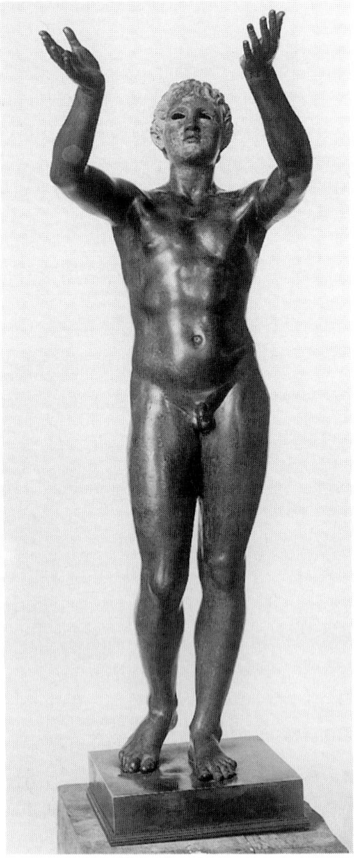

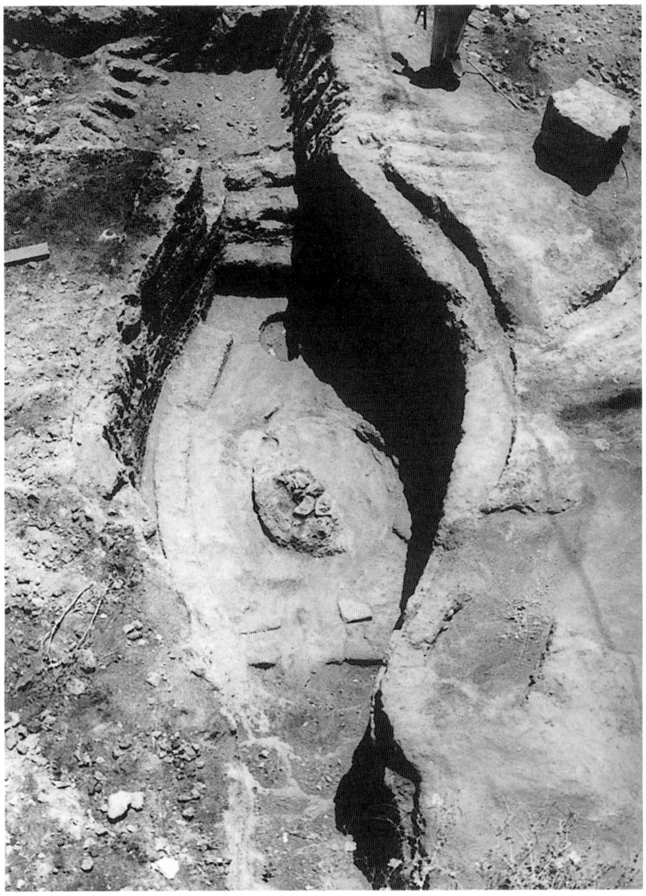

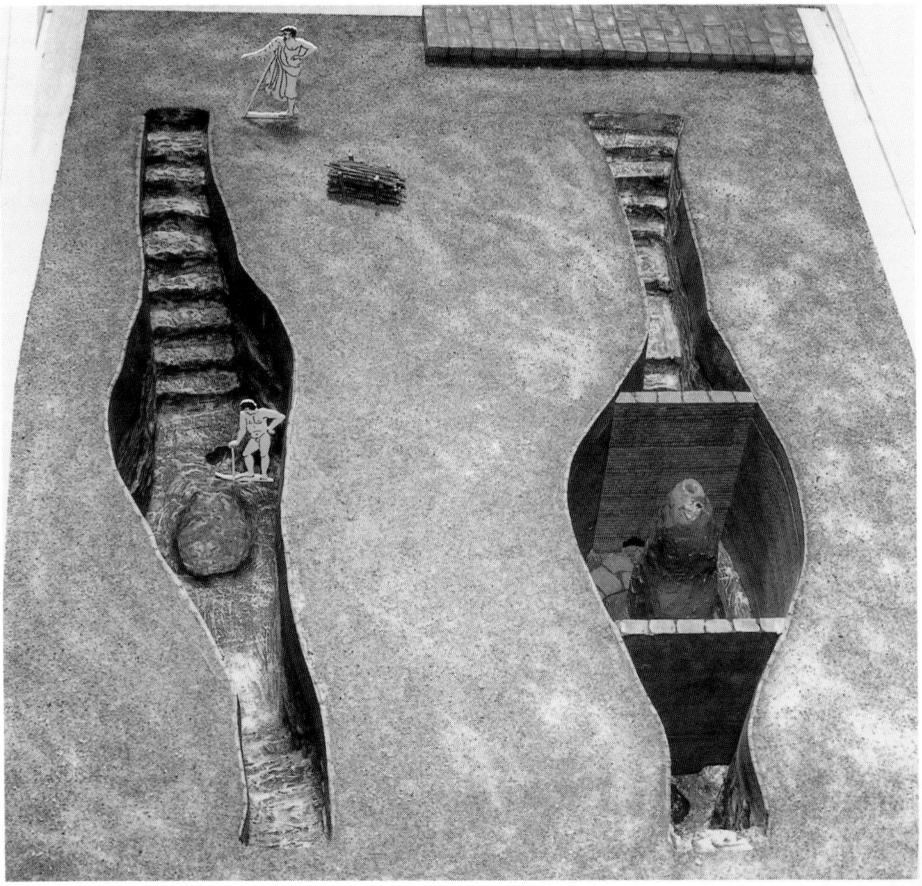

Fig. 1 (top left). The Praying Boy. Bronze, h 1.28 m. Berlin, Staatliche Museen zu Berlin, Preußischer Kulturbesitz, Antikensammlung Sk 2. (Photo: Antikensammlung.)

Fig. 2 (top right). The Mylonas property foundry during the excavations in 1974. (Photo: Ephoria Rhodos.)

Fig. 3 (right). Reconstruction of the Mylonas foundry. (Photo: J. Laurentius.)

The Praying Boy and the Rhodian bronzecasting industry

Gerhard Zimmer

From the time the bronze statue called the Praying Boy came into the possession of Frederick the Great in 1747, after a long journey through several European collections, and found its ideal place of exhibition on the terrace of Sanssouci in the square encircled by a rose trellis, it has played an outstanding rôle in Berlin's collection of antiquities. But, as is frequently the case with famous works of art, so far a thorough examination has been missing (fig. 1).[1] A series of coincidences recently caused the Praying Boy to become the center of a scientific project that may provide the key to reconstruct the technology used in Greek bronzecasting foundries.

The starting point was the newly found bronzecasting foundries in Rhodes, above all the large foundry on the Mylonas property at Odos Diagoridon on the east slope of Monte Smith.[2] The center of this work area is a gigantic casting pit that came to light in 1975 during the construction of a new building (fig. 2). Originally the pit was about 3.6 m deep. In it the mold for a monumental casting was formed and baked. Features in the walls of the pit showed that for this work cross-walls were erected to facilitate the heating of the pit and to provide even heat. The floor and the side walls of the pit were lined with mud bricks. Basically, the pit functioned like an oven. Discoloration during firing and similarities in contemporaneous casting pits point to openings in the side walls to permit the regulation of the temperature. This pit and another slightly smaller pit of the same date formed the core of a large bronze foundry. A model in the scale of 1:20 demonstrates the huge size of the dimensions (fig. 3).

Accompanying finds dated the installation in the first quarter of the 3rd c. B.C. Most interesting was the foot of a small vessel that had the name Eubulos scratched in the bottom, a nice parallel to the Pheidias mug in Olympia.[3]

The pit on the Mylonas property allows us to understand the functioning of such an installation very precisely. We are also aided by the results of other salvage excavations in Rhodes during recent years. An installation from about the same time on the Tzedakis property not only pointed to the use of crucibles and bellows nozzles but also provided a number of fragments of the mold casing from which we could take samples (fig. 4).[4] Analysis of these clay fragments furnished information about the composition of the material, its heat conductivity, and its plasticity, i.e., about its potential usability. Thus we are now well informed about the workshop situation in Rhodes at the beginning of the 3rd c. B.C.

The statue of the Praying Boy belongs to the same Early Hellenistic period. From our examination of the statue, we now know that a classicizing Early Imperial interpretation of the statue can no longer be considered.

That the statue was found in Rhodes is clear. That it was also made there could be shown after comparing mold material from the Rhodian foundries with samples from the statue's core.

---

1 Das Projekt zur Erforschung antiker Gießtechnik am Beispiel des Betenden Knaben ist Gegenstand einer ausführlichen Dokumentation: G. Zimmer and N. Hackländer (edd.), *Der Betende Knabe — Original und Experiment* (Frankfurt 1997). Here I shall use a lecture format, and keep notes and illustrations to a minimum. For previous research, see R. Kabus-Preißhofen, "Der 'betende Knabe' in Berlin. Schicksal einer antiken Großbronze und das Problem ihrer Deutung," *AA* (1988) 679-99. For additional reports on this project, see Ratka und Sahm below p. 197 and Hackländer p. 201.

2 Preliminary report: C. Kantzia and G. Zimmer, "Rhodische Kolosse: eine hellenistische Bronzeguß-werkstatt," *AA* 1989, 497-523.

3 A. Mallwitz and W. Schiering, *Die Werkstatt des Pheidias in Olympia* (*OF* 5, 1964) 169, no. 1 and pl. 64; W.-D. Heilmeyer, *AA* 1981, 447 f.

4 J. Nicolaidou, *Arch. Delt.* 42 (1987) *Chron.* 587 ff.

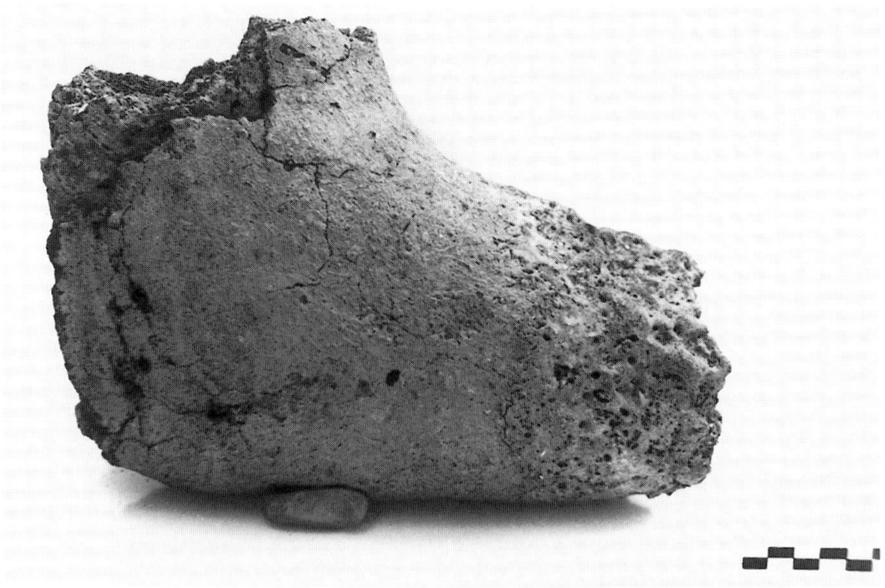

Fig. 4. Bellows nozzle from the Tzedakis property foundry. (Photo: author.)

Thus we have a complex of information on an ancient workshop situation that is unparalleled and that almost completely corresponds, as it were, to the demands of ancient tragedy for unity of place and time.

Earlier descriptions and reproductions show that the boy was originally found without arms. They were most likely added in the 17th c. in France. Also restored are toes and the front part of the right foot. The restored parts could be identified by an eddy current reading. They consisted of a brass alloy containing 10.5-23% zinc. The original parts, however, are of homogenous tin-bronze whose tin content varies between 9.3 and 13.8% and which contains hardly any lead.

Pictures taken with an intense light source and computerized axial tomography furnished information about the great and variable wall thickness. This technique sets the boy apart from classicizing Early Imperial sculptures. The extent of the modern lead casting also became obvious during our examination.

Further information was obtained from endoscopic pictures. By inserting the smallest tube through the eye opening and passing the modern support plates in the neck and chest area, it was possible to reach the inside and obtain information about the construction and also about restorations performed in previous centuries.

A focal point of the work was the exact microscopic examination and mapping of the exterior surface. The casting of the bronze did not come out very well (fig. 5). Numerous little air bubbles or shrink holes weaken the metal in various concentrations. Parts of the surface were repaired with small plates in antiquity. The rest remained beneath the surface and became visible only after a mechanical cleaning during which the patina was blasted off. The date of this cleaning cannot be determined. The surface also showed sections of greater density where in all probability the gates had been attached.

The thorough scientific examination of the Praying Boy in 1995 furnished clues to the endangerment of the statue caused by the restoration performed a hundred years ago. In particular the enormous amount of lead with which the arms were fastened caused the upper part of the body and the shoulder parts to suffer extreme tension, which might have had a negative effect whenever the boy was moved. Above all, a crack in the right shoulder threatened to open wider (fig. 6). The restorers reached the conclusion that any movement of the statue should be avoided and that the crack should be observed closely, because no new restoration and mounting of the statue could be contemplated because of the museum's financial limitations.

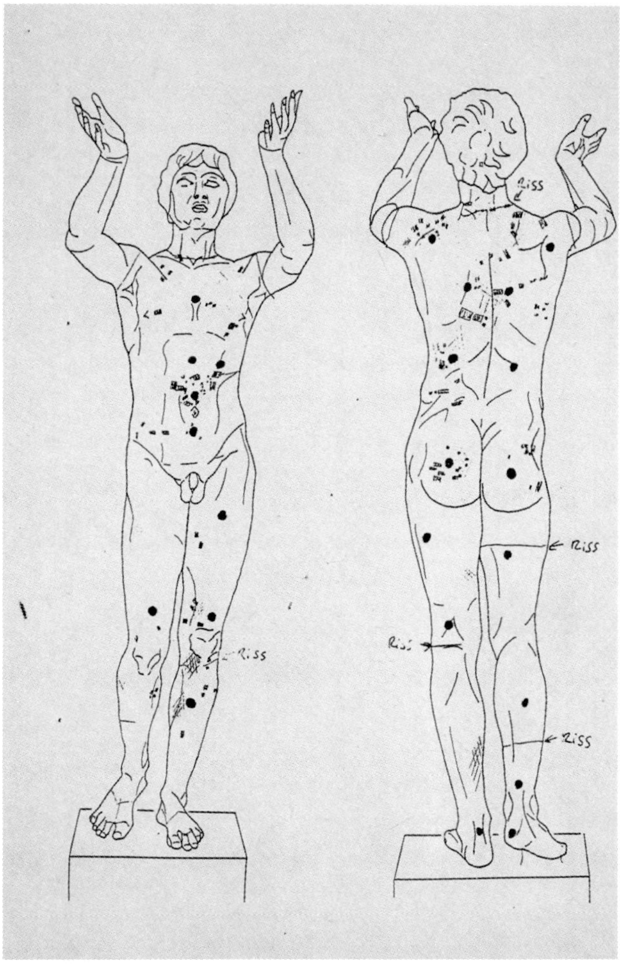

Fig. 5. The Praying Boy: map of the surface. (Drawings: author.)

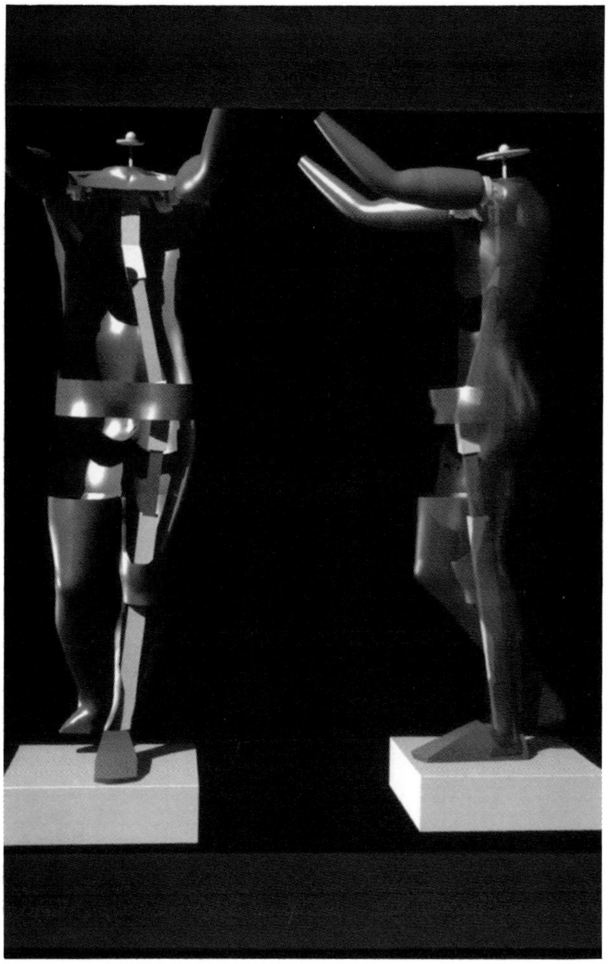

Fig. 7. The Praying Boy: construction of the new mounting. (Photo: U. Schramm.)

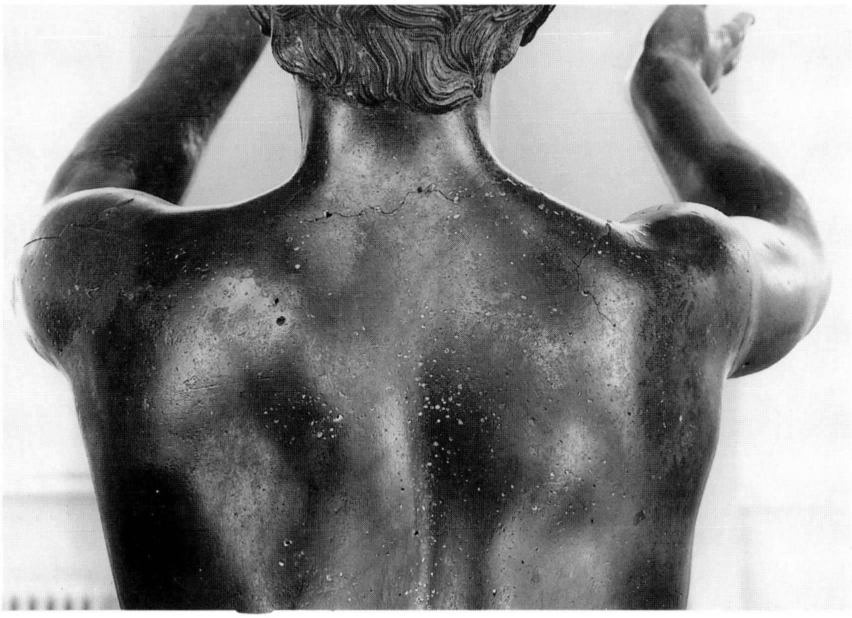

Fig. 6. The Praying Boy: crack in the right shoulder. (Photo: J. Laurentius.)

However, luck would have it that the request to send the Praying Boy on loan to the important exhibition in Atlanta on the occasion of the 1996 Olympic Games produced private donations which allowed us to begin with the restoration. Removal of the arms turned out to be difficult and laborious. U. Rohnstock, restorer with the Collection of Antiquities, had to remove the lead mechanically with a drill and chisel. Removal of the squared rod in the weight-bearing leg caused a particular problem. Here the corroded iron had bonded so solidly with the lead that it had to be cut away piece by piece. To extricate the rod by means of heating the lead proved to be impractical.

Our hopes of finding parts of the original casting core in the free leg were not fulfilled. Only greater amounts of plaster and the fireclay-like core of the repair work performed in modern times were found.

The new mounting for the statue has now been completed, based on a complicated calculation of the weight-bearing ability (fig. 7). It was mandatory that the arms be carried by the steel support without putting pressure on the ancient bronze. Thus, moving the Praying Boy became possible once again.

The data gained from the technical examination and the restoration allowed us to perform a reconstruction of the casting process modeled after the excavated Rhodian foundry pits. Previous attempts to reconstruct the ancient casting process based on the evidence of workshop remains and miscasts as well as on finished works always encountered obstacles that could not be overcome without a costly series of experiments.

Accurate knowledge of the conditions of the Early Hellenistic Rhodian casting process allowed us to plan an experiment with the aim of finding an answer to a specific question regarding the firing technique of such pits and ventilation of the mold. The way was paved to imitate the actual casting with the help of a computer simulation (see Ratka and Sahm, below p. 197 ff. In this way the following questions could be answered: At what temperature could the mold be filled? What were the characteristics of the solidification of the metal? What size was required for the gates and vents? The project, financed by the Volkswagen Foundation, enabled us to reconstruct a Hellenistic foundry in Rhodes complete in every detail (see Hackländer, below p. 201 ff.).

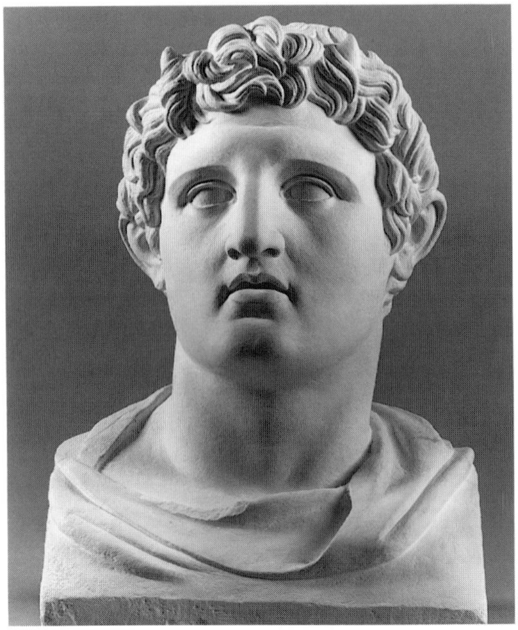

Fig. 8. Bust of Demetrios Poliorketes (cast), Naples. (Photo: J. Laurentius.)

The closest stylistic parallel to the Praying Boy is the head of Demetrios Poliorketes, dated to around 300 B.C. The artist of that portrait was Teisikrates, a grandson of Lysippos. I think the same artist could have created the Praying Boy (fig. 8).

In contrast to the date and the casting process, we were not able to come to a definite conclusion concerning the interpretation of the boy. So far, all interpretations have been governed by the spirit of the age. The earliest interpretation as Ganymede, longingly stretching out his arms to Zeus, corresponded to the baroque way of thinking in the 17th c. Interpretation of the Boy as a worshipper arose from the prevailing taste of the 19th c. Perhaps now in the sports-minded 20th c. the interpretation of the statue as a young athlete in the process of putting the winner's fillet around his head will again be met with approval. This would certainly be a fine contribution to the 100th Olympiad of modern times.

Katholische Universität, D-85072 Eichstätt

Numerical simulation of historical bronzecasting

Markus Ratka and P. R. Sahm

Introduction

Interdisciplinary co-operation between trained foundryworkers and archaeologists offers new methods of answering questions about ancient casting processes. In particular, the use of numerical simulation of filling and solidification processes, a new tool for production design in foundries, accompanied by experimental castings, provides many new insights. Numerical simulation is a quick and inexpensive method to try out all the parameters probably used by ancient foundrymen. It clearly minimizes the number of expensive test castings, limiting them to those necessary to verify the results of the simulations and the cases in which it is impossible to simulate, such as the production of molds.

Interdisciplinary co-operation and the use of numerical simulation have already yielded new knowledge about the casting of Etruscan bronze hand-mirrors and various bronze axes and swords.[1] The Gießerei-Institut, RWTH-Aachen, in tandem with the Berlin Antikensammlung, has been working on an archaeometallurgy project about casting methods and workshop organization for casting large bronze statues. The object investigated was the so-called Praying Boy (see Zimmer, above p. 192 ff.; fig. 1). Certain casting parameters, such as casting and mold temperatures and the construction of the gating system that could have been used by the ancient foundrymen, were the focus.

Numerical simulation: state of the art

Today numerical simulation is the state of the art in progressive foundries.[2] Modern programs are designed to simulate many phenomena in castings and related manufacturing processes;[3] they include

- fluid dynamics
- heat flow
- microstructure
- segregation
- shrinkage and porosity
- stress/strain and structure deformation

In addition, numerical simulation has no limitations concerning the type of material or casting process used.[4] The range of possible applications runs from scrap material reduction for

---

1 C. Eibner and D. Wald, "Computersimulation von gegossenen Bronzeschwerten" and "Der Zweikampf zwischen Paris und Menelaos bei Homer," *Giesserei* 77 (Bericht Nr. 10, Düsseldorf 1990); K. Moeinipour *et al.*, "Bestimmung historischer Gießtechnik mittels numerischer Simulation am Beispiel etruskischer Handspiegel," *Berliner Beiträge zur Archäometrie* 13 (1995); M. Ratka *et al.*, "Numerical simulation of historical casting processes for bronze," *International Symposium on the beginning of metallurgy, 26th-28th April 1995* (Deutsches Bergbaumuseum Bochum) passim; P. R. Sahm *et al.*, "Numerical simulation of casting and solidification of ancient bronze axes and mirrors," *Proceedings of the third int. conference on the beginning of the use of metals and alloy, BUMA-3*, Sanmenxia, China (1994); D. Wald und P. R. Sahm, "Die numerische Simulation des Gießens und Erstarrens als neuartiges Werkzeug zur Erforschung der historischen Gießereitechnik," *Giesserei* 79 (Düsseldorf 1992). See also Zimmer, above p. 192 ff. and Hackländer, above p. 201 ff.

2 P. R. Sahm, "Formfüll- und Erstarrungssimulation — Eine Übersicht," *Guss-Produkte* (1994) 237-51.

3 P. R. Sahm and P. Hansen, "Numerical simulation and modeling of casting and solidification processes for foundry and cast-house," *Comité int. des associations techniques des fonderies* (Zürich 1984).

4 MAGMA GmbH, *"Calculation Pays" — MAGMASOFT simulation tool for quality improvement and cost saving in foundries* (MAGMA Gießereitechnologie GmbH, Aachen 1995).

gray iron series castings, and planning of feeding and gating systems for huge steel castings, to die and process layout for non-ferrous parts. Such 'cold casting' at the computer shows all the effects the foundryman can achieve through various processing conditions and different casting designs. In this manner, simulation helps in a quick and inexpensive way before beginning production. The benefits of numerical simulation can include:

- minimization of feeding and gating systems
- optimal planning of process conditions
- casting accommodated construction
- increased die life of permanent molds
- reduction of lead times

In short, numerical simulation is a comprehensive and powerful tool to help the founder improve his casting quality and save substantial costs in the foundry.

Numerical simulation can also be a useful tool for extrapolating backward to provide a better understanding of historical casting practices. The variation of casting and/or mold materials and temperatures, funnel and gating systems, and geometry helps one assess the techniques used by ancient foundrymen.

Before starting numerical simulation, it is essential to have accurate thermophysical data as a function of temperature and exact initial and boundary conditions. These are necessary to describe the thermophysical properties of all materials involved and the heat flow between them. After providing these data, casting and solidification are calculated in three steps:

I. Pre-processing: generation of the grid
II. Main processing: calculation of filling and solidification
III. Post-processing: visualization and evaluation of the results of the Main processing

Simulation of the Praying Boy

In order to render a precise simulation, the first step is to examine carefully the bronze. Evaluation of this kind offers preliminary insights into the casting process used. Examination of the Praying Boy provided information that corresponded with previous archaeological findings on large bronze statues: the arms, the head, and the front sections of the feet had been cast separately and attached to the body later.[5] In addition, the entire body had obvious, approximately round, symmetrically located patches that had a coarser grain structure than the rest of the surface. These hinted at what kind of gating system had been used. The casting material was denser at the points where the gating system was connected to the thin-walled casting and, due to greater heat accumulation, patches of grain enlargement developed.

After collection of all possible information from the bronze and after obtaining the necessary thermophysical data, a first attempt at numerical simulation was made. The section of the Praying Boy that was probably the largest to be cast in one piece (the torso and the two legs) was selected for simulation. This was also the section that was examined in actual casting experiments (see Hackländer above, p. 201 ff.).

Mesh generation: the surface of the bronze

Because of the complicated surface envelope of the Praying Boy, which consists entirely of ill-defined surface geometry and therefore is extremely difficult to reconstruct, it had to be measured by an automatic mechanical point-measuring machine.

First, measurements were taken from a plaster cast of the Praying Boy, cut into several sections. The torso and legs were measured separately from the rest. These data were fed into the computer (fig. 1a). Using these measured points, it was possible to generate a closed surface with a CAD (Computer Assisted Drafting and Design) program (fig. 1b). It was also possible to

---

5 U. Rohnstock, "Die am 'Betenden Knaben' angewendeten Technologien nach seiner Ausgrabung," *Vortrag im Rahmen des Seminars "I Grandi Bronzi Antichi"* (Siena 1995).

construct a small-scale core geometry. This was inserted into the surface geometry so that a core-volume could be cut out to obtain the required hollowness of the statue. The remaining wall thickness of about 6 mm corresponds approximately to that of the original bronze (all figures, in colour, are placed following p. 96).

Construction of the gating system was also carried out by CAD. This very probably corresponds to the gating system used in the original, as was deduced from observations made of the statue during restoration.

The CAD data were transferred to the gating simulation program by means of an STL (stereolithography) interface (fig. 1c). This allowed for easy transfer of the data produced by CAD into the preprocessing module of the simulation program. Then a mold was constructed by the preprocessor. Experiments have shown that the thickness of the casting is of little significance if the mold is preheated to a sufficiently high temperature, the mold material being a poor heat conductor. As a result, it was not necessary to construct a mold especially adapted to the shape of the casting.

The subsequent graphing of the geometry was carried out automatically after the enmeshment parameters had been entered (fig. 1d). Two contradictory requirements had to be taken into consideration. On the one hand, the number of enmeshment elements had to be less than 7.5 million so as not to exceed the capacity of the hardware. On the other hand, a sufficiently accurate calculation of the mold filling requires subdividing the wall thickness of the casting into at least three element layers. Consequently, the size of the individual simulated elements is limited to a maximum of 2 square mm.

Simulation of the mold filling

A simulation of the filling sequence can be seen in figs. 2-3. The casting time was calculated as 18 seconds at a casting temperature of 1080° C and a mold temperature of 500° C. The illustrations show a distinct difference between the gating systems at the front and at the back of the statue. The gating channel at the front is nearly vertical, with a small bend in the middle. The rear gating channel, on the other hand, has several sharp bends. This difference in geometry has a definite effect on the filling. The vertical gating channel allows the molten bronze to flow directly to the bottom of the gating channel, where it flows into the lower regions of the statue. Gradually, as the level of the filling rises, the higher gates are activated. This shortens the distance the molten bronze must flow through the cavity, and each part of the figure is filled with sufficiently hot metal. However, this only functions when the dimensions of the gating channel and the gates are appropriate to the wall thickness of the cavity. A further advantage of the gating system we have chosen is that no metal flows through already filled areas. This allows the melt to solidify in the lower regions of the casting although filling of the upper regions has not yet been completed. The simulation pictures of the rear of the statue show that melt already flows into the cavity in the region of the buttocks and the waist at a very early stage. That is due to the sharp bends in the gating channel, which hinder the free flow of the melt. The result is that the molten metal jams and the following metal flows into the cavity through higher gates. This presents a certain danger for the casting. The molten metal which enters the cavity too early flows through it too long and so loses its portion of overheating. If the melt front cools too much, it is no longer able to fuse completely with any other melt front it runs into. This produces undesirable divisions in the material, called cold laps.

The effect of the number and position of the gates is also shown by this filling sequence. The front of the torso has only single gates. This forces the metal to flow a long way to the sides of the statue, and there is a danger that the metal will cool too quickly (fig. 4). Cold laps, or even unfilled areas within the casting, may cause flaws in the mold filling. The rear shows the effect of different placing of the gates. The widely separated gates at the waist allow even filling with short flow distances to this area of the casting. The gates in the back and shoulder regions, which are placed close together, cause the same problems as a single gate, but to a smaller degree.

The simulation shows that the geometry of the gating channel and the number and placement of the gates have a strong effect on the filling process. Strong bends in the gating channel must be avoided if a smooth uphill casting is to be attained (fig. 5). The number and the placement of the gates must be appropriate to the flow distances in the cavity. Further gates, especially on the sides of the torso, would be of advantage. It must be considered, however, that the volume of the gating system had to be kept to a minimum because the melting and casting of bronze in antiquity was very laborious.

Simulation of the solidification

Temperature distribution in the statue during solidification is shown by the solidification sequence illustrated in fig. 6. The homogeneity of the temperature distribution in each of the illustrated steps is particularly noticeable. This is due to the combination of two factors: a mold material that has good insulation properties, and the release of the main part of the latent heat when solidification begins. The conversion of a tin bronze from its liquid to its solid phase releases heat in addition to that which escapes due to the cooling process. A solid aligned crystal structure is more efficient than an unaligned liquid structure. Thermophysical data show that the main part of the latent heat is released at the beginning of the solidification interval. Because the metal is an efficient heat conductor and little heat passes into the mold, which is a good insulator, the temperature distribution is very even.

The solidification velocity is strongly influenced by the heating of the mold. While the first 50% of the melt requires 2:39 minutes to solidify, the second 50% needs 11:31 minutes. This results in a total time for solidification of 14:10 minutes.

The degree and location of the heating in the mold material is shown in fig. 7. It becomes obvious here that a thin, hot outer layer forms around the casting material. It is the low conductivity of mold material that is especially responsible for this effect. The high heat in the metal/mold boundary areas reduces the temperature difference between these two components. As a result, the heat energy flows only slowly from the casting material into the mold.

The effect of the gating system on the temperature balance of the mold can also be seen in fig. 7. The closer the gate is to the cavity, the higher the local heating in the area near the cavity. As a result, cooling is slower in this area. Shrinkage and porosity may occur in the casting due to feeding processes and grain enlargement due to prolonged growing time for the crystal grains. This applies to the gating points of the casting and to the areas in which the gating channel is very near the casting. An evaluation according to a solidification criterion confirms this conclusion (fig. 8).

Giesserei-Institut Aachen

Casting a new Praying Boy

Nele Hackländer

In the last 40 years, new discoveries of ancient bronze statues, excavations of casting pits, and new research methods have helped us understand the casting processes of ancient statues. The lost-wax method now seems well known, but many questions concerning the practical aspects of the casting process in antiquity are still not resolved. In 1995, the Foundry Institute of the University of Aachen, the Antikensammlung in Berlin, and E. Formigli worked together on the Praying Boy project,[1] a foundry experiment that aimed at obtaining new insights into the methods and procedures of the lost-wax casting process in antiquity. The bronze statue of the so-called Praying Boy at the Pergamon Museum in Berlin[2] seemed to meet the requirements for the experiment. The bronze, dated on stylistic grounds to Early Hellenistic times, and attributed, according to new analysis of the core material produced at its place of discovery, to the city of Rhodes, is one of the few large-scale bronzes that provide evidence for this important Hellenistic bronze casting center;[3] further evidence is provided by literary sources[4] and by the important finds of several Hellenistic casting pits.[5]

The casting experiment, which took place at Murlo in Tuscany, involved the construction of a wax model of the Praying Boy and the casting of a new statue by the lost-wax method in a replica of an ancient casting pit. The casting pit was modeled after the 3rd c. B.C. pit excavated in 1988 at Rhodes by C. Kantzia (see Zimmer, above pp. 192 ff.).[6] The pit was oval in shape and had steps leading down into it on two sides. The bottom and the walls were lined with clay bricks. In the middle of the pit there was a pedestal on which the mold containing the wax model was placed for firing. The kiln could be closed around the form by means of brick walls at the bottom of the steps. During the melting process, the wax flowed out through a channel into a collection hole in the floor of the pit.

In our small-scale replica of this pit (dimensions 2 x 5 x 2.5 m) a wax model of the Praying Boy was constructed (figs. 1-2). The wax model was filled with core material and provided with a gating system and finally with a mantle of clay that became progressively coarser and leaner from inside to outside due to the inclusion of hair and other organic materials. Then the mold was left in the pit to dry for two months (fig. 3).

The actual firing experiment took place in July 1995. First, the wax was melted out at a temperature of about 80° C. Then the pit was heated to 600-700° C for 4 days and 3 nights until the firing was completed (fig. 4). Finally, about 6 kg of molten bronze were poured into the mold to see whether all of the metal would flow through and come out of the wax extraction channel.

---

1 For discussion of other parts of the research project, see Zimmer, above p. 192 and Ratka and Sahm, above p. 197.

2 Berlin, Antikensammlung Sk 2: A. Conze, "Der betende Knabe in den königlichen Museen zu Berlin," *JdI* 1 (1886) 1-39; *Beschreibung der antiken Skulpturen in den Königlichen Museen zu Berlin* (Berlin 1891) no. 2; L. Franzoni, *La Galleria Bevilaqua a Verona e l'Adorante di Berlino* (1964); L. Franzoni, *Per una storia del collezionismo. Verona. La galleria Bevilacqua.* (Milan 1970) 111-41; M. Perry, "A Greek bronze in Renaissance Venice," *BurlMag* 117 (1975) 204-11; G. Heres and M. Kunze, *Staatliche Museen zu Berlin. Antikensammlung* I (Berlin 1984) no. 63, figs. 31, 33; R. Kabus-Preishofen, "Der 'betende Knabe' in Berlin. Schicksal einer antiken Großbronze und das Problem ihrer Deutung," *AA* 1988, 679-99.

3 The life-size statue of a sleeping Eros in the Metropolitan Museum of Art is also said to have come from Rhodes: M. Söldner, *Untersuchungen zu liegenden Eroten in der hellenistischen und römischen Kunst* (Frankfurt am Main 1986) 11 ff., 291, 605 n.17; J. R. Mertens, *Greek bronzes in the Metropolitan Museum of Art* (= MMA Bulleti*n* 43.2, 1985) 55-53; Mattusch, *Classical bronzes* 161 ff.

4 Pliny, *NH* 34.36; 34.41.

5 Zimmer, *Bronzegußwerkstätten* 91-97.

6 C. Kantzia and G. Zimmer, "Rhodische Kolosse," *AA* 1989, 497-523; Zimmer, *Bronzegußwerkstätten* 91-97.

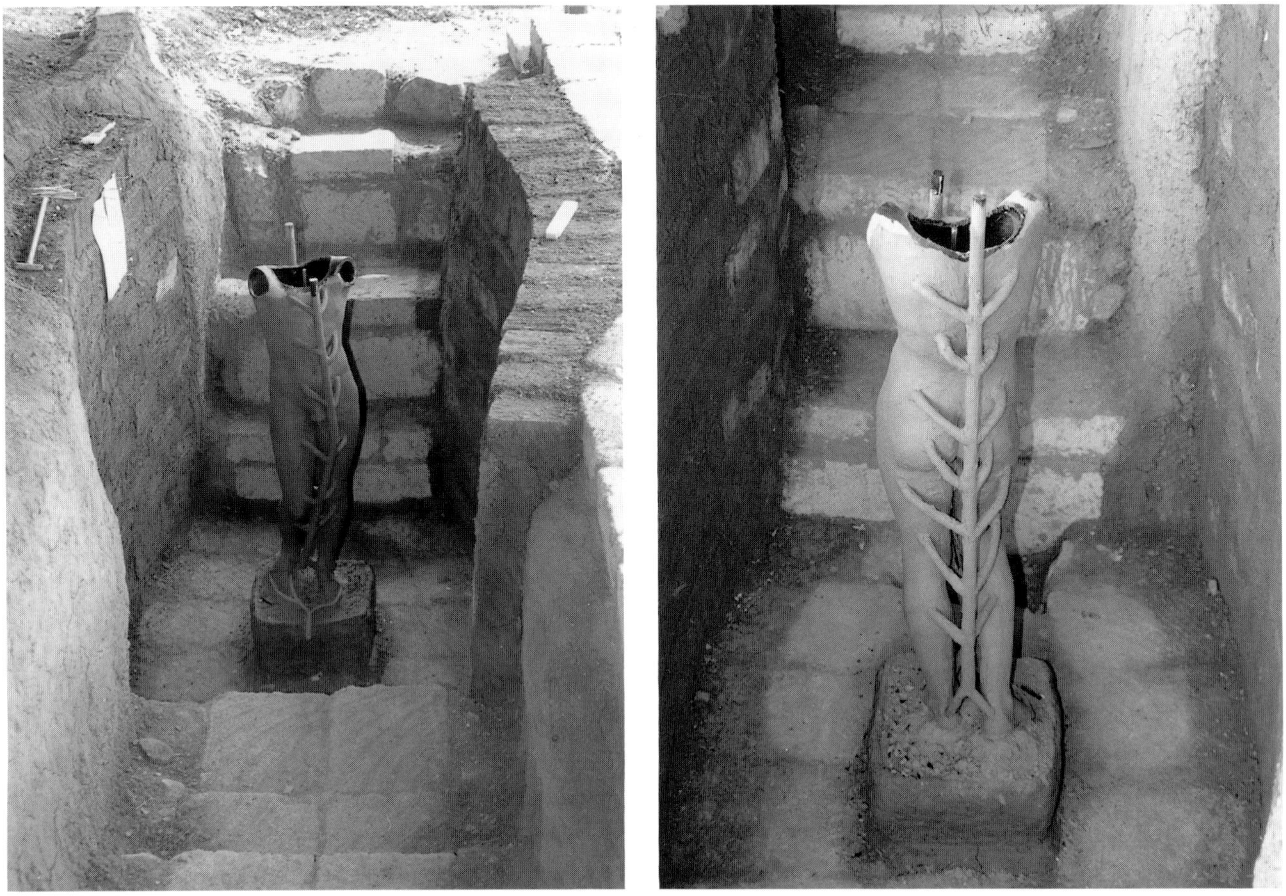

Figs. 1-2. Wax model of the Praying Boy in the small-scale replica of the Rhodes Hellenstic casting pit. (Photos: author.)

Unfortunately, due to technical reasons, it was not possible to recast the entire statue. That would have required pouring about 80 kg of bronze into the mold.

The results of our experiment are as follows:

1. The choice of location for the construction of a casting pit depends not only on the future location of the finished statue or on who commissions it: certain prerequisites, including the availability of materials, must be fulfilled by the site. Among the materials needed are *water, wood, wax,* and *earth*:

Water is necessary for producing the bricks, for mixing the various layers of the mold mantle, and for extinguishing the fire in case of an emergency. It is not just by chance that ancient casting pits are often found near rivers or wells.[7]

Large quantities of *wood* are needed for casting. For our experiment we used about 75 kg of charcoal and 5 cubic meters of firewood. In addition, wood is needed for the construction of a roof over the pit. Every ancient pit needed a roof to protect the model from the weather, i.e., from moisture during the drying process, but also from extreme sun, which could soften the wax and cause deformations or crack the mantle. In order to keep the workload to a minimum, ancient casting pits were often set up in unfinished or abandoned buildings. The ancient Greek casting pits in Demetrias, for example, made use of the peristyles of what is known as the Anaktoron.[8]

Wax and *earth* were certainly among the materials that were closely guarded secrets of the individual craftsmen using their own personal methods. They were used for the core material

7 Zimmer, *Bronzegußwerkstätten* 157.

8 Zimmer, *Bronzegußwerkstätten* 106-15.

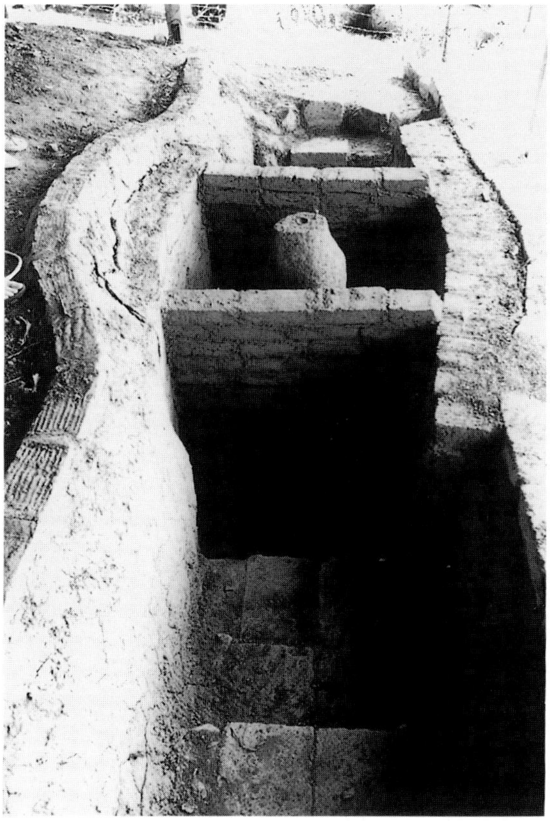

Fig. 3. The wax model, filled with core material and surrounded by a mantle of clay, left to dry in the pit. (Photo: author.)

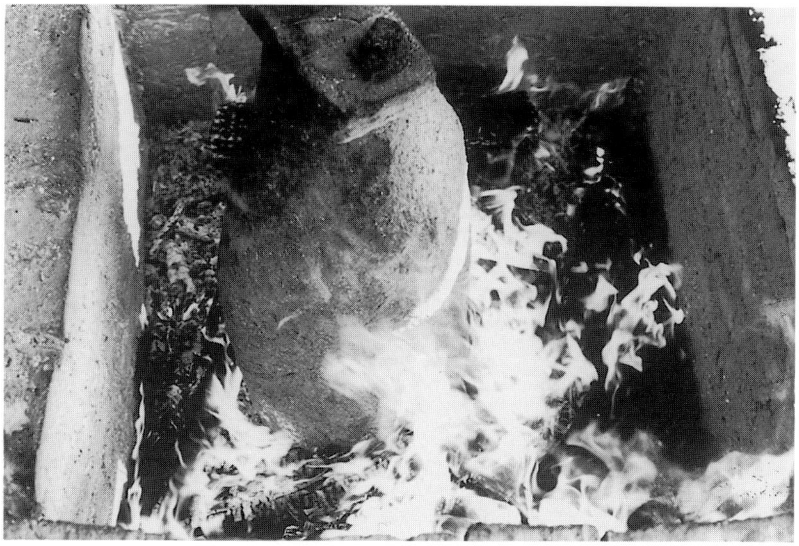

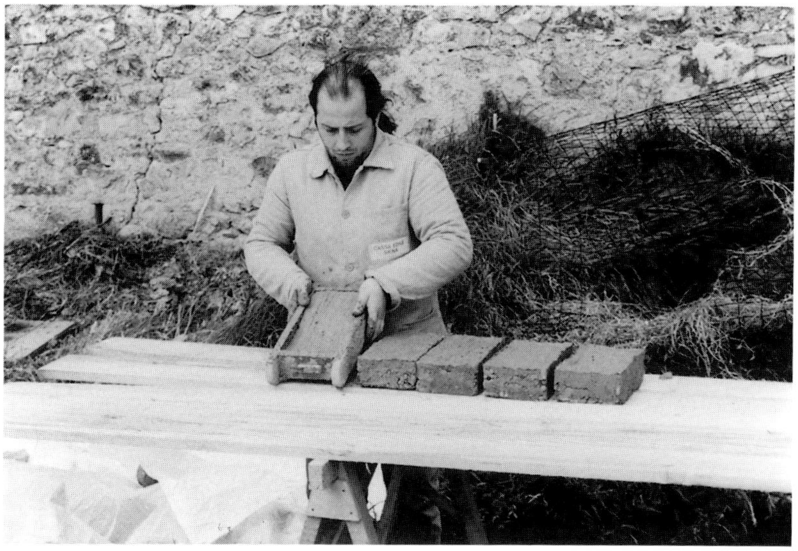

Fig. 4 (above). Firing the mold in the pit. (Photo: author.)
Fig. 5 (below). Making bricks to line the casting pit. (Photo: author.)

and for the innermost layers of the mantle around the mold. The kind of earth that was needed could not be found just anywhere: it had to be very fine on the one hand, but it also had to be compacted and be subject to only minimal shrinkage. Thus, it either had to be brought in by the master craftsman or obtained from local potteries and properly prepared for use.

2. With regard to the amount of labor required to cast a statue, we found that a lot of work could be carried out by ordinary craftsmen and unskilled assistants. This included digging the pit, making the bricks — we produced about 300 of them (figs. 5-6), building the roof, chopping wood, firing the kiln 4 days at a time, and finally clearing out the pit. Certainly there would have been two or three other workers, probably hired locally, to assist the master craftsman by carrying out these jobs according to his instructions. To economize on labor, the pits would have been used a number of times for a number of castings.

3. The third and most important finding is probably the insight that the model must be constructed directly in the casting pit. The wax model of the statue, which has very thin walls —

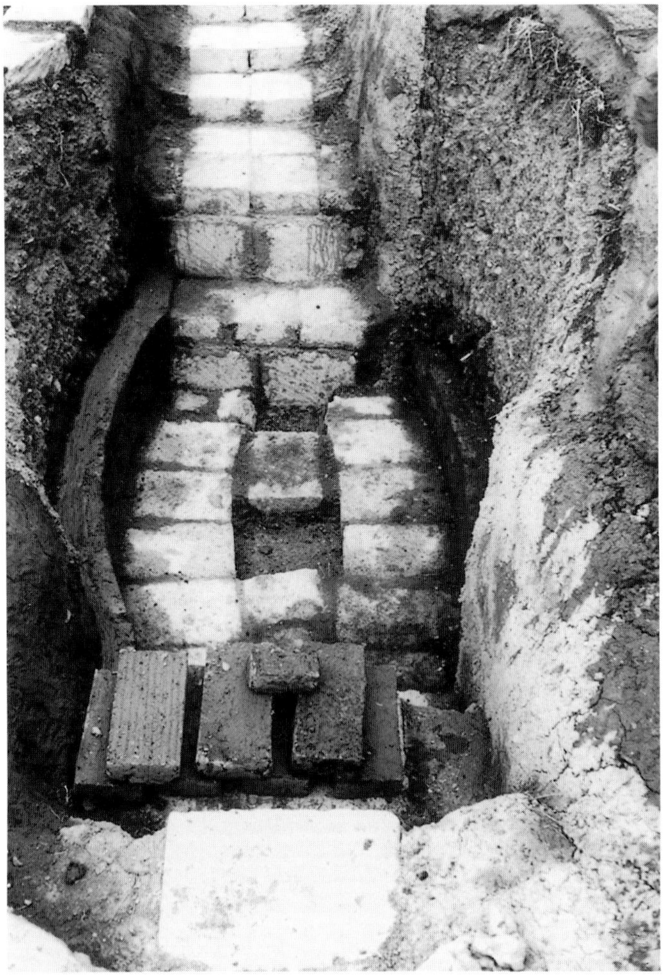

Fig. 6. Bricks lining the casting pit. (Photo: author.)

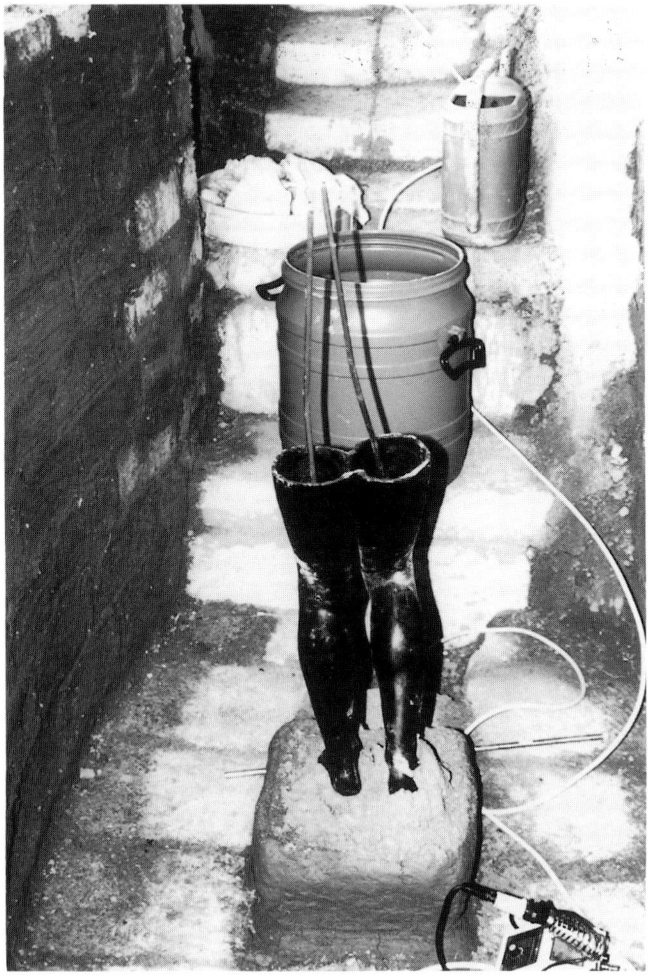

Fig. 7. Assembling the wax model around an inner framework of iron rods anchored in a clay base. (Photo: author.)

only a few mm thick like the subsequent bronze casting — is very fragile and extremely heavy due to the core material. Any movement whatsoever carries the risk of deforming or tearing the wax. This must have been even worse with the wax used in antiquity, which must have been relatively soft compared to the synthetic wax used today.[9] The mantle, consisting of several layers of clay, could not have been put on the model before it was in the pit, and it is also very susceptible to damage if it is moved. That means that possibly the odd individual piece of the mold could have been prepared off site, but the master craftsman himself must have put everything together on location.

The wax model was constructed bit by bit around an inner framework of iron rods anchored in a clay base: first, the leg it stands on, then the other leg, and finally the torso (fig. 7). The construction of the wax model was interrupted regularly to fill the individual sections carefully with core material. A large section of the shoulder area had to remain open until the end when the entire torso had been filled (figs. 8-9). The x-ray pictures of many large bronze statues show a seam in this area.[10]

The actual experiment took place as follows. The first step was to extract the wax by means of melting. That took about 8 hours. Glowing charcoal was placed all around the form. Particu-

9 *RE Suppl.* 13 (1973) 1347 ff., s.v. Wachs (R. Büll and E. Moser).

10 G. Althaus, E. Formigli, and B. von Zelewsky, in *Akten der 10 int. Tagung über antike Bronzen, Freiburg, 18-22 Juli 1988* (Stuttgart 1994) 23-28; H. Born in W.-D. Heilmeyer, *Der Jüngling von Salamis* (1996) 17.

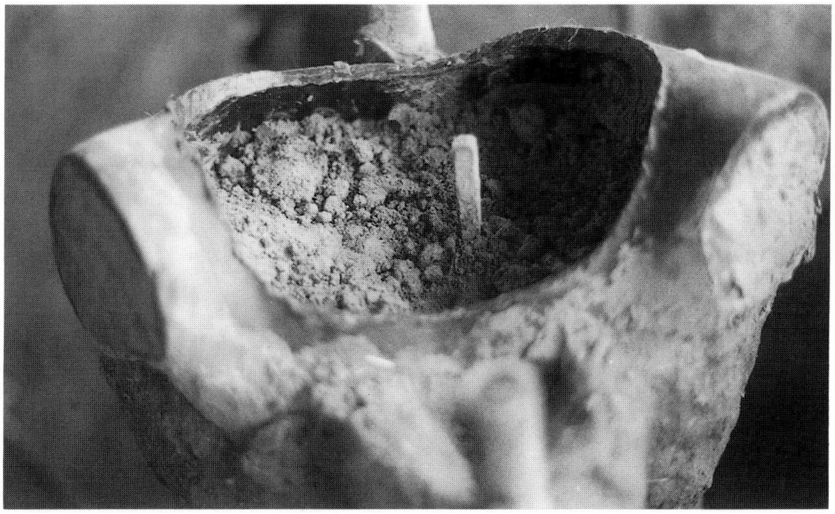

Fig. 8. Shoulder area of the wax model left open to receive core material. (Photo: author.)

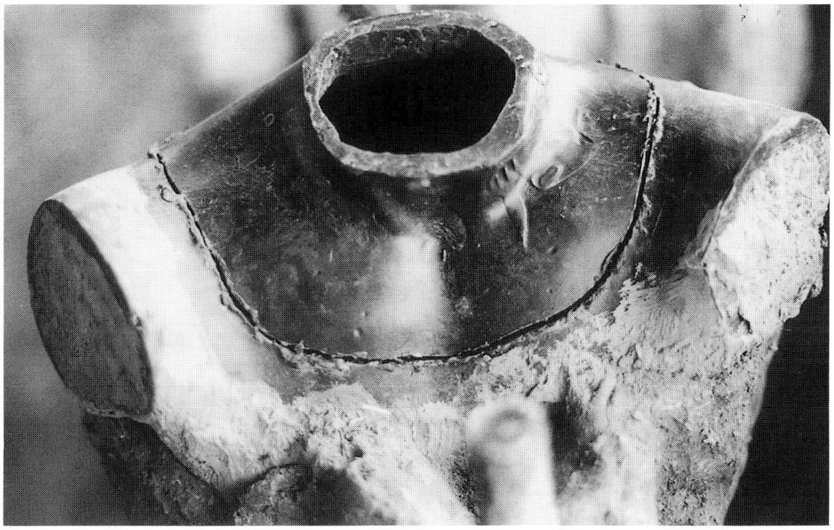

Fig. 9. Addition of the neck and shoulders to the wax model. (Photo: author.)

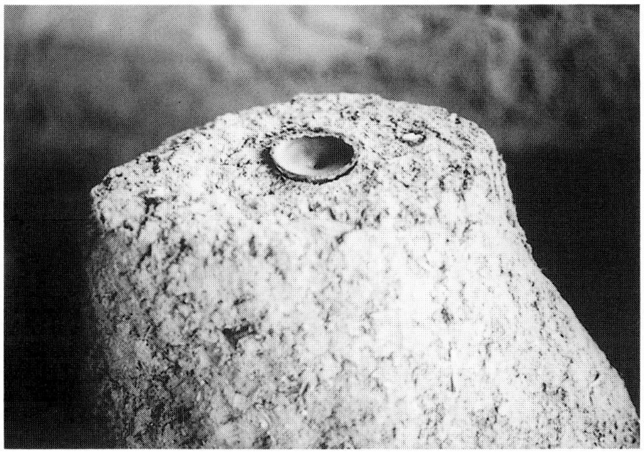

Fig. 10. Molten wax rising in the filling funnel as the heating began. (Photo: author.)

lar attention had to be paid to melting the wax in the extraction channel first, so that the wax could not look for other places to escape and then cause the fire in the pit to get out of control. The heating process caused the wax to expand. The increase in volume was clearly visible in the funnel, where the wax rose slightly as the heating began (fig. 10). After about 5 hours, the wax started to flow out of the form into the collection hole in large spurts. Finally, the air pipes and the funnel of the gating system sank down. The total amount of wax that came out was only a fraction of the original wax model. A large amount of the melted wax penetrated the clay mantle and burnt away during the firing which followed.

The firing of the clay mantle took 4 days and 3 nights (fig. 4). It was fired at temperatures of about 600-700° C obtained by throwing well-dried firewood into the pit at regular intervals. The air intake and the intensity of the fire could be regulated constantly by means of two air ducts in the walls.

During the firing, the funnel and the gates were covered by a tile to prevent any impurities from entering the mold. Due to the high temperature, first some dark smoke, caused by the burning of the leftover wax, was emitted through the funnel. The color of the smoke changed after about 48 hours. By that time the organic material left in the mold had largely been burnt out. All that escaped now was a little steam, mainly from the core material. After 72 hours there were no more emissions. This indicated that the clay mold around the cavity had completely dried out. The foundryworkers knew that the time had come to stop the baking and pour in the bronze.

A copy of the Praying Boy produced in Aachen bears witness to a successful casting. Today it stands beside our replica casting pit in Murlo to show visitors what a successful statue would look like as it came out of the mold after an ideal casting.

Korsörer Str. 22, D-10437 Berlin

Radiographic examination of ancient bronzes: the applicability of industrial casting standards

Jeffrey Maish

The investigation of bronzecasting has benefited from the increased availability of more powerful x-ray units. New radiographs have helped identify a variety of features that relate to the modeling, investing, casting, joining, and repair of ancient bronze. Although these features tell us the "how" of casting, a secondary consideration is the question "how well." Understanding the quality of casting may help us not only better understand the proficiency of the founder but also lead to a better understanding of the casting process of a sculpture's individual components.

The industrial approach

Within the metal casting industry, radiographers use sets of standard practices and reference materials to estimate casting quality. Committees have developed standard reference films for certain bronze alloys. Consistent means of radiographic practice have developed, as have specific practices for comparing film densities to known alloys and metal thicknesses. The approaches strive for consistency and in many instances are regulated in order to catch potentially dangerous flaws. Although such radiographic film interpretation is usually applied to ferrous alloys and aluminum castings, bronzecasting has found a small niche in marine applications. No one standard method has developed for the description of features and flaws although, in the United States, the American Society for Testing Materials (ASTM) standards have been the most used. Specifications were developed first within the military, primarily the U.S. Navy.[1] The American Foundrymen's Society has developed categories in addition to those developed by the ASTM (Committee E.7.0.2).[2] For example, radiographs found in ASTM document E310 are based on slightly leaded bronze. These radiographs could differ, however, from those of a highly leaded bronze. Document E310 also provides comparisons for evaluating gas porosities, inclusions, and shrinkage.[3]

Qualitative study of ancient material

Safety and qualitative inspection have been the driving factors in industrial inspections, and the latter has not been applied rigorously to the examination of ancient metals. To a great extent the success of this application in industry has been due to the availability of large bodies of consistent castings which create an equally large body of comparative material. This situation is rare if not non-existent in the study of ancient material. Categorization of ancient metal flaws is rendered even more difficult when taking into account the degradation of ancient alloys,[4] dealloying (decuprification, dezincification, destannication),[5] and variations due to the subject matter, practices in different casting localities, and variable time-frames for comparative material.

---

1 S. Goldspiel and H. W. Lloyd, "Radiographic indications and mechanical properties of bronze castings," *Modern casting* 49 (1966) 81.

2 M. Rowley, *International atlas of casting defects* (American Foundrymen's Society, Des Plaines, IL 1974). See also *Casting defects handbook* (America Foundrymen's Society, Des Plaines, IL 1984).

3 T. Jones and S. Goldspiel, "Reference radiograph standards: past, present and future," *Nondestructive testing standards - present and future, ASTM STP 1151* (H. Berger and L. Mordfin, edd.) (Philadelphia 1992) 24.

4 R. F. Tylecote, "The effect of soil conditions on long term corrosion of buried tin bronzes and copper," *JArchSci* 6 (1979) 345-68.

5 T. S. Weisser, "The de-alloying of copper alloys," in *Conservation in archaeology and the applied arts, Stockholm congress, 2-6 June 1975* (Int. Inst. Conservation Historic & Artistic Works, 1975) 207.

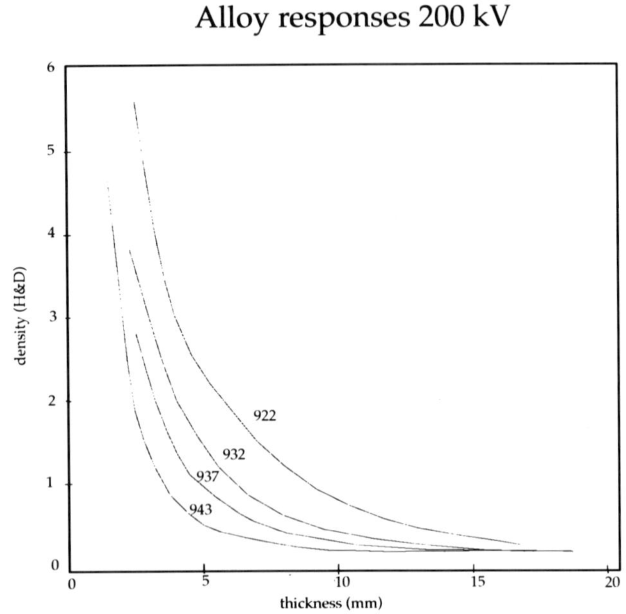

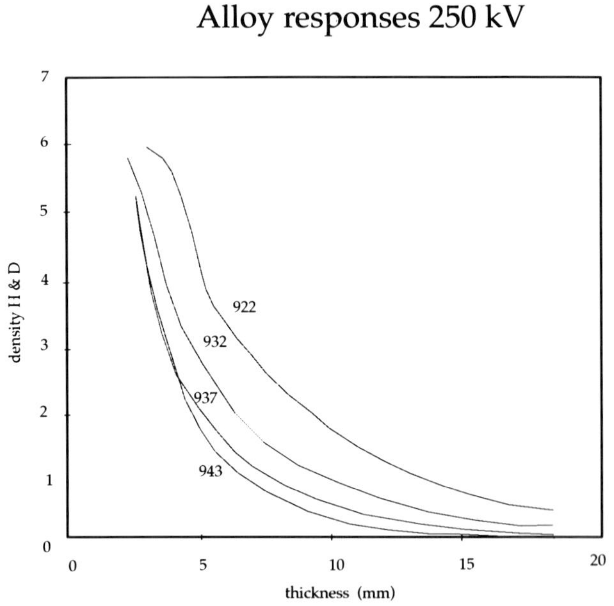

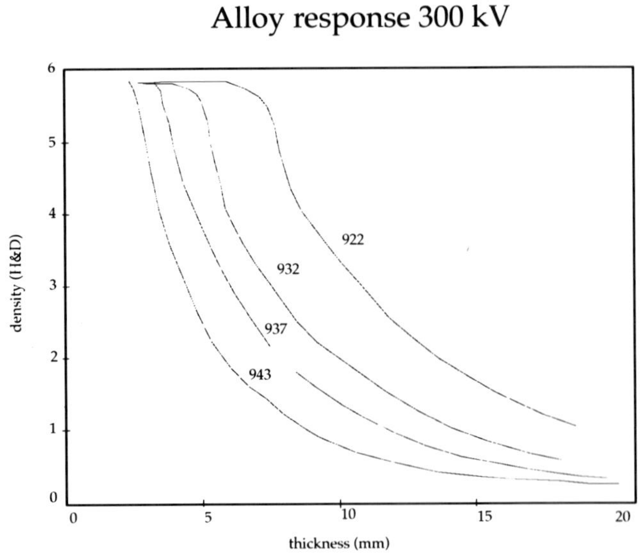

Fig. 1. Three graphs of alloy/thickness and radiographic density. Step wedges were fabricated from four modern bronze alloys (922, 932, 937, and 943) and radiographed under standardized conditions at 200, 250, and 300 kilovolts. The resulting films were measured for darkening (density), yielding results for darkening as compared to alloy thickness. At 300 kV the curves clearly separate for the different alloys. It can also be noted that, as might be expected, high lead alloy 943 is more opaque to x-radiation and consistently produced curves below and to the left of the others (tin may have a lesser effect). Conversely, the curves for alloy 922, with 1.5% lead, were consistently to the upper right in each group.

I would like to acknowledge the kind help of J. Davies, Getty Conservation Institute, for fabricating the step wedges, and of A. Bezur, Museum Research Laboratory, GCI, for plotting the densitometric information.

Alloy	%Pb	%Sn	%Cu	%Pb/Sn
922	1.5	6	88	0.25
932	7	7	83	1
937	10	10	80	1
943	25	5	70	5

Potential application may therefore be found in the consistency of the industrial methods which identify features and flaws by type and degree. Part of this approach may include the simple categorization of features of technical joins, further elaborated by the description of flaw features. Analyses of casting[6] might be amplified by correlating visually observed technical features with radiographic images. Within industry, flaws are evaluated according to whether they are inherent, that is, existing at the time of manufacture, or "in service," from

6 Mattusch, *Greek bronze statuary.* See also Bol, *Bronzetechnik.*

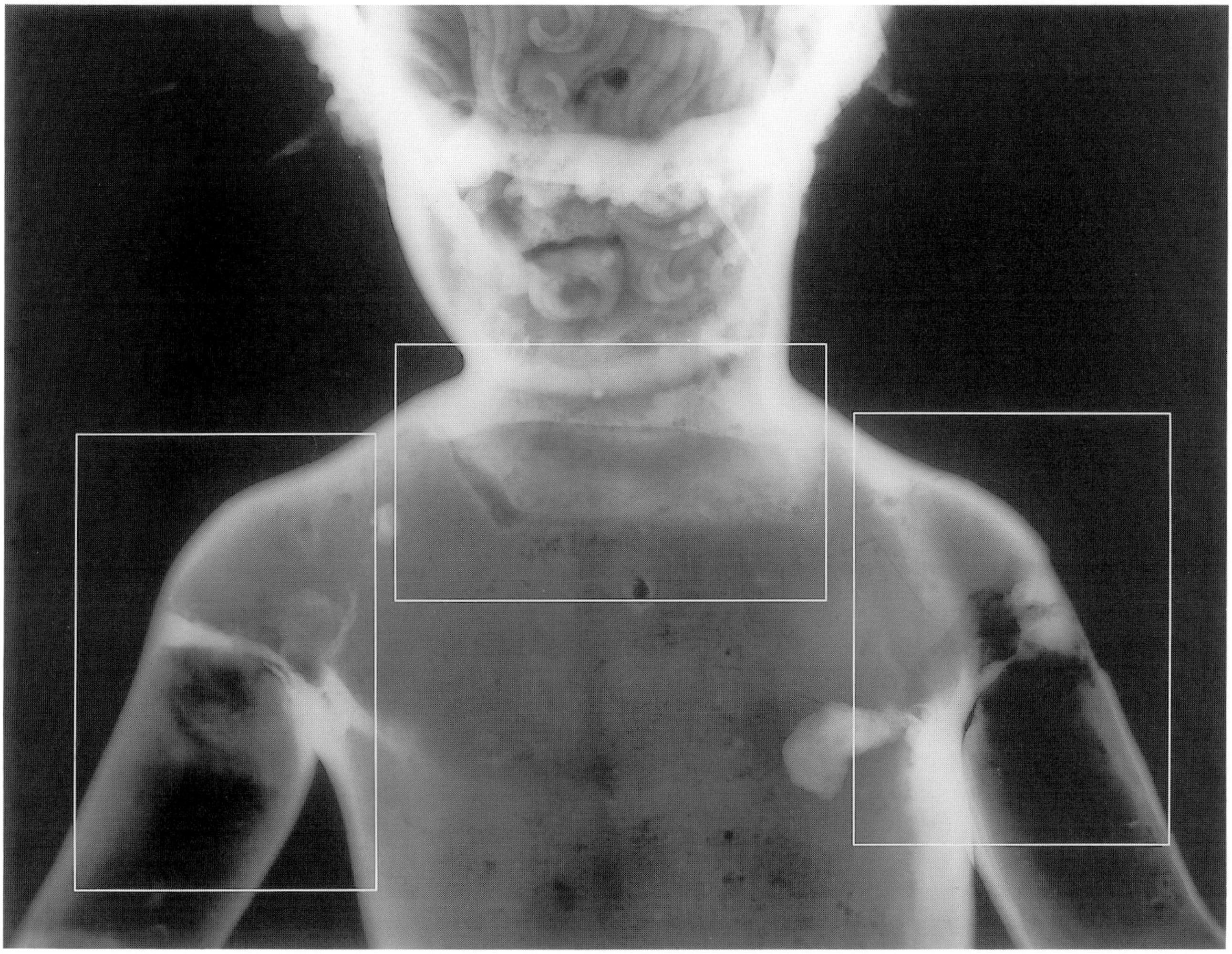

Fig. 2. X-ray detail of statue of the child Dionysos. Roman, 1st c. A.D. Bronze, h. 0.64 m. The J. Paul Getty Museum 96.AB.53. A significant and sharp wall/film density difference can be noted between the arms and torso (left and right boxes). Greater manipulation of the wax can be noted in the neck walls visible at the center.

use. Within ancient metallurgy the latter category may include evidence of ancient use, re-use, or deterioration from burial.

Preliminary application of industrial methodology

1. Thickness measurement

Variation in x-ray film density is based on alloy composition and thickness (fig. 1); the more opaque areas are therefore either thicker or more leaded. In a controlled situation, for example, one might tell whether more lead is present in one area than another *if the walls are of the same thickness.* This methodology has been applied to the examination of ancient coins with limited success.[7] In this example the investigators could not discern lead content from thickness, especially considering that "thickness" may include non-metallic crust and thin metal cores. Another example is provided by the child Dionysos where large density shifts can be noted in the arms (fig. 2) as compared to the torso.[8] This can also be noted in the neck walls. The

7 G. Foster and J. MacIsaac, "Application of xeroradiography to the study of bronze coins," *JFA* 16 (1989) 245-49.

8 J. Paul Getty Museum 96.AB.53: see also *Fire of Hephaistos* no. 26.

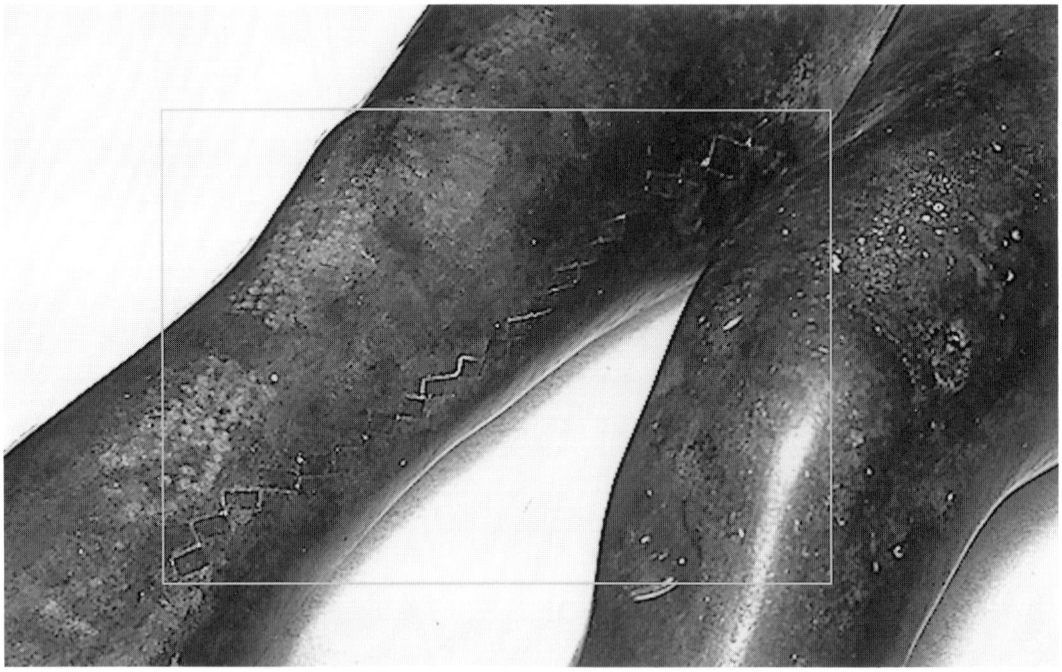

Fig. 3. Detail of legs of standing nude statue of a prince. Roman, second quarter of the 3rd c. Bronze, h. 1.20 m. The J. Paul Getty Museum 71.AB.454. A series of rectangular patches spans a probable hot tear in the leg.

sharp density shift at the shoulders and unusual join suggest metallurgical attachment. In the case of the head join, the walls at the neck have a variable thickness as compared to the walls of the upper torso. This suggests greater manipulation of wax in this area, supporting the idea of a wax-to-wax join.

2. Hot tearing

A series of patch repairs (fig. 3) can be noted extending down the right leg of the Standing Male Nude,[9] covering what appears to be a long flaw. The extensive patching may be a repair to a "hot tear," in which the metal shrank around a core inside the leg. This example is consistent with a cylindrical casting rupturing parallel to the cylindrical axis, due most probably to a too-rigid core. Hot tearing can also occur where there are large differences in section thickness, around rough mold surfaces, where there is insufficient flow of metal, and in tin bronzes where lead has segregated.

3. Segregation

Segregation (and microsegregation) occurs when one constituent of an alloy separates from another if the cooling time is sufficient to allow for separation. This may present a problem in highly leaded bronzes, containing from 15 to 27% lead. The ability to detect this radiographically is questionable, and further evaluation would be needed to clarify whether gravity segregation of lead could happen, for example, in a crucible where a highly leaded alloy was left unmixed. Although not conclusive, this feature may be present in the walls of the highly leaded Herm, which show a fair degree of nonhomogeneity (fig. 4).[10]

4. Porosity

Published examples of porosity may be noted in the statue of Hypnos in the White–Levy collection[11] and the head of one of the Four Horses of St. Mark's Basilica, Venice.[12] Extensive

9 JPGM 71.AB.454: J. Frel, *Roman portraits in the Getty Museum* (Malibu 1981) 103, no. 85.

10 JPGM 79.AB.138: *Fire of Hephaistos* 186-91, no. 3; Mattusch, *Classical bronzes* 168 ff.

11 *Fire of Hephaistos* 242-47, no. 27.

12 A. Gilardoni *et al.*, *X-rays in art — physics, technique, applications* (Como 1977).

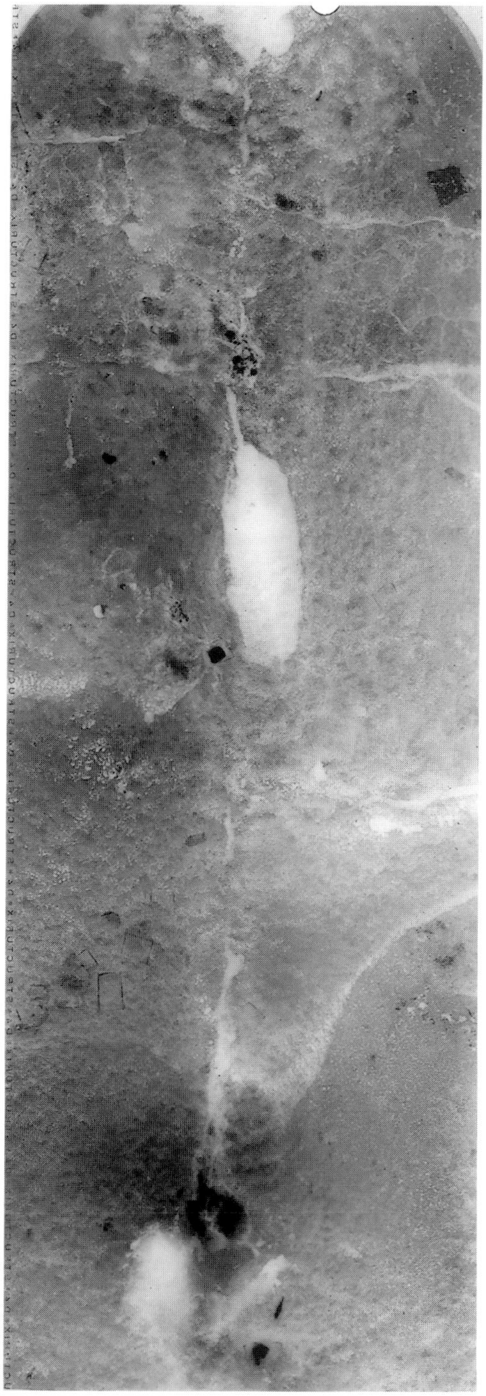

porosity may also be noted in a furniture support (JPGM 79.AC.140; fig. 5), which probably resulted from turbulence of the metal near the pouring funnel. In contrast to "artesian well" system of upward bronze flow in the mold, this pattern suggests the introduction of gas from pouring into an inverted mold.

Localized porosity can also be noted in the leg of the child Dionysos (fig. 6).[13] An initial evaluation would suggest that the differential porosity in the left and right legs was the result of two castings. However, a spongy shrinkage in the groin area (fig. 7) suggests that the torso and legs were cast as one section, and the differential porosity is due more to the direction of the flow of bronze within the mold.

5. Core shift

Uniform thinness of a bronze wall on one side of a casting, contrasting with uniform thickness on the opposite side, indicates that the chaplets did not hold the core securely in place during casting. This example of core shift can be noted in the wall thicknesses of the portrait head of an emperor (Kluge Collection; fig. 8).[14] In this particular case, a thin but acceptable wall resulted on one side; this may not have been perceived by the maker and apparently was not critical to the final product.

Further developments: digitization

The examination of ancient bronzes may be aided not only by industrial flaw analysis but also by recent technical and methodological developments in radiographic imaging. Most of these revolve around the increased use of digital methods. Digitization is approximating and should strive to match the resolution and density of film in order to aid in accurate interpretation.[15] The development of atlases of features may aid in providing a uniform source for identifying features in bronzes.[16] Digital radiograph data-bases in industry often include defect types as well as information on the object, recording system as

Fig. 4. Detail of Herm of Dionysos. Greek, 100–50 B.C. Bronze, h. 1.04 m. The J. Paul Getty Museum 79.AB.138. Detail of wall nonhomogeneity possibly due to lead segregation in a highly leaded bronze.

---

13 See supra n.8.

14 *Fire of Hephaistos* 339-43, no.53.

15 W. A. Graeme, A. C. Eizember, and J. Douglas, "Digital image analysis of non-destructive testing radiographs," *Materials Evaluation* 48 (Feb. 1990) 117-20.

16 C. Hellier and S. Wenk, "Radiographic interpretation," in P. McIntire and L. Bryant (edd.), *Nondestructive testing handbook on radiography and radiation testing* (ASNT, Columbus, OH 1985) 38.

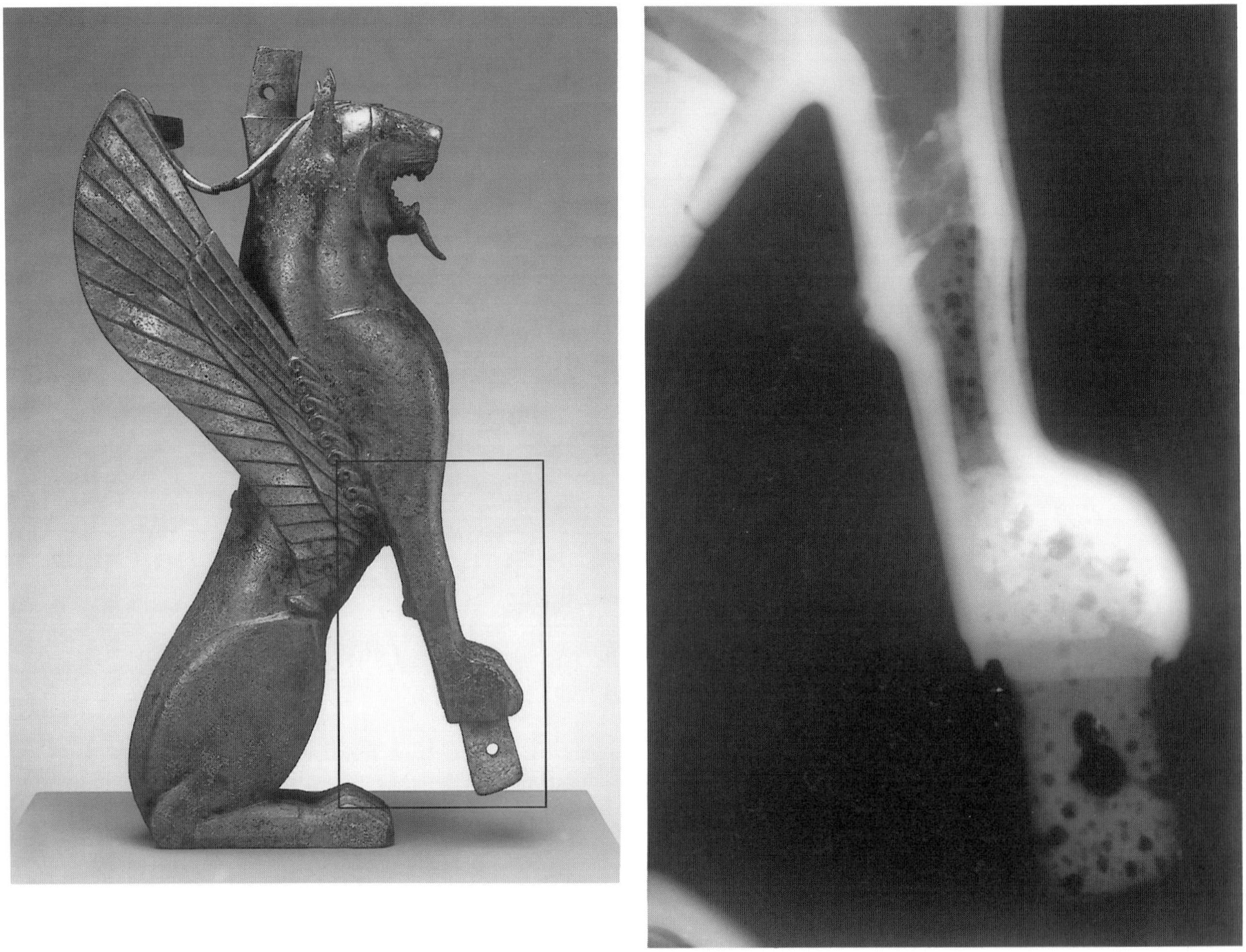

Fig. 5. Detail of furniture support cast in the shape of a winged feline. Phoenician (Tartessian), 7th to 6th c. B.C. The J. Paul Getty Museum 79.AC.140. Radiographic detail showing extensive localized porosity in the feet and lower legs.

well as quantitative information about defects.[17] Although real-time evaluation has increased the reliability of identification of defects in standardized objects,[18] this type of evaluation may be of limited use with highly individualized ancient casts. While methods in industry may gradually shift toward the inspection of other materials, such as ceramic and fiber composites, the examiner of ancient metals may benefit from greater implementation of established radiographic methods such as stereo and single wall radiography. Basic image enhancement and filtration methods may also aid in elucidating information.[19] Finally, good correlation to endoscopic information would help in clarifying interior wall features.

Conclusions

Industrial methods and standards have some application to the examination of ancient bronzes, although not on the level of their application in industry. This is due largely to the state of preservation and uniqueness of ancient artifacts. Benefits may be derived, however, sim-

17 P. Rose, J. H. Builtjes, W. Daum, and H. Heidt, "Digital image data base for flaw classification in radiographs," in J. M. Farley and R. W. Nichols (edd.), *Nondestructive testing* 3 (British Institute for NDT, London 1988) 1564-67.

18 W. Daum, H. Heidt, P. Rose, and J. H. Builtjes, "Real time evaluation of weld radiographs by digital image processing," ibid. 1568-74.

19 Jones and Goldspiel 1992 (supra n.3) 30.

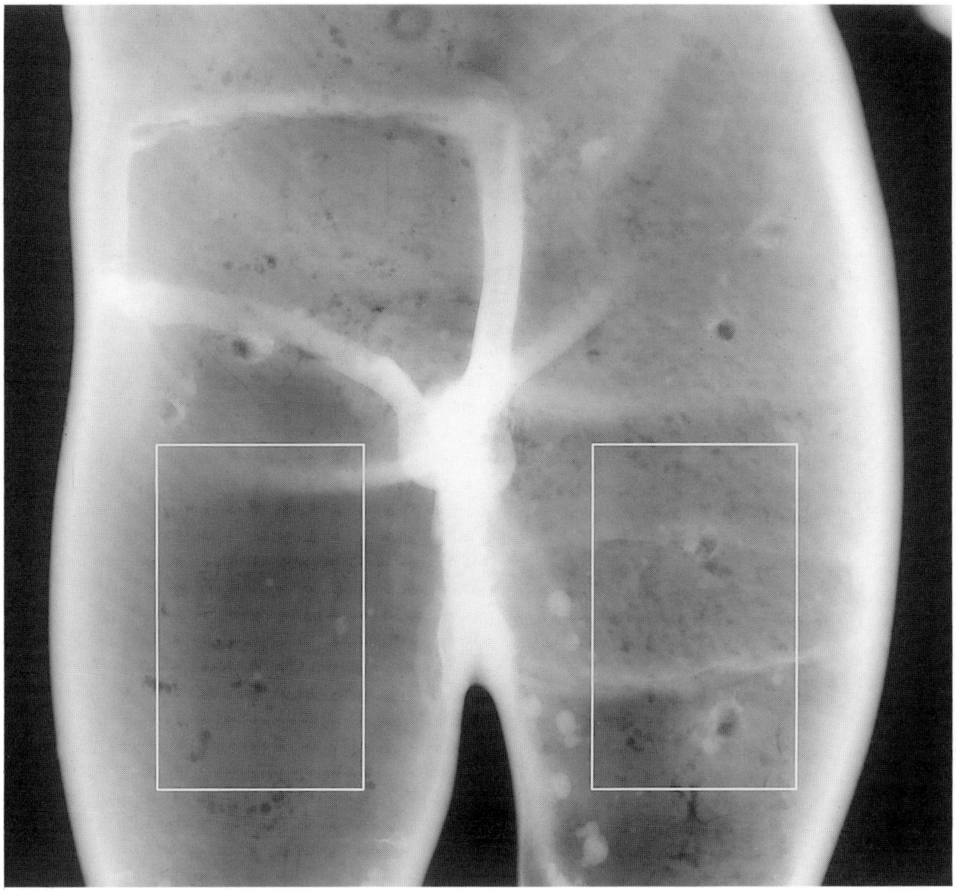

Fig. 6. Detail of statue of the child Dionysos (see fig. 2). Differential porosity in left and right leg. (J. Maish, Antiquities Conservation, JPGM.)

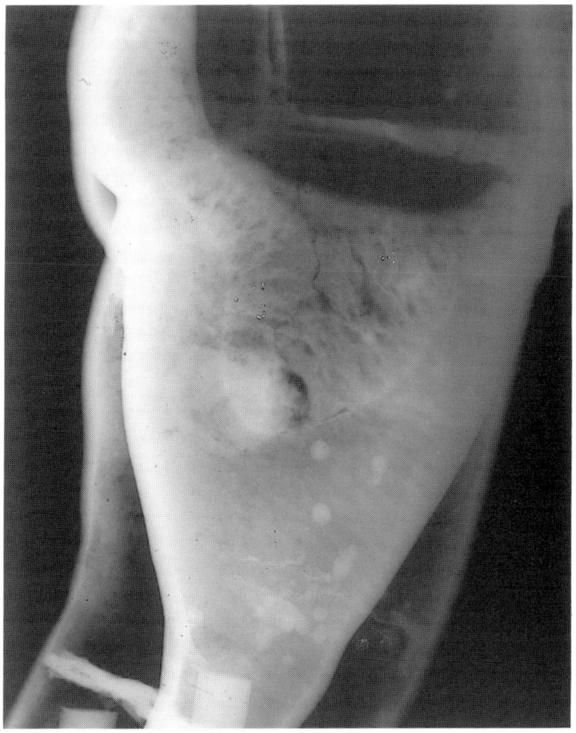

Fig. 7. Same (see fig. 2). Spongy metal between left and right legs. (J. Maish, Antiquities Conservation, JPGM.)

ply from the use of the established industrial flaw vocabulary and by a concerted effort to identify examples of casting flaw types. An added level of description may therefore help the investigator of ancient bronze technology in furthering technical understanding. An additional refinement may be a set of radiographs that provides clear examples of not only flaw types but also technical features such as joins. Finally, refinements in radiographic method may further aid in the structural analysis of ancient cast bronzes.

Antiquities Conservation Department,
J. Paul Getty Museum

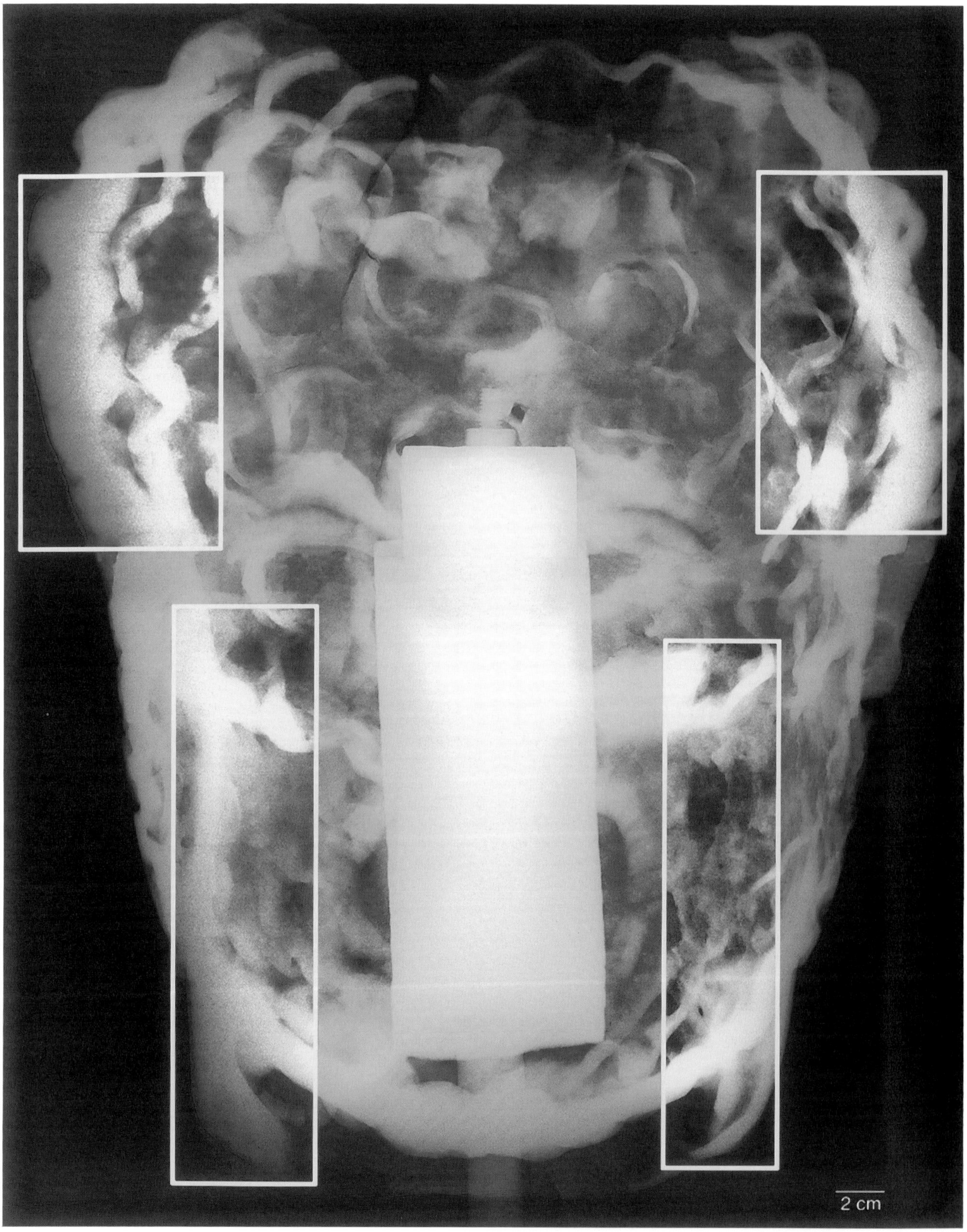

Fig. 8. Image of portrait head of an emperor (John K. Kluge collection no. 88-46, by permission). Differential wall thicknesses (most notable in neck) illustrate core shifting (scanned image sharpened and grey scale enhanced). (Radiography and observations courtesy of H. Lie, Harvard Univ. Art Museums.)

Ptolemaios III. Murray — Eine Neuerwerbung der Antikensammlung Berlin

Wolf-Dieter Heilmeyer

1993 konnte die Berliner Antikensammlung zwei erst neuerdings zusammengesetzte Fragmente einer Bronzegruppe kleinen Formats erwerben, die ursprünglich vermutlich den siegreichen Herrscher Ptolemaios III. (König von Ägypten 246–221 v. Chr.) und seinen unterlegenen Feind dargestellt hat. Die beiden Fragmente sind um 1882 in Alexandria von David Murray entdeckt und über England nach Adelaide in Südaustralien verbracht worden. Dort waren sie im Mai 1886 Mittelpunkt einer Hellseher-Sitzung, über die ihr damaliger Besitzer im April 1891 in einer von dem Londoner Verleger John Murray herausgegebenen Zeitschrift berichtet hat.[1]

Diese Story ist bei der Statuette geblieben und mit ihr in einer einfachen Photokopie 1992 auf einer Auktion bei Phillips in London verkauft worden als "an account of an eccentric experi-

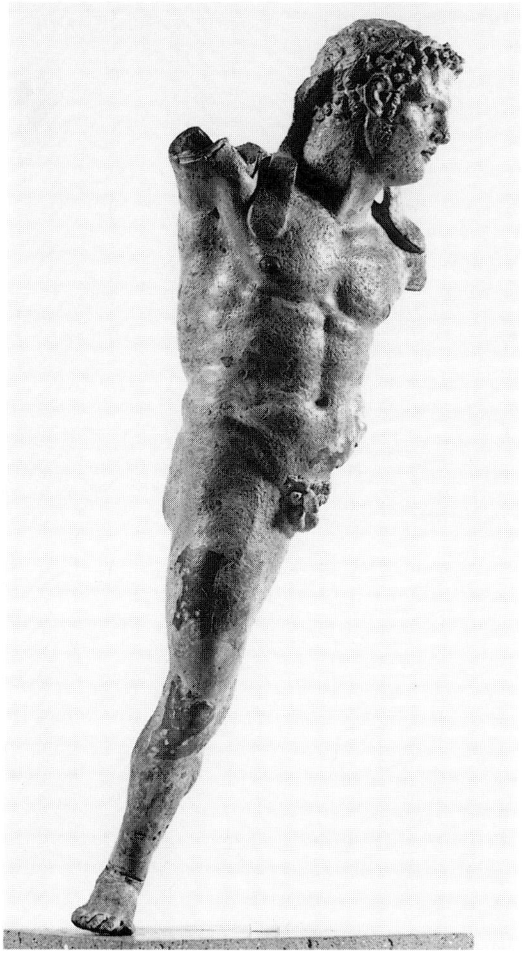

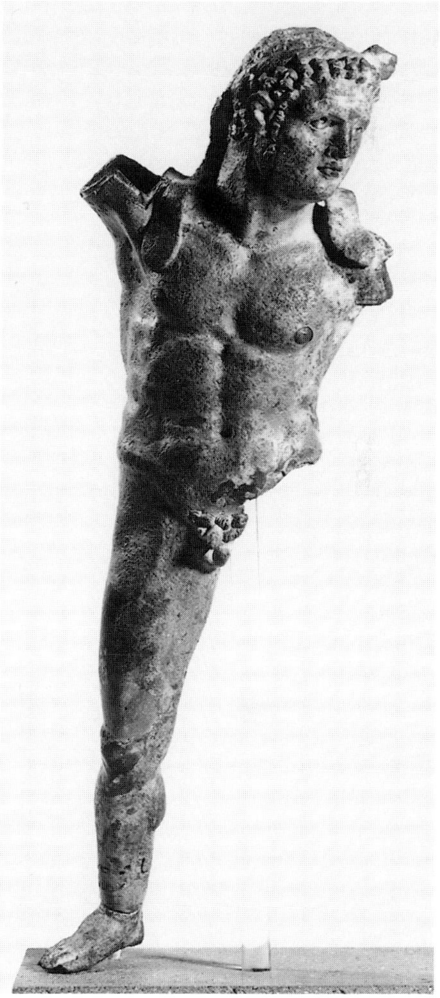

Abb. 1-2. Ptolemaios III. Murray. Ansicht von rechts und von vorne. 3 Jh. v.Chr. Bronze, h. 0,327 m. Berlin, Antikensammlung 1993,2. (Photos: J. Laurentius; Berlin, Antikensammlung.)

1 D. Murray in *Murray's Magazine* 62.9 (1891). Die Statuette tauchte wieder auf in Phillips West Two, *Cat. tribal art and antiquities, Auktion 8.7.1992*, 36 Nr. 226 Taf. 13 und Titelblatt. Eine ausführlichere Publikation des Autors in: *Jahrbuch Berliner Museen* 39 (1997) 7-22.

ment devised by the author, the components being a local Australian girl, a hypnotist and the detached foot of the present bronze." Über Basel, wo die Statuette gereinigt worden ist, hat sie 1993 Berlin erreicht. Die zu steile Baseler Montage, aber auch die Frage nach den Gründen für das Abbrechen des rechten Beines machten eine neue Restaurierung notwendig.

Die Statuette, die wir Ptolemaios III. Murray nennen, ist nur als Torso auf uns gekommen (Abb. 1-2). Ihre Bewegung erklärt sich daraus, daß die Figur das linke Bein vorangestellt hatte und sich auf dem seitwärts stehenden rechten Bein aufrichtet. Der linke Arm war im Ansatz (wie die unverlötete Achsel zeigt) nahe am Körper gehalten, folgte dann aber nach links unten vorne dem dort wahrscheinlich aufgestemmten linken Bein. Der rechte Arm war nach rückwärts hoch erhoben und sicher mit einer Stoßwaffe ausgerüstet. Die Bewegung des somit in voller Breite dargebotenen Körpers und des konzentriert nach vorne links gewendeten Kopfs weist auf einen Gruppenzusammenhang, in dem ein Gegner etwa dreiviertel links vor Ptolemaios zu ergänzen wäre. Wie der König ihn packte, wie er ihn endgültig zu besiegen trachtete, bleibt ungewiß: nach der Neigung des Körpers und der Blickrichtung des Kopfes war der Gegner bereits derart unterworfen, wie alt-ägyptische Reliefs die Feinde des Pharao niedersinken und um Gnade flehen ließen. Beide Arme der Statuette und ihr linkes Bein sind an den kantig zugeschnittenen Lötstellen herausgebrochen und fehlen heute. Der Körper ist ganz nackt; den Kopf ziert ein Blattkranz, um den eine Binde rechtsläufig derart geschlungen ist, daß ihre beiden abgerundeten Enden in langen Wellen auf die Schultern des Trägers fallen und daß ursprünglich sechs, heute nur noch drei Blätter (auf der linken Seite) in großen Abständen aus der Umwicklung ragen. Soweit sich noch erkennen läßt, sind es die geschwungenen und spitz zulaufenden Umrisse von Efeublättern.

Die Statuette ist, richtig aufgerichtet, heute 32,7 cm hoch. Sie wiegt in ihrem torsohaften Zustand nur noch 1280 gr.

Die vom Rathgen-Forschungslabor (Chr. Goedicke, 21.3.1996) mitgeteilte Materialzusammensetzung schien zunächst recht eigentümlich: zur Kontrolle wurden zwei weit voneinander entfernte Stellen beprobt, die dies zuließen, an der Ferse (Probe 1) und an der Innenkante des rechten Glutäus (Probe 2).

Element	Probe 1	Probe 2
Cu	62.54	62.63
Sn	6.128	5.102
Pb	30.927	31.555
Zn	0.0304	0.0297
Fe	0.162	0.482
Ni	0.0510	0.047
Ag	0.0763	0.0906
Sb	0.082	0.066
As	< 0.1	< 0.1
Bi	< 0.025	< 0.025
Co	< 0.005	< 0.005
Au	< 0.01	< 0.01
Cd	< 0.001	< 0.001

Nach der Definition von J. Riederer handelt es sich um eine Blei-Zinn-Bronze mit selten hohem Bleigehalt, wie er aber verschiedentlich bereits nachgewiesen ist.

Dank der Hilfe der Bundesanstalt für Materialforschung und -Prüfung (J. Goebbels, 22.4. 1996) konnten Radiogramme und Computertomogramme hergestellt werden, die die Besonderheiten der Herstellung enthüllten (Abb. 3-4).

Der Guß der Statuette erfolgte nach Abnahme der Arme und des linken Beins vom Wachsmodell in einem Stück, weist aber erhebliche Fehler auf: einerseits lief offensichtlich mehr Gußmasse als nötig in Lücken und Grate der Kernoberfläche im Inneren des Hohlgußes, ander-

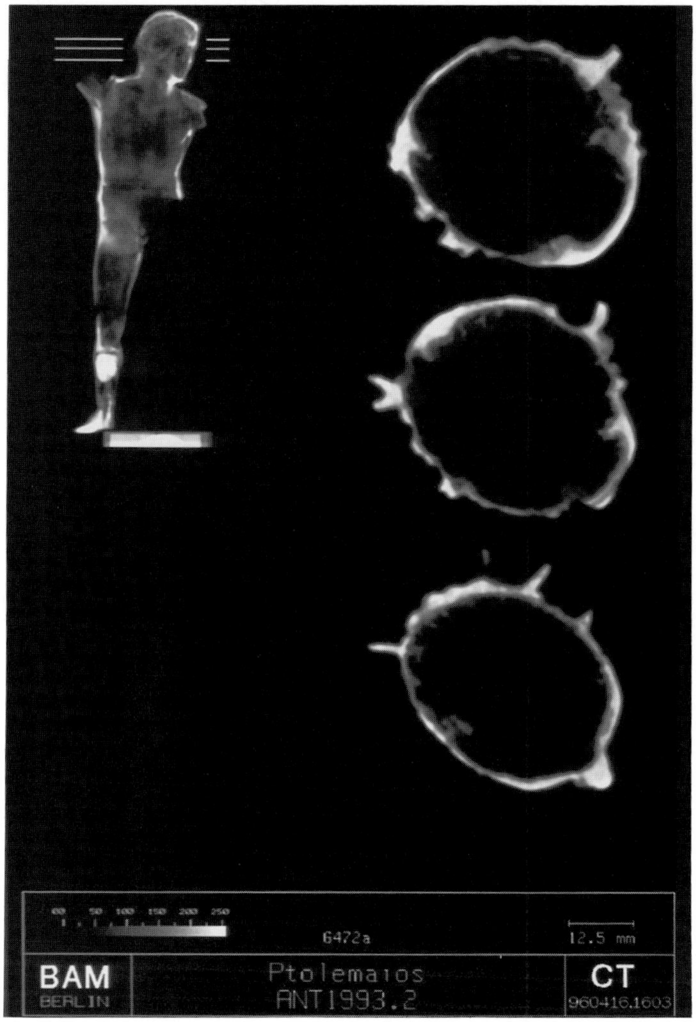

Abb. 3. Computertomogramme des Kopfes. (Photo: Berlin, BAM.)

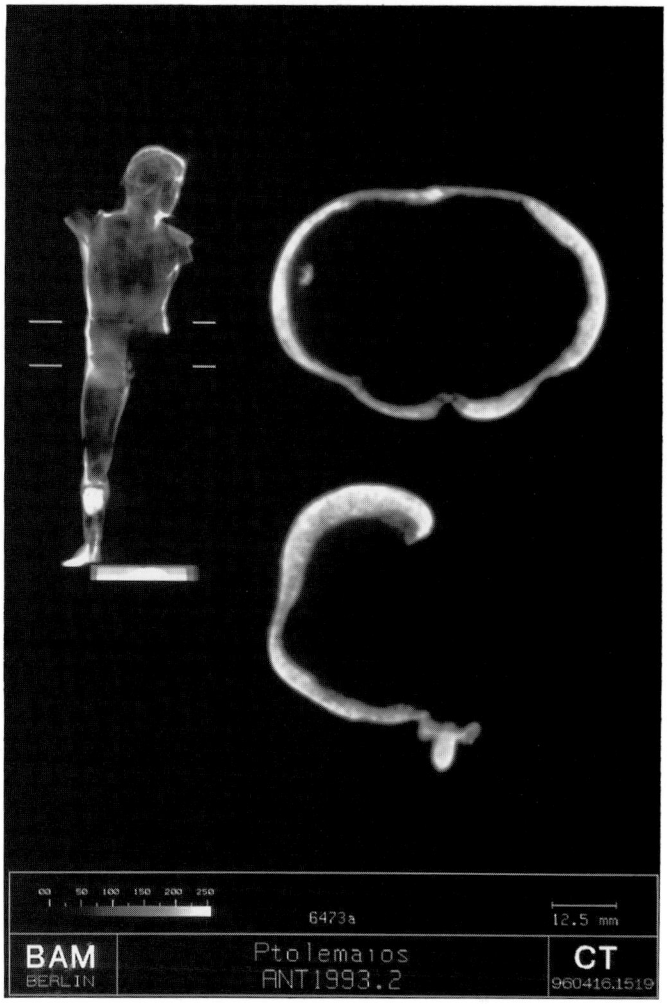

Abb. 4. Computertomogramme des Bauchs und der Hüfte. (Photo: Berlin, BAM.)

seits lief die Wandung an Stirn und Schläfe, an Nabel und Rücken zu dünn und schloß sich am rechten Knöchel so unvollkommen, daß der Fuß schon antik eigens angesetzt bzw. repariert werden mußte. Eine sehr unregelmäßige Stelle der Rückenwand, die innen leicht vorsteht und daneben an zwei Stellen Löcher läßt, interpretiert B. Niemeyer als Anschnitt, vielleicht des Haupteingußkanals.

Der rechte Fuß ist in seinem Ansatz rundum rißartig abgetrennt, teils vielleicht als Bruch, teils aber sicher als durch Kaltfluß entstandene Naht: an der Fersensehne sind die Ränder dieser Naht kugelig stehengeblieben. Ein herausgefallener Flicken sollte die Fuge decken. Es scheint, als sei der Fuß zwar im Guß gekommen, aber nicht ganz bindend, sodaß er eine interessante, erst durch die Radio- und Tomogramme enthüllte Reparatur nötig gemacht hat, und zwar nach der gleichen Art der Patina am Fuß und Körper der Statuette vermutlich schon bald nach dem Guß: Zwei kleine Bleiklumpen, von denen einer im Waden-, der andere im Knöchelbereich fest sitzt, ummanteln einen vierkantigen Kupferstab, der fast genauso lang ist wie die Verbleiung (5,7 mm), aber oben und unten von ihr eingehüllt wird. Höchstens Reste des Kerns könnten daneben noch vorhanden sein. Hohe Qualität bei Modell- und Wachsarbeit, gesicherte Tradition bei Lötfugenschnitt und nachträglicher Oberflächenbearbeitung sowie die Hinnahme und umfangreiche Ausbesserung der Gußfehler sprechen für eine Werkstatt von hohem Rang und gesicherter Auftragslage, mithin im Kontext des alexandrinischen Königsbilds von einer mit dem ptolemäischen Hof verbundenen Kunst.

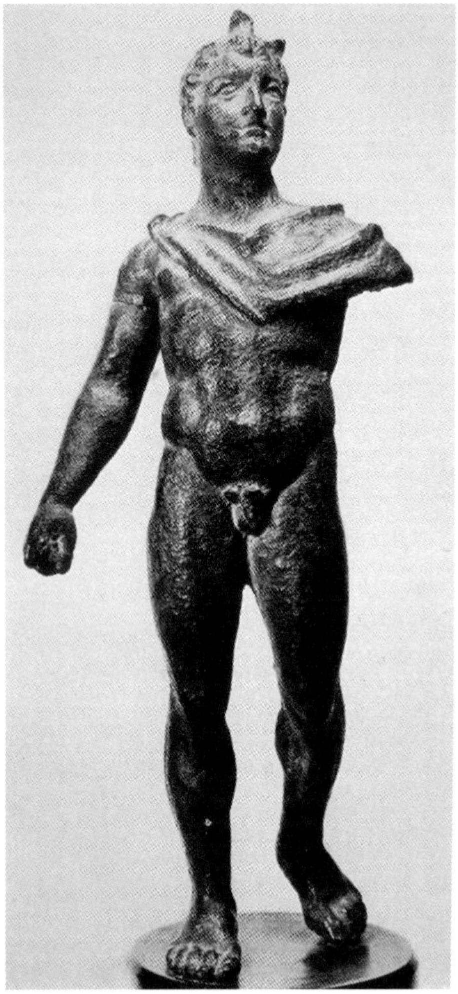

Abb. 5. Ptolemaios III Euergetes. Bronze. Bonn, Akademisches Kunstmuseum Inv. C 301. (Photo: Akademisches Kunstmuseum.)

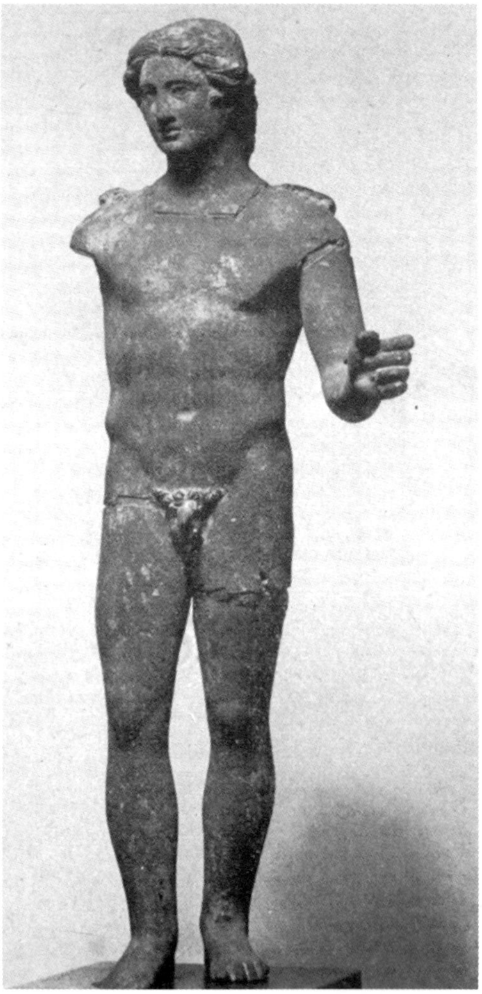

Abb. 7. Apollo. Bronze. Baltimore, Walters Art Gallery, Inv. 54.757. (Photo: Walters Art Gallery.)

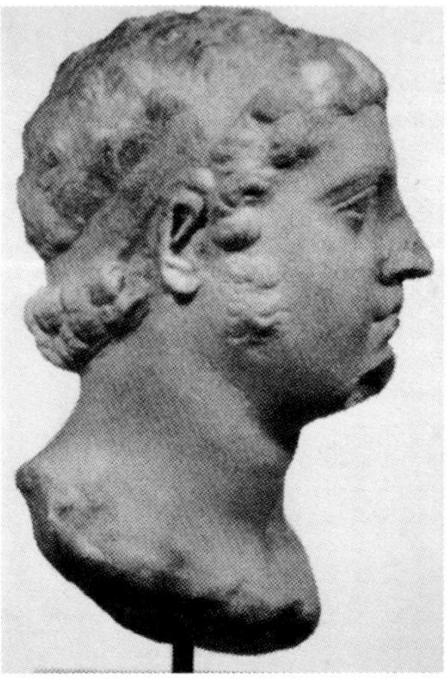

Abb. 6. Ptolemaios III Euergetes, 3. Jh. v.Chr. Marmor, H. 34,5 cm. Schweiz, Privatbesitz. (Photo: J. Zbinden, Bern.)

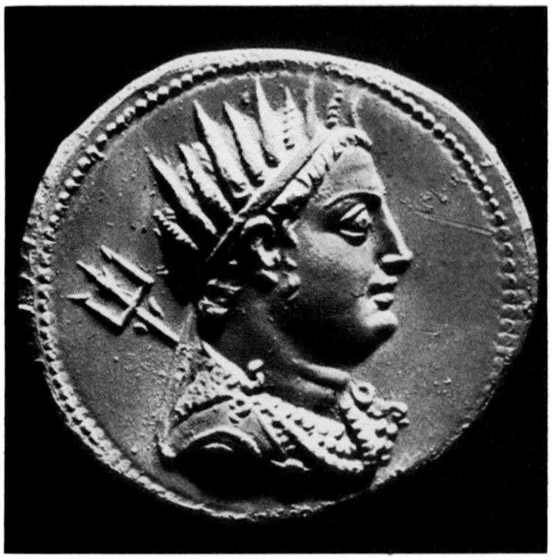

Abb. 8. Goldoktadrachmon des Ptolemaios III Euergetes. London, British Museum. (Photo: Athen, DAI Neg. 77/936.)

Ein guter Vergleich zu unserer Statuette ist dem Kopftypus nach, dem Körperbau und der Stück-Technik nach der "Ptolemaios III. Euergetes als Hermes" aus Ägypten in Bonn (Abb. 5). Schon die verschiedenen von ihm publizierten Photos zeigen den allein erhaltenen rechten Arm mit einer ähnlichen zungen- und stufenförmigen Lötfuge, die heute anscheinend nicht mehr ganz fest ist. Weitere Beispiele schließen sich an, schließlich, technisch besonders gut zu vergleichen, der "Jüngling" oder "Apollo" aus Suez in Baltimore (Abb. 7): bei ihm sind beide Beine und Arme sowie der Kopf gesondert gegossen und angelötet und die Lötfugen teilweise ebenfalls gestuft. Zur Identifizierung Ptolemaios' III. Murray gibt sein fülliger Kopf den Ausschlag: deutlicher als bei den Bonner und Stuttgarter Vergleichsstücken ist hier der auf Münzen charakterisierte "Euergetes" und "Tryphon" zu erkennen (Abb. 8). Ein Marmorkopf in Schweizer Privatbesitz, der 1982/83 in Bern ausgestellt war und von Ines Jucker beschrieben worden ist (Abb. 6), stimmt bis auf die Augen (denen bei unserer Statuette eine motivlich bedingte Bedeutung zukam) völlig mit dem soviel kleineren Bronzebild überein.

Der bindenumwundene Efeukranz im Haar gleicht den siegenden Ptolemaios Euergetes dem Gott Dionysos an. Über die Beziehungen der Ptolemäer zu diesem Gott ist schon viel gehandelt worden; der Gegensatz der damit verbundenen Tryphe zum römischen *mos maiorum* hat die Überlieferung des hellenistischen "Dionysosglaubens" (Wilamowitz) vermutlich verdunkelt. Ob Ptolemaios hier als Dionysos kämpfend siegte oder ob der Pharao-Basileus durch seinen Sieg dem Dionysos glich? Der Indienzug des Dionysos war jedenfalls sein "Triumphzug" (Kerényi), und die Gleichsetzung des Dionysos mit Osiris praedestinierte ihn für den ägyptisch-hellenistischen Herrscherkult. Sollte die Gruppe, aus der unsere Statuette stammt, einen orientalischen Sieg als Grundlage der üppigen Wohltaten Ptolemaios' III. feiern, dann wäre an die ersten Erfolge im Laodikekrieg und an den Frieden mit den Seleukiden 241 v.Chr. zu denken, der als Triumphzug bis nach Baktrien/Afghanistan gefeiert wurde.

Staatliche Museen zu Berlin, Antikensammlung

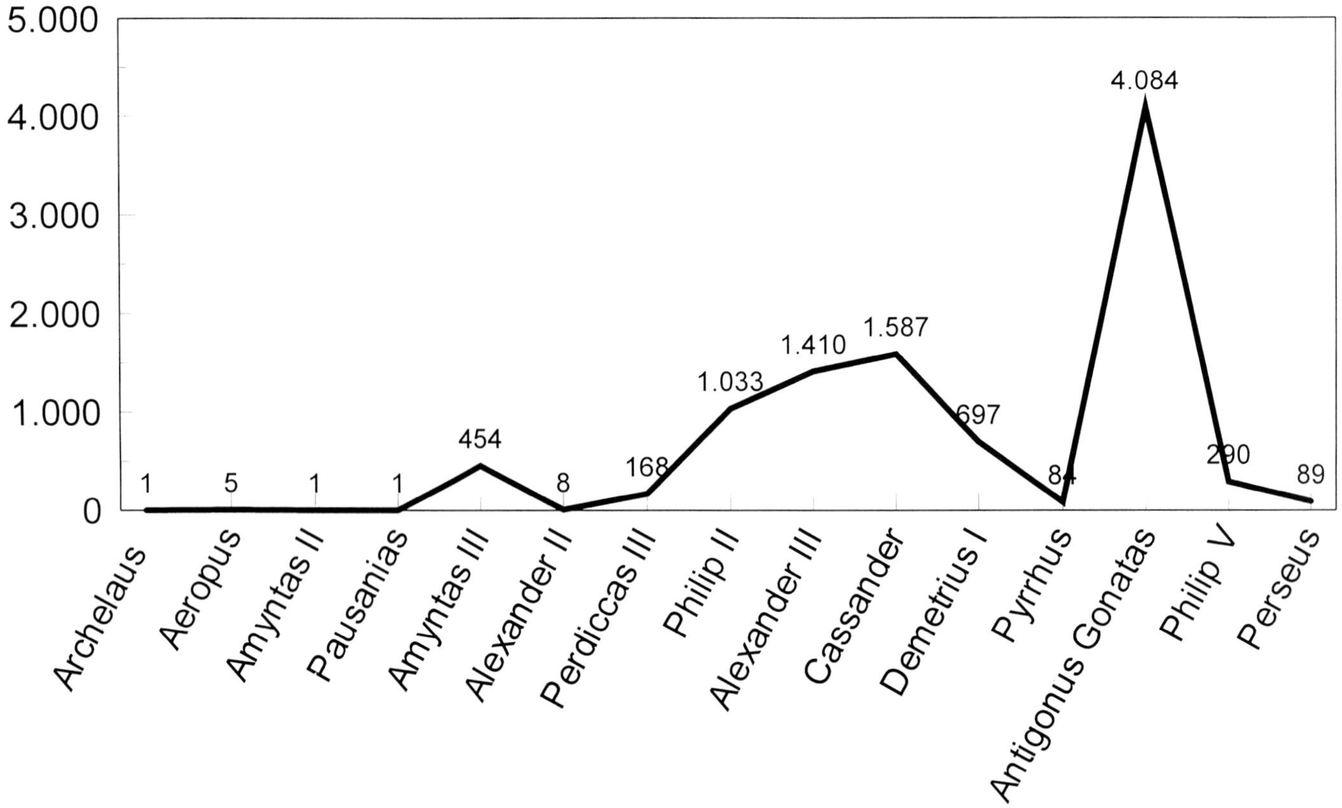

Table 1. Numbers of Macedonian royal bronze coins found in Thessaly, by king.

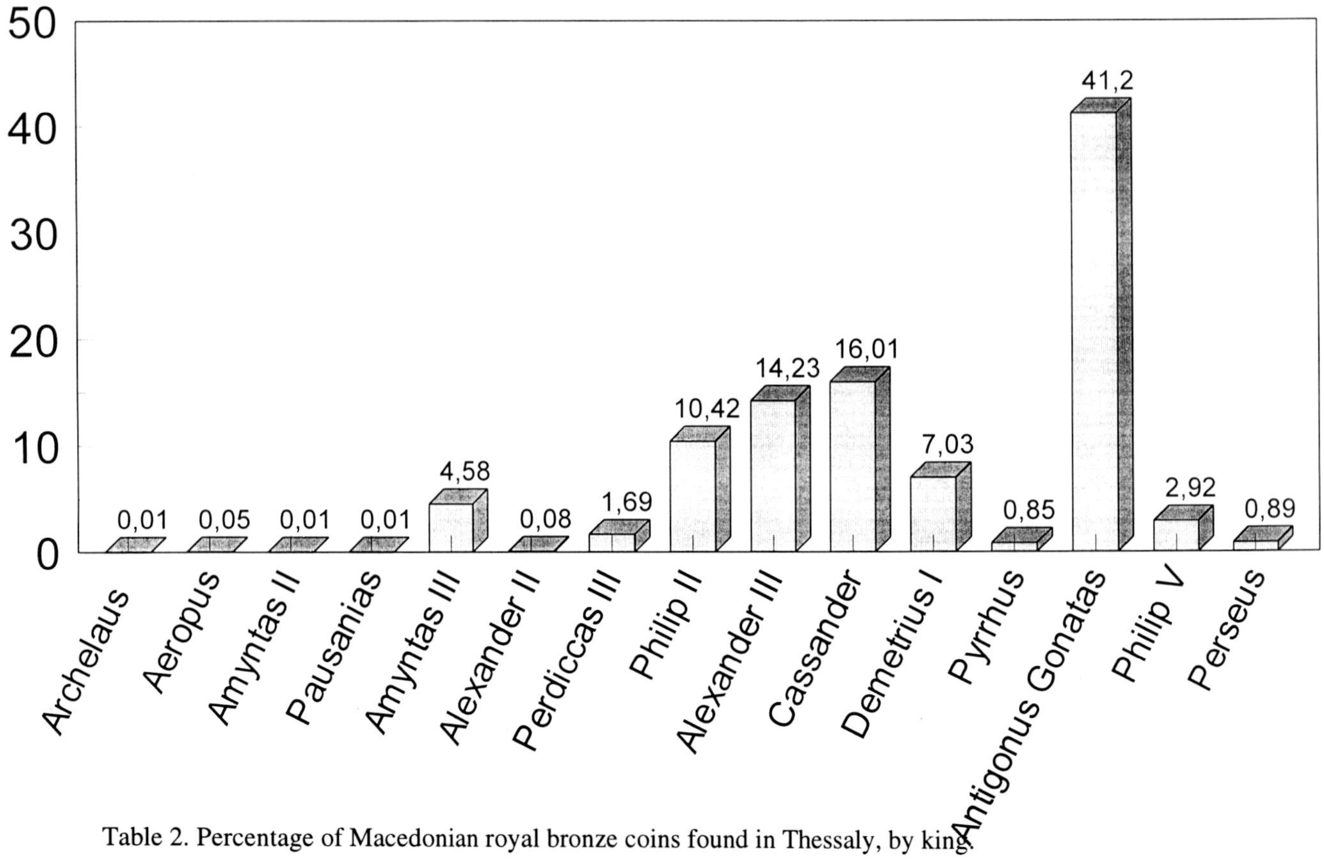

Table 2. Percentage of Macedonian royal bronze coins found in Thessaly, by king.

The circulation of bronze Macedonian royal coins in Thessaly

Katerini Liampi

Royal Macedonian bronze coinage made its way into neighboring Thessaly quite early, even before the ultimate political and military interference of the Macedonians in the region under Philip II. A different situation persisted in the other neighboring regions, such as Epeiros, Thrace, or the area north of Macedonia, where far fewer examples of this coinage have come to light.

The wide circulation of these bronze issues attests the various relationships that existed between Macedonia and Thessaly and underlines Thessaly's position as the gateway to Macedonia, her natural outlet to Greece further south. The vast numbers of royal bronze coins in Thessaly are best explained in the framework of Philip II's establishment of permanent Macedonian garrisons in strategic positions in Thessaly and by the founding of Demetrias as the seat of the Macedonian kings by Demetrius Poliorcetes. Indeed, a continuous Macedonian presence in Thessaly was demanded by the wars (especially the Chremonidean War) waged — one after another — between the Macedonians and southern Greeks. Supplies for the army, and the movement of Macedonian troops to the south, all explain the finding in Thessaly of so many Macedonian coins, especially of that period.

It is worth noting that the Thessalian cities never stopped issuing their own coins. Recent studies have shown that after the Lamian War (322 B.C.) Larisa reduced but did not altogether stop issuing silver coinage.[1] At the same time the other Thessalian cities continued their bronze coinage.

For the present study some 10,000 coins were examined from published material and from private collections, all certified to be of Thessalian origin[2] but without information on the exact place of finding. The number of coins, to be sure, is not conclusive evidence. Yet it gives a significant picture of the spread of Macedonian bronze coinage into Thessaly proportionately king by king. This general picture will not be changed by future study of coins from excavations.

As the tables show (Tables 1 and 2), the bronzes of the first Macedonian kings to appear in the Thessalian commercial market came there probably through chance and circumstance. Coins of Archelaus,[3] Aeropus II, Amyntas II,[4] and Pausanias have been identified:

---

1 T. Martin, *Sovereignty and coinage in classical Greece* (Princeton 1985) 89-152.

2 The archaeological areas in Thessaly where royal coins have been found and published are Demetrias, which yielded 1 bronze of Alexander III, 11 bronzes of Antigonus Gonatas and 2 bronzes of Perseus, see *Demetrias* I (Bonn 1976) 73, 140 f. and *Demetrias* IV.I (Bonn 1981) 17 f., 23 f.; Pherai, which yielded a bronze coin of Amyntas III, see A. Dougleri-Intzesiloglou, "Τα ελληνιστικά λυχνάρια των Φερών," *Γ' Επιστημονική Συνάντηση για την Ελληνιστική Κεραμική. Χρονολογημένα Σύνολα-Εργαστήρια, 24-27 September 1991 Thessaloniki* (Athens 1994) 386; Halos, which yielded 1 coin of Alexander III, 3 of Cassander, and 1 of the "anonymous" type which is attributed to Demetrius Poliorcetes by H. Reinder Reinders, *New Halos, a Hellenistic town in Thessalia, Greece* (Utrecht 1988) nos. 51.12-13; 52, 37; 54, 99; SF 150; SF 152. To Callithera 54 of the 110 identified coins have been attributed by B. Intzesiloglou, "The contribution of coins to the study of ancient topography. A first assessment: the case of Callithera," in Διεδνές Συνέδριο για την αρχαία Θεσσαλία στη Μνήμη του Δημήτρη Ρ. Θεοχάρη (Athens 1992) 425 f. The coins have been attributed to Amyntas III (1), Philip II (3), Alexander III (5), Cassander (10), Demetrius Poliorcetes (2), Pyrrhus (4), with most belonging to Antigonus Gonatas (29).

3 U. Westermark, "Remarks on the regal Macedonian coinage *c.* 413-359 B.C.," *Numismatic studies in memory of C. M. Kraay and O. Mørkholm* (Louvain-la-Neuve 1989) 301-15.

4 H. Gaebler, *Die antiken Münzen Nord-Griechenlands* 3.2 (Berlin 1935) 157 f.

Archelaus	(413-399)		
	head of lion/forepart of boar	Westermark pl. 69, 10 f.	1
Aeropus II	(396-393)		
	male head with *petasos*/forepart of lion with bone	Westermark pl. 69, 17	3
	male head with *petasos*/forepart of lion	ibid. pl. 69, 18	1
	male head with *petasos*/horse	ibid. pl. 69, 16	1
Amyntas II	(393-392)		
	head of Pan/forepart of wolf	Gaebler pl. 29, 28	1
Pausanias	(393-392)		
	male head/forepart of lion	Westermark pl. 69, 30	1

Macedonia at this time was in a state of upheaval at home, and her problems with enemies were even greater. There was thus no serious overture of any sort in the direction of Thessaly.

During the reign of Amyntas III there appears to have been the first notable influx of coins into Thessaly, with all types of his bronze coinage being represented:

Amyntas III	(393-370)		
	head of Heracles/eagle with snake	Westermark pl. 70, 34	449
	head of Heracles/eagle in incuse	Gaebler pl. 30, 1	1
	head of Heracles /forepart of boar	ibid. pl. 30, 4-5	2
	(without identification of the type from Callithera=1)		

The quantities of Amyntas's bronze coins in circulation no doubt reflect the friendly relations developed by the king with the Thessalians, who helped him in his struggle against the Chalcidians.

The coins of Alexander II are insignificant in number, whereas those of Perdiccas III evidently circulated in greater quantities:

Alexander II (370-369/8)			
	male head /horse	Westermark pl. 70, 39 f.	8
Perdiccas III (365-360/59)			
	head of Heracles /lion with spear	Westermark pl. 70, 46 f.	163
	head of Heracles /bull	ibid. pl. 70, 49	3
	head of Heracles /eagle	ibid. pl. 70, 50	2

Under Philip II the picture of royal bronze coinage in Thessaly changes decidedly. Nearly all of his issues are represented. The so-called small size predominates, but there is also a considerable series of the large size with the head of a youth/horseman.

Philip II (360/359-336)			
	a) head of Heracles/thunderbolt	Gaebler pl. 31, 17	11
	head of Heracles/club	ibid. pl. 31, 10	61
	head of Heracles/horseman	ibid. pl. 31, 16	6
	head of Heracles/his weapons	ibid. pl. 31, 11	2
	b) male head/horseman	ibid. pl. 31, 9, 12 f.	950
	(without identification of the type, from Callithera=3)		

This sudden increase of coins in the Thessalian market reflects the period when Philip II became *archon-hegemon* and established Macedonian garrisons in Thessaly to control the region.

In slightly greater numbers the bronzes of Alexander III also circulated in Thessaly. Practically all issues of his Macedonian mints are represented, and in comparable numbers the so-called anonymous coins with the Macedonian shield[5] and the coins with the horseman.[6] The

5 K. Liampi, "Zur Chronologie der sogenannten "anonymen" makedonischen Münzen des späten 4. Jhs. v. Chr.," *JNG* 36 (1986) 41-65.

6 M. J. Price, *The coinage in the name of Alexander the Great and Philip Arrhidaeus* (Zurich-London 1991).

bronzes with Heracles's weapons with the king's royal title or name occur in vast quantities:

Alexander III (336-323)

Macedonian shield/helmet

a) with thunderbolt	Liampi nos. 1 f.	233
b) with gorgoneion	ibid. nos. 170 f.	27
c) with head of Heracles	ibid. nos. 95 f.	12
d) with omphalos	ibid. nos. 160 f.	3
e) with caduceus	ibid. nos. 79 f.	1
head of Heracles/his weapons	Price nos. 266 f.	697
male head/horse	ibid. nos. 338 f.	396
head of Heracles/eagle with reverted head	ibid. nos.18, 27 f., 91	34
head of Apollo/thunderbolt	ibid. no. 19	2

(without identification of the type, from Callithera=5)

It is especially noteworthy that, apart from Macedonia, some types of the king's coins circulated in great numbers in Thessaly. These are issues a) with a Macedonian shield with thunderbolt as emblem, and b) with an eagle with head reverted.

With the reign of Cassander, the mass of coins entering Thessaly markedly increased. Of the various royal issues, the ones that circulated in Thessaly are those found in great numbers in Macedonia itself:

Cassander (315-297)

head of Heracles/lion seated	Gaebler pl. 32, 6	280
head of Apollo/tripod	ibid. pl. 32, 10	149
head of Heracles/lion running	ibid. pl. 32, 8	6
head of Heracles/horseman	ibid. pl. 32, 7	1142

(without identification of the type, from Callithera=10)

This marked accumulation of royal coins in Thessaly accompanies the king's commercial interests in the south, particularly in central Greece, and his interest in maintaining fortifications in Thessaly.

With Demetrius Poliorcetes a different picture emerges: far fewer of his coins circulated in Thessaly than did those of his predecessors. Moreover, only two of the many types of coins he issued made their way to Thessaly:[7]

Demetrius I (306-283)

Macedonian shield/helmet

a) with the monogram of king's name	Newell nos. 125 f.	536
b) with a star	ibid. nos. 181 f.	1
head of Athena/prow	ibid. nos. 162 f.	158

(without identification of the type, from Callithera=2)

Although Demetrius Poliorcetes established in Thessaly an important harbor for the Macedonians, simultaneously founding Demetrias as royal seat, his coins, while circulating in large enough numbers, are fewer than those of the preceding monarchs. This is related to the fact that his main efforts were devoted to southern Greece.

The Molossian king Pyrrhus, during his second short reign over Macedonia (274-272), used the Macedonian shield as a field for his emblem, an abbreviation of his name:

Pyrrhus (274-272)

Macedonian shield with monogram/helmet	Gaebler pl. nos. 33, 22-24	84

Considering the quantity issued and the brevity of his reign, the number of his coins taken to Thessaly is considerable.

---

7 E. T. Newell, *The coinage of Demetrios Poliorketes* (London 1927; repr. Chicago 1978).

Under Antigonus Gonatas there was an astonishing influx of coins into Thessaly (well demonstrated in Tables 1 and 2). Indeed, there are 4 times as many of his coins as those of Philip II and Alexander III, and they are found in greater numbers than any of the preceding coinages. All of his numismatic types are represented in Thessaly:

Antigonus Gonatas (276-239)		
Macedonian shield with monogram/helmet		
a) crested helmet	Gaebler pl. 34, 11	249
b) helmet with feathers	ibid. pl. 34, 12	6
head of Heracles/horseman	ibid. pl. 34, 8-10	646
head of Athena/Pan with *tropaion*	ibid. pl. 34, 4-7	3154
(without identification of the type, from Callithera=29)		

Some of the coins with horseman and Pan raising a *tropaion* are countermarked. Particularly in Thessaly it was surprising to discover that, on about half of the coins with heads of Athena and Pan, the helmet of Athena has various countermarks. The coins of this same type that are without countermarks are in fairly good condition, whereas those with countermarks are so badly worn that only the countermark can be detected.

The picture changes completely with the last two Macedonian kings, Philip V and Perseus. Although they minted plentifully, very little of their coinage reached Thessaly. The interpretation is simple enough. The unstable political situation, their disagreements with the Romans, and their confrontation with the alliance of southern Greeks and Antiochus III obliged them to reduce the number of garrisons in Thessaly, even though they appeared there often enough with their troops. Thus, only a limited number of their coins are found in that region.

All the coin types issued by Philip V are in evidence, though some are represented by only a few examples.

Philip V (222/21-179)		
Macedonian shield/helmet		
a) with head of Perseus	Gaebler pl. 35, 19-20	8
b) with omphalos	ibid. pl. 35, 21	3
c) with strovilos	ibid. pl. 35, 22	4
head of Zeus/Pan with *pedum*	ibid.. pl. 35, 1	2
head of Zeus/Athena Itonia	ibid. pl. 34, 22	111
head of Zeus/horseman	ibid. pl. 34, 21	2
head of Poseidon/prow	ibid. pl. 34, 24	40
head of Helios/thunderbolt	ibid. pl. 35, 5	11
head of Artemis/eagle	ibid. pl. 35, 3	2
head of Heracles/horseman	ibid. pl. 34, 25-26	45
head of Heracles/harpe	ibid. pl. 35, 6	10
head of Heracles/two goats	ibid. pl. 35, 2	11
head of Perseus/harpe	ibid. pl. 34, 29	23
head of Perseus/eagle	ibid. pl. 35, 4	5
head of Perseus/horse	ibid. pl. 35, 12	7
head of Perseus/harpe and club	ibid. pl. 34, 30	1
head of Pan/horseman	ibid. pl. 34, 27	5

Found in greater numbers is the series with an entirely Thessalian theme: a diptych of the head of Zeus and the Thessalian Athena Itonia, fully armed. The purpose of this bronze issue may well have been political, showing Philip V's desire for *rapprochement* with the Thessalians, relations with whom had deteriorated.

With Perseus, the number of Macedonian coins circulating in Thessaly was smaller still. Here too all the numismatic types the king produced during his brief reign are represented:

Perseus (179-168)		
Macedonian shield with strovilos/harpe	Gaebler pl. 36, 5	7

head of Perseus/eagle	ibid. pl. 36, 2-3	76
head of Heracles/horseman	ibid. pl. 36, 1	6

Almost all the coins of the Macedonian kings have seen considerable use and are much worn. Clearly they were in circulation for a long time.

In Thessaly bronze coins of the Macedonian kings turn up only occasionally in hoards, of Philip II, Cassander, Pyrrhus, and Antigonus Gonatas.[8] Instead, silver coins of these kings are found more frequently in the Thessalian hoards.[9] In contrast to this notable dearth under the first Macedonian kings, excepting the tetrobols of Perdiccas II,[10] the hoards contain a wealth of silver coins of Philip II and, especially, of Alexander III. Also represented is the silver coinage of Philip III, Demetrius Poliorcetes, Antigonus Gonatas, Antigonus Doson, Philip V, and finally Perseus.[11] Clearly, after Philip II the silver coinage of the Macedonian kings made its way continuously into Thessaly.

The continuous presence of Macedonian soldiers in the Thessalian garrisons at strategic points, as well as the frequent passage of the Macedonian army through Thessalian territory, fully explains the presence there of so many Macedonian bronze coins. There are also coins minted by other Greek cities, but these cannot compete numerically with the royal Macedonian coins. Indeed, no other foreign coinage is found in such great numbers; not even the bronzes of the Macedonian cities of the 2nd c. B.C. can compete. All indications are that the coins were used by Macedonian soldiers, and through their transactions entered the wider circulation of the Thessalian commercial market.

Xenophon and, more fully, Demosthenes and other authors provide important information about the economic situation of the soldiers. Both soldiers and sailors received a monthly salary and with this they also received provision money (σιτηρέσιον).[12] This money was given them apart from their salary to cover daily food expenses, so that their salary remained in its entirety (ἐντελής). This custom continued into Byzantine times, the allowance being known as σιτηρέσιον or οψώνιον.[13] There has been some discussion as to whether the actual amount of the σιτηρέσιον equaled that of the salary, but no ancient source tells us whether or not the σιτηρέσιον was given to the soldiers in the form of bronze coins.

Yet it is likely that when bronze coins replaced the smaller monetary subdivisions generally throughout the Greek world, the army did receive its σιτηρέσιον in the form of bronze coins. The discovery in Thessaly of such quantities of royal Macedonian bronzes, especially during periods of intense political dealings with the southern Greeks, is evidence that the Macedonian soldiers received their σιτηρέσιον in monetary form. We know from ancient sources that they bought their food supplies from local stores or from the commissary that accompanied the army during a campaign. As a matter of course the money then flowed into the Thessalian commercial market where it circulated together with Thessalian coinage.

National Hellenic Research Foundation, Research Centre for Greek and Roman Antiquity, Athens

8 *IGCH* 116, Thessaly (?) 1925: of Philip II and Cassander; 118, Karditsa 1955: of Cassander; 159, Phayttus 1956: of Antigonus Gonatas; 162, Karditsa 1930: of Philip II and Antigonus Gonatas.

9 M. Oeconomidou, "'Θησαυροί από το Νομισματικό Μουσείο. Μαρτυρία για την κυκλοφορία των μακεδονικών νομισμάτων," *Parnassos* 35 (1993) 541 f.

10 *CH* VIII, 76, Homolion 1993.

11 See *IGCH* and *CH* I-VIII under the names of the Macedonian kings.

12 H. Berve, *Das Alexanderreich auf prosopographischer Grundlage* (Munich 1926) 191 f.; O. Schulthess, s. v. σιτηρέσιον, in *RE* III.A.1 (1927) 382-88 (with the ancient sources); J. Kromayer and G. Veith, *Heerwesen und Kriegsführung der Griechen und Römer* (Munich 1928) 78, 111, 125 with n.4; G. T. Griffith, *The mercenaries of the Hellenistic world* (Cambridge 1935) 264-94; W. Kendrick Pritchett, *The Greek state at war I* (Berkeley 1971) 3-52.

13 *Oxford Dictionary of Byzantium* 3 (1991) 1529 s. v. *opsonion* (E. McGeer); J. Durliat, *De la ville antique à la ville byzantine. Le problème des subsistances* (Rome 1990) 191 f., 324 f., 441 f.

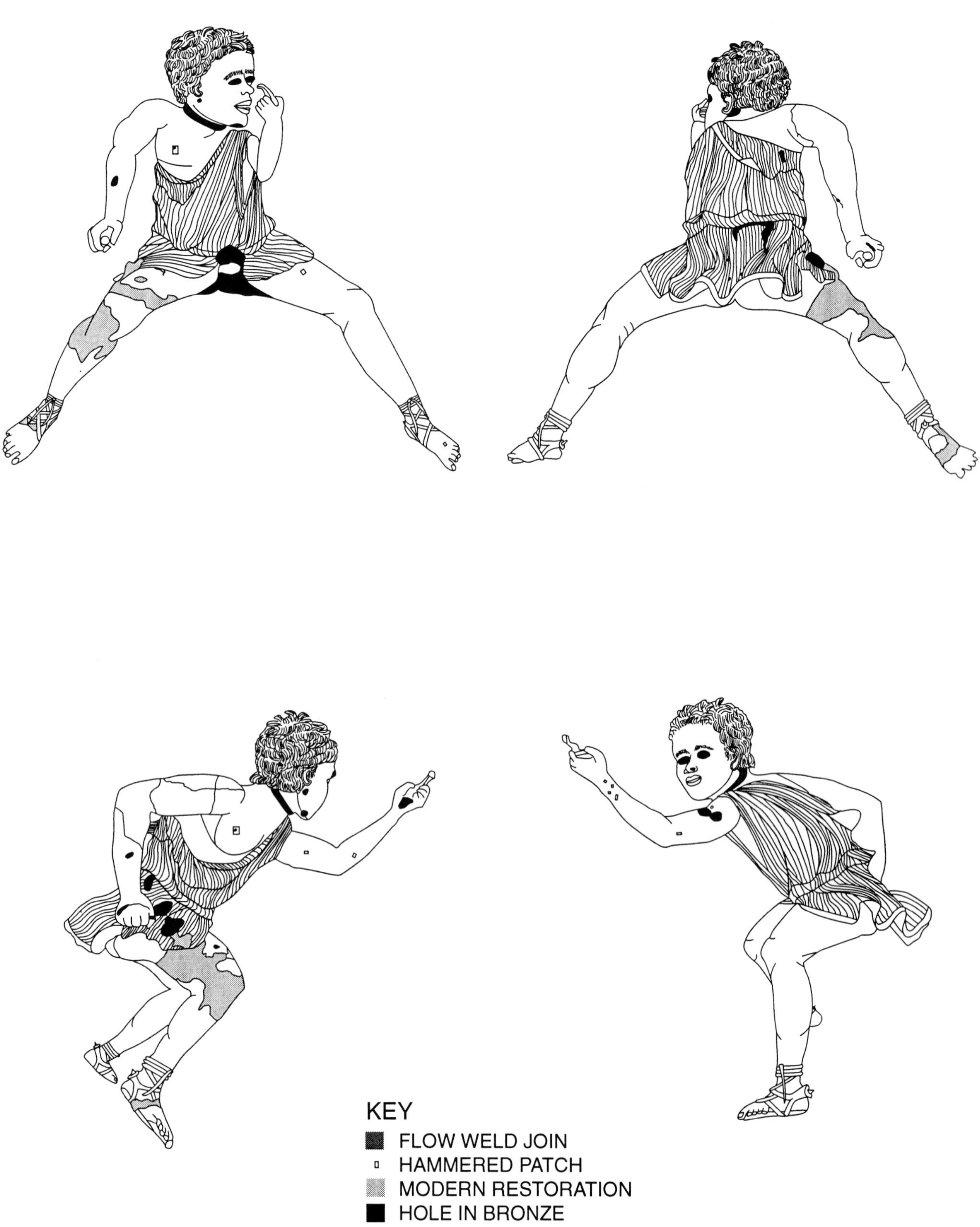

Fig. 1. Jockey from Artemision: front, back, and profile (1:10). (Drawing: author.)

A technical analysis of the bronze Horse and Jockey group from Artemision

Seán A. Hemingway

Introduction

In 1926 the arm of a large-scale bronze statue was discovered by fishermen at Cape Artemision just off the northwest coast of the island of Euboia. Two years later, the rest of this statue of a monumental striding god was pulled from the sea at the same location. After this remarkable discovery, an archaeological expedition was launched, under the direction of N. Bertos of the Greek Archaeological Service, to see what else from this apparent ancient shipwreck could be recovered. Bertos's brief investigation of the site yielded two more significant finds: the forepart of a large-scale bronze horse and a nearly complete jockey.[1] A short expedition in the spring of 1929 yielded the other foreleg of the horse and most of the right leg of the jockey.[2] These statues were the most significant to appear since the underwater excavation of the Antikythera shipwreck.[3]

All of the pieces were brought to the National Archaeological Museum in Athens for conservation and study. The Early Classical striding god, frequently referred to as the Artemision Zeus, and the Hellenistic boy jockey were put on display in the museum shortly after their discovery. Due to its more fragmentary state, the horse was kept in storage. Physical separation and an apparent discrepancy in scale and style between horse and jockey fueled the theory that the two statues might not belong together.[4] The fortuitous salvage of the horse's hindquarters in 1937 spurred a restoration project by the National Museum under the direction of Y. Panayotakis.[5]

In 1972 an extremely careful restoration was completed, utilizing a one-to-one plaster cast of the entire horse and an elaborate interior frame to stabilize and unite the fragments.[6] The plaster cast of the horse is restored in an elevated posture, as if jumping, reminding us that the pose of the bronze horse in the National Archaeological Museum in Athens is only one possible restoration.[7] Also in 1972, horse and jockey were reunited and placed on permanent display in the museum.[8] The horse and rider are among the few original large-scale Hellenistic bronze statues in existence today. Recent examination has revealed much about their technique of manufacture and consequently about the techniques employed to produce a large-scale equestrian sculptural group of the Hellenistic period.

Technical examination

In 1994, with the permission of the Greek Ephoria and the National Archaeological Museum in Athens, I undertook a systematic visual examination of the bronzes. This paper presents

---

1 N. Bertos, "Ἔκθεσις περὶ τῆς ἐξερευνήσεως τοῦ Βυθοῦ τῆς θαλλάσσης Ἀρτεμισίου," *Deltion* 10 (1926) 87-95.

2 H. Payne, "Archaeology in Greece, 1929-1930," *JHS* 50 (1930) 244.

3 On the 1st c. B.C. Antikythera shipwreck, which many consider to be the beginning of marine archaeology, see the excavation report in *Arch. Eph.* 1902, 146-71. See also P. Throckmorton, *Shipwrecks and archaeology: the unharvested sea* (Boston 1969) 113-68.

4 E. Buschor, *Die Plastik der Griechen* (Berlin 1936) 69.

5 P. Lemerle, "Chroniques des fouilles et découvertes archéologiques: musées et collections," *BCH* 60 (1936) 452, pl. 49.

6 V. Kallipolitis, "Ἀνασυγκρότησις τοῦ χαλκοῦ ἵππου τοῦ Ἀρτεμισίου," *AAA* 5 (1972) 419-26.

7 University of Athens Cast Gallery inv. no. 55. I am grateful to O. Palagia, Acting Curator, for showing me the cast in June 1995.

8 They share the same museum inventory number, Athens NM Br 15177.

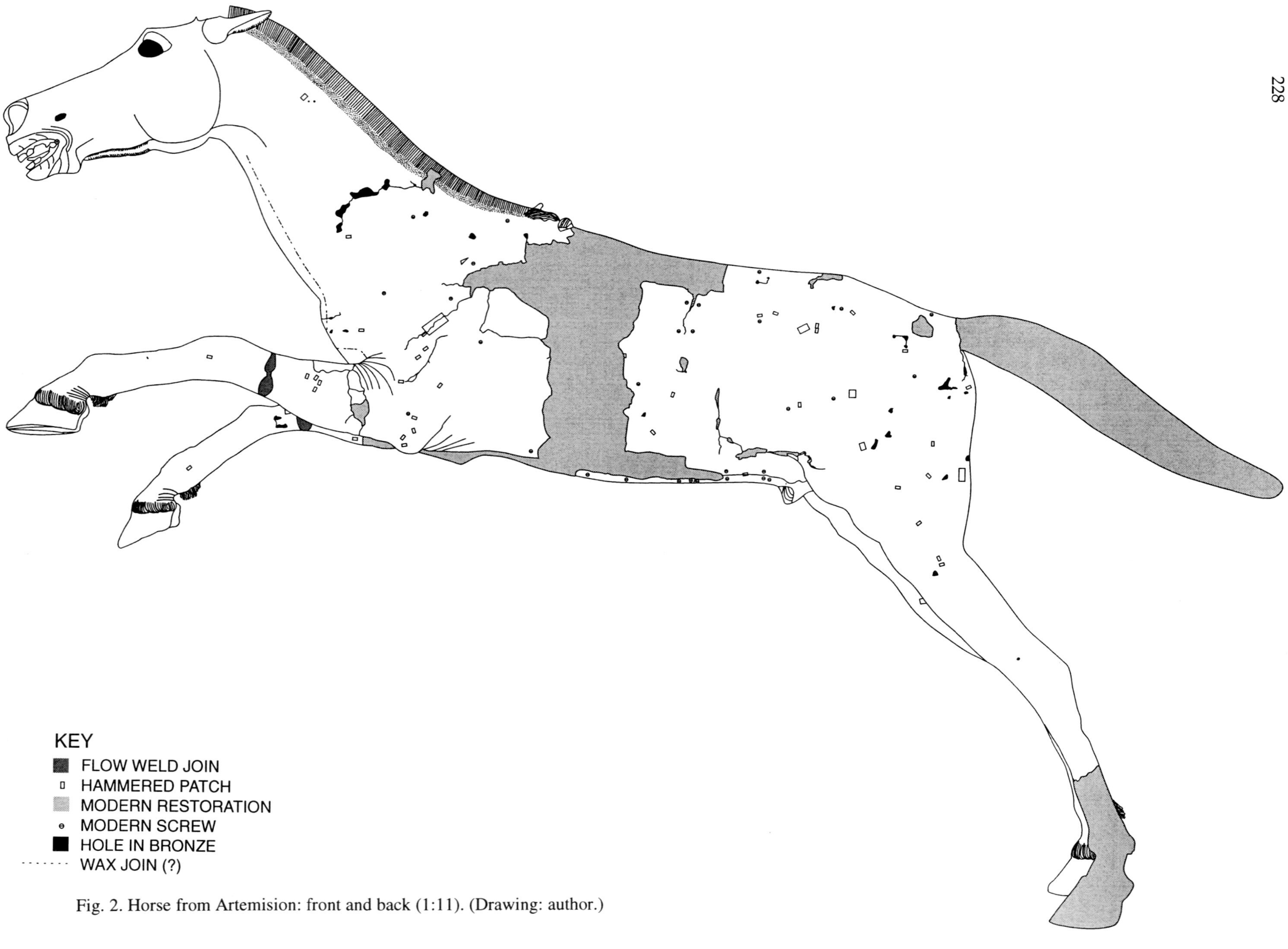

Fig. 2. Horse from Artemision: front and back (1:11). (Drawing: author.)

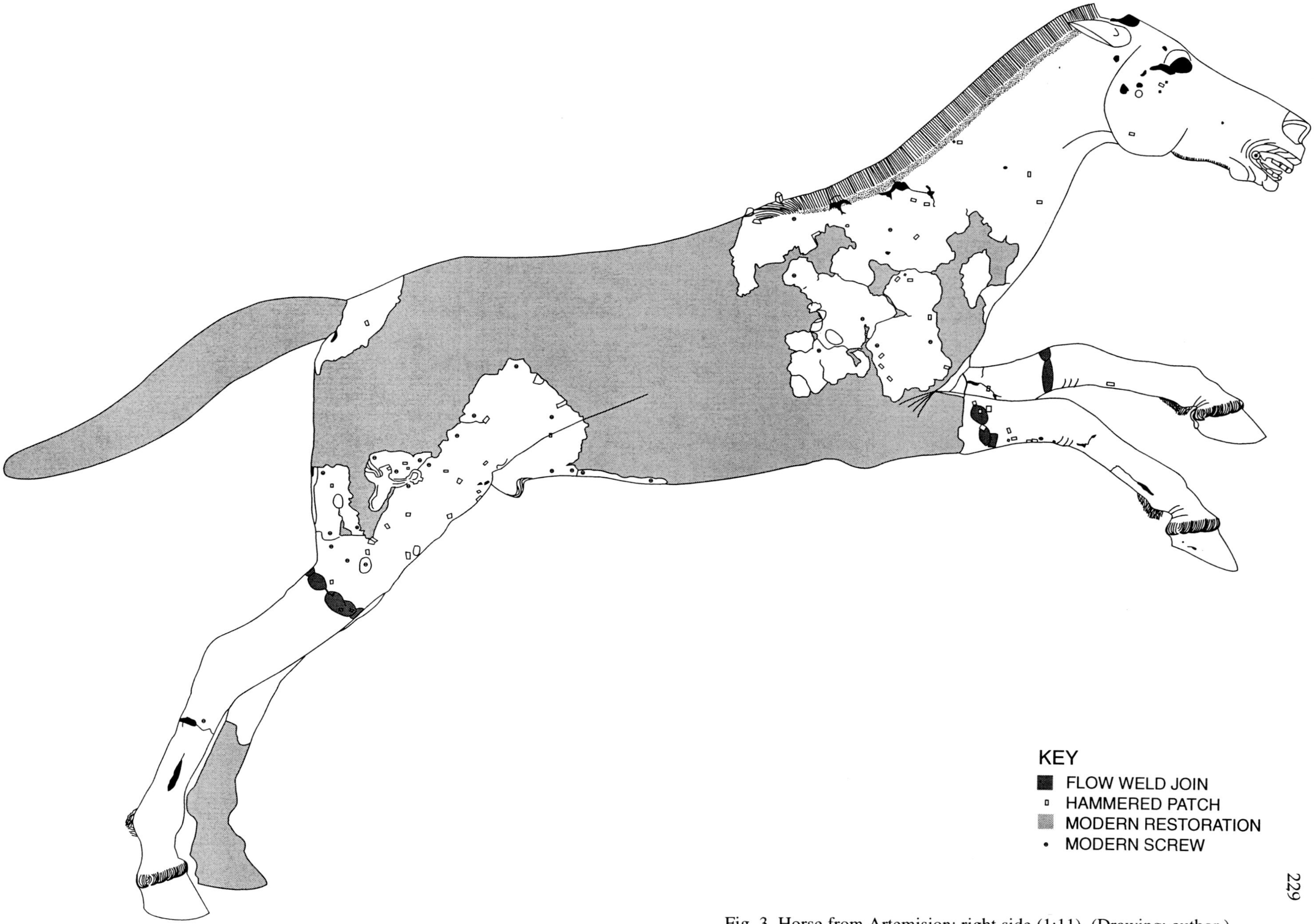

Fig. 3. Horse from Artemision: right side (1:11). (Drawing: author.)

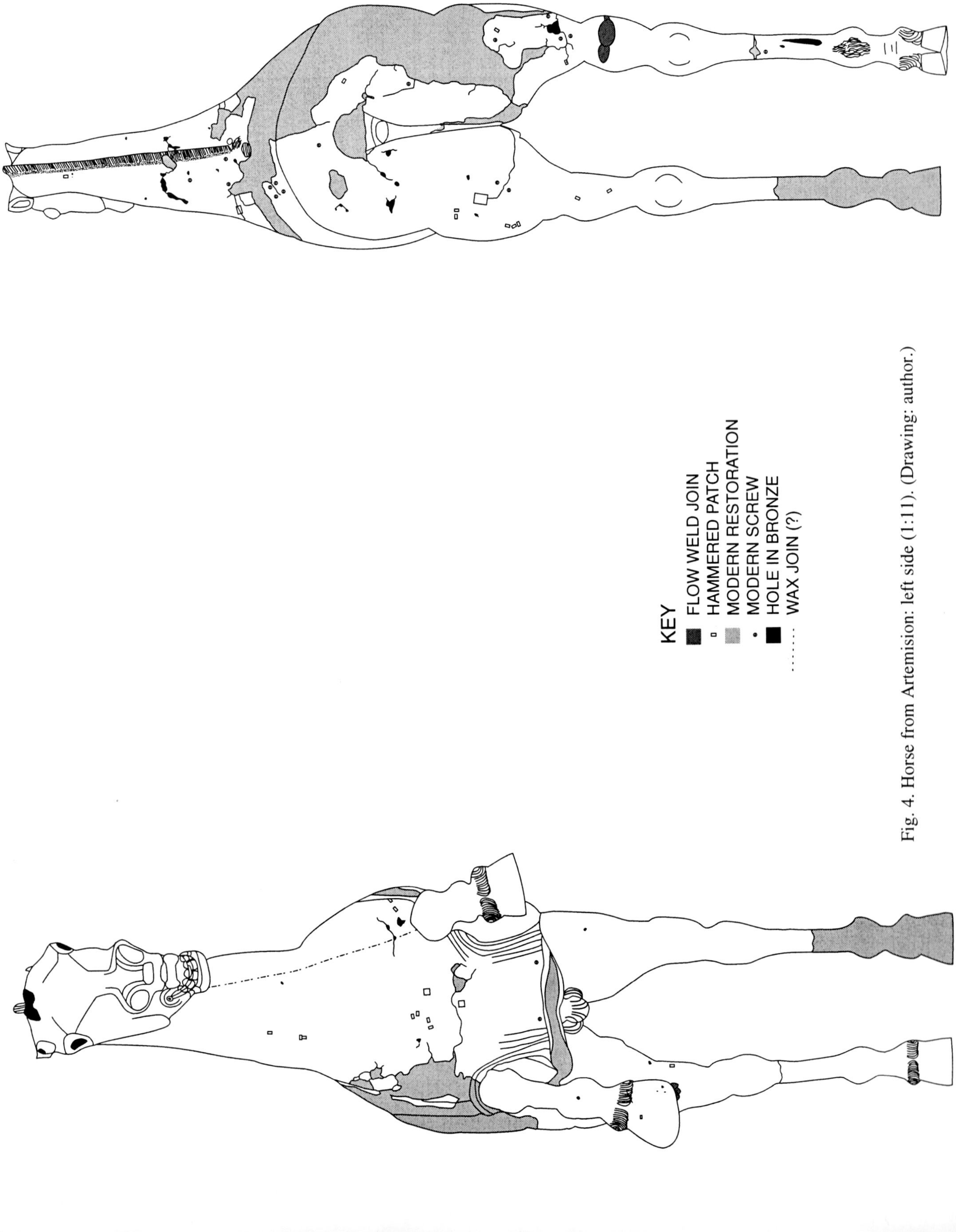

Fig. 4. Horse from Artemision: left side (1:11). (Drawing: author.)

observations from my investigation of these statues that document their state of preservation and yield new information about their technique of manufacture. The text is supplemented by a series of detailed technical illustrations that indicate prominent features visible on the surface of the bronzes.[9] Drawings of the left, right, front, and back views of both jockey (fig. 1) and horse (figs. 2-4) distinguish between preserved fragments and restored sections, and identify metallurgical joins and hammered patches.

The jockey

The statue is nearly intact except for the upper right thigh and the lower edges of the garment (see fig. 1). A deep brown with a greenish tinge in places characterizes the color of the bronze. The roughened and mottled state of the surface, an unfortunate result of corrosion products that were removed when the statue was first conserved, gives little indication of the original patina.

Although the statue was hollow cast, the completeness of the figure makes it difficult to examine the interior. However, holes in the head, chest, left hand, regions of the thighs, and back of the tunic do allow the thickness to be measured. It is between 3 and 5 mm, a relatively uniform and thin casting.[10] Certain features, such as the ears, nose, feet, and hands, are probably thicker. This is especially noticeable at the break through the right thumb that reveals a solid bronze interior. In the few places where it is visible, the interior surface closely follows the outer contours of the figure. This feature, as well as the thin casting, strongly suggests that the statue was made using the indirect lost wax process.

It is difficult to determine the location of joins between the separately cast pieces by examining only the exterior surface. Given the statue's relatively small size, there may have been very few joins. Two lines are clearly visible at the point where the head joins the neck (see fig. 1) and most likely indicate a flow weld. The construction of this join (or joins) could be better understood by examining the interior of the statue.[11] Certainly, the neck is a logical place for a join since it allows the head to be cast separately. At the back of the head, the hair overlays the neck and at certain points is not even attached. It is possible that the arms and legs of the jockey were cast separately and joined inconspicuously where they meet the drapery. However, there are no signs of this on the exterior surface of the bronze.[12] The underside of the jockey's buttocks and crotch, which are overshadowed by his garment but left open underneath, clearly indicate that he was made to fit onto another sculpture.[13]

Hammered patches used to cover chaplet holes and imperfections in the original casting of the statue are evident. There are considerably fewer patches on the jockey than on the horse, although the general characteristics of the patches are the same. These patches, a typical feature of large-scale classical bronzes, tend to be rectangular and small, with the greatest

---

9 Due to the careful attempts of the restorers not to draw attention to their work, it is often very difficult to distinguish from photographs exactly what is original and what is restored. Accurate drawings of all the fragments of the horse were achieved by close visual examination and through the assistance of a series of photographs in the archives of the German Archaeological Institute in Athens, which show the horse post-conservation and pre-restoration.

10 Haynes, *Technique* 68 also gives a thickness of 3 mm for the jockey, although he does not specify where he took his measurements.

11 These features could delineate a ring of bronze used to attach the head to the neck as in the life-size, Classical bronze statue of a veiled woman in the Izmir Museum of Archaeology, inv. no. 3544. See B. Ridgway, "The lady from the sea: a Greek bronze in Turkey," *AJA* 71 (1967) 329-34, and Mattusch, *Classical bronzes* 11-12, fig. 1.10.

12 In any event, the arms and legs are places where the wax model was likely to have been pieced together. Evidence for such wax joins might also be visible on the interior of the bronze.

13 The practice of not rendering sections of a sculpture not meant to be seen occurs in other Hellenistic bronzes: see, for example, the Sleeping Eros in the Metropolitan Museum of Art, New York, inv. no. 43.11.4.

concentration visible on the jockey's arm (fig. 1).[14] The largest patch is on the jockey's left breast.

A number of features were added separately after the main parts were cast and joined. The hollow eyes originally held life-like irises and pupils of stone or glass, encapsulated in bronze eyelashes.[15] Narrow shelves visible inside the eyelids supported the inlaid eyes once they were in place and provided a place for the fixative that secured them. The teeth, which may have been added in another material, are not preserved.[16] The lips do not appear to be cast separately, and the one visible nipple was cast together with the body. The jockey firmly grasps the remains of a bronze rod that was cast separately and then inserted into his right hand. This must have been the connector for a crop or whip. Fragments of two reins adhere to the palm of the left hand and may have been cast together with the arm. Much of the reins, however, are likely to have been cast separately and then joined. In its present state of preservation, it is difficult to assess how much cold working was done to the statue. It is conceivable that it involved portions of the hair and eyebrows, given the careful cold working that is detectable on the horse.

The horse

The greatest areas of restoration on the horse are the lower left hind leg, mid-section of the body, and tail (figs. 2-4). Brass screws used to attach the horse to its modern interior framework are identified in the illustrations. The surface of the front half of the horse is better preserved than the back half. Its rich brown color on the front may be very close to its original state, unlike the mottled dark brown and green on the back. The left front hoof is almost black.[17] The two halves do not join, but they are of the same style, scale, and technique.

Like the jockey, the horse is hollow cast. Open holes in the top of its head, eyes, right cheek, left side of muzzle, upper left neck, lower right neck, left hind buttock, and along the cannon bone of its right hind leg allow the thickness of the bronze to be measured. It is between 2 and 5 mm, a relatively thin and uniform casting of a similar thickness to the jockey.[18] Features such as the eye sockets, ears, teeth, tongue, and the bases of the hind legs, which were important areas of support for the statue, are thicker. Where it is possible to see the interior surface, it closely follows the exterior contours. It seems clear that this statue was also made using the indirect lost wax process. In the original report of the 1928 expedition, Bertos mentions that he found parts of the clay core inside the forepart of the horse while he was undertaking the initial cleaning of the statue.[19]

---

14 For an illustration of how these patches were executed, see Bol, *Bronzetechnik* 140, fig. 93A-B.

15 Compare, for examples of anthropomorphic inlaid eyes, a pair of eyes in Metropolitan Museum of Art in New York, inv. no. 1991.11.3ab, and an eye in the J. Paul Getty Museum in Malibu, inv. no. 84.AI.625. For eyes *in situ* on a Hellenistic bronze, see the portrait head of a man from Delos, in the National Archaeological Museum Athens, inv. no. 14.612. See also the discussion in Haynes, *Technique* 106-8. For an animal eye of similar design from Pergamon, see F. Winter, *Die Skulpturen mit Ausnahme der Altarreliefs* (Berlin 1908) 368, no. 466, fig. 466.

16 Teeth were often added in silver: see Mattusch, *Classical bronzes* 25.

17 In an early article on the conservation of Greek bronzes, C. Zenghelis, a chemist at the University of Athens and the conservator of the Horse and Jockey group from Artemision, analyzed samples from a hoof of the horse to determine if an artificial patina had been applied in antiquity to give it its deep black color. Based on the results of his analyses, he believed that the hooves had been subjected to fire in the presence of hydrosulphuric vapors, giving them their rich black color. See C. Zenghelis, "Bronzes antiques (Contribution à l'étude des)," *Mouseion* 3 (1929) 113-27, esp. 123. For more recent research on patination of ancient bronzes, see H. Born, "Patinated and painted bronzes: exotic technique or ancient tradition?" in *Small bronze sculpture* 179-96.

18 G. Dontas, "'Ο χάλκινος 'Απόλλων τοῦ Πειραῖα," in H. Kyrieleis (ed.), *Archaische und klassische Plastik* I (Mainz 1986) 183, n.6 lists the thickness of the horse as 2 mm.

19 Bertos 1926 (supra n.1) 91.

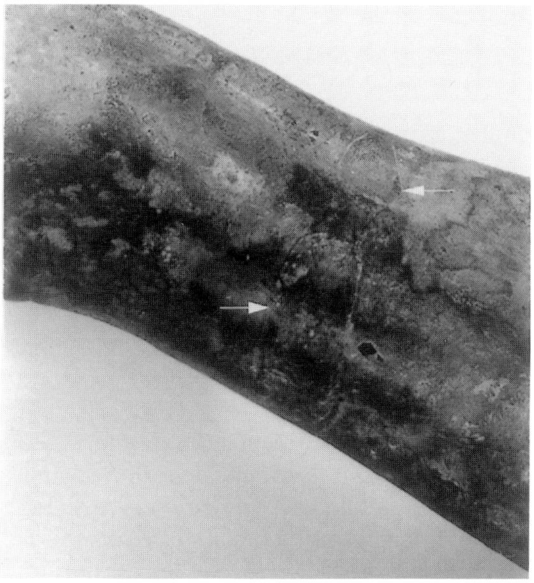

Fig. 5. Detail of outer left foreleg of Horse from Artemision; arrows point to flow weld. (Photo: author.)

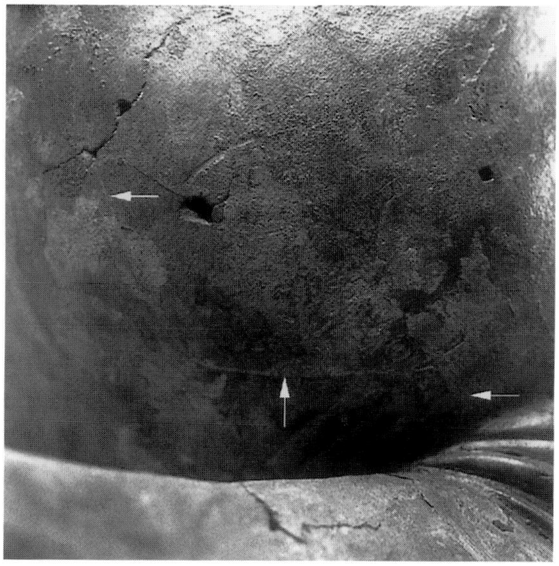

Fig. 6. Detail of left shoulder of Horse from Artemision; arrows point to line of join (?). (Photo: author.)

Some indications of metal-to-metal joins are visible on the exterior surface of the bronze. Most noticeable are the series of oval shapes on the forearms and right hind leg of the horse (figs. 2-5).[20] They represent a series of flow welds used to join at least three of the legs to the body. The process involved pouring molten bronze onto the two separately cast pieces at the point of juncture. The degree of metallurgical fusion, and hence the strength of the bond between the pieces, depended on the heat achieved. The actual line of the join has been obscured by these ovals, implying a high degree of metallurgical fusion. Further testimony to the strength of the joins is the fact that both front legs broke at places other than the joins. X-radiography and endoscopic examination of the interior of the left hind leg might reveal a join that is not visible on the exterior surface. Close examination of the horse's mouth indicates that the teeth, palate, and tongue were cast as a separate piece and then attached to the lips. A narrow sleeve on the edge of the scrotum is visible through a hole in the bronze. It suggests that the scrotum and perhaps the penis were cast separately and then attached.

Other markings on the exterior are more enigmatic and open to a number of interpretations. The most noticeable of these is a thin line along the horse's lower left shoulder (fig. 6). It becomes visible at the folds of skin on the left foreleg and continues in a straight line just above the foreleg where it makes a nearly 45° jog, to become horizontal. After several centimeters, this line, which is now primarily distinguished by its much lighter color, continues up the front of the neck. It is possible that this feature is the trace of a join in the wax model.[21] Examination of the interior of the bronze would quickly establish the accuracy of this identification.

Numerous small rectangular hammered patches, used to cover imperfections in the surface of the bronze, are clearly identifiable on the surface of the bronze (figs. 2-4). The thinness of the body of the horse, *c.*2 mm, may account for the greater number of patches in this area. Larger patches are noticeable on the horse's left side. One unusually large patch on the left shoulder, of which only the outline remains, was used to cover a long crack in the bronze.

A variety of other finishing touches were added to the horse. Its eyes, no longer preserved, would have been inset in the same fashion as the jockey's. An inlaid brand of a winged Nike

---

20 It is very likely that these are the joins that A. Steinberg refers to as spot welds in "Joining methods on large bronzes: some experiments," in W. J. Young (ed.), *Application of science in examination of works of art* (Boston 1973) 103-38. The statues are identified incorrectly as the Horse and Jockey from Antikythera, but it is clear that he is referring to the Horse and Jockey from Artemision.

21 It is also possible that it is a join, a later repair, or some feature not directly related to the manufacturing process. Further technical examination will surely help to determine its significance.

bearing a wreath, probably in silver or gold, originally adorned its lower right thigh.[22] The use of inlaid detail to heighten the realism of sculpture can be seen on other Hellenistic bronzes, such as the Terme Boxer.[23] An elaborate bridle, fashioned separately and attached to the horse, can be reconstructed from wear marks on the bronze. The cannon of the bit is still preserved in the mouth, and a lead(?) pin under the chin was used to secure the nose band in place.[24] Cold working is evident on the underside of the horse's cheek, where individual hairs are carefully incised, on the mane, and on the fetlocks of the hooves.

Conclusions

Close observation of the exterior surfaces of the Cape Artemision Horse and Jockey reveals much about the method of manufacture. Metallurgical joins visible on the exterior surfaces confirm that both statues were piece-cast, a technique widely used by Greek bronzeworkers to cast large-scale statuary. Some features of the exterior surface are subject to a number of interpretations, none of which can be confirmed until the interior surface is examined and scientific analyses are performed. The statues exhibit great attention to detail, evident in the careful modeling of the figures, fine cold-working preserved on the horse, and the additional features made from other materials. The inset eyes, inlaid brand, bridle, and whip are all identifiable, but now lost. Such workmanship is characteristic of the finest bronzes of the Hellenistic period.

Department of Greek and Roman Art, The Metropolitan Museum of Art, New York 10028

Acknowledgements

I would like to thank O. Tzachou-Alexandri of the National Archaeological Museum in Athens for permission to study and photograph the Horse and Jockey Group from Artemision, and I gratefully acknowledge the assistance of the late A. Onasoglou and the staff at the museum during my many visits in 1994 and 1995. The staff and facilities at the American School of Classical Studies were all very helpful during my two years spent there in 1994 and 1995. I especially thank A. Brauer, C. S. Czapski, H. Lie, C. C. Mattusch, D. G. Mitten, and B. S. Ridgway for their assistance with various aspects of the research and editing. The opinions expressed in this paper, of course, remain my own. This work was part of my dissertation research for the Department of Classical and Near Eastern Archaeology at Bryn Mawr College.

---

22 See Kallipolitis 1972 (supra n.6) 426, fig. 6.

23 Rome, Museo Nazionale Romano, inv. no. 1055. See N. Himmelmann, *Herrscher und Athlete: Die Bronzen vom Quirinal* (Milan 1989) 170-71.

24 For a detailed discussion of the evidence for the bridle, see S. Hemingway, "A bridle for the bronze horse from Artemision," in K. J. Hartswick and M. C. Sturgeon (edd.), *STEFANOS: studies in honor of Brunilde S. Ridgway* (Philadelphia 1998) 115-18.

Conservation in 1994 of the so-called Agon, the life-size bronze statue from Mahdia

Frank Willer

The Mahdia shipwreck, discovered in 1907, is the most spectacular shipwreck known from antiquity, comparable only with that of Antikythera discovered a few years later.[1] Among the objects discovered in the wreck, the life-size statues of a nude winged youth and a bronze herm inscribed with the name of the sculptor Boethos of Chalcedon were the most sensational.[2] During conservation at Bonn, interpretation of the youth and the herm underwent some changes. Examination revealed that neither the youth nor the herm showed any traces of having been united as a group (fig. 1), as had long been thought.[3] Both had come aboard the ship as 'antiques', as both still contain the lead that had been used to fasten them to their marble bases. Lead isotope analyses proved that lead of different origins had been used,[4] additional evidence that the two statues were not mounted at the same time or in the same place.

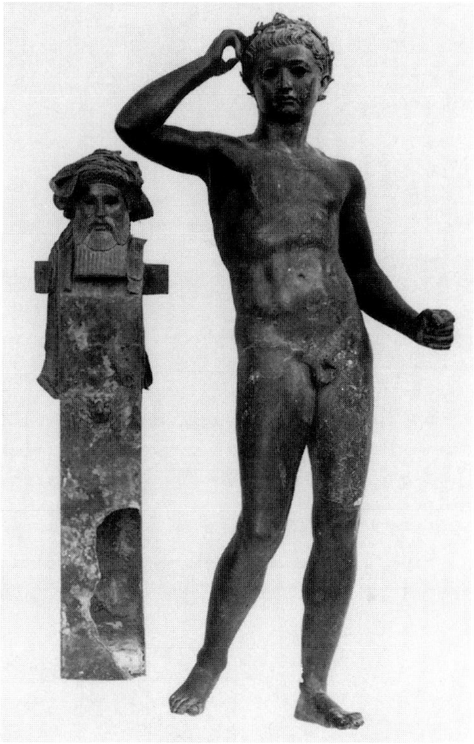

Fig. 1. Herm and Eros. Bronze, H (herm) 1.03 m; H (Eros) 1.37 m. Tunis, Bardo Museum, inv. no. F 107 (herm) and F 106 (Eros). (Photo: H. Lilienthal; Rheinisches Landesmuseum Bonn.)

The statue of the youth (fig. 1), 1.37 m in height and about 72 kg in weight (without the modern fill), can be dated by style to the last quarter of the 2nd c. B.C.[5] The youth wears a wreath, which he has just placed on his head with his raised hand. In combination with the herm, the wreath suggested an interpretation of the youth as Agon, the personification of contest. New archaeological and scientific analyses suggest that the youth is Eros.[6] The remains of an attribute in the youth's left hand are clearly to be interpreted as a bow and arrow, not a palm branch as was favored by the Agon interpretation.[7]

Different methods were used to reconstruct the ancient casting process as well as to investigate the inside of the statue for features, e.g., the inner construction made for its support àt the time of the first conservation in the early 20th c. Endoscopy, radiography, and computer tomography revealed that early in this century the fragments of the youth were fixed by iron rods and by a cement filling reaching up to the waist. These examinations also showed that in some areas the bronze was extremely corroded and a number of fragments had been lost, such as the complete upper part of the engaged leg. Most of these parts were then reconstructed with cement and plaster, painted green to

---

1 A full bibliography of the ship is given in *Das Wrack* 1107-17.

2 For Agon, see M. Söldner, "Der sogenannte Agon" in *Das Wrack* 399-429. For the herm, see C. C. Mattusch, "Bronze herm of Dionysos" ibid. 431-50.

3 Söldner ibid.

4 F. Begemann and S. Schmitt-Strecker, "Das Blei von Schiff und Ladung: Seine Isotopie und mögliche Herkunft" ibid. 1073-76.

5 Söldner ibid. 417.

6 Ibid. 399 ff.

7 F. Willer, "Die Restaurierung des 'Agon'," ibid. 971-84.

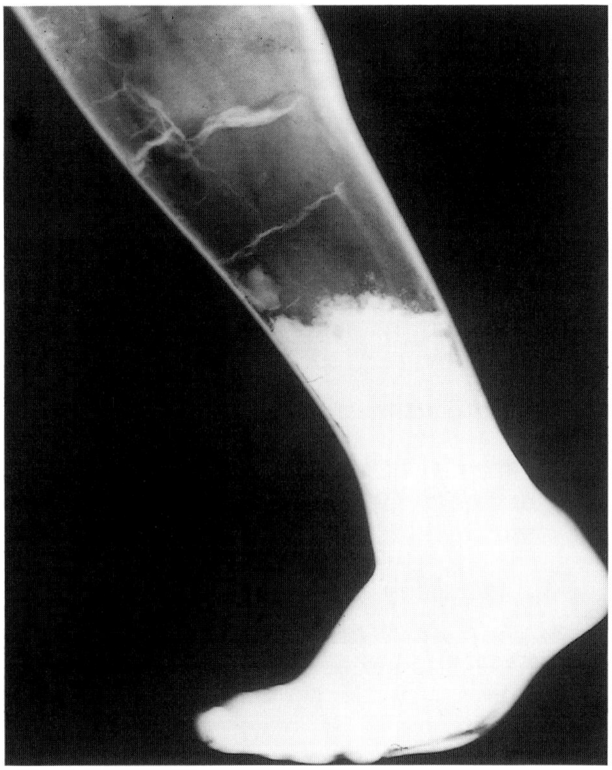

Fig. 2. Radiograph showing the lead filling the right leg. (Photo: author.)

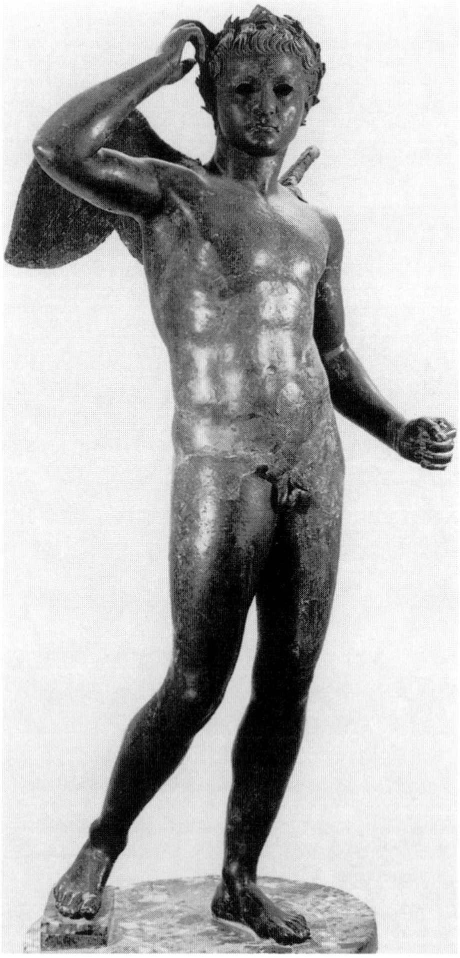

Fig. 3. Eros, as previously reconstructed with a wedge under the right foot. (Photo: Deutsches Archäologisches Institut, Rome.)

look like bronze.

Because Agon and herm were interpreted as a group, about 3 cm of plaster was added to a missing part of the thigh to set the free leg onto the reconstructed base of the herm without unbalancing the figure.[8]

The level of the ancient lead poured into both legs to mount the statue to its stone base was an important clue in establishing the youth's original posture (fig. 2).[9] The level of the upper surface of the lead has to have been parallel to the surface level of the ancient base, because the soles of the feet are parallel to the cast lead surface. In the early 20th c. reconstruction they were not parallel. So it was certain that the posture had to be modified. The reconstructed, engaged left thigh was too long, consequently the free leg was later supported by a wedge-shaped base (fig. 3) when the two figures were separated.

The ancient bronzecaster had to balance the statue to compensate for the 13.2-kg wings. He used the attributes (reconstructed as bow and arrow) in the statue's outstretched left hand. In addition, x-ray photos show a lead filling in the same hand.

As a result of examination, I decided to develop a new interior support system of high-grade steel, V2A (fig. 4). The fragile condition of the bronze made it necessary to experiment with the

8 Söldner ibid. 399 ff.

9 F. Willer, "Beobachtungen zur Sockelung von bronzenen Statuen und Statuetten," in "Neue Forschungen zum Schiffsfund von Mahdia," *BJb* 196 (1996) 337 ff.

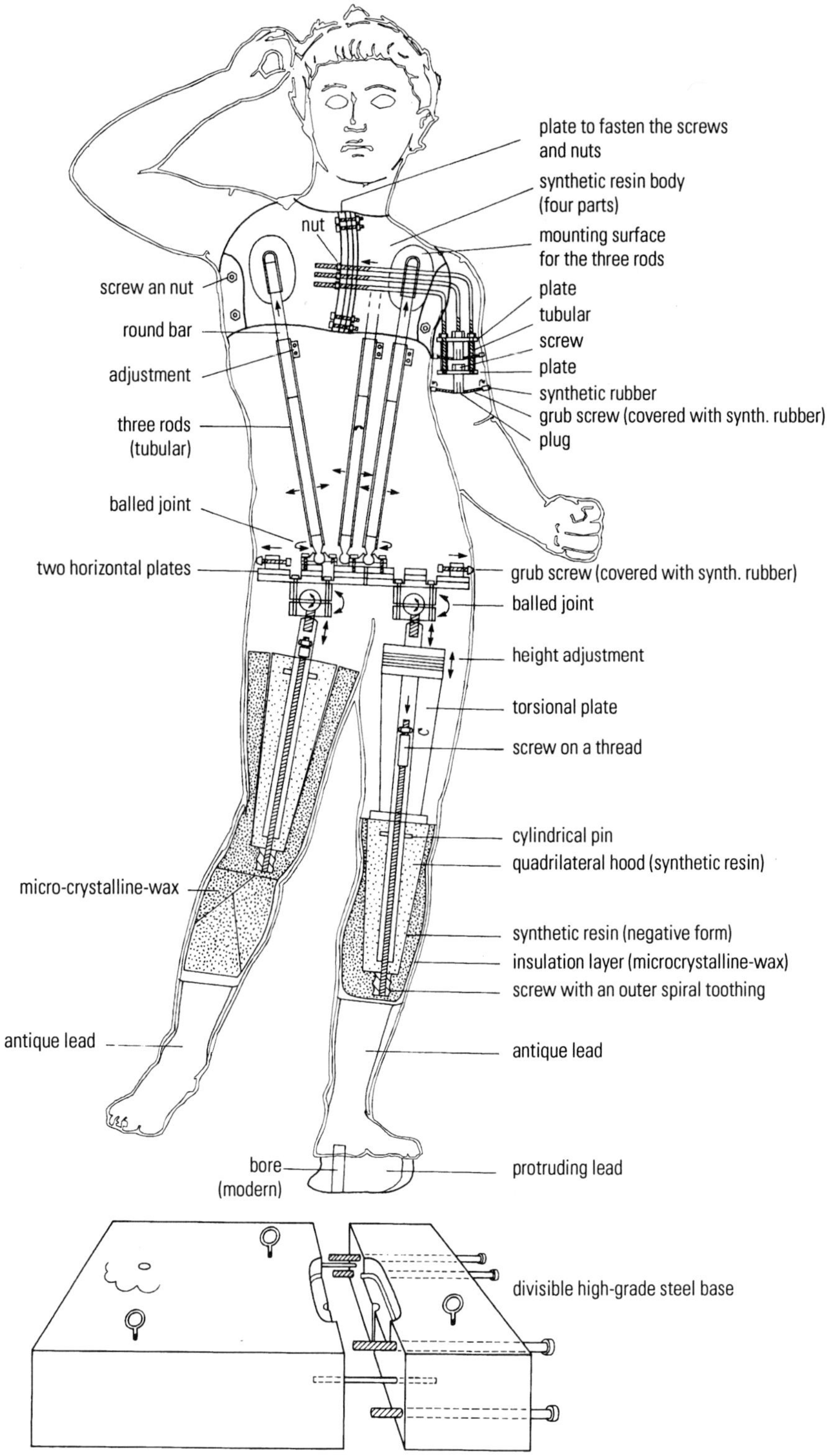

Fig. 4. Drawing of the new support system for the Eros. (Drawing: author.)

correct position of the statue by using casts of the original parts. These casts were assembled in a box frame developed for this special task. An adjustable system held the torso and allowed the reconstruction of the original position. The right leg was adjusted to the body in order to join the extant original parts. Then the other leg was added. The missing parts were molded with clay. Long, adjustable screws helped to fix the position of the statue. This system made it possible to avoid optical mistakes. It also helped in reconstructing the original appearance of the statue without any danger to the original parts. In contrast to the first reconstruction, the body

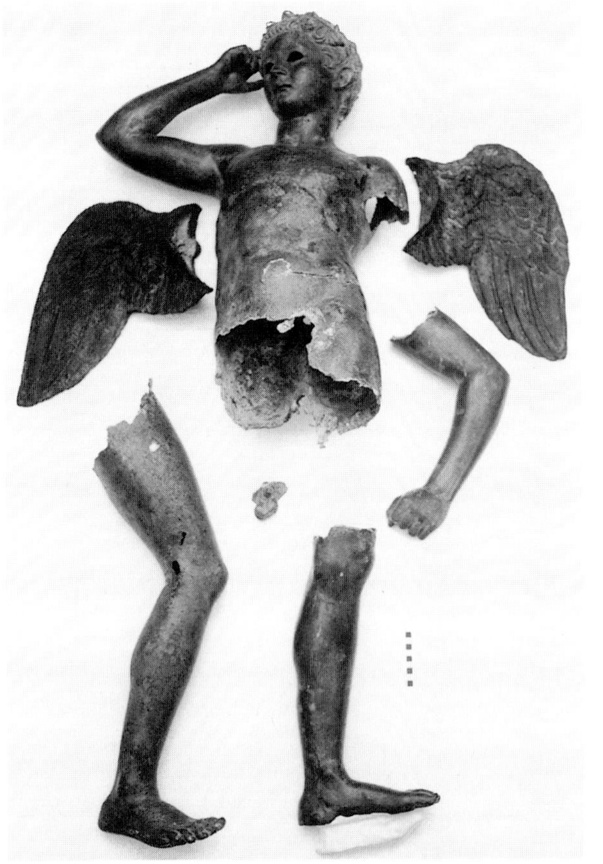

Fig. 5. The Eros disassembled during conservation. (Photo: author.)

of the statue is now balanced more forward, with the center of gravity of the statue shifted from the wings to the middle of the figure. I calculated that the mounting system could be used without exterior support.

A micro-pneumatic chisel was used to remove the cement and the iron rods used for the statue's first conservation (fig. 5). This tool is best known for its usefulness in uncovering fossils.

The new mounting system — consisting of 58 steel elements together weighing 18.5 kg — was manufactured and mounted with the addition of epoxy resin (Araldit XW 396/H397). Ball joints allowed the legs to be moved into their correct positions. The joints hold two horizontal plates, the mounting surface for three rods fastened to a synthetic resin body consisting of four different parts. This design supports the torso in the shoulder area. The complete system can be moved or removed at any time.

Then all original fragments were assembled in the box frame (fig. 6). Its adjustable features helped to obtain the same position as with the copies. Two ancient crack lines between the right leg and the torso helped to locate their original positions. At this time the mounting platform of the box frame had to be horizontally adjusted to ensure that the inner lead fill surface was parallel to the mounting platform, just as it was parallel to the base in ancient times.

The lead poured into the legs in order to set up the statue protrudes from the bottom of the left foot. Before it was set into a separable high-grade steel base weighing 114 kg, it had to be insulated with silicon and a layer of epoxy resin (Araldit XW 396/H 397). Here the center of gravity of the statue is physically displaced toward the base, thus ensuring that the figure stands securely.

The missing parts of the statue were reconstructed in epoxy resin (Araldit XW 396/H 397) and fixed with magnetic clips so that they could be removed at any time. They were painted with oil paint, so that they could be recognized as reconstructions (fig. 7).

The statue was cast by the indirect lost-wax process.[10] This means that it was cast with the help of a detailed wax working model made from two main piece molds taken from the original model. In most areas the foundry used wax sheets that were between 2 and 4 mm thick. Only some parts that needed static support were up to 8 mm thick, such as the upper legs. The wax sheets were laid into the negative form and pressed into it firmly. Areas with curves or bends had to be made in several sections. They were simply jointed together by using a hot spatula. This can be seen in the shoulder, back, legs, and arms (figs. 8-9). Only the head seems to have been made by pouring liquid wax inside it, probably with the help of a brush, for instance to obtain all the details of the hair. Then the sections were taken out of the negative forms and jointed together with a spatula, but this time from the outside. The inside does not seem to have been important in this case, so we can see the join lines there. The left and right sides

10 C. C. Mattusch in E. Formigli (ed.), *I grandi bronzi antichi* (Siena 1999) 75 ff.

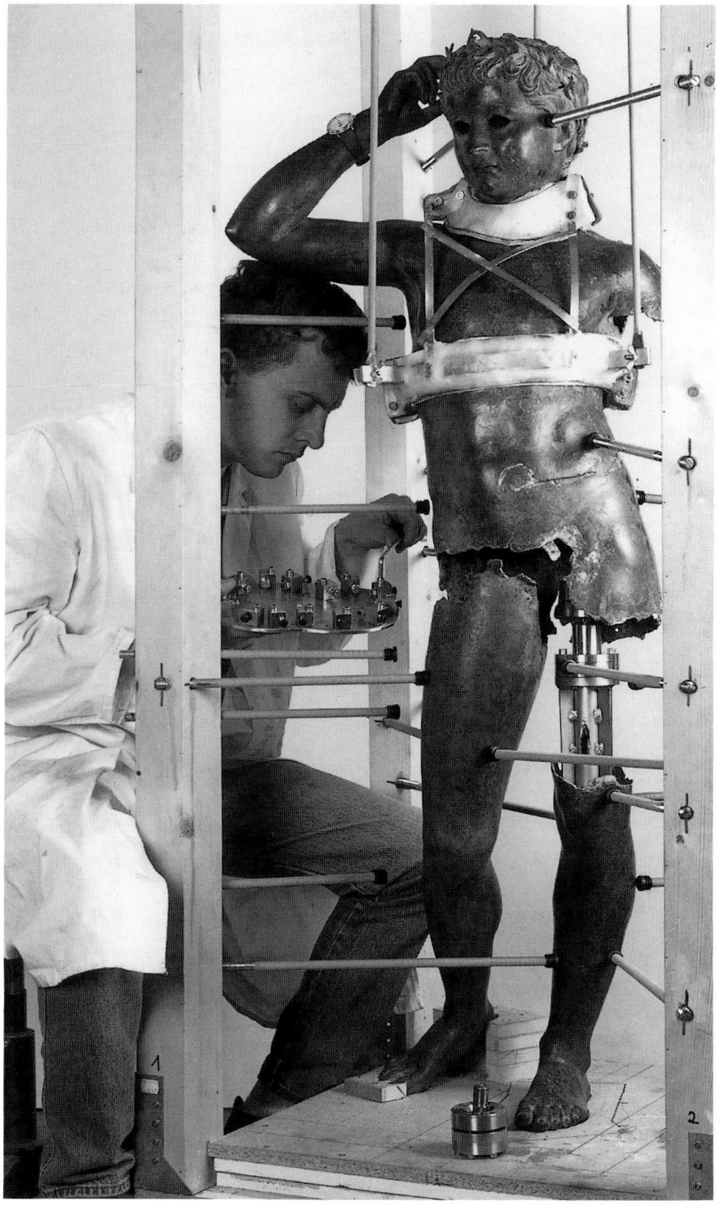

Fig. 6. The Eros reassembled in the box frame during conservation. (Photo: T. Schläger, Köln.)

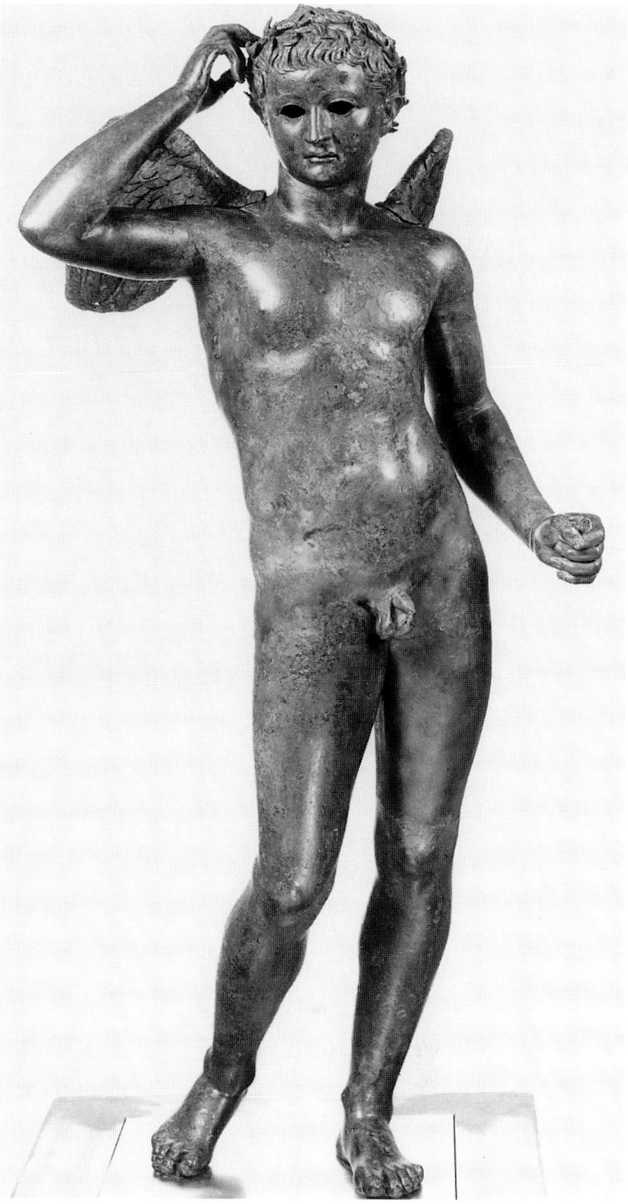

Fig. 7. The Eros as conserved. (Photo: G. Detloff; Forschungsarchiv für Römische Plastik, Köln.)

where the front and the back parts of the torso were joined were overlaid on the inside with a hot, soft wax rod. The rod was pressed in place firmly by fingers. The marks of the fingertips can be seen on the inside of the bronze (fig. 10). The use of wax sheets provided control over the wall thickness, and sheets could be removed more easily from the negative forms than would be the case when working with liquid wax. This procedure was also used for the Mahdia herm.[11]

The wax model consisted of 15 parts (torso, head, wings, the two arms, both legs and the left foot [fig. 1 left]). After being cast, the parts were soldered with a copper alloy (fig. 11 right).[12] The wings and attributes were cast separately and also soldered, but with a soft lead alloy solder. Each wing weighs 6.6 kg. The bronze used to cast the statue has a remarkably high lead and tin content. This alloy probably ensured the safe casting of large, thin forms.[13]

Rheinisches Landesmuseum Bonn

11 F. Willer, "Zur Herstellungstechnik der Herme" in *Das Wrack* 959-70.

12 E. Formigli in *Atti XII Convegno Studi Etruschi e Italiani* (Siena 1979); Mattusch, *Classical bronzes* 170 ff.

13 E. Pernicka and G. Eggert, "Die Zusammensetzung der Bronzeobjekte von Mahdia" in *Das Wrack* 1047-61.

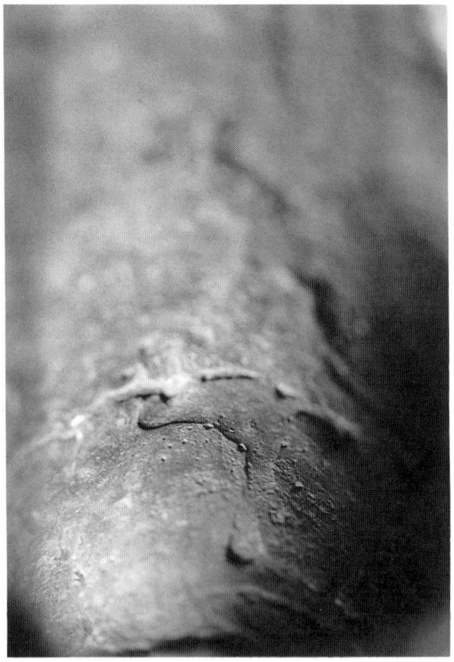

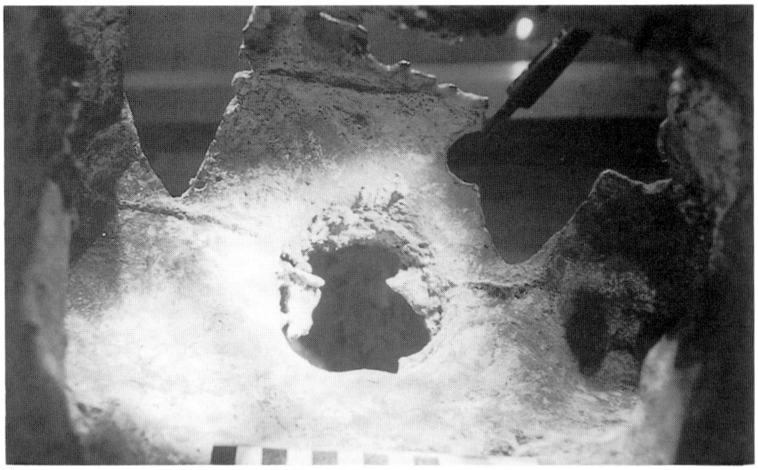

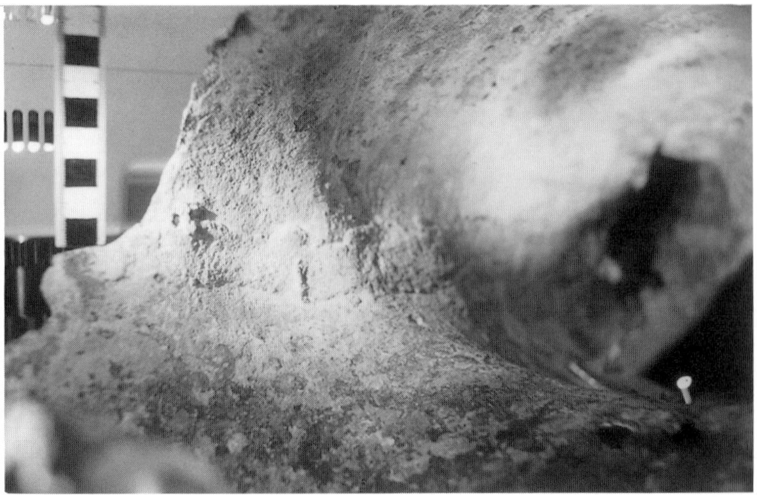

Fig. 8 (top left). Interior of the left arm.
Fig. 9 (top right). Interior of the shoulder.
Fig. 10 (lower right). Interior, showing finger marks. (All photos: author.)

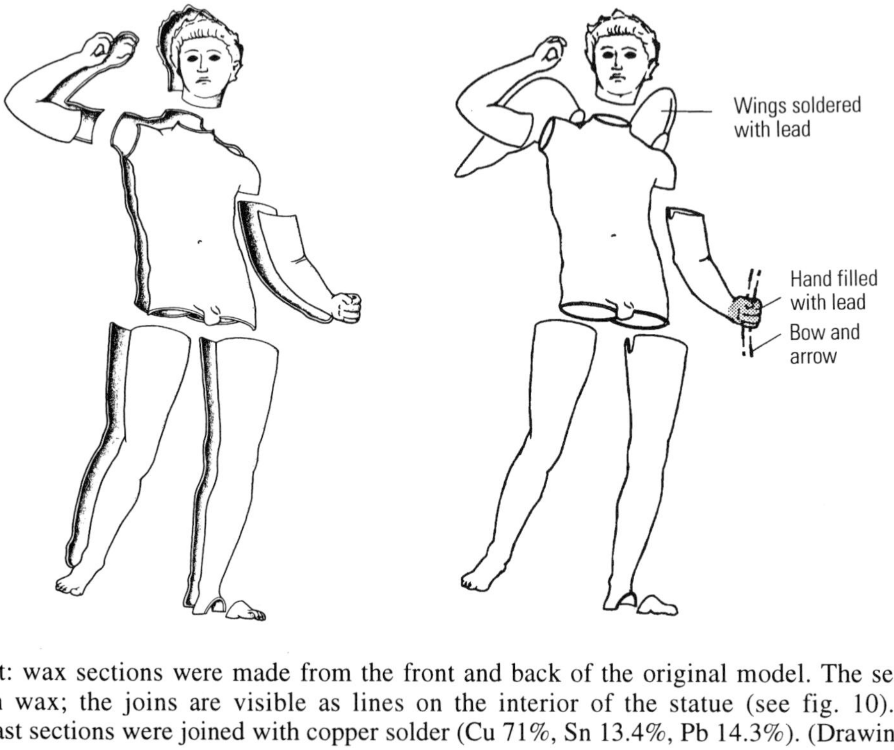

Fig. 11. Left: wax sections were made from the front and back of the original model. The sections were jointed with wax; the joins are visible as lines on the interior of the statue (see fig. 10). Right: the separately cast sections were joined with copper solder (Cu 71%, Sn 13.4%, Pb 14.3%). (Drawings: author.)

A bronze lebes in the light of the Mahdia wreck

Ariel Herrmann

The Late Hellenistic bronze lebes from the Fleischman collection[1] (figs. 1a-c, 3, 5, 7, and 8), now in the J. Paul Getty Museum,[2] clearly warrants more study than could be given it in the brief entry for the exhibition catalogue. In particular, the new publication of material from the Mahdia shipwreck[3] has revealed parallels for several parts of the vessel. In the course of his recent work on the conservation of the Mahdia finds, F. Willer of the Rheinisches Landesmuseum, Bonn, made many of the same observations as the present author.[4]

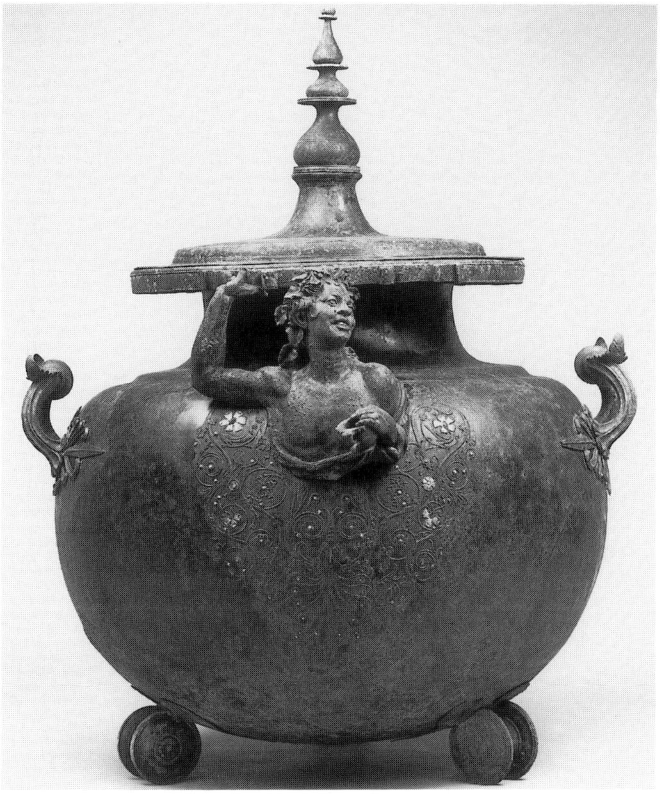

Fig. 1a. Lebes, front. Bronze with silver, h. 0.58 m. The J. Paul Getty Museum 96.AC.51. (Photo: courtesy The J. Paul Getty Museum.)

---

1 A. Herrmann in M. True and K. Hamma (edd.), *A passion for antiquities: ancient art from the collection of Barbara and Lawrence Fleischman* (Exhib. cat., The J. Paul Getty Museum, Malibu 1994) 258-62, no. 130. My thanks to Barbara and the late Lawrence Fleischman for the opportunity to study the lebes while it was in their collection.

2 Acc. no. 96.AC.51.

3 *Das Wrack.* This catalogue, published in connection with the conservation and exhibition of the Mahdia finds at the Rheinisches Landesmuseum Bonn, is a full presentation of material from the wreck, including hitherto unknown fragments and new technical observations, along with a series of interpretative essays. It expands on the earlier publication by W. Fuchs, *Der Schiffsfund von Mahdia* (Tübingen 1963), so long indispensable to scholars of Hellenistic art.

4 I would like to thank F. Willer for very helpful and collegial discussions. My thanks as well to the late G. Hellenkemper Salies for a most cordial reception in Bonn, and to H.-H. von Prittwitz und Gaffron and R. Petrovszky. The Rheinisches Landesmuseum Bonn has been generous in providing photographs of the Mahdia material.

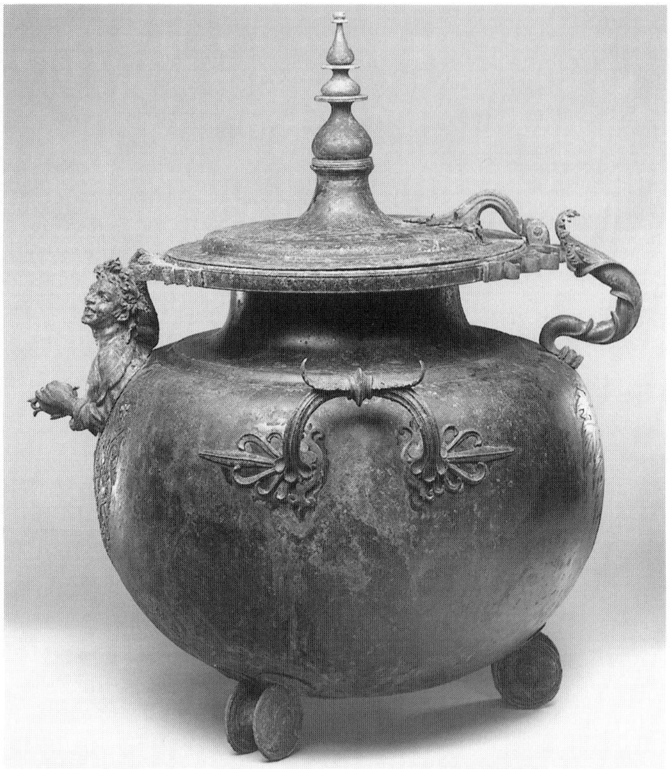

Fig. 1b. Lebes, profile. (Photo: courtesy The J. Paul Getty Museum.)

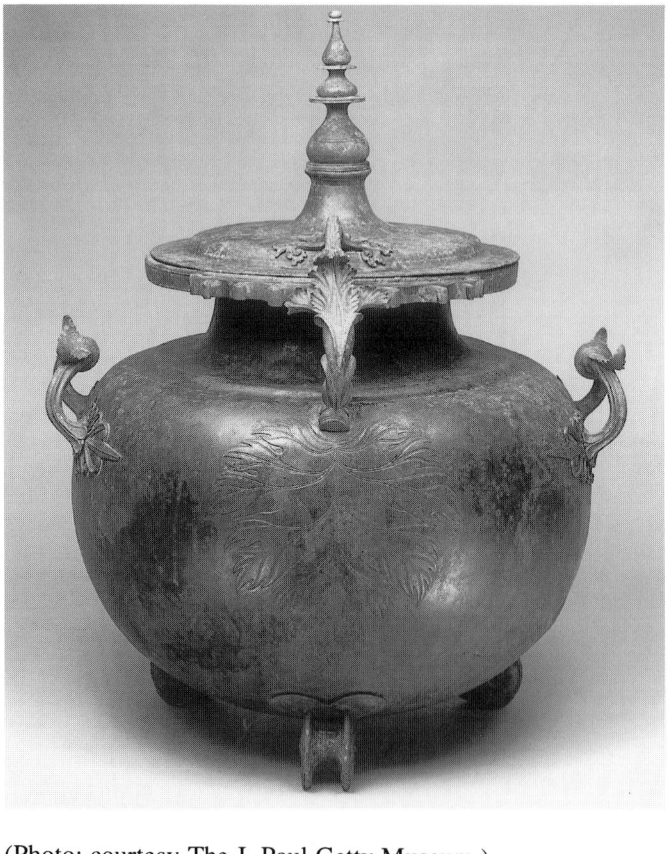

Fig. 1c. Lebes, handle. (Photo: courtesy The J. Paul Getty Museum.)

A tiny vessel from the wreck repeats, in miniature, the overall shape of the lebes's body and lid.[5] The griffin protomes now shown to join the Mahdia piece make explicit the form's descent from the great Archaic votive cauldrons. Such griffin cauldrons, always with tall conical lids, appear frequently in architectural or sacro-idyllic wall-paintings from the Vesuvian sites.[6] The basic shape, with globular body, short wide neck, and everted rim, topped by a conical lid, is well attested in real vases of the 1st c. B.C.–A.D. The monumental bronze vase body from Anzio in the Palazzo dei Conservatori,[7] which bears an inscription of Mithridates Eupator to the *eupatoristai* of a gymnasium at some unspecified site, is compromised by Renaissance foot and handles but remains an imposing Late Hellenistic example. Like many but not all versions of the shape, the Conservatori vase is fluted. The form is adapted in various permutations for Roman marble cinerary urns and decorative vases.[8]

The form of the lebes owes its energized appearance largely to the way the body is set not on the expected profiled base but on three roller-like spool feet. Spool feet, not at all common, are sometimes used on basins[9] and situlae.[10] Like the disc feet occasionally seen on Canosan pyxides,[11] the spools give a sense of potential movement, as if to evoke the magically self-propelled rolling tripods made by Hephaistos.[12] Normally spool feet are attached to a base ring. Those of the lebes, however, are joined directly to its globular body by way of ivy-leaf–shaped reinforcing plates (fig. 3), a very unusual solution also adopted in a small bronze vase from Pompeii.[13]

Two spool feet were found by the conservators among the Mahdia material sent to Bonn and were added at the last minute to the catalogue (fig. 4).[14] Petrovszky noted the unusually careful workmanship of the Mahdia examples, which closely resemble the feet of the lebes. The Mahdia and Fleischman feet agree not only in their fine craftsmanship but in their large size and their relatively tall proportions; ordinarily the spool is longer and lower. The preparation of the Mahdia feet for joining to another element — a small flattened area with a central prong — appears to have been used for the lebes feet as well.

A link between the lebes and the Mahdia material was first suggested to the writer by the similarity of two bronze foliage attachments from the wreck, illustrated in Fuchs's 1963 publication (fig. 2),[15] to the foliate back handle of the lebes (figs. 1b and 5). The resemblance of these elements is striking as to style and basic conception, although the curvatures of the pieces

---

5 R. Petrovszky, "Die Bronzegefässe," in *Das Wrack* 663-700, 673 and Abb. 12, 693 nos. 36-37 and Abb. 50-51.

6 A. E. Riz, *Bronzegefässe in der römisch-pompeianischen Wandmalerei* (Mainz 1990) 96 ff., Taf. 55-57.

7 H. Stuart-Jones, *A catalogue of the ancient sculptures in the Palazzo dei Conservatori* (Oxford 1926; repr. Rome 1968) 175, no. 10. The fluting on the vase body is interrupted in such a way as to show that the piece did originally have side handles.

8 A. M. Mlasowsky, "Die Aschenurne des Germanicus," *RömMitt* 98 (1991) 223 ff., esp. 225 n.8. See A. Giuliano (ed.), *Museo Nazionale Romano: le sculture* I.1 (Rome 1979) 150 f. for an ash urn that originally did have griffin protomes.

9 I. Vokotopoulou, *'Οδηγὸς Μουσείου 'Ιοαννίνων (Guide of the Ioannina Museum)* (Athens 1973) 52, pl. 17A for a bronze basin with spool feet from Metsovo, datable in the late 6th or 5th c. B.C. A basin with spool feet attached to a base ring appears in the Capitoline version of Sosos's mosaic: see M. Donderer, "Das kapitolinische Taubenmosaik: Original des Sosos?" *RömMitt* 98 (1991) 189 ff. and Taf. 49.

10 E. Pernice, *Die hellenistische Kunst in Pompeii: Gefässe und Geräte aus Bronze* (Berlin–Leipzig 1925) 29 and Abb. 40; Petrovszky (supra n.5) 679 f.

11 M. E. Mayo (ed.), *Vases from Magna Graecia* (Exhib. cat., The Virginia Museum of Fine Art, Richmond 1982) 299 f., no. 153.

12 *Iliad* 18, 373-77, as M. Schmidt has reminded the author.

13 *Real Museo Borbonico* VI (Naples 1830) Tav. 31,1.

14 Petrovszky (supra n.5) 679 f., 695 nos. 44-45 and Abb. 55; *Das Wrack* 2, Farbtaf. 35.4.

15 Fuchs, *Schiffsfund* (supra n.3) 26, no. 25, Taf. 34.

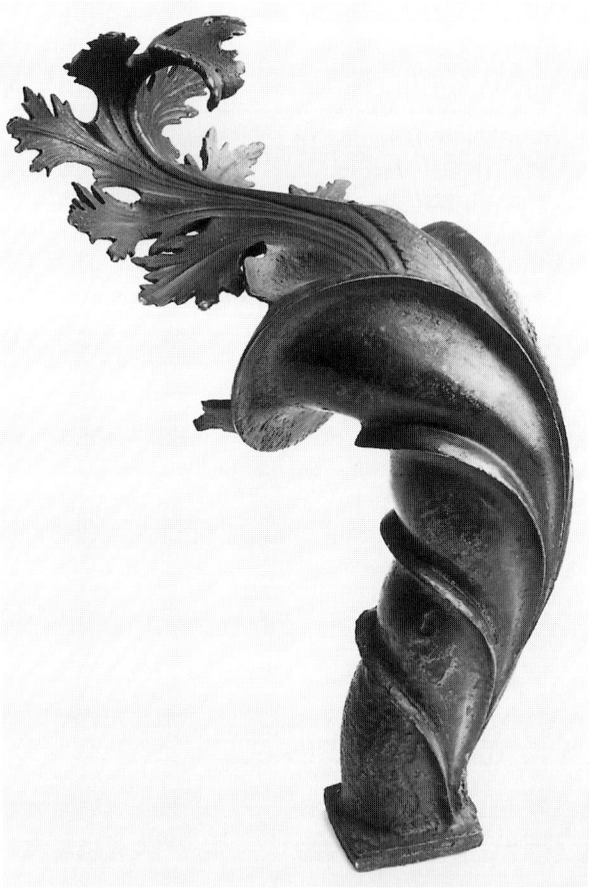

Fig. 2. Foliate attachment from the Mahdia wreck. Bronze, l. 0.26 m. Tunis, Bardo Museum F 303 or 304. (Photo: H. Lilienthal; courtesy Rheinisches Landesmuseum Bonn.)

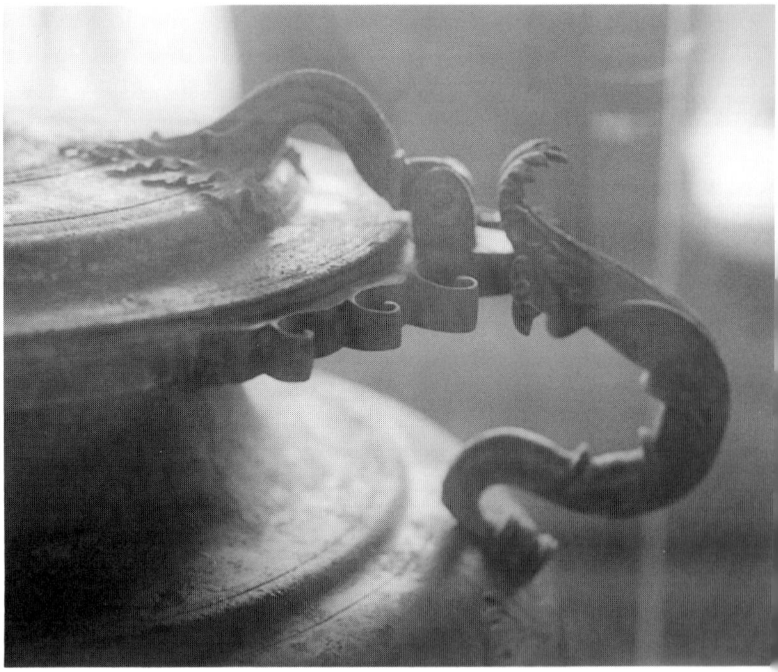

Fig. 5. Lebes, detail of scrollwork and back handle. (Photo: author.)

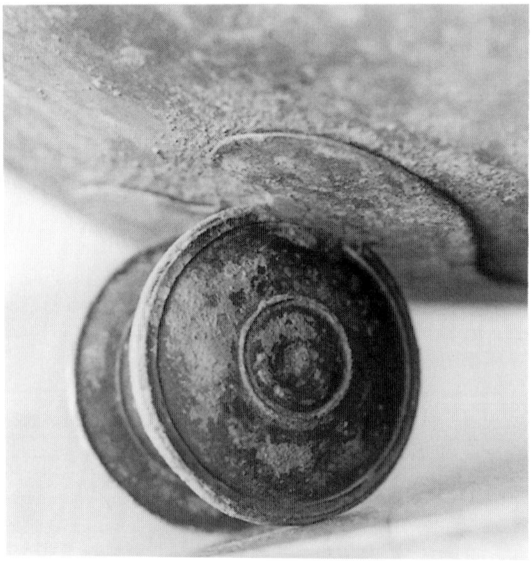

Fig. 3. Lebes, spool foot. (Photo: author.)

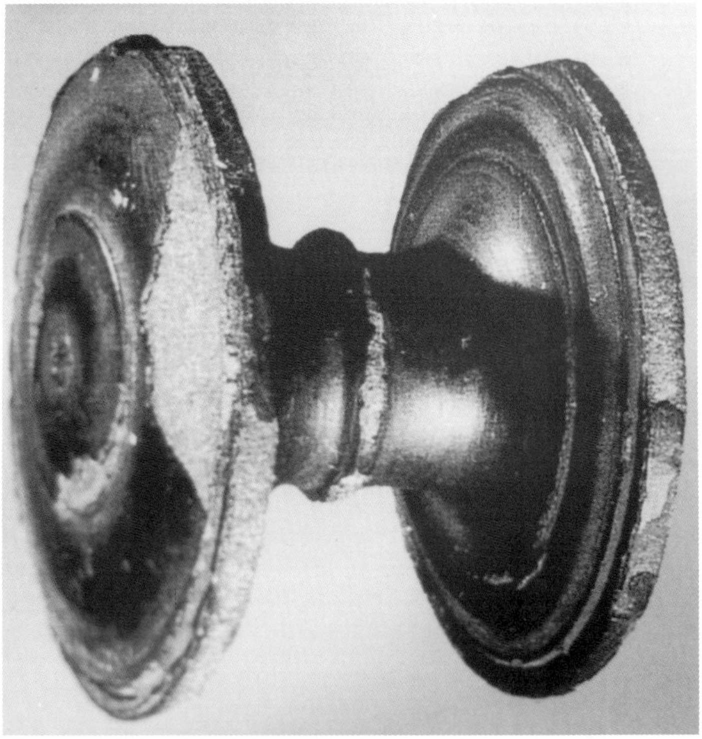

Fig. 4. Spool foot, from the Mahdia wreck. Bronze, diam. 1.9 cm. Tunis, Bardo Museum F 295 or 295bis. (Photo: courtesy Rheinisches Landesmuseum Bonn.)

are somewhat different. It has been tentatively suggested that the Mahdia branches supported two small statuettes of satyrs, and that they may have formed part of an ornate lighting apparatus along the lines of the famous one in Vienna from Ephesos.[16] The physical join is possible although not inevitable. One of the two satyr statuettes preserves its base, and this base can be fitted into an open-ended notch, apparently to hold some attachment, in the foliage. The correspondence, then, involves only one dimension that is not an unusual one. Functionally and compositionally the reconstruction is rather unconvincing[17] and should perhaps be reconsidered. The disproportion between the tiny statuette and the large, powerful acanthus leaf is awkward, as is the way the tiptoe position of the satyr's feet, so important to an understanding of his pose, would be hidden by the foliage. More promising is the conservators' association of the Mahdia branches with elements of low-relief foliage that may have served to attach them to the curving body of a large vessel.

Fluted handles from the wreck[18] are of a very old and well-known type that was also common at the Vesuvian sites.[19] The side handles of the lebes are a flamboyant variation on the theme, bursting into leaf at either side of their central beads. This variant appears on a Hellenistic hydria in the Metropolitan Museum of Art; a similar, stray example with leaf attachment plates, datable to Roman times, is in the same museum,[20] and other apparently Roman examples, like one on the New York market (Fortuna Fine Arts Ltd., 1994), are known. The treatment of the exuberant turned-up leaves on the lebes handles is in the spirit of vegetation seen on lampstand branches from Pompeii.[21] While the handles on the lebes transform the conservative model of the Mahdia handles, they are similar in their basic fluted elements and especially in their very careful many-part construction. On the lebes, the handles have attachment plates in the form of openwork palmettes. Among the other fragments from the Mahdia wreck is an attenuated openwork palmette of related form, combined with acanthus foliage in what looks like part of an ornate handle.[22]

The plates of cut-out scrollwork adorning the rim of the lebes (fig. 5) also have close parallels among newly published finds from Mahdia (fig. 6).[23] The wreck contained at least two sets of similar scrollwork, tentatively identified by the cataloguers as mirror surrounds. Cut and curled work like this reaches its apogee in tableware of the 1st c. B.C. Early examples seem to be characterized by large, tightly rolled spirals, as on the jug and strainer from the Arcisate find,[24] datable around 75 B.C., or on two skyphoi from a Late Hellenistic group once in the Fleischman collection.[25] Scrollwork is still conspicuous on Tiberian pieces from the Bosco-

16 F. Naumann-Steckner, T. Raeder, and F. Willer, "Ein Kandelaber mit Akanthusranken?" in *Das Wrack* 629-38, Abb. 2 for the lighting device from Ephesos in Vienna.

17 Ibid. 631, Abb. 4 for the join; *Das Wrack* Taf. 26 for a telling view of the reconstruction.

18 Petrovzsky (supra n.5) 680 f., nos. 1-6, Abb. 1719.

19 Pernice (supra n.10) 1517.

20 New York, MMA 66.11.12; *Sotheby's, London, auction catalogue, Antiquities, July 25, 1966,* lot 267 (the hydria). MMA 66.119.1; *Parke Bernet, New York, auction catalogue, The collection of Florence L. Rauh, December 4-6 1940,* part of lot 72 (the stray handle).

21 *Das Wrack* 634, Abb. 7-8.

22 Rheinisches Landesmuseum Bonn, photo 2470/94X (6-9) shows this fragment, apparently not included in the exhibition catalogue. The surviving part of the palmette looks as if it is meant to be overlaid with another piece. The form is difficult to interpret, especially without knowing the dimensions, but suggests the upper part of a very ornate skyphos handle with thumb-plate.

23 B. Päffgen and W. Zanier, "Kleinfunde aus Metall," in *Das Wrack* 111-30, 117 f. nos. 14-15, Abb. 8-9. A similar scrollwork border comes from the Spargi shipwreck off Sardinia, datable *c.* 120-100 B.C. See R. D'Oriano in G. Lilliu (ed.), *L'Antiquarium arborense e i civici musei archeologici della Sardegna* (Sassari 1988) 48 ff. and fig. 24.

24 D. E. Strong, *Greek and Roman gold and silver plate* (London 1966) 115 f., pl. 34.

25 Now J. Paul Getty Museum 96.AM.162.7-8: A. Oliver in *A passion for antiquities* (supra n.1) 231 f., no. 115 G-H.

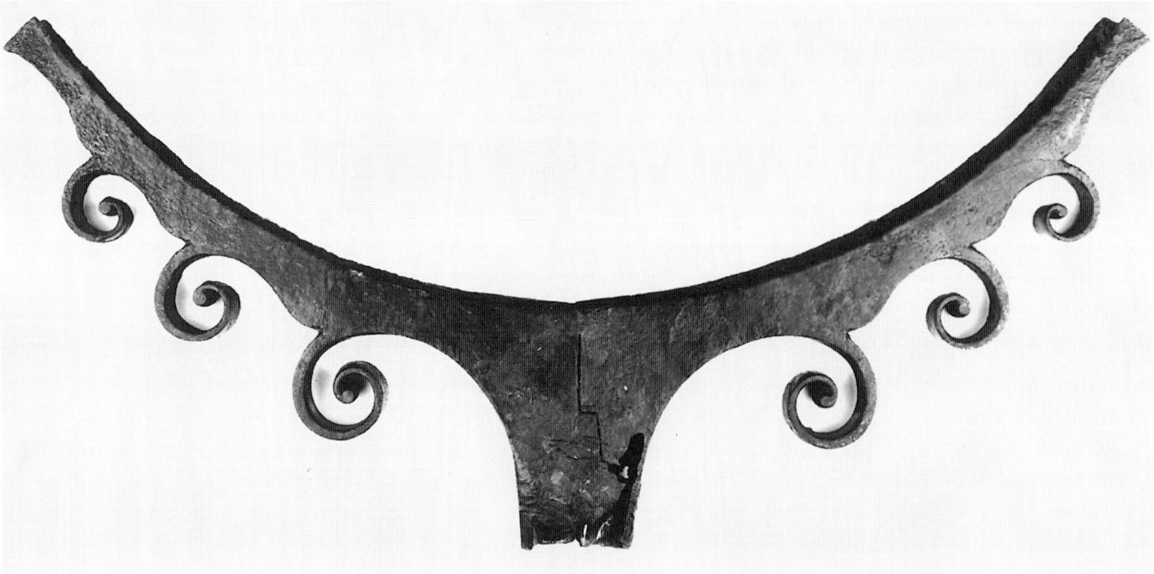

Fig. 6. Scrollwork from the Mahdia wreck. Bronze, l. 0.51 m. Tunis, Bardo Museum F 339 and 340. (Photo: H. Lilienthal; courtesy Rheinisches Landesmuseum Bonn.)

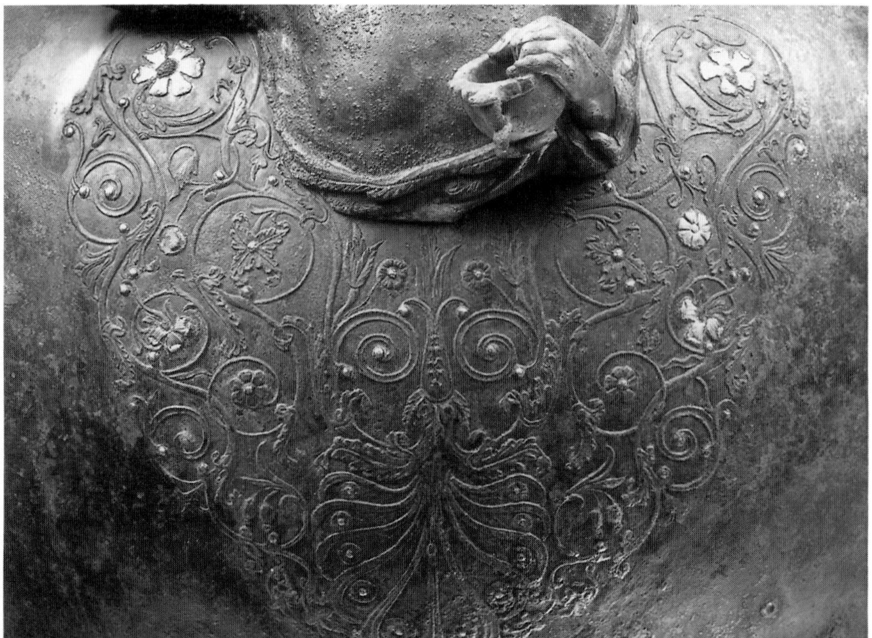

Fig. 7. Lebes, detail of low relief foliate decoration. (Photo: courtesy The J. Paul Getty Museum.)

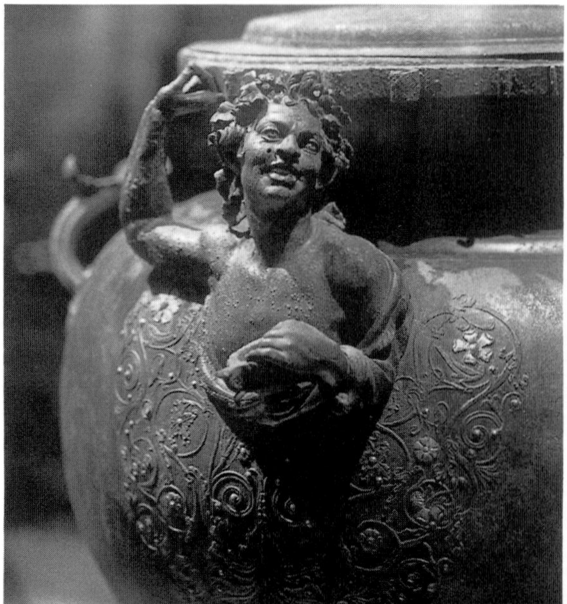

Fig. 8. Lebes, bust of a youthful Pan and foliate decoration. (Photo: author.)

reale treasure,[26] but thereafter cut-out ornament was at first complemented and then replaced by more plastic decoration.

26 F. Baratte, *Le trésor d'orfèvrerie romaine de Boscoreale* (Paris 1986) passim, 22-23 for an illustration that shows this feature, often minimized by strict profile photographs of vessels.

We have seen that many details of the lebes have parallels in materials from the wreck. However, one feature appears to be considerably later; this is the foliate design beneath the bust of a young Pan (figs. 7-8). At first glance it recalls the low-relief decoration of early Hellenistic situlae,[27] and like many of the situla ornaments emanates from an inverted palmette.

The foliage on the lebes, however, has its closest relatives in Roman architectural ornament of the second half of the 1st c. B.C. Its wiry stems and jagged, crisp-looking leaves recall the fragments attributed to the Temple of the Divus Iulius, dedicated in 29 B.C.[28] What seems most telling, though, is that the overall design is organized in the same way as the tree of scrolls of the Ara Pacis Augustae, constructed between 13 and 9 B.C.[29] The arrangement, perfectly symmetrical for all its apparent lushness and developing vertically as well as horizontally, is composed around a candelabrum-like vertical axis of stacked vegetal forms. Regularly spaced acanthus scrolls, each encircling a frontally seen blossom, are the basic unit of construction; among the blooms, rosettes predominate. Other, asymmetrical flowers are flattened as if pressed between an invisible front and back plane. As in the vegetation decorating the seat of the Augustan goddess from Cuma,[30] the continuity and linear energy of the stems is emphasized. The tendency, beginning in late Augustan times, to concentrate on the plasticity of leaves and blooms while dissolving the stems, seen for example on the Hildesheim krater,[31] has not yet appeared.

In the lebes ornament some elements are naturalistic, while others are stylized or completely abstract. Ribbon-like, slightly concave strips end in volutes rolled around silver buttons. These ribbon tendrils, of Classical derivation, are a favorite Augustan motif, appearing on Campana reliefs[32] as well as in the relief ornament of the sphinx tripod from Pompeii.[33]

The foliate design on the lebes seems very comparable to some of the standardized decorative patterns for the bases of marble candelabra, recently studied by Cain.[34] In type II, created around the middle of the 1st c. B.C., the forms of some flowers, leaves, and stems recall the lebes. All of the arrangements are axial, and Types III, IVa, and IVb develop according to the tree-of-scrolls system. Types III and IVb, both classified by Cain as Augustan inventions, include palmettes in the central arrangement. In IVb, the palmette has thin undulating lobes with inward-curling ends, much like the lobes, accentuated by minuscule silver-centered rosettes, of the palmette on the lebes.

---

27 P. J. Riis, "The Danish bronze vessels," *ActaA* 30 (1959) 1 ff.; 18 ff. for bell situlae, esp. 21, section C; 23 for the suggestion that type C is western. E. Paunov and N. Torbov presented a spectacular 4th c. example from Vratsa in Bulgaria at this Congress (see Paunov and Torbov, above p. 163). See Comstock and Vermeule, *Bronzes* 338 f., no. 477 for a version datable 50 B.C. -A.D.50.

28 M. A. Zagdoun, *La sculpture archaïsante dans l'art hellénistique et dans l'art romain du haut-empire (BEFAR* 269, 1989) fig. 159, no. 378.

29 E. La Rocca, *Ara Pacis Augustae* (Rome 1983) passim; D. Castriota, *The Ara Pacis Augustae and the imagery of abundance in later Greek and early Roman imperial art* (Princeton 1995) passim. Useful modern discussions of Late Republican and Early Imperial foliate ornament include: C. Börker, "Neuattisches und pergamenisches an den Ranken der Ara Pacis," *JdI* 88 (1973) 283 ff.; W. von Sydow, "Die Grabexedra eines römischen Feldherren," *JdI* 89 (1974) 187 ff.; G. Sauron, "Les modèles funéraires classiques de l'art décoratif néo-attique au Ier siècle av. J.C.," *MEFRA* 91 (1979) 183 ff.; id., "Le message esthétique des rinceaux de l'Ara Pacis Augustae," *RA* 1988.1, 3 ff.; E. Ghisellini, "Modelli ufficiali della prima età imperiale," *RömMitt* 95 (1988) 187 ff.

30 P. Zanker, *Augustus und die Macht der Bilder* (Munich 1987) fig. 245.

31 L. Pirzio Biroli Stefanelli (ed.), *L'argento dei Romani* (Rome 1991) 69, figs. 45-47. See also the cup from Boscoreale ibid. 140, fig. 106.

32 Castriota (supra n.29) figs. 73, 77.

33 L. Pirzio Biroli Stefanelli (ed.), *Il bronzo dei romani* (Rome 1990) fig. 110.

34 H.-U. Cain, *Römische Marmorkandelaber* (Mainz 1985) passim, esp. 38-59 and Beilage 3.

Many flower petals and centers on the lebes are picked out in silver for a starry, highly decorative effect. Some blossoms, symmetrically placed, have a copper color that contrasts with the background and may well be the result of deliberate treatment of the metal, a question that awaits technical investigation.[35]

The large vine leaf under the back handle of the lebes has obviously been worked up in repoussé and is visible on the vessel's interior. Derived from the more usual applied vine-leaf attachment plates, it has the look of an improvisation to compensate for the handle's somewhat abrupt join to the body at this point. The foliage under the bust, however, seems to have been made by a different technique, as no trace of it is apparent within.[36] Pfrommer has made the same observation about the elegant low-relief ornament of an oinochoe in the Getty Museum, which despite the thinness of its body must have been cast.[37] The oinochoe, dated by Pfrommer to Augustan times, is comparable to the lebes in the delicacy of its ornament, picked out in silver, and in its sophisticated reproduction of Hellenistic motifs.

A further hint that the lebes is somewhat later than the Mahdia material comes from the style of the applied bust (fig. 8). Its careful, refined small-scale modeling has an almost academic precision, quite different from the nervous energy and, even allowing for the effects of corrosion, the rather sketchy, impressionistic surface treatment of all the figural decorative elements from the Mahdia wreck. The eyeballs and teeth of the young Pan are silvered, a feature seen in fine bronzes of many periods but less common in the rather relaxed productions of Hellenistic times than in elegant work of the 1st c. B.C.–A.D.

The bust of a youthful Pan or satyr in the same pose as the one on the lebes, snapping the fingers of his raised right hand while cradling a wine cup in his left, exists in at least two other examples — a bizarre appliqué in Bonn[38] and a much more normal if rather crude version superimposed on the vine-leaf attachment plate of an oinochoe handle in the White–Levy collection.[39] These agree in composition and iconography with the lebes bust but are very different from it, and from each other, in style. The relatively early dates that have been assigned to both should perhaps be reconsidered. The Bonn piece has a wild spontaneity that certainly belongs somewhere in Hellenistic times but is hard to pin down more precisely, while the style of the White–Levy handle is not without parallels among the finds from the Vesuvian sites.[40] The much more finely executed bust on the lebes seems to make it clear that the type is derived, in a rather literal-minded way, from a Late Hellenistic model closely related to the Invitation to the Dance satyr and the Young Centaur.[41] He holds a miniature

---

35 A number of essays in *Das Wrack* study related issues in connection with the Mahdia bronzes: B. Cuppers, "Metalleinlagen als farbige Ziertechnik," 1013-16; F. Willer, "Fragen zur intentionellen Schwarzpatina an den Mahdiabronzen," 1023-31; G. Eggert, "Schwarzfärbung oder Korrosion? Das Rätsel der schwarzen Bronzen aus chemischer Sicht," 1033-39.

36 This is not quite certain, because although the lebes is in general very well preserved, there has presumably been some repair to the body, and details of the interior may be obscured by material added to reinforce or disguise restorations. A more thorough technical investigation would be useful.

37 M. Pfrommer, "Kopie oder Nachschöpfung. Eine Bronzekanne im J. Paul Getty Museum," *GettyMusJ* 15 (1987) 15 ff. For the probability that the piece is cast, see p.15, and for the Augustan date, n.3.

38 B. Barr-Sharrar, *The Hellenistic and Early Imperial decorative bust* (Mainz 1987) 57, no. C95ter.

39 D. von Bothmer in *Glories of the past: ancient art from the Shelby White and Leon Levy collection* (Exhib. cat., The Metropolitan Museum of Art, New York 1990) 186, no. 133.

40 The peculiarity of the bust being superimposed on a leaf is paralleled by *Bronzo dei Romani* (supra n.33) fig. 80, its coarse and bold style by Vesuvian pieces such as fig. 77. Wide-mouthed jugs, although not normally as large as the one to which the White–Levy example belonged, are a common type at Pompeii and Herculaneum. See S. Tassinari, "Pots campaniens à décor bacchique," in *Actes du Ve colloque int. sur les bronzes antiques* (Lausanne 1979) pl. 64.2 for a small example whose handle has a leaf attachment plate; a similar, unpublished jug is in the Metropolitan Museum of Art, 21.88.164. For a wide-mouthed jug with much more pretentious ornamentation, cf. *Bronzo dei Romani* fig. 70.

41 J. J. Pollitt, *Art in the Hellenistic age* (Cambridge 1986) figs. 139, 145.

Late Hellenistic skyphos with scrollwork around its ring-and-thumb-plate handles, possibly a further hint as to the date of the model. High-quality Pompeiian works make sparing use of such roccoco types, but the brazier with the youthful Pan figures[42] would be an example, as would some of the silenus, satyr, or triton heads on elegant vessel handles.

Taken as a whole, the lebes is a hybrid object that combines elements originally associated with other vessel types. This aspect too seems Roman, recalling pieces from the Vesuvian sites like the famous 'samovar,'[43] with its volute-krater handles and table- (or basin-) legs. The way the lebes, a two-handled vase, sprouts further excrescences front and back is paralleled in the 'samovar.' So is the penchant for placing three feet under a body with a four-sided arrangement of ornamentation.

This writer's first inclination, then, was to view the lebes, with its eclectic decoration, additive composition, and tree-of-scrolls ornament, as a work of early Augustan date produced in Italy. On becoming aware how many correspondences there are between finds from the Mahdia wreck and details of the lebes, one is prompted to reconsider. It still seems difficult to accept the ornament as pre-Augustan. However, the *impasse* is less serious than it seems at first. The Mahdia ship's last voyage was probably in the 70s B.C. Most of the decorative objects in its cargo, whether new or second-hand, were recent productions by workshops that were presumably still in business. Some of these ateliers doubtless continued to manufacture the same line down into the middle of the 1st c. B.C. and beyond. Copyists could revive the models even later. The long subsequent history of Neo-Attic marble kraters and candelabra and of bronze couch fulcra belonging to the same types as those from the wreck is a perfect illustration of how such luxury objects continued to be made according to standardized designs — but with slight modifications to suit changing fashion or individual preferences — for several generations.

Whether the Mahdia ship's cargo came entirely from Attica or partly from other places such as Delos, it is fairly certain to represent workshops active in Greece proper. Recent studies of Late Hellenistic and Early Imperial decorative objects conclude that many of the types were formulated in the artistic centers of the Greek world, but were specifically designed for export to a clientele of wealthy villa owners in Rome and Campania.[44] The tree of scrolls seems an explicitly western design, rarely seen in the Greek East. Can it nonetheless have been created there, for export only? Or can it have been transmitted, for reproduction, from West to East? Is such metalwork an immediate forerunner, or a manneristic slightly later reflection, of the marble foliate reliefs of the Ara Pacis? Would a later generation of the Mahdia workshop have been this tuned in to artistic trends in the land for which their production was destined? Or had their activity, like that of the expert Greek stone carvers who helped transform Augustan Rome from a city of brick to a city of marble, been transplanted to Italy? All these and other questions remain to be answered.

New York, NY

---

42 *Bronzo dei romani* (supra n.33) fig. 109.

43 *Bronzo dei romani* (supra n.33) fig. 207.

44 See the essays in *Das Wrack*, for example H.-U. Cain and O. Dräger, "Die Marmorkandelaber," 239-57, esp. 251 ff.; Cain and Dräger, "Die sogenannten neuattischen Werkstätten," 809-29; D. Grassinger, "Die Marmorkratere," 259-83, esp. 275 f.; T. Hölscher, "Hellenistische Kunst und römische Aristokratie," 875-88, esp. 881 ff.

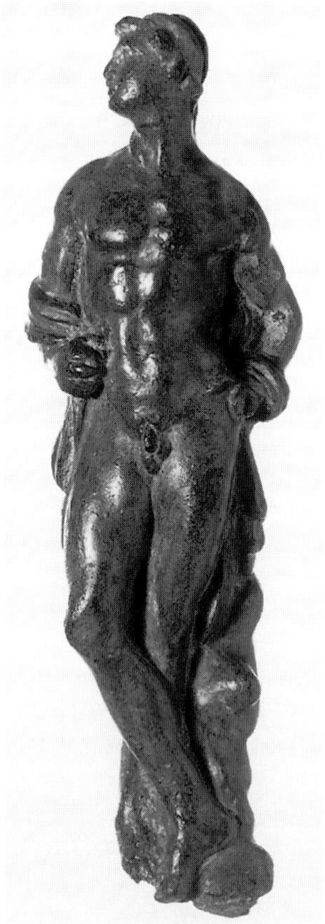

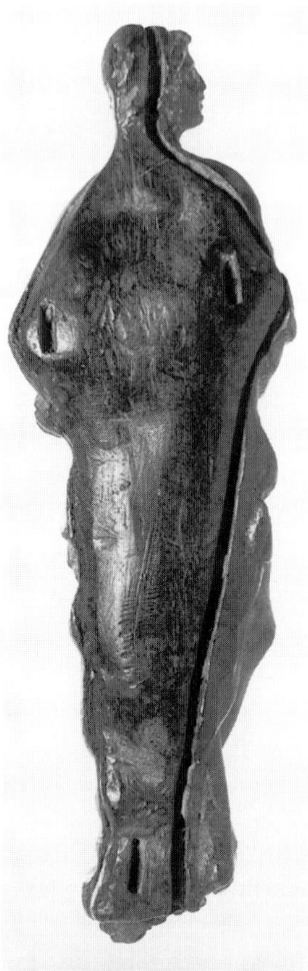

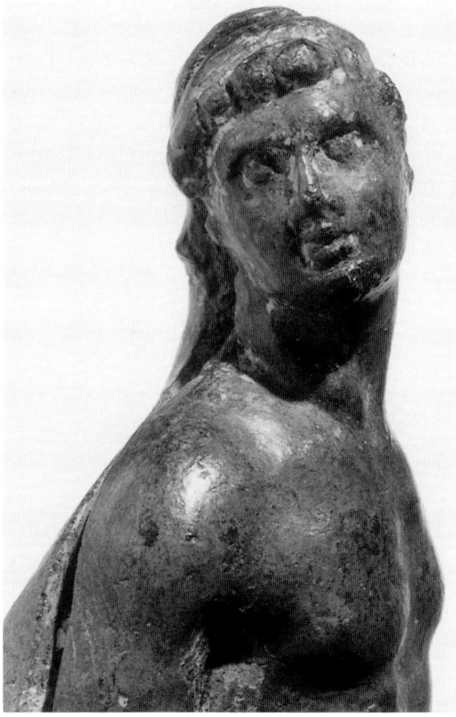

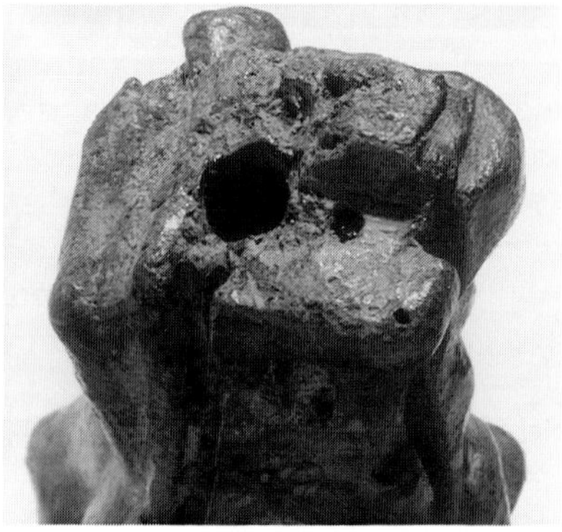

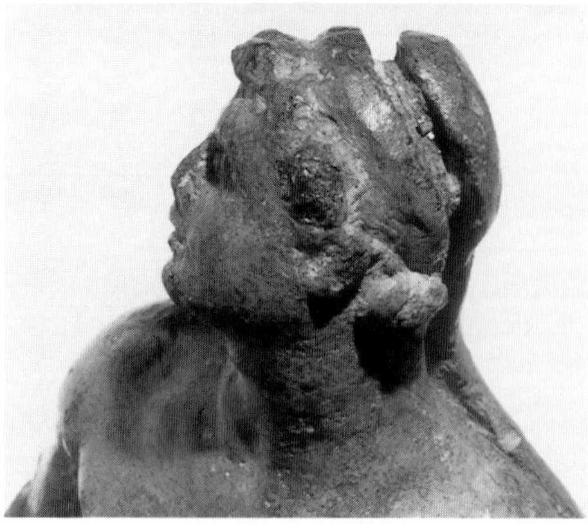

Fig. 1 (top). Youth. Bronze, h. 0.115 m. Bloomington, Indiana University Art Museum, gift of Burton Y. Berry, 76.34.50.
Fig. 3 (below). Detail of head.

Fig. 2 (top). Back.
Fig. 4 (middle). Detail of base.
Fig. 5 (below). Detail of head. (All photos: courtesy Museum).

A rare Hellenistic bronze in the Indiana University Art Museum

Heather F. Sharpe

Recent discussions of foil-gilded bronze sculpture from the Greek world have been hindered by the fact that only two examples were known to have survived: a head of a Nike[1] and the remains of an equestrian statue,[2] both excavated in the Athenian Agora.[3] Now a third example can be added to this group, a solid-cast statuette of a youth (figs. 1-5) in the Indiana University Art Museum, Bloomington, which bears similar grooves and traces of gold that indicate it was once gilded in the same manner as the two Athenian bronzes.[4] The statuette was acquired in 1976 as part of a larger gift bequeathed to the museum by Burton Y. Berry, whose collection was assembled principally in the Eastern Mediterranean. The focus here is primarily on the bronze's technical features. Research on the statuette's style and specific origins must await a future date.

The youth stands in a languid pose with legs casually crossed, leaning against a knotted tree trunk. His arms are slightly bent and partly covered with a length of cloth that wraps around his right elbow, disappears behind his lower back, and twists over his left wrist. His hands rest on his hips, the left one slightly lower with two fingers spread across the crest of his hip and the right clenched in a fist. Resting on a tall, slender neck, the small head twists sharply and is tilted upward and canted slightly to the right (fig. 3). Clumps of hair frame the well-modeled face. Below a bulging forehead lie deep-set eyes, of which only the right remains clearly indicated. The iris protrudes strongly and the pupil is indicated by a small punched dot. Subtly arching brows lead down to a fine straight nose, below which is a loosely modeled mouth.

By contrast, the back of the figure (fig. 2) is only cursorily modeled, with little regard for anatomical details. The surface, not entirely flat, is gently undulating and relatively smooth. There are also 4 rectangular cuts, measuring *c.*1 x 5 mm, and 1-1.5 mm in depth, located behind the head, feet, and elbows. More obvious, however, is a continuous groove, *c.*2 mm wide and 1-1.5 mm deep, that runs along the back outer edge of the figure.

The statuette is intact and in good condition. Except for a few small slightly corroded areas, the surface is smooth and has an olive green patina. The bottom of the statuette is pierced by two holes (fig. 4), the smallest of which measures just over 1 mm in diameter and may date to the time of production. The larger hole, *c.*4 mm in diameter and 15-20 mm in depth, is apparently a modern alteration, judging by the relatively pristine condition of the bronze revealed. It appears that a portion of the left side of the base was broken off, perhaps in antiquity, considering the incrustations and wear. One should imagine that in its original state the base had a rectangular plinth just below and slightly recessed from the ground upon which the figure stands.

Judging from the 4 cuts located on the back of the statuette, it is more than likely that the figure originally served as an appliqué. In Classical and Hellenistic times, bronze appliqués could be attached to a variety of objects. Appliqués on metal vessels and mirrors are well known and were customarily produced in one of two forms. Hollow bronze reliefs, executed in repoussé, were applied to the surface of an object. Solid cast figures could function as handles or as

---

1 T. L. Shear, "The campaign of 1932," *Hesperia* 2 (1933) 519-27; D. B. Thompson, "The golden Nikai reconsidered," *Hesperia* 13 (1944) 173-209; H. A. Thompson, "A golden Nike from the Athenian Agora," *HSCP Suppl.* 1 (1940) 183-210.

2 T. L. Shear, Jr., "Sculpture in the Athenian Agora: excavations of 1971," *Hesperia* 42 (1973) 165-68.

3 For a recent discussion of the Nike head and equestrian statue, see Mattusch, *Classical bronzes* 121-29.

4 IUAM 76.34.50. H. 0.115 m; l. 0.036 m; w. (at shoulders) 0.021 m; maximum depth 0.02.1 m.

decorative appliqués. However, it is unlikely that the bronze youth was utilized in either of these ways. The back of the figure is neither flat nor curving as it should be in order to conform to the contour of a vase, nor is it sculpted in the round as a vessel handle would be. Instead, it appears that this statuette once served as an appliqué for furniture.

Unfortunately, few complete examples of furniture are known from the ancient world, particularly Greece, due to the perishable materials from which they were made. Some bronze examples have survived, yet their numbers are small compared to the great quantities which must have disappeared into ancient and mediaeval melting pots. Roman furniture is better known, due in particular to discoveries at Pompeii and Herculaneum, and it is to these examples that I now turn for suggestions regarding the bronze youth. A statuette from Pompeii of Fortuna seated on a throne, with appliqués decorating the backrest, armrests, and corners of the footstool, gives a tantalizing glimpse of how an actual throne might have appeared.[5] A 1st c. A.D. tripod from Turin,[6] richly decorated with busts of youths, striding Nike figures, crouching sphinxes and kneeling satyrs, and a table from Pompeii[7] with a cupid riding a dolphin adorning its leg, suggest that less grandiose items were also adorned with decorative appliqués.

The methods of manufacture and assemblage of these bronze objects are generally not well understood, and certainly whatever information has been gathered is not readily accessible. This makes it difficult to find comparanda for the Bloomington bronze with respect to its specific function and means of attachment.

The groove along the outer edge of the figure was not used for attaching but rather for gilding the statuette. This technique, termed foil gilding, was rarely used in the ancient Greek world and, as mentioned above, is documented on only two other extant Greek bronzes: a late 5th c. B.C. head of a Nike, and the remains of an equestrian portrait dated towards the end of the 4th c. B.C.[8]

Briefly, the process of foil gilding is as follows: a piece of gold foil is applied to the statue and pressed onto the surface; the edges of the gold foil are tucked into the grooves and then either locked into place with a length of wire[9] or the edges hammered closed.[10] In the case of the Bloomington bronze, fixing the gold in place with gold wire is more conceivable, as there is no evidence of hammering along the edges of the groove. The Agora bronzes also have such grooves on their surface, and although they have lost much of their gold foil, small vestiges are still visible in the grooves where the gold was difficult to remove. On the bronze youth, small flecks of gold are noticeable in the groove running across the top of the head (fig. 5).[11]

Given the small size of the statuette, it is conceivable that some of the more delicate areas were refinished after the gold foil was applied, otherwise the finer details would have been lost.[12] That such a process was possible is supported by the examination of a foil-gilded Egyptian statuette of a smiting god in the Los Angeles County Museum of Art. The Smiting God measures *c.*18 cm in height (not much taller than the Bloomington statuette) and is dated

---

5 G. M. A. Richter, *The furniture of the Greeks, Etruscans and Romans* (London 1966) no. 487.

6 L. Pirzio Biroli Stefanelli (ed.), *Il bronzo dei Romani* (Rome 1990) 147, no. 98.

7 Richter, *Furniture* (supra n.5) no. 565.

8 For information on various gilding techniques, see W. A. Oddy, "Gilding: an outline of the technology of the plating of gold on to silver or copper in the Old World," *Endeavour* n.s. 15.1 (1991) 29-33; W. A. Oddy *et al.*, "The gilding of bronze sculpture in the classical world," in *Small bronze sculpture* 103-24; W. A. Oddy, "The gilding of Roman silver plate," in F. Baratte (ed.), *Argenterie romaine et byzantine* (Paris 1988) 9-25.

9 Shear 1973 (supra n.2) 167.

10 Oddy *et al.* (supra n.8) 106.

11 Traces of gold are also apparent in some of the cuts located on the back of the statuette and on the surface of the back of the figure. Some of the gold was detectable only with the aid of a microscope, and I am most appreciative of the help and advice given by D. Thimme on this subject.

12 I am grateful to W. A. Oddy for his comments and suggestions.

c.1550-1150 B.C.[13] Much of the gold foil used to cover the statuette is still preserved, and the grooves used to anchor the foil are clearly visible on the back of the legs, arms, kilt, and crown of the figure. It is also readily apparent that, after the foil was applied, some of the more delicate areas such as the facial features and folds in the kilt were carefully incised, presumably with a pointed instrument, in order to highlight these smaller details.

In summary, it is clear that the Bloomington bronze, in appearance and function, is substantially different from the Athenian Nike head and equestrian statue. First of all, its origin in Pergamon indicates that the process of foil gilding was not confined to Athens. In fact, the technique was probably imported to Greece from the East.[14] The Egyptian Smiting God is said to have come from either Syria or Palestine, and the Persians also used this technique. Two surviving examples, both small in size, are the lion pedestal excavated at Persepolis[15] and an Achaemenid silver bowl from the 5th c. B.C.[16] Second, and more important, the bronze youth is quite small, indicating that the process of foil gilding was not restricted to larger sculpture, as the Athenian bronzes have led us to believe. Furthermore, the Bloomington bronze probably adorned a piece of furniture meant for an interior space, in contrast to the Nike head and equestrian statue, which were outdoor public monuments. Therefore, we have before us a truly important piece of bronze workmanship that will compel many scholars to adjust their view of foil-gilded bronzes in the Greek world.

Fine Arts 132, Indiana University, Bloomington, IN 47405

Acknowledgements

I would like to thank A. Calinescu of the Indiana University Art Museum for allowing me to publish this object and for her guidance and valuable insights. Special thanks go also to W. Rudolph who first encouraged me to pursue this topic and provided constant support and editorial assistance. I am also much indebted to K. Glowacki, K. Ros, T. Sabatos, and N. Alexander for their aid in preparing earlier drafts of this paper.

Since presenting my paper, it has come to my attention that the bronze figure in the Indiana University Art Museum was in fact excavated from the Asklepieion in Pergamon in 1938: see O. Deubner, "Eine hellenistische Bronzefigur aus dem Asklepieion von Pergamon," in N. Basgelen and M. Lugal (edd.), *Festschrift für Jale Inan* (Istanbul 1989) 13-16. The IUAM has taken steps toward the restitution of the bronze to the Bergama Museum.

---

13 LACMA M.45.3.121. J. A. Bisno, "A bronze figure of Ba'al in the Los Angeles County Museum of Art," *JNES* 29.2 (1970) 78-79.

14 H. Thompson 1940 (supra n.1) 191.

15 D. Thompson 1944 (supra n.1) fig. 5.

16 Oddy 1991 (supra n.8) fig. 2.

On the Capponi grotesque in the Metropolitan Museum of Art

Maria Teresa Marabini Moevs

This bronze statuette of a grotesque male figure (figs. 1-2) was originally in the Roman collection of the marquis Alessandro Gregorio Capponi,[1] "curator and lifetime president of the Capitoline Museum." After his death in 1746, it was bequeathed to the Kircher Museum of the Collegio Romano,[2] where it remained at least until 1877.[3] When at the end of the century the Kircher Museum was dismantled, the statuette apparently never reached its likely destination, the newly instituted Museo Nazionale Romano. Instead it appeared in 1912 in New York, when it was acquired by the Metropolitan Museum of Art and published shortly thereafter by Gisela Richter.[4]

"It was found in Rome, in the excavations on the Esquiline in 1727,"[5] a precise reference befitting the diligence of Capponi, who habitually captioned the etchings of the objects in his collection with information about their acquisition.[6] The find can be very likely located in the eastern section of the hill, where excavations had started as early as the beginning of the 16th c., culminating from 1872 to 1887 in the grand project connected with the urban development of the entire area. Reclaimed by Maecenas in the years between 42 and 35 B.C. from its primeval use as potter's field to a region radiant with villas and gardens, abode of the privileged and sophisticated, it was, under Tiberius, annexed to the imperial properties.[7] The Italian provenance of the statuette, therefore, loses its significance because of the cosmopolitan character of the region.

The statuette is 0.10 m high and solid-cast. The partially cleaned surface is marred by corrosion pits where cuprite and, above it, malachite have formed. Missing are the right forearm and, from above the elbow, the left arm extended sideways, which had been made separately and inserted. A depression along the right side of the chest with a large spot of cuprite seems to indicate that the forearm adhered to it, possibly holding an object in between.

---

1 F. Ficoroni, *Le maschere sceniche e le figure comiche d'antichi Romani, descritte brevemente da Francesco de' Ficoroni* (Rome 1736) 49-50, pl. 9.2: "figura delineata dall'originale del Signor Marchese Capponi, che la conserva nel suo Museo ... Vedasi la spiegazione in stampa pubblicata dal detto Signor Marchese." For a brief biography of Capponi, see *I codici capponiani della Biblioteca Vaticana descritti da Giuseppe Salvo Cozzo* (Rome 1897) x-xi, n.2.

2 *Francisci Ficoronii dissertatio de larvis scaenicis et figuris comicis antiquorum Romanorum ex italica in latinam linguam versa* (Rome 1750) 25, pl. 9.2: *persona, e prototypo delineata est, qui in Museo RR. PP. Societatis Jesu, olim Marchionis Capponi asservatur.*

3 "Atellanae fabulae," *DarSag* 1 (1877) 514-15, fig. 597, n.30: "Le petit bronze du musée Kircher a été publié par Ficoroni."

4 Rogers Fund, 1912, no. 12.229.6; G. Richter, "Grotesques and the mime," *AJA* 17 (1913) 149-56, pls. 5-6, and in abbreviated form in *The Metropolitan Museum of Art. Greek, Etruscan, and Roman bronzes* (New York 1915) 81-84, fig. 127. L. Pollak, in his *Römische Memoiren* (M. Guldan [ed.], (Rome 1994) 131, says that the Jesuits shortly before September 20, 1870, had set aside from their collection in the Kircher Museum many important antiquities (mostly bronze and gold objects), which 30 years later were sold privately through the mediation of a Roman painter (Guerrini), who later retired to Viterbo. Among them was the grotesque acquired by the Metropolitan Museum (I owe this reference to J. Mertens).

5 *DarSag* (supra n.3) 515, n.30: "Il fut trouvé à Rome dans les fouilles du mont Esquilin, en 1727." The source for this information presumably was Capponi's publication, quoted by Ficoroni (supra n.1); *The Gods delight* 164-67, no. 28.

6 *I codici capponiani* (supra n.1) no. 224.

7 For a survey of the excavations and finds in this region of the Esquiline, see *Le tranquille dimore degli dei. La residenza imperiale degli Horti Lamiani* (Venice 1986), especially 167-72 for the excavations before 1870.

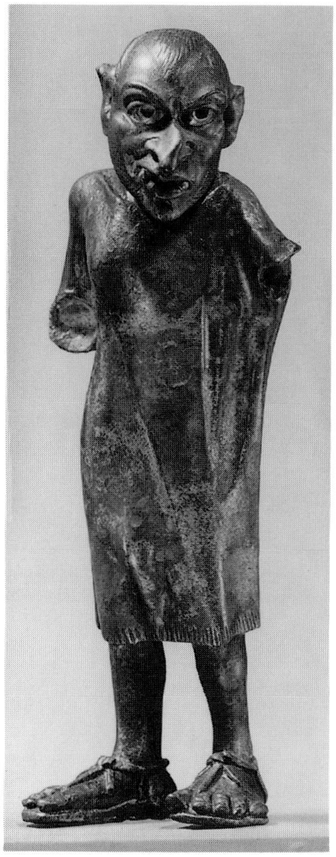
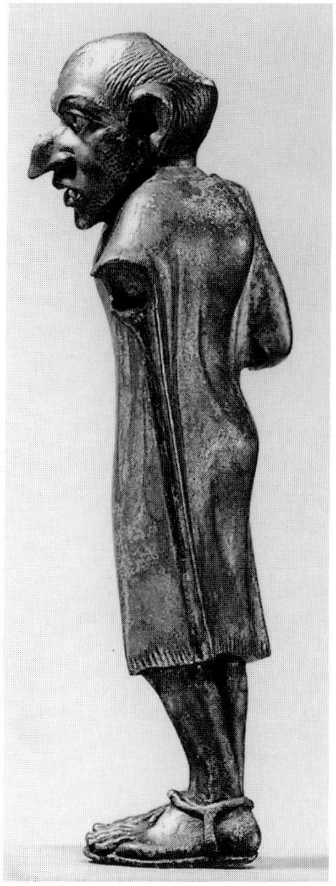
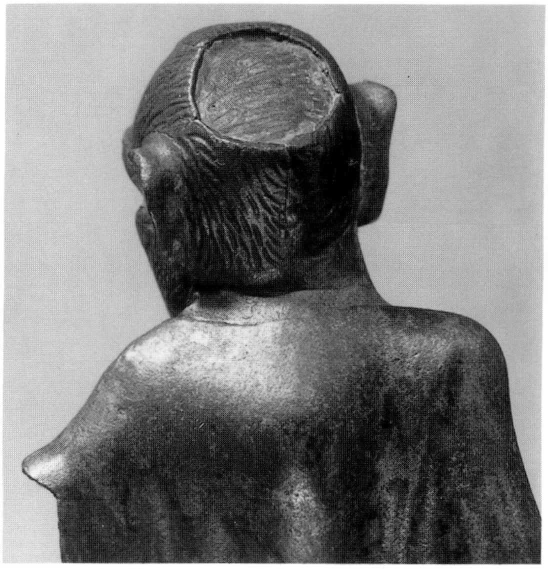

Fig. 1 (left). Statuette of a grotesque male figure, front. Bronze, h. 0.10 m. Found on the Esquiline, Rome; originally in the Capponi collection. New York, The Metropolitan Museum of Art, Rogers Fund, 1912, 12.229.6. Fig. 2 (center). Left side. Fig. 3 (right). Back of the head (All photos: courtesy The Metropolitan Museum of Art.)

Balancing the weight of his spindle-legged body on both feet, the right slightly advanced, the miserable creature sinks his enormous head into his chest, humped on the right side. A second hump on his left shoulder and a large, pendulous phallus are revealed from under the fabric of the garment, marked by essential and sharply defined folds. On the legs, shinbones and peroneal muscles are summarily indicated, but the structure of the feet is detailed and accurate.

The head is a rare achievement of expressiveness and technical virtuosity.[8] Egg-shaped with fan-like ears, it has cavernous eye sockets under sharply arched brows, a big hooked nose, and a crooked mouth. The fang-like canines and the whites of the eyes are of silver; the conical holes at the centers of the eyes were not cut to receive an inlay. A foil sheet made of an alloy of copper, silver, and gold, originally velvety black, covers in sections the whiskers and the hair, where a thin seam is visible at the back and above the left ear. On this foil, which recedes on each side of the forehead from a central peak, the hair is indicated by short strokes, the whiskers by stipples. Richter imprecisely called this foil a niello.[9] It is in truth a technique similar

---

8 Richard Stone had Mark Wypyski do a complete re-analysis of the statuette, with the following results: "The bronze of the figure itself is a leaded tin bronze of typical composition: 7.6% tin, 7.7% lead. The eyes are indeed silver, but with a small addition of copper (9.3% copper). The hair and beard are a different matter entirely. They seem to be made of a *shakudo* type alloy as they are both copper with the addition of both silver and gold. The hair has 2.5% silver and 2.7% gold. There is also about 2% lead, which is probably adventitious. The beard has 2.3% silver and 0.7% gold (as well as 0.6% zinc, again probably adventitious). The grayish material present at the site of the missing patch of hair contains both tin and lead and is clearly the remains of heavily corroded soft solder.
It would seem that both the hair and beard would have originally been the velvety black color typical of *shakudo* after mild acidic oxidation. Also, the hair was attached, at least in part, by soft soldering."

9 Richter 1913 (supra n.4) 150; ead., *The Metropolitan Museum of Art. Handbook of the classical collection* (New York 1917) 161, fig. 101; ead., *The Metropolitan Museum of Art. Handbook of the Greek collection*

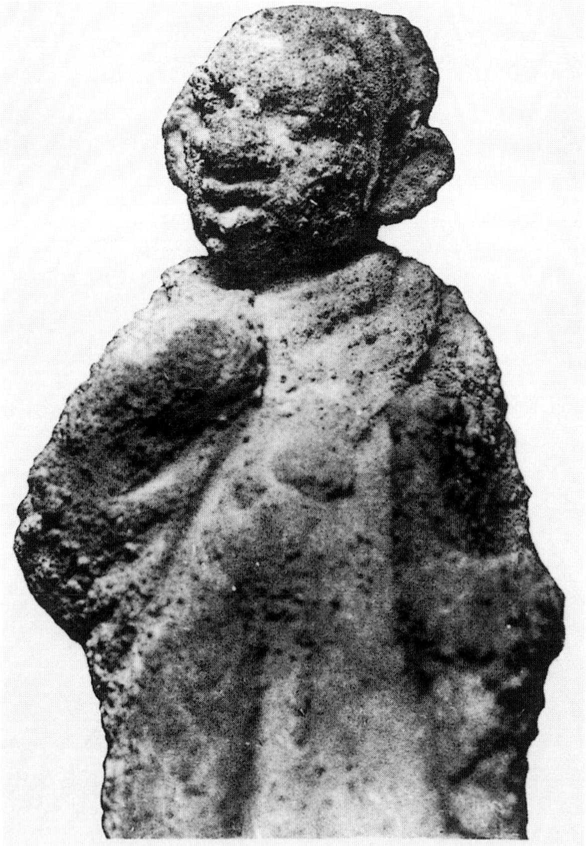

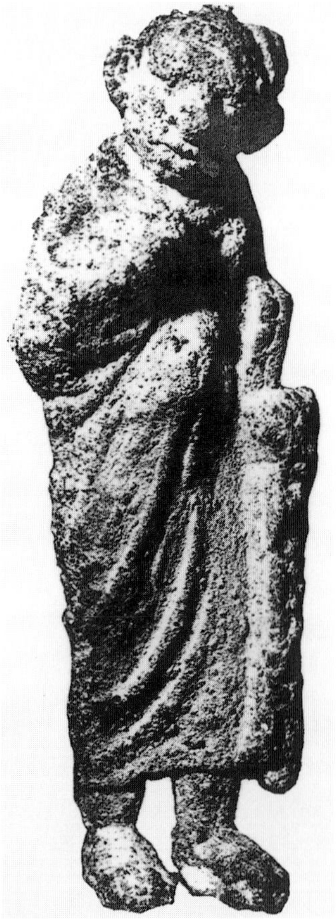

Figs. 4-5. Statuette of grotesque scholar. Bronze, h 0.10 m. Found at Begram, Afghanistan. Paris, Musée Guimet 19844. (Photos: Réunion des Musées Nationaux.)

to the one frequently mentioned as 'black bronze' in Egyptian texts from Dynasty 18 through the New Kingdom and later. Though the last reference to it is in Dynasty 30, it has been suggested that 'black bronze' continued to be used in the Ptolemaic period.[10] Indeed, the most exhaustive description of this technique in antiquity can be found in Book 33 of Pliny's *Natural History*:

> The people of Egypt ... do not engrave but paint their silver ... The method adopted is as follows: with the silver is mixed one third its amount of the very fine Cyprus copper ... and the same amount of live sulfur as of silver, and then they are melted in an earthenware vessel ... Silver is also turned black by means of the yolk of a hard-boiled egg.[11]

A round shallow depression on the crown of the head (fig. 3), which has been interpreted as intended to receive a silver inlay simulating a tonsure or simply another section of the sheet,[12] may be suited rather to receive a *cirrus in vertice,* cast separately and applied to the flat, roughened surface of the bronze by soft soldering, like a skullcap. The weight of this solid piece would explain its later dislodging.

(Cambridge, MA 1953) 126, no. 2, pl. 105A. Afterwards the statuette "has been cleaned by D. von Bothmer, which brought out the contrast of the inlays": *The gods delight* 167.

10 J. D. Cooney, "On the meaning of bi3," *ZAS* 93 (1966) 43-47; R. Bianchi, "Egyptian metal statuary of the Third Intermediate Period (*c.*1070-656 B.C.) from its Egyptian antecedents to its Samian examples," in *Small bronze sculpture* 69-72. Black bronze is discussed by P. T. Craddock and A. Giumlia-Mair in the *Acta of the 12th bronze congress* 137-47, and by Giumlia-Mair in *AntW* 27.4 (1996) 313-21.

11 33.46.131.

12 The first restoration is suggested by Richter 1913 (supra n.4) 149; the second is offered in *The gods delight* 165.

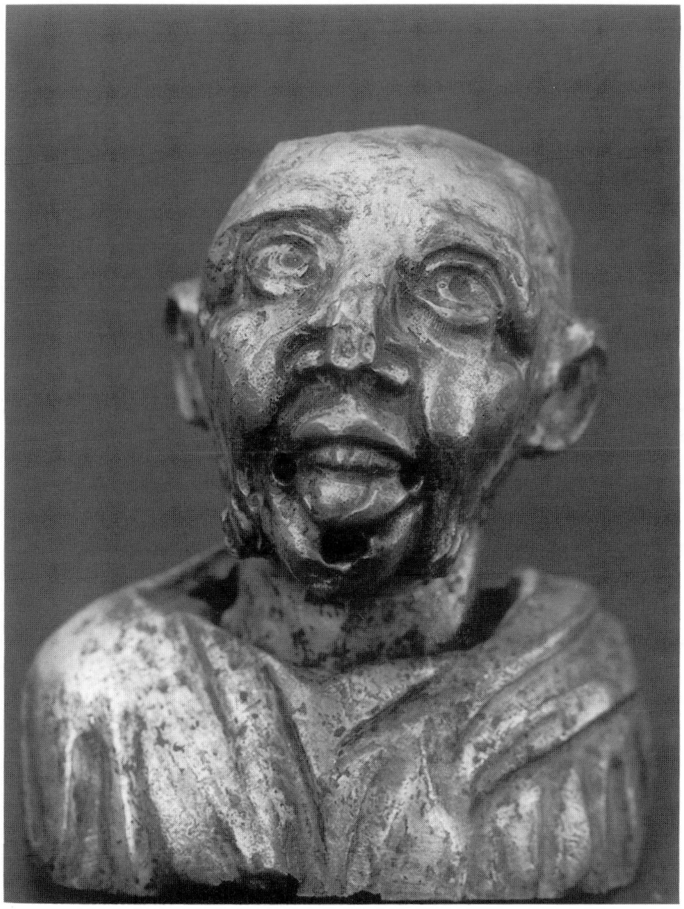
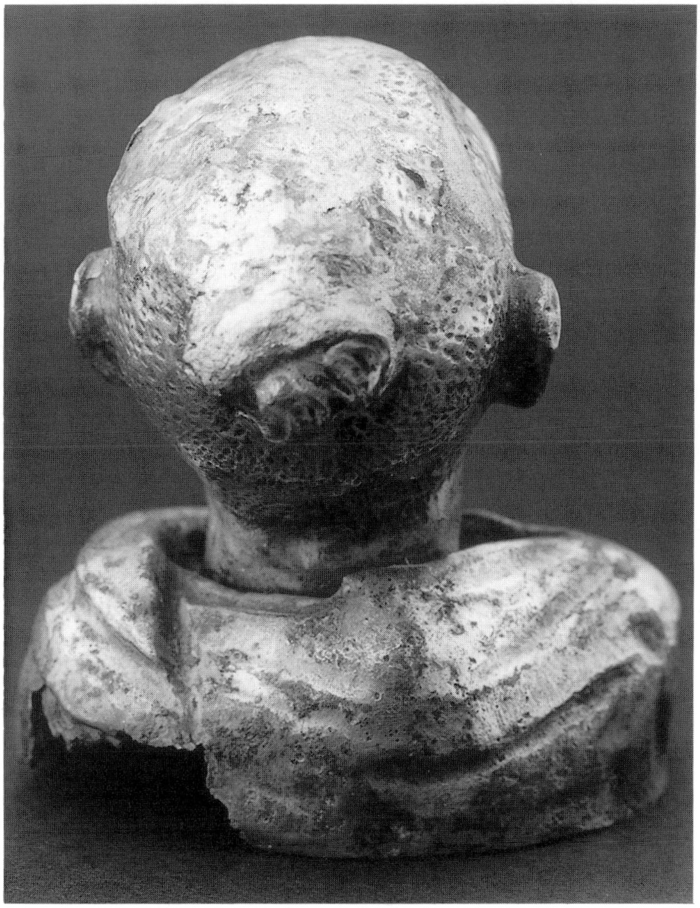

Figs. 6-7. Bust of a grotesque male figure, front and back. Found at Sainte-Colombe-lès-Vienne (Rhône). Silver, h. 5.5 cm. Lyon, Musée de la Civilisation Gallo-Romaine E 176. (Photos: Ch. Thioc, courtesy Museum.)

A *cirrus in vertice,* surrounded by very short hair, appears, it seems, on the head of a bronze statuette from Begram (figs. 4-5), quite possibly from Alexandria.[13] Although wearing a mantle rather than only a tunic, this personage shares many similarities with the Metropolitan statuette: thin hunched body, enormous head on a very short neck, and exaggerated features such as the large protruding ears, broad forehead, big hooked nose, and crooked mouth. The mortified expression that underlines the misery of the body is created in both by the inclination of the head. The diptych held close to his side by the Begram figurine suggests that a similar attribute was held in the same position by the Metropolitan bronze.

The celebrity of this personage in antiquity is confirmed by the preservation of his basic features on a small silver bust found near Lyon (figs. 6-7), a 2nd c. A.D. provincial adaptation of an Alexandrian original.[14] Two holes at the corners of the mouth suggest the original presence of fang-like canines, while the protruding tongue may be a faulty interpretation of the thick,

13 R. Ghirshman, *Mémoires de la délégation archéologique française en Afghanistan* XII: *Bégram. Recherches archéologiques et historiques sur les Kouchans* (Cairo 1946) 68, pls. 12, 24 B.G.9.

14 S. Boucher, *Bronzes grecs, hellénistiques et étrusques des musées de Lyon* (Lyon 1970) 48, no. 27; ead. *Recherches sur les bronzes figurés de Gaule pré-romaine et romaine* (BEFAR 228, 1976) no. 341, pl. 70; on the Egyptian influence on the bronzes found in Gallia, see ibid. 186-202.

drooping lip seen on the Metropolitan statuette. The *cirrus in vertice*, short and curly, rises from a skull covered with incisions, similar to the small strokes depicting the hair of the Capponi figure. A *cirrus* limited in size to the surface of the lost inlay may also be suggested here, since no traces of attachment are preserved elsewhere.

Although the *cirrus in vertice* is Pharaonic, and Greek Egypt is mostly associated with the side-lock version typical of the Child-Horus and in the Roman world with the topknot seen on figures of athletes,[15] it seems to have an ethnic African origin, particularly evident if associated with short, curly hair,[16] as for instance on a stele of the Meroitic period in the Cairo Museum.[17] The egg-shaped skull of the Capponi bronze and the superficially marked hair adhering to it like a cap are common features of late Egyptian heads.[18]

The unbelted tunic open on both sides and sewn on the shoulder, with stitches meticulously marked along the sleeves, is fringed at the bottom. It is a Hellenized version of the conventional Egyptian costume described by Herodotus (2.81): "They wear linen tunics with fringes hanging about the legs, called 'calasiris'."[19] To the same tradition belong the linen garments worn by the Egyptians on the Caeretan hydria by the Busiris Painter,[20] or those appearing in the Egyptian processional scene painted by a provincial Greek artist on a wooden panel from Saqqâra, both dated to the end of the 6th c. B.C.[21]

In their attempts to find a suitable interpretation for this figure, scholars have been misled by its Italian provenance and have, at the same time, either ignored the precise location and date of the find or simply dismissed it.[22] It became commonly identified as an actor of the mime and, more specifically, of the Atellan farce, possibly a Dossenus. The masterly execution was tentatively credited to a Greek artist of the 2nd c. B.C., evidently from South Italy.[23] In a more far-fetched explanation, the bronze was seen as a Roman Late Republican or Early Imperial version of the Etruscan Charun.[24] Richter envisaged him as a performer[25] in a scene like those represented in the figurative cycle Dragendorff XXIV by the Arretine potter M. Perennius Bargathes.[26] Indeed, a striking resemblance exists between this bronze and the four personages

---

15 B. Gassowska, "Cirrus in vertice — one of the problems in Roman athlete iconography," in *Mélanges offerts à K. Michalowski* (Warsaw 1966) 421-27.

16 On the Egyptian connotation of this type of coiffure and its ethnic origin, see V. von Gonzenbach, *Untersuchungen zu den Knabenweihen im Isiskult der römischer Kaiserzeit* (Antiquitas 1, vol. 4; Bonn 1957) 39-50.

17 T. Säve-Soderbergh (ed.), *Temples and tombs of ancient Nubia: the international rescue campaign at Abu Simbel, Philae, and other sites* (London–Paris 1987) pl. 36.

18 R. S. Bianchi, "The Pharaonic art of Ptolemaic Egypt," in *Cleopatra's Egypt: age of the Ptolemies* (Exhib. cat.., Brooklyn Museum of Art 1988) 55-59, 65.

19 E. Capps, T. Page, and W. Rouse (edd.), *Herodotus* I (LCL, London 1926) 367.

20 J. M. Hemelrijk, *Caeretan hydriae* (Mainz am Rhein 1984) 173-74, pls. 118a, 119-21: "The picture seems inspired by Egyptian reliefs which the Busiris Painter must have admired when staying in Egypt as a boy."

21 Ibid. 201-2, no. 2; G. T. Martin, *The tomb of Hetepka* (London 1979) 74-78, no. 284, pl. 1 (frontispiece).

22 As happens in *The gods delight*, in spite of the fact that provenance and date are mentioned for the first time since *DarSag* (supra n.3).

23 The Italian connection of the personage was already evidence in Ficoroni's evaluation (supra n.1): "Il suo volto ... è a guisa di Buffone, e di Pulcinella, che è solito introdursi nei nostri teatri." He had become an actor in the Atellan farce in F. Wieseler, *Theatergebäude und Denkmäler des Bühnenwesen bei den Griechen und Römern* (Göttingen 1851) 92, no. 10, pl. 12.10, and later in *Dar Sag* (supra n.3). He was called first an actor in the mime by Richter 1913 (supra n.4) and later (1953) more specifically in the Atellan farces of South Italy (supra n.9). He was seen as a possible image of Dossenus of South Italian provenance by M. Bieber, *The history of the Greek and Roman theater* (Princeton 1961) 247-48, fig. 817.

24 *The gods delight* 166.

25 Richter 1913 (supra n.4) 155.

26 H. Dragendorff and C. Watzinger, *Arretinische Reliefkeramik* (Reutlingen 1948) 107-9, "Karikaturen und Possenfiguren"; *M. Perennius Bargathes* (Rome 1984) 64-77.

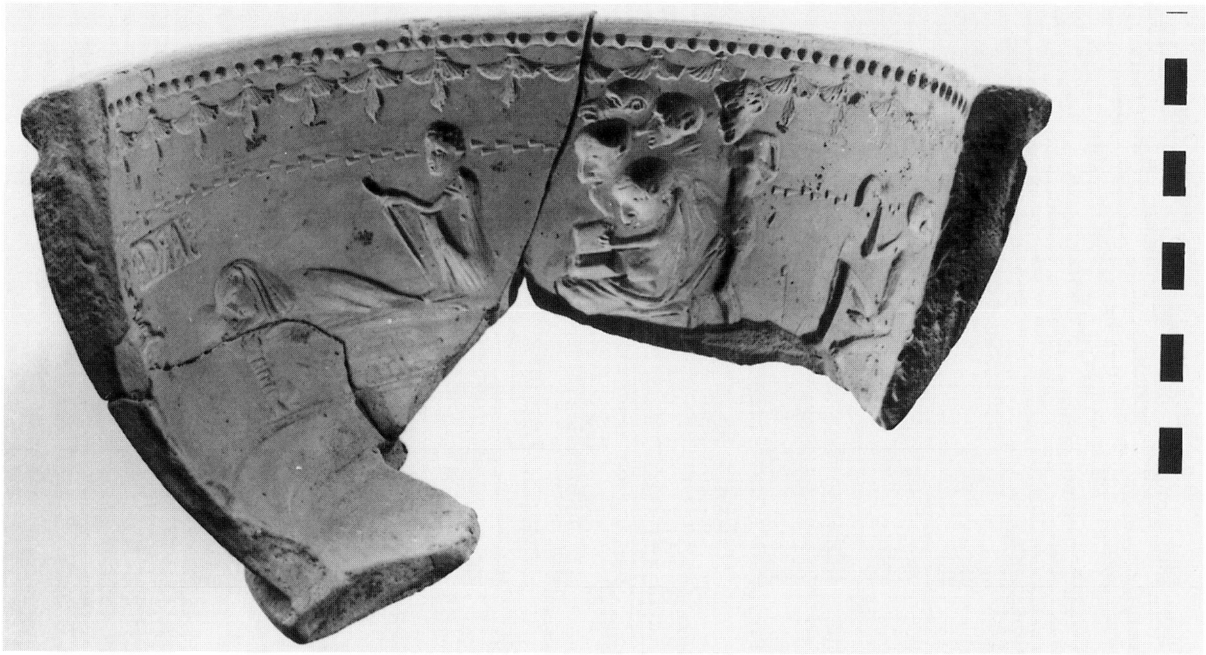

Fig. 8. Arretine mold by M. Perennius Bargathes. Scene derived from an illustrated edition of the *Silloi* by Timon of Phlius. Arezzo, Archaelogical Museum 4957. (Photo: courtesy Soprintendenza alleAntichità d'Etruria, Florence, 39372/1.)

represented on mold inv. 4957 (fig. 8) in the Archaeological Museum, Arezzo.[27]

My interpretation of the scene,[28] however, diverges from the common assumption that a theatrical performance is represented.[29] I have identified it, and the rest of the cycle, as reproductions from an illustrated edition of the *Silloi* by the Sceptic philosopher and satirist Timon of Phlius (320-230 B.C.).[30] The work was a satire on past and contemporary worlds of learning, and the illustrations were presumably created by an Alexandrian artist in the 3rd c. B.C. The presence of a crouching Cyclops among the characters confirms Timon's authorship, since Diogenes Laertius (9.112) informs us, "I have heard that he had only one eye; indeed he used to call himself a Cyclops."[31]

This particular vignette, a parody of the scholarship promoted in the Museum at Alexandria, is a direct commentary on Timon's verses: "In the cosmopolitan land of Egypt many are they who get fed, cloistered bookworms, endlessly arguing in the bird cage of the Muses."[32] Also from Diogenes Laertius (9.113) we learn that the Homeric studies cultivated by the literati of the Museum were a favorite target of Timon. In this scene, Homer himself, stultified

---

27 Ibid., Dragendorff and Watzinger, 107 nos. 8-12; *Bargathes* 66-67, no. 49.

28 "Philosophers and scholars in Roman caricatures of Alexandrian origin," in *L'Egitto in Italia dall'antichità al medioevo* (Rome 1998) 439-47, figs. 1, 2, 4.

29 U. Pasqui, "Nuove scoperte di antiche figuline della fornace di M. Perennio," *NSc* 1896, 458; K. Hähnle, *Arretinische Reliefkeramik* (Stuttgart 1915) 73-74; Dragendorff and Watzinger (supra n.26) 109; P. Porten Palange, "M. Perennius Bargathes," in *Bargathes* (supra n.26) 17.

30 The principal source on Timon is Diogenes Laertius's *Lives of eminent philosophers*, 9.109-16. On his life and work, see G. Voghera, *Timone di Fliunte e la poesia sillografica* (Padua 1904); A. Long, "Timon of Phlius: Pyrrhonist and satirist," *ProcCambPhilSoc* 204 (1978) 68-91.

31 R. D. Hicks (transl.), *Diogenes Laertius: lives of eminent philosophers* 2 (LCL, Cambridge, MA 1925) 523.

32 H. Diels, *Poetarum philosophorum fragmenta* (Poetarum graecorum fragmenta 3.1, Berlin 1901) 187, no. 12; the text is preserved in a quotation by Athenaeus of Naucratis (*Deipn*. 1.22 D). My translation is based on that of P. M. Fraser, *Ptolemaic Alexandria* 1 (Oxford 1972) 317.

by inane scholarship to the condition of a mummy, with his Muse at the brink of starvation,[33] is visited in vain by a peacock, symbol of resurrection.[34] In the meantime, he is worshipped by four scholars and watched by a poor passer-by, with Negroid features and no clothes, who tries to participate, *suo more,* in their scholarly excitement.[35] The diptych in the hands of the scholar in the foreground recalls the attribute of the statuette from Begram. The deformed thinness of this man and the grotesque features of the entire group, particularly the rooster-like man in the middle ground,[36] match the absurdity of the Metropolitan figure. I tentatively identify the scholar with the diptych as Philetas of Cos, tutor to the future Ptolemy II and laughing-stock of contemporary comedy because of his pedantic Homeric expertise and proverbial thinness.[37]

The Capponi grotesque in the Metropolitan Museum finds, I believe, its place in this tradition of parodied scholarship. The many Egyptian connotations — cultural, stylistic, and technical—, as well as the superb quality of the execution, qualify it as a product of the best period of Alexandrian art, not later than the beginning of the 2nd c. B.C.

Department of Classics, Rugers the State University of New Jersey, New Brunswick, NJ

Acknowledgements

I wish to thank J. R. Mertens, Curator of Greek and Roman Art at The Metropolitan Museum of Art, New York, for her invaluable help and keen observations. R. E. Stone of the Sherman Fairchild Center for Objects Conservation in the same museum has shared his great knowledge of ancient bronze technique and had a complete re-analysis done of the statuette.

---

33 She is crouching at the foot of the bed in a manner recalling the *ba*-bird of the Egyptians perched at the foot of the mummy's bier, as in C. Andrews and R. O. Faulkner, *The ancient Egyptian Book of the Dead* (London 1985) 85.

34 The long arched beak, elongated eye socket and, above all, the nail-like growths of its crest secure the identification. Already in the Early Hellenistic period this Dionysian bird had acquired that symbolic meaning of resurrection and immortality which explains its familiar presence in Early Christian art. Two colossal groups of the infant Dionysos riding a sacred peacock were found in the Serapeion of Memphis: J. P. Lauer and C. Picard, *Les statues ptolémaiques du Sérapieion de Memphis* (Paris 1955) 194-209, pls. 19-20. Live peacocks in cages were carried in the Dionysian section of the Grand Procession of Ptolemy Philadelphos: Athenaeus, *Deipn.* 5.201 B.

35 The state of erection, representing sexual excitement in Old Comedy, is ironically transferred here to a depiction of the intellectual enthusiasm of the populace.

36 A small bronze head from Lower Egypt, with very similar features, is topped by a rooster crest: P. Perdrizet, *Bronzes grecs d'Égypte de la collection Fouquet* (Paris 1911) 60, no. 97, p. 28 (middle). Animal likeness in human characterization gained philosophical recognition in the works of Aristotle and became under his successors an integral part of the empirical science of physiognomics: see E. C. Evans, *Physiognomics in the ancient world* (TransAmPhilSoc n.s. 59, 1969). The presence of a rooster-like man in this context underlines the garrulous and litigious habits of the Museum scholars. The similar features of the Metropolitan piece very likely indicate the same intent of characterization.

37 Plutarch, *An Seni* 791 E. Athenaeus describes him with lead balls bound to his feet to keep him from blowing away (*Deipn.* 12.552 B) and worn out by his studies of linguistics (*Deipn.* 9.401 E). Ridiculed in Attic comedy of the 3rd c. B.C., particularly in the *Phoenicides* by Strabo (*Deipn.* 9.382-83 B), Philetas of Cos must have been rather popular with Athenian audiences.

The Harvard fulcrum attachment: a problem in dating

Natalie Taback

This paper offers a close reading of the Harvard fulcrum attachment[1] (fig. 1), a fine bronze example of an S-shaped attachment designed to decorate a Hellenistic or Early Imperial Roman couch. The piece would have been affixed to the side of a curved wooden headboard (*fulcrum*) of the same S-shape, and may have served as an elbow-rest for a diner. The attachment is on display in the Arthur M. Sackler Museum, where it is labeled as a Roman work of c.A.D. 100-150. After providing a detailed description of selected iconographic and technical aspects of the attachment, I advance a somewhat earlier dating based on two models of dating proposed by S. Faust and B. Barr-Sharrar.

The Harvard fulcrum attachment is intact. The surface is slightly rough with incrustation and has a green patina, with a reddish-brown layer of cuprite visible where the patina has worn away. Iron nails are visible on the sides of the attachment, suggesting that it was affixed to the headrest by means of a perpendicular shelf on the back, following the silhouette of the piece. The shelf enabled the attachment to fit like a bracket onto the edge of the headrest and then to be secured on its sides with nails (see fig. 2).[2]

The Harvard fulcrum attachment, including its decoration, was solid-cast as a single piece. Such attachments would have been cast using the indirect lost-wax process, allowing them to be

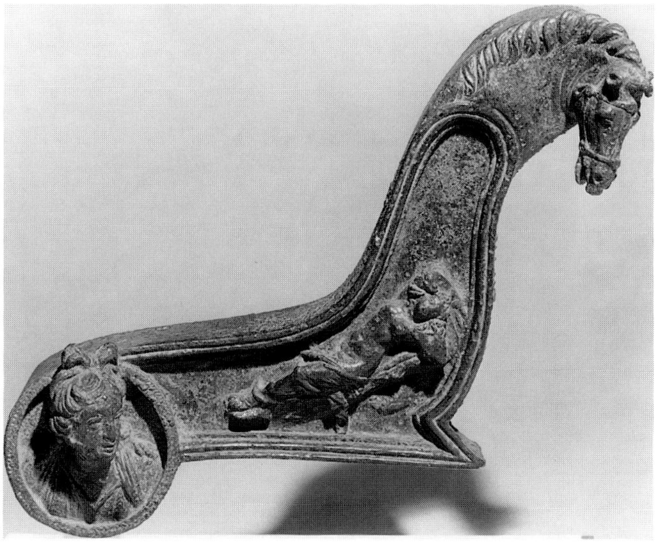

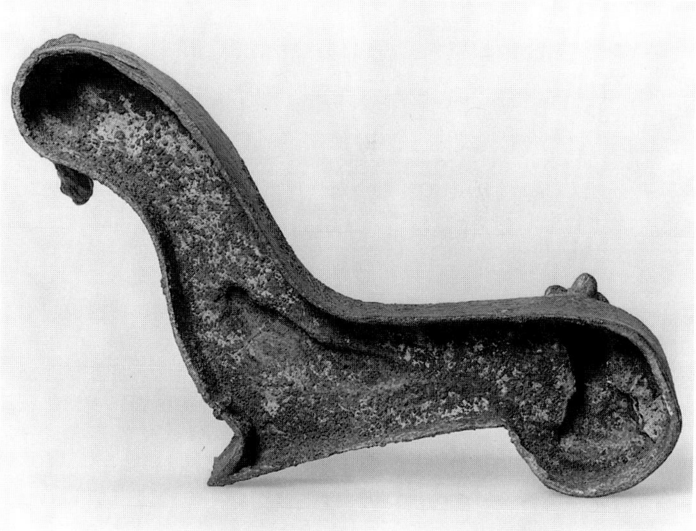

Figs. 1-2. Fulcrum attachment, front and back. Hellenistic, late 2nd/early 1st c. B.C.- early 1st c A.D. Bronze, l. 0.22 m. Cambridge, Mass., Arthur M. Sackler Museum, Harvard University Art Museums, 1987.130. (Photos: courtesy Arthur M. Sackler Museum.)

---

1 Acc. no. 1987.130. Purchased by the Ancient Art Acquisitions Fund through the generosity of William Collins Kohler in memory of Dr. Elaine Humphreys Kohler. H. 0.184 m., w. 0.056 m, and l. 0.22 m. Following Barr-Sharrar, we will take fulcrum to denote "headrest," as it is used in ancient literary sources; this term is to be distinguished from fulcrum attachment, which adorned the sides of a headrest and may have served as an elbow-rest. See B. Barr-Sharrar, *The Hellenistic and Early Imperial decorative bust* (Mainz 1987) 4.

2 Such a method of attachment was in use by the end of the 1st quarter of the 2nd c. B.C.: see B. Barr-Sharrar, "The bronze fulcrum attachment: some clarifications in the chronology of solutions to this problematic format" in K. Gschwantler and A. Bernhard-Walcher (edd.), *Griechische und römische Statuetten und Großbronzen. Akten der 9. int. Tagung über antike Bronzen 1986* (Vienna 1988) 280.

produced serially from a model. The waxes could have been worked over to provide some distinctive qualities for a given piece.[3] Because they could be produced serially, fulcrum attachments were common in the Hellenistic and Early Imperial periods. The Harvard attachment might therefore have been displayed in the *triclinium* of a Roman villa belonging to a person of the middle or upper stratum of society.

The Harvard fulcrum attachment consists of three principal components, a medallion at the lower left, a slanted central section, and a protome at the upper right. Each component has distinctive iconographic elements, all Hellenistic in style. Furthermore, as is characteristic of many extant fulcrum attachments, the piece is decorated with a Dionysian theme, an appealing subject for a dining couch.

The medallion at the lower left corner of the Harvard attachment contains a high relief bust of a female figure, a maenad or nymph, depicted with frontal chest, head in three-quarter view to her left, chin raised, mouth slightly open. A *mitra* adorns her forehead; the hair, piled high on her head and fastened in a Hellenistic top-knot *(krobylos)*, extends above the confines of the roundel; ivy or thick clumps of hair hang over her shoulders. The figure is clad in a *chiton* with a particularly sharp V-fold below the throat and, over it, a *himation*. The roundel is decorated with a vine pattern.

The slanted central portion depicts a reclining figure in relief, either a sleeping maenad or Ariadne. The woman's body is twisted, with right arm placed behind the head, head and torso twisting to her left, lower body twisting to her right, left leg crossed over the right. The figure is unclothed save for some drapery over the lower body and genitalia that still reveals the contour of the legs. The head is adorned with a garland and several bunches of grapes; long curly locks of hair fall over the shoulders. The woman appears to recline on a sloping rock. A curvilinear decoration in low relief below her body may represent a cornucopia.

The upper part of the attachment ends in a horse protome, one of the most common on fulcrum attachments.[4] The horse is represented with mouth gaping, head down and turned to its right, as if in motion; three horizontal folds of skin on the neck show compressed flesh as the horse turns its head. The mane, in low relief, consists of locks falling in a pattern of undulating waves which culminates in a tuft arching forward between the small, pointed ears. The horse's bridle has round *phalerae* where the browband and the noseband join the cheekpiece.

As with the majority of such attachments, the orientation, with medallion at the lower left and protome at the upper right, suggests that this bronze decoration would have been attached to a dining couch so as to support the elbow of a diner reclining on his left side. This was undoubtedly the preferred side on which to recline, freeing the right hand to hold refreshment. Some scholars, in fact, suggest that left-oriented fulcrum attachments, and perhaps the entire left side of a dining couch, would have been more elaborately decorated than their right-oriented counterparts, which probably faced a wall.[5] Since headrests could be found at one or both ends of a couch,[6] with one or two fulcrum attachments at each end, a given couch could have as many as four fulcrum attachments.[7] Although fulcrum attachments are often found in pairs, sometimes mirror images of each other,[8] it is not possible to determine whether the Harvard attachment was part of a matching set.

A precise dating for the Harvard fulcrum attachment, as for the majority of such attachments, is problematic. Currently it is dated *c.*A.D. 100-150. One method of dating utilizes a

---

3 C. Mattusch, "The production of bronze statuary in antiquity," in *Das Wrack* 791.

4 Barr-Sharrar, *Bust* (supra n.1) 4.

5 Barr-Sharrar 1988 (supra n.2) 279.

6 According to Richter, couches with both headrests and footrests were probably not used for dining: see G. M. A. Richter, *The furniture of the Greeks, Etruscans, and Romans* (London 1966) 107.

7 See Barr-Sharrar, *Bust* (supra n.1) 6 n.11.

8 Particularly in the Early Roman period: see Barr-Sharrar 1988 (supra n.2) 279.

stylistic development of the shape of fulcrum attachments from the Hellenistic through Early Imperial periods based upon changes in two particular characteristics — massiveness, and the angle of incline. Fulcrum attachments are believed to have become larger in the Roman period, growing more massive and more upright as couches, including headrests, grew larger and higher.[9] This development has been investigated by B. Barr-Sharrar[10] using a series of 10 securely dated attachments, that is, those for which a *terminus ante quem* and/or a *terminus post quem* exists, derived from sites with known destruction dates, from tombs, from shipwrecks, and from identifiable portrait busts depicted on the attachments. Barr-Sharrar reports, however, that the increases in massiveness and uprightness are far from consistent and cautions against dating fulcrum attachments on the basis of these characteristics alone.

Faust utilizes still another tool in dating fulcrum attachments, the character of the inner angle formed where the horizontal bottom edge meets the adjacent sloping side, an area she terms the 'Zwickel,' or triangular insert.[11] She posits that the inner angle at the 'Zwickel' progressed, between the late 3rd c. B.C. and the early 1st c. A.D., from the development of a volute to a sharp, acute, inwardly directed angle, a change accompanied by a lengthening of the lower edge.[12] Thus, two acute angles at the 'Zwickel' were eventually formed, the basis of Faust's conceptualization of 'Doppelspornfulcra'[13] or double-spur fulcrum attachments. Faust in fact defines four principal classifications of fulcrum attachments. Form I attachments are slender and solid-cast, with relief decoration on their mid-section and high-relief busts at both finials; they date from the late 3rd/early 2nd c. B.C. through the early 1st c. B.C. Form II attachments have frames with inset panels and volutes at the 'Zwickel', and date from the first half of the 2nd c. B.C. through the early 1st c. B.C. Form III attachments have the same open frames but are double-spur fulcra, and date from the late 2nd/early 1st c. B.C. through the first half of the 1st c. A.D. Form IV attachments are fully upright, undecorated, and were produced from the second half of the 1st c. B.C. to the middle of the 1st c. A.D.[14]

The Harvard attachment, with two acute angles at the triangular insert, is clearly a double-spur fulcrum attachment and falls into Faust's Form III. If we survey the published double-spur fulcra, it is noteworthy that for the most part (although not without exception) they follow a general progression from slimmest to most voluminous and bellied-out.[15] The Harvard attachment is on the slender side of Form III attachments, not very bellied-out, and has an inner angle at the 'Zwickel' that is neither particularly sharp nor long. Furthermore the Harvard fulcrum is far from upright. Such features might indicate that the piece is among the early Form III attachments.

The size of the Harvard fulcrum attachment, measuring *c.*0.287 m along the diagonal, makes it difficult to determine the chronological placement of the piece within Faust's Form III. Most of the attachments from the end of Form III measure *c.*0.40 m along the diagonal.[16] The relatively small size of the Harvard attachment might suggest that it dates somewhat earlier than these pieces, since fulcrum attachments are generally believed to have become larger in the Roman period. Yet the Harvard attachment is virtually identical in size to the pair of fulcrum attachments (measuring 0.28 m) found in a tomb in Amiternum and now housed in the

---

9 Barr-Sharrar, *Bust* (supra n.1) 7. See also Richter, *Furniture* (supra n.7) 107.

10 Barr-Sharrar 1988 (supra n.2) 279-83.

11 S. Faust, *Fulcra: Figürlicher und ornamentaler Schmuck an antiken Betten* (Mainz 1989) 41.

12 The change is ascribed to the introduction of larger and more solid furniture: see Barr-Sharrar 1988 (supra n.3) 282.

13 Faust, *Fulcra* (supra n.11) 50.

14 For the above, see Faust, *Fulcra* (supra n.11) 34-39, 40-49, 50-54, 54-57.

15 B. Barr-Sharrar, review of Faust, *Fulcra*, in *BJb* 94 (1994) 635. Barr-Sharrar also suggests that the variations may sometimes be attributable to regional preferences: see Barr-Sharrar 1988 (supra n.2) 281.

16 See measurements supplied at ibid. 284.

Palazzo dei Conservatori,[17] attachments that Barr-Sharrar dates to the Tiberian era (*c.*A.D. 14-37) — occurring near the end rather than the beginning of Form III.[18] Thus we should be reluctant to restrict the Harvard attachment to a specific date within the chronological range of Form III. Furthermore, it should be recognized that couches of varying sizes were probably produced throughout the Hellenistic and Roman periods; also, the Harvard attachment might have decorated a child's couch.[19]

Several additional features of the Harvard attachment are useful in helping to establish a dating earlier than *c.*A.D. 100-150. It is solid-cast as a single piece with a central section decorated with a reclining figure in relief, reminiscent of the earliest surviving cast bronze fulcrum attachments (Form I). The piece, however, employs the shelf method of attachment, characteristic of Form II, originating in the first half of the 2nd c. B.C.[20] Also occurring at this time was a change in decoration from busts at both terminals (characteristic of Form I) to a single bust in the lower terminal and a protome at the upper terminal (characteristic of Form II and continuing through Form III). The Harvard attachment employs the latter method of decoration but, on the other hand, it fails to reflect certain changes that began to appear at this time, namely the replacement of the central section by an inlaid panel, allowing easier casting and the potential for a more elaborately decorated attachment.[21]

An attachment similar to the Harvard piece, located in the Staatliche Museen zu Berlin,[22] is helpful in assessing an earlier dating for the Harvard piece. The Berlin attachment depicts on its slanting central section a sleeping Ariadne in relief, not unlike the reclining figure on the Harvard piece. Ariadne reclines on a grapevine, her left arm supporting her tilted head, her right arm arched behind her head, a mantle wrapped over her lower body; the figure-type is based on the Hellenistic Sleeping Ariadne. Although the piece is currently dated to the 3rd c. B.C., Barr-Sharrar believes it is more likely to date within the first half of the 1st c. A.D. She has shown that not all fulcrum attachments with solid-cast fields and relief decoration are Hellenistic but that some were produced in the Roman period.[23] This could be the case with the Harvard attachment, since the piece is undeniably characterized by its double-spur angles.

In short, it seems reasonable to suggest a date for the Harvard fulcrum attachment within the span of Faust's Form III double-spur fulcra (late 2nd/early 1st c. B.C. to the early 1st c. A.D.). It is not possible to narrow this range on the basis of traits of massiveness, uprightness, and size, since Form III attachments varied considerably. Some scholars have asserted that the slanting fulcrum attachment largely went out of use after the Julio-Claudian period, at which time dining couches began to resemble the more modern sofa with three sides and a straight back,[24] perhaps suggesting that diners did not recline as before.[25] In light of these points, the current dating of *c.*A.D. 100-150 seems somewhat late and narrow. While the possibility exists that the Harvard piece might have been made at that time, the attachment may well date to a somewhat earlier period: the late 2nd/early 1st c. B.C. to the early 1st c. A.D.

Department of History of Art and Architecture, Harvard University, Cambridge, MA

Acknowledgements

For advice and encouragement I am grateful to K. Welch, D. G. Mitten, B. Barr-Sharrar, as well as to A. Brauer, S. Hemingway, and A. Paul. I thank Harvard University Art Museums for allowing me to publish the piece.

---

17 Ibid. fig. 10.
18 Ibid. 283.
19 I owe this suggestion to D. G. Mitten.
20 Faust, *Fulcra* (supra n.11) 40.
21 Barr-Sharrar 1988 (supra n.2) 280.
22 Inv. no. 30167, said to be from Ionia. Barr Sharrar, *Bust* (supra n.1) C 104, pl. 34. At the time of publication, the piece was in the Antikenabteilung, Berlin-Charlottenburg.
23 Barr-Sharrar, *Bust* (supra n.1) 60, 101.
24 Barr-Sharrar 1988 (supra n.2) 281, 283 n.4.
25 Barr-Sharrar 1994 (supra n.15) 636.

A bronze plaque to Apollo Praenos in Boston

Annewies van den Hoek and Sarolta A. Takács

The problem

An inscribed bronze votive plaque was acquired by the Museum of Fine Arts, Boston, in 1983 and published subsequently in the annual report and in the museum's 1988 catalogue *Sculpture in stone and bronze*.[1] M. P. Speidel briefly discussed the piece in his *Roman army studies* since the inscription mentions *Legio XXII*.[2] The inscription itself was published in 1994 in the *Supplementum Epigraphicum Graecum*.[3]

The rectangular plaque (fig. 1) has the remains of a bronze strap for attachment pulled through a hole at the top center and twisted. An inscription of three lines covers the full width of the lower part of the plaque; above the inscription is a drawing of Apollo riding a horse. Both drawing and lettering appear to have been incised in the wax model before casting. The god holds a laurel branch in his right hand; his left hand is placed beside the horse's head. The god rolls his eyes backward, and a laurel wreath crowns his head. He is nude except for a *chlamys* fastened in front by a round fibula and open-toed boots made of straps. The horse, which gallops to the right, has a bridle, a saddlecloth with fringe, a decorated breastband (poitrel), and a crupper decorated with tassels that passes underneath his tail.

The reason for taking up the plaque again is a discrepancy in dating. C. C. Vermeule and J. J. Herrmann dated it to the 3rd c. A.D. on the basis of the style of the incised drawing.[4] One of the prime arguments for this date was the cartoon-like rendering of the rider-god, his expressive eyes, and the way his attention is disconnected from his action (of riding). Herrmann compared the treatment of the face of Apollo and of his horse to that of a Victory and a horse on incised silver plate of Constantine II (mid 4th c.).[5] Another late-looking feature is the treatment of the horse's harness: some of its ornaments, such as the tassels hanging from the crupper, have parallels in coinage of the Late Empire, in particular of Constantinian times.[6]

M. P. Speidel, on the other hand, dated the plaque to a much earlier period, the 1st c. A.D., and even to its first half (the Julio-Claudian period). He supported his dating from Roman military history. There were two legions with the number *XXII*, located in different geographical areas. *Legio XXII Deiotariana* was stationed in Egypt and supposedly was disbanded in the course of the 2nd c. *Legio XXII Primigenia* was located at Mainz in Germany and continued to exist in subsequent centuries. Speidel connected the Boston plaque's inscription with the relatively early Deiotariana, apparently discarding the possibility of a connection with the Primigenia. In his view the careful drawing of the letters, use of the Greek language, the name of Marc Antony, and occurrence of the *tria nomina* all pointed to an early date.

In response to these differing opinions we will try to introduce some new arguments and see if the gap of two centuries can be bridged.

---

1 MFA, *The Museum Year 1982-83* (Boston 1983) 42; C. Vermeule, *Numismatic art of the Greek imperial world: interactions between Rome, Greece, Asia Minor, Syria, the Holy Land and Egypt* (Cambridge, MA 1986) 125, fig. 118; C. C. Vermeule III and M. B. Comstock, *Sculpture in stone and bronze in the Museum of Fine Arts, Boston* (Boston 1988) 99-100, no. 131.

2 M. P. Speidel, *Roman army studies* 2 (Stuttgart 1992) 304-5; we are grateful to the author for sending us his article.

3 *SEG* 41 (1991) 561, no. 1702.

4 Vermeule and Comstock (supra n.1) and J. J. Herrmann (pers. comm.).

5 St. Petersburg, Hermitage Museum; found at Kertch: J. P. C. Kent and K. S. Painter (edd.), *Wealth of the Roman world* (Exhib. cat., British Museum, London 1977) 25, no. 11.

6 For the horse trappings, see below.

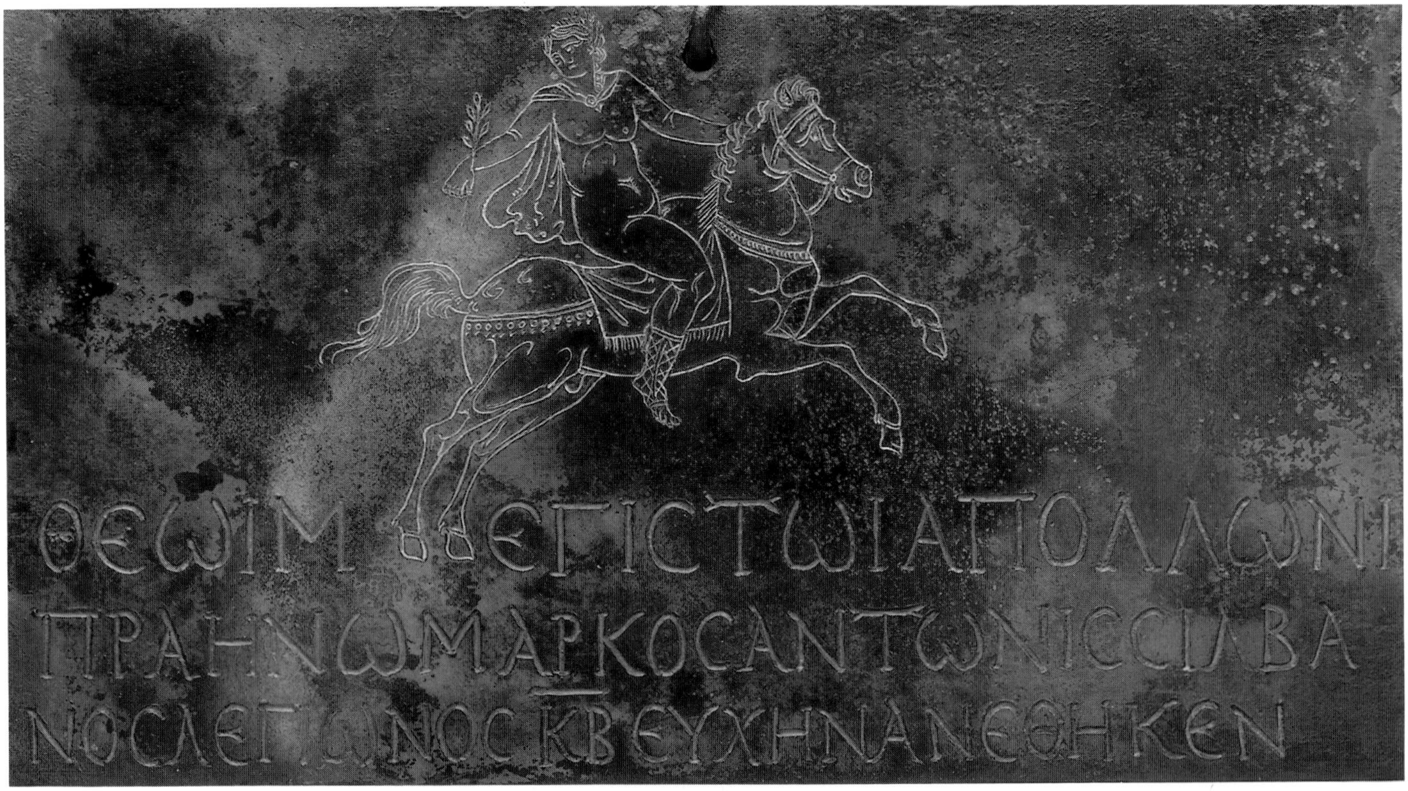

Fig. 1. Votive plaque. Roman, first half of the 3rd c. Bronze, h. 0.13 m; w. 0.234 m. Boston, Museum of Fine Arts, Edwin E. Jack Fund, 1983.222. (Photo: courtesy Museum of Fine Arts, Boston.)

The inscription

ΘЄωΙΜЄΓΙϹΤωΙ ΑΠΟΛΛωΝΙ

ΠΡΑΗΝω ΜΑΡΚΟϹ ΑΝΤωΝιϹϹΙ ΛΒΑ

ΝΟϹΛЄΓΙωΝΟϹΚ̅Β̅ЄΥΧΗΝΑΝЄΘΗΚЄΝ

θεῶι μεγίστωι Ἀπόλλωνι Πραηνῷ Μᾶρκος Ἀντώνις Σιλβανὸς λεγιῶνος κβ' εὐχὴν ἀνέθηκεν

"To the greatest god Apollo Praenos. Markos Antonis Silvanos of the twenty-second legion dedicated (this) as a votive gift."

The letters are carefully drawn in a fluid style, the sigmas are lunate and the omegas cursive. The upper bars of the tau and the middle bars of the epsilon split like the tongue of a serpent. The alphas have straight bars and a slight overhang to the left on top; the second loop of the omega is bent inward. The iotas in θεῶι μεγίστωι are postscript, but πραηνῶ lacks a iota. The letters range from 12 to 10 mm in height.

θεῶι μεγίστωι

The epithet μέγας or μέγιστος often appears in invocations to gods and can occur either with or without θεός. The term originally seems to have derived from oriental (Babylonian and Egyptian) cult language and expresses the great power of a deity. Many Greek gods (or oriental gods perceived as Greek) may receive the epithet: above all Zeus, but also Apollo, Ares, Asklepios, Dionysos, Helios, Herakles, Hermes, Pluto, Poseidon, Aphrodite, Artemis, Demeter, Hekate, Nemesis, Nike, Nymphai, Tyche. For Greek female deities the epithet seems to be attested primarily in Asia Minor, and for Greek male gods it occurs in that area as well as in Egypt and Syria. In Roman times the divinised emperors, following the custom of the Ptolemies, are addressed with the epithet, which is equally used in Jewish and Early Christian cult language.[7]

---

7 See B. Müller, *Μέγας θεός* (Halle 1913); also *RE* XV (1932, Kazarow) s.v. μέγας, 221-30. For other examples of the epithet in connection with Apollo, see *CIG* 4860; *IGRR* I 1286, from Ombos in Egypt, dated to A.D. 79-81; another inscription from Egypt (*CIG* 4716e) dedicated to Apollo reads θεῷ μεγίστῳ

It is worth noting that in Thrace, where depictions of rider-gods are abundant, the epithet μέγας occurs only rarely, and the superlative μέγιστος is even rarer.[8] Thus we can virtually exclude Thrace as the place of origin of our plaque.[9]

Iota adscriptum

The iota adscriptum in θεῶι μεγίστωι is an interesting feature which occurs mostly during the Early Empire (and before). The inscription is not entirely consistent in this respect since Πραηνῶ does not have a iota. To our surprise we did find groups of inscriptions of later date with the iota adscriptum. They turned up in clusters in geographically defined areas, such as Thrace, Moesia Inferior, the north shore of the Black Sea, and Thyatira in Lydia (a very good example);[10] the late group consists of some 30 inscriptions, all belonging to the time of Alexander Severus. They showed that specific formulae were favorite recipients of the iota adscriptum, formulae such as Ἀγαθῆι Τύχηι and Θεῶι Ὑψίστωι at the beginning, or ἐπ' ἀγαθῶι, at the end of an inscription.[11] Our inscription has an equally formulaic beginning, and this may explain why the two first words have the iota, while Praenos (a much less common word) lacks it.

It has been pointed out that the iota adscriptum disappears in the course of Severan times in inscriptions from Syria,[12] and the same may be true during post-Severan times in Asia Minor, since most of our late examples date to the reign of Alexander Severus and very few thereafter. Thus a date around the middle of the 3rd c. may serve as a tentative *terminus ad quem* for our inscription.

Apollo Praenos

The most notable word in the inscription is the epithet for Apollo, namely Praenos. Like many epithets in Asia Minor and Thrace connected with Apollo, this nickname with the ending on -ηνος probably had geographic or ethnic connotations.[13] We were unable to connect Praenos to any known place-name.[14] However, it is not at all unusual for new names to turn up; the *SEG* produces several examples every year.[15] We therefore propose a new toponym of unknown locality: Πρα(α) or Πρα(ον) or a similar name of the same root.

---

but without the name Apollo. For the epithet on papyri, see *SB* 12438, and *SB* 12439, dated to A.D. 235. In all these instances the word order is different: Ἀπόλλωνι θεῷ μεγίστῳ...

8 See M. Tačeva-Hitova, "Über die Götterepitheta in den griechischen Inschriften aus Moesia Inferior und Thracia," *Bulgarian Historical Review* (1978/3) 52-65. This observation is confirmed by other studies, see *Corpus cultus equitis thracii (CCET)* I, II 1/2, IV, V (Leiden 1979-84) passim.

9 For a comparison in terms of object, see a bronze plaque with a loop for hanging from Syria: *IGLS* 4041, also H. Seyrig, *Syria* 28 (1951) 191-228, and *SEG* 32 (1982) no. 1445. It also has the initial words θεῷ μεγίστῳ, after which the name of a Syrian god follows. The Syrian plaque, however, is very dissimilar in shape, since it is a *tabula ansata* and lacks an image.

10 See *IGRR* IV passim, nos. 1215-67 (*TAM* V/2); for Thrace, *IGRR* I 685 ff.; for Moesia Inferior, *IGRR* I 574 ff.; for Panticapaeum on the Bosporus, *IGRR* 886 ff.

11 See also L. Threatte, *The grammar of Attic inscriptions* (Berlin–New York 1980) 362-65.

12 See H. Seyrig, *Antiquités syriennes* 4 (1953) 155-56 and n.5.

13 M. Speidel refers to the article "Thrake" in Pauly Wissowa, in which many local names of Apollo ending in -ηνος are listed: *RE* VI B (1937, Kazarow) esp. 501-2. For epithets with a similar ending, see the study of E. N.Lane on the Phrygian god Men in his *Corpus monumentorum religionis dei Menis* (*CMRDM*) III (Leiden 1976) 67-80; Lane also lists a number of unattested place-names.

14 Speidel suggests Bria, a place that was located in Phrygia, somewhere between Sebaste and Eumeneia and near the present town of Burgaz. L. Zgusta lists this place as Βρίανα· *Kleinasiatische Ortsnamen* (Heidelberg 1984) par. 171-2. The vowel changes, however, are hard to explain and the hypothesis is therefore unconvincing.

15 Lane's listing (supra n.13) shows that our knowledge of ethnic names is rather limited. Another example is a document from Ephesus that contains a list of communities in Asia Minor: see C. Habicht, "New evidence on the province of Asia," *JRS* 65 (1975) 64-91. Some of the names in this inscription were

Tria nomina

The dedicant fully spells out his three common Latin names: Markos Antonis Silvanos (or Marcus Antonius Silvanus in Latin). Although the inscription is in Greek, it is not clear whether the dedicant of our plaque was a Latin or Greek speaker. The spelling Antonis instead of Antonios cannot serve as a marker for a more precise dating, since it occurs already in Greek papyri from the 1st c. A.D. onward.[16] The same argument is valid for Silvanos written with a beta.[17]

Speidel connects the names of our dedicant with the triumvir Mark Antony, and he stresses the idea that the fully-written first name Markos points to an early date.[18] A quick check in P.-W. shows that the name Mark Antony continued to be used long after the 1st c. (2 times in the 1st c. B.C. and 8 times in each of the next three centuries).[19] This is not, of course, a statistically valid survey but it does give some insight into the occurrence of the name. The name of the emperor Gordianus who came to power in 238 was also Marcus Antonius Gordianus, as were the names of his father and his son, and possibly he, rather than the triumvir of almost three centuries earlier, was the point of reference.

The fully spelled-out *praenomen*, Markos, is admittedly more common in the 1st and 2nd c. A.D. but there are examples to be found in the later Empire.[20] It is also significant to notice that in bilingual inscriptions the Latin version often has the *praenomen* abbreviated while the Greek is spelled out. A vivid example of this can be seen on a sarcophagus in the Cortile del Belvedere in the Vatican, where Julia Soaemia Bassiana made a dedication to Sex(tus) Varius Marcellus, whose *praenomen* was abbreviated in Latin but is complete in Greek.[21] This inscription is firmly dated to the 3rd c., since the people involved happened to be the parents of the (later) emperor Elagabalus.[22] Thus, although not typical for its time, the fully spelled-out *praenomen* in the *tria nomina* does not necessarily exclude a later date, particularly as it is written in Greek.

---

familiar either through literary sources or other inscriptions; other names, however, were totally unknown, and the inscription provided the only surviving testimony to their existence.

16 See D. J. Georgacas, "On the nominal endings -i, -in, in later Greek," *CP* 43 (1948) 243-60, esp. 245. Of the 15 occurrences of the name Ἀντώνις on stone and in papyri that we could find, one was dated to the 1st c. A.D. (*PMich*. 3.201); 7 to the 2nd c. (*IG* II/2. 2097 B from Attica; *IG* V. 2. 55 Peloponnesos, Tegea; *PHamb*. 1.39; *PPetaus*. 92; *PWisc*. 2.69; *SB* 1.5124; *SB* 6.9017[?]), 2 to the 2nd-3rd c. (*PCustoms*. 573/596; *O Oasis.Bahria* 21), 3 to the 4th c. (*PRossGeorg*. 5.558; *SB*.3.6965; *OLeid*.344); 1 to the 6th-7th c. (*SEG* 8.230 Bittir, Palestine); and one Early Christian from Rome (*CIG* 9676, ην πακη Ἀντώνις ...).

17 Names such as Λειβία, Βεργίλιος and Φλάβιος could all be written with a β from the Early Empire onward: see K. Meisterhans, *Grammatik der attischen Inschriften* (Berlin 1900) 77-78, no. 666; Threatte, *Grammar* (supra n.11) 442.

18 Speidel, *Studies* (supra n.2) 2, 305.

19 See *RE* I (1894, von Rohden) s.v. Antonius.

20 There also seem to have been fashions in specific traditions. On military diplomas, for example, the *praenomina* of the witnesses are always abbreviated.

21 This difference could also be observed on a bilingual grave monument of a soldier of *Legio II* (*Parthica*) from Perugia, who died in Apamea toward the middle of the 3rd c. The Greek adaptations of his name and of his heir's are more fully spelled out than the Latin version: Baeb(ius) Severus and Valer(ius) Respectus receive their full names in Greek as Βαίβιος Σεουῆρος and Οὐαλέριος Ρεσπέκτος; see W. Van Rengen and J. C. Balty, *Apamea in Syrië. Winterkwartieren van Legio II Parthica* (Brussel 1992) 37, no. 15.

22 *IG* XIV 911. Other examples of fully spelled-out *tria nomina* of this time can be found in *IGRR* III 481 (Devijver V 39) and *IGRR* IV 635. In the 3rd c. the full *tria nomina* seem to be more common in papyri than on stone, e.g., *POxy*. 34.2710, and *BGU* IV 1074. Bilingual papyri show the same characteristics as bilingual inscriptions, e.g., *SB* 1 1010 (Latin) and *SB* 6 9298 (Greek), in which Greek and Latin versions of the same document occur; the Greek has Marcus Aurelius Chaeremon fully spelled out, while the Latin has only M. for Marcus.

Legio XXII

Neither the rank of the dedicant nor the epithet of his legion is spelled out in the inscription; it therefore remains open which of the two twenty-second legions is meant. The Deiotariana originated in the time of Augustus. While there is testimony for its existence in Hadrian's time,[23] by the time of Antoninus Pius the Deiotariana was no longer on the official list of legions.[24] It might have been a casualty of the Jewish revolt under Simon Bar Kokhba,[25] but this remains uncertain. Up to the year 69, the majority of recruits for the Deiotariana were Greek speakers from Asia Minor (the inscriptions point especially to Ancyra). In subsequent periods, however, the recruits seem to have come from Egypt itself, while their inscriptions are predominantly in Latin.[26]

The other legion, *XXII Primigenia*, was stationed in *Moguntiacum* (Mainz) and its origins date either to the time of Caligula or Claudius. From the legion's beginnings up to 193, its area of recruitment included Italy, Gallia Narbonensis, and Spain.[27] From the Severan period to *c.*300, the recruits (in addition to those born in the camp) came from Gaul, the German *limes*, Thrace, and Syria.[28]

Ritterling noted that the legion's epithet was omitted in the early existence of the *Deiotariana*, before there was a Primigenia and (more frequently) in later periods, that is, after the disappearance of the *Deiotariana*.[29] Speidel identified the legion in which Markos Antonis served as the Egyptian-based *Deiotariana* in its earliest phase. However, this choice is not inevitable. The fact that the Boston inscription is Greek need not exclude a dedication by a member of the Mainz-based legion. Not only would recruits from Syria and Thrace be Greek speakers, but the *Primigenia*'s assignments sent it to the East on at least two occasions.[30] Lucius Verus employed *Legio I Minervia*, another German-based legion, in his campaign against the Parthians,[31] and he probably brought a *vexillum* of *legio XXII* with him as well. On the same model, it seems likely that Severus Alexander took elements of the legion with him on his own expedition against the Persians. An eastern campaign is particularly likely in this case since the legion had a close connection with the Severan house, beginning when the Pannonian legions proclaimed Septimius Severus emperor in Carnuntum and *legio XXII* followed suit.

Speidel's early date based on Markos Antonis's legionary affiliation is not binding, and since art-historical considerations suggest the plaque is later, one should be aware of the epigraphical and historical possibilities for a later 2nd or especially 3rd c. date for the Silvanos dedication. An antiquarian detail also argues in favor of a later rather than an earlier date:

Horse trappings

The trappings of Apollo's horse are embellished with a dense row of tassels. This kind of ornament is not easy to find in the 1st c. B.C. and A.D. The reverse of a silver *denarius* of

---

23 A.D. 122; *BGU* I 140.

24 *ILS* 2288.

25 A.D. 132-135.

26 J. C. Mann, *Legionary recruitment and veteran settlement during the Principate* (Institute of Archaeology Occasional Publication 7, 1983) 44-46 and 154-55. In addition, M. D. Parker, *The Roman legions* (Oxford 1928) 182: "Lesquier has shown that of 61 soldiers in the 1st c. 8 come from Italy, Gaul, or Africa, and 53 from Asia Minor, Syria, and Egypt, in the proportion of 29 from Asia Minor, chiefly from Galatia, to 24 from Syria and Egypt (*L'armée romaine d'Egypte*, 206)."

27 Mann, *Recruitment* 28-30, 100-6; Parker, *Legions* 175.

28 Mann, *Recruitment* 105-6.

29 *RE* XII (1925, Ritterling) s.v. legio, 1820: "Ohne jeden Beinamen nur als LEG XXII bezeichnet (...) begegnet sowohl in früher (...) wie besonders in späterer (...) wie spätester Zeit nicht selten."

30 Ibid. 1812-15, for the legion's movement outside Germania Superior.

31 This is based on an inscription from Ancyra (*CIL* III 269 = 6765).

Labienus dated to 40 B.C., for example, shows a saddled and bridled horse.[32] Two big *phalerae* are visible, one in front dividing the poitrel, the other at a triple junction of the crupper. Excavations in France and England have confirmed the use of these *phalerae* in the 1st c. A.D., and several places of production of military equipment have been identified, such as Alesia.[33] A number of *cippi* of *equites* of Roman auxiliary troops, all dated to the 1st c. A.D. (early and middle), show horses and their riders;[34] as on the Labienus coin, the large *phalerae* in front and back of the horse are prominent, even more accentuated in stone than on silver. A reconstruction of a harnessed cavalry horse in the middle of the 1st c. A.D., made by M. C. Bishop and P. Connolly, shows small *phalerae* in between the large ones.[35] However, depictions of 1st c. gear, whether on coins or stone, do not show the densely packed pendants hanging from the crupper of our plaque. Something more similar appears on the Column of Trajan, where a horse has a crupper with three acorn-like pendants and similar pendants on the front strap. Pendants of various shapes have been excavated, for example at Xanten.[36] They also are represented on grave monuments in that area, like the one of T. Flavius Bassus who died in Cologne toward the end of the 1st c. Other funerary reliefs from Cologne show similar features.[37] These hanging ornaments are visually different from the ones on the Boston horse, however, since they have the shapes of flowers, leaves, and crescent moons and are not very numerous or densely packed.[38]

The Dacian Wars seem to have started new fashions in military equipment.[39] The metopes of the victory monument in Adamklissi (A.D. 109) show riders and horses with tassels on the crupper — apparently for the first time.[40] These pendants are more elongated than the tassels on our plaque, but they do show that variations not unlike the arrangement on our plaque could appear on the outskirts of the empire.[41] They probably reflect local traditions and reflect influences from other horse-riding cultures.[42]

Monuments and coinage of the 3rd c. do not provide much information on horse trappings,[43] but 4th c. coins show many innovations. Some features of the earlier Roman trappings are still visible but now modified. A gold medaillon of 313 shows Constantine making his entry into Rome;[44] his horse has broad straps in front and back in which the round disks are enclosed. Their function, therefore, seems different from the *phalerai* of earlier times, changed, as it were, from strap holders and connectors to mere strap ornaments.[45]

---

32 London, *BMCRR* II 500, no. 132. See also J. P. C. Kent *et al.*, *Roman coins* (London 1978) no. 101R.

33 See E. Rabeisen, "La production d'équipement de cavalerie au 1er s. après J.-C. à Alésia (Alise-Sainte-Reine, Côte-d'Or, France)," *JRMES* 1 (1990) 73-98.

34 See P. A. Holder, *Studies in the auxilia of the Roman army from Augustus to Trajan* (BAR Int. Ser. 70, Oxford 1980) pls. 1B, 3C, 5C, 6A-B.

35 Rabeisen 1990 (supra n.33) 76.

36 See I. Jenkins, "A group of silvered bronze horse-trappings from Xanten," *Britannia* 16 (1985) 141-64.

37 See M. Feugère, *Les armes des Romains* (Paris 1993) 173-81.

38 See also the representations in M. C. Bishop and J. C. N. Coulston, *Roman military equipment* (London 1993) 27.

39 For a discussion of the armor in this period, see R. MacMullen, *Barbarian cavalry in the Roman army: from 69 to 268 AD* (Diss., Harvard Univ. 1950) 17.

40 F. B. Florescu, *Monumentul de la Adamklissi Tropaeum Traiani* (Bucarest 1959) figs. 132-38.

41 Other monuments, such as the relief of the Palmyrene rider-gods, Abgal and Asar, dated to A.D. 154, show round crupper pendants: see R. Ghirshman, *Iran: Parthians and Sassanids* (London 1962) pl. 86. Compare also the trappings of the Sassanian rider-kings of the 5th c. A.D. (Kent and Painter, *Wealth* [supra n.5] 146-47, nos. 307-8).

42 On the question of interaction with other peoples, see Bishop and Coulston, *Equipment* (supra n.38) 205.

43 Bishop and Coulston ibid. 23 comment on the absence of representations in the 3rd c.

44 Kent, *Roman coins* no. 629 R.

45 Similarly on other coins of later date, for example, of Valentinian I and Valens, dated *c.*A.D. 370; Kent, *Roman coins* nos. 669 R, 676 R, 704 R, 707 R.

A closer parallel to the horse trappings on the Boston plaque occurs on a rare gold medallion from Nicomedia of Constantine, dated to 330; it shows a dense row of tassels on the back strap of the emperor's horse.[46] This iconographic tradition continues throughout the 4th c. On a gold triple *solidus* of 350 showing Magnentius on horseback,[47] the horse's crupper still has one phalera, but small pendants are also visible, and there are pendants on the horse's breastband. A later gold coin of Valens, dated to 373/4, shows the emperor's horse with broad crupper and breastband equipped with small dangling pendants.[48] Other objects made of precious metal confirm this development. The gilded silver Conçesti amphora, dated to *c.*400, from the Black Sea region, shows horses with decorated straps in front and back with pendants that are very similar to the tassels on the back strap of Apollo's horse.[49]

Although the images are far from identical, due in part to the different media and the different workmanship, the horse trappings on the Apollo plaque seem to relate to those of the Adamklissi monument of the early 2nd c. but are closer still to those of the 4th c. coins and the Conçesti amphora. This pattern reinforces a date for the Boston plaque later than the 1st c., and the first half of the 3rd c. seems the most likely.

Harvard Divinity School (A vdH.); Department of the Classics, Harvard University (S.A.T.)

Acknowledgements

Our thanks go to M. B. Comstock, D. Feissel, J. J. Herrmann, C. P. Jones, and K. A. Worp for their willing ears, their critical eyes, and their much valued comments.

---

46 See *Giessener Münzhandlung, auction catalogue 56* (October 7, 1991) no. 628*.

47 *Coin catalogue Hess-Leu* (1961) no. 434; P. Bastien, *Le monnayage de Magnence* (Wetteren 1964) 302.

48 Kent, *Roman coins* no. 704 R.

49 See L. Matzulevitch, *Byzantinische Antike. Studien auf Grund der Silbergefässe der Ermitage* (Berlin–Leipzig 1929) 132, 134, pls. 36-43.

L'impiego epigrafico di lamine e tavole di bronzo e di piombo nella Sicilia antica

Giacomo Manganaro

Il materiale scrittorio impiegato dai Greci fu vario nel corso della loro lunga storia culturale: innanzitutto, alle origini e ancora fino in età classica, si sarà scritto, dipingendo i caratteri alfabetici, su tavolette di legno e su membrane di pelle, anche se questo era per Erodoto un costume dei barbari;[1] quindi su papiri, importati dall'Egitto, naturalmente un prodotto costoso,[2] per documenti quotidiani o di pubblico interesse, utilizzati in un ristretto ambiente. Invece per la "pubblicazione" nell'ambito della comunità cittadina di atti pubblici o privati era scelto materiale non deperibile: lastre di marmo, di calcare, lastre più o meno sottili di bronzo, di piombo, mattoni (o vasi di argilla, specie cocci).

In Sicilia, priva di marmo, che doveva essere importato e perciò impiegato piuttosto in casi particolari, si ricorse per iscrizioni pubbliche, e tali sono anche le iscrizioni funerarie, al calcare locale, non dappertutto di buona grana. Una tale circostanza avrebbe dovuto incrementare l'impiego per documenti pubblici, anche sacrali, di lamine appositamente preparate.

In realtà si registra un numero maggiore di lamine di piombo, a partire almeno dal VI secolo a.C.[3] fino all'epoca imperiale e tardoantica,[4] e ancora per il genere di preghiere propiziatrici, da deporre in tomba, fino in età araba.[5] Una ricca documentazione di "tessere" di piombo inscritte, databili al V a.C., coi nomi dei partecipanti alle assemblee cittadine, ai quali spettava una indennità, è stata scoperta a Camarina.[6] Per un'età post timoleontea in area sud-orientale si annoverano alcune decine di contratti di acquisto di terreni e di case e una lista civica,[7] qualche documento di garanzia, di deposito di valuta e con annotazioni di spese, sempre su lamine di piombo[8] e naturalmente *defixiones*.[9]

Rare l'impiego epigrafico di lamine di argento. Tuttavia da rillevare per la Sicilia un contratto con πρᾶσις ἐπὶ λύσει inciso su lamina di argento da Morgantina,[10] e la dedica di un lingotto di argento a Zeus Lykaios, rinvenuto a Himera.[11]

---

1 Hdt. 5.58.3; cfr. rispettivamente L. H. Jeffery, *The local scripts of Archaic Greece* (Oxford 1961) 51-55; A. Miller, *Studies in early Sicilian epigraphy: an opistographic lead tablet* (diss., University Microfilms 1973) 20, n.1; G. Pugliese Carratelli, "Cadmo: prima e dopo," *PP* 31 (1976) 11 ss.

2 Jeffery ibid. 56-57; P. Page, "Archilochus and the oral tradition," *Archiloque* (EntrHardt X, 1964) 163-79.

3 Cfr. M. H. Jameson, D. R. Jordan, R. D. Kotansky, *A lex sacra from Selinous* (=GRB Mon. 11, Durham, NC 1993). La lamina evoca le *kyrbeis* soloniane. Per l'impiego del piombo in Sicilia, cfr. G. Manganaro, "La Sicilia da Sesto Pompeo a Diocleziano," *ANRW* II.11.1 (1988) 28.

4 Vedi G. Manganaro, "Iscrizioni esorcistiche della Sicilia bizantina," in *Scritti classici e cristiani in onore di Francesco Corsaro* (Catania 1994) 457-64.

5 Cfr. G. Manganaro, "Nuovo manipolo di documenti magici della Sicilia tardoantica," *RendLinc* 391 (1994) 485-517, 511-17.

6 F. Cordano, *Le tessere pubbliche del tempio di Atena a Camarina* (Roma 1992): osservazioni nel G. Manganaro, "Sikelikà I," *QUCC* 78 (1995) 99-102. Esempi di tessere simili già in Miller, *Studies* (supra n.1) 8 s., che la Cordano avrebbe fatto bene a consultare. Per quelle di Styra cfr. *Bull. Ép.* 1993, 396.

7 Cfr., oltre ai G. Manganaro, "Case e terre a Kamarina e Morgantina nel III-II sec. a.C.," *PP* 246 (1989) 189-216, e "Nuove tavolette di piombo inscritte siceliote," *PP* 52 (1997) 305-48, L. Dubois, *Inscriptions grecques dialectales de Sicile* (CollEFR 119, 1989) 131 ss.

8 Cfr. rispettivamente Miller, *Studies* (supra n.1) 38 s. (R. Arena, *Iscrizioni greche arcaiche di Sicilia e Magna Grecia* I [Milano 1989] 81, no. 77); Dubois, *Inscriptions* (supra n.7) 13-14 (un messaggio).

9 Vedi ora Manganaro, "Nuove tavolette" (supra n.7) 332-34.

10 Dubois, *Inscriptions* (supra n.7) 231-32.

11 *IG* XIV (1890) 412: cfr. G. Manganaro, "Due studi di numismatica greca," *AnnPisa* 20 (1990) 425-27.

L'uso di laminette d'oro attestate altrove per incidervi testi religiosi — basta pensare alle laminette orfiche — o tradizionali *phylakteria* magici, di cui uno in ebraico databile al V sec. d.C. fu scoperto a Comiso (Sicilia),[12] mi risulta indirettamente da una notizia fornitami anni fa da un antiquario gelese, il quale mi trascrisse in maiuscola il testo, che egli avrebbe letto su una laminetta aurea una serie di nomi, tipicamente sicelioti.[13]

Invece, l'impiego epigrafico di lamine di bronzo, assai frequenti in varie regioni di Grecia,[14] la preparazione delle quali anche in Sicilia si associava ovviamente all'arte della toreutica e alla confezione di statuine in bronzo destinate alle offerte in santuari o, in epoca romana, in *lararia*, e anche per il corredo di tombe, come nel caso di animaletti c.d. 'siculi' e cinturoni "siculi" caratterizzati da figurazioni antropomorfe,[15] non trova per la Sicilia larga documentazione: alla scomparsa di molti esemplari avrà contribuito la sottigliezza di tali lamine, rinvenute quasi sempre in frammenti.

Comunque, tavole di bronzo, anche per ragioni pratiche e per rispondere alle esigenze dell' εἰς ἀεί, erano usate per consacrare accordi politici, stipulati tra gruppi civici o tra città, in santuari: così nel caso della *Lex de exsulibus restituendis* di Zancle, di quella relativa agli esuli selinuntini, rinvenute in frammenti a Olimpia, databili nel VI sec. a.C. e di una legge di Himera del 500 a.C. circa;[16] per le tavolette in frammenti da S. Mauro (Euboia, *chorion* dei Leontinoi) con disposizioni giuridiche, scritte in alfabeto calcidese e databili nel VI sec. a.C., recentemente ripresentate[17] senza nuovi apporti rispetto alle edizioni di P. Orsi e di V. Arangio Ruiz e alle considerazioni di G. Vallet;[18] così per le otto lastre di Entella (la IX, come in questo convegno è stato ulteriormente dimostrato, è un falso moderno), certamente databili nel decennio anteriore alla fine della prima guerra romano-punica (241 a.C.), le quali, almeno quelle a noi pervenute, saranno state esposte in un santuario federale, quello di Zeus Olympios, oltre che nel *bouleuterion* o nel santuario cittadino di *Hestia*.[19]

In edifici pubblici saranno stati affissi, per la pubblicazione, appunto le lamine, di cui si sono ritrovati quattro frammenti a Morgantina, interpretate come *rationes quaestorum* da V. Arangio Ruiz;[20] la tavoletta di Kasmenai, conservata al Metropolitan Museum di New York,

---

12 Cfr., ad es., C. A. Faraone e R. D. Kotansky, "An inscribed gold phylaktery in Stamford, Connecticut," *ZPE* 75 (1988) 257-66; S. Calderone, "Per una storia dell'elemento giudaico nella Sicilia orientale," *RendLinc* 10 (1955) 489-502.

13 ΑΡΧΙΑΣ | ΚΑΙΕΝΟΙ | ΜΟΣΚΑΙΑ | ΠΕΛΟΣ ΠΥ | ΡΙΝΟ, cioè Ἀρχίας καὶ Ἔνθιμος καὶ Ἄπελος Πυρίνō.

14. P. Charneux, "En relisant les décrets argiens," *BCH* 114 (1990) 396 s.; *Bull. Ép.* 1976, 255, 290.

15 Cfr., ad es., G. Manganaro, "Sikelikà I" (supra n.6) fig. 26; "Culti privati nella Sicilia Romana," *Mélanges M. Le Glay = Latomus* 226 (1994) 831 ss.; "Per una storia della chora Katanaia," *Stuttgarter Kolloquium zur historisches Geographie des Altertums* 4 (1990) 134-35; altresì St. Vassallo, "Lamina bronzea con decorazione antropomorfa da Terravecchia Li Cuti," *Sic. Arch.* 54-55 (1984) 137-42. In Sicilia attestato in area etnea un χαλκότυπος: A. Brugnone, "I Mestieri," *Atti XI Congr. Int. Studi Antropologici Siciliani* (Palermo 1981) 21, no. 34.

16 *Inschr. von Olympia* 24; 22 (cfr., anche per la bibliografia recente, G. Manganaro, "Studi di epigrafia greca," *RendLinc* 393 [1996] 45-51); A. Brugnone, "Legge di Himera sulla ridistribuzione della terra," *PP* 52 (1997) 262-305 (vedi le mie osservazioni in "Revisione ... di un decreto frammentario di Himera," in *Atti III Giornate Int. Studi Area Elima, 1998).* .

17 F. Cordano, "Le leggi calcidesi da Monte S. Mauro di Caltagirone," *Decima miscellanea greca e romana* (Roma 1986) 33-60 con tavv. I-X.

18 *Rhégion et Zancle. Histoire, commerce et civilisation* (Paris 1958) 318.

19 Cfr. G. Manganaro, "Metoikismos — Metaphora di *poleis* in Sicilia: il caso dei Geloi di Phintias e la relativa documentazione epigrafica," *AnnPisa* 20 (1990) 391-408. Rilevo che I. B. Curbera, "Sulla cronologia relativa dei decreti di Entella," *AnnPisa* 24 (1994) 883, ha inserito erroneamente tra i casi di normali patronimici al genitivo dopo il nome personale al nominativo due esempi di nomi personali al genitivo seguiti dal patronimico al genitivo, che avrebbe dovuto essere preceduto dall'articolo τοῦ.

20 V. Arangio-Ruiz e A. Olivieri, *Inscriptiones graecae Siciliae* (Milano 1925) 128-29, no. 14: cfr. G. Manganaro, *Sikelika. Studi di antichità e di epigrafia della Sicilia greca.* B, *QUCC* 8, Pisa 1999, 61-62.

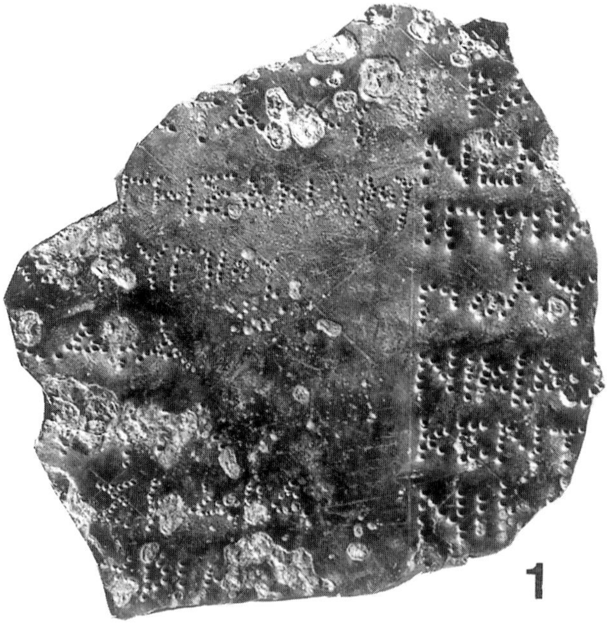

1

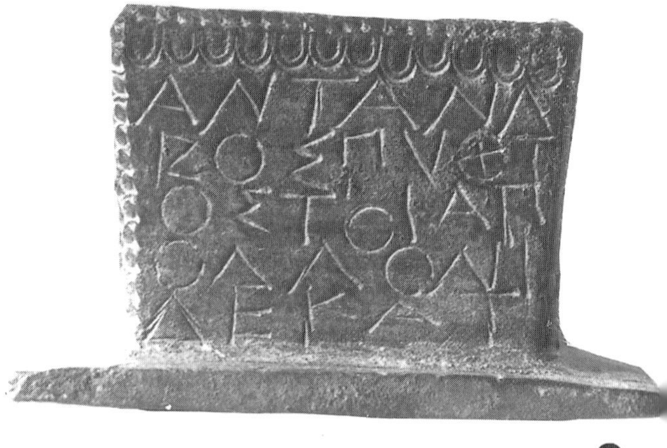

2

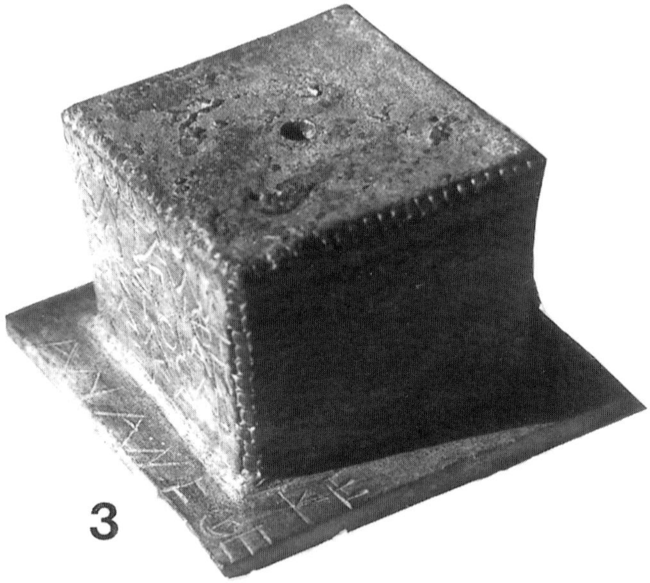

3

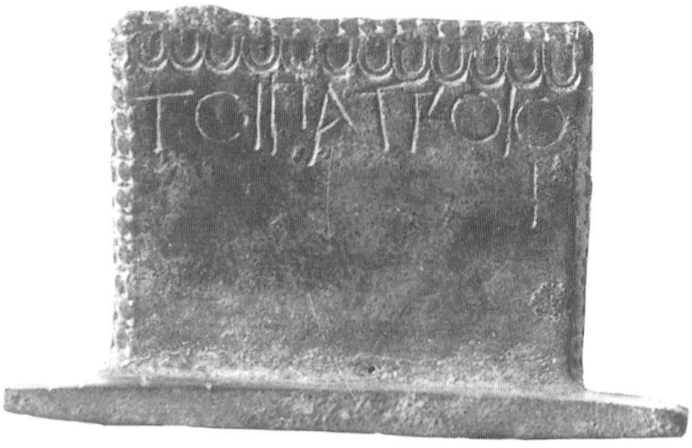

4

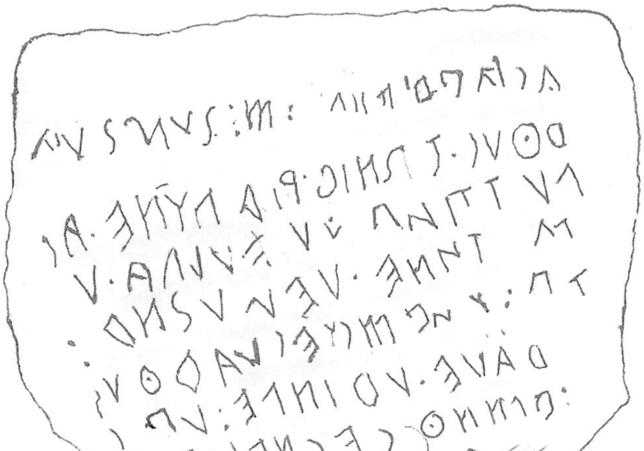

5

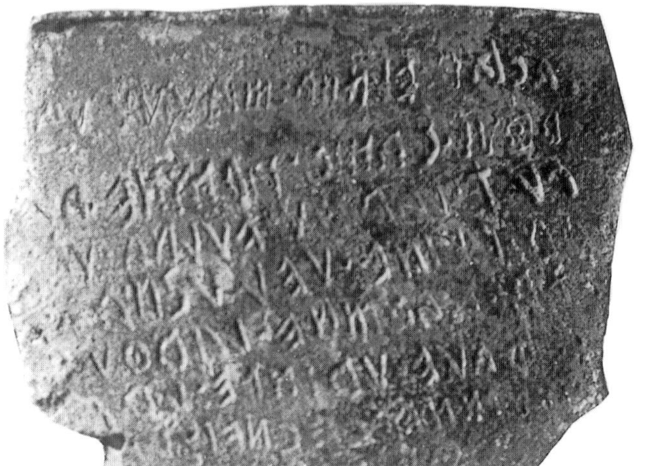

Fig. 1. Frammento di lamina di bronzo, inscritta con lista di nomi personali. Collez. privata, Catania. Figg. 2-4. Altarino di bronzo, con dedica ad Apollo Patroios. Collez. privata, Catania. Figg. 5-5a. Disegno e foto di iscrizione, forse etrusca, su tavoletta frammentaria di bronzo. Collez. privata, Catania.

con concessione di privilegi politici ad un qualche esule;[21] le lamine frammentarie contenenti decreti per *euergetai*, come quella, ridotta a grattugia, pare da Morgantina, edita da P. Orsi; e un'altra, in collezione, forse da Morgantina;[22] una lamina (fig. 1), in collezione, sulla quale è incisa con lettere di III-II sec. a.C. a 'pointille' su due colonne una lista di nomi, probabilmente di efebi, in parte integrabili, e con patronimico (alla colonna A), alcuni dei quali interessanti come Ἡ]γησάνδρου, Κυπίου, Καρᾶ, [? Π]υρρία, [?Γ]υρίνου e, sulla colonna B, Γρα[ῖκος?], Ἱππία[ς], Νικίας, Κέντ[ος].[23]

Non mancano laminette inscritte con il nome del dedicante.[24] Da ricordare ancora, anche se piuttosto di I sec. a.C., due tavole di bronzo con decreti di *proxenia* per un agrigentino, e altre due ritagliate, certamente provenienti dalla Sicilia.[25]

Merita di essere presentato un altarino di bronzo, da Camarina, di forma cubica, vuoto all'interno, con foro sulla base superiore (per innalzarvi il donario), alto cm 3,6, profondo cm 5, largo cm 6, il quale aggetta nel bordo inferiore su ogni lato cm 1 sulla faccia anteriore e su quella destra, entro un contorno dentellato che circonda un fregio a mezzo scudo ovale, oltre che sul bordo aggettante, si legge a lettere alte cm 0,5 la dedica Ἄντανδ|ρος Πύθι|ος τôι Ἀπ|όλλōνι δεκάτ (sul bordo aggettante) αν ἀνέθε̄ (sull'angolo destro dello stesso) κε (sulla faccia destra) τôι Πατρôιοι (figs. 2-4).

Per confezionare questo altarino — un vero gioiello — e la probabile statuina, verosimilmente di Apollo 'ancestrale,' che su esso era stata sistemata, il dedicante avrà speso la decima, forse della produzione del suo lotto di terreno, assegnatogli come colono di Camarina rifondata nel 461 a.C.[26]

Anche se in un'epoca, in cui prevale, per la categoria delle iscrizioni 'magiche,' l'impiego di lamine di piombo,[27] si rilevano in Sicilia almeno due lamine di bronzo con iscrizioni dello stesso genere: una da Akrai,[28] e una da Sofiana.[29]

Presento per l'occasione una lastrina di bronzo (cm 4,8 x 3,8) spessa oltre cm 0,1, leggermente convessa, con punti di saldatura al R, conservata in collezione siciliana, unica presunzione per un rinvenimento locale, sulla quale si legge una iscrizione sinistrorsa, a lettere alte cm 0,3, di tipo etrusco: ne presento foto e apografo (figs. 5-5a), e ne lascio a specialisti l'ardua decifrazione.

Dipartimento di studi antichi e tardoantichi, Università di Catania

21 Cfr. Arena, *Iscrizioni greche* (supra n.8) 79-80, no. 76.

22 Cfr. *RivStorAnt* 5 (1900) 54, no. 25; *Sikelika* (supra n.20) 62 nrr. 51-52.

23 L'iscrizione illustrata in *Sikelika* (supra n.20) 62-63, nr. 53.

24 Cfr. "Sikelikà I" (supra n.6) 103-4.

25 *IG* XIV 952-955: cfr. G. Manganaro, "Tre tavole di bronzo con decreti di *proxenia*," *Kokalos* 9 (1963) 205-20 con tavv. 63-67.

26 "Sikelikà I" (supra n.6) 98-99.

27 Vedi indietro alle nn. 4-5.

28 *IG* XIV 2413.17: L. Bernabò Brea e G. Pugliese Carratelli, *Akrai* (Catania 1956) 170 s., no. 52; G. Manganaro, "Nuovi documenti magici della Sicilia orientale," *RendLinc* 18 (1963) 70-71; F. P. Rizzo, "I Formulari di Mosè in un documento acrense: Paure e speranze dell'uomo tardo-antico," *Atti Acc. Sc. Lettere e Arti, Palermo* 1994-95, 6-41, e anche R. D. Kotansky, *Greek magical amulets* (Opladen 1994) 126-54, no. 32 (The Phylaktery of Moses) (per segnalazione di R. Merkelbach).

29 S. Sciacca, "*Phylakterion* con iscrizione magica greco-ebraica," *Kokalos* 28-29 (1982-83) 87-104 [cfr. mie osservazioni di lettura in *RendLinc* 391 (1994) 506, n.52]; Kotansky (supra n.28) 155 ss., no. 33 (Jewish amulet with angel-names). Aggiungerei, ad es., il *phylakterion* su lastra di bronzo da Avignone (*IG* XIV 2481).

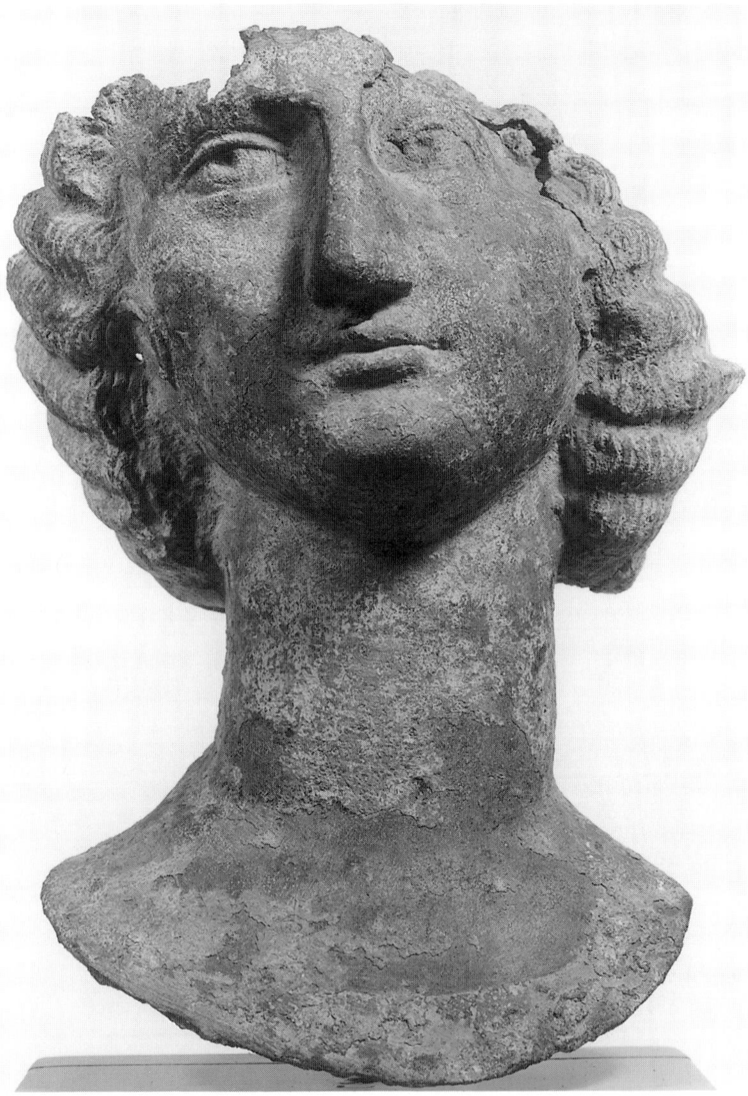

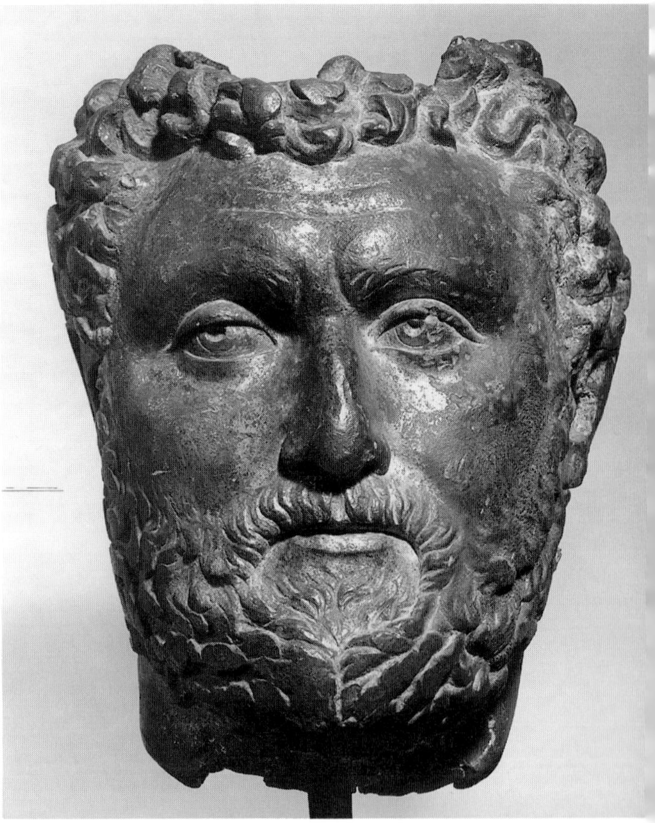

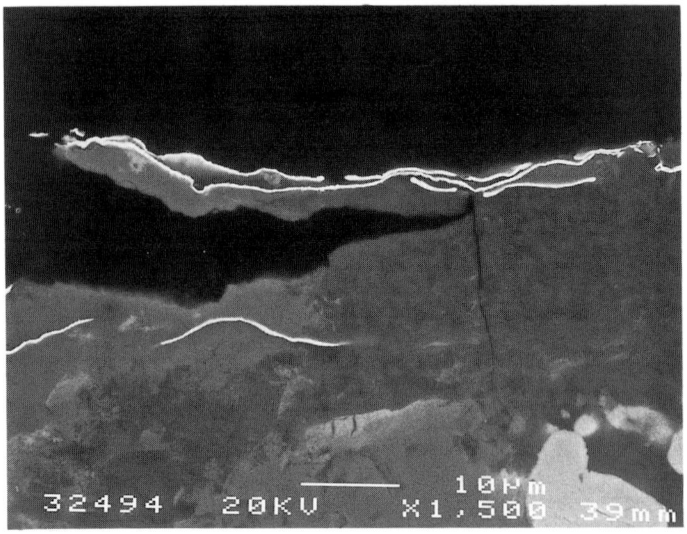

Fig. 1 (top left). Portrait head of the empress Julia Domna. Gilded bronze, h. 0.36 m. Cambridge, MA, Arthur M. Sackler Museum, Harvard University Art Museums, Gift of C. Ruston Love, Jr., 1956.19. (Photo: courtesy Harvard University Art Museums.)

Fig. 2 (bottom left). Cross section from the portrait of Julia Domna, showing multiple layers of gold leaf interspersed with corrosion and burial clay. (SEM photo: author, mag. x 1,500.)

Fig. 3 (top right). Portrait head of an emperor. Gilded bronze, h. 0.44 m. Charlottesville, VA, John W. Kluge 88-46. (Photo: courtesy Harvard University Art Museums.)

Analysis of gilding and other decorative metals from selected bronzes in the exhibition *The Fire of Hephaistos*

Amy Snodgrass

The exhibition *The fire of Hephaistos: large classical bronzes from North American collections*[1] explored the rôle of technology in Greek and Roman bronzes. In preparation for the exhibit, 52 large-scale statues and fragments were examined for their casting and joining technology, methods of ornamentation and repair, and the alloys used to produce them. Close examination of the bronzes raised questions about the use of gilding and other decorative metals. How was gilding applied to these bronzes? What other metals were used for decoration?

To investigate gilding, the portrait head of Julia Domna (cat no. 42), the portrait head of an emperor (cat. no. 53), the head of a horse (cat. no. 20), and the sword (cat. no. 21) were selected for analysis. A life-size statue of Dionysos as a youth (cat. no. 23) and one (cat no. 33) of three statuettes of Aphrodite in the exhibition were selected for analysis of metal overlay on features such as the eyes. Minute samples of gilding and overlay were removed from the objects for microscopic examination. Most of the samples were taken from the surface and do not include the underlying metal. The samples were examined with a metallographic microscope. They were also viewed with a scanning electron microscope (SEM), and their elemental composition was analyzed using an energy dispersive spectrometer (EDS).

The first object examined was the portrait head of Julia Domna (fig. 1). It has minute traces of gold leaf on the back of the neck and a sample of gilding was taken from this area. Viewed in cross section with the SEM and analyzed by EDS, the cross section showed up to 6 layers of pure gold leaf, each about 1 micron thick, applied directly onto a bronze substrate without the use of a gesso underlayer (fig. 2). A fine red clay was observed between some of the layers. At first, it was thought that the clay might be a preparatory layer, but the small amount of material and the discontinuity of the layer suggests, instead, that it was an accretion during burial.

The portrait head of an emperor with a battered and abraded appearance (fig. 3) was reportedly pulled from the Tiber in Rome after being submerged for centuries. Many of the details of the hair and beard are lost, but enough gilding remains to show that the entire head — including the hair, face, and eyes — was once gilded. A sample was removed from the hair, and viewed in cross section with the SEM it showed two layers of gold leaf, each about 2 microns in thickness, with a white material between the layers. EDS analysis showed the gilding layers to be pure gold, and the white material to be a lead compound. The lead compound is probably a corrosion product from the bronze, which contains 17% lead.

The head of a horse (fig. 4) and the sword (fig. 5) were also selected for analysis. These two objects had long been assumed to be part of the same gilded equestrian monument. Although the two were purchased together and have been displayed together, there is no good evidence that they are part of the same monument. The composition of the bronze for these two pieces was compared. They are somewhat close, but not similar enough to have been cast from the same pour. With the hope that analysis of the gilding could provide additional clues to their history, samples were removed from under the horse's neck and from the back of the sword. Viewed in cross section with the SEM and analyzed by EDS, each of the two samples showed 3 layers of gold leaf. The presence of three layers on both objects lends credence to the hypothesis

---

1 Curated by C. C. Mattusch, the exhibit was shown successively at the Sackler Museum, Harvard University, the Toledo Museum of Art, and the Tampa Museum of Art in 1996 and 1997.

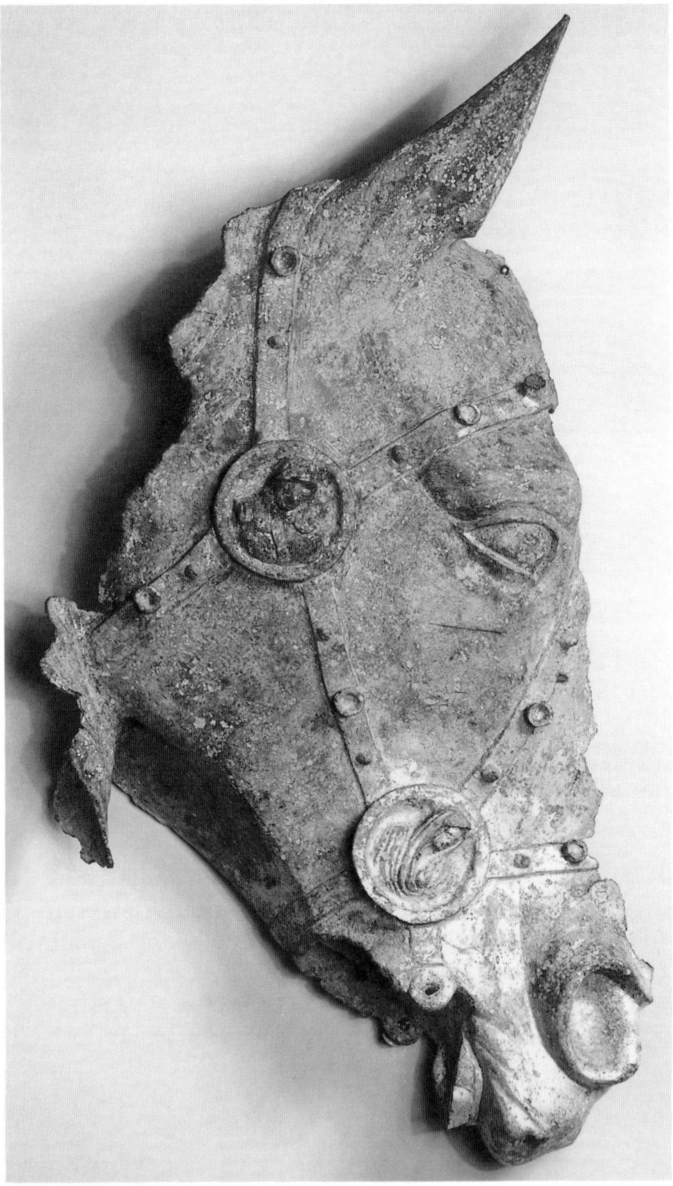

Fig. 4. Head of a horse. Gilded bronze, l. 0.545 m. Baltimore, Walters Art Gallery 54.759. (Photo: courtesy Walters Art Gallery.)

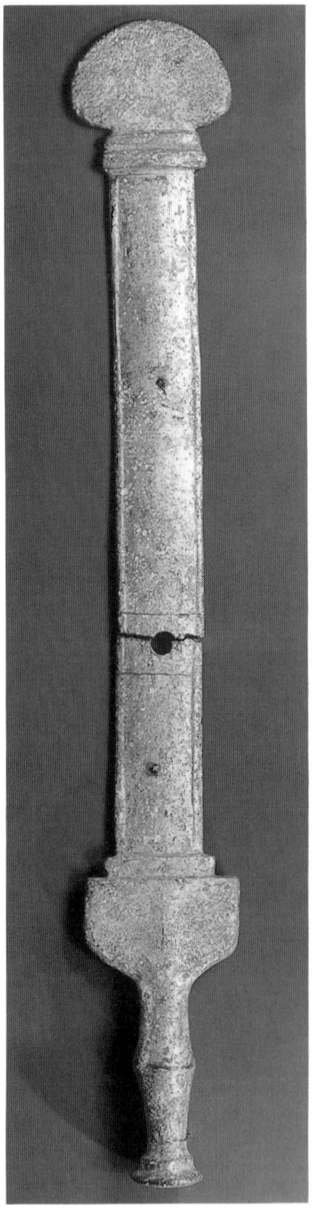

Fig. 5. Sword. Gilded bronze, l. 0.71 m. Baltimore, Walters Art Gallery 54.761. (Photo: courtesy Walters Art Gallery.)

that these two pieces are from the same monument and shared the same gilding history, but it was possible to remove only one sample from each object and since gilding is applied in overlapping sheets the number of gilding layers may vary by location. Thus, multiple samples would be needed to confirm the number of layers present on each object.

In their publication on gilding in the classical world, Oddy *et al.*[2] described a relationship between the type of gilding and the composition of the bronze on which it is found. Fire gilding is an amalgam of mercury and gold, which was applied to the bronze as a paste. Heat was applied until most of the mercury was driven off, leaving a well-adhered but porous layer of gilding. This type of gilding is found on bronzes with a composition approaching pure copper. Leaf-gilding was applied in sheets of extremely thin gold and bonded in place with heat or adhesive. This type of gilding is found on bronzes having a composition high in lead and tin. On the ternary diagram (fig. 6), fire-gilded bronzes are clustered at the top of the triangle,

2 W. A. Oddy *et al.*, "The gilding of bronze sculpture in the classical world," in *Small bronze sculpture* 103-24.

representing 100% copper. The leaf-gilded bronzes are spread throughout the rest of the diagram. All the gilt objects in the exhibition are leaf-gilded and have a bronze composition high

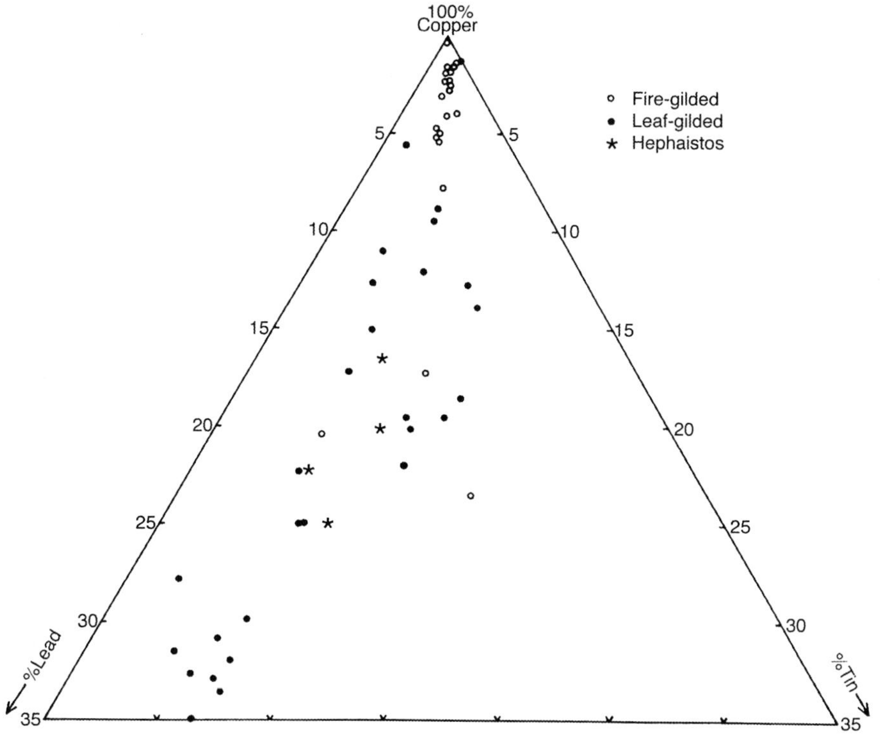

Fig. 6. Composition of gilded Roman bronzes. (Diagram: after Oddy *et al.* 1990.)

TABLE 1. BRONZE ALLOYS FOR FOUR GILDED OBJECTS IN *THE FIRE OF HEPHAISTOS* (%)

Object	*Copper*	*Tin*	*Lead*	*Total*
Sword	83.02	5.31	10.97	99.30
Horse head	79.59	6.75	12.71	99.05
Emperor	77.57	5.07	16.98	99.62
Julia Domna	74.67	7.54	17.44	99.65

in lead and tin (Table 1). In accordance with Oddy's findings, the *Fire of Hephaistos* bronzes, shown as asterisks on the diagram, fall into the same region on the graph with the other leaf-gilded bronzes.

Traces of a black material on the right eye of the Aphrodite (fig. 7) raised questions about the use of decorative metals on this object. When analyzed by EDS, the eye and lip showed silver as a major element, which suggests that these features were once overlaid with silver metal. The lower of the two headbands was once overlaid with decorative metal as well (fig. 8). Analysis of the metal near the left ear confirmed that the band was silver.

The statue of Dionysos as a youth (fig. 9) was also examined for the use of decorative metal. Since this object has been cleaned conservatively, it provided a rare opportunity to examine relatively thick layers of undisturbed corrosion. Close inspection of the eyes and the decoration on the front of the headband revealed a discontinuous black layer. Fragments of this layer can be seen just to the left of the pupil (fig. 10). Analyzed by EDS, the material showed a significant amount of tin. Since this finding is unusual, a second sample was taken from the eye and viewed in cross section. EDS of the cross section showed relatively pure tin throughout the layer. X-ray diffraction analysis identified the tin-containing material as tin oxide (cassiterite).

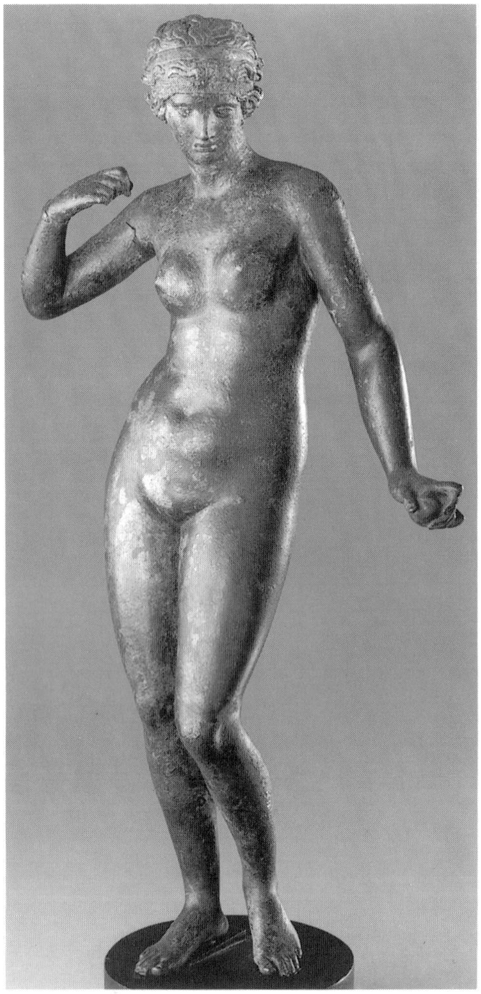

Fig. 7. Aphrodite. Bronze, p.h. 0.47 m. Providence, Museum of Art, Rhode Island School of Design, Museum Appropriation and Special Gift 26.117. (Photo: courtesy Museum.)

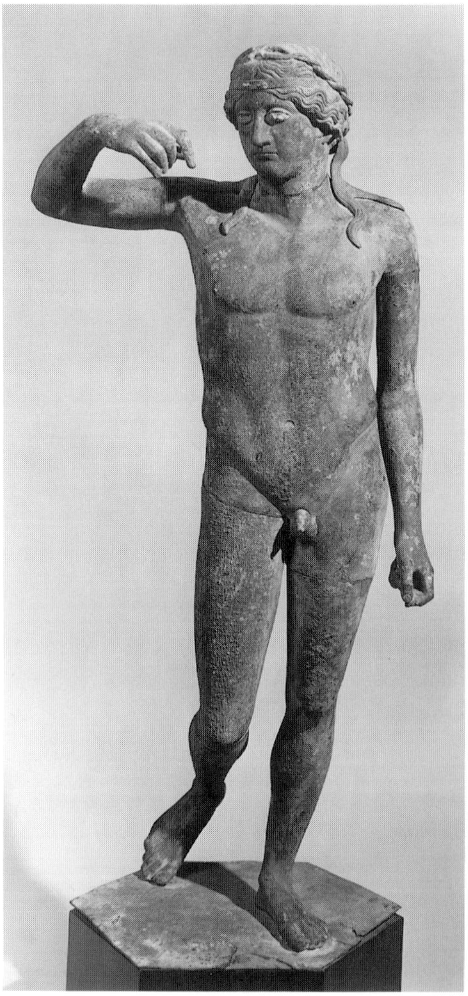

Fig. 9. Statue of Dionysos as a youth. Bronze, h. 1.285 m. Washington, D.C., Susanne K. Bennet. (Photo: courtesy Harvard University Art Museums.)

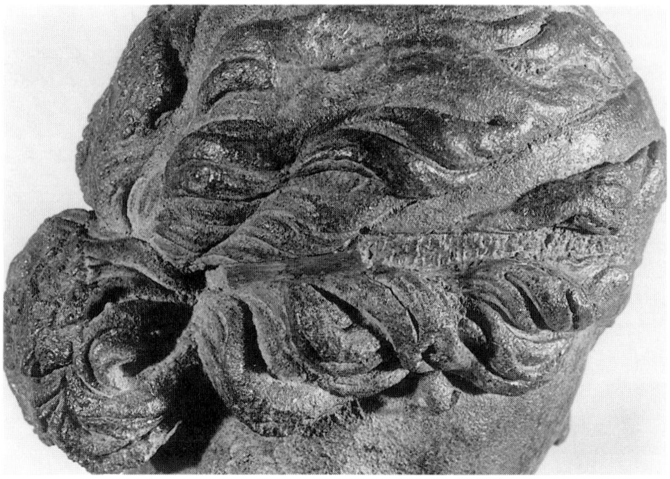

Fig. 8. Detail of Aphrodite's silver headband and the textured bronze surface once covered with silver sheet. (Photo: H. Lie.)

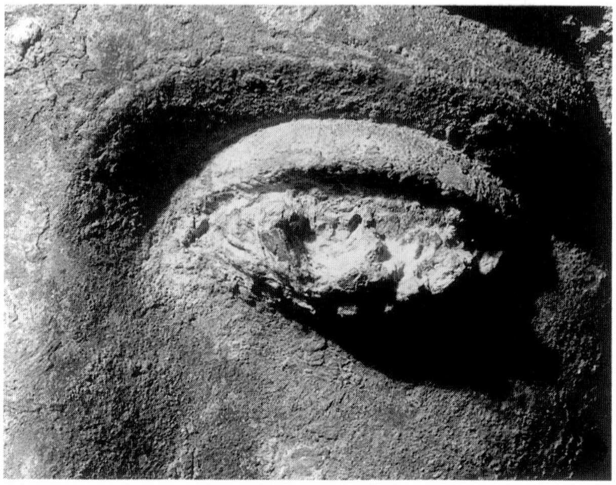

Fig. 10. Detail of the right eye of the Dionysos statue. (Photo: H. Lie.)

Several mechanisms have been proposed for the formation of a tin layer on the surface of bronze.[3] During casting of a high-tin bronze, tin may segregate on to the surface. After casting, copper may corrode preferentially from the surface, leaving a layer of tin. The tin on the Dionysos could have formed by either of these mechanisms; however, because of its thickness (200 microns) and location on the decorative elements, it is more likely to be the oxidized remains of an applied layer of tin sheet. This finding leads one to question why tin was used to decorate this statue instead of silver. Perhaps the artisans chose tin because it tarnishes more slowly than silver, or as a less costly substitute for the precious metal. Economy seems to have been a concern in the manufacture of this statue, which has unusually thin walls, and exhibits extensive flaws and ancient repairs.

In conclusion, the four bronzes selected for analysis showed leaf-gilding applied without the use of a preparatory layer. The presence of up to 6 layers of leaf indicates that the statues were gilded more than once. The presence of burial clay and corrosion observed between and on top of the layers of leaf provides evidence that the gilding is original and not a later restoration. The alloys used to cast the statues are similar to those reported for other leaf-gilded classical bronzes. None of the objects examined was fire-gilded. The Aphrodite has silver overlay on its eyes, lips, and headband, while the Dionysos has oxidized remains of tin sheet on its eyes and headband.

Straus Center for Conservation, Harvard University Art Museums, Cambridge, MA

Acknowledgements

I would like to thank H. Lie for suggesting this investigation and providing me with samples. I also thank A. Oddy for sharing his expertise.

---

3 W. A. Oddy and N. D. Meeks, "Unusual phenomena in the corrosion of ancient bronzes," in *Preprints of the contributions to the Washington Congress, September 3-9, 1982* (The International Institute for Conservation of Historic and Artistic Works, London 1982) 119-24.

Trace elements in Roman copper alloys

Josef Riederer

Chemical analysis of archaeological bronzes provides two entirely different types of information. In the first place, there are the three main elements — tin, lead, and zinc — which have been used since the Roman period to alloy copper. Their amounts were chosen by the bronzecaster to obtain an alloy with the specific technological properties needed or wanted to produce a certain type of object. The large number of analyses now available shows convincingly that nearly standard copper alloys were used: for instance, lead-tin bronzes with high amounts of lead for larger sculptures, pure tin bronzes with *c.*10% tin for vessels, and special types of brasses for groups of fibulae. In the second place, in addition to the 4 main elements of copper, tin, lead, and zinc, there are trace elements which were not added intentionally but came into the alloy as impurities of the base metals. Most of the trace elements, especially antimony, arsenic, bismuth, nickel, and cobalt, as well as part of the silver and most of the iron, entered the alloy with the copper ores. Silver also came with the lead ores, while cadmium and sometimes iron entered with the zinc ores. From experience we know that the concentrations of trace elements vary widely in archaeological objects made of copper alloys. This variation is due to the use of ores from different mines. Though this is well known, until now there has been almost no convincing evidence from the analysis of trace elements of copper alloys that the deposits which provided the copper could be precisely identified. Up to now, the main importance of the trace elements has been information about the homogeneity or heterogeneity of a group of objects that belongs together archaeologically. By now so many analyses of Roman bronzes, and of bronzes from earlier or later periods or from neighboring cultures, have been accumulated that we can discuss which concentrations of trace elements occur in Roman bronzes and whether they are the same or different in other regions or other periods.

To discuss the significance of the different trace elements for Roman objects made of copper alloys, the analyses of the following larger groups of objects are compared among themselves and with other groups of more or less contemporary objects from other regions, such as Etruscan, Late Egyptian, or Middle European Bronze Age objects. The following list describes the 21 groups of objects which have been analyzed at the Rathgen-Research Laboratory and which have been used to discuss the relevance of trace elements in copper alloys.

group number	*group of objects*	*provenance*	*number of analyses*
1	horse 1 (Roman)	Augst	228
2	horse 2 (Roman)	Augst	155
3	Bronze sculptures (Roman)	various	14
4	Statuettes (Roman)	Augst Museum	24
5	Statuettes (Roman)	Heddersheim	14
6	Statuettes (Roman)	Straubing	16
7	Statuettes (Roman)	Cologne Museum	11
8	vessels (Roman)	Neupotz	312
9	vessels (Roman)	Cologne Museum	25
10	fibulae (Roman)	Kempten	110
11	fibulae (Roman)	Saalburg	21
12	railing from boat (Roman)	Lake Nemi	10
13	handles (Roman)	Rome	64
14	coins, sesterces (Roman)	Rome	140
15	Etruscan mirrors	Corpus Speculorum Etr.	150
16	Etruscan bronzes	Karlsruhe Museum	400
17	Sardinian bronzes	Various collections	80
18	Egyptian stauettes	German museums	1300
19	Bronze Age daggers I	East Germany	226
20	Bronze Age daggers II	East Germany	154
21	Luristan objects	German museums	320

The concentrations of iron, nickel, silver, antimony, arsenic, and bismuth in Roman copper alloys are discussed below.

Iron

Iron is found in Roman objects usually in a very broad range of concentrations but with a relatively low average value of around 0.1%. This is also the usual concentration in bronzes from other cultures, though there are exceptions with higher concentrations like bronzes from Sardinia or bronzes from Luristan, where local ores of a peculiar type have been used. But among Roman bronzes there are also exceptions. The fibulae from Campodunum or the Saalburg and a group of vessels in the Museum of Cologne contain around 0.3% iron, which might indicate a local production with local ores.

Nickel

CHART 1. CONCENTRATION OF NICKEL (see also in colour after p. 96)

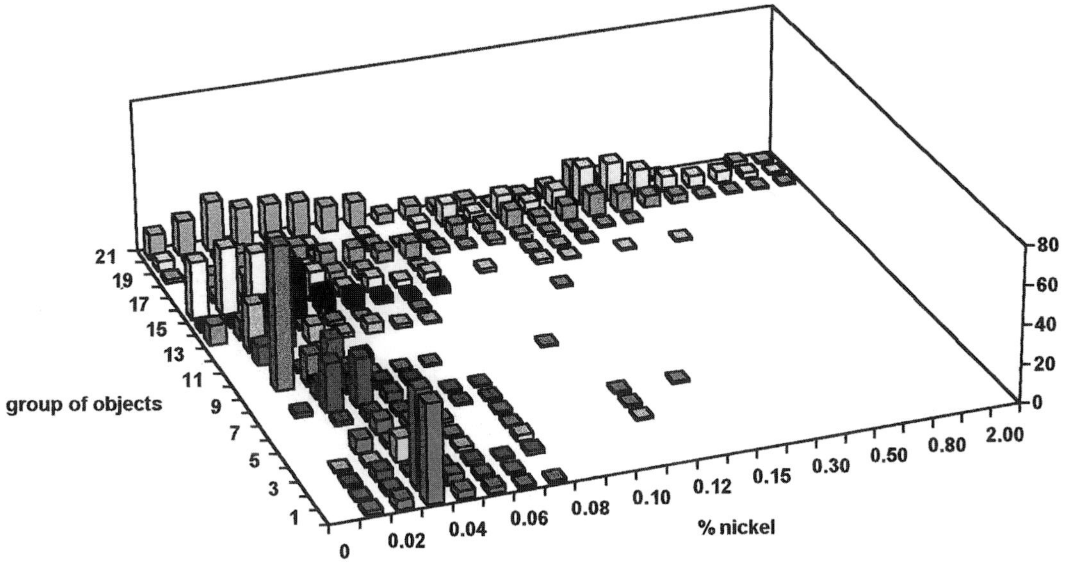

To demonstrate the use of the discussion of trace element concentrations, the values of nickel for the 21 groups of bronzes are shown in the three-dimensional chart 1. The horizontal rows 1-14, at the front of the diagram, are Roman objects. They all have a maximum concentration in the range of 0.02-0.04%. Some objects of the different Roman groups, like rows 4-6, statuettes from different museums, contain nickel up to 0.12-0.14%, and this may indicate a provenance which is different from the mass of the objects. In bronzes of other cultures the concentrations of nickel are considerably higher, and values up to 1% are not uncommon, especially in Bronze Age objects from Middle Europe. By that it is obvious that for the production of Roman bronze statuettes no copper was used from these mines, which were extensively exploited during the Bronze Age.

Silver

Silver is more or less untypical in bronzes from all regions and periods. Both in Roman bronzes and in bronzes from surrounding cultures the concentration of silver is between 0.04 and 0.06%. Sometimes a group of objects has slightly exceptional compositions, like the fibulae of the Saalburg with 0.07% silver. This might be due to the use of peculiar ores, which is probable in this case, or of remelted objects with silvered surfaces or partially made of silver.

Antimony

In most groups of Roman bronzes the concentration of antimony is amazingly stable at around 0.06%, while the average of bronzes from other cultures is somewhat lower — around 0.03-0.04%. Again the fibulae from the Saalburg have considerably higher concentrations at around

0.09%. An as-yet-unexplained phenomenon has been observed with Roman sesterces, among which early casts are relatively poor in antimony (0.08%), then the concentration of antimony increases abruptly up to 0.20% in the period from Titus to Hadrian; finally, after Antoninus Pius the concentration of antimony goes up to the relatively high value of 0.30%.

Arsenic

CHART 2: THE CONCENTRATION OF ARSENIC (see also in colour after p. 96)

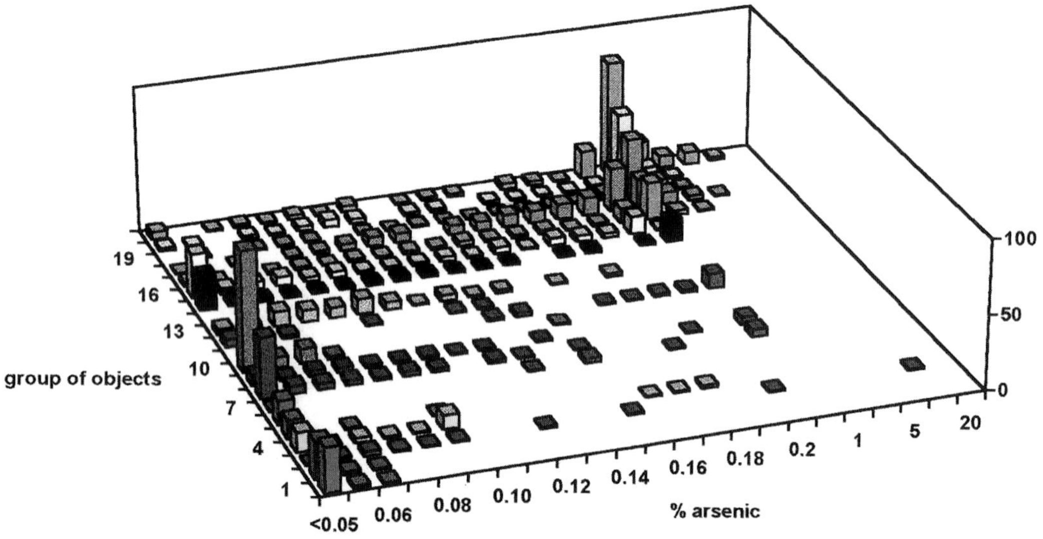

The concentration of arsenic in Roman bronze is so exceptional that it is detailed in chart 2. All the Roman objects in the front from rows 1 to 13 are characterized by extremely low concentrations of around 0.05%, while it is normal for bronzes of other cultures to contain much higher concentrations of arsenic, from 0.2% to several percent. This observation, that Roman bronzes are so different from bronzes of other origin with respect to their content of arsenic, was the reason to postulate a) that the Romans used copper ores from a mine which was not exploited by other cultures, and b) because of the homogeneity of all Roman bronzes with respect to their arsenic content, that the copper ores from just one mining area were used by the Romans.

Cobalt

The concentration of cobalt in Roman copper alloys is extremely low. Normally the concentration is below 0.005%, the detection limit of atomic absorption spectroscopy. In larger series of objects, about 5% of the objects have more than 0.005% of cobalt, but almost no concentrations of over 0.01% are found. Compared with copper alloys from other regions and periods, this concentration is relatively low, and in that respect also characteristic for Roman copper alloys.

Gold

Gold is found in Roman copper alloys normally in concentrations below 0.01%. If the concentration of gold is higher than 0.01%, it could be possible that the object was gilded or that a gilt object had been melted to produce a new object.

Cadmium

Cadmium is geochemically connected with zinc. In bronzes where the copper is alloyed with tin and lead, the concentration of this element is below 0.001%. In brasses, such as brass fibulae or in brass ornaments, the concentration of cadmium goes up.

From these data it becomes obvious that Roman objects made of copper alloys are characterized by almost identical concentrations of trace elements, so that it looks as if during the whole Roman period just one type of copper ore was used. Completely independent of the type of alloy

— pure copper, tin-bronze, lead-tin bronze, or any type of brass — the trace elements vary within extremely narrow concentration ranges, which in some cases are different from the concentrations of trace elements in copper alloys from other cultures. This amazing fact can be shown by comparing the analysis of objects belonging to different groups of Roman artefacts that are made of copper alloys:

	No	*Cu*	*Sn*	*Pb*	*Zn*	*Fe*	*Ni*	*Ag*	*Sb*	*As*
sculptures	1	69.22	5.96	24.42	0.11	0.08	0.02	0.06	0.06	0.07
	2	71.47	6.97	21.31	0.06	0.05	0.03	0.05	0.06	0.05
	3	77.25	9.00	13.40	0.02	0.05	0.04	0.06	0.05	0.07
	4	64.90	7.05	27.57	0.28	0.09	0.03	0.05	0.05	<0.05
	5	66.27	7.22	25.97	0.32	0.09	0.03	0.05	0.06	<0.05
	6	69.81	8.31	21.44	0.20	0.08	0.03	0.05	0.06	<0.05
statuettes	7	76.06	8.53	13.26	1.81	0.06	0.03	0.05	0.06	0.15
	8	77.10	6.92	13.03	2.29	0.26	0.03	0.05	0.09	0.23
	9	61.78	11.48	21.80	4.36	0.31	0.02	0.05	0.06	0.13
	10	71.09	7.41	20.57	0.51	0.15	0.04	0.06	0.07	0.10
	11	79.69	9.66	10.10	0.40	0.02	0.03	0.04	0.05	<0.05
	12	82.64	4.53	10.90	1.73	0.07	0.03	0.05	0.06	<0.05
	13	73.10	5.56	20.76	0.10	0.24	0.04	0.05	0.06	<0.05
	14	77.51	5.20	16.33	0.56	0.29	0.03	0.05	0.07	<0.05
	15	71.66	8.70	19.23	0.09	0.21	0.02	0.05	0.05	<0.05
	16	80.95	10.01	8.47	0.22	0.14	0.05	0.06	0.05	<0.05
	17	77.40	9.19	12.91	0.23	0.08	0.05	0.06	0.06	<0.05
	18	79.42	10.13	10.17	0.03	0.07	0.04	0.05	0.09	<0.05
fibulae	19	82.56	1.14	0.32	15.35	0.48	0.03	0.07	0.05	<0.05
	20	81.07	<0.02	1.07	17.46	0.25	0.01	0.05	0.09	<0.05
	21	80.73	3.74	0.16	15.08	0.16	0.03	0.05	0.05	<0.05
	22	68.40	7.65	21.87	0.72	0.88	0.04	0.07	0.10	0.26
	23	69.13	6.32	23.45	0.69	0.11	0.03	0.05	0.08	0.14
	24	70.40	7.79	21.22	0.13	0.02	0.03	0.07	0.08	0.20
vessels	25	86.36	12.43	0.66	0.18	0.06	0.03	0.05	0.06	0.07
	26	87.62	11.35	0.49	0.32	0.10	0.03	0.05	0.05	<0.05
	27	92.89	5.84	0.82	0.23	0.06	0.03	0.06	0.06	<0.05
	28	96.22	2.65	0.54	0.26	0.17	0.02	0.06	0.08	<0.05
	29	90.31	9.38	0.02	0.03	0.16	0.01	0.05	0.04	<0.05
	30	83.44	10.29	5.89	0.09	0.07	0.02	0.05	0.06	0.09
	31	77.16	2.17	0.45	19.56	0.52	0.03	0.06	0.05	<0.05
	32	79.22	3.79	1.77	14.69	0.38	0.02	0.07	0.06	<0.05
	33	82.77	8.15	1.50	7.09	0.21	0.05	0.08	0.09	0.06
handles	34	84.29	10.75	4.81	0.08	0.03	0.02	0.06	0.07	0.09
	35	75.35	6.64	17.82	0.01	0.02	0.03	0.06	0.07	<0.05
	36	72.97	8.24	18.26	0.03	0.15	0.03	0.05	0.07	0.20
	37	76.53	10.22	12.68	0.04	0.35	0.03	0.05	0.04	0.06
	38	91.98	6.16	0.23	1.30	0.16	0.03	0.04	0.05	0.06
	39	88.79	10.85	0.05	0.01	0.03	0.11	0.02	0.06	0.08
coins	40	86.51	<0.25	0.12	13.07	0.15	0.02	0.04	0.09	<0.05
	41	85.79	<0.25	0.04	13.94	0.11	0.02	0.06	0.06	<0.05
	42	88.50	0.50	0.10	10.20	0.23	0.03	0.06	0.16	<0.05

Sculptures:
1. Father of Trajan, Museum, Belgrade
2. Head of a boy, Allard Pierson Museum, Amsterdam
3. Head of a child, Casa dei Vettii, Pompeii
4-6. Horse, Augst (Riederer 1996a)

Statuettes:
7-9. Jupiter statuettes, Museum of Cologne
10-12. Museum Augst: Venus 60.2561 (10), Minerva 67.53 (11), Minerva 71.3248
13-15. Treasure from Straubing: Mars (13), Mercury (14), god (15)

	16-18. Frankfurt-Heddersheim: Genius 22864 (16), Genius 3501 (17), Mercury 9385 (189)
Fibulae:	19-21. Kempten–Campodunum
	22-24. Saalburg
Vessels:	25.-27. Neupotz: Inv.Nos. E 35 (25), E 2 (26), E 107 (27)
	28-30. Museum of Cologne: Inv.No. N 3763 (28), 44.1 (29), 118 (30)
Hemmorer Eimer:	31-33. Museum of Cologne: Inv.No. 793, 25.379 66.6
Handles:	34-36. Museum of Cologne: Inv. Nos. 118 (34), 44,5 (35), 67,537
	37-39. Rome: Nos. 10, 40, 43
Coins:	40-42. Sesterces, Rome: Tiberius (40), Trajan (41), Antoninus Pius (42).

This list shows convincingly that the same concentrations of trace elements occur, though the main elements differ considerably according to the type of object.

That there is no relationship between the main elements and the trace elements has also been shown by the analysis of unfinished objects of copper alloys from Augst. These unfinished objects consist of all the different alloys known at the time, but the trace elements are the same in all alloy groups and the trace elements are in the same range of concentrations as those in all groups mentioned above:

	Cu	*Sn*	*Pb*	*Zn*	*Fe*	*Ni*	*Ag*	*Sb*	*As*
copper	99.40	0.34	0.07	0.02	0.12	0.03	0.03	0.04	<0.05
copper with impurities	96.47	2.88	0.23	0.06	0.23	0.02	0.05	0.06	<0.05
tin bronze	89.38	9.73	0.39	0.25	0.11	0.03	0.05	0.06	<0.05
tin-lead bronze	74.06	8.78	16.54	0.28	0.13	0.04	0.08	0.10	<0.05
brass	79.91	0.54	0.19	19.07	0.21	0.02	0.03	0.04	<0.05
tin-brass	81.94	3.40	0.49	13.62	0.39	0.03	0.04	0.05	<0.05
lead-tin brass	78.94	5.67	6.31	8.28	0.36	0.02	0.07	0.05	<0.05

Based on a large number of about 2,000 reliable analyses of Roman objects made of copper alloys, in spite of the fact that a large variety of alloy types was used, it seems that all these objects are characterized by a very similar and homogeneous pattern of trace elements from whatever region or period of Roman civilization they come. This pattern of trace elements has peculiar characteristics, like the extremely low concentrations of most of the trace elements, especially arsenic, which distinguish Roman copper alloys more or less clearly from the copper alloys used by neighboring cultures. Based on these data, a typically Roman type of ore can be defined which provides copper alloys that contain about 0.03% nickel, 0.05% silver, 0.06% antimony, 0.05% arsenic, and 0.01% cobalt. Bases on this, it looks as if during the Roman period in the whole of the Roman world copper ores from only one mining area were used for the production of the different bronze alloys. At present there is no chance to identify a copper district with this peculiar composition and large enough to provide the immense quantities of copper used in Roman times. Neither bronze objects from different periods from Cyprus nor Spain have similar trace-element patterns to Roman objects, since normally they are rich in arsenic. Closest to the Roman trace-element pattern are the trace elements in bronzes from the Late Bronze Age in SE France and Switzerland — regions where there are no larger copper deposits.

The fact that Roman bronzes are characterized by an almost unique trace-element pattern provides the possibility of recognizing Roman bronze objects found outside the borders of the empire. On the other hand, imports from outside into the Roman empire also can be identified because of the characteristic concentrations of their trace elements.

From the large number of metal analyses of groups of related Roman objects of copper alloys, it becomes obvious that:

1. A large variety of copper alloys with different technical properties was used in the Roman period.
2. For the production of a certain type of object well-defined alloys were generally used, such as lead bronzes with a high content of lead for bronze sculptures; tin bronzes with a high amount of tin for bronze vessels; and brass rich in zinc for certain types of fibulae.

3. The type of alloy was chosen according to its technical properties by the founder or the smith to produce a particular object.
4. In spite of the large variety of copper alloys, the trace elements of nickel, silver, antimony, and arsenic vary in extremely narrow ranges; it is therefore possible to define a typical Roman type of copper alloy.
5. The concentration of trace elements in Roman copper alloys is different from copper alloys used earlier or at the same time in neighboring regions. By this means possible to distinguish products made of Roman metals from those of other cultures.
6. The low concentration of arsenic is a characteristic feature of Roman bronzes. Arsenic concentrations as low as those in Roman bronzes are extremely rare in bronzes from other cultures.
7. It is not yet possible to identify an ancient copper mining district with similar trace-element patterns to those of the Roman bronzes that provided copper ores for bronzes.

Rathgen-Forschungslabor, Schlass-Str. 1a, D-14059 Berlin